Mastering Skills for the TOEFL® iBT

Advanced

Mastering Skills for the TOEFL® iBT: Advanced

Patrick Yancey • Moraig Macgillivray • Casey Malarcher

© 2006 Compass Publishing

Acquisitions Editor: Casey Malarcher
Development Editors: Garrett Byrne, David Charlton, Chan-hee Park
Contributing Writers: Dean Beckman, Lark Bowerman, Kayang Gagiano,
                      Rob Jordens, Terry Jordens, Mike Pederson,
                      Eric Williamson, Adam Worcester
Cover/Interior Design: Design Plus

email: info@compasspub.com
http://www.compasspub.com

ISBN: 978-1-59966-053-0

20 19 18 17 16 15 14 13 12 11 10 9 8 7 6 5 4
09 08 07

Photo Credits
• Cover ©JupiterImages Corporation

Reading
• p. 11, 19, 45, 57, 107, 169, 183 ©JupiterImages Corporation

Listening
• pp. 203, 209, 241, 279, 287, 313, 351, 365 ©JupiterImages Corporation

Speaking
• pp. 373, 435, 441, 491, 501 ©JupiterImages Corporation

Writing
• p. 511, 519, 571, 577 541, 615, 625 ©JupiterImages Corporation

Practice Test
• p. 643, 668, 670, 677, 684, 689 ©JupiterImages Corporation
• p. 660, 662, 664, 666, 680, 682 ©iStockphoto Inc.

Mastering Skills for the TOEFL® iBT

Advanced

Compass Publishing

Table of Contents

Introduction

What to Expect on the TOEFL® Test

The TOEFL® test (Test of English as a Foreign Language) is an Internet-based test designed to assess English proficiency in non-native speakers who want to achieve academic success as well as effective communication. Most people take the TOEFL® test to gain admission into universities and colleges where instruction is in English. Additionally, many employers, government agencies, etc. use the scores to determine a person's English ability. It is not meant to test academic knowledge or computer ability, and as such, questions are always based on materials found in the test (computer tutorials are available for those not familiar with the PC). We have designed this practice book to be as similar as possible to the actual computer-based test in format and appearance in order to better prepare you for the TOEFL® test.

The TOEFL® test, like this series, is divided into four sections: reading, listening, speaking, and writing.

Major Changes in the Internet-Based TOEFL® (iBT)

- **General**
  - ⇨ The test measures all four language skills equally; a speaking section is included.
  - ⇨ The Test of Spoken English® (TSE®) will now be part of the TOEFL® test. Test takers will no longer take the TSE® as a separate test.
  - ⇨ The order of sections in the test are as follows:

    Reading
    Listening
    (10-minute break)
    Speaking
    Writing

  - ⇨ The test is approximately four hours long and can be taken in one day.
  - ⇨ Tests are administered through the Internet in test centers around the world.
  - ⇨ Unlike past tests, there is no structure section.
  - ⇨ Note-taking is allowed in every section.
  - ⇨ The test is a linear exam, not computer adaptive; each test taker receives the same range of questions.
  - ⇨ The scores will be viewed online.

- **Reading/Listening**
  - ⇨ Passages for Reading and Listening are longer than those in the CBT (See introduction of individual sections for further details).

- **Speaking/Writing**
  - ⇨ Tasks for Speaking and Writing include integrated questions that require more than one skill to complete, i.e., reading and/or listening, then speaking or writing.
  - ⇨ For the speaking section, test takers speak into a microphone, and their responses are digitized and sent to the ETS Online Scoring Network.
  - ⇨ For the writing section, test takers must type their responses.

The New Test Format

Section	Number of Questions	Time (minutes)	Score
Reading	3–5 passages • 12–14 questions each • 700 words per passage	60–100	30 points
Listening	4–6 lectures • 6 questions each • 500–800 words (4–6 min.) 2–3 conversations • 5 questions each • 400–500 words (2–3 min.)	60–90	30 points
BREAK		10	
Speaking	2 independent tasks • 1 personal experience • 1 preference/choice 2 integrated tasks (Read-Listen-Speak) • Reading 100 words • Conversation 200 words (1–2 min.) • Lecture 200–300 words (1–2 min.) 2 integrated tasks (Listen-Speak) • Conversation 200 words (1–2 min.) • Lecture 200–300 words (1–2 min.)	20	30 points
Writing	1 independent task (same as TWE®) 1 integrated task (Read-Listen-Write) - Reading 250–300 words - Lecture 250–300 words (2 min.)	50	30 points

How this book is organized

There are four main sections and one practice test in this book.

Introduction	Understanding what each section requires you to do
Chapter 1	Practicing organizing and synthesizing information
Chapter 2	Developing coherence
Chapter 3	Focusing on clarity of speech
Practice Test	Practicing with questions designed according to the real test format

Test-taking and study tips

The only way to be certain of an excellent TOEFL® test score is to be able to read, write, understand, and speak English like an educated native speaker. You have no doubt been developing your ability in these areas for many years now. Unfortunately, this is not something one can accomplish by studying in the traditional way. However, research conducted over the years by applied linguists, psychologists, and educators has yielded a considerable amount of information on the best methods for refining these skills for the purposes of standardized tests. By keeping the following test-taking tips in mind, you can optimize your study habits and achieve the highest possible scores with the level of language proficiency you have developed.

General study tips:

- Prepare a study area for yourself. This should include the following:
  - ⇨ A comfortable chair and spacious table/desk
  - ⇨ Suitable lighting
  - ⇨ Good ventilation and air quality; an open window or a house plant are good ideas
  - ⇨ An area free of distractions such as outside noises/television/radio (unless of course you are using the television/radio to study listening)
  - ⇨ Proper space to keep all the materials you will need when studying, such as books, paper, pens/pencils, a tape recorder or other recording device, and if possible, a computer with Internet access

- Study regularly over a long period of time. Do not study to the point of physical/mental exhaustion, as this has been shown to be ineffective in retaining information.

- "Cramming," i.e., studying intensely for long periods before an exam, is less effective, as it strains your general health and well-being and does not lead to good long-term retention of information/skills.

- Psychologists have discovered a principle called "state-specific memory." This means you remember things better in the same conditions that you learned them. So, for example, if you always study math at night, you will do better on a math exam at night. Use this concept to your advantage. If you know when and under what conditions you will take the TOEFL® test, simulate these in your study environment and habits. For example, if you will take the TOEFL® test on a Sunday afternoon from your computer at home, then make it a point to study at this computer on Sunday afternoons.

- Be well rested on the day of the exam. Do not stay up all night studying. Also, eat healthy foods including fruits and vegetables.

- Be relaxed and confident. Do the best that you can and do not worry excessively about any mistakes or uncertainties.

Registering for the TOEFL® test

Students must get registration information for the TOEFL® test. Registration information can be obtained online at the ETS website. The Internet address is www.ets.org/toefl. The website provides information such as testing locations, costs, and identification requirements. The website also provides other test preparation material.

The registration information, such as the test center location, identification requirements, and costs, will vary depending on the country in which you take the test. Be sure to follow these requirements carefully. If you do not have the proper requirements in order, you may not be able to take the test. Remember that if you register online, you will need to have your credit card information ready.

What TOEFL® test scores can be used for

The primary use of TOEFL® test scores is for acceptance into institutions such as universities and colleges in which English is the primary language of instruction. As noted earlier in this introduction, a great number of universities and other institutions require a certain TOEFL® test score for admission. In fact, it is estimated that as many as 4,400 such institutions require TOEFL® test scores for admission.

The exact calculation of a TOEFL® test score is complicated and probably not necessary for the student to understand. It is helpful to know, however, that each section of the Internet-based test is worth the same amount of points. The highest possible score on the iBT is 120 points. Each particular institution, for example, a university, will have its own score requirements for admission. For that reason, it is very important to check with each institution individually to find out what its admission requirements are. For example, a passing score at one university may not be a passing score at another university. It is the responsibility of the student to find out what the requirements are for each institution.

Although the primary use of TOEFL® test scores is for admission into English language institutions, there are a number of other places that require TOEFL® test scores. For example, many government agencies require TOEFL® test scores to evaluate an applicant's English ability for employment. In addition, many companies and corporations worldwide may also request TOEFL® test scores for similar uses. Even language institutes may request TOEFL® test scores for use in placing students in the appropriate level of English instruction.

Certainly, doing well on the TOEFL® test is important in many ways. Remember, practice makes perfect. We hope that you will take full advantage of this practice book and study hard. Your hard work and dedication will provide you with the best opportunity to do well on the TOEFL® test and to meet your goals for the future.

Mastering Skills for the TOEFL® iBT

READING

READING Table of Contents

How the reading section is organized

There are four main parts in the reading section.

Introduction   Understanding what each section requires you to do
Chapter 1   Practicing necessary skills with short reading passages
Chapter 2   Mastering the skills with longer reading passages
Chapter 3   Improving on summarizing skills

Reading

In the reading section of the TOEFL® test, you will be required to read three to five passages on varying topics. After each passage, you will answer twelve to fourteen questions that test your ability to understand vocabulary, sentence structure, and factual information as well as implied information and the writer's intention. You will not be permitted to see the questions until after you have read the passage. While answering the questions, you will be permitted to look back at the reading. You do not need any previous knowledge on the topic in order to answer the questions correctly.

- **Passage Types:**
  1. Exposition — Material that provides information about or an explanation of a topic
  2. Argumentation — Material that presents a point of view about a topic and provides supporting evidence in favor of a position
  3. Narrative — An account of a person's life or a historical event

- **Question Types:**
  Questions 1 through 10 will be multiple-choice questions much like those found on older versions of the TOEFL®. The following list explains the types and number of each type of question on the test. Questions will not necessarily appear in this order.

Question Type	Number	Task
Vocabulary	2	choose the best synonym
Pronoun Reference	1	identify the noun to which a pronoun is referring
Factual Information	4	select details or facts provided in the passage, including one (1) negative fact question identifying something that is not in the passage, or not true according to the passage
Organization and Purpose	1	identify the writer's method in explaining his or her point, or tell why the writer has mentioned something
Inferences	1	draw an inference from the passage by choosing an answer that is something not actually said in the passage, but is implied or can be inferred
Paraphrase	1	choose the best paraphrase to demonstrate your understanding of part of the passage or a sentence and your ability to analyze the meaning of the designated part of the passage

The 11th and 12th questions for each passage are not multiple-choice and are question types not found on older versions of the TOEFL®. The 11th question is a sentence insertion activity, and the 12th question can be one of two types of activities: either a chart or a summary question.

Sentence Insertion

This question shows you a sentence that could be added to the passage. You must decide where the sentence would best fit in the passage. While you are reading you will notice several icons that look like this ■ on the actual Internet-based test. You will be required to click on the square [■] where you feel the new sentence should be added. For the purposes of this practice test, you can simply choose the letter beside the appropriate square. This question tests how well you understand the organization of the passage.

Category Chart

In passages on topics that explain groups or categories of information, you will most likely be asked to demonstrate your understanding of the groups or categories mentioned in the reading by completing a chart. There will be two or three categories and six to nine choices. Four to seven of these choices should be placed in a chart or table listing characteristics of the groups or categories. Two choices will not be used.

● **Example:**

Frogs	**Toads**		
_____	_____	(A)	bumpy, dry skin
_____	_____	(B)	eggs in a chain
_____	_____	(C)	build nests
_____		(D)	shorter legs
		(E)	eggs in a bunch
		(F)	have live babies
		(G)	longer legs
		(H)	smooth, wet skin
		(I)	bulging eyes

● **Correct answers:**

Frogs	**Toads**
smooth, wet skin	bumpy, dry skin
longer legs	shorter legs
eggs in bunches	eggs in a chain
bulging eyes	

● **Not used:** build nests, have live babies

The chart questions are worth up to 3 points if there are five key items and 4 points if there are seven key items. Partial credit is given for this question format.

Summary

In this type of question, you will be presented first with an introductory sentence for a possible summary of the passage. You will then find a set of additional sentences. Three of these sentences belong in a summary paragraph, and the others do not. Your job is to decide which sentences belong. Incorrect choices will either present ideas that are not in the passage or ideas that do not belong in the summary because they are only minor ideas.

● **Example:**
First sentence of introduction:
Animals in the desert have different ways to live with little water.
⇨ Camels can live for a long time without water.
⇨ Desert plants do not need much water.

⇨ Desert reptiles and birds don't sweat.

⇨ Larger animals get the water they need from things they eat.

⇨ At night, desert temperatures can drop below 10 degrees Celsius.

⇨ Some animals stay underground to keep water in their skin.

● **Correct answers:**

First sentence of introduction:

Animals in the desert have different ways to live with little water.

⇨ Desert reptiles and birds don't sweat.

⇨ Larger animals get the water they need from things they eat.

⇨ Some animals stay underground to keep water in their skin.

● **Not used:**

⇨ Camels can live for a long time without water. (minor detail)

⇨ Desert plants do not need much water. (incorrect information)

⇨ At night, desert temperatures can drop below 10 degrees Celsius. (minor detail)

The summary questions are worth up to 2 points each.

Study Tips for Reading

- Practice reading passages of academic English regularly (the Internet can be a great source of practice materials).
- Become a master of vocabulary and constructions:
  ⇨ Make it your goal to understand all the words you come across when studying.
  ⇨ Keep a vocabulary notebook listing new terms and their definitions. Write out the definitions in English. Only refer to bilingual dictionaries as a last resort. Set aside a period of time every week to review your new vocabulary. Practice it by writing out your own sentences using the words.
  ⇨ Master any and all grammatical and rhetorical constructions you encounter. Discover their meanings and uses by asking a teacher or doing an Internet search and viewing multiple examples of their use. You can keep a notebook of constructions as well.
- Learn how to take notes. You are permitted to take notes during the reading section of the TOEFL®. Note-taking is NOT writing down every word of the reading. A good idea is to note the main idea, and then note the information that supports this main idea. Note-taking must be learned, and it takes time. The better your note-taking skills, the easier you should find the TOEFL® reading section, as well as other sections of the iBT TOEFL®.
- Do not use a pencil or your finger when you are reading. Your eyes move faster than your finger, so you slow yourself down if you trace lines with a pencil or finger while reading.

Test management:

- Questions cannot be viewed until after the passage has been read.
- You will be allowed to study the reading as you attempt the questions.
- Use the Review icon at the top of the screen to return to previous questions you may wish to revise or recheck.
- There is a glossary available. Simply select the particular word with the cursor to find its meaning.
- When reading passages, ask yourself the following questions:
  ⇨ What is the main idea of the passage?
  ⇨ How is the main idea developed/supported in the passage?
- For each paragraph/new point in the passage, ask yourself why the author mentions this and how it relates to the main idea.
- Keep in mind that you have about 60 minutes to read 3 passages and answer 12 questions per passage. This means roughly 20 minutes per set of passage and questions. Try to pace yourself accordingly. For each set of questions, first answer all of the questions that you can answer easily. You can then go back and answer more difficult questions. If you find that you have exceeded 20 minutes for a particular section, it is best to guess an answer and move on to the next section rather than remain on a particularly difficult question for several minutes.

Chapter 1

Short Passage Skill Practice

Skill A Understanding Details

Necessary Skills

Identifying Facts

- Comprehending important information and facts that are stated in a passage
- Locating a specific piece of information in the passage quickly
- Using examples and descriptions to find information
- Understanding the distinction between main ideas and supporting details
- Using transitional expressions to locate details such as examples, time, reasons, or results

Identifying Negative Facts

- Recognizing incorrect information as well as information not mentioned in the text
- Identifying paraphrases that do or do not correctly summarize information from the text

Example Questions

- According to the passage, who/when/where/what/how/why _____?
- According to paragraph _____, _____ because
- In paragraph _____, the author states that
- In paragraph _____, what does the author say about _____?
- The author mentions _____ as an example of
- According to the passage, which of the following is true about _____?

Negative Facts Questions

- All of the following are mentioned in paragraph _____ EXCEPT
- According to the passage, which is NOT _____?

Skill A 01 Ear Infections

One of the more prevalent illnesses in children under three is ear infections. These can be quite painful and will often result in incessant crying. Ear infections are caused when bacteria or viruses get into the inside of the ear. The Eustachian tubes, which supply the ear with air, become swollen or inflamed. The adenoids, cell clusters near these tubes that fight infections, can also become infected and block the tubes. Children's Eustachian tubes are smaller and straighter, and their adenoids are larger. This means that the tubes do not drain as well, which often results in the adenoids impeding flow through the tubes.

prevalent (adj):
common

incessant (adj):
without end; going on and on

inflamed (adj):
swollen and red

cluster (n):
a small group of things that are connected or are very close together

impede (v):
to block; to cause resistance

1. According to the passage, what is the cause of an ear infection?

   (A) A virus spreading from the throat
   (B) Painfulness and incessant crying
   (C) A bacteria or virus in the ear
   (D) A bacteria blocking the adenoids

3. The word "block" in the passage is closest in meaning to

   (A) a square made of wood
   (B) stand in the way of
   (C) a neighborhood
   (D) stop up

2. Why are young children more susceptible to ear infections than adults?

   (A) Their ears and nostrils are smaller and contain less natural defenses.
   (B) Their tubes are shorter, and their adenoids are not fully developed.
   (C) They often cry incessantly, causing damage to the tubes in the ear.
   (D) Their Eustachian tubes are naturally blocked by their adenoids.

4. Which sentence(s) in the passage helped you answer question 2 above?

   _____
   _____
   _____
   _____

Skill A **02** Symbolism

READING

LISTENING

SPEAKING

WRITING

PRACTICE TEST

The idea of symbolism is simple enough: an object in reality takes on an abstract meaning. For example, a large bridge may symbolize humankind's progress, or the Titanic disaster takes on a symbolism similar to the myth of Icarus. Authors often use symbolism in literature to make broad, comprehensive statements about life that are implicit in their writings. For instance, in the myth of Sisyphus, a man is condemned by the gods to roll a great rock up a hill every day, only for it to roll back down at night. This has been viewed as symbolizing the futility of humankind's pursuits.

abstract *(adj)*:
not concrete; impossible to touch or see in reality

comprehensive *(adj)*:
general; universal

implicit *(adj)*:
indicated; inferred

condemned *(adj)*:
found guilty of some crime or offense and put under punishment

futility *(n)*:
worthlessness

1. According to the passage, what is symbolism?
   (A) An object being used for an abstract meaning
   (B) The making of a symbol from a non-symbol
   (C) Two objects being linked by a literary idea
   (D) A book that captures the heart of a generation

3. The word "great" in the passage is closest in meaning to
   (A) powerful
   (B) old
   (C) large
   (D) wonderful

2. What is true of the myth of Sisyphus?
   (A) The prison of Sisyphus symbolizes humankind's limitations.
   (B) Sisyphus's rock symbolizes the pointless toil of daily life.
   (C) Sisyphus's myth symbolizes his love of dreams over reality.
   (D) The gods symbolize the cruelty of tyrants at that time.

4. List three symbols mentioned in the passage? What do these symbols represent?

   _____

   _____

   _____

   _____

Most countries set an age at which its young people become adults in the eyes of the law. This age is called the age of majority. When people reach this age, usually 18, they become entitled to certain inalienable rights from which they were precluded as minors, such as the right to vote. Before becoming adults, minors are not able to enter into legal contracts. This is seen as being for their own protection. They are also protected from statutory rape, from being exploited in the labor market, and from having to go through the same penal system as adults.

in the eyes of (*prep phrase*): under; by

inalienable (*adj*): not capable of being taken or given away to another person

precluded (*adj*): excluded from

exploit (*v*): to take advantage of

penal (*adj*): related to punishment or prison

1. Which of the following would be an example of a protection granted specifically to minors?
   (A) The right to vote
   (B) Child labor laws
   (C) Pursuit of employment
   (D) The right to a fair trial

2. Which of the following would be an example of a right denied to minors?
   (A) The right to vote
   (B) The right to a fair trial
   (C) Child labor laws
   (D) Separate penal system

3. The word "statutory" in the passage is closest in meaning to
   (A) part of a statue
   (B) punishable under the law
   (C) said or stated
   (D) not very serious

4. List two things that minors are not allowed to do, but adults are allowed to do.

   _____

   _____

   _____

   _____

Skill B — Identifying Topics and Paraphrasing

Necessary Skills

- Understanding the meaning of the highlighted sentence correctly
- Using the context to understand the highlighted sentence clearly
- Identifying a paraphrase that most accurately restates the key information in the original sentence
- Recognizing different sentence structures that keep the meaning of the original sentence
  Ex. Australia is the world's smallest continent, but it is one of the most fascinating.
  Changed sentence structure: One of the most fascinating continents, Australia, is also the world's smallest continent.
- Recognizing different vocabulary words that keep the meaning of the original sentence.
  Ex. Australia is the world's smallest continent, but it is one of the most fascinating.
  Changed wording: Australia is the smallest large landmass on the planet; however, it is among the most interesting.
  Changed structure and wording: Though it is the smallest continent on the planet, Australia is among the most interesting.

Example Questions

Which of the following best states the essential information in the highlighted sentence in the passage? Incorrect choices change the meaning in important ways or leave out essential information.

Normal breathing involves drawing air into the lungs through the nose using the diaphragm. The chest expands, and then the air is forced out again through the nose. Special breathing techniques that deviate from normal breathing have been developed for a variety of purposes. Singers must learn special breathing techniques to avoid damaging their vocal chords. These techniques involve expansion of the entire torso and deeper, more diaphragmatic breathing. Many forms of Eastern philosophy and religion also use special breathing for meditation, manipulation of energies, and spiritual enlightenment. These involve such techniques as abdominal breathing, reverse breathing, and nose-mouth breathing.

draw (v):
to pull; to take

diaphragm (n):
a muscular membrane that separates the upper and lower organs of the torso, used in breathing

deviate (v):
to differ from

vocal (adj):
related to the voice

manipulation (n):
control

1. Which of the following sentences best expresses the essential information of the highlighted sentence? Incorrect choices change the meaning in important ways or leave out essential information.
   (A) It is much healthier in general to use a special breathing technique in everyday life.
   (B) Singing while breathing will typically cause damage to your vocal chords.
   (C) In addition to normal breathing, there are special techniques for other purposes.
   (D) The most spiritually-enlightened people breathe using several special techniques.

2. Which of the following is NOT mentioned in the passage?
   (A) Reverse breathing used in Eastern religious practices
   (B) Breathing deeper in order to sing properly
   (C) Breathing used in sports to boost strength and endurance
   (D) Breathing used for meditation and manipulation of energies

3. The word "forms" in the passage is closest in meaning to
   (A) kinds
   (B) shapes
   (C) documents
   (D) bodies

4. Which words in the highlighted sentence helped you choose the right answer for question 1?

   _____

   _____

   _____

   _____

Skill B 02   The Rings of Saturn

Galileo was the first to detect a disc around Saturn. This was done in the year 1610. Since then, progressively more powerful telescopes and space probes have refined our original conception of this disc. Saturn's disc is actually many thin rings, mostly made of particles of ice and rock. The largest rings, A and B, are separated by the Cassini division. The fainter C and D rings are inside the B, and the F ring lies beyond the A. The **gaps** are created by the paths of Saturn's moons: the Cassini division by Mimas, the smaller Encke gap by Pan. The gaps on either side of the F ring are made by Prometheus on the inside and Pandora on the outside.

space probe (n):
an unmanned space craft used to collect data

refine (v):
to change to a more developed or more useful state

conception (n):
an understanding

fainter (adj):
less bright; harder to see

lie (v):
to be located

1. Which of the following sentences best expresses the essential information of the highlighted sentence? Incorrect choices change the meaning in important ways or leave out essential information.

   (A) The larger the ring or division, the more moons found within the gap.
   (B) The F ring needs two moons due to its relatively enormous size.
   (C) The moons prevent the A and B rings from colliding and disintegrating.
   (D) Saturn's rings are separated from each other by the planet's moons.

2. According to the passage, which moon divides the A ring from the F ring?

   (A) Pan
   (B) Mimas
   (C) Prometheus
   (D) Pandora

3. The word "gaps" in the passage is closest in meaning to

   (A) differences
   (B) blanks
   (C) pauses
   (D) separations

4. Which of the following best states the topic of the passage?

   (A) What people once thought was a disc around Saturn is really a group of rings.
   (B) Galileo discovered both the rings and the moons of Saturn.

   Why? _____

   _____

Skill B 03   Materials from the Colonies

Some areas of colonial America grew cotton and flax. However, the British would not allow the colonists to weave this material into cloth. Instead, they forced them to sell the raw material to Britain, where it would be woven; then the colonists would buy it back. In this way, the British made more of a profit off the fabric industry than did the colonists themselves. Despite these rules, though, many colonists did weave their own cloth. They mainly used plain weaves and then dyed the material using berries or other natural materials that could be gathered in the vicinity of their homes.

weave (v): to make cloth from thread

raw (adj): unprocessed

fabric (n): a cloth produced by weaving

colonist (n): a person who leaves his or her native country to live in a colony

vicinity (n): an adjacent or local area

1. Which of the following sentences best expresses the essential information of the highlighted sentence? Incorrect choices change the meaning in important ways or leave out essential information.

   (A) Colonists sold crops to Britain and then bought back the finished product.
   (B) Britain sold crops to the colonists and then bought back the finished product.
   (C) Colonists forced the British to pay high prices for the clothes that they had manufactured from American cotton and flax.
   (D) Britain forced colonists to pay high prices for the clothes that they had manufactured from British cotton and flax.

2. Which of the following is NOT mentioned in the passage?

   (A) Weaving methods
   (B) Weaving restrictions
   (C) Methods for coloring fabric
   (D) Cloth materials

3. The word "flax" in the passage refers to

   (A) something that the colonists ate
   (B) a tool used in the weaving process
   (C) a crop useful for making fabric
   (D) a part of a cotton plant

4. Which of the following best states the topic of the passage?

   (A) Fabrics in the early American colonies
   (B) Differences between British and American cloth

   Why? _____

   _____

Necessary Skills

- Identifying logical connections within a passage
- Producing a passage that is ordered and consistent
- Recognizing transitional words that show the connections among sentences
- Using pronouns to figure out the order of ideas and sentences

Example Questions

Look at the four squares [■] that indicate where the following sentence could be added to the passage. Where would the sentence best fit? Click on a square [■] to add the sentence to the passage.

Skill C 01 Greek Philosophers

■ **A)** The Ancient Greeks believed in five virtues: justice, strength, temperance, courage, and wisdom. Socrates tried to show that all of these virtues were merely different kinds of wisdom. According to him, the greatest wisdom was to know the limits of one's own knowledge. Plato, his student, recorded Socrates's dialogues and went on to philosophize on politics and just government. ■ **B)** Aristotle, Plato's student, was highly analytical and began to approach abstract questions from a rigorous, logical standpoint, thus planting the seeds of modern theoretical inquiry and scientific research methods. ■ **C)** Aristotle's student, Alexander the Great, ended up turning toward military conquest rather than philosophy. ■ **D)**

temperance *(n)*:
moderation or restraint

analytical *(adj)*:
based on reason or logic as a way to understand reality

rigorous *(adj)*:
very strict; precise

plant the seeds *(v. phrase)*:
to do some work that will develop into something later

conquest *(n)*:
the act of taking control of other nations by force

---

1. Which of the following sentences best expresses the essential information of the highlighted sentence? Incorrect choices change the meaning in important ways or leave out essential information.

   (A) Merely possessing wisdom was good enough, according to Socrates, because the other virtues were not as important.
   (B) Socrates was the first person to define the virtue of wisdom.
   (C) One of the main teachings of Socrates was that wisdom should be understood as separate from the other virtues.
   (D) Socrates worked toward a way to prove that the five virtues could all be understood as parts of a single whole.

2. The word "just" as used in the passage is closest in meaning to

   (A) a moment ago (B) fair or right
   (C) only   (D) simply

3. Look at the four squares [■] that indicate where the following sentence could be added to the passage:

   After the Ancient period, philosophers began to be persecuted by the Church, and philosophy lay largely dormant in Europe until the Renaissance.

   Where would the sentence best fit? Choose the square [■] where the sentence should be added to the passage.

   (A) Line 1   (B) Line 6
   (C) Line 9   (D) Line 10

4. Which of the following sentences could best replace the first sentence of the reading and maintain the coherence of the passage?

   (A) Socrates, Aristotle, and Plato were all Greek philosophers, but each had his own unique approach to the discipline.
   (B) Although the three great Greek philosophers disagreed about many things, they all enjoyed teaching.

   Why? _____

   _____

Skill C 02 Wildfires

A wildfire is an uncontrolled fire occurring in forests, grasslands, or any other area with natural fuels. They are not planned, but occur due to natural phenomena such as lightning and volcanic activity or due to human carelessness. ■ **A)** Though wildfires can be devastating, some species of trees and brush are dependent on them. For example, the Giant Sequoia needs the heat that fire generates to procreate. ■ **B)** For this reason, planned fires are common in places with fire-dependent species. ■ **C)** Likewise, natural wildfires are a natural phenomenon that have always occurred and can be beneficial to an ecosystem because they create change. ■ **D)**

phenomena (n): occurrences; events
devastating (adj): destroying everything
dependent (adj): relying on
procreate (v): to multiply by reproducing
beneficial (adj): producing a useful result; advantageous

1. Which of the following sentences best expresses the essential information of the highlighted sentence? Incorrect choices change the meaning in important ways or leave out essential information.
   - (A) Lightning and volcanic activity are natural phenomena that cannot be planned for, much like wildfires.
   - (B) Natural events that can cause fires include lightning and volcanic activity.
   - (C) The carelessness of some people may cause natural disasters to occur, and such disasters are impossible to plan for.
   - (D) Wildfires can be caused by natural events or by careless people.

2. The word "brush" in the passage is closest in meaning to
   - (A) clean
   - (B) comb
   - (C) lightly touch
   - (D) plants

3. Look at the four squares [■] that indicate where the following sentence could be added to the passage:

   With careful planning, a controlled fire can be very useful to an ecosystem.

   Where would the sentence best fit? Choose the square [■] where the sentence should be added to the passage.
   - (A) Line 4
   - (B) Line 6
   - (C) Line 8
   - (D) Line 10

4. How did you choose the answer for question 3 above? Explain how you found the right answer, or write the words that gave a clue to the answer.

   _____

   _____

   _____

   _____

Skill C 03 Infant Communication

Infants, despite their inability to speak, are excellent communicators. ■ **A)** Their primary means of communication is crying. Several things could be wrong with the baby to make him cry: he may be hungry, cold, tired, or want to be held. ■ **B)** Parents learn quickly that their baby has different cries for different needs. ■ **C)** For example, his hungry cry may be short and low-pitched. Babies are also receptive to speech, even if they cannot understand the words. They can distinguish between a human voice and other noises and tend to listen attentively to their parents' voices. ■ **D)**

inability *(n)*:
a lack of ability

pitched *(adj)*:
having a particular musical sound

receptive *(adj)*:
able and willing to receive

distinguish *(v)*:
to tell apart; to discriminate

attentively *(adv)*:
with attention

1. Which of the following sentences best expresses the essential information of the highlighted sentence? Incorrect choices change the meaning in important ways or leave out essential information.

   (A) Although the meaning of words may be unknown to babies, they do recognize and respond to them.

   (B) Babies will try to speak because they hear other people around them using words.

   (C) Even if some words are too difficult for babies to understand, parents continue to use such words to talk to babies.

   (D) When babies receive input from parents who talk to them, the babies fail to understand their parents' messages.

2. The word "short" in the passage is closest in meaning to

   (A) not enough   (B) not full
   (C) not long   (D) not tall

3. Look at the four squares [■] that indicate where the following sentence could be added to the passage:

   In fact, many parents report that when their baby is crying, he begins to calm down as he hears his parent's voice approaching.

   Where would the sentence best fit? Choose the square [■] where the sentence should be added to the passage.

   (A) Line 2   (B) Line 4
   (C) Line 5   (D) Line 9

4. Which of the following sentences could best replace the first sentence of the reading and maintain the coherence of the passage?

   (A) Babies can effectively send and receive messages without speaking.

   (B) Parents should not worry if their babies are not speaking by the time they are 12 months old.

   Why? _____

   _____

Necessary Skills

Vocabulary

- Understanding the meaning of a word as it is used in the passage
- Using context clues (synonyms, antonyms, examples) to figure out the meaning of a word
- Applying knowledge of word parts (roots, prefixes, suffixes, etc.) to help understand the meaning
- Applying knowledge of grammar clues such as the verb "be" (for giving definitions), conjunctions, and punctuation marks (dash, colon, parentheses, etc.) to help understand connections and context

Referents

- Recognizing a noun that is being referred to by a pronoun or other reference word. (This noun is known as the "referent.")
- Understanding the different kinds of pronouns and reference words

Example Questions

Vocabulary

- The word/phrase _____ in the passage is closest in meaning to
- The word _____ could best be replaced by which of the following?
- The phrase _____ in the passage means

Referents

- The word _____ in the passage refers to
- What does the word _____ in paragraph _____ refer to?
- What does _____ in paragraph _____ refer to?
- What is the meaning of the word _____ in paragraph _____?
- The phrase _____ in the passage refers to

Starting at Lake Itasca in Minnesota, the Mississippi River flows south through ten states before it reaches the Gulf of Mexico. ■ **A)** It was formed about 10,000 years ago when the Ice Age was coming to an end. At this time, glacier deposits created the upper Mississippi Valley. As these glaciers melted, the water carved its way through the debris, creating the upper Mississippi and the rivers that flow into it. ■ **B)** The lower Mississippi gets its water from the Ohio and Missouri rivers. ■ **C)** The Missouri River is actually longer than the Mississippi. Collectively, they make up the fourth longest river in the world. ■ **D)**

deposit *(n)*:
a layer of material left from some natural process

upper *(adj)*:
higher; above some lower part

glacier *(n)*:
a huge mass of ice that moves over land

debris *(n)*:
broken pieces of something that are scattered over an area

collectively *(adv)*:
taken together

1. Look at the four squares [■] that indicate where the following sentence could be added to the passage:

   Only the Nile, the Amazon and the Yangtze are longer.

   Where would the sentence best fit? Choose the square [■] where the sentence should be added to the passage.
   (A) Line 2
   (B) Line 6
   (C) Line 7
   (D) Line 9

2. The word "it" in the passage refers to
   (A) the glacier
   (B) the debris
   (C) the upper Mississippi
   (D) the rivers

3. The word "carved" could best be replaced by which of the following?
   (A) Cut
   (B) Pressed
   (C) Fixed
   (D) Set

4. The word "its" appears twice in the reading. What does each pronoun refer to?

   First "its" — _____   Second "its" — _____

The job of your computer's memory system is to store your OS (Operating System), programs, and files, and to supply information to the CPU (Central Processing Unit) so it can be modified. ■ **A)** It is like a pyramid, with the CPU at the top, the hard disk at the bottom, and intermediary memory in between. ■ **B)** Data that is in use, e.g. the OS, and opened program/files, is passed to the RAM (Random Access Memory). ■ **C)** Information is passed from the RAM up to the cache for modification by the CPU. Although it is small, the cache provides the best access for the CPU. ■ **D)**

store (v):
to keep for future use

modified (adj):
changed

intermediary (adj):
existing between

cache (n):
a place to keep valuable or important things; a fast storage buffer

access (n):
a way to get to or make use of

---

1. Look at the four squares [■] that indicate where the following sentence could be added to the passage:

   After the CPU modifies data from the cache, it is passed back to the RAM and written to the hard disk when saved.

   Where would the sentence best fit? Choose the square [■] where the sentence should be added to the passage.

   (A) Line 3
   (B) Line 5
   (C) Line 7
   (D) Line 9

2. What does the word "it" in line 8 refer to?

   (A) The cache
   (B) The OS
   (C) The CPU
   (D) The information

3. The word "passed" in the passage is closest in meaning to

   (A) skipped
   (B) given
   (C) deleted
   (D) charged

---

4. Draw a line from "it" in sentence 1 of the reading to the word or phrase it refers to.

   _____

   _____

   _____

   _____

The oldest known string instrument is the harp. ■ **A)** It seems that it may have been inspired by the hunter's bow in primitive times. ■ **B)** Rock paintings of harp-like instruments have been found in France that date back to 15,000 B.C. ■ **C)** Images of harps have also been identified in Egyptian hieroglyphs on the tomb of Pharaoh Ramses III. ■ **D)** Harps were also in widespread use in Scotland and Ireland. The word "harp" can be traced back to words in Anglo-Saxon, Old German, and Old Norse. These all aptly appertain to a single meaning, "to pluck."

inspire *(v)*:
to cause; to be the source of an idea

bow *(n)*:
a tool made of curved wood and string, used to shoot arrows

widespread *(adj)*:
common

appertain to *(v phrase)*:
to relate to

pluck *(v)*:
to pull and release in order to start vibrating

1. Look at the four squares [■] that indicate where the following sentence could be added to the passage:

   Many different cultures had different versions of this instrument.

   Where would the sentence best fit? Choose the square [■] where the sentence should be added to the passage.
   (A) Line 1
   (B) Line 2
   (C) Line 4
   (D) Line 5

2. What does the word "that" in line 3 refer to?
   (A) France
   (B) A belief
   (C) The harp
   (D) Paintings

3. The word "aptly" in the passage is closest in meaning to
   (A) oddly
   (B) appropriately
   (C) precisely
   (D) tastelessly

4. Find the word "These" in the passage. What does this word refer to?

   _____

   _____

   _____

   _____

Skill E   Making Inferences and Establishing Purpose

Necessary Skills

Making Inferences

- Perceiving ideas that are suggested but not directly stated within the text
- Drawing conclusions based on the information given within a statement or section of the text

Establishing Purpose

- Understanding the role of a certain statement in the passage
- Inferring the author's intention for mentioning certain information
- Relating specific information to the main ideas to understand the purpose of the information

Example Questions

Making Inferences

- From the passage, it can be inferred that
- Which of the following can be inferred from paragraph _____ about _____?
- Based on the information in paragraph _____ and paragraph _____, what can be inferred about _____?
- It is implied in paragraph _____ that
- According to paragraph _____, with which statement do you think the author would most probably agree?

Establishing Purpose

- Why does the author mention _____ in paragraph _____?
- Why does the author introduce _____?
- The author mentions _____ in paragraph _____ in order to
- What is the main purpose of paragraph _____?
- Why does the author give details about _____?
- Why does the author refer to _____?

Skill E 01 Ernest Hemingway

Ernest Hemingway often signed his books with the French expression "il faut d'abord durer," which means "first, one must last." This seems ironic because Hemingway killed himself on July 2, 1961. However, the saying is appropriate because Hemingway's legacy endures through his works, some of which are considered the most important works of 20th century fiction. Hemingway also wrote non-fiction pieces such as *The Sun Also Rises*, but he is most well-known for his novels, *For Whom the Bell Tolls*, which depicts events from the Spanish Civil War, and *The Old Man and the Sea*, which garnered the Pulitzer Prize for fiction in 1953.

ironic (adj):
stating something, while meaning the opposite, i.e. saying "you did well" while actually meaning that the person did NOT do well

legacy (n):
that which a person leaves behind them when they die

endure (v):
to put up with; to bear; to continue to do

depict (v):
to describe; to give a description of

garner (v):
to collect; to gain

---

1. What does "which garnered the Pulitzer Prize" refer to?
   (A) Ernest Hemingway
   (B) Ernest Hemingway's novels
   (C) *For Whom the Bell Tolls*
   (D) *The Old Man and the Sea*

2. It can be inferred from the passage that
   (A) Ernest Hemingway grew up speaking both French and Spanish.
   (B) Ernest Hemingway wasn't famous while he was alive.
   (C) Ernest Hemingway's fiction was more popular than his non-fiction.
   (D) Ernest Hemingway taught writing.

3. The word "last" in the passage is closest in meaning to
   (A) be behind others
   (B) have the only one
   (C) continue
   (D) end

4. Explain how you chose your answer for question 2 above. Refer to key words or phrases in the passage that helped you choose your answer.

   _____

   _____

   _____

   _____

Skill E 02   Body Language

Body language imparts meaning without the use of words. It is a type of non-verbal communication. There are certain recognized distinctions between types of body language: voluntary/involuntary and universal/cultural. The first distinction is often fuzzy. For instance, a smile can be voluntary or involuntary. However, by the second distinction, smiles are universal. They are interpreted the same across all cultures. Nodding and head shaking, however, are cultural. In Turkey, the former is replaced by raising the eyebrows. It is thought that body language has its roots in animal communication. Indeed, great apes raised in captivity are quite proficient at reading human body language.

impart (v):
to communicate; to convey

distinction (n):
a difference

voluntary (adj):
done by free choice; on purpose

former (n):
the first of two things mentioned

proficient (adj):
adept; skillful at doing something

READING   LISTENING   SPEAKING   WRITING   PRACTICE TEST

1. The word "They" in the passage refers to
   (A) distinctions
   (B) cultures
   (C) smiles
   (D) people who smile

3. The word "fuzzy" in the passage is closest in meaning to
   (A) unclear
   (B) hairy
   (C) solid
   (D) inverted

2. What can be inferred from the passage about nodding?
   (A) It will be understood everywhere.
   (B) It will not be understood in Turkey.
   (C) It will not be understood by an ape.
   (D) It will be understood if it is voluntary.

4. Explain how you chose your answer for question 2 above. Refer to key words or phrases in the passage that helped you choose your answer.

   _____

   _____

   _____

   _____

The jingle dress dance is a traditional dance of the Ojibwa people that originated in Minnesota. The dresses are adorned with metal cones or jingles that are not only decorative, but jingle during the dance. One particular legend recounts how a medicine man helped his very sick daughter. One night, a spirit wearing the jingle dress appeared to him in a dream. She told him that he could cure his daughter by making one of these jingle dresses for her. When he woke up, he and his wife crafted a jingle dress according to the spirit's instructions, and their daughter was cured.

adorn (v):
to decorate; to add decorations to

medicine man (n):
among certain peoples, a person believed to have magic powers often used for healing

recount (v):
to tell; to relate

spirit (n):
a ghost; a supernatural creature

craft (v):
to make

1. What does "that" in line 2 refer to?
   (A) The jingle dress
   (B) The jingle dress dance
   (C) The Ojibwa people
   (D) Minnesota

2. It can be inferred from the passage that
   (A) the jingle dress dance can cure diseases
   (B) the jingle dress is no longer used
   (C) the Ojibwa people believed in the supernatural
   (D) the Ojibwa people suffered an epidemic

3. The word "jingles" in line 3 is closest in meaning to
   (A) decorations
   (B) songs
   (C) movements
   (D) people

4. Which sentence in the passage helped you choose the answer to question 2 above?

   _____

   _____

   _____

   _____

Necessary Skills

Completing Summaries

- Recognizing the organization and purpose of a passage
- Recognizing the relationship between main ideas and details
- Recognizing the difference between key points and details
- Omitting insignificant details from the summary chart
- Identifying which sentences are proper paraphrases of the text

Completing Tables

- Recognizing the overall organization to quickly find the major points of the passage
- Distinguishing between major and minor points of the passage
- Placing concepts within a certain category
- Identifying statements in the answer choices that are not mentioned or not true

Example Questions

Completing Summaries

- An introductory sentence for a brief summary of the passage is provided below. Complete the summary by selecting the THREE answer choices that express the most important ideas in the passage. Some sentences do not belong in the summary because they express ideas that are not presented in the passage or are minor ideas in the passage. **This question is worth 2 points.**

Completing Tables

- Complete the table below about _____ discussed in the passage. Match the appropriate statements to the _____ to which they are associated.
- Complete the table by matching the phrases below. Select the appropriate phrases from the answer choices and match them to the type of _____ that they describe. TWO of the answer choices will NOT be used. **This question is worth 3 (or 4) points.**

Skill F 01 Non-native Plant Species

When a species occurs in an area naturally, or without human interference, it is called a native or indigenous species. It evolves in response to natural conditions in its location. Non-native species are those that live in an area in which they did not originally evolve. They have been introduced to the area by humans. In North America, a species is considered native if it existed there before Europeans settled in the area. When European settlers arrived, they brought many species of plants to be used for food, medicine, and decoration. Though they have since lived in North America for hundreds of years, the plants are still classified as non-native.

indigenous (adj):
belonging to a particular area

location (n):
a place; a position

introduce (v):
to bring in

settle (v):
to establish a home in a new area

classify (v):
to put into a particular group or class

1. **Directions:** *Select the appropriate phrases from the answer choices and match them to the type of category of plants to which they relate. TWO of the answer choices will NOT be used.*

Native	Non-native
_____	_____
_____	_____
_____	

(A) Decorative or medicinal plants for settlers
(B) Do not grow well; die easily
(C) Evolve through natural conditions
(D) Existed prior to arrival of settlers
(E) Introduced by humans
(F) May kill other plants
(G) Occur without human interference

2. From the passage, it can be inferred that a plant that is found in North America but not in Europe is probably
(A) native to North America and non-native to Europe
(B) native to Europe and non-native to North America
(C) native to both Europe and North America
(D) non-native to both Europe and North America

3. The word "occurs" in line 1 of the passage is closest in meaning to
(A) is found
(B) happens
(C) results
(D) takes place

4. In question 1 above, how did you know which of the answer choices should NOT be used?

_____

_____

_____

_____

Skill F 02 The Marathon

The Marathon is the longest footrace competition, consisting of 26.2 miles (42,195 m). The name comes from the Greek legend of Pheidippides, who died after running from the city of Marathon to Athens to report the Greek triumph over Persia so that the Athenians would not surrender. Modern historians say the legend is likely to have been embellished or fabricated; a man named Philippedes did make a similar run from Athens to Sparta, but did not perish from the effort. The winner of the first modern marathon in the 1896 Olympics was Spiridon "Spiros" Louis. An interesting side note about his victory is that he stopped during the course of the race for a glass of wine at a local inn.

triumph (n):
a win

likely to be (adj phrase):
probably

embellish (v):
to make a story more interesting by adding facts and details that may not be true

largely (adv):
mostly; mainly

perish (v):
to die

READING | LISTENING | SPEAKING | WRITING | PRACTICE TEST

1. **Directions:** *An introductory sentence for a brief summary of the passage is provided below. Complete the summary by selecting the THREE answer choices that express the most important ideas in the passage. Some sentences do not belong in the summary because they express ideas that are not presented in the passage or are minor ideas in the passage.*

First sentence: **The marathon is a famous Olympic event with an interesting history.**

(A) It was based on the Greek legend of a famous runner.
(B) The runner died after saving his civilization from the Persians.
(C) The real name of Pheidippides was probably Philippedes.
(D) The legend is probably loosely based on a similar occurrence.
(E) Spiridon Louis enjoyed drinking wine at local inns.
(F) Today, there are marathons in major cities all over the world.

2. It can be inferred from the passage that
   (A) it is physically impossible for a man to run from Marathon to Athens
   (B) the Greeks in Marathon successfully defended the city
   (C) it is traditional to drink a glass of wine during a marathon
   (D) the modern Olympics were started in honor of the marathon

3. The word "fabricated" in the passage is closest in meaning to
   (A) manufactured
   (B) unknown
   (C) cherished
   (D) false

4. Which sentences in the passage contain the main ideas listed in the summary?

_____

_____

_____

_____

Skill F 03   Slang

Slang is a form of speech used by socially marginalized groups so that members of mainstream society will not understand them. Slang typically involves the replacement of nouns or the heavy use of idiomatic expressions. These often refer to matters that are taboo, such as sexuality, drugs, or crime. As colloquial slang expressions become part of everyday speech, the slang communities replace them with new expressions.

Some forms of slang are actually encrypted versions of normal speech. In Pig Latin, for example, the initial consonants of a word are moved to the end followed by the "ay" sound. So "book" becomes "ook-bay."

marginalized (adj): lesser and unimportant

mainstream (adj): popular

taboo (adj): forbidden; not socially acceptable

colloquial (adj): conversational; familiar

encrypted (adj): coded

1. **Directions:** *Select the appropriate phrases from the answer choices and match them to the form of speech to which they relate. TWO of the answer choices will NOT be used.*

Slang	Mainstream Speech
_____	_____
_____	_____
_____	

(A) Taboos
(B) Adverbs
(C) Pig Latin
(D) Borrows expressions from the other
(E) Used for general purposes
(F) Spoken in the home
(G) Marginalized groups
(H) Understood by most people

2. Based on the information in the passage, what can be inferred about slang?
  (A) It changes slowly over time.
  (B) It can describe illegal activities.
  (C) It is only used by criminals.
  (D) It is illegal in many societies.

3. The word "expressions" in the passage is closest in meaning to
  (A) actions
  (B) body language using the face
  (C) words or phrases
  (D) characteristics

4. In question 1 above, how did you know which of the answer choices should NOT be used?

_____

_____

_____

_____

Review A – F

Vocabulary Review

Skill Review

Vocabulary Review

Instructions: Choose the word or phrase to complete each sentence.

1. The _____ rain caused the river to overflow its banks.
   (A) abstract
   (B) indigenous
   (C) hollow
   (D) incessant

2. With its _____ engine, the car performed better than we had hoped.
   (A) marginalized
   (B) rigorous
   (C) modified
   (D) garner

3. A heavy object will _____ other objects toward it by its gravity.
   (A) drain
   (B) draw
   (C) exploit
   (D) colloquial

4. Over the sounds of the storm, she could not hear the _____ sound of footsteps outside her bedroom door.
   (A) acclaimed
   (B) condemned
   (C) eternal
   (D) fainter

5. Through his _____, the billionaire will be remembered for many centuries.
   (A) binary
   (B) ordeal
   (C) taboo
   (D) legacy

6. Several individuals from _____ groups of society protested in front of the government offices today.
   (A) encrypted
   (B) incessant
   (C) marginalized
   (D) inalienable

7. Providing an excellent view of the landscape up to 120 miles in all directions, the mountain _____ over the surrounding countryside.
   (A) deviates
   (B) lies
   (C) portrays
   (D) towers

8. Some career choices are better suited for individuals with good problem-solving skills and _____ minds.
   (A) analytical
   (B) beneficial
   (C) dependent
   (D) epic

Instructions: Choose the word or phrase closest in meaning to the underlined part.

9. The people of that particular village are famous for the goods they <u>create</u>.
   (A) depict
   (B) impart
   (C) adorn
   (D) craft

10. He focused his telescope on a small <u>group</u> of stars high in the night sky.
    (A) cluster
    (B) memory
    (C) temperance
    (D) colonist

11. It is my great privilege to accept this <u>important</u> award on behalf of my colleague.

    (A) acrobatic
    (B) devastating
    (C) implicit
    (D) prestigious

12. The pot holds enough water for <u>approximately</u> four cups of tea.

    (A) attentively
    (B) respectively
    (C) roughly
    (D) widely

13. With most advertisements, the <u>suggestion</u> is that newer is better.

    (A) conception
    (B) triumph
    (C) implication
    (D) manipulation

14. That is considered a <u>forbidden</u> subject in my family's household.

    (A) taboo
    (B) prestigious
    (C) rigorous
    (D) marginalized

15. Not so long ago, eye surgery of any kind was often a difficult <u>experience</u> for the patient.

    (A) circuit
    (B) mime
    (C) ordeal
    (D) set

Instructions: Write the missing words. Use the words below to fill in the blanks.

recite	contend	composing
distinguish	inability	

Does the **(16)** _____ to see or hear allow some musicians or poets to **(17)** _____ themselves in their fields? For example, Beethoven was deaf, yet this did not hinder his **(18)** _____. Homer is another good example. Some scholars **(19)** _____ that the Greek bard could **(20)** _____ the episodes of his epic poems vividly because of his blindness.

Instructions: Choose the one word that does not belong.

21. craft   depict   perish   compose
22. access   alter   modify   refine
23. conquest   perish   triumphant   victory
24. attentive   aware   proficient   receptive
25. explain   impart   preclude   recount

Water makes up seventy percent of the Earth's surface, and people rely on it to sustain life. Rainfall nurtures crops and restores water supplies. The amount of water on the Earth is constant, meaning that we can neither create more water, nor get rid of it. We can, however, interfere with the water cycle. Water has several forms — liquid, vapor, and ice — and is constantly changing and being recycled through a process known as the hydrologic cycle. ■ **A)**

The hydrologic cycle involves inflows, outflows, and storage. ■ **B)** When water moves from the ground, for example, into a river, it is called an outflow for the ground and an inflow for the river. ■ **C)** Water is stored when it rests somewhere with relatively little movement. ■ **D)**

There are six components to the hydrologic cycle: evapotranspiration, condensation, precipitation, run-off, infiltration, and percolation. Evapotranspiration is the combination of evaporation and transpiration. Evaporation occurs when the sun warms surface water and transforms it into water vapor. Transpiration is the same thing, but involves plants. Plants soak water up from the ground and then return it to the cycle via the pores in their leaves. Once again, the sun turns this water into vapor. Once the water has been evaporated, it rises into the atmosphere. As the air gets colder at higher altitudes, the water vapor condenses and clings to particles in the air. This is called condensation and is how clouds are formed. When the clouds get too heavy, droplets fall back to the earth through a process called precipitation.

Now that the water has been returned to the earth, it can either be intercepted by a water source, or it can land on the ground. For the water that lands on the ground, one of several things can happen. If there has been a heavy rain, or if it has rained for a long time, a lot of the water will return to the streams, lakes, and oceans as run-off. Run-off also depends on the slope of the ground. A steep slope will cause more movement of water. Conversely, if water movement is minimized, much of the water will infiltrate the soil. Gravity forces the water lower and lower into the ground through a process called percolation. The permeability of the soil determines the rate at which percolation occurs. If the soil is very dense, it will hold less water. If it is porous, on the other hand, it will store more water. The amount of water that can be held in the soil is called its porosity.

The water will continue to move downward until it reaches saturated soil. This means that there is already so much water in the soil that it

nurture (v):
to nourish and tend to; to care for

component (n):
any of the parts that make up a machine

pore (n):
a small round opening in the surface of a living organism

vapor (n):
gas

condense (v):
to decrease the volume or size of a substance

cling (v):
to stick to

intercept (v):
to stop something going from one point to another

infiltrate (v):
to get through; to pass through

permeability (n):
the ability to allow liquids to pass through

dense (adj):
closely packed

saturated (adj):
wet; full of liquid

can't hold any more. An aquifer is any geologic material that can hold water or allow water to transmit through it. Even solid rock can be an aquifer because water can move through its cracks and pores.

Ground water is returned to the earth via vegetation. Plants soak up water through their roots and, as mentioned, return the water to the atmosphere. Outflows also occur naturally via springs. Humans can extract ground water using wells. Ground water mining can cause problems for the water table, which is the measure of water in the ground. Taking too much water not only reduces the water supply, but it affects the soil. When water is withdrawn, the pores that hold the water collapse, altering the make-up of the soil. Further, contamination from landfills and septic systems cause serious problems for the soil and for the plants that rely on it.

contamination (n):
pollution caused by unwanted substances

1. Which of the following is closest is meaning to "extract" in paragraph 6?
   (A) Exact
   (B) Intact
   (C) Take out
   (D) Dig up

2. Which of the following means most nearly the same as "collapse" as used in paragraph 6?
   (A) Cave in
   (B) Tumble
   (C) Shut down
   (D) Open up

3. What word does "it" in paragraph 6, line 10 refer to?
   (A) The soil
   (B) The plants
   (C) The septic systems
   (D) The landfills

4. Why does the author mention vegetation?
   (A) To show how important water is for yielding a good crop
   (B) To show how crops can be harmed by contamination
   (C) To show how the roots of plants help to hold the soil together
   (D) To show how ground water is used in the hydrologic cycle

5. According to the passage, what is percolation?
   (A) The process of water seeping into the soil
   (B) The process of water turning to vapor
   (C) The process of water vapor forming clouds
   (D) The process of water falling to the Earth

6. According to the reading, which of the following would cause run-off?
   (A) Heavy rain
   (B) A steep slope
   (C) Both A and B
   (D) Neither A nor B

7. According to the passage, what is an "inflow"?
   (A) When water is removed from a place
   (B) When water is added to a place
   (C) When water is stored in a place
   (D) When water falls from the sky

8. Based on the information in paragraph 1, which of the following best explains why the Earth doesn't run out of water?
   (A) Water gets recycled.
   (B) We get plenty of rain.
   (C) We have plenty of sources of water.
   (D) When we run out, we can melt ice.

9. Look at the four squares [■] that indicate where the following sentence could be added to the passage:

   When the river reaches the sea, it is an outflow for the river and an inflow for the sea.

   Where would the sentence best fit? Choose the square [■] where the sentence should be added to the passage.

   (A) Paragraph 1, line 7
   (B) Paragraph 2, line 1
   (C) Paragraph 2, line 3
   (D) Paragraph 2, line 4

10. Which of the following is NOT mentioned in the passage?

(A) The world's water supply is diminishing.

(B) Plants are involved in the hydrologic cycle.

(C) People should be careful not to damage the soil.

(D) Solid rock can be on aquifer.

11. From the passage, it can be inferred that

(A) there is an unlimited amount of water available

(B) porous soil stores less water

(C) human interference can affect the stability of the soil

(D) water continues to move downward after it reaches saturated soil

12. Directions: *Complete the table by matching the phrases below. Select the appropriate phrases from the answer choices and match them to the section of the reading to which they relate. Decide if the word in italics is experiencing an inflow or an outflow. TWO of the answer choices will NOT be used.*

Inflow	Outflow
_____	_____
_____	_____
_____	_____

(A) Water being evaporated from the surface of a *lake*

(B) Water infiltrating the *ground*

(C) Water being *contaminated*

(D) Run-off entering a *river*

(E) *Plants* returning water to the atmosphere

(F) Plants soaking water up from the *ground*

(G) *Soil* collapsing

(H) Water moving through cracks in *rock*

In 1831, a young student of botany named Charles Darwin accepted an invitation to act as a traveling companion to a sea captain on a three-year scientific expedition. Nearly four years later, in 1835, the ship came to a group of islands about 400 miles west of South America called the Galapagos archipelago. The islands had long been a hideout for pirates and were known as a popular hunting ground for whalers and seal hunters. But to Darwin's highly trained eye, the islands were a unique and fascinating opportunity.

During his five weeks on the islands, he observed a remarkable variety of flora and fauna as well as the many interesting non-living, geological aspects of the islands. Each island seemed to have slightly different variations of the same animals and plants. The particular features of these animals and plants were perfectly suited to the environment of their respective islands. His experiences on the Galapagos Islands would later bring Darwin to write his famous work *On the Origin of Species*, in which he proposed the ideas that led to the theory of evolution.

Today, the Galapagos Islands are a protected natural park under the Ecuadorian government, and they are a UNESCO world heritage site. They are perhaps best known for their 14 subspecies of giant tortoise, which can weigh up to 250 kilograms and live for over 100 years. The islands actually take their name from the tortoises: "galapagos" is the Spanish word for these tortoises, perhaps coming from a word meaning "saddle."

Scientists theorize that normal-sized tortoises originally floated to the islands long ago on water currents from mainland South America. ■ **A)** They grew to their enormous size because the islands lacked any kind of natural predators. ■ **B)** It is estimated that there were originally about 100,000 tortoises living in Galapagos. ■ **C)** The tortoises can go for months without food or water. ■ **D)** Unfortunately, this made them an attractive source of food for pirates and whalers in the 18th and 19th centuries because the tortoises were simple to capture, they provided a lot of meat, and they could be stored alive on ships over long voyages.

Today there are only about 15,000 giant tortoises left alive. Three of the fourteen subspecies are now completely extinct. A fourth subspecies has only one single member left, who is known as "lonesome George." Efforts to find a female mate for George have thus far been unsuccessful. When George dies, it will likely mark the extinction of a fourth species.

expedition *(n)*:
an organized journey with a purpose

respective *(adj)*:
belonging to or relating to each person or thing mentioned

evolution *(n)*:
the change in living organisms — changing to suit the environments or surroundings

predator *(n)*:
an animal that hunts or eats other animals

whaler *(n)*:
a person or ship that hunts and kills whales

George lives at the Charles Darwin Research Station on Santa Cruz Island, an environmental preservation center established in 1959. One of their major goals is to safeguard the populations of giant tortoises on the islands. Many populations are still under threat from foreign animals that were introduced to the islands by the Europeans. Dogs, rats, and pigs eat their eggs and young. Larger animals, such as donkeys, cattle, and goats step on their nests and eat their food sources. There are even still instances of humans killing the tortoises: roughly 120 tortoises have been poached from the island of Isabella since 1990.

To combat this, the Research Station runs a repopulation program. Eggs are taken from the wild and hatched at the Research Station. The young are released back into the wild after they are big enough to survive attacks from other animals. The program has enjoyed some success and has safeguarded the populations of several of the islands. However, the future of the Galapagos Islands and its unique forms of life is far from certain. Non-native animal species and human activities, such as fishing, continue to threaten this once isolated ecosystem.

preservation (n):
a place that protects endangered and rare animals

safeguard (v):
to protect; to ensure the safety of

instance (n):
an example

hatch (v):
to break out of an egg

isolated (adj):
remote; standing alone or apart

1. Which of the following could best replace the word "ground" as used in paragraph 1?

   (A) Dry land
   (B) Area
   (C) Floor
   (D) Soil

2. The expression "flora and fauna" in paragraph 2 is closest in meaning to

   (A) hills and mountains
   (B) rivers and lakes
   (C) birds and mammals
   (D) plants and animals

3. The word "that" in paragraph 6 line 4 refers to

   (A) the animals introduced by Europeans
   (B) the Galapagos Islands
   (C) the threat to the tortoises
   (D) the populations of tortoises

4. Why does the author mention that there were originally 100,000 tortoises?

   (A) To emphasize the surprising number that led to Darwin's theory
   (B) To contrast it with the small number alive today
   (C) To point out the breeding capabilities of the tortoise
   (D) To indicate their high value as a food source

5. How long was Charles Darwin a visitor on the Galapagos Islands?

   (A) About 4 months
   (B) 12 days
   (C) 5 weeks
   (D) Over 3 years

6. According to the passage, why were tortoises hunted by pirates and whalers?

   (A) Because they lasted a long time on boats
   (B) Because their meat was prized as a delicacy
   (C) Because they were exciting to hunt
   (D) Because the pirates used their shells as shields

7. Which predators still eat the giant tortoises?

   (A) Dogs, cats, wolves, and seals
   (B) Humans, rats, goats, and hawks
   (C) Pigs, goats, seals, and cats
   (D) Dogs, rats, humans, and pigs

8. What does the last paragraph in the passage mainly discuss?

   (A) Efforts to protect the giant tortoises
   (B) Dangers to the giant tortoises
   (C) Tourism and giant tortoises
   (D) The mating habits of the giant tortoises

9. Look at the four squares [■] that indicate where the following sentence could be added to paragraph 4:

   Also, larger male tortoises usually win in the competition for female mates.

   Where would the sentence best fit? Choose the square [■] where the sentence should be added to the passage.

   (A) Line 3
   (B) Line 4
   (C) Line 5
   (D) Line 6

10. Based on the information in paragraph 1, what can be inferred about the ship's voyage?

(A) The ship's mission was to chart the Pacific Ocean.

(B) The voyage lasted longer than was originally planned.

(C) The ship was attacked by pirates on the voyage.

(D) Charles Darwin was a famous scientist at the time.

11. According to the passage, which is NOT true?

(A) The Spanish used the tortoise shells to make saddles.

(B) Horses sometimes step on the nests of giant tortoises.

(C) Darwin based his theories on his observations in Galapagos.

(D) There is only one survivor of the fourth tortoise subspecies.

12. Directions: *An introductory sentence for a brief summary of the passage is provided below. Complete the summary by selecting the THREE answer choices that express the most important ideas in the passage. Some sentences do not belong in the summary because they express ideas that are not presented in the passage or are minor ideas in the passage.*

First Sentence: **Charles Darwin, upon visiting the Galapagos islands in 1831, observed the slight differences in species native to the area and came up with the idea of evolution.**

(A) Pirates had long used the archipelago as a hideout.

(B) These days, the Galapagos are a government-protected natural park, ensuring the survival of many unique species including the giant tortoise.

(C) These giant tortoises can weigh as much as 250 kilograms.

(D) Scientists estimate that more than 100,000 tortoises lived in the Galapagos at the time of Darwin's arrival.

(E) In the years since Darwin arrived on the island, the population of the giant tortoises has decreased dramatically.

(F) To help protect the animals, the Charles Darwin Research Station runs a repopulation program.

Chapter 2

Long Passage Skill Practice

Understanding Details

Strategy

- Within the text, there is usually a paraphrase of a sentence with different wording but a similar meaning. Try to find the paraphrase by looking at the meaning of the sentences.
- Look for sections in the text that use similar language or expressions to the question choices. Read the sentences around these sections.
- It is important to look at the transitions within the passage. They can give you key information within the text and point you toward the answers.
- Choose the statement that is definitely mentioned in the passage. Though another statement may be based on fact, it is not the correct answer unless it is explicitly stated in the passage.
- Eliminate the obviously incorrect answer choices when you have difficulty finding the correct answer.

Transitions

Explanation	in fact, in this case
Cause	because of, since, for, due to, owing to
Clarification	for example, as in the case of, such (as), most, some, others
Comparison	both, the same, similar to, like, as ___ as
Contrast	but, however, although, even though, while, whereas, in contrast, conversely, on the other hand
Result	consequently, subsequently, therefore, then, hence, as a result
Addition	also, too, as well as, furthermore, moreover, in addition, what's more, additionally
Time or Duration	during the 1980s, in the mid-'20s, for many decades, until the end of the century

The Industrial Revolution was not a war, although it can certainly be argued that there were casualties of this revolution much like in other revolutions. Rather than a war, the Industrial Revolution was a period of social change in England that marked a major turning point in the country's history. It was a stage during which English society shifted from an agricultural and labor-based economy to an industrial and manufacturing economy.

It is actually more precise to think of the Industrial Revolution as occurring in two waves. The first wave, known as the First Industrial Revolution, began in the late 1700s and ended around 1830. Key developments during this time were innovations that boosted production in textiles and the first coal-powered steam engines used in iron production. The ending date of the First Industrial Revolution cannot be pinpointed because the second wave, the Second Industrial Revolution, came out of the first and blurs the cut-off between the two. It is definite, however, that by 1850 the Second Industrial Revolution was gaining momentum, and this later revolution would continue through the second half of the 19th century. Differences that marked this second revolution as distinct from the first were the introduction of steam-powered forms of transportation (both ships and trains), followed by the development of internal combustion engines and electrical generators.

In studying the Industrial Revolution, a natural question one might begin with is, "Why did the Industrial Revolution occur in England rather than in another country?" Although the question itself is simple enough, the answer is far from easy to establish. Historians continue to debate the primary cause (or causes) that triggered the Industrial Revolution in England.

As a method of examining some of the causes that historians believe played a critical role in setting events in motion in England as opposed to somewhere else, consider the differences that existed in the late 1700s between England and France. Probably three of the most important differences that appear directly linked to the Industrial Revolution are each country's cities and resources, agricultural production, and local and international markets.

The late 1700s was a time of turmoil in Europe, especially in France. In fact, the end of the 18th century and beginning of the 19th century was a period of over 20 years of continuous warfare in France, including fighting during the French Revolution followed by the battles of the

casualty *(n)*:
a victim; a death

wave *(n)*:
a spreading trend that involves many people

boost *(v)*:
to make higher or greater

textiles *(n)*:
fabrics, especially of the kinds used for clothes

pinpoint *(v)*:
to locate or indicate exactly

blur *(v)*:
to make unclear or difficult to see

momentum *(n)*:
the driving force behind a course of events or an idea

combustion *(n)*:
the process of burning

trigger *(v)*:
to set off; to begin

turmoil *(n)*:
a state of extreme confusion or disorder

agricultural *(adj)*:
related to farming

Napoleonic Wars. Not only were cities and the countryside of France damaged by these wars, but many other parts of Europe suffered as well. England, on the other hand emerged from this bloody period of European history relatively unharmed. Therefore, England, unlike the other countries across Europe, did not need to divert its resources toward rebuilding cities or otherwise repairing the wartime damage to its farmlands or forests. Instead, England was in a position to take full advantage economically of the latest industrial innovations that came to light at that time.

A major change in England's agricultural production is also believed to have been a catalyst for the Industrial Revolution. At the beginning of the 1700s, as new ideas in farming were implemented in England, food production became much more efficient. Additionally, one aspect of these new ideas involved "enclosing" farmland owned by poor farmers as part of larger farms in order to grow more crops more efficiently. The poor farmers who lost their lands found themselves out of work; thus, there came into existence in England a ready population suitable for employment in the new factories that would spring up across the country. Also, as food production became more efficient, food prices dropped, and more and more middle-class families found themselves with money to spend on manufactured goods, further fueling the growth of factories. In France, by contrast, taxes required of farmers simply to move goods from region to region within the country kept food prices high and agricultural innovation minimal. Such conditions in France did nothing to support industrial development.

A third notable difference between England and France at the time of the First Industrial Revolution was England's ability to ship goods to other markets. Due to the wars in Europe, England had the only useful merchant fleet worth mentioning at the time. This allowed England's economy to build even greater momentum with regard to the country's industrial growth. As new industrial technology produced more goods more efficiently, exports kept the money flowing in; money which could then be utilized to research and develop even better technology.

come to light (v phrase): to come to public attention

catalyst (n): something that triggers a process or an event

implement (v): to use

fuel (v): to support or stimulate

1. The author mentions the change in England's agricultural production as an example of
   (A) a possible cause of the First Industrial Revolution
   (B) a result of innovations introduced during the First Industrial Revolution
   (C) the biggest advantage for the country by the end of the Second Industrial Revolution
   (D) the event that marked the transition between the First and Second Industrial Revolutions

2. According to the passage, which of the following is true about France in the early part of the 19th century?
   (A) It had a large merchant fleet and exported many products to other countries.
   (B) It was more advanced than England.
   (C) It had certain laws for farmers that England didn't have.
   (D) It was expanding its power and adding colonies faster than England at that time.

3. The phrase "spring up" in the passage is closest in meaning to
   (A) appear suddenly
   (B) become upright
   (C) grow out of the ground
   (D) jump up

4. The word "natural" in paragraph 3 of the passage means
   (A) expected
   (B) not artificial
   (C) primitive
   (D) produced by nature

5. **Directions:** *Complete the table by matching the phrases below. Select the appropriate phrases from the answer choices and match them to the country that they describe. TWO of the answer choices will NOT be used.*

England	France
C, E, F, G	
	B-D-H

   (A) 20 years of continuous production
   (B) damaged farmlands and forests
   (C) First Industrial Revolution
   (D) little money to invest in innovations
   (E) many out-of-work farmers
   (F) merchant fleet
   (G) Second Industrial Revolution
   (H) taxes to move products between regions
   (I) the most advanced universities

Two significant terms associated with computers are "bit" and "byte." These refer to the numbering system computers use to translate digits into letters and characters. Bit is an abbreviation of "binary digit," referring to the base-2 system used in computer coding. Instead of the decimal digits 0 through 9 that comprise a base-10 system, computer code consists of only two digits: 0 and 1. Each of these digits is a bit — the smallest unit of information that can be stored or manipulated on a computer. By combining bits in thousands of different ways, computer programmers direct computers to process words, calculate numbers, and perform various other functions.

Computers are composed of digital electronics, so they respond to two kinds of electrical states. These states could be called "on" and "off," true and false, positive voltage and negative voltage, or some other paired combination of terms. It doesn't matter, as long as there are two conditions. The bits 0 and 1 represent these conditions. Two bits can combine to represent up to four different decimal numbers. Imagine bits in terms of switches. Two switches can yield the following: 0 0 (off off) = decimal number 0; 0 1 (off on) = decimal 1; 1 0 (on, off) = decimal 2; and 1 1 (on on) = decimal 3. Adding a third bit (another 1) to the left-hand side produces eight different decimal numbers: 0 through 7 (100 = 4; 101 = 5; 110 = 6; 111 = 7). Four bits can represent 16 numbers (0 through 15). Five bits can represent 32 numbers (0 through 31). Each added bit doubles the number of possible combinations of 0s and 1s. Eight bits are called a byte, which represents 256 numbers (0 through 255).

A byte usually represents a single character of data in a computer. Grouping bits into bytes enables the computer to more easily interpret the continuous string of information it receives. A byte is also the amount of bits needed to represent letters of the alphabet and other characters. Special codes enable the computer to recognize eight-digit binary strings as letters of the alphabet. For instance, under a common computer code called ASCII (American Standard Code for Information Interchange), the letter "A" is expressed as 65. This converts to the binary number 01000001. Computers recognize these eight bits, or one byte, as "A."

Computers interpret any character typed on the keyboard as a byte. Each byte is assigned a specific ASCII character, such as 65 noted above for "A." Computers store text documents, both in memory and

digit (n):
a symbol used in a system of counting

comprise (v):
to make up; to compose

state (n):
a condition; a mode of being

voltage (n):
a measure of electrical force or difference between positive and negative charges

switch (n):
a device which turns a machine or electrical equipment on and off

enable (v):
to supply with a means; to make able

string (n):
a series of similar related things

express (v):
to communicate; to depict

READING

LISTENING

SPEAKING

WRITING

PRACTICE TEST

on disk, using these ASCII character codes. For each letter typed into a text file, the computer uses one byte of memory — including one byte for each space between the words (ASCII character number 32 represents a space). So, for instance, the sentence "I am studying for the final exam," consists of 32 bytes: 26 letters and six spaces between the words. When the sentence is stored on a file on disk, the file will also contain 32 bytes.

One area in which it's easy to confuse bits and bytes is monitoring data transfer speed. For example, when you download a file from the Internet, your browser indicates the transfer rate in KBps (kilobytes per second). Note that the letter "B" is capitalized. This indicates kilobytes. Many computer modems have a speed of 56K. The K stands for Kbps. But note that the "b" in this instance is lower case. This means kilobits per second. Since eight bits equals one byte, we can divide 56 by eight to derive a maximum download speed: 7 Kilobytes per second (7KBps). Thus, if you download a document at a transfer rate of 3.5 KBps, you are using 50 percent of the maximum transfer speed.

Another area where bits and bytes are often confused is measuring computer memory storage capacity. Early computer manufacturers stated memory capacity in terms of kilobytes. However, they were using kilo as a decimal system prefix, in which it means 1,000. In a binary system, the prefix kilo means 1,024. Bearing this distinction in mind, a computer described as having 64K (64 Kilobytes) of memory can actually store 655,360 bytes (640 x 1,024) of data. Those extra bytes may come in handy for people who need to create and store a large number of computer documents.

transfer *(v)*:
to send

browser *(n)*:
a program that locates and displays sites or information on the Internet

lower case *(adj)*:
small letter; not capital

capacity *(n)*:
the amount that can be contained

bear in mind *(v phrase)*:
to remember; to keep in mind

1. According to the passage, which of the following is true about bits?

   (A) They are larger than bytes.
   (B) They are the digits 1 and 2.
   (C) They are units of information.
   (D) They are an abbreviation of decimal digits.

2. According to the passage, how does a computer recognize the letter "A"?

   (A) As 65
   (B) As a binary number
   (C) As 01000000
   (D) As a group of bytes

3. The word "derive" in the passage is closest in meaning to

   (A) obtain
   (B) invent
   (C) purchase
   (D) guess

4. The word "data" could best be replaced by which of the following?

   (A) Code
   (B) Number
   (C) Material
   (D) Information

5. **Directions:** *Complete the table below about bits and bytes discussed in the passage. Match the appropriate statements to the category to which they are associated. TWO of the answer choices will NOT be used.*

Bit	Byte

   (A) consists of 8 digits
   (B) binary digit
   (C) represents 256 numbers
   (D) single character of data in computer
   (E) base-10 system
   (F) helps hold and store text documents
   (G) smallest unit of information in a computer

Ansel Adams was born in San Francisco, California in 1902. Although he became famous as a photographer and visual artist, he showed an early talent for music. In fact, in his youth, he taught himself to play the piano. As a child, Adams had difficulty adapting to the structure of formal education, and he actually dropped out of school for a year when he was in middle school. During this break from schooling, Adams spent his time at the World's Fair, which was being hosted in San Francisco that year. His father bought Adams a pass so that he could attend the fair as many times as he liked during the year. Adams put the pass to good use, repeatedly visiting the modern art exhibit and musical performances at the fair.

In 1916, Adams visited Yosemite National Park on a trip with his family. Although none of Adams's family realized it at the time, it would be this park that Adams's name would forever be associated with. On the trip, Adams took his first pictures of the natural beauty of Yosemite. In particular, the mountain range running through the park drew the young photographer's eye. From that summer on, Adams visited the park every year. Somewhat surprisingly, by the time he was 23, Adams had decided to become a concert pianist, though his life would eventually take a very different course.

In 1930, a meeting with the photographer Paul Strand inspired Adams to dedicate the rest of his life to photography and environmental preservation. Looking back now from the vantage point of today, this was obviously the right choice for the young man. To this day, Adams's most famous photos are of natural, sweeping landscapes of the American West, especially his photographs of Yosemite. Adams was highly praised for the technical quality and detail of his photographs. He attributed these to his special approach to photography, the Zone System.

The Zone System is undeniably Adams's greatest contribution to fine art photography. This calculated and highly controlled system allows photographers to plan the final composition of a shot before taking a picture. Photographers could then become more "creatively expressive," in Adams's words, rather than simply recording the scene that the camera was aimed at. The Zone System allows photographers to manipulate color tones without distorting the essential image. For example, a photograph of a sand dune could be altered to become, in effect, a sharply contrasting black-and-white abstract composition. Or a lonely tree along the shore of a lake could be brought into high contrast

adapt *(v):*
to change to fit a particular environment

structure *(n):*
the way something is set up to operate

exhibit *(n):*
a public showing

vantage point *(n):*
the place one looks from

technical *(adj):*
related to the use of science or a scientific method

attribute *(v):*
to relate to a particular source or cause

approach *(n):*
a method; a way of doing

contribution *(n):*
a benefit or useful thing that is added

distort *(v):*
to change from the natural or original state

manipulate *(v):*
to control

abstract *(adj):*
not of the physical world; not concrete

with its background. It could appear as if in a spotlight against a dimmer, floating background. Through development of the Zone System, Adams provided photographers finer control of both the optical and mechanical aspects of photography, on par with the control painters have through their brushes and palettes.

Adams went beyond simply contributing new ideas to the art and process of photography. He also made many concrete contributions to the field. Adams helped found several departments of artistic photography at museums and universities across the US. In fact, Adams was the co-founder of the world's first museum department of photography at the Museum of Modern Art, or MoMA, in New York. Additionally, he was the driving force behind the establishment of the photography program at the San Francisco Museum of Modern Art, SFMoMA. Adams was also founder and president of the f/64 photographer's group. Along with his continued work as a professional photographer, Adams also served as a university lecturer, member of President Johnson's Environmental Task Force, and a fellow in the American Academy of Sciences.

Adams died in 1982 at the age of 80. On the one-year anniversary of his death, an 11,760-foot mountain on the southwestern border of Yosemite National Park was officially named Mount Ansel Adams in honor of his life-long dedication to the preservation of nature.

aspect *(n)*:
a feature or element

founder *(n)*:
a person who establishes an institution or organization

establishment *(n)*:
the setting up; the founding

task force *(n)*:
a group that is given the job to accomplish a certain job or solve a certain problem

1. According to the passage, what did Adams dedicate his life to?

   (A) Exploration and chemistry
   (B) Modern art mountaineering
   (C) Education and technical perfection
   (D) Nature and photography

2. According to the passage, which is NOT true?

   (A) He won photography competitions at a young age.
   (B) He left school for a year at the age of thirteen.
   (C) He loved music and taught himself to play the piano.
   (D) He visited Yosemite National Park with his family.

3. What is the meaning of the word "sweeping" as used in paragraph 3?

   (A) Dusting
   (B) Vast
   (C) Dangerous
   (D) Flying

4. Which of the following is closest is meaning to "found" in paragraph 5?

   (A) Implement
   (B) Discovered
   (C) Establish
   (D) Salvaged

5. **Directions:** *An introductory sentence for a brief summary of the passage is provided below. Complete the summary by selecting the THREE answer choices that express the most important ideas in the passage. Some sentences do not belong in the summary because they express ideas that are not presented in the passage or are minor ideas in the passage.*

   First sentence: **Ansel Adams was both an influential photographer and conservationist.**

   (A) Adams developed the Zone System for photographers.
   (B) He never achieved his dream of becoming a musician.
   (C) Adams worked for one summer in Yosemite National Park.
   (D) He learned the art of photography from Paul Strand.
   (E) Adams was instrumental in setting up photography departments in both museums and universities.
   (F) His most famous photos are of natural objects and landscapes.

Stress caused by worry is both useful and problematic for people. How can it be both useful and problematic? Consider the stress some people feel when they worry about the future. Worrying about the future, though unpleasant, motivates us to get things done. We strive to accomplish certain tasks today in order to avoid unpleasant outcomes later. This would be an example of how stress actually serves a useful purpose.

However, sometimes worry can have the opposite effect. Let us again take the example of worrying about the future. As discussed above, a certain level of worry can help us accomplish the tasks at hand. But some people experience a significantly higher level of stress brought on by worry. This is when worry turns into fear or anxiety, and although many people might understand fear and anxiety as the same thing, psychologists define these two emotions differently.

Basically, fear can be understood as a normal, healthy reaction to one's situation. Anxiety, on the other hand, is typically associated with an unhealthy mental state. An additional distinction between fear and anxiety can be seen in their sources. The source of fear can be named or described. It might be an important test that is coming up, or it could be a large black spider on the wall. In contrast, anxiety is not based on a describable source. When you ask a person exhibiting the symptoms of extreme stress or worry about the cause of their distress, they cannot name it. Needless to say, such imagined, indefinable causes of anxiety and any effort to solve or avoid these problems are a waste of energy.

Other than such negative effects as consuming energy and causing distraction, too much anxiety can cause people to feel overwhelmed. A person's anxiety might actually hinder his or her ability to take any action, and in severe cases, the person may be unable to even leave home. When the quality of a person's life is seriously affected by their feelings of anxiety, they are said to be suffering from an anxiety disorder. There are several types of disorders, the most common being specific phobias such as fear of spiders or fear of heights. This is not a really big problem, so long as the feared situation is not important to the person's life. However, more serious anxiety disorders can be accompanied by symptoms that affect a person's physical health.

When someone suffers severe physical symptoms of anxiety, it is called a panic attack. A panic attack is a sudden and intense onset of fear. As for the symptoms that accompany such an attack, the person

outcome *(n)*:
a result

significantly *(adv)*:
considerably; quite

mental *(adj)*:
related to the mind

distinction *(n)*:
a difference; a point of uniqueness

source *(n)*:
the origin; the cause

exhibit *(v)*:
to show

indefinable *(adj)*:
not able to be defined or described

symptom *(n)*:
a sign of an illness or problem

intense *(adj)*:
very strong; extreme

onset *(n)*:
the beginning; the first stage

disorder *(n)*:
a problem that affects the mind or body

accompany *(v)*:
to appear with; to be associated with

may experience shortness of breath, sweating, trembling, or even an irregular heartbeat. These symptoms may cause the panic to become worse because the symptoms are so frightening for the individual. Obviously, a panic attack is a very unpleasant experience that the person does not want to repeat. For this reason, the individual develops even greater anxiety about having another panic attack.

Anxiety disorders are serious conditions. They are not only unpleasant emotionally for the individual, but they also make it very difficult for the person to have relationships and to maintain employment. Anxiety disorders can have disastrous effects on a person's life and the way that the person functions in society. However, the good news is that, of all mental disorders, anxiety disorder has the highest rate of effective treatment.

maintain (v):
to keep; to continue

1. Which of the following is NOT a symptom described of panic attacks?

(A) Shortness of breath
(B) Shaking
(C) Sweating
(D) Nausea

2. What is anxiety, according to the passage?

(A) Worry about the future
(B) Fear of certain situations
(C) Fear of panic attacks
(D) Irrational fear

3. Which of the following is closest in meaning to "motivates" in paragraph 1?

(A) Causes
(B) Prompts → want to do it.
(C) Persuades
(D) Discourages

4. Which of the following could best replace the word "consuming" as used in paragraph 4?

(A) Destroying
(B) Eating
(C) Producing
(D) Draining

5. Directions: *Complete the table below about the mental states discussed in the passage. Match the appropriate statements to the feeling with which they are associated. TWO of the answers will NOT be used.*

Fear	Anxiety
B	E

(A) cannot be treated
(B) is healthy
(C) source can be named
(D) is unhealthy
(E) source cannot be named
(F) is used to treat panic attacks
(G) wastes energy

Industrialized nations are typically divided into three main groups: the US, Western Europe, and East Asia. The group defined as Western Europe includes such countries as England, France, and Germany while East Asia includes highly developed Asian countries such as South Korea and Japan. Other nations around the world do not fit so easily into these three groups. For example, one might expand "the US" group to become North America, and thus include Canada in industrialized countries of that region. However, what should one do with such countries as Australia and Singapore? For all intents and purposes, both of these countries should be classified together with other industrialized countries of the world. However, Australia in particular seems an oddity when lumped together with the other industrialized countries of East Asia. It is not so much the level of industrialization that sets Australia apart. Rather, it is Australia's social similarity with the countries of Western Europe that marks it as different within the region. When viewed collectively by groups, the societies of these three groupings of industrialized countries differ markedly in many respects.

Consider, for instance, the role of women in society within each of the three groups: the US, Western Europe, and East Asia. East Asia has the highest rate of gender integration in the workforce, meaning women can be found working alongside men in more types of occupations. This is attributed to a tradition from the past of women in East Asian societies participating in manual labor. On the other hand, East Asia also has the greatest disparity between men's and women's wages. Although women may work alongside men in a certain occupation, men are typically paid higher wages than women doing the same job. Western Europe is the opposite. Workplace statistics indicate that across Europe there exists the best gender pay ratio between men and women; however, Europe also has the lowest level of workforce integration for women. In other words, men and women in the same occupations can expect to receive the same wages, but in reality, there are far fewer women than men in the European workforce. The US falls in the middle. The rate of gender integration in the workforce is higher than Europe's rate but lower than East Asia's rate, and disparity between wages for men and women is less than that found in East Asia but greater than the disparity found in Europe.

In general, Female LFP (Labor Force Participation) has been on the rise in all industrialized countries for quite some time, while male LFP

expand *(v)*:
to increase; to widen

region *(n)*:
an area

role *(n)*:
a position; a function

gender *(n)*:
either male or female

integration *(n)*:
the act of placing or bringing into

alongside *(prep)*:
beside; with

occupation *(n)*:
a job; paid work

tradition *(n)*:
thoughts or behaviors followed by a group of people generation after generation

participate *(v)*:
to take part; to do together

manual labor *(n)*:
work done with the hands

has been declining. One factor to account for this change would be the improvement in social support for working women in industrialized countries. Women receive the best system of social support in Western Europe, led by Sweden where they receive one year of maternity leave with 75% pay. By comparison, working women in the US typically receive twelve weeks of maternity leave with no pay. It should be noted, however, that the greater social support for women in Western Europe may also be linked to the lower rate of workforce integration of women. This is due to the fact that social security nets for maternity often affect women's chances of employment or career advancement. A company is less likely to hire a female for an important position since they may be forced to replace her and give her extended paid leave if she becomes pregnant.

Surprisingly, the United States, in many senses the most industrialized country, has more in common with less industrialized countries (also called Third World countries) than with the industrialized nations of Western Europe and East Asia. The US has some of the highest rates of unwanted pregnancy, sexually transmitted diseases, and abortions in the world. This is attributed to such characteristics of US society as its unequal distribution of wealth, and its lack of access to health care for the poor. These conditions are also commonly found in Third World countries.

link (v):
to connect; to associate with

social security (n):
a government program that helps people who lose their jobs or who can't work for some reason

maternity (adj):
related to the time that a woman is pregnant or the first months of motherhood

transmitted (adj):
passed; caused to spread

abortion (n):
the ending of a pregnancy before a baby is able to survive outside of the mother

1. According to the passage, what is the reason for greater East Asian work force integration?

   (A) A reaction to European policies
   (B) A strong women's right movement
   (C) A gap in the labor market
   (D) A tradition of integration

2. Why is it more difficult for women to find upper level jobs in Western Europe?

   (A) Traditional social prejudices against female working ability
   (B) Outdated laws giving preference to male job candidates
   (C) Fewer of these positions are available in general in Europe
   (D) Laws requiring companies to give women extended maternity leave

3. Which of the following means most nearly the same as "markedly" as used in paragraph 1?

   (A) Visibly
   (B) Distinctly
   (C) Surprisingly
   (D) Considerably

4. The word "disparity" in paragraph 2 could best be replaced by which of the following?

   (A) Hopelessness
   (B) Difference
   (C) Injustice
   (D) Authority

5. **Directions:** *An introductory sentence for a brief summary of the passage is provided below. Complete the summary by selecting the THREE answer choices that express the most important ideas in the passage. Some sentences do not belong in the summary because they express ideas that are not presented in the passage or are minor ideas in the passage.*

First sentence: **Industrialized countries may be categorized into three large groups, and the countries included within each group share certain similar characteristics.**

   (A) Australia is not classified as an industrialized country because it is different from other countries in Asia.
   (B) Industrialized countries in East Asia have high gender integration in the workforce but large wage disparities between men's and women's wages.
   (C) Industrialized countries of Western Europe have low gender integration in the workforce but small wage disparities between men's and women's wages.
   (D) The US shares some striking similarities with Third World countries, unlike other industrialized countries.
   (E) Industrialized countries of East Asia have low gender integration in the workforce and large wage disparities between men's and women's wages.
   (F) Industrialized countries of Western Europe have high gender integration in the workforce and excellent social support for working women.

Strategy

- Understand the original sentence accurately.
- Read around the original sentence for clear understanding. The sentences before or after the original sentence often contain key words or phrases that the original sentence refers to.
- Learn to recognize what makes a paraphrase a paraphrase.
  ⇨ Paraphrases are usually shorter than the original sentences from the passage.
  ⇨ Paraphrases should include all of the essential information from the original sentence.
  ⇨ In paraphrases, it is uncommon to use the same vocabulary as in the original. Choices that use the same vocabulary as the original, then, are NOT proper paraphrases.
  ⇨ Paraphrases often change the structure of a sentence. Learn to recognize when the structure has changed but the original meaning has remained.
  ⇨ In paraphrases, pronouns are often changed into the nouns they refer to in the original sentence. Look carefully at each noun in the paraphrase and decide which pronoun in the original text refers to it.

  Example: It exports ninety-seven percent of its wool to Japan, Europe, and China.

  Paraphrase: European countries, along with Japan and China, import 97 percent of Australia's wool.

  "It" and "its" in the original sentence refer to Australia, so the paraphrase replaces these words with "Australia."

Listed among the endangered bird species of North America is the whooping crane. This species of crane is actually the tallest bird in North America, at 1.5 meters. The birds get their name from their distinctive "whooping" call.

Biologists estimate that originally there were about 1,500 cranes living in the southern United States in the late 1800s. However, by the 1940s, this number had dwindled to a mere 16! The dramatic decrease in the number of whooping cranes in North America was linked to a number of reasons. During the late 1800s and early 1900s, more and more immigrants were pouring into the United States and settling across the southern and western parts of the country. The encroachment of human populations into the wetland habitats destroyed much of the whooping cranes' feeding grounds. The birds were also easy targets for hunters before they were placed on the US endangered species list. Finally, there is the natural limitation of cranes hatched each year. Female whooping cranes lay only two eggs per year. Typically, only one of these manages to survive the first stages of life and the long migration south to the cranes' winter feeding grounds. Because a female crane may only produce a single offspring each year, should any of the offspring die, the total population of cranes suffers.

It is interesting to consider that, for a long time, no one knew much about whooping crane reproduction simply because biologists could not find their nests. The whereabouts of the cranes' nesting grounds wasn't discovered until 1954. By luck, a pilot spotted two cranes in northern Canada, and the nesting grounds of the cranes were finally located. Amazingly, whooping cranes make a 4,000 kilometer journey every year from Texas to Canada in order to summer and nest in the north. Today, a network of people communicating via the Internet continues to monitor and track whooping crane migration every year.

Since being placed on the endangered species list, the whooping crane population of North America has increased. However, the fate of the species is still at great risk. Today, only one wild flock of whooping cranes exists in the whole of North America. The main concern for conservationists is that a disease or disaster could wipe out this flock, and then only human-bred, non-migrating groups of whooping cranes would remain. In order to breed more whooping cranes, scientists took eggs from crane nests in Canada and hatched the young in Florida. Part of this human-bred flock in central Florida is currently being

distinctive (adj):
characteristic; distinguishing

dwindle (v):
to decrease almost to zero

dramatic (adj):
surprising; startling

trace (v):
to follow clues to the source or cause

immigrant (n):
a person who moves to settle in a new country

encroachment (n):
the act of advancing beyond a border or limit

hatch (v):
to cause to produce eggs and young

migration (n):
a journey to seasonal feeding grounds

offspring (n):
young

network (n):
an interconnected group of people who are in communication with each other

via (prep):
by way of; by means of

monitor (v):
to watch in order to note changes in

conservationist (n):
a person who works to save or conserve natural resources

breed (v):
to cause to reproduce

flock (n):
a group of birds

trained to migrate in an attempt to develop a second migrating flock of cranes. Biologists dress in crane costumes to work with the birds. Then, each summer, a small, light plane leads the cranes to a nesting ground in Wisconsin. The plane also leads the cranes back to Florida during the winter migration. It is hoped that in the future, the older cranes of the flock will train the younger cranes to follow this migration pattern without the aid of the plane.

Through the efforts of biologists over the past fifty years, whooping cranes have made progress, though much work remains to be done. The two migrating flocks of cranes, the eastern migratory flock in Florida and the wild western migratory flock from Texas, still number less than 350. The fate of the wild North American whooping crane remains at risk.

1. What does the last paragraph mainly discuss?
   (A) The creation of the Eastern flock of whooping cranes
   (B) Projections for the future of whooping crane survival
   (C) The dangers posed by humans to crane populations
   (D) The use of aircraft in wildlife conservation projects

2. Which of the sentences below best expresses the essential information in the highlighted sentence in the passage? *Incorrect* choices change the meaning in important ways or leave out essential information.
   (A) In most cases, one of the young whooping cranes begins its first stage of life during the migration to the winter feeding grounds.
   (B) In order to survive the first stages of life, a young whooping crane often must first travel from the winter feeding grounds south.
   (C) Of the two offspring, one usually dies either during the first weeks or during the difficult migration south for the winter.
   (D) One egg does not hatch because the mother crane migrates before the egg matures.

3. The expression "wipe out" in paragraph 4 is closest in meaning to
   (A) purify
   (B) disperse
   (C) infiltrate
   (D) eradicate

4. The word "remain" in paragraph 4 is closest in meaning to
   (A) inhabit
   (B) linger
   (C) survive
   (D) wait

5. **Directions:** *Complete the table below about the crane flocks discussed in the passage. Match the appropriate statements to the category with which they are associated. TWO of the answer choices will NOT be used.*

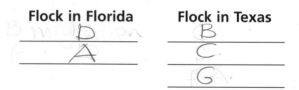

Flock in Florida	Flock in Texas
D	B
A	C
	G

   (A) All female
   (B) Migrating
   (C) Nesting grounds in Canada
   (D) Nesting grounds in Wisconsin
   (E) Non-migrating
   (F) Used to make costumes
   (G) Wild

READING

LISTENING

SPEAKING

WRITING

PRACTICE TEST

Laissez-Faire is a French phrase meaning literally "let do, let pass," which has been applied to the principles of economics. Laissez-faire economic theory holds that individuals should be allowed to pursue their own interests with as little government intervention as possible. It was popularized in English-speaking countries in the 18th and 19th centuries by Adam Smith (1723-1790), who was both a philosopher and economist and is considered to be the "father of modern economics."

Smith sought to understand and explain the market system of his time. He felt that a majority of people saw confusion when they observed economic activity in England during the middle of the 18th century. At the time it seemed that almost everyone was doing, economically, whatever they pleased and deemed necessary. Businesses produced whatever they wanted to make. Consumers purchased whatever they wanted to buy. People didn't tell each other what had to be bought and what had to be sold, especially not the government. And yet, somehow, businesses seemed to be providing the goods and services that consumers wanted and needed. Some might have called this luck; Adam Smith called it an "invisible hand." Today, this economic concept is called the laissez-faire economy.

The "invisible hand" is a term for the unseen process of co-ordination which ensures consistency of individual plans in a decentralized market economy. Adam Smith introduced this phrase in his book, *An Inquiry into the Nature and Causes of the Wealth of Nations*, in which he stressed the role that the invisible hand played in attaining a harmony of interests.

Imagine this invisible hand suspended above everyone. This invisible hand encourages businesspeople to pursue profits, and it pushes consumers to buy goods and services. And at the same time, that invisible hand discourages government from directing the economic activity.

The invisible hand that Adam Smith referred to as a guiding force was the people and their attitudes. It all started with profit-seeking individuals. Using self-interest to feed their drive, people started businesses. When a business would become successful, others would notice and enter into the same field. As a direct result, growing consumer demand was satisfied while competition controlled rising prices. As demand grew, businesses were established in which workers shared tasks. This is called division of labor, in which one worker handled the first stage, another the second, and a third finished the product. The result was mass production, more efficiency, and lower costs. Mass production meant

intervention (n):
the act of coming between in order to control or help

popularize (v):
to make popular; to increase acceptance of

ensure (v):
to guarantee; to make certain

decentralized (adj):
having power or control spread among several points

attain (v):
to get; to reach

drive (n):
a force that pushes or gives power to something

that people no longer had to grow their own food and remain on the farm; there would be enough to supply a large workforce. Paying all those laborers resulted in an army of consumers with money to spend.

Adam Smith argued that an individual acting purely out of self-interest would be a progressive force for the maximization of the total wealth of a nation. He maintained that the role of the government should be permissive; creating a legal defensive setup sufficient to allow individual action. Interference with the free working of this natural order, he felt, would reduce the growth of wealth and misdirect resources.

Though Smith argued for laissez-faire, he recognized the need for minimal government intervention, for example, a tariff for infant industries and for the three functions of the state: security, justice, and certain public works. However, he strongly opposed any direct government intervention into business affairs. Trade restrictions, minimum wage laws, and product regulation he viewed as detrimental to a nation's economic health. Smith believed that competition, the market's invisible hand, would lead to proper pricing, and this played a large role in his economic policy recommendations.

His support of competition remained contingent on the fact that it encouraged economic growth, something Smith felt would benefit all members of society. He proposed that, as long as markets grew, an increased demand for labor would prevent owners from exploiting their workers. But he failed to consider that the process of urbanization would wreak havoc on the labor market, and his optimism about growth seemingly ignored the possibility that capitalists might disproportionately consume the benefits of expansion. The inability of growth to substantially increase general living conditions became the primary concern of Smith's intellectual descendants. Despite these concerns, his laissez-faire policy of government non-intervention remained popular throughout the Victorian Era and still plays an important part in present-day economic policy of many countries.

maximization (n):
the act of raising to the highest point or condition

maintain (v):
to say; to declare to be true

permissive (adj):
tolerant; allowing

tariff (n):
a fee or tax applied to certain goods or industries

wage (n):
the money paid to an employee

detrimental (adj):
causing damage or harm

contingent (adj):
dependent; conditional

urbanization (n):
the building of cities or urban areas

wreak havoc (v phrase):
to damage; to disrupt

disproportionately (adv):
to a disproportionate degree; too great or too small when compared to something else

Victorian Era (n phrase):
a period in British history during the reign of Queen Victoria (1837-1901)

Italian mob

1. According to the passage, what are most individuals concerned with?
   - (A) The power of the "invisible hand"
   - (B) The government's role in the distribution of wealth
   - (C) Their own economic self-interests
   - (D) The division of labor

2. Which of the sentences below best expresses the essential information in the highlighted sentence in the passage? *Incorrect* choices change the meaning in important ways or leave out essential information.
   - (A) Despite any rules or regulations, the economy seemed to be functioning effectively.
   - (B) Businesses produced only what was needed.
   - (C) Rules and regulations made it possible for producers and consumers to co-exist.
   - (D) Business dictated the economy.

3. The word "deemed" in paragraph 2 is closest in meaning to
   - (A) conceived
   - (B) made
   - (C) estimated
   - (D) considered

4. The expression "an army" in paragraph 5 is closest in meaning to
   - (A) a mob — *angry / violent.*
   - (B) a large group
   - (C) soldiers
   - (D) a crowd

5. **Directions:** *An introductory sentence for a brief summary of the passage is provided below. Complete the summary by selecting the THREE answer choices that express the most important ideas in the passage. Some sentences do not belong in the summary because they express ideas that are not presented in the passage or are minor ideas in the passage.*

   First sentence: **Adam Smith argued that an economic system functions best when there is little or no interference by the government.**

   - (A) Capitalists consumed most of the benefits of economic expansion.
   - (B) People acting purely out of self-interest would help maximize the total wealth of a nation.
   - (C) Urbanization created a large work-force.
   - (D) The "invisible hand" plays an important part in economic growth.
   - (E) Trade restrictions were not conducive to economic growth.
   - (F) Competition encouraged economic growth.

Perhaps one of the most influential musicians to emerge from the New Orleans jazz scene was Louis Armstrong. Growing up in New Orleans, Armstrong was exposed at an early age to all of the innovative sounds that were coming out of the city. Though he was too poor to buy an instrument, he still listened with fascination to the music around him and was active in the music community. With a small group of other boys, Armstrong would sing on the street for pennies from passersby.

At the age of twelve, Armstrong was arrested for a minor offense, firing a gun into the air in celebration of New Years Eve. As a result, he was sent to a reform school. For most, this kind of experience would have been a tragedy, but for Armstrong it was the beginning of a successful career. In reform school, he learned how to play cornet. For the two years that he was confined to the reform school, he had access to musical instruments and was instructed in the basics of brass technique. This education gave him an "in" to the music scene when he was released two years later. While working in various jobs such as selling papers or loading and unloading trucks, Armstrong managed to save enough to buy an instrument. At that point, he was ready to try his hand at becoming a musician.

Armstrong was fortunate enough to find guidance and support from a professional musician at one of the musical venues he frequented as an audience member. The musician, Joseph "King" Oliver, took a shine to the young Armstrong and helped him both develop his technique as well as get gigs around town. Armstrong played in various bands in a wide range of venues, from popular concert halls to Mississippi riverboats and, of course, jazz bars. In 1919, the young musician's big break came. His old mentor, Joseph Oliver, sent him a letter asking Armstrong to join Oliver's band in Chicago. Armstrong jumped at the chance and soon became the talk of the town in Chicago. From there, he moved to New York, where in addition to playing live in front of audiences, he took jobs recording with famous blues singers of that time. It was in New York, while working with a band called Fletcher Henderson, that Armstrong became renowned for his style, intensity, and innovation. The next step in his career came when Armstrong returned to Chicago and recorded with a studio band he formed, called the Hot Five. This record is considered by many to be the preeminent piece of work in jazz of the 20th century.

What made Armstrong's music so revolutionary was his groundbreaking

emerge (v):
to come out of

expose (v):
to be introduced; to experience

innovative (adj):
new and progressive

community (n):
a social group formed of people with similar interests

confine (v):
to limit; to restrict in some place

release (v):
to set free

venue (n):
a designated place for a performance

gig (n):
a contractual job for a musician

mentor (n):
an elder or more knowledgeable person who train or teaches a novice

renowned (adj):
famous; well-known

intensity (n):
a powerful focus; a discernable energy

preeminent (adj):
best; most exemplary

use of his instrument. But there was more to Armstrong's influence than just his innovative jazz style of playing music. He also used an innovative arrangement of players. Traditional New Orleans style jazz bands used a front line of players composed of a clarinet, a trumpet, and a trombone player. Armstrong rejected this line up in favor of a single front instrument, allowing that player greater freedom for improvisation and individual creative interpretation of a musical piece. Other jazz bands of the time were quick to adopt this new arrangement of a single front horn, and even today this type of band arrangement remains the convention.

Finally, there is the legacy of Armstrong's incorporation of vocal improvisation in jazz music. In particular, Armstrong is cited as introducing "scat" to the music scene of the 1920s and 30s. Scat is singing without using real words. For example, a singer might fill a musical phrase using invented words or simply sounds such as "be-bop-a-do-wop." There are some who claim that Armstrong invented scat; however, recordings of other singers incorporating scat into songs from the 1910s prove this was not true, and Armstrong himself never claimed to have invented scat. He just showed other musicians of his time how effectively it could be used, especially in jazz.

The list of singers and musicians who could trace influences back to Armstrong would certainly fill volumes. Performers ranging from Billie Holiday to Bing Crosby used techniques borrowed from Armstrong, and even modern rock-and-roll and rap performers incorporate elements of this great performer's innovative style.

interpretation (n):
an understanding; a personal take

convention (n):
a standard practice

improvisation (n):
an unpracticed or unplanned performance

cite (v):
to reference

volume (n):
a thick written work

1. What does the second paragraph mainly discuss?

   (A) Armstrong's family life
   (B) Armstrong's school life
   (C) Armstrong's first job
   (D) Armstrong's development as a musician

2. Which of the following best expresses the essential information in the highlighted sentence? *Incorrect* choices change the meaning in important ways or leave out essential information.

   (A) Armstrong had a good opportunity in 1919.
   (B) In 1919, something terrible happened to Armstrong.
   (C) The young musician had a serious accident in 1919.
   (D) 1919 was the year that Oliver and Armstrong quit working together.

3. The phrase "rejected this line up" in the passage refers to the fact that Armstrong

   (A) did not accept the traditional idea
   (B) fired the players
   (C) did not take the job that was offered to him
   (D) refused to perform with the group

4. As used in paragraph 2, line 8, what is the meaning of the word "in"?

   (A) Fashionable
   (B) Access
   (C) Indoors
   (D) Reputation

5. **Directions:** *Complete the table by matching the phrases below. Select the appropriate phrases from the answer choices and match them to the category that they describe. TWO of the answer choices will NOT be used.*

Early jazz musicians	Armstrong's innovations
C	B
F	D
G	

   (A) Incorporated the Hot Five
   (B) New style of playing
   (C) Played cornet
   (D) One front player
   (E) Recorded volumes
   (F) Three front players
   (G) Used scat

Criminal behavior is a social ill that has inspired a great deal of research and debate. The issues of debate can be categorized under two areas: how society should deal with criminals and why certain individuals resort to criminal behavior. In actuality, these two issues are closely connected. This information is based on statistics that report that *how* criminals are rehabilitated influences the likelihood of repeat offenses upon release from prison. Thus, the methods employed in treatment or rehabilitation of criminals seem to have a causal relation to repeat offenses. Additionally, the rehabilitation methods utilized within the prison system are based on society's generally held beliefs about why certain citizens become criminals in the first place. It is important, therefore, to first try to understand the dominant perspective held by a society regarding the origin of criminal behavior. Several possible theories to explain the origin of criminal behavior have been suggested.

One of the most widely held beliefs about crime claims that criminal behavior has a biological origin. For example, one particular biological theory claims that criminal behavior is linked to body type. Researchers interested in criminal behavior observed that criminals had certain physical characteristics in common. Researchers also theorized that these traits predisposed people to criminal behavior. Over the years, this theory has lost credibility. It is probably more likely that people have different social experiences because of their body types. It is then these experiences that predispose individuals to criminal behavior. As an example, consider skin color. In a society where racism tracks some people of one color into higher levels in society and people of other colors into lower levels, one would logically predict a higher tendency toward criminal behavior among races tracked into the lowest levels of society. It is the effect of social stratification that predisposes people of a particular race to criminal behavior, rather than a biological factor connected with race.

As illustrated above, society, rather than biology, has also been suggested as a powerful influence on the individual's tendency toward crime. In a classic study of criminal behavior, Clifford Shaw, in 1929, noticed that there were clusters of crime in certain areas. For instance, inner city slums that are characterized by poverty were found to yield a high rate of delinquency. It did not matter if the slums were populated by blacks, Hispanics, or whites.

There is also the theory of "differential association," put forth by Edwin Sutherland in 1950. This theory suggests that criminal behavior

rehabilitate *(v)*:
to restore to normal life through therapy and education

likelihood *(n)*:
a probability

causal *(adj)*:
relating to or involving a cause

predispose *(v)*:
to make one inclined or susceptible to

credibility *(n)*:
an amount of reliability; a level to which something can be believed

stratification *(n)*:
a condition of being layered or arranged in levels

slum *(n)*:
an area of poverty marked by substandard housing

yield *(v)*:
to produce or give forth naturally

delinquency *(n)*:
a failure to follow the law

is learned rather than spontaneously developed. The name of this theory relates to Sutherland's observation that no matter what group you look at, you will find both criminals and non-criminals. Therefore, certain factors at the individual level must exist that differentiate criminals and non-criminals. Sutherland suggested that the key factor for individuals related to contact and communication with people already engaged in criminal behaviors.

Based on Sutherland's claim that a person's criminal behavior increases in conjunction with the person's contact with criminals, one must naturally question the practice of incarcerating large numbers of offenders together. Although it may be easier for society to control such individuals under such a system, Sutherland's theory suggests that this would promote future offenses. With regard to young offenders, Sutherland would argue that prison exposes youth to a wide range of criminal behavior. Instead of being rehabilitated, the young person learns more about being a criminal.

By looking at this research, society can create new policies to reduce crime. Programs that aim to reduce poverty might decrease people's need to engage in crime. A restructuring of the prison system in such a way that pro-social behavior is learned and rewarded might counter the effects of exposure to more criminals. Through incorporation of research findings, better ways of both dealing with the causes of criminal behavior and rehabilitating individuals who engage in such practices may be developed.

spontaneously (adv):
automatically; without a visible cause

differentiate (v):
to distinguish; to tell apart

engage (v):
to do; to participate

in conjunction with (prep phrase):
together with; in connection with

incarcerate (v):
to put into prison

1. Which statement best reflects the author's opinion?
   - (A) Research is needed into genetic screening of potential criminals.
   - (B) Policy makers should consider theories of criminal behavior.
   - (C) Rehabilitation programs need to consider race as a factor affecting behavior.
   - (D) Young offenders should not be sent to prison.

2. Which of the following best expresses the essential information in the highlighted sentence? *Incorrect* choices change the meaning in important ways or leave out essential information.
   - (A) Because criminals typically commit crimes again after they get out of prison, society attempts to rehabilitate criminals in prison.
   - (B) Criminals who undergo methods of treatment during rehabilitation commit fewer crimes after they are released.
   - (C) The way criminals are rehabilitated affects the likelihood of further criminal behavior upon release from prison.
   - (D) There is a causal relationship that exists between criminal treatment and criminal rehabilitation.

3. Which of the following could best replace the word "ill" as used in paragraph 1?
   - (A) Idea
   - (B) Disease
   - (C) Behavior
   - (D) Problem

4. The word "tracks" in paragraph 2 is closest in meaning to
   - (A) follows
   - (B) directs
   - (C) connects
   - (D) traces

5. **Directions:** *An introductory sentence for a brief summary of the passage is provided below. Complete the summary by selecting the THREE answer choices that express the most important ideas in the passage. Some sentences do not belong in the summary because they express ideas that are not presented in the passage or are minor ideas in the passage.*

   First sentence: **Social research has attempted to explain criminal behavior by various theories.**

   - (A) Criminal behavior has been explained as developing out of biological factors.
   - (B) Different societies have their own ways of rehabilitating criminals.
   - (C) Sutherland said that people learn how to be criminals from other criminals.
   - (D) Prisons are one place where criminals come into contact with other criminals.
   - (E) Social factors may cause individuals to resort to criminal behavior.
   - (F) Statistics indicate that there is a lower rate of criminal behavior in higher levels of society. ACE

Perspective plays a large role in modern art. To understand this, the invention and development of the principles of perspective must be examined. The earliest contribution to this principle came from Ibn al-Haytham in 1000 A.D. He gave the first correct explanation of vision, showing that light is reflected from an object into the eye. He studied the complete science of vision, called "perspectiva" in medieval times, and although he did not apply his ideas to painting, the Renaissance artists later made good use of al-Haytham's optics.

The early Greeks are also known to have used some notion of perspective in their architecture and design of stage sets. However, while these early theatrical painters could create an illusion of depth in their works, there is no evidence to suggest that they understood the precise mathematical laws which govern correct representation.

The problem faced by these artists and architects was one of representing the three-dimensional world on a two-dimensional canvas. There were two aspects to this problem. First, how could one use mathematics to make realistic paintings? Second, what was the impact of these ideas on geometry and architecture?

It was not until the 1400s that mathematics was systematically applied in art in order to present objects with accurate perspective. While artists such as the 13th century painter Giotto di Bondone seemed to be using modern perspective, they, in fact, weren't. Giotto only used a form of perspective utilizing inclining, declining, and converging lines to indicate items in the painting that were further away from the observer, and to give the impression of depth. This was not the precise mathematical formulation that would later be developed and used.

Where Giotto had failed, Filippo Brunelleschi is the person credited with achieving the first correct formulation of linear perspective. He understood that there should be a single vanishing point to which all parallel lines in a plane converge. Rather than using simply inclining and declining lines, he made all lines converge to a central point. He also considered scale to accurately depict objects on the canvas in relation to their actual size.

How did Brunelleschi achieve this milestone in perspective where others had failed? His training in geometry and interest in surveying methods and instruments helped him discover and understand the concepts of perspective. However, while it is clear that he understood the mathematical rules involving the vanishing point, he didn't write

medieval *(adj)*:
of or relating to the Middle Ages (450-1450)

optics *(n)*:
the science of lenses, prisms, mirrors, etc.

notion *(n)*:
an idea

set *(n)*:
the scenery constructed for a theatrical performance

govern *(v)*:
to serve as a guiding or determining principle

canvas *(n)*:
a piece of heavy fabric on which artists paint

converge *(v)*:
to come together; to meet

linear *(adj)*:
of or relating to a line

plane *(n)*:
a flat or level surface

scale *(n)*:
a proportion used in determining size or dimensions

depict *(v)*:
to represent; to show

milestone *(n)*:
a turning point; an important event

down an explanation of how the rules of perspective work. The first person to do that was Leon Battista Alberti in his treatise on painting in 1435, *De pictura*.

The first part of *De pictura* gives the mathematical description of perspective, which Alberti considered necessary to properly understand a painting. Alberti claimed that painting is completely mathematical. A painting is the intersection of a visual pyramid at a given distance, with a fixed center and a defined position of light represented by the artist through the use of lines and colors on a given surface. Alberti also provided background on the principles of geometry and on the science of optics. He provided very detailed proofs regarding both perspective and the vanishing point.

Lorenzo Ghiberti used Alberti's new ideas on perspective to construct a second set of doors for the famous baptistery in Florence, Italy. Ghiberti is also famous for his compilation of medieval texts on the theory of vision such as that by al-Haytham. This is notable, as, until this point, there had been no connection made between the concepts of optics and vision to those of art. Ghiberti showed the relevance of earlier ideas on optics to the world of art.

The most mathematical of all of the books on perspective was published in the middle of the 15th century by Piero della Francesca. This was not surprising since, as well as being one of the leading artists of the time, Piero was also one of the leading mathematicians. With remarkable detail, Piero included many diagrams of solid figures in his work, all drawn in perspective. This serves art historians as an indication that the principles of perspective were being accepted and used.

treatise *(n)*:
a systematic, usually long written explanation on a subject

baptistery *(n)*:
a part of a church where baptisms are done

1. In paragraph 5, the author states that

   (A) Giotti was successful in inventing perspective.
   (B) Giotti helped Brunelleshi invent perspective.
   (C) Giotti didn't invent perspective.
   (D) Giotti was a great man.

2. Which of the following best expresses the essential information in the highlighted sentence? *Incorrect* choices change the meaning in important ways or leave out essential information.

   (A) Ghiberti was the first to relate ideas about optics and vision with ideas about painting.
   (B) Notable works produced at this time connected optics with the vision of great artists.
   (C) Painting of this time did not show lines related to optics and vision connecting at a point.
   (D) Until this time, Ghiberti was unable to connect his personal theory about optics and vision with artistic methods.

3. The word "form" in paragraph 4 is closest in meaning to

   (A) basic structure
   (B) shape
   (C) document
   (D) variety

4. The word "single" could best be replaced by which of the following?

   (A) Unmarried
   (B) For one person
   (C) One
   (D) Between only two people

5. **Directions:** *Complete the table below about the history of perspective discussed in the passage. Match the appropriate statements to the time period to which they are associated. Two of the answer choices will NOT be used.*

Ideas Before 1300	Ideas After 1300
_____	_____
_____	_____
	_____

   (A) A painting is purely mathematical.
   (B) Optics and vision are connected to art.
   (C) The first correct explanation of vision is given.
   (D) Paintings should incorporate a single vanishing point.
   (E) Paintings should focus on religious topics.
   (F) Alberti shows the problem in al-Haytham's work.
   (G) Perspective can create the illusion of depth on a theater stage.

Recognizing Coherence

Strategy

- Learn to recognize what the passage is doing, whether it's comparing, explaining, etc. This will help you see whether the sentence belongs in a particular section.
- It is important to look for the transitional words to see how they order and structure the sentences in the passage.
- Look at how the sentence changes or interrupts the flow of each section of the text.
- Be aware of pronouns in the inserted sentences. They are likely to refer to a noun in the sentence before the proper insertion point.
- On the actual test, when you click on a square, the sentence will be added to that section of the passage. You can then study the passage to see if the sentence is appropriate for that section. You may continue to click on the squares until you have chosen a position.

Transitions

Cause	because of, since, for, due to, owing to
Example	for example, for instance, such (as), most, some, others
Comparison	both, the same, similarly
Contrast	however, although, while, whereas, on the other hand
Result	consequently, subsequently, therefore, then, hence, as a result
Addition	also, too, as well as, furthermore, moreover, in addition

The Dead Sea, as the name suggests, has no living creatures in it. It has no fish, seaweed, algae, or life of any kind. This is because it is so salty. If a fish accidentally makes its way into it, it will die instantly.

The Dead Sea is also interesting in that it is a very low lake. In fact, the Dead Sea is the lowest exposed place on Earth. Its surface is more than 390 m below sea level!

The water in the Dead Sea has a higher concentration of salt than any other body of water. From the surface down to about forty meters, there are about three hundred and fifty grams of salt per kilogram of water. That gives the water a salinity of 35%! Additionally, the water in the Dead Sea becomes even saltier at lower depths. By comparison, sea water in the oceans around the world has, on average, about thirty-five grams of salt per kilogram of water, or a salinity of 3.5%.

Because the Dead Sea has such a high salinity, some interesting effects can be noticed by those who visit the lake. The Archimedes principle states that an object that is immersed in a fluid is buoyed up by a force equal to the weight of the fluid displaced by the object. Because salt water is heavier than fresh water, objects in salt water are more buoyant and so float more easily. ■ **A)** This is why it is easier to swim in salt water; it takes less energy to displace it. The water in the Dead Sea is so heavy that a swimmer does not need to use any energy at all in order to stay afloat. ■ **B)** A person can simply jump in and lie back, as if lying on an air mattress!

The main reason that the Dead Sea is so salty is that, although it has one primary and many secondary sources of water flowing into it, no water flows out of it. ■ **C)** The only way for water to escape the Dead Sea is to evaporate. ■ **D)** However, from time to time, the salinity of the lake is reduced due to flooding. During periods of heavy rain, runoff water pours into the lake, dropping the water's salinity from its usual level of 35% down to 30%. At such times, algae and certain types of bacteria can actually thrive in the lake. Most recently, this situation occurred in 1980. The dark blue water of the lake turned red from the bacteria teeming in the water. However, after the lake returned to its normal salinity, the algae and bacteria died off, and the Dead Sea's waters changed once again to blue.

Just before the floods of 1980, another significant change affected the waters of the Dead Sea. For thousands of years, the waters of the lake were actually stratified into two distinct layers, a dense lower layer

algae (n):
any of a type of primitive plant that grows underwater but lacks true stems, roots, and leaves

salinity (n):
a concentration of salt in a solution

immerse (v):
to put below the surface of water

buoy (v):
to keep afloat; to maintain or support near the surface of water

fresh water (n):
water that is not salty

buoyant (adj):
tending to float on water

afloat (adj):
in a floating position or condition

lie back (v phrase):
to recline; to get into a lying position

evaporate (v):
to change from a liquid to a gas

runoff (n):
rain water that is not absorbed by soil and flows to a lower area

thrive (v):
to grow vigorously; to flourish

teem (v):
to abound; to swarm

and a less dense upper layer.

The less dense layer of water measured from the Dead Sea's surface to approximately 35 m below the surface. As mentioned previously, the salinity of the top layer typically measured around 35%. The temperature of the upper layer of water ranged anywhere from 19°C up to 37°C, depending on various climatic conditions. In contrast, the denser lower layer of water in the sea had a much higher salinity than the top layer. This lower layer also maintained a steady temperature throughout the year, a consistent 22°C.

Those were the conditions of the lake for thousands of years leading up to the 20th century. During the 1960s, water was drawn from the Jordan River to irrigate crops of surrounding farms; thus, less water was fed into the Dead Sea. ■ **A)** On top of that, the entire region went through a dry period of low rainfall. Over the course of a decade, these conditions caused the upper layer of lake water to increase in salinity. ■ **B)** However, because the upper layer was still warmer than the lower layer, it remained suspended on the dense, cold lower layer. It was not until the winter of 1978 that the upper layer cooled enough to mix with the lower layer. ■ **C)** From that time until the present, researchers have noted the slow progress of re-stratification of the water. ■ **D)**

climatic *(adj)*:
relating to climate

steady *(adj)*:
fixed; unchanging

irrigate *(v)*:
to water an area by means of ditches, pipes, or streams

suspended *(adj)*:
supported or kept from sinking

homogenous *(adj)*:
all of the same kind or nature

READING

LISTENING

SPEAKING

WRITING

PRACTICE TEST

1. Look at the four squares [■] that indicate where the following sentence could be added to the passage:

When water evaporates, it leaves the salt behind.

Where would the sentence best fit? Choose the square [■] where the sentence should be added to the passage.

(A) Paragraph 4, line 6
(B) Paragraph 4, line 9
(C) Paragraph 5, line 3
(D) Paragraph 5, line 4

2. Look at the four squares [■] that indicate where the following sentence could be added to paragraph 8:

The Dead Sea finally became a homogenous body of water.

Where would the sentence best fit? Choose the square [■] where the sentence should be added to the passage.

(A) Line 4
(B) Line 6
(C) Line 10
(D) Line 11

3. Which of the following is closest is meaning to "concentration" in paragraph 2?

(A) Attention
(B) Density
(C) Retention
(D) Absorption

4. The word "displaced" in the passage is closest in meaning to

(A) banished
(B) moved
(C) removed
(D) restored

5. **Directions:** *An introductory sentence for a brief summary of the passage is provided below. Complete the summary by selecting the THREE answer choices that express the most important ideas in the passage. Some sentences do not belong in the summary because they express ideas that are not presented in the passage or are minor ideas in the passage.*

First sentence: **The Dead Sea is a fascinating and unique body of water that researchers continually study.**

(A) The Dead Sea has an extremely high concentration of salt in its water.
(B) The salinity of the Dead Sea gives the water in the lake some interesting properties.
(C) Both the climate and human interference have affected the lake's salinity.
(D) Even poor swimmers can float easily in the Dead Sea.
(E) The salinity of the lake and its size make it unique among the lakes of the world.
(F) The water in the Dead Sea is warmer on the top of the lake than on the bottom.

If one were to take a survey of passersby on the street, the majority of people surveyed could not explain the difference between herbs and spices. No doubt, this is due in part to the fact that people commonly use the two terms interchangeably. However, just because many people do it, this does not alter the fact that they are different. There are, in fact, several factors that differentiate herbs from spices.

Herbs and spices both come from plants. ■ **A)** Herbs typically come from plants with green stems, whereas spices typically come from plants with woody stems, like shrubs and trees. Additionally, herbs are made from the leaves of the plants. Spices, on the other hand, can be made from a plant's roots, bark, seeds, or flowers. ■ **B)** That being said, one might be confused by a plant such as *Coriandrum sativum*. The leaves of this plant are used as an herb (cilantro), while the seeds are used as a spice (coriander)! ■ **C)** Does that make *Coriandrum sativum* an herb or a spice? The answer to this question would be, "neither." It is the products of the plant that become herbs or spices. ■ **D)**

A second general distinction between herbs and spices can be drawn from where herbs and spices originate. Herbs typically come from temperate regions, such as Italy, France, and England. Spices come from the tropics.

There is a third test that can be used to differentiate herbs and spices. This test involves considering how much of the substance is used in cooking, which is the most common use of herbs and spices today. In most cases, a greater amount of an herb is used to flavor foods compared to the amount of a spice used. A recipe for a certain sauce may call for a few teaspoons of an herb but only a pinch or two of a spice.

Recalling the first point, that herbs come from the leaves of a plant and spices from other parts, it makes sense that more people grow their own herbs but buy their spices from stores. The leaves of a plant can be picked fresh and crushed right into a dish. Spices generally require more processing before they are ready to be added to foods.

In the past, herb gardens were quite common. In fact, just about every house had one! Unlike growing flowers, people grew herbs for practical reasons. They needed the herbs that were grown for cooking and home remedies. It is interesting to note that people who choose to grow herbs today rarely include medicinal plants in their gardens.

---

interchangeably *(adv)*:
in a manner that can be changed or switched

stem *(n)*:
a main, central support of a plant

woody *(adj)*:
like wood

shrub *(n)*:
a bush; a low, woody plant having several stems growing from a base but no single trunk

temperate *(adj)*:
characterized by moderate temperatures

tropics *(n)*:
the region on Earth lying between 23° north and 23° south of the equator

flavor *(v)*:
to add taste to

pinch *(n)*:
a small amount that can be held between a finger and the thumb

dish *(n)*:
a food

remedy *(n)*:
a medicine or therapy used to relieve pain or cure disease

medicinal *(adj)*:
relating to medicine

READING

LISTENING

SPEAKING

WRITING

PRACTICE TEST

Herb gardens today include almost exclusively plants used in cooking.
■ **A)** A few of the most popular herbs grown in gardens include oregano, basil, rosemary, and cilantro. Oregano, basil, and rosemary are commonly used in Italian cooking. ■ **B)** Cilantro looks similar to parsley, but it has a strong, distinct flavor. Each of these herbs is easy to care for. ■ **C)** In addition, they sprout again quickly after they are cut, or their leaves are harvested. ■ **D)**

Gauging from descriptions found in most books, herb gardens appear to be grown exclusively in temperate regions. Books about herb gardening rarely include information on tropical herb gardens. Thus, people mistakenly assume that herb gardens do not grow well in such regions. Herb gardens can in fact be grown just about anywhere. However, gardeners use different methods depending on where they live.

In temperate regions, like most of Europe and North America, gardeners work indoors in winter. First, they plant seeds in pots or flats indoors. In the spring, the gardeners move the seedlings to garden beds outdoors. Gardeners working in warmer and wetter climates can work with plants outdoors all year long.

sprout *(v)*:
to begin to grow; to appear just above the soil

harvest *(v)*:
to collect ripe grains or fruits

gauge *(v)*:
to judge

flat *(n)*:
a square container holding a dozen or more young plants in small pots or holders

seedling *(n)*:
a young plant that is grown from a seed

bed *(n)*:
a section of a garden where certain plants or flowers are grown

1. Look at the four squares [■] that indicate where the following sentence could be added to paragraph 2:

In the same way, orchids are not labeled as a spice simply because vanilla is produced from these plants' undeveloped fruit.

Where would the sentence best fit? Choose the square [■] where the sentence should be added to the passage.

(A) Line 1
(B) Line 5
(C) Line 8
(D) Line 11

2. Look at the four squares [■] that indicate where the following sentence could be added to paragraph 7:

Cilantro is typically added to Mexican salsa or Vietnamese soups.

Where would the sentence best fit? Choose the square [■] where the sentence should be added to the passage.

(A) Line 1
(B) Line 3
(C) Line 5
(D) Line 6

3. The word "exclusively" in paragraph 6 is closest in meaning to

(A) especially
(B) only
(C) privately
(D) selectively

4. The word "flats" in the passage refers to

(A) a type of gardening tool
(B) apartments
(C) something to grow plants in
(D) the shape of a plant's leaves

5. **Directions:** *Complete the table below about the differences between herbs and spices discussed in the passage. Match the appropriate words and phrases to the category to which they are associated. Two of the answer choices will NOT be used.*

Herbs	Spices
_____	_____
_____	_____
_____	_____
_____	

(A) Bitter flavor
(B) *Coriandrum sativum*
(C) Green stemmed plants
(D) Leaves
(E) Come from temperate regions
(F) Come from tropical regions
(G) Use a little
(H) Use a lot
(I) Fruits and seeds

■ **A)** Jack Fenn, an analyst at the Gartner Research Institute, presents his description of the process that a technology goes through from the moment of its release to its eventual end. Although any new form of technology enters the market in basically the same way, relatively few products reach a level of accepted everyday use. ■ **B)** Rather, the vast majority of products eventually disappear entirely from the market. ■ **C)** In considering any new gadget introduced to the market, Fenn noted a common series of stages through which the product develops. He outlines the five specific stages, labeling each stage as follows: the technology trigger, the peak of inflated expectations, the trough of disillusionment, the slope of enlightenment, and finally the plateau of productivity. ■ **D)**

Fenn terms the first stage of the technology hype cycle as "the technology trigger." This is when a media story or publicized event introduces the new technology to the public. The media then typically hypes the technology causing unreasonably high public expectations in the peak of inflated expectations. A good example of this would be the Segway scooter. Before anyone even knew what the device was, the manufacturing company released "hints" to the press that a major breakthrough in transportation technology was on the way. No pictures or descriptions of the device were released to the public. The company ran their promotional campaign for months before the official unveiling of the device in December of 2001.

After it hits the market, a product enters the second stage of the hype cycle, the peak of inflated expectations. To this point, the flames of public interest have been fanned into a full blaze. Now the public has the product in hand, and they can test its usefulness for themselves. More often than not, this stage of the cycle ends in disappointment when the public realizes the new technology is not all it's cracked up to be. At this point, the technology descends into the trough of disillusionment. A perfect example of this would be the laserdisc, the precursor to the DVD. A laserdisc was as large as a phonograph record, and the players cost upwards of $500. This bulky and expensive product never escaped from the trough of disillusionment.

Other technologies, for instance cell phones and personal computers, survived long enough and received enough investment for researchers to develop second and third generations of the devices in order to climb the slope of enlightenment. In this phase, the technology is made more

gadget *(n)*:
a device; a small machine

trigger *(n)*:
a mechanism that activates something

inflated *(adj)*:
unduly enlarged; raised beyond a reasonable level

trough *(n)*:
the lowest part of a U curve

disillusionment *(n)*:
disappointment; being freed from a false belief

enlightenment *(n)*:
education that results in understanding

plateau *(n)*:
a level period or state

publicized *(adj)*:
made widely known

hype *(v)*:
to promote through excessive publicity

scooter *(n)*:
a child's vehicle with two wheels and a tall upright handle

unveil *(v)*:
to disclose; to reveal

blaze *(n)*:
a big, bright fire

descend *(v)*:
to go down

precursor *(n)*:
a sign or an object that indicates or announces something to come

bulky *(adj)*:
of a large, unmanageable size; difficult to hold or carry

practical and affordable and is developed toward specific real world applications. In the case of personal computers, the evolution of a more practical device has involved the expansion of memory capacity, the reduction of space taken up by the device (through thinner monitors and smaller hard drives), and user-friendly accessories incorporating plug-and-play installation.

■ **A)** As the public is gradually reintroduced to the next generation of a device, it becomes more ubiquitous and widely accepted. ■ **B)** Such products are set to enjoy an extended existence in this final stage of the technology hype cycle, the plateau of productivity. ■ **C)** Nowadays, the cell phone is viewed by many in the industrialized world as a basic life necessity. From here, the technology may continue in the plateau of productivity until it is replaced by a more advanced device. However, such new, advanced devices must enter the technology hype cycle at the first stage and survive in the market long enough to reach at least the slope of enlightenment. At that point, they may realistically pose a challenge to existing products. ■ **D)** Recent products that have made it through the first stages of the hype cycle and now seek to challenge the cell phones' present position in the market include Palm Pilots and Blackberries.

pose *(v)*:
to present; to put forth

Palm Pilot *(n)*:
a trademark for a handheld digital organizer or personal digital assistant

1. Look at the four squares [■] that indicate where the following sentence could be added to paragraph 1:

   As a whole, these stages are known as the technology hype cycle.

   Where would the sentence best fit? Choose the square [■] where the sentence should be added to the passage.
   (A) Line 1
   (B) Line 5
   (C) Line 6
   (D) Line 12

2. Look at the four squares [■] that indicate where the following sentence could be added to paragraph 5:

   There was a time when a person with a cell phone was probably a stockbroker.

   Where would the sentence best fit? Choose the square [■] where the sentence should be added to the passage.
   (A) Line 1
   (B) Line 2
   (C) Line 4
   (D) Line 11

3. Which of the following means most nearly the same as "ubiquitous" as used in paragraph 5?
   (A) Commonplace
   (B) Powerful
   (C) Practical
   (D) Popular

4. The expression "not all it's cracked up to be" in paragraph 3 is closest in meaning to
   (A) unreliable
   (B) coherent
   (C) beneficial
   (D) overrated

5. **Directions:** *An introductory sentence for a brief summary of the passage is provided below. Complete the summary by selecting the THREE answer choices that express the most important ideas in the passage. Some sentences do not belong in the summary because they express ideas that are not presented in the passage or are minor ideas in the passage.*

   First sentence: **New products go through a series of stages called the Technology Hype Cycle.**

   (A) After people buy them and use them, they may be disappointed.
   (B) Cell phones ended up doing better in the market than laserdiscs.
   (C) Jack Fenn was an employee of the Gartner Research Institute.
   (D) At first, people have high expectations about the product because advertising has hyped them.
   (E) People lost interest in the Segway even before the devices were unveiled for the market.
   (F) Products that are developed through further research and new designs might eventually reach a steady level of sales.

There are many great literary figures that have shaped the way that we view the arts. Homer was one of these great individuals. He paved the way for epic poetry and created the roots for the great innovation of theater.

Homer was a Greek poet who lived around 1200 B.C., or was he? For over three centuries, scholars have debated whether or not Homer even existed. No one knows exactly who Homer was. What is known for sure is that Homer's stories and poems were handed down orally for centuries before ever being recorded on paper.

There are at least three schools of popular thought about the identity and existence of Homer. ■ **A)** Some people think that Homer didn't exist at all. ■ **B)** Others believe that Homer was actually a group of people, called the Homeridae, who wrote and interpreted the poetry that has been passed down through history. ■ **C)** The final school of thought is the scholars who believe that Homer was real. ■ **D)** They believe that one man named Homer, who was probably a minstrel, traveled around ancient Greece telling poems and entertaining audiences. These scholars say that Homer, as the original creator of the poems, was a literary genius. They state that Homer was way ahead of his time, citing that his poems had a beginning, middle, and ending, which was extraordinary for this time.

Whether or not an individual named Homer ever lived and wrote poetry, the fact remains that the works that have come down to us under Homer's name are literary masterpieces. Homer is the composer of the two famous poems *The Iliad* and *The Odyssey*. These are the only two complete surviving works from Homer.

The Iliad is based on actual events occurring around 1000 B.C. It describes the misfortune of the city of Troy, which was rebuilt numerous times due to war and fire. Whether all the events in *The Iliad* are true is still an unknown fact, but the descriptions of Troy at the time and geographical references given by Homer in the poem are near the truth.

The plot of *The Iliad* follows a simple theme: the wrath of Achilles. At the start of the poem, we meet Achilles, who is a great warrior. He is in a state of misery about his personal life. Achilles is wrathful because Agamemnon has taken his beautiful girlfriend, Briseis, from him. Agamemnon has claimed Briseis as a prize of war. Instead of living up to his reputation as a warrior, Achilles is sitting in his tent sulking and letting his beloved Greece fall around him. After many detailed and

---

hand down *(v phrase)*:
to give or pass to a younger generation

orally *(adv)*:
by means of voice

literary *(adj)*:
related to literature

misfortune *(n)*:
unfortunate trouble; bad luck

wrath *(n)*:
punishment inflicted with anger

misery *(n)*:
mental or emotional unhappiness

live up to *(v phrase)*:
to act in accordance with

sulk *(v)*:
to show disappointment through silent, resentful protest

---

colorful events are described by Homer in *The Iliad*, we find Briseis back in the arms of Achilles.

By contrast, *The Odyssey* is a work of pure fiction not based on any real historical figures or events. It is a poem of the fantastic adventures of the great Odysseus as he takes a ten-year journey home to Ithaca after the Trojan War. At the beginning of the poem we meet Penelope, the wife of Odysseus. Penelope has had a hard time in the absence of her husband. She has been harassed by many men, who have abused her servants and taken all of her wealth, leaving her in a state of despair. ■ **A)** As Odysseus's journey home is a long one, his appearance has changed and his fortune has diminished. These changes are so dramatic, in fact, that he is mistaken for a beggar by the people of Ithaca. Even his own wife fails to recognize him. ■ **B)** However, all is not lost for Odysseus. As the poem continues, an announcement for a contest to string the Great Bow of Odysseus is made. In the end, Odysseus himself is the only man with enough strength to complete the task. ■ **C)** Odysseus then takes his revenge. Using his bow, he kills Penelope's suitors and takes her back as his wife. ■ **D)** This is certainly an example of an epic adventure/romance. Additionally, *The Odyssey* has been hailed as the first science fiction novel. This in itself is quite a tribute to the genius of Homer.

Who was Homer? When did he write? What did he actually write himself? These difficult questions have puzzled scholars since the 6th century B.C. and still do so today. However, though these questions may remain unanswered, a certain truth is that the beginnings of literature, theater, and science fiction all lie in Homer. Whoever Homer was or wasn't, readers today can still enjoy his works and appreciate his legacy.

---

harass *(v):*
to annoy or trouble persistently

despair *(n):*
complete loss of hope

beggar *(n):*
a poor person who begs for money as a living

string *(v):*
to put string on an instrument or device

suitor *(n):*
a man who seeks to marry a woman

hail *(v):*
to acclaim

tribute *(n):*
a declaration of respect or admiration

puzzle *(v):*
to confuse; to baffle

1. Look at the four squares [■] that indicate where the following sentence could be added in paragraph 3:

   They claim that the writings attributed to Homer were not written by Homer, but by another poet or poets.

   Where would the sentence best fit? Choose the square [■] where the sentence should be added to the passage.

   (A) Line 2
   (B) Line 3
   (C) Line 5
   (D) Line 6

2. Look at the four squares [■] that indicate where the following sentence could be added in paragraph 7:

   The happy pair were reunited in love.

   Where would the sentence best fit? Choose the square [■] where the sentence should be added to the passage.

   (A) Line 8
   (B) Line 11
   (C) Line 15
   (D) Line 16

3. The word "minstrel" could best be replaced by which of the following?

   (A) An actor
   (B) A writer
   (C) A traveling musician
   (D) A poet

4. The expression "prize of war" in the passage is closet in meaning to

   (A) trophy
   (B) money
   (C) wife
   (D) treasure

5. **Directions:** *An introductory sentence for a brief summary is provided below. Complete the summary by selecting THREE answer choices that express the most important ideas in the passage. Some sentences do not belong in the summary because they express ideas that are not presented in the passage or are minor ideas in the passage.*

   First sentence: **The question of Homer's existence has been debated by scholars for three centuries.**

   (A) There are three main schools of thought about the existence of Homer.
   (B) Homer as the creator of *The Iliad* and *The Odyssey* is considered a literary genius.
   (C) Homer may have been married and may have had 3 children.
   (D) Achilles was a great warrior, who Homer wrote about in *The Iliad*.
   (E) The "Homeric Question" is a group of debatable questions that still puzzle scholars today.
   (F) Anyone can enjoy reading Homer's work.

Acting is often thought of as the process of giving birth to a human soul through art. Yet, if everything in film or on stage is nothing more than a lie or an invention, how can an actor find truth there? Film and theatre are filled with falsehoods — mere imitations of life. How can actors believe where no truth exists? How do great actors, such as Marlon Brando, Robert De Niro, or Meryl Streep, create the most complex characters ever conceived? And how do the events on a stage appear as if happening for the first time? Are some actors merely inspired to greatness? From where do their creations come? How do gifted actors know what will happen next, and yet their characters do not know? Is great acting only limited to those who are gifted enough to summon inspiration upon demand? These were some of the questions that Constantin Stanislavski dedicated his life to exploring.

Born in Moscow in 1863, Stanislavski, a Russian actor, director, and co-founder of the Moscow Theatre of Art, was especially obsessed with discovering the mystery of inspiration for the actor. ■ **A)** He believed that actors could not create inspiration by artificial means, and therefore, sought to find technical means for the manufacturing of art so that this inspiration would appear more often than not. ■ **B)** Stanislavski created a favorable condition for the appearance of inspiration by means of the will. ■ **C)** He produced a positive environment for the inception of artistic stimulation during the creation and performance of a role. For stage characterization and behavior which appeared as spontaneously and naturally as in real life, he designed a "system" of actor training. ■ **D)**

The Stanislavski System, or "the Method," as it has become more popularly known, held that an actor's main responsibility was to be believed rather than recognized or understood. ■ **A)** Stanislavski asserted that if the theatre was going to be meaningful, it needed to move beyond the external representation that acting had primarily been. ■ **B)** He believed that actors needed to take their own personalities onto the stage when they began to play a character. ■ **C)** This was a clear break from previous modes of acting that held that the actor's job was to become the character and leave their own emotions behind. ■ **D)**

To reach this "believable truth," Stanislavski first employed methods such as "emotional memory." For example, to prepare for a role that involves fear, the actor must remember something frightening and attempt to act the part in the emotional space of that fear they once

mere *(adj)*:
only; just

conceive *(v)*:
to think of first

dedicate *(v)*:
to devote

obsessed *(adj)*:
excessively preoccupied

will *(n)*:
the power a person has to make deliberate choices about actions done or not done

inception *(n)*:
the beginning or first stage

hold *(v)*:
to assert; to affirm

assert *(v)*:
to state positively; to affirm

felt. Later, Stanislavski concerned himself with the creation of physical entries into these emotional states, believing that the repetition of certain physical acts and exercises could bridge the gap between life on and off the stage.

By the 1940s, the Stanislavski System had found its way to America, where it was further adapted and explored by one of Stanislavski's most famous students — Lee Strasberg. Strasberg was a teacher and theorist of acting and a leader of the Actors Studio, an organization that has been home to some of the most talented and successful actors of our time, including the previously mentioned Brando, De Niro, and Streep as well as Julia Roberts, Russell Crowe, Leonardo DiCaprio, and Dustin Hoffman, to name only a few.

At the Actors Studio, Strasberg continued on with the Stanislavski System of encouraging actors not to emote in the traditional manner of stage conventions, but to speak and gesture in a manner one would use in private life. The Actors Studio, like Stanislavski himself, emphasized an individualized, psychological approach to acting that required a performer to draw on personal experiences, memories, and emotions that could inform a characterization and shape how a character might speak or move. Characters were thus shown to have an interior life, rather than being stereotyped figures representing a single concept, such as a heroine or a villain. They could become complex human beings with multiple and contradictory feelings and desires. It is this ability to convey the complexity — indeed, the confusion — of inner feelings that has made many of the Actors Studio-trained actors such emblematic figures for over sixty years.

gap *(n):*
a difference

emote *(v):*
to express emotions, especially when acting

gesture *(v):*
to motion with the body as a means of communication

contradictory *(adj):*
involving or being opposites, where both cannot be true at the same time

convey *(v):*
to communicate; to make known

emblematic *(adj):*
symbolic

1. Look at the four squares [■] that indicate where the following sentence could be added in paragraph 2:

This system is as relevant to twenty-first century actors trying to establish a career on stage or in film or television as it was to actors one hundred years ago.

Where would the sentence best fit? Choose the square [■] where the sentence should be added to the passage.

(A) Line 3
(B) Line 6
(C) Line 8
(D) Line 12

2. Look at the four squares [■] that indicate where the following sentence could be added in paragraph 3:

It was a complex method for producing realistic characters.

Where would the sentence best fit? Choose the square [■] where the sentence should be added to the passage.

(A) Line 3
(B) Line 5
(C) Line 7
(D) Line 9

3. The word "manufacturing" in paragraph 2 is closest in meaning to

(A) building
(B) structuring
(C) creation
(D) establishment

4. The phrase "draw on" in paragraph 6 is closest in meaning to

(A) paint
(B) make use of
(C) configure
(D) copy

5. **Directions:** *An introductory sentence for a brief summary of the passage is provided below. Complete the summary by selecting the THREE answer choices that express the most important ideas in the passage. Some sentences do not belong in the summary because they express ideas that are not presented in the passage or are minor ideas in the passage.*

First sentence: **Stanislavski created a system of actor training that has helped actors achieve a more genuine, naturalistic performance.**

(A) An actor's main responsibility is to be believed.
(B) Lee Strasberg was a student of Stanislavski and an American.
(C) An actor should use their own feelings and emotions when they perform.
(D) Stanislavski believed that fame was the ultimate goal of an actor.
(E) An audience will be able to detect when an actor performs in a traditional manner.
(F) Stanislavski and the Actors Studio stressed both the psychological and the physical aspects of acting.

Review A – C

Vocabulary Review

Skill Review

Vocabulary Review

Instructions: Choose the best answer to complete each sentence.

1. The government continues to disparage smoking because of its _____ effects on the body.
   - (A) distinctive
   - (B) detrimental
   - (C) preeminent
   - (D) emblematic

2. The woman filed a law suit after her ex-husband continued to _____ her.
   - (A) immerse
   - (B) wreak havoc
   - (C) harass
   - (D) manipulate

3. Winning him over was no difficulty. He already seemed _____ to our ideas.
   - (A) predisposed
   - (B) permissive
   - (C) contradictory
   - (D) dramatic

4. He was _____ toward her bad manners, but he couldn't accept her constant swearing.
   - (A) unsure
   - (B) contradictory
   - (C) tolerant
   - (D) literary

5. With the destruction caused by hurricane damage, the government needed to _____ some swift procedures.
   - (A) implement
   - (B) ensure
   - (C) enable
   - (D) attribute

6. His promotion to vice executive marked a distinctive _____ in his career.
   - (A) gesture
   - (B) outcome
   - (C) onset
   - (D) milestone

7. Even with their persistent attempts to _____ him, his drug habit could never be shaken.
   - (A) manipulate
   - (B) rehabilitate
   - (C) predispose
   - (D) incarcerate

8. Without their direct _____, this company would have collapsed under all the current economic pressure.
   - (A) improvisation
   - (B) intervention
   - (C) encroachment
   - (D) inception

9. The company expects all senior management at the convention when we _____ our new range of products.
   - (A) insulate
   - (B) popularize
   - (C) pinpoint
   - (D) unveil

10. The company's sales have increased significantly after their _____ advertising campaign.
    - (A) instrumental
    - (B) innovative
    - (C) buoyant
    - (D) preeminent

11. They are so similar, you would need an expert to _____ them.
    - (A) trace
    - (B) pinpoint
    - (C) differentiate
    - (D) dedicate

12. He is a very _____ individual. He needs to relax a little.
    - (A) intense
    - (B) emote
    - (C) distinctive
    - (D) tolerant

13. As a lawyer, he shouldn't make so many _____ statements in his cases.
    - (A) instrumental
    - (B) emblematic
    - (C) climatic
    - (D) contradictory

14. Since its _____ in the late 90s, the company's growth has surpassed all expectation.
    - (A) inception
    - (B) improvisation
    - (C) outcome
    - (D) distinction

15. He was _____ after finally being caught for bank fraud.
    - (A) incarcerated
    - (B) harassed
    - (C) manipulated
    - (D) released

Instructions: Choose the word closest in meaning to the underlined word or phrase.

16. He is <u>famous</u> for his grace and eloquence in public speaking.
    - (A) exhibited
    - (B) depicted
    - (C) renowned
    - (D) immersed

17. Because of the <u>disturbance</u>, all hotel guests were advised to remain in their rooms.
    - (A) misery
    - (B) momentum
    - (C) wrath
    - (D) turmoil

18. They were unhappy about the <u>intrusion</u> of the squatters on their land.
    - (A) misfortune
    - (B) integration
    - (C) encroachment
    - (D) disparity

19. After meeting the famous actor in the flesh, they felt a sense of <u>disappointment</u>.
    - (A) disillusionment
    - (B) improvisation
    - (C) encroachment
    - (D) establishment

20. Because of their <u>fundamental difference</u>, they would never be close friends.
    - (A) contradictory
    - (B) disparity
    - (C) delinquency
    - (D) intensity

21. The stadium doesn't have the <u>capability</u> to hold one hundred thousand supporters for the game.

(A) maximization
(B) contingent
(C) capacity
(D) source

22. I think the professor failed me because my <u>understanding</u> of the play differed so much from hers.

(A) interpretation
(B) improvisation
(C) inception
(D) contribution

23. His <u>reliability</u> has gone down in my eyes, ever since he lost that big account with the advertising firm.

(A) likelihood
(B) credibility
(C) delinquency
(D) distinction

24. He was fired because his ideas were always too <u>vague</u> and incomplete.

(A) general
(B) distinctive
(C) homogenous
(D) inflated

25. We were very pleased with the substantial <u>donation</u> that was made to our organization.

(A) milestone
(B) momentum
(C) intervention
(D) contribution

26. I don't like her. She always tries to <u>influence</u> all the other employees in her favor.

(A) maintain
(B) manipulate
(C) pinpoint
(D) adapt

27. The lecturers in our university are quite <u>liberal and broad minded</u>.

(A) preeminent
(B) obsessed
(C) renowned
(D) permissive

28. Her <u>knowledge</u> of the theory leaves a lot to be desired.

(A) tribute
(B) grasp
(C) gauge
(D) wrath

29. The promoters of the event are still unsure of the <u>location</u>.

(A) source
(B) tariff
(C) venue
(D) convention

30. When choosing your future career, you would do well to <u>remember</u> that you will probably be engaged in that particular field for the rest of your life.

(A) maintain
(B) express
(C) bear in mind
(D) assert

Instructions: Write the missing words. Use the words below to fill in the blanks.

exposed	misery	comprised	link	occupation
likelihood	ensure	enables	social security	immigration

A US investigation in 2004 into **(31)** _____ policies showed that there was an increased **(32)** _____ of domestic violence against South Asian women moving to the States. These policies, preventing women on spousal visas from having an **(33)** _____ or **(34)** _____ card, may have constituted a violation of human rights. The survey, which was **(35)** _____ of approximately 200 married South Asian women, showed that those women who held certain visas were more **(36)** _____ to violence and abuse. The **(37)** _____ between the visa status and abuse **(38)** _____ officials to recognize the need to expand the definitions of domestic abuse to include government-related policies for newcomers, in order to prevent more suffering and **(39)** _____ and to **(40)** _____ the safety of these women.

Instructions: Choose the one word that does not belong.

41. outcome	motivation	result	consequence
42. transfer	cite	convey	release
43. descend	buoyant	afloat	weightless
44. indefinable	abstract	innovative	vague
45. preeminent	distinctive	prominent	exclusively

Instructions: Match the words that are opposites.

46. thrive	(A)	release
47. confine	(B)	outcome
48. interchangeably	(C)	mumble
49. onset	(D)	exclusively
50. emote	(E)	dwindle

For many students, the college years are a trying time. While academic challenges are an expected part of higher learning, students can face personal challenges as well. One common problem is that of isolation. ■ **A)** To feel isolated is to feel absolutely alone, with no feelings of connection to others. Of course, in a literal sense, students are not alone, as they are surrounded by other students all the time. ■ **B)** It is very easy to feel lost among a large group of many different sorts of people. This can intensify the normal barriers between people, making them seem much larger and more complicated. For students that are naturally introverted or overly attached to their families, it can be a very complicated problem. ■ **C)** If a student does not take part in any student activities, spends most or all of his or her time alone, and has no meaningful relationships with other students, that student can be considered isolated. Of course, there are certain students who may prefer this sort of condition. ■ **D)** Some may feel more comfortable having few or no relationships at school so that they can focus more intensely on their studies. However, studies show that the vast majority of students who find themselves isolated do not enjoy this condition.

Freshmen normally experience the most extreme feelings of isolation. They are suddenly in an unfamiliar environment away from relatives and friends, where everyone seems to be a stranger. Naturally shy students or those with strong family ties may not only feel homesick, but also threatened. There is also the added pressure to perform well academically. A student may feel judged by his or her peers as well as professors. He or she may feel like everyone is watching and evaluating, ready to criticize or accuse. All of this may cause a student to emotionally and socially withdraw as a defense mechanism. Instead of thinking of other students as potential friends, they imagine them as potential enemies. Those freshmen who deeply miss their friends from before college may cling to those old friendships. This makes establishing new friendships all the more difficult and the feelings of isolation more pronounced.

To make matters worse, isolation can lead to other emotional problems, primarily depression. Loneliness and other negative feelings are only deepened and reinforced by the fact that there is no one with whom the isolated student can share his or her feelings. Depression can drain a student's energy and initiative, resulting in poor academic performance. In addition, it can damage what relationships the student may already have. Finally, it can also lead to more serious problems such as alcoholism

literal *(adj)*:
conforming to the exact meaning of a word

intensify *(v)*:
to make more intense

introverted *(adj)*:
shy; tending to keep to oneself

peer *(n)*:
an equal; a person of the same standing

evaluate *(v)*:
to judge the value or quality of

cling *(v)*:
to stay close to; to depend on emotionally

deepen *(v)*:
to make stronger and more intense

reinforce *(v)*:
to make stronger

initiative *(n)*:
the desire to work; a plan of action

and, in some cases, suicidal feelings.

Universities can take various initiatives to prevent students from becoming isolated. One of the most effective and common methods is to require students to share a dormitory room. ■ **A)** Having a roommate makes it very difficult to be isolated since a student must interact with this person regardless of how shy he or she may be. Although a determined student can still manage to be isolated, even in such a situation, few students have both the will and the desire to do so. ■ **B)** Another method is to encourage a student to join in some sort of activity immediately after entering university. This can include joining a club, a student association, or a study group. ■ **C)** There are also student groups designed to ease freshmen into university life, giving them opportunities to meet other new students through various social activities, such as lunches or day trips. ■ **D)** Finally, a university can provide professional counseling for students with personal problems.

However a university attempts to help, the fact remains that the cause of isolation among students is personal. Unlike health and academic problems, there are few resources to conclusively treat the problem of isolation, since much of the problem lies in the individual student's personality. This does not mean that such a student deserves to feel bad or suffer, but it does mean that, in the end, the student is the one who has the ultimate power to improve the situation.

interact *(v)*:
to communicate with

ultimate *(adj)*:
last; of greatest strength or importance

1. The expression "more pronounced" in paragraph 2 is closest in meaning to
   (A) clearer
   (B) louder
   (C) more talked about
   (D) more intense

2. The phrase "defense mechanism" in paragraph 2 is closest in meaning to
   (A) tool for distraction
   (B) reason for withdrawing
   (C) method of protection
   (D) device for resolving disputes

3. In paragraph 1, the author explains the concept of isolation by
   (A) giving examples of how schools can help isolated students
   (B) characterizing the type of students who cause isolation in their classmates
   (C) providing a definition of the concept and examples of those prone to it
   (D) discussing factors affecting the barriers between students

4. According to the passage, what types of students most typically experience isolation?
   (A) Students who prefer to focus on their studies rather than socialize
   (B) Students who are surrounded by large amounts of other students
   (C) Students who view others as potential enemies or accusers
   (D) Freshman students who are shy or overly attached to their families

5. Which of the following sentences best expresses the essential information of the highlighted sentence? Incorrect choices change the meaning in important ways or leave out essential information.
   (A) There are several ways in which universities can initiate feelings of isolation in the students.
   (B) There are several strategies that universities can implement in order to reduce the chances of students becoming isolated.
   (C) Isolated students can be prevented from entering certain universities.
   (D) Students can start the process of avoiding isolation by suggesting strategies to their university.

6. Look at the four squares [■] that indicate where the following sentence could be added to the paragraph 1:

   However, this can actually aggravate one's sense of isolation.

   Where would the sentence best fit? Choose the square [■] where the sentence should be added to the passage.
   (A) Line 4
   (B) Line 6
   (C) Line 11
   (D) Line 15

7. The word "higher" in paragraph 1 could best be replaced by which of the following?
   (A) taller
   (B) more expensive
   (C) longer
   (D) advanced

8. What does the third paragraph mainly discuss?

(A) The reasons why students should make an effort to meet new people.

(B) Things the students can do to free themselves from isolation.

(C) The negative effects of isolation on the student.

(D) Ways in which the university contributes to isolation.

9. Look at the four squares [■] that indicate where the following sentence could be added to the paragraph 4:

These organizations give the student a sense of belonging and self-worth.

Where would the sentence best fit? Choose the square [■] where the sentence should be added to the passage.

(A) Line 3

(B) Line 7

(C) Line 10

(D) Line 13

10. Directions: *Select the appropriate phrases from the answer choices and match them to the category to which they relate. TWO of the answer choices will NOT be used.*

Causes of Isolation	Effects of Isolation	Ways to Prevent Isolation
_____	_____	_____
_____	_____	_____

(A) Join a club

(B) Live with family

(C) Alcoholism

(D) Poor academic performance

(E) Being away from family and friends

(F) Live with a roommate

(G) Talk to professors

(H) Being around large groups of people

Jane Austen was born in 1775 in a small village in the English countryside. Her father was a reverend and teacher, and she was the seventh of his eight children. ■ **A)** Although she would later gain renown for her numerous novels featuring illuminating insight into morality, sociology, friendship, and courtship, she led what would most likely be considered a sheltered life. ■ **B)** She never once left the south of England, received little formal education, and was not in touch with the literary community. ■ **C)** In spite of her many novels regarding the dynamics of courtship and happy marriage, she herself never married. ■ **D)**

Austen's literature is generally regarded as marking the transition into the 19th Victorian romanticist style. It is typified by realistic human characters struggling between the opposing forces of romantic love and morality and prudence. Her novels feature strong, intelligent female protagonists who struggle to balance their emotions against their intellectual judgments in their relations with male suitors, while working towards the ultimate end of achieving a happy marriage. The happy marriage, however, is not always found. Some of her characters end up unhappy by marrying for security, social status, convenience, or in the case of one male character, beauty alone. Characters that do succeed in finding a happy marriage do so on the basis of friendship and respect.

One of the major criticisms of Austen's work is that her characters are too flawed to be admirable. For instance, they take wrong turns and make unadvisable decisions. Interestingly, it is this very aspect of her work that appeals to many readers. They contend that these flaws make Austen's characters more human, and therefore easier to relate to.

Austen's best-known works include *Sense and Sensibility*, *Pride and Prejudice*, and *Emma*. *Sense and Sensibility* is the story of two sisters: one who balances the stress of her romantic relationship with restraint and good judgment, and the other who responds to her difficulties by acting melodramatically. Ultimately, the first ends up in a happy marriage while the second loses her first suitor and must fall back on a boring alternative suitor. The first sister possessed "sense," or good judgment, in addition to "sensibility," or emotions.

Pride and Prejudice centers on a family with several daughters, all of whom are in search of the perfect husband. The protagonist, Elizabeth, and her suitor both possess the virtues of intelligence and romanticism. In the end, they discover that they must get over their

reverend (n):
a minister of a church

renown (n):
the quality of being widely admired

illuminating (adj):
creating clarity and understanding

sheltered (adj):
innocent; not exposed to different aspects of life

dynamics (n):
the way in which things work together

prudence (n):
the state of acting wisely and carefully, especially so as not to do anything immoral

protagonist (n):
the main, heroic character in a story

restraint (n):
the condition of being in control of emotions

melodramatically (adv):
with excessive emotion

"pride," or their high images of themselves, and their "prejudice," or their scrutiny of the other, in order to achieve a happy marriage. Many regard *Pride and Prejudice* as Jane Austen's masterpiece.

Emma is a later work, which incorporates a slightly different tone. It details the progression of a non-virtuous character into a virtuous one. The title character, Emma, is helped along her path by her suitor, Mr. Knightly. For example, he helps her give up her past habits of playing childish games with romance. This novel is remarkable in its elaboration on personal development and the transition to self-knowledge.

Many of these characters or themes may sound familiar to avid readers. ■ **A)** In addition, four of Austen's novels have been made into popular Hollywood movies. ■ **B)** Other popular Hollywood movies have borrowed heavily from Austen's style, themes, and characters, such as *Clueless* and *Bridget Jones' Diary*. The latter actually borrowed the name of the male suitor, Mr. Darcy, from *Pride and Prejudice*. ■ **C)** Although her novels are immensely popular in our time, Austen was not a well-known author in her own time. ■ **D)** All of her novels were published anonymously under the simple heading "By a Lady."

scrutiny *(n)*:
a close, careful examination

incorporate *(v)*:
to include

avid *(adj)*:
enthusiastic; with strong interest

1. The phrase "in touch with" in paragraph 1 means
   (A) being close to
   (B) communicating with
   (C) causing an emotional response
   (D) playing

2. As used in paragraph 2, what is the meaning of the word "end"?
   (A) Despair
   (B) Goal
   (C) Finish
   (D) Consequence

3. The phrase "fall back on" in paragraph 4 means
   (A) fail to accomplish
   (B) slip and hit the ground
   (C) change seasons
   (D) accept a second choice

4. Which of the following is NOT mentioned in the passage?
   (A) The presence of Austen's work in Hollywood
   (B) The reason why Austen never got married
   (C) The struggle between judgment and emotion
   (D) The book which is considered Austen's masterpiece

5. According to the passage, one male character found in Austen's work had an unhappy marriage for what reason?
   (A) He married only for beauty.
   (B) He married only for companionship.
   (C) He married only for money.
   (D) He married only for social status.

6. Which of the following sentences best expresses the essential information of the highlighted sentence? Incorrect choices change the meaning in important ways or leave out essential information.
   (A) Many critics consider Austen's novels to contain too many errors to be considered admirable literature.
   (B) One prominent criticism of Austen is that her personality was too flawed for people to admire her.
   (C) The tendency for Austen's characters to display flaws too strong to be considered heroic is one of the prominent criticisms of her novels.
   (D) Austen's work has been criticized for admiring characters with too many personality problems.

7. Look at the four squares [■] that indicate where the following sentence could be added to the paragraph 1:

   Austen died at the age of forty-one from what modern doctors suspect was Addison's disease, then an incurable disorder of the kidneys.

   Where would the sentence best fit? Choose the square [■] where the sentence should be added to the passage.
   (A) Line 3
   (B) Line 6
   (C) Line 8
   (D) Line 10

8. The main purpose of the passage is to

   (A) introduce the reader to the themes in Austen's work
   (B) discuss the life and experiences of Austen
   (C) respond to common criticisms of Austen's work
   (D) show the impact of Austen's work on society

9. Look at the four squares [■] that indicate where the following sentence could be added to the paragraph 7:

   Austen is generally regarded as having influenced Margaret Mitchell's classic novel _Gone with the Wind_.

   Where would the sentence best fit? Choose the square [■] where the sentence should be added to the passage.

   (A) Line 2
   (B) Line 3
   (C) Line 6
   (D) Line 8

10. **Directions:** _An introductory sentence for a brief summary of the passage is provided below. Complete the summary by selecting the THREE answer choices that express the most important ideas in the passage. Some sentences do not belong in the summary because they express ideas that are not presented in the passage or are minor ideas in the passage._

    First sentence: **Jane Austen was an influential novelist who wrote about the moral and emotional aspects of courtship.**

    (A) Austen was the daughter of a reverend and grew up in a small village in southern England.
    (B) Austen's novels feature strong female characters who have to balance the forces of judgment and emotion to end up happily married.
    (C) Some of Austen's characters do not end up happily married due to their poor choices during courtship, such as marrying for convenience, social status, or beauty.
    (D) Her three most renowned works are _Sense and Sensibility, Pride and Prejudice_, and _Emma_, of which _Pride and Prejudice_ is considered her masterpiece.
    (E) _Emma_ was a remarkable novel in that it gave the reader an overview of the transition from a non-virtuous to a virtuous character.
    (F) Though she died a little known author, her works have achieved great fame in our time, even appearing as Hollywood movies.

Understanding Referents and Vocabulary

Strategy

Vocabulary

- It is important that the meaning of the word fits the meaning in context and not just a general meaning of that particular word, e.g., "It was a very *basic* question, and so, very *easy* to answer." Fundamental is one meaning for basic; however, it is not suitable as a replacement in this case.
- Try to guess the meaning from your understanding of the sentence.
- If you are unfamiliar with a word, look for examples, antonyms, or adjective clauses in the text around it for any clues to its meaning.
- Guess from word parts such as pre- (before), anti- (against), dis- (not), etc.

Word Part	Example	Word Part	Example
anti- (against)	antibiotic	pre- (before)	prehistoric
bio- (living)	biology	post- (after)	postwar
co- (together)	cooperate	sub- (under)	submarine
dis-, im-, in-, un- (not)	disagree, immature, incorrect, unhappy	trans- (across)	transmission
		-able (can be done)	readable
inter- (among)	international	-ology (study)	archaeology
multi- (many)	multimedia	-ship (being, art)	membership, penmanship
over- (too much, beyond)	overcooked, overflow		

Referents

- Usually, the pronoun appears AFTER its referent. Look at nouns that come before the highlighted pronoun.
- Look at the form of the pronoun and identify whether it refers to a person, a thing, or an idea. This will make it easier to match the pronoun to the correct referent.
- Identify whether the pronoun is singular or plural.

Reference Words and Phrases

Personal Pronouns	Singular: *I, you, he/she/it* and the possessive, objective forms Plural: *we, you, they* and the possessive, objective forms
Demonstrative Pronouns	*this, that, these, those*
Relative Pronouns	Personal: *who, whose, whom, that* Non-personal: *which, that* Previous statement: *which* (used with a comma)
Indefinite Pronouns	Singular: *one, another, either, each* Non-count/Plural: *some, any, all, none, both, neither*
Quantifiers	Count: *most, many, half, (a) few, several* Non-count: *most, much, half, (a) little*
Paired Pronouns	*one/another/the other, some/(the) others, the former/the latter*
Cardinal/Ordinal Numbers	*one, two/the first, the fourth, the last*
Adverbs	Place: *here, there, where* Time: *then, in those days, when*

Human understanding of the universe is limited. We are biased because of our physical position in space, because of limits in our ability to perceive, and because of our relatively short life spans. As a result, our knowledge of the universe is severely hindered because of our transience and our limited, though developing, potential.

Though advanced technology has only been made available to us in recent centuries, astronomy is still one of the oldest sciences with a scientific methodology that had already been developed by the time of the ancient Greeks. There is also evidence to suggest that advanced observation techniques had been established well before this time. Historically, astronomy is a field where amateurs have, even to this date, contributed to many important astronomical discoveries. It is one of the few sciences where amateurs can still play an active role, especially in the discovery and observation of transient phenomena.

The science of astronomy is the observation and explanation of events that occur outside the Earth and its atmosphere. Its study encompasses the origins, evolution, and physical and chemical properties of objects and phenomena that can be observed in the sky (and that are outside the Earth), as well as the processes involving them. In early civilizations, the practice of astronomy consisted mainly of astrometry, measuring the positions of celestial bodies. It was the work of later astronomers such as Newton and Kepler that eventually led to the development of celestial mechanics. Newton was responsible for uniting the sciences of astronomy and physics. His laws of motion and theory of universal gravitation provided a physical basis for the purely descriptive laws of Kepler. Celestial mechanics is the mathematical science that can predict the movements of planets, asteroids, and other celestial bodies. This is most applicable to the objects within our own solar system. Motions and positions of objects have become easier to determine, and modern astronomy now focuses more on the observation of celestial objects as well as gaining an understanding of their physical nature.

Until science gave us the technology to look into space, people thought that the sun revolved around the Earth. This was a natural assumption; they saw the sun come up in the east and go down in the west. They had no way of knowing that the Earth spins on its axis, or that it orbits the sun. The fact that the Earth spins on its axis also causes problems because when the sun lights up the sky, we cannot see the stars. Aristotle was one of the more famous advocates of this theory.

biased *(adj)*:
predisposed to favor one side; having an inclination to favor something

hinder *(v)*:
to obstruct; to hamper or slow down

transience *(n)*:
the condition of lasting for only a short period

methodology *(n)*:
a system of methods or principles

phenomenon *(n)*:
an event or action perceived through the senses

encompass *(v)*:
to include

evolution *(n)*:
the process whereby organisms develop or change from generation to generation

celestial *(adj)*:
belonging to or relating to the sky

nature *(n)*:
essential characteristics

As a result, many people in the following centuries assumed that the Earth was the center of the universe.

Even under perfect conditions, human visual perception is limited. Our eyes are imperfect and are able to see only a small fraction of the light in the universe. We cannot detect radiation outside the range of the light spectrum, including radiation of the following wavelengths: radio, infrared, ultraviolet, x-ray, or gamma ray. Just as we are developing technology to overcome our positional bias, we are also "seeing" more of the universe through these other wavelengths with the help of various technological advances.

Another problem limiting our understanding of the universe is that we don't live very long. The universe, it is believed, is about fifteen billion years old. So, in our short life spans, we don't see many of the changes that occur in the universe. It can be thought of as trying to understand what happens in the course of a whole year by only looking at what happens within one second. Though we may be able to see stars and other phenomena at different stages in their development, we cannot measure the course of many cosmic phenomena through their life spans. We cannot have a comprehensive knowledge of the universe if we have only been aware of it for such a short time, relatively speaking. However, technology is improving our pursuit, as modern computers are able to simulate changes in the universe occurring over billions of years.

Technology is helping us overcome our limitations, but our location, our limited eyesight, and our short time on Earth still hinder a complete grasp of the universe.

spectrum (n):
the band of colors visible to the eye

infrared (adj):
light with a wavelength beyond the red end of the visible spectrum

ultraviolet (adj):
light with a wavelength between violet (in the visible spectrum) and x-rays

gamma ray (n):
electromagnetic radiation of very high frequency

cosmic (adj):
relating to the universe

grasp (n):
an understanding

READING

LISTENING

SPEAKING

WRITING

PRACTICE TEST

1. Who does "we" in paragraph 1 refer to?
   (A) Earth
   (B) Astronomers
   (C) Scientists
   (D) Humans

2. What word does "it" in paragraph 6 refer to
   in the passage?
   (A) The snapshot of space that a human sees
   (B) The snapshot of space that the human
       race has seen
   (C) The belief that the universe is 15 billion
       years old
   (D) The belief that humans went to space
       before recorded history

3. The word "limited" could best be replaced by
   which of the following?
   (A) Focused
   (B) Infinite
   (C) Growing
   (D) Restricted

4. Which of the following is closest is meaning
   to "course" in paragraph 6?
   (A) Class
   (B) Development
   (C) Age
   (D) Range

5. **Directions:** *An introductory sentence for a
   brief summary of the passage is provided below.
   Complete the summary by selecting the THREE
   answer choices that express the most important
   ideas in the passage. Some sentences do not
   belong in the summary because they express
   ideas that are not presented in the passage or
   are minor ideas in the passage.*

   First sentence: **Humanity's understanding
   of the universe has developed over the
   centuries.**

   (A) Astronomy is an ancient science which
       had established systems more than two
       thousand years ago.
   (B) A number of new instruments have been
       developed to improve our view of space.
   (C) The Earth spins on its axis, which causes
       problems.
   (D) Over time, theories that explain astronomical
       observations have become more
       sophisticated.
   (E) Because a human life span is short on an
       astronomical scale, human understanding
       of changes in space is naturally limited.
   (F) Aristotle's ideas and theories hindered
       the development of astronomy for many
       centuries.

In China, the practice of acupuncture has been traced back to approximately the 1st millennium B.C. Some evidence has placed the practice of acupuncture within the period of the Han dynasty (from 202 B.C. to 220 A.D.). Its origins are somewhat uncertain. The earliest Chinese medical texts (68 B.C.) do not mention acupuncture, though some hieroglyphics have been found dating back to 1000 B.C. that depict an early type of acupuncture. Sharp pointed stones, believed to have been used to treat certain diseases in ancient times, were discovered amongst some ruins. Some scholars argue that the manner in which these stones were used was not dissimilar to certain acupuncture techniques.

Acupuncture is understood to be a procedure for regulating the circulation of gi (vital energy) and blood. Approximately 2,000 years ago, a text describing the usage of gi was written, titled *Huangdi Neijing (Yellow Emperor's Classic on Internal Medicine)*. This text explained how holes, put into the energy paths of the body, called meridians, could treat various physical problems. In some cases, holes into a meridian would let out blood without releasing gi. Other holes into meridians would let out gi without releasing blood. The basic understanding of gi and blood within the body was based on observations of water in nature.

Over time, the focus of acupuncture shifted from releasing gi and blood to regulating the flow of gi within the body. Physicians believed that, just as water could be blocked from its natural flow, gi could be blocked within the body. The physician's job was then to determine where meridians were blocked, and through acupuncture, to clear the blockage. In a blocked stream, creating a small hole or crevice in a blockage may clear the entire path of the stream. The force of the water penetrating the hole will widen it until the normal flow is restored. Physicians then reasoned that, in the human body, inserting a small needle into the blocked meridian would have a similar effect.

Although this description of the basic concept behind acupuncture is overly simplified, it still conveys the essence of how acupuncture works. Even today, students of traditional acupuncture are taught to locate the areas of disturbance, to isolate the main blockage points, and to clear the blockage. But that is only the tip of the acupuncture iceberg. Other factors which must be considered in acupuncture therapy include where needles are put into meridians, how deeply the needles are

hieroglyphics (n):
a form of writing using pictures as symbols

circulation (n):
flow or movement

vital (energy) (adj):
life (energy)

blockage (n):
something which blocks or prevents something from passing

crevice (n):
a narrow opening

penetrate (v):
to get through; to find a way through

essence (n):
the basic or fundamental part of something

iceberg (n):
a huge mass of ice that floats in the sea

inserted, and even what the needles are made of.

In the Western world, many arguments have been made against acupuncture. One such argument is that traditional Chinese medicine is not based on knowledge of modern physiology, biochemistry, nutrition, anatomy, and any of the known mechanisms of healing. Nor does it have any basis in cell chemistry, blood circulation, nerve function, or the existence of hormones and other biochemical substances. There is no relationship between the meridians that are used in this form of medicine and the layout of the organs and nerves in human physiology. Nor can it be demonstrated that unblocking gi by any means is effective in the treatment of disease. Many scientists and doctors continue to make this argument in opposition of acupuncture, trying to prevent it from becoming an established form of medicine. Because it has no strong scientific foundation or basis, there are those who would continue to discredit it.

Though it has continued to be regarded with some level of skepticism and mistrust, acupuncture is gradually becoming accepted in the Western world as a form of medicine. In 1994, between ten and fifteen million people in the United States tried it as a form of treatment. Furthermore, in 1996, the FDA changed the status of acupuncture needles. With the needles now regarded as class 2 medical devices, it meant that acupuncture was now considered safe when performed by a licensed practitioner. Acupuncture can also be found on many college curriculums today.

mechanism *(n)*:
a means; an action

hormone *(n)*:
a chemical made and released in the body by special glands

biochemical *(adj)*:
relating to chemical compounds and reactions in the body

discredit *(v)*:
to cause to be regarded with doubt and suspicion

1. What does "its" in paragraph 3 refer to?

   (A) Acupuncture
   (B) Blood
   (C) Gi
   (D) Water

2. What does the pronoun "it" in line 5 of the last paragraph refer to?

   (A) Acupuncture
   (B) The needle
   (C) The FDA
   (D) The change in medical status

3. The phrase "a similar effect" in the last line of paragraph 3 refers to

   (A) creating more flow through opening a small hole first
   (B) inserting needles into crevices
   (C) locating blocked points that need to be opened
   (D) testing the amount of flow through different points of the body

4. Which of the following means most nearly the same as "clear" as used in paragraph 3?

   (A) Clean
   (B) Go beyond
   (C) Remove
   (D) Successfully pass through

5. **Directions:** *An introductory sentence for a brief summary of the passage is provided below. Complete the summary by selecting the THREE answer choices that express the most important ideas in the passage. Some sentences do not belong in the summary because they express ideas that are not presented in the passage or are minor ideas in the passage.*

First sentence: **The practice of acupuncture has existed for over two thousand years.**

   (A) It regulates the flow of energy through the body by removing blockages.
   (B) References to acupuncture can be found in the earliest Chinese medical texts.
   (C) Many arguments have been made to discredit acupuncture as a form of medicine.
   (D) Over ten million people tried acupuncture in the United States in 1994.
   (E) The treatment of the meridians is based on nerve function and blood circulation.
   (F) Acupuncture is considered a safe treatment when practiced by a qualified professional.

   A - C - F

Robert Frost was a legendary 20th century American poet. Though he did not begin his career as a writer until later in life, by the time of his death in 1963, he had achieved fame on both sides of the Atlantic, had been appointed to the position of Poet Laureate, and had won four Pulitzer prizes. Frost was highly-acclaimed for mastering the ability to combine a range of genres and styles. He was best known for his simple poems about nature and New England farm life.

Frost drew his images from typical New England countryside scenarios, and his language reflected the characteristics of New England speech. Although the images and voices that Frost depicts often seem familiar and old, it is not unusual to see an edge of skepticism or irony in his work. While his poetry can at first appear old-fashioned, easy, or carefree, on re-examination, it can distinguish itself from traditional poetry. Though it does maintain a sense of tradition, his skepticism and the wider range of emotions that are evoked help provide a link between the American poetry of the 19th century and that of the 20th century.

Though free verse had become a popular form during his time, Frost preferred to write using traditional metrical and rhythmical schemes. (He once said he would as soon play tennis without a net as write free verse.) He would often write in the standard meter of blank verse (lines with five stresses) but would run sentences over several lines to allow the poetic meter to play subtly under the rhythms of natural speech. He remained apart from the typical poetic forms of his time.

Much of his poetry deals with the interaction between people and nature. His poems are often a dark and ironic meditation on universal themes, expressed in a way that is faithful to spoken language. His poetry is infused with layers of ambiguity and irony. His impression of nature is that it is beautiful and yet perilous, descriptors which later critics and writers equated with the tragic circumstances which would affect his family and life. He often writes of woods, birds, and other parts of a simple living that surrounded his everyday life in New England.

His childhood, however, must have been quite distinct from the country living and meditations for which he would later be known. Frost was born in San Francisco, California in 1885 and lived there until the age of eleven when his father died. The family then moved to Massachusetts, where Frost attended high school. He was co-valedictorian of his high school along with his future wife, Eleanor White. He later attended Dartmouth and Harvard Universities, though he never completed a

legendary *(adj)*:
relating to a famous person or thing from the past

poet laureate *(n)*:
an officially appointed poet commissioned to write for state occasions

acclaimed *(adj)*:
praised; commended

reflect *(v)*:
to consider; to think about

irony *(n)*:
a type of humor that takes its effect from stating the opposite of what is meant

distinguish *(v)*:
to mark or see as different

evoke *(v)*:
to bring out

form *(n)*:
a type or variety

meditation *(n)*:
a thought about a subject

infuse *(v)*:
to fill with

ambiguity *(n)*:
the state of having mixed or uncertain meanings

perilous *(adj)*:
dangerous

paralleled *(adj)*:
corresponding with; similar to

valedictorian *(n)*:
the student with the highest academic grade in a graduating class

degree at either. He settled on a farm in New Hampshire which his grandfather had bought for him. In 1912, he sold the farm and moved to England to dedicate himself entirely to his writing, which soon brought him both fame and fortune.

Frost spent three years in England, where two books of his verse, *A Boy's Will* and *North of Boston,* were published. He also became acquainted with the poet F. S. Flint, who introduced him to Ezra Pound. When he returned from England, he was able to purchase a new farm in Franconia, New Hampshire with the money from his poetry. By the 1920s, he was firmly established as a great literary figure. The pivotal change of direction in Frost's life, at the age of 53, seems to be reflected in perhaps the best known passage from any of his poems, the ending from "The Road not Taken" (1915), the words of which reflect that sometimes the more difficult route in life can be the one that brings a greater reward or perhaps a deeper understanding:

"Two roads diverged in a wood, and I —
I took the one less traveled by,
And that has made all the difference."

figure *(n)*:
individual; person

pivotal *(adj)*:
crucially important

diverge *(v)*:
to split; to go separate ways

1. The word "which" in the first sentence of paragraph 5 refers to

   (A) country living and meditations
   (B) the distinctiveness
   (C) his childhood
   (D) Robert Frost

2. What does "that" in the last line of the passage refer to?

   (A) The path that was less traveled by
   (B) The lack of travel on the path
   (C) The divergence of the paths
   (D) Frost's taking of the path

3. The expression "on both sides of the Atlantic" in paragraph 1 is closest in meaning to

   (A) with both the general public and intellectuals
   (B) with both English and non-English speakers
   (C) in both the United States and England
   (D) for both his poetry and his prose

4. The word "skepticism" in paragraph 2 could best be replaced by which of the following?

   (A) Cynicism
   (B) Disbelief
   (C) Suspicion
   (D) Disagreement

5. **Directions:** *Complete the table by matching the phrases below. Select the appropriate phrases from the answer choices and match them to the category they belong to. Two of the answer choices will NOT be used.*

Traditional Poetry	Non-traditional poetry
B	A
D	C
E	

   (A) Skepticism
   (B) Rhythmical schemes
   (C) Free verse
   (D) Form
   (E) Blank verse
   (F) Country imagery
   (G) Genre and style

James Madison, born March 16, 1751 in Westmoreland County, Virginia, is considered by many to be the father of the Constitution. This, of course, isn't without good reason, as he was instrumental in the development and ratification of the United States Constitution. He also spearheaded the drive to create the Bill of Rights and to include it in the Constitution. Why he did this, and the hurdles that he overcame in achieving this goal, would secure his place in American history.

Madison was born into a wealthy family. His wealth afforded him many luxuries, such as attending and graduating from what is today known as Princeton University. Following this, his social status, intelligence, and innate leadership abilities allowed him to secure positions of power and prestige. He was a popular and gifted leader, even at a young age. He was soon elected to the Virginia Convention (1776). Its responsibility was to consider the relationship of the US colonies to Great Britain, pondering the possibility of an independent America. Madison, being a staunch patriot, was in firm support of US independence from Britain.

Subsequently, he was selected as a member of the Governor's Council (1777-1780) and then elected to a 3-year term in the Continental Congress (1780-1783). Madison's popularity was apparent, as he was quickly elevated to a position of power within the Congress. This was quite surprising given that he was the youngest person in the Congress. While an unsuccessful bid along with Alexander Hamilton to strengthen the power of Congress (allowing it to tax and regulate trade) may have proven disheartening to some, Madison forged ahead. He moved to the Virginia legislature (1783) and fought for the complete separation of church and state. His efforts proved successful as the legislature adopted the Statute of Virginia for Religious Freedom drafted by Thomas Jefferson.

Finally, Madison and his associates, with a goal toward increasing the power of a central government, were able to convince the Congress to summon the May 1787 Constitutional Convention in Philadelphia. Its purpose was to revise some of the articles contained in the federal Constitution. This was a pivotal meeting not only for the country, but for securing Madison's legacy in history. Madison's leadership and persuasive abilities were vital to his accomplishments at this convention. These included drafting the Virginia Plan, fighting to ensure that the federal constitution included separation of the powers of church and state,

instrumental *(adj)*:
being an important factor in or to something

ratification *(n)*:
a confirmation; a formal consent

spearhead *(v)*:
to lead a movement or campaign

hurdle *(n)*:
a problem; an obstacle

innate *(adj)*:
of a natural gift or ability within a person; not learned

prestige *(n)*:
fame; reputation

staunch *(adj)*:
loyal; faithful

apparent *(adj)*:
obvious

legislature *(n)*:
the section of the government which has the power to make laws

and creating a plan to establish a strong executive with a veto and a judiciary able to override state laws. He was also forced to defend his position on a strong central government against those fearful of such a thing. His prophetic letters defending the Constitution have been proven true throughout the experiences of history.

As suggested, James Madison was also responsible for the inclusion of the Bill of Rights into the US Constitution. It was at the same Constitutional Convention in 1787 when Madison made his successful push for the Bill of Rights. While opposition to this was strong, Madison and his supporters continued to insist on its inclusion. Many, in opposition to strong, centralized power, were strong supporters of the Bill of Rights, since it served as a safety net, preventing the potential abuse of power by a strong centralized government.

Thanks to Madison's fortitude and persistence, Congress was forced to debate his list of Congressional amendments, despite a general disinterest. He successfully defended them, and as a result, the Bill of Rights was created. Madison's direct involvement in its creation is apparent in its language, which is said to be very close, if not exactly the way Madison himself wrote it.

Perhaps more than any other member of the founding generation, Madison played a major role in forming America's political institutions. It has been said that Madison's Constitution was instrumental in creating a balance of order and liberty, national pride and rational principle, as well as faith and reason. He understood that restricting any human freedom, whether it is political, economic, intellectual, or religious, is equivalent to restricting them all.

Following the ratification of the Constitution, Madison went on to serve in the House of Representatives (1789-1797), as Secretary of State under Jefferson (1801-1809), and then as the fourth President of the United States (1809-1817). He lived a truly outstanding life.

veto (n):
the right to formally reject a proposal or to forbid an action

judiciary (n):
the branch of the government concerned with the legal system and the administration of justice

prophetic (adj):
foretelling the future

fortitude (n):
uncomplaining courage in the face of problems or adversity

1. In paragraph 2, what does the pronoun "its" refer to?

   (A) James Madison
   (B) The Virginia Convention
   (C) The Constitutional Convention
   (D) Great Britain

2. What does "these" refer to in paragraph 4?

   (A) The United States
   (B) The amendments to the U.S. Constitution
   (C) Madison's accomplishments
   (D) Madison's ideas

3. In paragraph 7, the word "equivalent" is closest in meaning to

   (A) different
   (B) the same
   (C) almost
   (D) unlike

4. The word "patriot" in paragraph 2 means

   (A) someone who proudly supports his/her country
   (B) someone who is ashamed of his/her country
   (C) a national hero
   (D) someone who loves politics

evil reader

5. **Directions:** *An introductory sentence for a brief summary of the passage is provided below. Complete the summary by selecting the THREE answer choices that express the most important ideas in the passage. Some sentences do not belong in the summary because they express ideas that are not presented in the passage or are minor ideas in the passage.*

First sentence: **James Madison was a key figure in establishing American political institutions.**

(A) He was selected or elected to several prominent political positions from which he supported many causes, particularly separation of church and state and a strong centralized government.
(B) Being born into a rich family, he was able to attend a prestigious university.
(C) Born into wealth, he used his power to rally for US independence from Britain.
(D) He served as the 4th President of the United States from 1809-1817.
(E) He played a pivotal role in the creation of the US Constitution and the Bill of Rights, all culminating in the Constitutional Convention of 1787.
(F) Even though he and his colleague, Alexander Hamilton, were unsuccessful in trying to strengthen the power of Congress, he kept going.

A C E

It was not until the 19th century that artists in America could credit themselves with developing a uniquely American school of art. Before that, artists in the young democracy of America based their techniques and content on the established schools of European art ideals. However, during the first half of the 19th century, a group of painters who came to be known as the Hudson River painters developed a truly American version of romantic realism depicting landscapes.

In order to appreciate the importance of the works of the Hudson River painters, one must first understand the distinction of romantic realism from other schools of realism. There are, after all, more than a dozen formalized ways to interpret realism in art. Some of the more familiar schools of realism would include classical realism, realist realism, photo realism, political realism, and social realism. For the sake of simplicity, examples from only classical and realist realism shall be covered.

Obviously, any artist seeking realism in his or her works hopes that people will recognize the subject of the work as something from the existing world. This does not mean, however, that the subject of the work must actually exist. For example, suppose a classical realist chooses a man's body as the subject of a work. The artist must necessarily make use of an existing model, living or inanimate, to base his work on. However, the aim of the piece for the classical realist is to create the "perfect" body a man rather than recreate the body of the actual model for the piece. On the other hand, an artist from the school of realist realism would attempt to recreate exactly the figure of the model, warts and all.

Where, then, does that leave the school of romantic realism? By comparison with the schools of classical and realist realism, one finds that neither of these schools deals with emotion. These schools both maintain an objective view of their subjects. The artist objectively attempts to create a perfectly imagined representation of a subject or a perfectly accurate representation of a subject. The romantic realist brings emotion into the work. The artist's subjective view of a subject is rendered in the work through strategic use of particular realist techniques.

Bearing these distinctions in mind, one may better grasp the efforts of the Hudson River painters in what they attempted to do, and in what they actually accomplished. At the time that this school of art evolved, America was mostly undeveloped wilderness. Large cities did

realism (n):
a realistic or lifelike representation in art or literature

inanimate (adj):
not living; inorganic

wart (n):
a small hard growth found on the skin

objective (adj):
of an opinion or view that is not related to a personal beliefs or ideals

subjective (adj):
of an opinion or view related to personal beliefs or ideals

render (v):
to cause to become

bear in mind (v phrase):
to remember; to keep in mind

wilderness (n):
a wild, uncultivated or uninhabited region

exist along the east coast; however, in less than a day's journey outside of any of these large metropolitan areas, one could easily enter forests and river valleys seemingly untouched by humans since the dawn of time. In fact, in the early 1800s, traveling north along the Hudson River, which happens to flow along the western edge of Manhattan Island in New York state, provided quick, easy access to the scenic wilderness of the Hudson River Valley. It was this area that the Hudson River painters used as the subject of many of their works. The Hudson River painters would enter the wilderness with sketchbook in hand to record the details of the landscapes and scenery that struck them. They would then return to their studios with their sketches in order to paint their masterpieces.

"But," some may argue, "romantic landscapes were not an invention of American artists." And this is true. In fact, a clear influence of 18th century European romantic landscapes is evident in the works of the Hudson painters. What is different about the Hudson painters' works is nature presented in its "uncivilized" glory. Whereas the landscape painters of Europe romanticized the tamed rivers and people-worn hills of Europe, artists of the American landscape were given the unique opportunity to interpret a more rugged environment. This uncivilized ruggedness spoke to Americans. This was a landscape that the Hudson River painters infused with a haunting loneliness as well as a reverence for nature, capturing two emotions close to the hearts of Americans of that era.

seemingly *(adv)*:
apparently

dawn of time *(n phase)*:
the beginning of time

rugged *(adj)*:
being rough and uneven

reverence *(n)*:
a great respect

1. The phrase "these schools" in paragraph 4 refers to
   (A) all of the schools of realism
   (B) art schools that taught realism
   (C) classical realism and realist realism
   (D) romantic realism and American realism

2. What does "them" in the next to the last sentence of paragraph 5 refer to?
   (A) Details
   (B) Landscapes
   (C) Painters
   (D) Sketchbooks

3. The word "aim" in paragraph 3 is closest in meaning to
   (A) accuracy
   (B) direction
   (C) pointing
   (D) purpose

4. The word "clear" in the last paragraph could best be replaced by which of the following?
   (A) Bright
   (B) Evident
   (C) Transparent
   (D) Without guilt

5. **Directions:** *Complete the table below about the different schools of realism discussed in the passage. Match the appropriate words or phrases to the type of realism to which they are associated in the passage. Two of the answer choices will NOT be used.*

Classical Realism	Romantic Realism
_____	_____
_____	_____
_____	

   (A) A human figure
   (B) Emotion
   (C) A landscape
   (D) Objective
   (E) Accuracy
   (F) Perfection
   (G) Warts

Skill E — Making Inferences and Establishing Purpose

Strategy

Making Inferences

- The questions in this section require more thought; therefore, you should spend more time on these questions.
- Understand the facts accurately. It makes inferring easier.
- Try to guess the meaning behind the information that is given.
- Read the key words and phrases in the question and answer choices. Look for those key words in the passage.
- Draw a conclusion based on the key words and phrases you have found.

Establishing Purpose

- Read the relevant information in the passage for accurate understanding.
- Think about the writer's purpose for putting the information in the passage.
- Do not choose answer choices that are too general or vague.
- It is important to get a clear image of the main idea.
- Using the main idea and development of the passage, infer the purpose.
- Looking at the development of the passage, identify whether the purpose will be to compare, contrast, or give a point of view.
- Words that appear in answer choices:
  ⇨ give examples, illustrate, describe, explain
  ⇨ prove, support, argue, persuade
  ⇨ introduce, emphasize, point out
  ⇨ compare, contrast

In the past, writing was considered exclusive and time-consuming. The advent of the printing press popularized the written word and ushered in the gradual rise in global literacy. The speed and legibility of writing was greatly improved by the typewriter. But all of these were eclipsed when the personal computer came of age as the standard tool for writing. But what new dimensions and drawbacks, if any, does it offer?

We can first consider the benefits of online resources that may be accessed while we are writing on our computers. By merely typing in a single word or sentence, we can gain access to hundreds of thousands, if not millions of essays, stories, guides, and articles on the subject we are writing about. These resources can encompass almost any aspect of research or information we can contemplate, as well as give us ideas we hadn't previously considered. Grammar resources, dictionaries, even translations can be readily available at the push of a button.

With regard to actual writing, the main innovation is that the information on the page can be infinitely modified. This has no doubt saved countless hours of time over the past two decades. The mastery of the functions of the word processing program is invaluable in today's world, and has now become a pre-requisite for many firms when taking on new staff. Knowledge of the many different types of computer software available has become a necessity in the workplace.

The Cut, Copy, and Paste functions, usually CTRL-X, C, and V respectively, can be seen as a prime example. These can be used to rearrange the structure of sentences, paragraphs, and whole essays, as well as to quickly transfer pieces of text from one document to another.

The Find/Replace function, CTRL-F, is also an indispensable tool. This allows us to scan the text for particular words and examine each instance of their use, replacing them with another term wherever we choose. Abbreviating is a handy method that goes along with this. For example, if writing about pollution, you can write "plt" instead, and later use Find/Replace to change them all to "pollution."

Having multiple screens open simultaneously can also facilitate cutting and pasting functions. This can also allow us to view the same text in two windows and to make slight modifications to each version so as to choose which one we prefer. We can then cut and paste the various sentences from each text to create new paragraphs.

Some word processing programs also include a thesaurus which

exclusive (adj):
involving the rejection or denial of something else

advent (n):
a coming; an arrival

legibility (n):
the ability to be read easily

dimension (n):
an aspect

contemplate (v):
to think about; to consider

innovation (n):
something new which has been introduced

pre-requisite (n):
something that is needed beforehand

respectively (adv):
referring to each person or thing separately and in order

indispensable (adj):
necessary; essential

facilitate (v):
to help or assist someone

can be useful for looking up synonyms for words that we may be using too often. These can often be a brief respite when our creativity has started to dull after long periods of writing. The use of basic functions such as Word Count and Spell Check can also save students valuable time when they have a deadline for a paper or essay.

Though the benefits of writing with computers are many, we also have to be aware of certain negative implications. For example, a writer must be careful with Autocorrection for spelling and grammar. Spellcheck does not catch mistakes like "form" instead of "from," and Grammar Check will overlook some bad sentences, while at the same time flagging all passive sentences — as if English had no passive voice!

One of the main criticisms of computers is that you cannot get a good overview of the text. But, if we consider the many improvements and changes to monitors in recent years, this is likely to improve in the future with larger screens and better zoom functions.

Unfortunately, one negative side-effect of this is the deterioration to a person's eyesight. Television and eye-related problems have been well documented; the effects of computers on eye strain are worse. This is due to the fact that computers require users to be closer to the screen. The problem is caused by long periods of time focusing on the screen. Computers can put stress on your eyes, causing headaches, blurred vision, tired eyes, and other symptoms of eye strain. There are measures to help prevent these symptoms, though many people remain unaware of them.

respite *(n)*:
a break; a period of rest

implication *(n)*:
an indirect indication

deterioration *(n)*:
the process of becoming weaker, or less effective

1. In paragraph 5, what does the author imply?

   (A) The Find/Replace function can result in errors if not used carefully.
   (B) The abbreviating method is superior to the Find/Replace function.
   (C) The purpose of abbreviating is to save time by not writing the full word.
   (D) The Find/Replace function often makes the Copy/Paste function unnecessary.

2. The author mentions Autocorrection tools in paragraph 8 in order to

   (A) show that they are extremely useful but require specialized software knowledge
   (B) show that they make knowledge of spelling and grammar effectively unnecessary
   (C) show that they should not be used by university professors or serious writers
   (D) show that they are useful, but we must be careful to double-check their results

3. The expression "ushered in" in paragraph 1 is closest in meaning to

   (A) hindered
   (B) instigated
   (C) procured
   (D) harmonized

4. Which of the following could best replace the word "eclipsed" in paragraph 1?

   (A) Taken over
   (B) Redeemed
   (C) Outshined
   (D) Reproached

5. **Directions:** *An introductory sentence for a brief summary of the passage is provided below. Complete the summary by selecting the THREE answer choices that express the most important ideas in the passage. Some sentences do not belong in the summary because they express ideas that are not presented in the passage or are minor ideas in the passage.*

   First sentence: **Personal computers have revolutionized the process of writing in the modern age.**

   (A) Numerous resources and sources of information have been made available through the Internet.
   (B) Personal computers come in a variety of models.
   (C) A good knowledge of word processing functions is essential.
   (D) Many new writing programs have been made available in recent years.
   (E) Autocorrection tools are very reliable and have made a good knowledge of grammar unnecessary.
   (F) Though there are numerous benefits, there are also certain physical side-effects to using computers.

Skill E 02   Problems with Meat Production

Most people in wealthy countries enjoy diets that are rich in meat and dairy products. But experts warn that we cannot continue in this trend for long. The current demand for food products that come from animals is not sustainable, and future generations are going to have to change their eating habits.

The problem is water. It takes a lot more water to feed animals than it does to grow grains. For example, fifteen cubic meters of water is needed to produce a kilogram of beef, whereas a kilo of cereals needs less than three cubic meters. It also takes more water to process the meat and to refrigerate it. The meat industry consumes over half of all water used for all purposes in the United States, and most of this water is used to irrigate cattle feedlots.

Not only does meat production use up a lot of water, it also causes water pollution and affects land. Waste from livestock contains high levels of nitrogen and phosphorus. These chemicals pollute the groundwater and waterways. The percentage of U.S. agricultural land used to produce meat is 56%. The strains on land include topsoil erosion and depletion of forested areas.

We see, therefore, that the cattle industry places a large strain on the environment. Not only is it energy inefficient, it also pollutes water, occupies large tracts of land, and has a negative effect on the health of the people who abuse its consumption. This industry is also subsidized by the government. Therefore, the price paid for meat doesn't reflect the environmental hazards involved in the process. As a result, most people are unaware of the negative impact the production of meat has on the environment, as well as how much it depletes the resources so badly needed for the future. Because it is not reflected in the cost, many people remain unaware of these facts. Furthermore, because it is not an immediate threat, relatively speaking, many producers tend to ignore these facts in order to continue making a profit.

In the recent past, the increases in food production have exceeded population growth, but because of dwindling water supplies, increases in food production cannot continue at the same pace. Population growth is increasing rapidly, and the world population is expected to grow to at least eight billion by 2025. Hunger and malnutrition are rampant in developing countries. The already scarce food supplies cannot keep up with population growth. The excessive production in the meat industry, now, is reducing the availability of water we will so desperately need

sustainable (adj):
being able to maintain a certain level

irrigate (v):
to supply land with water

depletion (n):
the reduction in number or amount of something

consumption (n):
the rate at which something is used

subsidize (v):
to provide financial support for

hazard (n):
risk or danger

impact (n):
an effect or influence

dwindling (adj):
lessening; decreasing

malnutrition (n):
the condition resulting from lack of food intake or an unbalanced diet

in the future.

While resources such as fossil fuels should be used conservatively for the future, they are being seriously depleted by the cattle industry. Currently, the most energy efficient meat processing procedure produces about 35 units of energy (available in the meat consumed) for every 100 units of fossil fuel energy spent in the production process. On the other hand, the least efficient plant processing procedure produces more than 300 units of energy for every 100 units of fossil fuel energy spent in the production process. This gives some indication of how wasteful, or inefficient, the beef industry actually is. Fossil fuel energy is utilized from before a cow is raised until it is eaten. This includes the energy necessary to clear land of its original vegetation, to grow cow feed, to operate slaughterhouses, and to transport the meat to market. Forty pounds of soybeans are produced by the same amount of fossil fuels required to produce one pound of meat.

The best way to ensure that everyone has enough to eat is to be more efficient about food production. Water supplies are limited, so we must make the best use of it. If we can feed more people by growing grain instead of meat, we should, as this also lessens the amount of fuels used to generate that amount of food. Meat and dairy products are a luxury that we can no longer afford to consume in the quantities we are accustomed to. A drastic change in our diets is going to be required to alleviate world hunger and to sustain population growth.

expend *(v)*:
to use up

utilize *(v)*:
to use

alleviate *(v)*:
to make less severe; lessen

1. Which of the following can be inferred from paragraph 1 about meat production?

(A) Meat production is likely to increase as the population increases.

(B) Meat production is likely to decrease as the population increases.

(C) Meat production is likely to have little effect on supplies of fresh water.

(D) Meat production is likely to diminish grain production.

2. Why does the author mention government subsidizing in paragraph 4?

(A) To show that the government supports the production of meat

(B) To show how population growth is putting a strain on fresh water supplies

(C) To show that the government has made people aware of environmental hazards related to the meat industry

(D) To show that the government does not want to promote grain and cereal production

3. As used in paragraph 1, what is the meaning of the word "rich"?

(A) Wealthy

(B) Developed

(C) Prosperous

(D) Plentiful

4. Which of the following could best replace the word "rampant" as used in paragraph 5?

(A) Disconcerting

(B) Widespread

(C) Problematic

(D) Improving

5. **Directions:** *An introductory sentence for a brief summary of the passage is provided below. Complete the summary by selecting the THREE answer choices that express the most important ideas in the passage. Some sentences do not belong in the summary because they express ideas that are not presented in the passage or are minor ideas in the passage.*

First sentence: **In the near future, it will be necessary to change eating habits because of the excess in food consumption.**

(A) It takes more than five times the amount of water to produce a kilo of beef than it does a kilo of cereal.

(B) The availability of beef has increased the number of fast food outlets in America.

(C) Beef production accounts for two thirds of agricultural land use.

(D) Government funding helps sustain low costs, as well as the current level of production in the beef industry.

(E) Because of population growth, the current rate of food production is unsustainable.

(F) In the future, it will be necessary to allocate more agricultural land for meat production.

"The Silk Road" is the Western name for the longest and most significant trade route in the history of the world. It effectively spanned the entire Eurasian land mass and carried with it the cultures and religions of the diverse peoples that it served. It was controlled, at various chronological and geographical points, by the Chinese, the Indians, the Greeks and Romans, the Muslims, the Mongols, and a miscellany of smaller tribes.

The term "Silk Road" is in fact largely a misnomer. Firstly, it was not one single road but several branching paths. This is due to the difficult terrain between China and western Asia, whose centerpiece is "the land of death," the Taklimakan desert. Secondly, many other items were traded besides silk, such as precious stones, metals, spices, and exotic animals and plants.

The Silk Road was first traveled by emissary Zhang Qian when he was sent on a diplomatic mission to the Western Regions in the Han Dynasty (206 B.C.-A.D. 220) for military and political reasons, not trade. His purpose was to seek allies against Xiongnu's repeated invasions. Although the mission failed in its original purpose, information Zhang Qian conveyed to China about Central Asia, and vice versa, made people in each area desire goods produced in the other. Silk, which was favored by Persians and Romans, inaugurated the trade along the Silk Road. Interestingly, Zhang Qian also returned with news of a larger type of horse that he had seen on his journey. The Han Dynasty later sent a number of expeditions to capture some of these horses in order to improve their cavalry. Images of these horses can be seen in Han art of that period.

The road brought Chinese inventions to Europe, such as silk, porcelain, and gun powder. It brought Greek culture as far as India under the reign of Alexander the Great and also brought the Chinese spices and wool. One Buddhist sect, imitating Greek sculpture, began to make statues of the Buddha. Statues such as these can now be found all over eastern Asia. Two of the most famous travelers on the road were Xuan Zhuang, who brought Indian priests to China, and Marco Polo, who reportedly brought porcelain and pasta to Europe.

Having examined the productivity of earlier dynasties, it was the Tang Dynasty that recognized the importance of internal stability and economic development. A number of favorable policies were implemented to stimulate and encourage trade between the East and the West. This

span *(v)*:
to extend to; to cover

diverse *(adj)*:
varied; various

miscellany *(n)*:
a mixture of various kinds

terrain *(n)*:
a stretch of land, especially with reference to its physical characteristics

emissary *(n)*:
a person sent on a mission, usually on behalf of the government

diplomatic *(adj)*:
concerned with making agreements, usually between governments

inaugurate *(v)*:
to mark the beginning of something

reign *(n)*:
a period of rule or control (by a king or leader)

implement *(v)*:
to put into place; to carry out

led to a quick expansion of the market and increased trade on the route. During this period, more and more missionaries traveled to the East. As a result, information and ideas were also exchanged.

With the spreading of various religions, more and more missionaries reached the East by this road. With the Silk Road acting as an information superhighway, the exchange of ideas grew to a larger scale than ever before. As a result, the Tang Dynasty fortuitously experienced the most flourishing period of the Silk Road. By 760 A.D., however, trade along the Silk Road began to decline. It revived tremendously under the Sung Dynasty in the 11th and 12th centuries when China became largely dependent on its silk trade. In addition, trade to Central and Western Asia as well as Europe recovered for a period of time from 1276-1368 under the Yuan Dynasty when the Mongols controlled China.

However, with the eventual decline of the Mongol Empire also came an end to the political, cultural, and economic stability of the Silk Road. With its disintegration came a cultural and economic separation of the political powers along the Road. A decline in nomad power, in part brought about by the devastation of the Black Death, the encroachment of settled civilians (now equipped with gunpowder), as well as the modernization of Europe, resulted in a steady decline in caravans and merchants attempting to ply their trade.

The road suffered many problems and periods of disuse. Bandits were a constant nuisance. Religious differences also inhibited trade, especially during the time of the Crusades. It was finally the opening of a sea route to China and increased Chinese isolationism that spurred the end of the golden age of the old Silk Road. Today, the Silk Road is a popular tourist destination in Western China, where travelers enjoy the artwork and ruins of the small trading communities that once populated the region.

flourish (v):
to prosper; succeed

disintegration (n):
to break up; to dissolve

encroachment (n):
a intrusion on another person's territory

isolationism (n):
the policy of not joining with other countries in international political affairs

1. Based on the information in paragraph 3, what can be inferred about the road?

    (A) Zhang Qian succeeded in his original task.
    (B) The Han Dynasty benefited from it by finding a military advantage.
    (C) The Xiongnu were the first to travel it.
    (D) The land route was superior to the sea route.

2. It is implied in paragraph 7 that

    (A) political factors were not a cause for instability on the route
    (B) the modernization of Europe saw a larger demand for imports from China
    (C) the availability of gunpowder was a strong factor in the decline of the Silk Road
    (D) increased robbery and theft led to the route being abandoned

3. The expression "chronological and geographical points" in paragraph 1 is closest in meaning to

    (A) directions and kingdoms
    (B) products and peoples
    (C) times and places
    (D) laws and commerce

4. Which of the following could best replace the word "misnomer" as used in paragraph 2?

    (A) Modern adaptation
    (B) Misleading name
    (C) Slang usage
    (D) Contradiction

5. **Directions:** *Complete the table by matching the phrases below. Select the appropriate phrases from the answer choices and match them to the category they belong to. Two of the answer choices will NOT be used.*

Chinese Imports	Chinese exports
_____	_____
_____	_____
_____	

    (A) Gun powder
    (B) Spices
    (C) Wool
    (D) Porcelain
    (E) Paintings
    (F) Greek sculpture
    (G) Horses

Skill E 04   Tracking

Most people believe that tracking animals is primarily a matter of following their footprints. This may be true in certain environments, such as sand and snow, but in forested landscapes, trackers cannot rely solely upon footprints to detect and interpret signs of wildlife passage. Finding a distinct set of footprints in dense forest is like finding $100 lying on the ground. It's wonderful, but it doesn't happen often.

Amazingly, most tracking field guides remain oblivious to this fact. Even field guides focusing specifically on forested environments place a heavy emphasis on the use of footprints for tracking. Based on my experience, I have identified three principal points for effective forest tracking: 1) Pay attention to signs other than footprints; 2) Erase images you have seen that pertain to searching in other environments; 3) Develop search images applicable to forests.

Sign tracking involves recognizing different clues of animal activity. All animals leave signs of their passage. A diligent tracker must learn to see beyond footprints. For instance, particular types of cuts on the branches of a bush might indicate that deer or snowshoe hare ate there. Tufts of fur clinging to trees might betray the passage of a cougar or bear. The number of different signs a tracker could discover in the forest is nearly infinite, but they can be grouped into five broad categories: feeding, feces, travel routes, shelters, and marking. Feeding signs could range from clipped vegetation to partially buried carcasses. Scat (or feces) signs are usually quite distinct. Different creatures deposit their scat in different places for various reasons. Travel routes could be indicated by packed-down trails through brush, or by places where vegetation does not grow in straight lines within areas of overall abundant growth. Shelters might include subterranean dens, a patch of grass under a tree, or a hollow log. Some shelters might be associated with a feeding sign or scat, while others might be carefully separated from these things. Marking signs could involve scent marking, scraping trees, and leaving scat in particular locations. Domestic dogs, for example, display marking activity by urinating on places they wish to designate as "their" territory.

Adjusting to forest tracking requires trackers to change their methods of observation. First, they must recognize and erase search images that might be acting as blinders to them. A search image is a picture in your head that you try to match with a similar image in the landscape. For example, close your eyes and imagine a horse footprint. This picture is

---

solely (adv):
alone; without others

interpret (v):
to construe or take a certain meaning from something

oblivious (adj):
unaware of

emphasis (n):
a special importance; significance

pertain (to) (v):
to be related to; concerned with

diligent (adj):
doing things with care and concern

tuft (n):
a small bunch of grass

clipped (adj):
shortened

subterranean (adj):
underground

designate (v):
to choose or specify; to assign

blinder (n):
an object used to prevent full vision

aspire *(v)*:
to have a desire to achieve

the one you would use when looking for horse tracks in the wilderness. Search images are vital tools for trackers, because the mental pictures help them quickly locate and recognize a variety of different animal tracks. Relying on search images can hinder the forest tracker, however. One reason for this is that most trackers train by developing search images of footprints, which are nearly useless in the forest. Another reason is that the tracking signs in the forest are so variable. Third, by focusing too heavily on a search image, trackers can miss many important details that don't fit their imagined picture. Effective trackers must learn to recognize the search image, then erase it and look for details that don't fit in with their mental picture. They need to practice seeing what is actually there, rather than what they want to see.

In addition to erasing inappropriate search images, forest trackers must develop new search images applicable to forests. This might prove difficult initially, as there are few books to assist them. How many field guides show pictures of a browse line created by deer, or a nest made by a Douglas squirrel? Some do, undoubtedly, but not nearly as many as those that emphasize the shape, size, and characteristics of animals' feet. Even so, aspiring forest trackers should not be discouraged. They should trust their lessons instead to that greatest of all teachers, experience. With time, they will learn to shift their focus from footprints on the ground to signs at all eye levels. Gradually, their mental file cabinet of search images will expand from footprints in sand to include branches, bushes, rocks, water, and grass: the sights and sounds of the forest.

1. It is implied in paragraph 2 that

    (A) the author is frustrated with field guides

    (B) footprints can be useful for tracking in forests

    (C) the author has written a book

    (D) the author is a novice tracker

2. According to paragraph 3, with which statement do you think the author would most probably agree?

    (A) Forest tracking is easy.

    (B) Good sign trackers are not very diligent.

    (C) Sign tracking offers a wide variability of clues.

    (D) Domestic dogs are different than wild animals.

3. The word "distinct" in paragraph 1 could best be replaced by which of the following?

    (A) Different

    (B) Unique

    (C) Clear

    (D) Unusual

4. The word "detect" in paragraph 1 is closest in meaning to

    (A) look for

    (B) find

    (C) demonstrate

    (D) document

5. Directions: *An introductory sentence for a brief summary of the passage is provided below. Complete the summary by selecting the THREE answer choices that express the most important ideas in the passage. Some sentences do not belong in the summary because they express ideas that are not presented in the passage or are minor ideas in the passage.*

First sentence: **Forest tracking challenges trackers to change their methods of observation.**

    (A) They must learn to pay attention to signs other than footprints.

    (B) Field guides emphasize tracking by footprints.

    (C) There are four broad categories of forest animal signs.

    (D) They need to erase inappropriate search images and develop new ones.

    (E) Relying too much on search images can be an inefficient way of tracking.

    (F) There are more different types of animals in a forest than in other environments.

The words culture and society are used interchangeably by many people, but their precise meanings are a little different. Society can be defined as the organized interaction among people living within a geographical or political boundary that is determined by culture. Culture, meanwhile, is the shared way of life of a particular group of people. It is composed of the values, beliefs, behaviors, and physical objects that the group shares.

Sociologists regard culture as possessing two distinct aspects: nonmaterial and material. The nonmaterial aspect is all of the intangible creations of a people. These are the culture's values, ideas, and beliefs. They can be anything from egalitarianism to Taoism. The material aspect, meanwhile, is all of the tangible things that a culture creates — anything from pyramids to lawn mowers. Looking more closely, we begin to see that culture is, in fact, a complete social heritage.

Since ancient times, human cultures have evolved in unique and astonishing ways. For many thousands of years this happened very slowly, but in recent times, it has been happening more quickly. A graph depicting the timeline of various world civilizations could show this clearly. Many of the recent changes are not a result of adaptation to environment, like the kind animals make. (Animals do not create culture.) These changes are the original and unique creations of particular groups.

Some groups, however, whose cultures have remained linked with the environment, have remained very stable and have continued to evolve slowly. The Hopi tribe in North America or the Wambuti in Africa are both examples. One instance of a gradual animal adaptation would be squirrels living at the Grand Canyon, in the Southwestern United States. Scientists have determined that it took thousands of years after the canyon opened for them to evolve into the separate species that live on either side of the rift today.

Culture programs not only our pace, slow or fast, but also our reasons for choosing the pace. Cultures which choose to evolve at the pace of the natural environment do so because they choose to conserve resources. Cultures which choose speed also choose unlimited use of resources. No culture is intrinsically "natural," but these two choices made by cultures in using resources produce groups of people whose lifestyles are directly at odds. One result of this is that we frequently hear of travelers today experiencing extreme culture shock.

intangible *(adj)*:
not able to be felt or perceived by touch

egalitarianism *(n)*:
the belief that all humans are equal and should enjoy the same rights

Taoism *(n)*:
a Chinese philosophy that advocates a simple life with non-interference in the natural course of events

adaptation *(n)*:
the process of changing to suit a particular need

intrinsically *(adv)*:
inherently; belonging to something as part of its nature

at odds with *(expression)*:
in opposition to

A modern person finding themselves in an environmentally-based culture may need, for example, to learn to accept nudity as a part of daily life or eat foods that are shockingly cathartic to a body accustomed to eating processed foods. A traditional person finding themselves in a modern culture will likely be overwhelmed at the dizzying pace of modern life and feel bereft of the supportive matrix of a close-knit community of people, plants, and animals.

In a modern culture, we are not likely to encounter behavioral demands that have environmental determinants. The required change has nothing to do with adjusting to the climate but has primarily to do with the need to find approval and a sense of belonging to the social group. Because human beings evolved over many thousands of years as a social animal, gathering and hunting, and banding together against common enemies, the need for approval from the group is in fact a very strong human instinct and should also link us to the environment.

Animals, whose instincts are directly linked to the environment for survival, experience extreme shock as well when exposed to modern cultures. A trail sign in a Canadian national park reads, "A Fed Bear Is A Dead Bear," meaning that once the animal has learned to rely on humans for food rather than getting its own from nature, it almost inevitably comes into conflict with humans and is killed by them. A city dwelling pet, on the other hand, once abandoned, is quite unlikely to survive in nature.

The need exists for modern humans to align culture to the natural environment. The key to this change lies in re-examining and re-formatting its nonmaterial aspects — its values, beliefs, and behaviors. It also involves managing the material aspects differently.

nudity *(n)*:
the condition of being naked

cathartic *(adj)*:
resulting in an emotional release

bereft of *(adj)*:
deprived of something; having something taken away

determinant *(n)*:
a factor or circumstance which determines an action or event

inevitably *(adv)*:
unavoidably

READING

LISTENING

SPEAKING

WRITING

PRACTICE TEST

1. In paragraph 2, what does the author imply?
    (A) There are two aspects of culture denoted by physical entities and concepts.
    (B) Culture is the sum total of objects and things made by people.
    (C) Culture is not related to the physical things produced by people.
    (D) The physical entities created are more important than the conceptual ones.

2. In which paragraph is it implied that our ancestors have a large part in creating the cultures we have today?
    (A) Paragraph 1
    (B) Paragraph 3
    (C) Paragraph 4
    (D) Paragraph 5

3. The word "determined" in paragraph 1 is closest in meaning to
    (A) convinced
    (B) decided
    (C) impressed
    (D) considered

4. The word "conserve" in paragraph 5 could best be replaced by which of the following?
    (A) Hoard
    (B) Complete
    (C) Prepare
    (D) Use cautiously

5. **Directions:** *An introductory sentence for a brief summary of the passage is provided below. Complete the summary by selecting the THREE answer choices that express the most important ideas in the passage. Some sentences do not belong in the summary because they express ideas that are not presented in the passage or are minor ideas in the passage.*

    First sentence: **It is culture that determines the physical and political boundaries of a society.**

    (A) Animals do not respond to instinct for their survival.
    (B) Although culture arose out of instinctive interactions to the environment, it is no longer directly linked to it.
    (C) Human beings do not have either instinct or the need to respond to it for survival.
    (D) Culture is the shared way of life of a particular group of people and comprises both tangible and intangible aspects.
    (E) Most animals create culture in much the same way that humans do.
    (F) Culture shock for both humans and animals can be one result of the misalignment of culture with environment.

Completing Summaries and Tables

Strategy

- Take notes of the information that you believe to be important during your first reading. It will save time in finding the key information while you are actually dealing with the question.
- Quickly read the text to gain an understanding of the overall passage. These two types of questions require you to find answers throughout the whole passage.

Completing Summaries

- Recognize the major point of each paragraph. The answer choices are likely to be a paraphrase of the main point of each paragraph.
- Read the introductory summary sentence given in the summary chart and the answer choices carefully. They will guide you to the section of the passage you need to look at again.
- Do not choose answer choices that contain insignificant details or points.
- Do not choose answer choices whose information is not included in the passage.
- Do not choose vague, general statements.
- Use the **View Text** icon to look at the passage again. The passage does not appear while you do this type of question.

Completing Tables

- Look for the main ideas while reading. Look at how the passage is organized.
- Be sure to recognize category names given in the table and identify the relevant information that fits each category.
- Use the category words to quickly find the section of the passage you need to look at again.
- The phrases for each category can generally be found after the topics and categories have been introduced. Read around the topic or category words to quickly find the information.

Ecology is the study of organisms, plants or animals, and their interactions with their environments. Organisms cannot exist independently; they all depend on factors in their ecosystems for survival. An ecosystem involves a delicate balance of activities, and disrupting this balance can cause major problems, especially in harsher environments with fewer species and severe weather conditions. For this reason, ecologists try to understand the complex interrelationships of an ecosystem.

■ **A)** One important aspect of ecology is the way that different organisms adapt to their environments. Types of environments can be widely grouped into biomes. ■ **B)** A biome is a major ecological community of organisms, occupying a large area. Three major biome types found here on earth are desert, forest, and tundra (with several subcategories for each type). ■ **C)** Because of the physical conditions of the different biomes, plants and animals have evolved in many different ways. ■ **D)**

The desert presents a particularly harsh environment for its inhabitants, as it tends to contain very little water. Life forms that evolve here are therefore usually good at retaining what little water they find. Cacti are a very good example of this. Most people are aware of their ability to survive in these harsh, unforgiving conditions where water is extremely scarce. Another common survival trait in the desert is the ability to burrow. In some deserts, animals must find a way to protect themselves from the hot sun and dry conditions. For this reason, most hot and dry desert predators are nocturnal. Surprisingly, in cold desert types animals must burrow for the opposite reason. With such a severe decrease in temperature, animals must find protection from the cold. Because of these similar survival skills, it is not unusual to find similar animals in different dessert types.

Another biome mentioned was the forest biome, of which there are three main types: boreal, temperate, and tropical rainforest. Boreal forests are cold, and the wildlife in this biome type has had to make significant adaptations to living there. For example, reptiles in boreal forests bear live young because there is not enough warmth to allow eggs to survive. Boreal forests are also populated primarily with cold-tolerant, evergreen trees. Temperate forests, on the other hand, have both deciduous and evergreen trees. Because sunlight easily reaches the forest floor, temperate forests are typically characterized by richly diversified undergrowth. Tropical rainforests have a warm damp climate

delicate *(adj)*:
easily damaged

disrupt *(v)*:
to disturb or interrupt

retain *(v)*:
to contain; to hold

tolerant *(adj)*:
capable of enduring difficult conditions

deciduous *(adj)*:
of trees or plants that shed their leaves at certain points during the year

that allows many different species to thrive; however, tropical rainforest canopies typically prevent light from reaching the undergrowth, resulting in less diversity than temperate forests.

The tundra is the coldest biome. Coming from a Finnish word meaning "treeless plain," the tundra offers very little protection from harsh winds and low temperatures. Despite the short growing season and bitter cold of the tundra, a surprising number of plants and animals thrive there. There are about 1,700 kinds of plants in the arctic and sub-arctic tundra. Animals have also adapted to the climate physically and behaviorally. Some store fat to insulate their bodies and, similar to the desert biome, some may burrow in the snow to provide shelter from the winds.

The balance found in ecosystems and biomes is fragile. When each species of flora and fauna depends on each other for survival, harm to one species affects every other species in the eco-system. While plants can create their own food supply, this is dependent on factors such as sunlight and moisture. When these factors are affected by human activity, plants can be displaced or even become extinct. When a plant is removed from a food chain, this can lead to other animals in that chain leaving that community, decreasing in number, or even dying off. With such strong interdependency within communities, the removal of a single link or factor can have enormous repercussions. The study of ecology can help us to be aware of the impact of our human activity on the environment.

canopy (n):
the top layer of a wood or forest consisting of the uppermost branches of trees

arctic (adj):
relating to the area around the North Pole

insulate (v):
to prevent the loss or passing of heat by covering with a certain material

fragile (adj):
easily broken; delicate

flora (n):
the wild plants in a particular region or time

fauna (n):
the animals associated with a particular region or time

repercussion (n):
a (usually indirect) result or consequence of an action

1. From the passage, it can be inferred that
   (A) human activity has negative effects on ecosystems
   (B) ecologists can save the planet by studying ecosystems
   (C) environmental agencies should listen to ecologists
   (D) animals can adapt to different climates

2. Look at the four squares [■] that indicate where the following sentence could be added in paragraph 2:

   They have developed physical characteristics as well as behaviors to adapt to varying environmental conditions.

   Where would the sentence best fit? Choose the square [■] where the sentence should be added to the passage.
   (A) Line 1
   (B) Line 3
   (C) Line 6
   (D) Line 8

3. Which of the following could best replace the word "diversity" in paragraph 4?
   (A) Variety
   (B) Difference
   (C) Species
   (D) Development

4. Which of the following is closest is meaning to "thrive" in paragraph 5?
   (A) Migrate
   (B) Function
   (C) Flourish
   (D) Weaken

5. **Directions:** *An introductory sentence for a brief summary of the passage is provided below. Complete the summary by selecting the THREE answer choices that express the most important ideas in the passage. Some sentences do not belong in the summary because they express ideas that are not presented in the passage or are minor ideas in the passage.*

   First sentence: **The study of ecology is an important endeavor.**

   (A) By understanding the complex relationships that exist in nature, we can better take care of the environment.
   (B) Ecologists are interested solely in how animals adapt to harsh environments by evolving special physical traits.
   (C) Ecologists are interested in the ways that animals have evolved to be able to survive in the different biomes.
   (D) The tundra is a very cold place where animals must migrate south during the winter in order to survive.
   (E) Plants in the desert are very good at retaining water because the desert is so dry.
   (F) Studying the ways in which flora and fauna adapt to their environments is one way to better understand how the elements of an ecosystem work together.

Skill F 02 Socialization

Socialization refers to the process by which we learn to interact with society. Professionals from many areas are interested in the study of socialization. Psychologists and sociologists are obvious, but the practical applications of the process are of great importance to politicians, marketers, public health professionals, and educators as well. The question of socialization, however, is so broad and all-encompassing that its definition, systematic study, and application are formidable tasks.

During socialization, we learn the language of the culture we are born into as well as the roles we are to play in life. For instance, girls learn how to be daughters, sisters, friends, wives, and mothers. In addition, they learn about the occupational roles that their society allows them. We also learn and usually adopt our culture's norms through the socialization process. Norms are the conceptions of appropriate and expected behavior that are held by most members of the society.

So, one of the primary questions about socialization is its actual scope: to what extent socialization determines who we are. This is the classic nature vs. nurture debate, one which usually ends in the refrain, "Personality is determined by an interaction between learned behaviors and biological predispositions." Further study of this question usually revolves around studies of twins separated at birth. But these too fail to offer much insight, as they can make strong cases either way. ■ **A)** There have been studies in which long-lost twins turned out to dress the same, like the same foods, and even make the same strange jokes. ■ **B)** Other studies include pairs in which one twin becomes a successful doctor, and the other a criminal.

■ **C)** The study of socialization has made progress in the categorization of agents of socialization. These include the family, the primary agent in most societies, as well as the school, peer groups, the media, religion, the work place, and the state. ■ **D)**

In the case of large-scale societies, such as the United States, communities are often formed from many different ethnic groups. As a consequence, early socialization in different families often varies in techniques, goals, and expectations, as these complex societies do not have unanimous agreement about what should be the shared norms. Not surprisingly, this national ambiguity usually results in more tolerance of social deviance — it is more acceptable to be different in appearance, personality, and actions in such large-scale societies.

If we consider other, less diverse societies, it is possible to see that

application *(n)*:
a use or relevance

formidable *(adj)*:
enormous; challenging

norms *(n)*:
the characteristics which are considered normal for a society

scope *(n)*:
a range; an extent

refrain *(n)*:
a repeated phrase

predisposition *(n)*:
the condition of being inclined to act in a certain way

unanimous *(adj)*:
in complete agreement

deviance *(n)*:
the condition of straying from the norm or accepted

very specific behavioral patterns are expected from individuals within that society, ones that may seem strange or unacceptable by other's standards. For instance, the Shiite Muslim men of Iran are expected at times to inflict severe pain and suffering on themselves in order to show their devotion and religious faith. This action in a Western society would seem very unusual.

Successful socialization may result in uniformity within a society. If children all receive the same socialization, it is not unlikely that they will share similar beliefs and expectations. In fact, national governments around the world are very aware of the implications of socialization and are being motivated to standardize education and make it compulsory. The ability to choose what and how children are taught is an effective political tool, one that is very useful for controlling people. By controlling what are thought of as standard norms for all individuals, society will decrease the likelihood of deviance from what is considered standard, acceptable behavior. Of course, there are always those who are considered "abnormally socialized," which means they don't accept the standard norms as their own. These people are often defined as deviants by the rest of society.

Socialization has also been broken down into various types. Primary socialization refers to basic behaviors across individuals within a culture. Anticipatory socialization is practicing a future social role. Gender socialization is learning behaviors specific to your sex in your society. Resocialization is when former behaviors are overwritten with new ones, for instance, in the army. A total institution is a closed society that controls all aspects of socialization, such as prisons, convents, and cults.

inflict (v):
to impose upon or cause to suffer

devotion (n):
a great dedication or loyalty to; a great love for

uniformity (n):
the condition of being similar or unchanging

implication (n):
an insinuation; an idea being hinted or suggested indirectly

convent (n):
a community of nuns and the building they occupy

1. Based on the information in paragraph 3, what can be inferred about personality?

   (A) It is determined primarily by gender.
   (B) It is determined by parents.
   (C) It is determined by a combination of social and physiological factors.
   (D) They are the most important agents.

2. Look at the four squares [■] that indicate where the following sentence could be added in the passage.

   There are some areas, however, in which studies of socialization have produced important results.

   Where would the sentence best fit? Choose the square [■] where the sentence should be added to the passage.

   (A) Paragraph 3, Line 7
   (B) Paragraph 3, Line 9
   (C) Paragraph 4, Line 1
   (D) Paragraph 4, Line 4

3. What word does "they" in paragraph 3 refer to in the passage?

   (A) The studies
   (B) The twins
   (C) The insights
   (D) The failings

4. Which of the following is closest is meaning to "all-encompassing" in paragraph 1?

   (A) Surrounding
   (B) Inclusive
   (C) Vague
   (D) Mystical

5. **Directions:** *Complete the table by matching the words and phrases below. Select the appropriate words and phrases from the answer choices and match them to the category to which they relate. TWO of the answer choices will NOT be used.*

Agents of Socialization	Types of Socialization
_____	_____
_____	_____
_____	

   (A) Religion
   (B) Anticipated
   (C) Gender
   (D) Politicians
   (E) Twin studies
   (F) Family
   (G) Primary
   (H) Media

Aristotle's *Poetics* is considered the first work of literary criticism in Western tradition. Aristotle, in his *Poetics*, looks at the form of tragedy in drama. He defined tragedy as an "imitation of an action that is complete and whole and of a certain magnitude." By this, Aristotle indicates that the medium of tragedy is not narrative, but drama. That is, tragedy must show us rather than tell us. An example we can consider is *Hamlet*. The serious action that the play centers around is Hamlet's quest to exact revenge for his father's death, and the play "shows" us the action through Hamlet's anguish, suffering, and paranoia. Rather than describe the action, Hamlet's actions and emotions reveal it.

One important aspect that Aristotle discusses is the plot. He places more significance on the plot than on any other aspect, such as character or diction, which he states stem from the plot itself. For the plot to be complete, he states, it must have "unity of action." The sequence of events should be logical and should not be episodic. The tension in the play must also come from a conflict, which is often condensed in the character of the antagonist. The plot should be aimed at working through this conflict.

To be whole, the tragedy must have a beginning, a middle, and an end. ■ **A)** This seems rather obvious, but Aristotle specified that there must be a cause and effect relationship between these parts. ■ **B)** That is, the beginning is the causal agent, and is not itself caused by anything occurring outside the realm of the play. Therefore, its effects are important, but its causes are not. ■ **C)** The middle, or climax, is caused by the beginning and is the cause of the end; therefore, the highest level of tension in the play should coincide with the actual middle of the play. The end, or resolution, is caused by the middle, but does not have any important effects. ■ **D)** This is the part of the play where the problem gets resolved.

By magnitude Aristotle includes both quantitative and qualitative aspects. The plot should neither be too great or too small in terms of length and complexity. Further, it should attain a certain universal significance. The ultimate goal is to bring events and themes together as an organic whole. Furthermore, the play should arouse a sense of pity and fear in the spectators, who must sympathize and identify with the hero. As a result of this, the spectators will appreciate the hero's predicament and after going through the hero's conflict with him, will feel a sense of cleansing or "catharsis." This catharsis is a kind of mental resolution or

imitation *(n)*:
the act of copying or repeating something

magnitude *(n)*:
a quantity; an extent; a proportion

narrative *(n)*:
an account (a telling) of an event or tale

paranoia *(n)*:
a strong emotion characterized by the feelings of suspicion and distrust

stem from *(v phrase)*:
to come from; to have its origins in

condense *(v)*:
to reduce in size

antagonist *(n)*:
an opponent or enemy

tension *(n)*:
a strain in relations or an underlying hostility between people

resolution *(n)*:
a conclusion

organic *(adj)*:
natural

predicament *(n)*:
a situation; a dilemma

closure. The aim of the play is to bring out this catharsis within the spectator.

Of course, for this catharsis to occur, the play and all its loose ends should be resolved in a believable manner. For the spectator to identify with the hero, the hero must display characteristics that the audience themselves experience, even if, like in *Hamlet*, the hero is a prince. Hamlet himself experiences strong emotions and feelings such as paranoia, confusion, and uncertainty, all of which are feelings the spectator can appreciate and relate to in some way.

Plots can be either simple or complex. Simple plots involve catastrophe, while complex plots add "reversal of intention" and "recognition." Reversal of intention occurs when a character causes an event to happen which is the opposite of what was intended. Recognition "is a change from ignorance to knowledge, producing love or hate between the persons destined for good or bad fortune." Again, we can see this in *Hamlet* when his uncle watches the play in which he sees very similar circumstances to those in which he killed Hamlet's father. These cause him to leave in distress, giving Hamlet strong evidence that his uncle did in fact kill his father, and strengthening his desire for revenge. Aristotle thought that the best plays were complex. They were only successful if all of the elements came together using cause and effect.

closure *(n):*
a sense of finality or completion

catastrophe *(n):*
a disaster

1. What can be inferred from paragraph 2 about Aristotle's breakdown of plot?

   (A) That it is overly simplistic
   (B) That it is more complex than it seems
   (C) That it is too complicated
   (D) That it wasn't well thought out

2. Look at the four squares [■] that indicate where the following sentence could be added in paragraph 3:

   He believed that the story should unfold through events that are connected to each other in a logical way and have obvious causes.

   Where would the sentence best fit? Choose the square [■] where the sentence should be added to the passage.

   (A) Line 2
   (B) Line 3
   (C) Line 6
   (D) Line 10

3. What word does "it" in paragraph 4 refer to in the passage?

   (A) The magnitude
   (B) The plot
   (C) The length
   (D) The complexity

4. The word "episodic" in paragraph 2 could best be replaced by which of the following?

   (A) Recurrent
   (B) Unusual
   (C) Sporadic
   (D) Dramatic

5. **Directions:** *An introductory sentence for a brief summary of the passage is provided below. Complete the summary by selecting the THREE answer choices that express the most important ideas in the passage. Some sentences do not belong in the summary because they express ideas that are not presented in the passage or are minor ideas in the passage.*

   First sentence: **Aristotle's view of tragedy was that it was an imitation of reality.**

   (A) Reality is chaotic, so this imitation should make order out of chaos.
   (B) To create an adequate imitation, the plot should be sequential.
   (C) It is of utmost importance that events occur for a reason.
   (D) Ideas of love and hate should be explored through poetry.
   (E) The best tragedies, according to Aristotle, have universal significance.
   (F) The best tragedies are simple ones that don't confuse the audience with too many events.

There are currently seven giant plates sliding across the Earth's surface, along with a few smaller ones. There may have been more or fewer plates in the past; scientists are not completely sure of the history of the continental plates. They do know that these plates are in continuous movement driven by the Earth's intense, internal heat. The deep heat within the Earth drives hot currents of gas and liquids upwards because they are less dense. In turn, the colder materials take a downward current because they are denser. This is the simple theory of how lighter substances float on top, and heavier substances sink to the bottom. Continents are considered the "scum of the earth," because they consist of mostly light minerals that can't sink in the Earth's mantle and instead float on the crust.

The continental plates slide, collide, and recede continuously. The plates move anywhere from 1 to 20 cm per year. Seafloor spreading is the cause of continental movement. It works like a giant conveyor belt moving the massive plates around like pieces of a puzzle. It is the movement and collisions of these plates that change the face of our planet by creating mountains and swallowing oceans.

Over 250 million years ago, before the age of the dinosaurs, the Earth was much different. The continents were fused as one super-continent called Pangaea. About 200 millions years ago, Pangaea broke into two separate continents: Laurasia, consisting of North America, Europe, and Asia, and Gondwanaland, consisting of South America, Australia, Antarctica, and India.

As India broke away from Gondwanaland, it moved 100 miles in 135 million years at the speed of 10 centimeters a year. It eventually collided with the continental plate of Asia. As the plate continued to move northward, it squashed and thickened the borders of the two continents. It was much like the process of pushing a rug against a wall. Out of this cataclysmic event, Mount Everest was born. All mountain ranges are made in much the same way. A crash between two plates causes the edges to buckle and fold, making mountains.

The collision of the Indian plate with the continent of Asia, about 100 million years ago, created the world's tallest mountain range, the Himalayas. The Himalayas span across the countries of China (Tibet), India, Nepal, Pakistan, and Bhutan. This mountain range is home to fourteen of the world's highest peaks, including of course Mount Everest, which is the tallest mountain in the world standing at 8,850 meters

plate *(n)*:
a large, rigid section that is part of the Earth's crust

continental *(adj)*:
relating to one of the continents of the world

mantle *(n)*:
the part of the Earth between the crust and the core

fuse *(v)*:
to join as a result of heat being applied between the two parts

squash *(v)*:
to crush by squeezing

cataclysmic *(adj)*:
disastrous; involving great change

buckle *(v)*:
to become bent as a result of pressure or heat

READING
LISTENING
SPEAKING
WRITING
PRACTICE TEST

above sea level.

The process of the collision between the Indian and Asian plates still continues today, which is why the Himalayas are still growing. ■ **A)** Over the next 5 to 10 million years, the continental plates will continue to move at the same rate they are moving today. ■ **B)** In 10 million years, India will push about 180 km into Tibet, which is about the width of Nepal. The mountain range itself will have much of the same profile, with taller mountains in the north and smaller ones in the south. ■ **C)** Scientific evidence predicts that the Himalayas are relentlessly progressing on India. ■ **D)**

Mount Everest is one of the most popular mountains for serious trekkers. It would probably be trendier if it were easier to get to. To get near Mount Everest, you have to either walk for 10 days or take a flight to Lukla, a remote mountain airstrip, which is known for its fallibility. Mount Everest sits on the border of Nepal and Tibet and can be climbed from both sides. Everest itself is a triangular pyramid with three ridges running up to the summit. These ridges provide the most frequently used trails for hikers. Naturally, only a few people have made it to the top of Mount Everest, but regular hikers can trek to Everest Base Camp. If you choose to do this, it is a three week trek to the base camp and then a half-an-hour flight back to Katmandu. After having exhausted themselves on a three-week hike, most people find it peculiar to get back to civilization in 30 minutes! Mount Everest has been conquered by more than 900 people, and it has claimed 150 lives.

relentlessly *(adv)*:
without sign of stopping; continuously

remote *(adj)*:
isolated; far from anything

airstrip *(n)*:
small field or piece of land where airplanes can take off and land

fallibility *(n)*:
the condition of being likely to make mistakes or have an accident

ridge *(n)*:
a long narrow raised area

1. According to paragraph 7, with which statement do you think the author would most probably agree?

   (A) Everyone can trek to the summit of Mount Everest.
   (B) Ordinary people can hike to Mount Everest Base Camp.
   (C) Most trekkers take only three weeks to summit Mount Everest.
   (D) Mount Everest is a great place for an easy, relaxing vacation.

2. Look at the four squares [■] that indicate where the following sentence could be added in paragraph 6:

   The future of the Himalayas can be predicted by scientists.

   Where would the sentence best fit? Choose the square [■] where the sentence should be added to the passage.

   (A) Line 2
   (B) Line 4
   (C) Line 8
   (D) Line 9

3. The word "scum" in paragraph 1 is closest in meaning to

   (A) light
   (B) heavy
   (C) salt
   (D) foam

4. The word "conquered" in paragraph 7 could best be replaced by which of the following?

   (A) Defeated
   (B) Victorious
   (C) Lost
   (D) Navigated

5. **Directions:** *Complete the table by matching the phrases below. Select the appropriate phrases from the answer choices and match them to the category to which they relate. TWO of the answer choices will NOT be used.*

Moving Plates	Forming Mountains
_____	_____
_____	_____
_____	

   (A) The collision of the Indian plate with the continent of Asia
   (B) Seafloor spreading
   (C) Pangaea broke into two separate continents
   (D) Conquered by 900 hikers
   (E) Earth's intense, internal heat
   (F) Across five countries
   (G) When plates collide and the edges buckle and thicken

Today in the West, we think of women's struggle for equality with men as beginning during the 1800s, but power struggle between women and men dates back to at least the time of the Greek Empire. ■ **A)** Grecian armies subdued and intentionally relegated to obscurity a Goddess-worshipping Mesopotamian empire. ■ **B)** Its leaders had been women, some of them quite brilliant military strategists. ■ **C)** Medusa, one of the most terrifying feminine archetypes, can be traced to one ruler who performed a dance wearing a headdress made of snakes. ■ **D)**

The Greek period of ascendancy ended the corruption of power prevalent during the decline of the culture of the Great Goddess, replacing it with the corruption of the patriarchal, God-worshipping culture still with us today. The great ideal of Grecian love was not that between a man and a woman, but that between an older man and a younger man. Some men during this era were determined to find a way to procreate without females. Obviously, this was not a good time for women. But did the situation for women improve much over the centuries that followed? Perhaps for a time. However, in more recent times, women's powers of self determination were being continually eroded in the West until the Women's Movement of the mid 1900s.

It is known that in 1737, in England, over 95% of married women had a trade and produced almost all the bread and beer sold at that time, among other things. Many women today, in less technologically advanced cultures, still have control of their resources in much the same way, even if they lack any official political voice.

In the 18th century in Europe, factories and mines hired entire families to work in them. The families received cash payment for their work. By 1835, it is estimated that something around 30 percent of textile workers were women, and that by 1841, one in three household servants were women. As one can see, it was not uncommon at that time for women to work outside the home. However, things were soon to change.

By the late 19th century, horrendous conditions in city slums and factories caused so much disease that it threatened, like an evil flood, to lap at the doors of the upper class. Domestic work among the working class had been reduced to an absolute minimum, crowded out by the demands of wage labor. The infant mortality rate soared. Factory machinery became more efficient, needing fewer workers to run it. The most cost-effective way of running a work force was to get women out of

subdue (v):
to overpower and bring under control

intentionally (adv):
deliberately

relegate (v):
to move to a lower position or level

obscurity (n):
the condition of being unclear or not well known

ascendancy (n):
the condition of being in control or having power

patriarchal (adj):
relating to male leadership or male control

horrendous (adj):
horrible; terrible

soar (v):
to increase rapidly; to become higher

the work place. The wealthy and the clergy colluded to enact laws preventing women from providing for themselves, confining them to unpaid domestic work. Both women and men protested, the rioting crowds led, more often than not, by women. By 1911, only one in ten wives in the UK worked for cash payments. In the US, only one in 20. Capitalism had effected a split between working-class men and women, making women wardens of their men, one on one, and making this guardianship into a burdensome duty.

The late 1800s and early 1900s found American and European suffragettes, including Susan B. Anthony, Elizabeth Cady Stanton, and Emmeline Pankhurst, lobbying for women's right to vote. Women also fought during this period for equal access to colleges and universities; but, ironically, it was the first and second World Wars that most effectively brought women back into the workplace. During the late 40s and 50s, women's roles in industry continued to expand in spite of the still prevalent attitude that home and child care should be women's work. Working women at this time experienced widespread gender discrimination, such as unequal pay and work opportunities, and sexual harassment. *The Second Sex*, by Simone de Beauvoir, published in 1949, was one of the first books analyzing the deep-seated fears and attitudes causing women to be discriminated against.

During the 60s and 70s, many women worked very hard to change attitudes toward the feminine, among them Gloria Steinem and Betty Friedan. Betty Friedan's book, *The Feminine Mystique*, joined de Beauvoir's in providing an intellectual foundation for the movement, or "women's lib" as it was called. Women succeeded in securing better and more varied work opportunities, better pay, equal access to education, the right to birth control, the right to divorce, equal treatment for women's athletics, and a greater role in political life.

To think, however, that gender discrimination has disappeared is quite unrealistic. The United States, the world's wealthiest nation, for example, has never had a woman president. Worldwide, fundamentalist regimes, along with socially sanctioned attitudes that consider women as inferior — or wives as servants or even property — still deprive many women of respect and resources.

suffragette *(n)*:
any of a group of women who campaigned for women's rights

lobbying *(n)*:
the process whereby attempts are made to influence elected representatives through personal contacts

1. According to paragraph 3, with which statement do you think the author would most probably agree?

   (A) Women need to be in control of their own resources.
   (B) Women should not be allowed to work.
   (C) Women should be the servants of men.
   (D) Women should not respect men.

2. Look at the four squares [■] that indicate where the following sentence could be added in paragraph 1:

   The fact that they did this so effectively is one reason why we know so little about this empire today.

   Where would the sentence best fit? Choose the square [■] where the sentence should be added to the passage.

   (A) Line 4
   (B) Line 5
   (C) Line 6
   (D) Line 9

3. What do the words "evil flood" in paragraph 5 refer to?

   (A) Men
   (B) Women
   (C) Disease
   (D) Factories

4. The word "colluded" in paragraph 5 could best be replaced by which of the following?

   (A) Worked
   (B) Gathered together
   (C) Cooperated
   (D) Rushed

5. **Directions:** *An introductory sentence for a brief summary of the passage is provided below. Complete the summary by selecting the THREE answer choices that express the most important ideas in the passage. Some sentences do not belong in the summary because they express ideas that are not presented in the passage or are minor ideas in the passage.*

   First sentence: **Western women have struggled for equality with men since the days of the Greek Empire.**

   (A) Some nineteenth-century women passively accepted laws preventing them from working.
   (B) Although women are still discriminated against, the Women's Movement of the 60s and 70s won many basic rights.
   (C) World Wars I and II brought women back into the workplace.
   (D) Men struggled for equal rights with women during the Goddess era.
   (E) Their struggle intensified at the end of the 19th century when laws prevented them from working for pay.
   (F) The culture of the Great Goddess prevented men from entering certain places in the temples.

Review A – F

Vocabulary Review

Skill Review

Vocabulary Review

Instructions: Choose the best word or phrase to complete each sentence.

1. They administered an injection which would help _____ the pain.
   - (A) interpret
   - (B) alleviate
   - (C) aspire
   - (D) hinder

2. Because of its _____, they were unsure of the significance of the letter.
   - (A) application
   - (B) closure
   - (C) ambiguity
   - (D) emphasis

3. With so much water having _____ its exterior, the engine was effectively ruined.
   - (A) pertained
   - (B) impacted
   - (C) evoked
   - (D) penetrated

4. He was a _____ conservative spokesperson, right until his death last year.
   - (A) vital
   - (B) staunch
   - (C) judiciary
   - (D) legendary

5. Had we been able to foresee the _____, we would never have begun the experiment.
   - (A) repercussions
   - (B) miscellany
   - (C) dimensions
   - (D) innovation

6. The party needed a representative to _____ their new campaign.
   - (A) subsidize
   - (B) render
   - (C) spearhead
   - (D) infuse

7. With such overwhelming evidence, the decision was always going to be _____.
   - (A) unanimous
   - (B) prophetic
   - (C) intangible
   - (D) indispensable

8. The witness stated he would never have _____ hurt his wife.
   - (A) intentionally
   - (B) relentlessly
   - (C) seemingly
   - (D) respectively .

9. The students had great difficulty trying to _____ the concept.
   - (A) evoke
   - (B) facilitate
   - (C) encompass
   - (D) grasp

10. Though he tried to remain _____, he was too personally involved in the issue.
    - (A) subjective
    - (B) objective
    - (C) indispensable
    - (D) diligent

11. The report was unsatisfactory, as it failed to _____ the key points mentioned.

   (A) pertain to
   (B) reflect on
   (C) evoke
   (D) collude

12. The director criticized his staff for not fully _____ the facilities available.

   (A) infusing
   (B) relegating
   (C) contemplating
   (D) utilizing

13. We were intimidated by such _____ opponents.

   (A) formidable
   (B) horrendous
   (C) rugged
   (D) diligent

14. Though no accusations were made, we could recognize the _____.

   (A) predispositions
   (B) implications
   (C) tensions
   (D) imitations

15. Channel 63 was granted a(n) _____ interview with the actor.

   (A) exclusive
   (B) apparent
   (C) resolution
   (D) narrative

Instructions: Choose the word or phrase closest in meaning to the underlined part.

16. His <u>loyalty</u> to the cause is unparalleled.

   (A) reverence
   (B) resolution
   (C) devotion
   (D) innovation

17. This philosophy paper is extremely confusing. Its key concepts are so <u>abstract</u>.

   (A) subjective
   (B) indispensable
   (C) intangible
   (D) unanimous

18. Mr. Ryan was <u>influential</u> in having the bill passed by congress.

   (A) legendary
   (B) diligent
   (C) formidable
   (D) instrumental

19. The prisoner was <u>apparently</u> unaffected by his unanimous conviction.

   (A) seemingly
   (B) relentlessly
   (C) intentionally
   (D) inevitably

20. Unfortunately, they were unaware of the <u>extent</u> of the damage.

   (A) fortitude
   (B) magnitude
   (C) essence
   (D) grasp

21. The translators disagreed about the writer's intention because of <u>vagueness</u> in the language used by the writer.

    (A) ambiguity
    (B) blockage
    (C) hurdles
    (D) phenomena

22. The police attempt to <u>overpower</u> the crowd resulted in a series of riots.

    (A) retain
    (B) render
    (C) evoke
    (D) subdue

23. The minister desired the position simply for the <u>status</u> associated with it.

    (A) reverence
    (B) prestige
    (C) scope
    (D) norms

24. The board is considering making 10 years of experience a <u>requirement</u> for the position.

    (A) determinant
    (B) repercussion
    (C) prerequisite
    (D) uniformity

25. He played a <u>crucial</u> role in the campaign's success.

    (A) pivotal
    (B) formidable
    (C) diplomatic
    (D) cataclysmic

26. He continued to <u>impede</u> their progress, even after he was cautioned.

    (A) utilize
    (B) render
    (C) infuse
    (D) hinder

27. As they were almost identical, we were unable to <u>differentiate</u> between the two.

    (A) interpret
    (B) distinguish
    (C) designate
    (D) contemplate

28. The new slogan for our company must <u>embody</u> all that we stand for.

    (A) encompass
    (B) inaugurate
    (C) condense
    (D) alleviate

29. The government <u>partially funded</u> the student exchange program in order to improve international relations.

    (A) infused
    (B) expended
    (C) subsidized
    (D) discredited

30. At the end of the year, the most <u>hardworking</u> students are rewarded.

    (A) diligent
    (B) acclaimed
    (C) formidable
    (D) instrumental

Instructions: Write the missing words. Use the words below to fill in the blanks.

diverse	inevitably	advent	diverge	adaptation
retain	discredit	evolution	essence	interpret

With the **(31)** _____ of modern science and more particularly the theory of **(32)** _____, a number of religious institutions became concerned that such a theory would **(33)** _____ the **(34)** _____ of biblical teachings, more particularly the Creation Myth recounted in Genesis. Several debates have arisen in which school boards have attempted to ban these teachings. **(35)** _____, the irrefutable logic and rationale of science have continued to see evolution's inclusion in the school curriculum of all but the most radical religious educational institutions. The theory depicts a significantly different account of life than that presented in Genesis. Its continuing support and proof will force many dogmatic thinkers to **(36)** _____ the Bible in a whole new way. Its central tenets are as follows.

Evolution is the process by which new characteristics develop in populations from one generation to the next. Its action over large periods of time explains the origin of new species and ultimately explains the existence of the many **(37)** _____ species in the biological world. Each generation slowly changes in order to suit its environment. These changes are referred to as **(38)** _____. As species **(39)** _____ over time, they start to distinguish themselves physically from their ancestors, though they continue to **(40)** _____ some of the traits that link them to a specific group. These simple scientific notions have contributed to large scale debates over teaching and education

Instructions: Choose the one word that does not belong.

41. catastrophe   hazard   obscurity   perilous
42. intrinsically   innate   mechanical   fundamental
43. prophetic   weak   fragile   delicate
44. subdue   reverence   depletion   relegate
45. spectrum   span   uniformity   scope

Instructions: Match the words that are opposites.

46. transience   (A) biased
47. expend   (B) importance
48. objective   (C) permanence
49. inflict   (D) protect
50. obscurity   (E) conserve

Shadow puppetry is a traditional art form that often goes unappreciated in modern times. A large part of the appeal of puppet shows is the craftsmanship behind the creation of the actual puppets. In shadow puppetry, on the other hand, the puppets remain unseen, so the real artistry is in the presentation. The combination of the puppet's shape, the background screen, and the light itself creates the overall effect of the shadow puppet show. The task of the director is to ensure these elements are working together harmoniously in order to produce the optimal experience for the audience.

The screen is the medium through which the audience experiences the performance, so selecting the best screen is essential. First, it must transmit as much light as possible to better capture the shape of the puppet. However, it shouldn't transmit so much light that the puppeteer is visible. The material should obviously be durable but thin. A thin material gives superior definition to the edges of the shadows. Traditionally, cotton was used for the screen, but it was very grainy. As new kinds of textiles have been developed, more suitable materials have become the standard. Silk works well but is expensive. A more affordable option is vinyl, which is thin and transmits light evenly. The only problem is that it stretches too easily. In order to allow the puppets to press up against the screen, it must be strung very tightly. If the material stretches too easily, it will sag.

One unique challenge for the puppet show director is that the presentation is two-dimensional. The screen is flat, so puppets can only move forwards and backwards. In order to create a three-dimensional appearance, directors often design a set in which the background is smaller than the foreground. Then, by using different-sized puppets at different heights on the screen, a more interesting scene can be created. If the script requires two puppets to pass by each other, it can be accurately reproduced on the screen. The "fade-out" is a common tool used by directors to avoid this problem. In this technique, the puppet is moved away from the screen, and the image becomes fuzzy before fading out altogether.

Having chosen a screen and designed the set, the next step is to determine the light that will be used. There are several factors to be considered: intensity, spread, and angle. Naturally, more light is required behind the screen than in front. The power or intensity of this light is best determined through experimentation. If the light is too bright, it

appeal *(n):*
the pleasing quality of something that attracts people to it

durable *(adj):*
long lasting or tough

definition *(n):*
the degree of clearness and preciseness of a form

grainy *(adj):*
not sharp or distinct

textile *(n):*
any cloth or fabric made by weaving or knitting

vinyl *(n):*
a tough type of plastic

sag *(v):*
to hang loosely or bulge downward

dimensional *(adj):*
having a certain number of dimensions

intensity *(n):*
the condition of being concentrated or extreme

will appear harsh to audience members positioned close to the screen. Dim light, though harder to see, can create an intimate mood. The intensity of the light can be manipulated throughout the performance by using a dimmer switch.

Spread describes how the intensity of light is dispersed over the screen. ■ **A)** If it is too focused on the center, it can leave dark areas at the edges. ■ **B)** In contrast, if the spread is too wide, light might spill over the edges of the screen, thus producing shadows of objects that aren't supposed to be part of the performance. ■ **C)** Additionally, the angle at which the light hits the screen will affect the spread. The director can manipulate the angle of the light in order to alter the shape and size of the puppets and to create dramatic effects. ■ **D)**

The shadow puppet show is an art that goes beyond the construction of the puppets and the performance of the script. Finding the optimal combination of light and shadow involves careful planning and meticulous design. Every detail must be considered and controlled in relation to every other detail, making shadow puppetry an art of precision.

intimate *(adj)*:
marked by close acquaintance or familiarity

dimmer switch *(n)*:
a switch that can control the level and brightness of light

disperse *(v)*:
to spread over a wide area

1. Which of the following is closest in meaning to the word "produce" as used in paragraph 1?
   (A) Fresh food
   (B) Create
   (C) Pay for
   (D) Oversee

2. The word "harsh" in paragraph 4 is closest in meaning to
   (A) very cold
   (B) crisp
   (C) insulting
   (D) severe

3. What word does "it" refer to in paragraph 2?
   (A) Option
   (B) Vinyl
   (C) Light
   (D) Problem

4. In paragraph 2, the author explains the importance of the screen by
   (A) showing how difficult it is to find good material
   (B) explaining the elements to be considered
   (C) saying what it is used for
   (D) giving examples of materials

5. According to the passage, which of the following can cause unwanted shadows?
   (A) A light that's too bright
   (B) A light that's not bright enough
   (C) A light that's too focused
   (D) A light that's not focused enough.

6. What does "this technique" refer to in paragraph 3?
   (A) Using different-sized puppets
   (B) The script
   (C) Using a smaller background
   (D) The "fade-out"

7. Which of the following sentences best expresses the essential information of the highlighted sentence? *Incorrect* choices change the meaning in important ways or leave out essential information.
   (A) Shadow puppetry, in contrast, is a truly artistic show.
   (B) Because the puppeteers remain out of sight in shadow puppetry, the presentation becomes more expressive.
   (C) In contrast, the true skill and appeal in shadow puppetry lies in the presentation, as the actual puppets are kept hidden.
   (D) Similarly, in shadow puppetry, the true skill is in the presentation of the show.

8. What is the main purpose of the passage?
   (A) To inspire people to become shadow puppeteers
   (B) To increase the popularity of shadow puppet shows
   (C) To show how shadow puppetry is better than regular puppetry
   (D) To demonstrate the challenges involved in shadow puppetry

9. All of the following are mentioned in the passage EXCEPT
   (A) color
   (B) intensity
   (C) spread
   (D) angle

10. Which of the following can be inferred from paragraph 1 about regular, non-shadow puppet shows?
    (A) They're not as good as shadow puppet shows.
    (B) They're easier to produce than shadow puppet shows.
    (C) Most of the work happens before the show.
    (D) It's not really an art form.

11. Look at the four squares [■] that indicate where the following sentence could be added to paragraph 5:

    It is the same effect as when a shadow appears differently at different times of the day, depending on where the sun is in the sky.

    Where would the sentence best fit? Choose the square [■] where the sentence should be added to the passage.
    (A) Line 2
    (B) Line 3
    (C) Line 5
    (D) Line 8

12. **Directions:** *Complete the table by matching the phrases below. Select the appropriate phrases from the answer choices and match them to the category to which they relate. TWO of the answer choices will NOT be used.*

Intensity	Spread
_____	_____
_____	_____
_____	_____

    (A) Experimenting with brightness of the light
    (B) Creating a 3-dimensional image
    (C) Unintentional shadows
    (D) Angle of the light
    (E) Crispness of shadows
    (F) Textile development
    (G) Creating an intimate feel
    (H) Dark areas around the edges

As more and more countries around the globe move towards industrialization in an attempt to compete in the global market, an environmental crisis over deforestation — the cutting down, burning, and general damaging of forests — is looming for mankind. Over the last several decades, environmental specialists have proposed various strategies aimed at slowing down this process of deforestation in developing countries. Many of these proposals are indeed valuable ideas in that they are realistic attempts to address some of the causes of deforestation, such as farming, cattle ranching, and commercial logging. All of them rely on government involvement of some kind.

There are three broad categories of solutions: state economic policies, internal agreements, and international programs. ■ **A)** Economic policies generally attempt to limit the activity of small farmers through government actions. ■ **B)** Government actions can include the clear and proper definition and enforcement of property rights, meaning that squatting, or illegally settling on land, would be more difficult. ■ **C)** Subsidies can be used to encourage conservation. That is, money may be paid to supplement the income of those farmers who make an effort to reduce the usual amount of damage to the forest that their farms cause. In addition, taxes can act as a deterrent to undesirable land use. ■ **D)** For example, certain kinds of agriculture, like the slash-and-burn method, as well as cattle ranching, may be taxed to discourage these activities.

An internal agreement may be made between governments and indigenous or native people living in the moist rainforests and open woodlands of the tropics, where the vast majority of this deforestation is occurring. Such an agreement would allow people to carry on traditional activities adapted for some economic benefit. One example is the rubber-tappers in Brazil. These native people draw sap from rubber trees in the rainforest, without damaging or killing the trees. The sap, in turn, is sold to rubber companies, thereby providing the native people with economic benefits.

Finally, international agreements usually involve the exchange of monetary aid in return for government action to protect its forests. One such plan seeks to help pay a nation's debt in exchange for restrictions on certain kinds of activities in rainforests. This is appealing for a poor country such as Brazil, which has an international debt of $160 billion. Instead of selling logging concessions to pay down that obligation, the government receives money for banning or restricting logging in its

supplement (v):
to add or make up a lack of

indigenous (adj):
native to a certain area

sap (n):
a liquid that circulates within a tree

forests. There is also the proposal of a global fund created in order to grant money to countries that choose to protect their environments. While all of these ideas could possibly work, it remains to be seen whether there will be any real progress in rainforest conservation.

It is clear that something must be done to protect the forests of the world. If the current rate of deforestation continues, the world's rainforests will vanish within 100 years, causing numerous adverse effects on global climate and eliminating the majority of plant and animal species on the planet. Deforestation significantly increases the amount of carbon dioxide (CO_2) released into the atmosphere each year, which in turn causes an increase in global temperatures. Also, scientists speculate that the tropical rainforests, though covering only seven percent of the Earth's dry surface, contain more than half of the 5 million to 80 million species of plants and animals that comprise the "biodiversity" of the planet. The loss of species resulting from radical climate change will have a drastic effect. The Earth is losing species every day that could potentially prevent cancer or lead to a cure for AIDS. In addition, other organisms are losing species they depend upon, and thus face extinction themselves. Unless some form of concrete solution for deforestation is enacted quickly, the survival of all creatures living on Earth could be in jeopardy.

adverse *(adj)*:
unfavorable or negative

speculate *(v)*:
to consider circumstances or possibilities without evidence or proof

drastic *(adj)*:
terrible; extreme

concrete *(adj)*:
specific; fixed or definite

in jeopardy *(prep phrase)*:
in danger of harm or loss

1. According to paragraphs 3 and 4, what is the main difference between an internal agreement and an international agreement?

(A) International agreements are more effective than internal agreements.
(B) An international agreement is between countries; an internal agreement is between a government and its people.
(C) Internal agreements benefit governments; international agreements benefit indigenous groups.
(D) Internal agreements are more effective than international ones.

2. The word "obligation" in paragraph 4 could best be replaced by

(A) promise
(B) relationship
(C) guarantee
(D) debt

3. In paragraph 1, what does the word "them" refer to?

(A) The causes of deforestation
(B) Decades
(C) Proposals
(D) Developing countries

4. Look at the four squares [■] that indicate where the following sentence could be added to paragraph 2:

Deforestation by a peasant farmer is often done to raise crops for subsistence and is driven by the basic human need for food.

Where would the sentence best fit? Choose the square [■] where the sentence should be added to the passage.

(A) Line 2
(B) Line 4
(C) Line 6
(D) Line 10

5. Why does the author mention rubber-tappers in paragraph 3?

(A) To provide an example of an internal agreement
(B) To provide an example of an international agreement
(C) To provide an example of a state economic policy
(D) To provide an example of why Brazil is a poor nation

6. According to the passage, what are the major adverse effects of deforestation?

(A) An increase in carbon dioxide and decrease in biodiversity
(B) Warmer weather and an increase in biodiversity
(C) Loss of plant and animal species and an increase in global debt
(D) An increase in global debt and human diseases

7. Which of the following sentences best expresses the essential information of the highlighted sentence? *Incorrect* choices change the meaning in important ways or leave out essential information.

(A) In coming decades, environmental scientists will suggest several strategies for stopping deforestation in third-world countries.
(B) Environmental scientists, in recent years, have suggested that deforestation slows down the process of development in various countries.
(C) In recent decades, several methods for countering deforestation in poor countries have been suggested by experts on the environment.
(D) Experts on the environment have been concerned about the impact of deforestation on the Earth's biodiversity in recent decades.

8. From the passage, it can be inferred that

(A) state economic policies are more effective than international agreements

(B) indigenous peoples in the tropics depend on forestry to make money

(C) the three types of solutions mentioned will save the rainforests

(D) deforestation is not a very serious problem

9. The word "deterrent" in paragraph 2 is closest in meaning to

(A) fine

(B) penalty

(C) incentive

(D) discouragement

10. The word "this" in paragraph 4 refers to

(A) a poor country

(B) a nation's debt

(C) an international agreement

(D) an obligation

11. The word "rate" in paragraph 5 is closest in meaning to

(A) price

(B) grade

(C) level

(D) evaluation

12. Directions: *An introductory sentence for a brief summary of the passage is provided below. Complete the summary by selecting the THREE answer choices that express the most important ideas in the passage. Some sentences do not belong in the summary because they express ideas that are not presented in the passage or are minor ideas in the passage.*

First Sentence: **Several plans for slowing down the adverse environmental effects produced from deforestation have recently been proposed by experts on the environment.**

(A) All of these strategies depend on funding and assistance from national governments around the world.

(B) One of these plans calls for governments to provide economic incentives for responsible land use and economic disincentives for harmful land use.

(C) Another plan suggests indigenous peoples and governments compromise and adapt traditional farming methods to modern environmental and economic situations.

(D) The rubber-tappers of Brazil are a good example of a native group adapting traditional practices to today's global economy.

(E) The Earth is constantly losing plant species that could one day lead scientists to cures for cancer or AIDS.

(F) A third strategy involves richer nations offering financial aid and incentives to poorer countries for protecting their own forests.

Chapter 3

Focus: Summarizing Information

Focus Summarizing Information

Tips

- Summarizing ideas is a new type of question in the reading sections, and it is also one of the skills you need for other new task types such as integrated speaking and writing. In this chapter, summarizing will be practiced in two ways — filling in a summary table for the reading sections and outlining a possible summary by creating a table or chart of the information in a reading passage.

Summarizing is putting the main ideas of a source into your own words.

- Summaries should include only the main points. Summaries, therefore, should be shorter than the original source and present a broad overview of the source.

A summary is different from a paraphrase.

- A paraphrase focuses on a specific part of a passage and rewords it, while a summary gives the general ideas of an entire passage. A summary avoids specific details or examples and should be more concise than the original source material.

When you look for and select information

- Skim the passage and make sure that you clearly understand its main points and purpose.
- Note the organization of the passage: contrast, comparison, etc.
- Take notes of the main ideas and key points.
- Choose the sentences that use words similar in meaning to those in the original source.
- Do not choose details or examples appearing in the options.
- Do not choose information that is not explicitly mentioned in the passage.

When you create your own table or chart

- Set up the table using the appropriate number of columns/topic.
- Place the column for a subcategory lower than a higher level category.
- Use single words or short phrases for the titles of each category in the table or chart.
- Include phrases to describe the key points in the passage.
- Look for unique information regarding each category.

Instructions: Read the passage and underline four key sentences or key ideas that would appear in a summary of the passage.

In China, the practice of acupuncture has been traced back to approximately the 1st millennium B.C. Some evidence has placed the practice of acupuncture within the period of the Han Dynasty (from 202 B.C. to 220 A.D.). Its origins are somewhat uncertain. The earliest Chinese medical texts (68 B.C.) do not mention acupuncture, though some hieroglyphics have been found dating back to 1000 B.C. that depict an early type of acupuncture. Sharp pointed stones, believed to have been used to treat certain diseases in ancient times, were discovered amongst some ruins. Some scholars argue that the manner in which these stones were used was not dissimilar to certain acupuncture techniques

Acupuncture is understood to be a procedure for regulating the circulation of gi (vital energy) and blood. Approximately 2,000 years ago, a text describing the usage of gi was written, titled *Huangdi Neijing* (*Yellow Emperor's Classic on Internal Medicine*). This text explained how holes, put into the energy paths of the body, called meridians, could treat various physical problems. In some cases, holes put into a meridian would let out blood without releasing gi. Other holes into meridians would let out gi without releasing blood. The basic understanding of gi and blood within the body was based on observations of water in nature.

Over time, the focus of acupuncture shifted from releasing gi and blood to regulating the flow of gi within the body. Physicians believed that, just as water could be blocked from its natural flow, gi could be blocked within the body. The physician's job was then to determine where meridians were blocked, and through acupuncture, to clear the blockage. In a blocked stream, creating a small hole or crevice in a blockage may clear the entire path of the stream. The force of the water penetrating the hole will widen it until the normal flow is restored. Physicians then reasoned that, in the human body, inserting a small needle into the blocked meridian would have a similar effect.

Although this description of the basic concept behind acupuncture is overly simplified, it still conveys the essence of how acupuncture works. Even today, students of traditional acupuncture are taught to locate the areas of disturbance, to isolate the main blockage points, and to clear the blockage. But that is only the tip of the acupuncture iceberg. Other factors that must be considered in acupuncture therapy include where needles are put into meridians, how deeply the needles are inserted, and even what the needles are made of.

In the Western world, many arguments have been made against acupuncture. One such argument is that traditional Chinese medicine is not based on knowledge of modern physiology, biochemistry, nutrition, anatomy, or any of the known mechanisms of healing. Nor does it have any basis in cell chemistry, blood circulation, nerve function, or the existence of hormones and other biochemical substances. There is no relationship between the meridians that are used in this form of medicine and the layout of the organs and nerves in human physiology. Nor can it be demonstrated that unblocking gi by any means is effective in the treatment of disease. Many scientists and doctors continue to make this argument in opposition of acupuncture, trying to prevent it from becoming an established form of medicine. Because it has no strong scientific foundation or basis, there are those who would continue to discredit it.

Though it has continued to be regarded with some level of skepticism and mistrust, acupuncture is gradually becoming accepted in the Western world as a form of medicine. In 1994, between ten and fifteen million people in the United States tried it as a form of treatment. Furthermore, in 1996, the FDA changed the status of acupuncture needles. With the needles now regarded as class 2 medical devices, it meant that acupuncture was now considered safe when performed by a licensed practitioner. Acupuncture can also be found on many college curriculums today.

Directions: Now complete the summary using three of the ideas that you underlined. The first sentence of the summary is written for you.

The technique of acupuncture has been used in China for over two thousand years to help people recover from illness.

_____

_____

_____

_____

Instructions: Read the passage and underline four key sentences or key ideas that would appear in a summary of the passage.

Capitalism is based on the firm belief that people are all responsible for their own lots in life. It dictates that opportunities exist for all people equally and that if a person does not succeed, it is due to his or her own shortcomings. This equal opportunity premise, however, is a faulty one. Because capitalism creates and maintains social stratification, it cannot be viewed as an equal-opportunity economic system. By and large, individuals are locked into a socio-economic class from birth and are kept there by social limitations.

Social stratification is the sociological term given to the hierarchical arrangement of social classes, castes, and strata within society. In a stratified society, certain groups of people are deemed more valuable and more worthy of commodities than others. In a capitalist society, this status is typically based on wealth. As such, the wealthy are granted more access to those resources that help them to maintain their wealth, such as education. A key tenet of social stratification is that status is inherited. This means that a child born into a certain class will usually remain in that class. For example, a person born to wealthy parents has better access to education, and as such, better access to high-paying jobs. Similarly, a person born to poor parents will have little access to education, and as such, is at a disadvantage when competing for high-paying jobs. This is not to say that social mobility is impossible. Indeed, in recent years, social mobility has increased greatly within some capitalist societies. However, achieving a higher social status remains difficult, and no capitalist country can yet claim complete equal opportunity within its society.

Wealth is not the only benefit for privileged members of a socially stratified system. Upper classes also have more political power, and so they are in a position to define the society's values according to their own beliefs. In fact, they are also able to use this power to maintain stratification. By setting their own values as those of the society, those who hold different beliefs are deemed less worthy as people.

Just as wealth is not the only benefit of social stratification, it is not the only determinant to a person's social standing. Social dominance theorists claim that humans have a natural tendency to form social hierarchies that are based on groups. The group can be defined by wealth and social status, but it is often also related to such factors as race, ethnicity, gender, age, and religion. For example, a dominant group may consist of Caucasian middle-aged men. This does not mean that every person in society who meets this description will be upper class. However, if you take, for example, an upper-class elderly woman of African descent with the same amount of money as a Caucasian man, she may still be valued less in society because of the age group and ethnic group that she belongs to. So, as can be seen by this example, the dynamics of social stratification involve more than just monetary assets.

Structural-functionalist theorists will argue that social stratification is beneficial to society because it provides stability. Their evidence to support this claim is simply this: all societies are organized by social stratification. This contention, however, is not true. Egalitarian societies have existed, and continue to exist, such as certain hunter-gatherer societies. While it is true that many of these societies from the past did not survive, it was because a stratified society arrived and used their power to dominate them. Further, history tells us that social stratification does not provide stability. Power struggles within societies and efforts by the powerful to deny privileges to certain groups have both resulted in severe disruptions in society, and in some cases have even led to genocide. These are the lengths that some powerful people will go to in order to maintain the status quo.

Equal opportunity is the tenet that capitalists use to justify the existence of social inequality. Upon close examination, however, this assertion is found to be faulty. Social stratification creates a societal structure in which people are valued based on their wealth and by their membership to the dominant group. Because it is in the interest of the powerful to prevent the less powerful from advancing their social status, they use their power to ensure that the social structure is kept intact.

Directions: Now complete the summary using three of the ideas that you underlined. The first sentence of the summary is written for you.

Social stratification is the hierarchical arrangement of society into social classes and strata that are very difficult for individuals to rise through.

_____

_____

_____

_____

Instructions: Read the passage and underline all of the key sentences or key ideas.

Aristotle's *Poetics* is considered the first work of literary criticism in the Western tradition. Aristotle, in his *Poetics*, looks at the form of tragedy in drama. He defined tragedy as an "imitation of an action that is complete and whole and of a certain magnitude." By this, Aristotle indicates that the medium of tragedy is not narrative, but drama. That is, tragedy must show rather than tell the audience. An example to consider is *Hamlet*. The serious action of the play centers around Hamlet's quest to exact revenge for his father's death. The play "shows" us the action through Hamlet's anguish, suffering, and paranoia. Rather than describe the action, Hamlet's actions and emotions reveal it.

One important aspect that Aristotle discusses is plot. He places more significance on plot than on any other aspect, such as character or diction, which he considers to stem from the plot itself. For the plot to be complete, he states, it must have "unity of action." The sequence of events should be logical and should not be episodic. Events should be connected to each other in a logical way and have obvious causes. The tension in the play must also come from a conflict, which is often condensed in the character of the antagonist. The plot should be aimed at working through this conflict.

To be whole, the tragedy must have a beginning, a middle, and an end. This seems rather obvious, but Aristotle specified that there must be a cause and effect relationship between these parts. That is, the beginning is the causal agent, and is not itself caused by anything occurring outside the realm of the play. Therefore, its effects are important, but its causes are not. The middle, or climax, is caused by the beginning and is the cause of the end; therefore, the highest level of tension in the play should coincide with the actual middle of the play. The end, or resolution, is caused by the middle, but does not have any important effects. This is the part of the play in which the chief problem gets resolved.

Additionally, Aristotle outlines both quantitative and qualitative aspects of the plot that tragedy should aim for. The plot should neither be too great or too small in terms of length and complexity. Further, it should attain a certain universal significance. The ultimate goal is to bring events and themes together as an organic whole. Furthermore, the play should arouse a sense of pity and fear in the audience, who must sympathize and identify with the hero. As a result, the audience will appreciate the hero's predicament and after going through the hero's conflict with him, will feel a sense of cleansing or "catharsis." This catharsis is a kind of mental resolution or closure. The aim of the play is to bring out this catharsis within the audience.

Of course, for this catharsis to occur, the play and all its loose ends should be resolved in a believable manner. For the audience to identify with the hero, the hero must display characteristics that people themselves experience, even if, like in *Hamlet*, the hero is a prince. Hamlet himself experiences strong emotions and feelings such as paranoia, confusion, and uncertainty, all of which are feelings the audience can appreciate and relate to in some way.

Plots can be either simple or complex. Simple plots involve catastrophe, while complex plots add "reversal of intention" and "recognition." Reversal of intention occurs when a character causes an opposite effect or outcome to what was intended. Recognition "is a change from ignorance to knowledge, producing love or hate between the persons destined for good or bad fortune." Again, this is evident in *Hamlet* when his uncle watches the play in which he sees very similar circumstances to those in which he killed Hamlet's father. These cause him to leave in distress, giving Hamlet strong evidence that his uncle did in fact kill his father, and strengthening his desire for revenge. Aristotle thought that the best plays were complex. They were only successful, though, if all of the elements came together using cause and effect.

Now write a summary using four of the ideas that you underlined.

_____

_____

_____

_____

Instructions: Read the passage and underline all of the key sentences or key ideas.

Why is it that some managers become successful and some do not? Naturally, the more talented ones will typically have more success, but among the talented ones, why do some move quickly to the top of the corporate ladder while others start out strong, and then fail somewhere along the way? Several studies have identified key mistakes that can impede a talented manager's career. By interviewing the co-workers of both successful managers, or "arrivers," and those who failed early in their careers, or "derailers," these studies outline five key mistakes that were common to the latter.

The first key mistake is insensitivity. Managers who do not respect their subordinates and who treat them with disdain are not exercising good managerial practice. Studies indicate that they will not go far in their careers. Bullying tactics and a disagreeable attitude do not create a healthy and productive workplace; therefore, managers who use this style of management often fail early in their careers.

Another somewhat related common flaw is arrogance. Again, the managers that were studied were very talented, and they were experts in their field. What distinguished the derailers from the arrivers was that they let this expertise go to their heads. As such, they treated non-experts with contempt, and did not take their input seriously. This attitude is clearly not conducive to teamwork, which is an important function in company operations.

Betrayal of trust is cited in the studies as a third common mistake. In the day-to-day running of a company, people often depend on others to do tasks for them. The importance of teamwork has already been mentioned. At times, a person will be unable to accomplish a task they had agreed to do. This is a common occurrence and not necessarily an indicator that one is set to become a derailer. Rather, the common trait to the derailers was that they would not inform others when they were unable to complete an assigned task. This leaves the others in a bind, because they were depending on the work being done. A betrayal of trust, then, arises when a manager commits to doing something, but then does not do so and does not inform colleagues about it. This betrayal of trust interrupts the smooth operation of the company, creates hostility, and indicates an inability to take responsibility for mistakes.

The next mistake commonly linked to derailers is over-ambition. Of course, there is nothing wrong with being ambitious. However, many of the derailers failed to establish positive working relationships with their co-workers because they were always thinking about the next job or always trying to be noticed by upper management. Again, this negates some important managerial principles such as teamwork and mutual respect. If the manager is more concerned with his or her own personal success than the success of the company, then he or she is not performing the function of a manager very well. Because the success of the company relies on highly effective teams of workers, any practice that does not encourage teamwork is not in the best interest of the company.

As with the above mistakes, the fifth and final key mistake of derailers relates to teamwork and the team operating under the manager. A good manager needs to delegate responsibility. Unfortunately, some talented managers are accustomed to doing everything themselves. The fifth key mistake identified in the research is that derailers do not effectively delegate. They are unable to trust their subordinates to do their jobs. Instead of doing their own jobs well, these managers would interfere with the tasks of subordinate workers. This tends to create hostility. It also takes time away from the manager's own workload. Because managers are so busy meddling in other people's jobs, they have less time to get their own jobs done.

In sum, effective managerial practice involves teamwork, respect, and effective time management. Five flaws that may hinder these principles are insensitivity, arrogance, betrayal of trust, over-ambition, and the inability to delegate responsibility. Studies show that many talented managers who failed in their careers were guilty of at least two of these flaws. As such, managers who intend to have successful careers would be well advised not to engage in any of these career-ruining practices.

Now write a summary using four of the ideas that you underlined.

_____

_____

_____

_____

Instructions: Read the passage and complete the table with key ideas or information from the passage.

Stress caused by worry can be both useful and problematic for people. How can it be both useful and problematic? Consider the stress some people feel when they worry about the future. Worrying about the future, though unpleasant, can motivate people to get things done. People strive to accomplish certain tasks today in order to avoid unpleasant outcomes later. This would be an example of how stress actually serves a useful purpose.

However, sometimes worry can have the opposite effect. Again, take the example of worrying about the future. As discussed above, a certain level of worry can help people accomplish the tasks at hand. Some people, however, experience a significantly higher level of stress brought on by worry. This is when worry escalates into fear or anxiety. Although many people might understand fear and anxiety as one and the same, psychologists define these two emotions differently.

Basically, fear can be understood as a normal, healthy reaction to one's situation. Anxiety, on the other hand, is typically associated with an unhealthy mental state. An additional distinction between fear and anxiety can be seen in their sources. The source of fear can be named or described. It might be an important test that is coming up, or it could be a large black spider on the wall. In contrast, anxiety is not based on a describable source. When you ask people exhibiting the symptoms of extreme stress or worry about the cause of their distress, they cannot name it. Needless to say, such imagined, indefinable causes of anxiety and any effort to solve or avoid these problems are a waste of energy.

Other than such negative effects as consuming energy and causing distraction, too much anxiety can cause people to feel overwhelmed. A person's anxiety might actually hinder his or her ability to take any action, and in severe cases, the person may be unable to even leave home. When the quality of a person's life is seriously affected by their feelings of anxiety, they are said to be suffering from an anxiety disorder. There are several types of disorders, the most common being specific phobias such as fear of spiders or fear of heights. This is not a really big problem, so long as the feared situation is not important to the person's life. However, more serious anxiety disorders can be accompanied by symptoms that affect a person's physical health.

When someone suffers severe physical symptoms of anxiety, it is called a panic attack. A panic attack is a sudden and intense onset of fear. As for the symptoms that accompany such an attack, the person may experience shortness of breath, sweating, trembling, or even an irregular heartbeat. These symptoms may cause the panic to become worse because the symptoms are so frightening for the individual. Obviously, a panic attack is a very unpleasant experience that the person does not want to repeat. For this reason, the individual develops even greater anxiety about having another panic attack, thus creating a vicious cycle.

Anxiety disorders are serious conditions. They are not only unpleasant emotionally for the individual, but they also make it very difficult for the person to have relationships and to maintain employment.

Anxiety disorders can have disastrous effects on a person's life and the way that the person functions in society. However, the good news is that, of all mental disorders, anxiety disorder has the highest rate of effective treatment.

_____

_____
_____
_____

_____

_____
_____
_____

_____

_____
_____
_____

Directions: Now write three more sentences to complete the summary of the passage using the ideas in the table. The first sentence of the summary is written for you.

Although many people think they are the same, psychologists differentiate between fear and anxiety.

_____
_____
_____
_____

Instructions: Read the passage and complete the table with key ideas or information from the passage.

The public prosecutor certainly wields a great deal of power in the application of the law. Before a case even appears before a judge, the prosecutor can decide to drop it for a wide variety of reasons. However, the most powerful tool of the public prosecutor is by far the plea bargain. This allows the prosecutor to offer the defendant a reduced sentence or reduced charges in exchange for a guilty plea.

A controversial practice by many accounts, the plea bargain's relatively recent introduction into the French legal system was met with social outcry and protest. Some legal theorists purport that it reduces justice to bartering and that a system depending on plea bargains denies defendants the right to a fair trial.

One main concern is that prosecutors will threaten the defendant with a large list of charges in order to scare him or her into pleading guilty to lesser charges. Thus, just like in bartering economies, in which a salesman may initially offer ten times the value of the product and then reduce the price in stages to five times the value of the product, so too a prosecutor might pressure a defendant into pleading guilty to crimes more serious than those actually committed by stacking up an excessive list of initial charges. This is especially true for cases in which the defendant cannot afford a defense attorney with strong influence or negotiating skills.

The criticisms of the plea bargain system, however, are countered by its advantages. It has been said that the US justice system, for example, would cease to function if plea bargaining were abolished. This is due to its effect on case loads. By cutting deals with defendants and foregoing lengthy and costly trials, the prosecutor is able to reduce the strain on the court system, and by extension, on the tax payer. Without plea bargaining, it is safe to say that the US court system would be hopelessly snowed under with pending cases.

It would be inaccurate, however, to maintain that plea bargaining is only advantageous to the prosecution. Often, defendants are eager to reduce the risk of receiving the maximum penalty for crimes they are accused of. In these cases, a plea bargain can both offer defendants a safe option for a reasonable sentence and save the justice system from expenditure of its resources.

In a special application, plea bargains are often offered to lower-level criminals in exchange for their testimony against higher-ups in organized crime or illegal drug trafficking organizations. In these cases, the sentence is often heavily reduced or eliminated altogether depending on the value of the defendant's testimony. In a sense, this may be criticized as unfair, since the defendant may end up not having to pay for his or her crime. However, such practices do serve the ultimate end of reducing overall crime in society, given that prosecution of major criminals is much more effective in breaking up such organizations.

Finally, prosecutors may choose to offer a plea bargain when they are themselves convinced of the defendant's guilt but doubt they have sufficient evidence for a conviction. Thus, the criminal will not get off scot-free and a lengthy, expensive, and most likely ineffective trial is avoided. Of course, these cases readily lend themselves to criticism. One may wonder: if there is not sufficient evidence to convict the defendant, then how can the prosecutor be so certain of the guilt of the accused? The argument that this system places undue disadvantage on the poorer members of society applies here as well. After all, a defendant who can afford a good defense attorney will likely be instructed not to accept such a plea, given that a trial would probably result in an acquittal.

Regardless of one's personal stance on the issue, it is undeniable that plea bargaining is a major source of power for prosecutors and a procedure that must be fully understood and applied with the best interests of society in mind. Though it may have its critics, plea bargaining will likely remain an integral part of judicial systems around the world for years to come.

_____

- _____
- _____
- _____

_____

- _____
- _____
- _____

Directions: Now write three more sentences to complete the summary of the passage using the ideas in the table. The first sentence of the summary is written for you.

Plea bargaining is a powerful tool for prosecutors, but there are both pros and cons related to this type of legal strategy.

_____

_____

_____

_____

Instructions: Read the passage and create a table with key ideas or information from the passage.

Two significant terms associated with computers are "bit" and "byte." These refer to the numbering system computers use to translate digits into letters and characters. Bit is an abbreviation of "binary digit," referring to the base-2 system used in computer coding. Instead of the decimal digits 0 through 9 that comprise a base-10 system, computer code consists of only two digits: 0 and 1. Each of these digits is a bit — the smallest unit of information that can be stored or manipulated on a computer. By combining bits in thousands of different ways, computer programmers direct computers to process words, calculate numbers, and perform various other functions.

Computers are composed of digital electronics, so they respond to two kinds of electrical states. These states could be called on and off, true and false, positive voltage and negative voltage, or some other paired combination of terms. It doesn't matter, as long as there are two conditions. The bits 0 and 1 represent these conditions. Two bits can combine to represent up to four different decimal numbers. Imagine bits in terms of switches. Two switches can yield the following: 0 0 (off off) = decimal number 0; 0 1 (off on) = decimal 1; 1 0 (on, off) = decimal 2; and 1 1 (on on) = decimal 3. Adding a third bit (another 1) to the left-hand side produces eight different decimal numbers: 0 through 7 (100 = 4; 101 = 5; 110 = 6; 111 = 7). Four bits can represent 16 numbers (0 through 15). Five bits can represent 32 numbers (0 through 31). Each added bit doubles the number of possible combinations of 0s and 1s. Eight bits are called a byte, which represents 256 numbers (0 through 255).

A byte usually represents a single character of data in a computer. Grouping bits into bytes enables the computer to more easily interpret the continuous string of information it receives. A byte is also the amount of bits needed to represent letters of the alphabet and other characters. Special codes enable the computer to recognize eight-digit binary strings as letters of the alphabet. For instance, under a common computer code called ASCII (American Standard Code for Information Interchange), the letter "A" is expressed as 65. This converts to the binary number 01000001. Computers recognize these eight bits, or one byte, as "A."

Computers interpret any character typed on the keyboard as a byte. Each byte is assigned a specific ASCII character, such as 65 noted above for "A." Computers store text documents, both in memory and on disk, using these ASCII character codes. For each letter typed into a text file, the computer uses one byte of memory — including one byte for each space between the words (ASCII character number 32 represents a space). So, for instance, the sentence "I am studying for the final exam," consists of 32 bytes: 26 letters and six spaces between the words. When the sentence is stored on a file on disk, the file will also contain 32 bytes.

One area in which it's easy to confuse bits and bytes is monitoring data transfer speed. For example, when you download a file from the Internet, your browser indicates the transfer rate in KBps (kilobytes per second). Note that the letter "B" is capitalized. This indicates kilobytes. Many computer modems have a speed of 56K. The K stands for Kbps. Note that the "b" in this instance is lower case. This means kilobits per second. Since eight bits equals one byte, we can divide 56 by eight to derive a maximum download speed: 7 Kilobytes per second (7KBps). Thus, if you download a document at a transfer rate of 3.5 KBps, you are using 50 percent of the maximum transfer speed.

Another area where bits and bytes are often confused is measuring computer memory storage capacity. Early computer manufacturers stated memory capacity in terms of kilobytes. However, they were using kilo as a decimal system prefix, in which it means 1,000. In a binary system, the prefix kilo means 1,024. Bearing this distinction in mind, a computer described as having 64K (64 Kilobytes) of memory can actually store 655,360 bytes (640 x 1,024) of data. Those extra bytes may come in handy for people who need to create and store a large number of computer documents.

Directions: Now write four sentences for a summary of the passage using the ideas in the table.

_____

_____

_____

_____

Instructions: Read the passage and create a table with key ideas or information from the passage.

One aspect integral to students of education is classroom technological aids. The main tool discussed in this chapter is the video projector, which allows instructors to project notes, images, sound, or video in the classroom. Some instructors feel that such tools are unnecessary and discourage student involvement in the class. This need not be the case. Indeed, engaging and effective multimedia lectures are possible if the following suggested framework for presentations is utilized.

The major criticisms of video projectors are that they inhibit student-teacher interaction, reduce classroom attendance, and distract the students from thinking critically and processing the lecture material. There is no doubt that some instructors do experience these effects, but this is primarily due to misuse of a video projector rather than the tool itself. The most common problem is that instructors go overboard by adding every detail of their lecture to the presentation. When this happens, the instructor merely rephrases what is already contained in the presentation slides. This reduces interaction because the professor becomes superfluous to the presentation. It reduces attendance because many students may be able to simply download the presentation instead of attending class. Finally, this approach tends to make students passive learners.

To avoid all of this, educators must use the technology strategically. One way to do this is to reduce the level of detail in the presentation outlines. If instructors only provide a broad outline of main points, this will leave room for the instructor to expound on the details, take the student out of the "read-and-copy" mindset, and, incidentally, solve the classroom attendance problem. As for the other two problems, instructors must design the presentation to be engaging and to encourage critical thinking and active information processing. In other words, they must become effective lecture writers. There are two key points in the structure of a lecture. It should be organized around a beginning, middle, and an end, and it should contain periodic pauses for active learning activities in order to engage the student.

The main objective in the beginning of the lecture is to spark the students' interest, command their attention, and clearly introduce the objective of the lecture. Video projectors can be particularly effective here with multimedia clips incorporating audio and/or video. Instructors should also present in the introduction a very broad enumeration of the main points that the lecture will cover. Many instructors like to use a "question of the day" to hone the students in on the lecture's motivation. The beginning is also a good time for a short brainstorming activity to further involve the students, such as a short discussion period. Now that the students have been introduced to the topic, its motivation, and the main points, it is time to move on to the "meat" of the lecture.

The middle of the lecture is basically the content of the lecture. The main idea here is to present all of the details without losing the students' interest. Psychologists have determined that the average person can remain focused on a lecture for approximately 12 to 15 minutes before mind-wandering ensues. The solution is simple: instructors must break the lecture somehow every 12 to 15 minutes, providing a pause for the processing of the information, during which instructors can re-engage the students and rekindle their attention. There are several options here. Instructors can have the students get into pairs and brainstorm or quiz each other on the information. Alternatively, instructors can have a free question/discussion period between the instructor and the class. More creative re-engagement tactics, involving the multimedia capabilities of video projectors and specifically-tailored to the topic, are of course highly effective as well.

The end of the lecture should rehash the information, address the initial motivation for the lecture, and help the students assimilate the material into their own experiences. Good techniques here are a closing summary and classroom assessment. The closing summary should reinforce the main points and overall structure of the lecture. The assessment aims to engage the students one last time and to give the instructor a means to measure the lecture's effectiveness. This could involve simply asking the students their thoughts on the lecture or whether any points are still unclear. Further, the instructor may ask the students a few assessment questions to evaluate their grasp of the content.

All in all, these techniques will motivate students to take an active role in class and will make video projectors a tool that enhances, rather than suffocates, the learning experience.

Directions: Now write four sentences for a summary of the passage using the ideas in the table.

_____

_____

_____

_____

Mastering Skills for the TOEFL® iBT

LISTENING

LISTENING Table of Contents

How the listening section is organized

There are four main parts in the listening section.

Introduction   Understanding what each section requires you to do
Chapter 1   Practicing necessary skills with short listening passages
Chapter 2   Mastering the skills with longer listening passages
Chapter 3   Improving note-taking skills

Listening

In the listening section of the TOEFL® test, you will hear a variety of conversations and lectures, each of which lasts from 3 to 6 minutes. A total of six listening passages will be presented. After each passage, you will then be asked to answer six questions about what you heard. Like the reading section of the TOEFL® test, the questions are designed to assess your understanding of the main idea, factual information, and inferences. You will not be asked questions regarding vocabulary or sentence structure.

- **Passage Types:**
    1. Conversations — Two people discussing a campus-related problem, issue, or process
    2. Lectures — A professor speaking a monologue, presenting information related to an academic topic
    3. Classroom interaction — Similar to the lecture passage type with some interaction between the professor and one or more students included

- **Question Types:**
    Questions for the listening section of the TOEFL® test typically appear in the following order:

Question	Type	Description
1	Main Idea	Choose the best phrase or sentence
2–3	Factual Information	Choose the statement that is true according to the listening Select multiple answers to complete a chart
4	Purpose / Inference / Organization	Recognize the speaker's purpose, draw an inference, or explain how the speaker communicated certain information
5–6	Repeated Listening Purpose / Inference / Attitude	Hear a particular portion of the listening passage again and recognize the speaker's purpose, attitude or the implied meaning of a statement

Study Tips for Listening:

- Practice listening to North American, British, and Australian English as much as possible. For the purposes of the TOEFL® test, educational programs, documentaries, and news programs are excellent sources.

- One lecture per test is spoken with a British or Australian accent, so practice listening to programs or news sources from the UK and Australia, as well as reports from the US and Canada.

- When you are practicing for the listening section of the TOEFL® test, listen to the material only once and then answer the questions. Then review the answers while listening a second or third time. Remember, though, on the real test you are only permitted to hear the conversation or lecture once before answering the questions.

- Pay attention to how pauses and intonation are used to organize the passage, emphasize important information, and show transition.

- Make a recording of the programs you use to practice listening. Replay any sections you have difficulty understanding.

- As suggested for reading, keep such things in mind as the main idea, the development/support of the main idea, and the speaker's reasons for mentioning certain points.

- Develop your note-taking skills. While you are listening to information, try to write down key words in an organized, graphic way that makes sense to you.

- Create a list of vocabulary words related to university campus life as well as various academic subjects.

Test Management:

- A visual image will be given on the screen to allow test takers to recognize each speaker's role and the context of the conversation. Along with this image, a subject title will be given for each lecture.

- Before you begin the listening section, listen to the headset directions. Pay particular attention to how you change the volume. It is very important that you be able to hear clearly during the listening section of the test.

- If you miss something that is said in a conversation or lecture, do not panic. Forget about it, and simply keep listening. Even native speakers do not hear everything that is said.

- Note-taking during the lecture is permitted. Paper will be provided by the test supervisor. These notes can be studied while answering the questions.

- Like the reading section, questions cannot be viewed until after the lecture/conversation has been completed.

- Do not leave any question unanswered. You are NOT penalized for guessing an answer.

Chapter 1

Short Passage Skill Practice

Understanding Main Ideas and Organization

Necessary Skills

Identifying Main Ideas

- Understanding the overall topic or basic idea of a lecture or a conversation
- Understanding the speaker's general purpose in giving a lecture or having a conversation
- Inferring the speaker's purpose or main idea when it is not directly stated

Understanding Organization

- Understanding why the speaker mentions a certain example or piece of information
- Recognizing how a particular statement connects to the whole passage
- Realizing the speaker's intention or purpose in an aside—a remark unrelated to the main subject of a conversation
- Recognizing a change in topic

Example Questions

Main Idea

- What are the speakers mainly discussing?
- Why does the man go to see his professor?
- What is the talk mainly about?
- What is the discussion mainly about?
- What aspect of _____ does the professor mainly discuss?
- What does the woman need from the _____?

Organization

- Why does the professor mention _____?
- How does the professor describe _____?
- In what order does the student tell his professor about _____?
- How does the professor emphasize her point about _____?

Notes

---

sign up *(v phrase):*
to officially register for a class or activity

intramural *(adj):*
between students and teams of one school, not with other schools

fill out *(v phrase):*
to write information and details on a form

free agent *(n phrase):*
a player who is available to any team that wants him or her

select *(v):*
to choose; to pick

---

1. What are the speakers mainly discussing?
   - (A) Getting a new room key
   - (B) Registering for classes
   - (C) The rules of a sport
   - (D) Joining a sports team

3. According to the man, how much does it cost to join a softball team?
   - (A) Three dollars
   - (B) Thirteen dollars
   - (C) Thirty dollars
   - (D) Three hundred and four dollars

2. How does the man help the woman?
   - (A) By letting her join his group
   - (B) By telling her about the procedure
   - (C) By giving her a phone number to call
   - (D) By explaining the physical requirements

4. Fill in the blanks to complete the organizer.

   The woman needs to:

   Go to room _____ in Withurst Hall

   Fill out a _____ and pay a _____

   The fee is _____ dollars for team players.

Notes

industrial *(adj)*:
related to the use of machinery and factories for production

mature *(adj)*:
well-established; fully developed

stable *(adj)*:
constant; not prone to large fluctuation

in theory *(adv phrase)*:
according to assumed facts; not necessarily true in practice

achieve *(v)*:
to do; to accomplish

---

1. What is the talk mainly about?
(A) India
(B) Population
(C) Disease
(D) Industry

2. What are two key features of a preindustrial population? Choose 2 answers.
(A) Agriculture
(B) Birth rate
(C) Death rate
(D) Employment
(E) Growth rate
(F) Location

3. In what order does the professor explain the categories?
(A) Mature industrial, early industrial, and preindustrial
(B) Preindustrial, early industrial, and mature industrial
(C) Preindustrial, mature industrial, and early industrial
(D) Early industrial, preindustrial, and mature industrial

---

4. Fill in the blanks to complete the organizer.

Stage of Industrialization	Death Rate	_____ Rate	Population
Preindustrial	High	High	_____
Early Industrial	_____	High	Explosion
Mature Industrial	Low	_____	Stable

Notes

fallacy *(n)*: an incorrect statement; a falsehood
sonnet *(n)*: a standardized form of poem with 14 lines
popularize *(v)*: to make popular
pastoral *(adj)*: related to an idealized, rural life
refine *(v)*: to change and improve

1. What is the talk mainly about?

(A) Poetry
(B) Shakespeare
(C) Geography
(D) Italian writers

2. How does the professor emphasize his point about sonnets?

(A) By stating the modern view of sonnets
(B) By explaining the personal relationship between Shakespeare and Petrarch
(C) By identifying the reasons why sonnets are written
(D) By comparing and contrasting Italian and English sonnets

3. According to the professor, where did sonnets exist before Shakespeare wrote them?

(A) In England
(B) In Petrarch
(C) In Italy
(D) In term papers

4. Fill in the blanks to complete the organizer.

Petrarch's sonnets	Shakespeare's sonnets
_____ parts	_____ parts
– _____ lines	– _____ 4-line parts
– _____ lines	– _____ couplet

Notes

require *(v)*:
to need; to demand

presume *(v)*:
to assume; to believe without strong evidence

given *(adj)*:
specified; particular

fulfill *(v)*:
to meet a requirement

permit *(v)*:
to allow; to grant permission

---

1. Why does the woman go to see the professor?

(A) To find out if he is teaching Chemistry 221

(B) To find out if she can take a class

(C) To find out the prerequisites for his class

(D) To find out how many students are in the class

2. How does the professor explain "prerequisite"? Choose 2 answers.

(A) He defines it.

(B) He explains the root and prefix of the word.

(C) He gives an example.

(D) He shows the woman a list.

3. According to the professor, why can the woman enroll in the course?

(A) Because it is full

(B) Because it isn't full

(C) Because it is a required course for the woman

(D) Because the woman has already taken Chemistry 221

4. Fill in the blanks to complete the organizer.

Enrolling in a class that is full

You may be able to enroll if it is a _____ course.

You may be able to enroll if you have the _____.

You can be put on a _____ list, if the previous two conditions do not apply.

Notes

erosion *(n)*:
the process by which solid material is worn away, or slowly broken down

abrasion *(n)*:
the process of breaking down by friction, or rubbing

bedrock *(n)*:
the solid rock that lies underneath looser material, such as soil, sand, and clay

backhoe *(n)*:
a machine used to dig and/or fill large holes; a type of tractor for digging

striation *(n)*:
a long line or scratch dug into the surface of a rock by the passing of another rock

1. What is the talk mainly about?

   (A) Plucking
   (B) Abrasion
   (C) Glacial erosion
   (D) Types of bedrock

2. How does the professor explain abrasion?

   (A) She demonstrates the process in class.
   (B) She brainstorms possible meanings.
   (C) She explains its chronological development through history.
   (D) She describes the process with a simple illustration.

3. What does the professor say about abrasion with coarse debris?

   (A) It creates long striations.
   (B) It works like a backhoe.
   (C) It creates a smooth surface.
   (D) It pulls rocks away from the bedrock.

4. Fill in the blanks to complete the organizer.

How glaciers erode bedrock

_____ causes large chunks to be detached.

Abrasion

_____ debris creates long grooves in the bedrock.

_____ debris creates a smooth surface.

READING

LISTENING

SPEAKING

WRITING

PRACTICE TEST

Notes

_____

_____

_____

_____

_____

_____

_____

_____

pasteurize (v):
to heat food in order to kill harmful microorganisms

bacteria (n):
one-celled microorganisms

procedure (n):
a way of doing something; a method

refrigerate (v):
to keep cool; to keep in a refrigerator

ultra (adj):
very; extreme

1. What aspect of pasteurization does the professor mainly discuss?

   (A) Inventor
   (B) First use
   (C) Purpose
   (D) Methods

2. How does the professor explain the effect of pasteurization on the shelf life of milk?

   (A) By explaining the relationship between bacteria and milk
   (B) By comparing HTST to UHT
   (C) By describing an experiment
   (D) By comparing it to other products

3. What are two key features of the ultra high temperature pasteurization process? Choose 2 answers.

   (A) Milk is heated to 72°C.
   (B) Milk is heated to 138°C.
   (C) It is kept at that temperature for two seconds.
   (D) It is kept at that temperature for 15 seconds.

4. Fill in the blanks to complete the organizer.

   Pasteurization

   _____
   • kept at 72°C for _____ seconds
   • can last for two or three _____

   _____
   • kept at 138°C for _____ seconds
   • can last for two or three _____

Notes

| | assess *(v)*: |
| to evaluate |
| note down *(v phrase)*: |
| to write on paper |
| grade *(v)*: |
| to assign a grade, or mark, on a student's work |
| eye contact *(n phrase)*: |
| the state of looking into another person's eyes |
| at all *(adv phrase)*: |
| in any way; to any extent |

1. What are the speakers mainly discussing?

   (A) Giving a psychological evaluation
   (B) How to assess a class presentation
   (C) Making categories for a lesson plan
   (D) Study notes for a test

2. How does the woman explain the procedure?

   (A) By referring to the handbook for the procedure
   (B) By quoting what the professor had said about it
   (C) By giving examples from when she did it
   (D) By comparing it to the old procedure

3. What is an example that the woman gives of a quality that earned a high grade?

   (A) Chewing gum during the presentation
   (B) Making eye contact during the presentation
   (C) Using an assessment form during the presentation
   (D) Summarizing the main ideas during the presentation

4. Fill in the blanks to complete the organizer.

   Notes: _____ ideas, strengths, one thing to _____

   Grading: from 1 to _____; best score = _____

∩ Skill A 08 Journalism

Notes

scholarly *(adj)*:
characteristic of scholars, that is, people whose job is to study and research a particular subject

analysis *(n)*:
an examination of a subject or event

interpretation *(n)*:
an explanation based on evidence

tertiary *(adj)*:
of third importance or rank

first hand *(adv phrase)*:
directly witnessed; in person

1. What is the talk mainly about?
   (A) The interpretation of diaries
   (B) Historical events
   (C) Scholars
   (D) Sources

2. How does the professor explain the different sources of information?
   (A) By highlighting key points in the textbook
   (B) By explaining the research process
   (C) By comparing categories
   (D) By pointing out good and bad sources of information

3. What is an example the professor gives of a primary source?
   (A) A newspaper article
   (B) A paper about a diary
   (C) A documentary film
   (D) A diary

4. Fill in the blanks to complete the organizer.

Where information comes from

_____	_____	_____
Ex: a diary	Ex: a scholar's interpretation of a _____ source	Ex: a document created from a _____ source

Understanding Main Ideas and Organization **219**

Understanding Details and Facts

Necessary Skills

- Taking notes of major points and important details of a lecture or conversation
- Listening for signal expressions that identify details, such as the following:
  for example, the reason is, on the other hand, I would say
- Eliminating incorrect answer choices
- Identifying a statement that is not mentioned

Example Questions

- According to the professor, what is _____?
- According to the professor, why/who/how/where/how many _____?
- What does the professor/woman/student say about _____?
- What is the evidence for _____?
- What is an example the professor gives of _____?
- What does the _____ want/suggest/advise the _____ to do?
- What are two key features of _____? Click on 2 answers.
- What are the reasons for _____? Click on 3 answers.
- What comparison does the professor make between _____ and _____?
- Why does the professor say this: ⌒ ?

Notes

audition *(v):*
to take part in a trial performance; to try to be accepted for a performing role
pointer *(n):* a tip; a piece of advice
dynamics *(n):* the relationship between two or more objects during change
scale *(n):* an ascending or descending order of pitches played at set intervals
warm up *(v phrase):* to prepare oneself for a performance

1. What does the man need from the woman?

(A) Information about jazz music

(B) Information about scales

(C) Information about how to prepare for an audition

(D) Information about when the audition takes place

2. What does the woman advise the man to do?

(A) Talk to a member of the band

(B) Concentrate on dynamics and tone

(C) Focus on scales and sight-reading

(D) Return early the next day

3. According to the man, what instrument does he play?

(A) Trombone

(B) Trumpet

(C) Saxophone

(D) Bass

4. Fill in the blanks to complete the organizer.

Jazz Band _____

Memorize _____

Practice _____ - _____

Allow plenty of time to _____

Notes

quest *(n)*:
a mission; a journey with a certain goal or purpose

charismatic *(adj)*:
very charming; having a compelling and attractive personality

foster *(v)*:
to assist; to create an environment conducive to a certain action

brutal *(adj)*:
violent and without compassion

strategist *(n)*:
a planner; a person who creates a strategy or plan

1. What aspect of Alexander's career does the professor mainly discuss?

(A) His childhood
(B) His empire
(C) His education
(D) His personal life

3. What are the characteristics for which Alexander is remembered? Choose 3 answers.

(A) He was a charismatic leader.
(B) He was a brutal killer.
(C) He was a loving father.
(D) He was a brilliant military strategist.
(E) He was a clever student.

2. Which empire is mentioned in the lecture?

(A) The Trojan empire
(B) The Persian empire
(C) The Egyptian empire
(D) The Greek empire

4. Fill in the blanks to complete the organizer.

Historians' perspective on Alexander the Great

| charismatic _____ | a brutal _____ | a brilliant military _____ |

fossilize (v):
to change from organic material into hard minerals over time

highly (adv):
very; quite

preservable (adj):
able to avoid decay and disintegration

sediment (n):
a layer of material placed atop another material

shoreline (n):
the land along the coast, or shore, of a body of water

---

1. What aspect of paleontology does the professor mainly discuss?

   (A) Chemical alteration of hard parts
   (B) Difficulties with excavating fossils
   (C) Fossil preservation
   (D) How to handle fossils

2. According to the professor, where do fossils usually form?

   (A) In dry climates
   (B) On mountains
   (C) In tropical jungles
   (D) Near bodies of water

3. What are two examples that the professor gives of preservable materials? Choose 2 answers.

   (A) Bones
   (B) Sediment
   (C) Fossils
   (D) Shells
   (E) Claws

4. Fill in the blanks to complete the organizer.

   Needed for preservation

   _____ substance
   – _____
   – _____

   Buried in _____

   Suitable _____
   – _____

READING
LISTENING
SPEAKING
WRITING
PRACTICE TEST

Notes

present *(v)*:
to give; to show for approval

authorize *(v)*:
to approve; to give permission

beforehand *(adv)*:
in advance; ahead of time

basis *(n)*:
a foundation; a basic principle or condition

appreciate *(v)*:
to value; to be thankful

1. What is the discussion mainly about?

(A) Buying uniforms
(B) Coaching a team
(C) Renting a locker
(D) Reserving a court

2. Where does the woman suggest the man go?

(A) The gym office
(B) The department office
(C) The court
(D) The sports center

3. According to the woman, what does a student need to show the office?

(A) A credit card
(B) A reservation number
(C) An ID card
(D) A gym card

4. Fill in the blanks to complete the organizer.

Court policy:

The maximum limit is one _____, _____ time(s) per week.

_____ are made one _____ beforehand.

Notes

formula *(n)*:
an equation or rule for performing a calculation

ravine *(n)*:
a deep, narrow valley

momentum *(n)*:
a measure of the motion of an object calculated by multiplying its mass by its velocity

principle *(n)*:
a basic truth or assumption; a guiding rule or standard

diffusion *(n)*:
the spread of particles from an area of high concentration to an area of low concentration

---

1. What is the talk mainly about?

(A) Applicability of concepts
(B) Requirements of the class
(C) Principles of motion
(D) Methodology of research

2. According to the professor, how should the subject matter be learned?

(A) As practical knowledge
(B) As a system, like mathematics
(C) As an art, like painting a picture
(D) As a skill, like learning an instrument

3. What are two examples the professor gives of situations in which physics is useful? Choose 2 answers.

(A) During an exam
(B) Memorizing formulae
(C) During a house fire
(D) When a person wants to jump far
(E) Heating things

4. Fill in the blanks to complete the organizer.

Example	Use of Physics
_____ over a ravine	calculate necessary _____
_____ in your house	use principles of _____ diffusion

Notes

_____

_____

_____

_____

_____

_____

ritual *(n)*: an act or sequence of acts as part of a ceremony
impersonate *(v)*: to pretend to be someone else
amplify *(v)*: to make louder or stronger
role *(n)*: a character or part played by an actor
medieval *(adj)*: relating to the Middle Ages period of European history (400-1500 A.D.)

1. What is the talk mainly about?

(A) The origins and influences of Greek theater

(B) The history of masks in theater

(C) The relationship between religion and theater

(D) The use of theater in religion

3. What is an example the professor gives of a way in which masks assisted Greek actors?

(A) Amplification of the voice

(B) Straightening of posture

(C) Invocation of the gods

(D) Interaction with the audience

2. According to the professor, how were medieval masks different from Greek masks?

(A) Size

(B) Colors

(C) Weight

(D) Materials

4. Fill in the blanks to complete the organizer.

```
                        ┌─── first used in _____
            ┌─ Greek ───┤
            │           └─── theater masks made of painted _____ or canvas
_____ ──────┤
            │           ┌─── used in morality plays
            └─ _____ ───┤
                        └─── made of paper mache
```

Notes

_____

_____

_____

_____

_____

_____

_____

_____

ensure *(v):*
to make certain of something

outline *(v):*
to provide the basic details of a procedure

absolutely *(adv):*
definitely; yes

flow chart *(n phrase):*
a diagram or visual representation of a sequence of actions

plagiarism *(n):*
the act of copying another person's work and claiming it as one's own

1. What aspect of the lab class does the woman mainly discuss?

    (A) The pre-lab report
    (B) The procedural flow chart
    (C) In-lab note taking
    (D) The post-lab report

2. What are two key features of the report mentioned in the discussion? Choose 2 answers.

    (A) Purpose
    (B) Hypothesis
    (C) Observations
    (D) Findings

3. According to the woman, what will be punished harshly?

    (A) Incorrect theory
    (B) Plagiarism
    (C) Mentioning past research
    (D) Using your own words

4. Fill in the blanks to complete the organizer.

The _____ report

Order of writing

_____   _____   procedure

Notes

_____

_____

_____

_____

_____

_____

sufficient *(adj)*:
enough to meet a requirement

interpreter *(n)*:
a person who changes another person's art to give it new meaning

facet *(n)*:
an element; a characteristic part

contend *(v)*:
to argue; to state strongly

collaboration *(n)*:
the act of working together

1. What is the talk mainly about?

(A) Performers
(B) Films
(C) Art
(D) Plays

2. According to the professor, what are the three kinds of art?

(A) Literary, visual, and performing
(B) Dance, music, and opera
(C) Poetry, painting, and music
(D) Dance, theater, and film

3. What are two key features of performing arts mentioned in the discussion? Choose 2 answers.

(A) A collaboration of many artists
(B) A creator, interpreter, and an audience
(C) Audience and interpreter in the same space
(D) Audience interpretation of a performance

4. Fill in the blanks to complete the organizer.

```
                    ┌─────────────────┐
                    │    _____     │
                    └────────┬────────┘
          ┌──────────────────┼──────────────────┐
    ┌──────────┐       ┌──────────┐       ┌──────────┐
    │ _____ │       │  Visual  │       │ Literary │
    └────┬─────┘       └────┬─────┘       └────┬─────┘
     ┌───┴────┐         ┌───┴────┐              │
┌─────────┐ ┌────────┐ ┌──────────────┐ ┌──────────────┐
│_____, │ │_____│ │Painting,     │ │Fiction,      │
│dance,    │ │        │ │sculpture,    │ │poetry        │
│opera,    │ │        │ │illustration  │ │              │
│music     │ │        │ │              │ │              │
└─────────┘ └────────┘ └──────────────┘ └──────────────┘
```

Skill C — Determining Reasons, Purposes, and Attitudes

Necessary Skills

Recognizing Reasons and Purposes

- Understanding what the speaker is trying to achieve throughout a whole lecture or conversation
- Understanding the speaker's reason for saying a certain sentence or phrase
- Using the context to figure out the real meaning of a sentence or phrase
- Recognizing the tone of voice, intonation, and the sentence stress that the speaker uses to show his or her intended meaning

Understanding Attitudes

- Understanding the speaker's general feeling about what is discussed
- Recognizing words or phrases that indicate the speaker's feeling or opinion
- Recognizing the tone of voice, intonation, and the sentence stress that the speaker uses to show his or her feeling or opinion
- Using the context to figure out the speaker's attitude that is not directly stated

Example Questions

Reasons and Purposes

- Why does the professor mention the _____?
- Why does the professor say this: ⌒ ?

Attitudes

- What is the student's attitude toward _____?
- What does the woman imply about the _____?
- What does the woman mean when she says this: ⌒ ?

Notes

> **pull off** *(v phrase)*:
> to do; to accomplish
>
> **display** *(v)*:
> to show; to project
>
> **screw up** *(v phrase)*:
> to make a mistake
>
> **reinforce** *(v)*:
> to strengthen by adding extra
> support
>
> **shortcoming** *(n)*:
> a weakness; a flaw

1. What does the woman want the man to do?

(A) Explain his technique

(B) Program her computer

(C) Help her with her homework

(D) Join a tutorial

2. Why does the man mention the verb "freeze"?

(A) To explain a problem with his computer

(B) To show an example of what the program does

(C) To describe the weather

(D) To test the woman's grammar

3. What is the man's attitude toward studying English?

(A) It is too hard.

(B) He wants to do better, but he doesn't have time to study.

(C) He seems to enjoy it.

(D) It is critical for his major, so he worries about it.

4. Fill in the blanks to complete the organizer.

Computer program → Shows a _____ → User _____ in past form → Mistakes are

_____ at the end

∩ Skill C **02** Sociology

Notes

encompass *(v)*:
to include

missionary *(n)*:
a person who works on a
religious mission to help others

order *(n)*:
a group of people united by a
common belief or social aim

abject *(adj)*:
miserable; suffering

abandon *(v)*:
to leave without help; to forsake

---

1. What are the people talking about?

(A) A country
(B) A historical event
(C) A social problem
(D) A historical person

2. Listen again to part of the conversation. Then answer the question. ∩
Why does the man say this: ∩ ?

(A) To correct a mistake he just made
(B) To give background information on India
(C) To test the woman's knowledge of the topic
(D) To correct a mistake the woman just made

3. What is the man's attitude toward Mother Teresa?

(A) He admires her helpful deeds.
(B) He is doubtful of her accomplishments.
(C) He is critical of her religious choices.
(D) He thinks she deserves a statue.

4. Fill in the blanks to complete the organizer.

_____

• Albanian, not _____

• worked as a _____

• received _____ in 1979

Notes

intertidal *(adj)*:
occurring in the period of time between two tides

bountiful *(adj)*:
plentiful; abundant

reservoir *(n)*:
a large or extra supply

poach *(v)*:
to hunt or kill an animal in a forbidden area or out of season

unaware *(adj)*:
not having knowledge of

1. What are the reasons for the low number of animals now found in California's intertidal pools? Choose 2 answers.

(A) Weather changes
(B) Poaching
(C) Lack of education
(D) Widespread disease

2. What does the professor imply about the situation?

(A) Poaching is becoming less frequent.
(B) People don't know the laws protecting the pools.
(C) The number of animals is increasing.
(D) The problems with the California coast are slowly being resolved.

3. What is the professor's attitude toward people who catch octopuses in the pools?

(A) He thinks they are uneducated.
(B) He thinks they are helping the situation.
(C) He thinks they are doing something bad.
(D) He thinks they don't have enough to eat.

4. Fill in the blanks to complete the organizer.

Problem: Hard to find _____ in intertidal pools

Cause 1: _____ = taking animals from pools
- _____
- octopuses
- barnacles

Cause 2: People don't know _____

Notes

_____

_____

_____

_____

_____

_____

illuminate *(v)*:
to show clearly; to illustrate

impetus *(n)*:
a stimulus; an impulse; a cause

incident *(n)*:
an occurrence; an event

touch off *(v phrase)*:
to start; to trigger

aggressive *(adj)*:
actively hostile; assertive

1. According to the student, what was one of the causes of the American Revolutionary War?
   (A) The Americans did not want British rule.
   (B) The tea was almost as expensive as gold.
   (C) The British started a revolution.
   (D) The ruling party in America did not want to buy British tea.

2. Why does the professor mention the Boston Tea Party?
   (A) To highlight the British role in the war
   (B) To describe American customs
   (C) To point out how tea causes aggressive acts
   (D) To demonstrate how tea played an important role in history

3. What does the woman mean when she says this: ( ) ?
   (A) She wants to add her own idea to the discussion.
   (B) She understood the situation differently.
   (C) She thought the British were doing the right thing.
   (D) She is not convinced about the facts.

4. Fill in the blanks to complete the organizer.

> _____ Revolution

> fought between US and _____

> started over tea in Boston

> Boston _____ Party: _____ aggressive act of war

Notes

bestow *(v)*:
to give; to provide

raise spirits *(v phrase)*:
to make happier

pertinent *(adj)*:
relevant; related to the topic

cohabit *(v)*:
to live in the same home

recover *(v)*:
to regain health after a sickness
or injury

---

1. What are examples that the professor gives of health benefits gained from owning a pet? Choose 2 answers.

(A) A lower risk of catching colds
(B) A lower rate of arthritis
(C) A lower risk of strokes
(D) A lower rate of heart disease

2. Why does the professor mention pets in Britain?

(A) That was where the study was done.
(B) People in Britain have more pets than people in other countries.
(C) People in Britain have fewer pets than people in other countries.
(D) There are many elderly people in Britain.

3. Why does the professor say this: ⌒ ?

(A) To convince students to buy puppies
(B) To demonstrate that elderly people should not live alone
(C) To point out that young people should always help their elders
(D) To show students that the lecture topic affects them personally

4. Fill in the blanks to complete the organizer. Use one of these words for each blank: *lowers* or *raises*.

| Elderly people | ▷ | pets | ▷ | _____ blood pressure
_____ spirits |

| Anybody | ▷ | pets | ▷ | _____ risk of heart disease
_____ speed of recovery from heart attacks
_____ cases of colds, headaches, fever |

Notes

---

clear up (v phrase):
to become sunny; to improve

after all (adv phrase):
nonetheless; despite factors to
the contrary

look forward to (v phrase):
to anticipate with excitement

arduous (adj):
very difficult

no sweat (adj phrase):
easy

---

1. What does the man say about the weather forecast?

   (A) It will start raining.
   (B) It will be very hot.
   (C) It will clear up.
   (D) It will be very cold.

2. Why are they happy to hear the weather forecast for Friday?

   (A) After class, they are planning to go skiing.
   (B) Class will be canceled because of bad weather.
   (C) The professor will hold class by the lake on campus.
   (D) They will be able to take a class trip.

3. What is the woman's attitude toward hiking in the mountains?

   (A) She's worried it will be too difficult for her.
   (B) She enjoys it.
   (C) She thinks it's too far to go.
   (D) She prefers the seaside.

---

4. Fill in the blanks to complete the organizer.

   The day of the trip: _____

   The weather forecast: _____

   The location: _____

   The student who went before: _____

Notes

ubiquitous *(adj):*
common; found everywhere

wipe out *(v phrase):*
to kill off; to destroy completely

colossal *(adj):*
very large

hurtle *(v):*
to move with great speed

subsist *(v):*
to maintain life

1. According to the professor, what does the meteor theory estimate?

(A) The location of the impact
(B) The size of the meteor
(C) The number of dinosaurs killed
(D) The weight of the meteor

2. Why does the professor mention a meteor?

(A) To interest her students
(B) To explain where dinosaurs came from
(C) To provide an alternative theory
(D) To show what lead to the dinosaurs' extinction

3. Why does the professor say this: ᘘ ?

(A) To help her students understand the effects of the meteor impact
(B) To correct a mistake she had just made
(C) To introduce a new concept to her students
(D) To help the class relax before introducing the next topic

4. Fill in the blanks to complete the organizer.

Meteor theory
1. _____ km meteor hit the Earth
2. Earth became _____ and cold
3. _____ died
4. _____-eating dinosaurs died
5. _____-eating dinosaurs died

Notes

---

allege *(v)*:
to claim; to assert as true

invalid *(adj)*:
not accurate; not in use

beats me *(phrase)*:
I don't know. I'm unsure.

procure *(v)*:
to get; to obtain

maiden name *(n phrase)*:
a woman's family name before marriage

1. What's the woman's problem?

   (A) She can't log in to the system.
   (B) She lost her credit card.
   (C) She forgot her username.
   (D) She needs to wait 180 days.

2. Why does the man ask this: ☊ ?

   (A) Because he thinks the woman has forgotten her password
   (B) Because passwords expire if they're not used for six months
   (C) Because the registrar's office closed for the day
   (D) Because she might still be logged in

3. Why does the woman say this: ☊ ?

   (A) To correct a mistake she just made
   (B) To express a positive opinion
   (C) To remind herself of information she had forgotten
   (D) To express her uncertainty

4. Fill in the blanks to complete the organizer.

   Problem: _____ isn't working

Possible cause:	Solution:
Hasn't logged in for _____ days	➤ Go to _____ and request a new one
Another student is using her _____ and password.	➤ Use _____, probably mother's maiden name

Review A – C

Vocabulary Review

Skill Review

Vocabulary Review

Instructions: Choose the best word or phrase to complete each sentence.

1. She is having trouble _____ which courses to study. She thinks they all sound interesting!
   - (A) requiring
   - (B) fulfilling
   - (C) popularizing
   - (D) selecting

2. It is safer to invest in _____ companies rather than new ones.
   - (A) intramural
   - (B) mature
   - (C) pastoral
   - (D) ultra

3. The idea that Dostoevsky invented the novel is a _____. Novels had been around long before his birth.
   - (A) fallacy
   - (B) sonnet
   - (C) backhoe
   - (D) pointer

4. Never _____ that your clients know everything about our products. Always give a brief presentation.
   - (A) presume
   - (B) refine
   - (C) achieve
   - (D) assess

5. Water and wind speed up the process of _____. One day, even this tall mountain will be a flat prairie.
   - (A) striation
   - (B) bacterium
   - (C) interpretation
   - (D) erosion

6. Sometimes, changing the seating arrangement of the students can help improve the _____ of a classroom.
   - (A) audition
   - (B) dynamics
   - (C) sediment
   - (D) diffusion

7. Since you don't have all the prerequisites for that course, you will have to get the professor to _____ your registration.
   - (A) appreciate
   - (B) illuminate
   - (C) pasteurize
   - (D) authorize

8. You must _____ that your essay covers all the important details or you won't receive an A.
   - (A) contend
   - (B) ensure
   - (C) poach
   - (D) bestow

Instructions: Choose the word or phrase closest in meaning to the underlined part.

9. He ordered more troops to <u>strengthen</u> the army in Africa.
   - (A) encompass
   - (B) illuminate
   - (C) touch off
   - (D) reinforce

10. She recommended that I read these books because they are <u>relevant</u> to the topic.
   - (A) invalid
   - (B) arduous
   - (C) pertinent
   - (D) sufficient

11. The company is trying to <u>accomplish</u> a high customer satisfaction rating.

(A) achieve
(B) fill out
(C) permit
(D) grade

12. I think I have to <u>change and improve</u> my study habits. My grades are not as good as they could be.

(A) fulfill
(B) audition
(C) refine
(D) present

13. Today, we have to <u>evaluate</u> our own progress in the class.

(A) foster
(B) impersonate
(C) assess
(D) amplify

14. Einstein's <u>reasoning</u> of how traveling at the speed of light affects objects changed the minds of many physicists.

(A) analysis
(B) quest
(C) basis
(D) ravine

15. I really <u>value</u> the help my professors have given me.

(A) outline
(B) display
(C) abandon
(D) appreciate

Instructions: Write the missing words. Use the words below to fill in the blanks.

foster	collaboration	sufficient
facets	contend	

There are three broad categories of art: literary, visual, and performing. A performing art has two necessary and **(16)** _____ conditions. First, it requires a creator, an interpreter, and an audience. Second, the audience and the interpreter must be in the same place. Three examples of performing arts are dance, music, and opera. Film contains **(17)** _____ of both visual and performing arts. Some critics **(18)** _____ that theater is not a pure art form, but a **(19)** _____ of various art forms involving many artists. This is not to say that theater is a lesser form. In fact, theater is an important form because it helps **(20)** _____ the growth of the other, pure arts.

Instructions: Match the words that are opposites.

21. stable   (A) rescue

22. abandon   (B) accurate

23. ubiquitous   (C) give

24. invalid   (D) changing

25. procure   (E) rare

Notes

---

administer (v):
to direct or supervise; to give

demonstrate (v):
to show; to prove

competence (n):
the condition of being qualified

attain (v):
to get; to reach a goal

sum up (v phrase):
to summarize; to provide an overview

matriculant (n):
a person who is admitted to a college

indicate (v):
to show; to state

eligibility (n):
a state of being entitled; the condition of meeting the requirements

criteria (n):
a set of standards upon which a judgment is based

valid (adj):
true; useful

1. What does the woman want?

    (A) She wants to take an English composition course.

    (B) She wants to earn credits for a university degree.

    (C) She wants to find out about the man's qualifications.

    (D) She wants to earn credits without taking exams.

2. How does the man explain credit-by-exam? Choose 2 answers.

    (A) He defines it.

    (B) He brainstorms other meanings.

    (C) He gives a quick demonstration.

    (D) He summarizes three key points.

    (E) He describes the process with a simple illustration.

3. According to the man, what is an example of a guest matriculant?

    (A) An alumni of the university

    (B) A student enrolled in the credit-by-exam system

    (C) A student who has not yet graduated from high school

    (D) A foreign exchange student

4. According to the woman, what might be a problem with earning credits this way?

(A) They will appear differently on her transcript.

(B) They will conflict with her graduate degree.

(C) They will affect her overall GPA.

(D) They will not count for as many credits as a normal class.

5. Why does the man tell the woman that she doesn't need to worry?

(A) There is a high likelihood that she will succeed in the tests.

(B) The university has strict regulations to maintain the quality of the credits.

(C) The woman is a matriculant, so she will not have any problems.

(D) He thinks that the woman won't need to attend any classes.

6. What does the woman mean when she says this: 🎧 ?

(A) She is completely unsure.

(B) She thinks she is right, but is not positive.

(C) She is absolutely certain that she is correct.

(D) She is making a wild guess.

Notes

Vocabulary
give a talk *(v phrase):* to speak in public on a given topic; to lecture
assemble *(v):* to gather; to collect
stem *(v):* to start from; to originate
gesture *(n):* a movement of the arms, legs, or body to express thought or feeling
scenario *(n):* a situation
competent *(adj):* capable; good enough for a given purpose
slouch *(v):* to stand or sit with the head and shoulders hanging down
irritable *(adj):* easily made angry
manipulate *(v):* to change or alter for one's own purpose

1. What aspect of communication does the professor mainly discuss?

(A) Public speaking
(B) Sending clear messages
(C) Body language
(D) Multimedia

2. How does the professor emphasize her point about the importance of posture and gestures?

(A) By identifying the different kinds of body postures
(B) By stating the dimensions of various gestures
(C) By comparing gestures in different cultures
(D) By explaining the relationship between body movements and other people's responses to them

3. According to the professor, how much of the information people receive when we talk to them comes from the words that we say?

(A) All of it
(B) 90%
(C) 50%
(D) 10%

4. According to the professor, why is it important to know and understand your own body language?

   (A) Because it often conflicts with spoken messages

   (B) So that students can feel more relaxed at an interview

   (C) Because people need to know what their body is saying if they want to succeed

   (D) Because people are not usually aware of informal body language

5. Why does the professor mention eye contact?

   (A) She wants the audience to look at her.

   (B) In her opinion, it is not necessary.

   (C) She uses it as an example of negative body language.

   (D) She believes that it causes complications.

6. What does the speaker imply when she says this: ( ) ?

   (A) The information she gives may surprise students.

   (B) The information she gives is false.

   (C) The information she gives is difficult to understand.

   (D) She is unsure of the information she gives.

Matching Words and Categories

Necessary Skills

- Understanding relationships between different pieces of information
- Identifying key category words in the lecture/conversation
- Understanding characteristics of each category
- Comparing characteristics of each category
- Putting information into the right category
- Determining whether a certain point is discussed in relation to the category

Example Questions

- Based on the information in the talk, indicate whether each phrase below describes _____ or _____.
- What is each type of _____? Click in the correct column.
- With what _____ are these _____ associated? Click in the correct column.
- Are these statements true about _____? Click in the YES or NO column.
- Is each of these _____ discussed in the lecture? Click in the YES or NO column.
- Match each _____ with the correct classification.
- In the lecture, the professor describes the steps in _____. Indicate whether each of the following is a step in the process. Click in the correct box for each phrase.

Notes

	campaign *(v)*: to try to get elected **senate *(n)*:** a group of students and faculty members that make decisions on university spending **eligible *(adj)*:** qualified; entitled **kick out *(v phrase)*:** to expel; to send away **mull over *(v phrase)*:** to consider; to think about

1. What are the two qualifications needed to run for a student senate position? Choose 2 answers.

(A) Must have paid a fee
(B) Must be a full-time student
(C) Must be a member of a university organization
(D) Must remain until graduation
(E) Must have at least a 2.0 GPA

2. What does the student mean when he says this: ∩ ?

(A) There is a lot more.
(B) For example.
(C) Nothing much.
(D) I don't know.

3. Are these statements about student senators true? For each phrase, mark the correct box.

	Yes	No
(A) Work with organizations at the university	✓	
(B) Earn a salary from student fees		✗
(C) Can be re-elected after a year	✓	
(D) Can be kicked out for not going to meetings	✓	

4. Fill in the blanks to complete the organizer.

Student Senators

Eligibility:
- _full time_ student
- _2.0_ GPA

Responsibility:
- decide what to do with _fees_
- deal with _organizations_

Notes

exchange *(v)*:
to trade one item or service for another

medium *(n)*:
a way or means for something to happen

barter *(v)*:
to trade goods or services without the exchange of money

asset *(n)*:
a useful or valuable quality or thing

put aside *(v phrase)*:
to save

READING

LISTENING

SPEAKING

WRITING

PRACTICE TEST

1. What are the uses of money mentioned in the lecture? Click on 3 answers.

   (A) A measure of value
   (B) A stored asset
   (C) A type of prestige
   (D) A medium of exchange
   (E) A way to gain power

2. What does the professor imply when she says this: ⌂ ?

   (A) Barter economies are more efficient than money-based economies.
   (B) Bartering is less practical than using money
   (C) People can earn more through bartering than through working for a salary.
   (D) Barter economies are superior to money-based economies.

3. Is each of these statements discussed in the lecture? For each phrase, mark the correct box.

	Yes	No
(A) Comparing costs and values	✓	
(B) Saving money	✓	
(C) Barter-based economies	✓	
(D) Governments and taxes		✓

4. Fill in the blanks to complete the organizer.

   Uses of _____
   1. medium of _____
   2. way to measure _____
   3. an _____ that can be saved

Notes

pitch *(n)*:
a tone; a frequency of sound

simultaneously *(adv)*:
at the same time

genre *(n)*:
a type; a style

distortion *(n)*:
a twisting of normal shape, form, or sound

surplus *(adj)*:
extra; more than needed or wanted

1. According to the professor, in which music genre are power chords commonly used?

   (A) Jazz
   (B) Classical
   (C) Blues
   (D) Hard rock

2. What does the professor mean when he says this: ∩ ?

   (A) Power chords help to create distortion.
   (B) Power chords create too much distortion.
   (C) Power chords sound good with distortion because they are not too noisy.
   (D) Power chords sound good with distortion because they create a lot of noise.

3. Based on information in the talk, indicate whether each phrase below describes chords or non-chords.

	Chords	Non-chords
(A) Three notes played at the same time	✓	
(B) Two notes played at intervals		✓
(C) Two different pitches played at the same time		✓
(D) Five notes played at the same time	✓	

4. Fill in the blanks to complete the organizer.

   Chords
   - combination of _____ or more different _____ played at the same time
   - only _____ note groups called chords
   - power chords involve only _____ pitch classes

Notes

---

syllabus *(n)*:
a list of lessons and materials needed for a class

half off *(adj phrase)*:
with the price reduced by 50 percent

label *(n)*:
a small sign giving information about a product

purchase *(n)*:
the act of buying

condition *(n)*:
state; shape

1. What are some of the conditions necessary for a student to get a refund on a textbook? Choose 3 answers.
   (A) The book must have a blue label.
   (B) The book must be returned within a week of purchase.
   (C) The student must have the receipt.
   (D) The book must not be damaged.

2. What does the woman mean when she says this: 🎧 ?
   (A) You don't want to have the wrong materials in class.
   (B) An incorrect purchase could cost you a lot of money.
   (C) Making such a mistake would be very embarrassing.
   (D) It's important to have the proper paperwork filled out.

3. Are these statements true based on the information in the conversation? For each phrase, mark the correct box.

	Yes	No
(A) Sometimes, textbooks listed in the course schedule are incorrect.	✓	
(B) Used books have a red label.		✓
(C) Books will be refunded within 2 weeks.		✓
(D) New and used books are not stacked together.	✓	✓

4. Fill in the blanks to complete the organizer.

   Required books:
   • refer to _____ to be sure about titles
   • used books are *less expense* and have a ___*blue*___ label
   • can be returned within _____ of purchase

Notes

_____
_____
_____
_____
_____
_____
_____
_____

major *(adj)*:
chief; principal; main

biome *(n)*:
a type of area characterized by its climate and life forms

go over *(v phrase)*:
to review

precipitation *(n)*:
a form of moisture, such as rainfall and snowfall

annually *(adv)*:
occurring every year

1. According to the professor, which biomes feature little precipitation? Choose 2 answers.

    (A) Tallgrass
    (B) Shortgrass
    (C) Tundra
    (D) Desert

2. Why does the professor say this: ∩ ?

    (A) To correct a mistake he just made
    (B) To introduce a new concept
    (C) To ensure students listen to important information
    (D) To announce the time and location of an exam

3. Are these statements true about shortgrass biomes? For each phrase, mark the correct box.

	Yes	No
(A) Located along the equator		
(B) Receive 15-30 inches of rain per year		
(C) Have thick, fertile soil		
(D) Have cold winters		

4. Fill in the blanks to complete the organizer.

Three Major Biomes

Tundra
- little _____
- cold _____
- from _____ to 24 hours of daylight

Grasslands
- located _____
- receive _____ inches of rainfall
- two types: _____ and _____

Deserts
- located within 20 to 30 _____ of equator
- _____ days and _____ nights
- less than _____ inches of rainfall

∩ Skill D 06 Religious Studies

morality *(n)*:
a system of ideas of right and wrong

ethical *(adj)*:
relating to behavior in accordance with an idea of right conduct

prescription *(n)*:
a set of rules or laws to follow

stance *(n)*:
an opinion or point of view

implication *(n)*:
a theoretical effect; an effect that might occur

1. According to the professor, where does a lot of our moral vocabulary originate?

(A) In religious institutions
(B) In university classes
(C) In the assumption of the existence of a single god
(D) In the assumption of the existence of no gods

2. What is the professor's attitude toward the subject he's teaching?

(A) He's enthusiastic about it.
(B) He is indifferent to it.
(C) He thinks it's not important.
(D) He thinks students will not enjoy it.

3. Match each phrase below with the correct classification.

First part of Course	Second part of Course	Entire Course

(A) Religion's effect on morality
(B) Assumption that there is no God
(C) Assumption that there is a God

4. Fill in the blanks to complete the organizer.

Class: _____ and _____

• discuss _____ between religion and _____

• assume _____ of God

• later, examine _____ assumption

Notes

_____

_____

_____

_____

_____

_____

drill *(n)*:
an exercise that is repeated many times in order to perfect a skill

overdo *(v)*:
to do something so much that a negative instead of positive outcome results

goal *(n)*:
an aim; a desired outcome

session *(n)*:
a period of time devoted to a specific activity

align *(v)*:
to arrange so that two or more parts are at a proper working orientation

---

1. According to the instructor, what is the main goal of the swimming session?

(A) To rotate the student's hips and chin
(B) To overdo it
(C) To improve fitness
(D) To achieve balance

2. Why does the man say this: ⌒ ?

(A) To show the instructor that he knows the purpose
(B) To show the instructor that he is enthusiastic about getting in shape
(C) To ask the instructor about his swimming technique
(D) To ask the instructor for assistance with his balance

3. Match each word with the correct classification.

Fitness		Recovery	
Heart Rate	Swim Speed	Heart Rate	Swim Speed

(A) Fast
(B) Slow
(C) High
(D) Low

4. Fill in the blanks to complete the organizer.

Goal of session: _____

Form: neck and spine should be _____

Technique: rotate _____ and _____

○ Skill D **08** Botany

Notes

enclose *(v)*:
to surround; to keep within

vital *(adj)*:
very important; necessary

evolve *(v)*:
to change and improve over time

cluster *(n)*:
a group of the same or similar items gathered together

inhibit *(v)*:
to prevent; to hinder

1. According to the professor, why have roses evolved thorns?

   (A) To hang on to other plants
   (B) To provide vitamin C for birds
   (C) To prevent sand erosion
   (D) To protect their seeds

2. Why does the professor mention that most rosehips are red?

   (A) To correct a mistake she has just made
   (B) To correct a mistake a student has just made
   (C) To provide a contrast with another type of rose
   (D) To provide a contrast to what students would expect

3. Match each word or phrase with the correct category.

Rose hips	Rose thorns

   (A) Hooked
   (B) Seeds
   (C) Some species lack them
   (D) Vitamin C

4. Fill in the blanks to complete the organizer.

   Rose Species

   Pimpinellifolia
   - dark _____ or black hips
   - tight cluster of _____ instead of thorns

   Canina
   - _____ high in vitamin C
   - _____ colored hips

   Rugosa
   - _____ high in vitamin C
   - tight cluster of _____ instead of thorns

Necessary Skills

Inference

- Guessing the implied meaning of a sentence or phrase
- Making a generalization from what is said
- Drawing a conclusion based on the main points of the lecture/conversation
- Understanding the relationship between a sentence or phrase and the overall topic
- Recognizing the intonation or stress that indicates what the speaker implies

Prediction

- Inferring what is likely to happen from what the speaker says
- Drawing a conclusion based on the main idea and what the speaker says

Example Questions

Inference

- What can be inferred about the students/the professor?
- What does the man imply about _____?
- What does the professor imply about the people who _____?
- How does the woman probably feel?
- Listen to part of the conversation. Then answer the question. ◯ What can be inferred about the student?
- Listen again to part of the conversation and answer the question. ◯ What does the speaker mean when he says this: ◯ ?
- What does the professor imply when he says this: ◯ ?

Prediction

- What will the man/woman/speaker probably do?
- Where will the man and woman look for the information the man needs?
- What will the professor discuss next?
- What will the man most likely do?

Notes

casual *(adj)*:
relaxed; not formal

tremendous *(adj)*:
very good; excellent

attraction *(n)*:
a fun or interesting place to visit

volunteer *(n)*:
a person who works without receiving money

adjust *(v)*:
to change to fit the situation; to adapt

1. Are these statements about what language partners do true? For each phrase, mark the correct box.

	Yes	No
(A) Help students practice casual conversation	✓	
(B) Charge a lot of money		✓
(C) Explain local culture to students	✓	
(D) Help students find suitable jobs		✓

2. What can be inferred about the woman?
   - (A) She is Canadian.
   - (B) She is staying in Vancouver.
   - (C) Her native language is Spanish.
   - (D) Her family is rich.

3. What does the woman imply when she says this: ∩ ?
   - (A) They are native English speakers.
   - (B) They are paid a high salary.
   - (C) They do not receive any payment.
   - (D) They are young people.

4. Fill in the blanks to complete the organizer.

   Language Partners

   • help foreign _____ practice English

   • are _____, not paid

   • explain language and _____

∩ Skill E 02   Physics

Notes

	hypothesize (v): to make a hypothesis; to postulate
	dense (adj): compact; having a high mass to volume ratio
	postulate (v): to make a guess; to hypothesize
	accurately (adv): with exactness
	contradiction (n): an inconsistency; a disagreement

1. Match each scientist to the theory his work supported.

	Wave Theory of Light	Particle Theory of Light
(A) Newton	✓	✓
(B) Christian Huygens		✓
(C) Leon Foucault	✓	
(D) Albert Einstein		✓

2. What will the professor probably discuss next?
- (A) 20th century work on light theory
- (B) Einstein's escape from Nazi Germany
- (C) Newton's early work on gravity
- (D) Other disagreements between Newton and Huygens

3. What does the professor imply when she says this: ∩ ?
- (A) Einstein probably marked his ideas in the laboratory.
- (B) Scientists refused to return to this theory.
- (C) After Einstein, scientists disagreed on the theory once more.
- (D) People cannot disagree with the theory.

4. Fill in the blanks to complete the organizer.

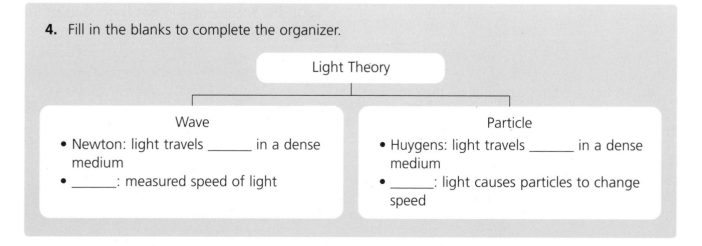

Light Theory

Wave
- Newton: light travels _____ in a dense medium
- _____: measured speed of light

Particle
- Huygens: light travels _____ in a dense medium
- _____: light causes particles to change speed

Notes

attached *(adj)*:
connected to

flanked *(adj)*:
surrounded

region *(n)*:
an area of land

instrumental *(adj)*:
vital; very important

transportation *(n)*:
the act of moving goods or
people over a distance

---

1. Is each of these subjects discussed in the lecture?
For each phrase, mark the correct box.

	Yes	No
(A) The origin of the name "Mediterranean"		
(B) The Mediterranean's location		
(C) The size of the Mediterranean		
(D) The first people to sail the Mediterranean		

2. What does the professor imply when he says
this: 🎧 ?
(A) His students have probably never heard of
the Mediterranean.
(B) His students probably do not know where
the Mediterranean is located.
(C) His students probably know that the
Mediterranean is part of an ocean.
(D) A lot of students do not know this fact.

3. What does the professor mean when he says
this: 🎧 ?
(A) History is studied by most people living near
the Mediterranean.
(B) People in this region are very civilized and
good-mannered.
(C) People have lived in cities in the region for
centuries.
(D) The Mediterranean has been studied for
many years.

4. Fill in the blanks to complete the organizer.

Location: bordered by Europe, _____, and Asia.

Origin of name: from _____ words
medi = _____, terra = _____

Notes

_____

head *(v)*:
to go in the direction

aspiring *(adj)*:
hopeful of becoming

certificate *(n)*:
a document proving a certain achievement

position *(n)*:
a job

automatically *(adv)*:
without a specific effort or request

1. Are these statements about the woman true? For each statement, mark the correct box.

	Yes	No
(A) She knows about the class.		
(B) She is looking for a new job.		
(C) She is taking a bar skills course.		
(D) She helps the man.		

2. Listen again to part of the conversation and answer the question. 🎧
What can be inferred about the woman?
(A) She is very busy.
(B) She just remembered some important information.
(C) She is curious about the man's job.
(D) She is about to take a lunch break.

3. What will the man most likely do next?
(A) Go to the 3rd floor of the student union building
(B) Help another student
(C) Take his resumé to the campus bar
(D) Register at the student employment office

4. Fill in the blanks to complete the organizer.

To register for student union class:
• go to _____ floor of _____ building

If course is _____ related:
• _____ at student _____ office

conflict (n):
an argument; a disagreement

ultimately (adv):
in the end; as a final result

enforce (v):
to compel others to follow a rule

reluctant (adj):
hesitant; unwilling

regime (n):
a government in power

1. Are each of these statements true about the League of Nations? Choose YES or NO.

	Yes	No
(A) It was established before World War II.		
(B) Its goal was to settle international conflicts.		
(C) It had a very strong army.		
(D) Fascist powers were members of the League.		

2. What does the professor imply when he says this: 🎧 ?

(A) Britain and France were ignorant about Hitler.

(B) Britain and France were the most powerful members of the League of Nations.

(C) Britain and France were responsible for World War II.

(D) Britain and France were not members of the League of Nations.

3. What will the professor discuss next?

(A) What replaced the League after World War II

(B) Cooperation between Britain and France

(C) What the League did during the 1920s

(D) Hitler's military regime after World War II

4. Fill in the blanks to complete the organizer.

League of Nations

- when established: after _____
- why established: to settle _____ peacefully
- why lacked strength: no _____
- powerful member countries: _____ and _____

∩ Skill E 06 Art History

Notes

---

depiction *(n)*:
a graphic or written description of something

portray *(v)*:
to show as; to describe

impact *(n)*:
an effect; an impression

maxim *(n)*:
a fundamental principle; a rule

literal *(adj)*:
realistic; life-like; stressing the physical over the emotional

---

1. Based on information from the lecture, indicate whether each phrase below describes impressionist or pre-impressionist work.

	Impressionist	Pre-impressionist
(A) Created life-like depictions		
(B) Used light and color to express feeling		
(C) Music composed as interpretation of paintings		

2. What does the professor imply about painters before the impressionist movement?
- (A) They thought realism was more important than emotion.
- (B) They painted interpretations of musical pieces.
- (C) They didn't include light or color in their work.
- (D) They tended to ignore musicians.

3. What will the professor discuss next?
- (A) Examples of pre-impressionist paintings
- (B) Examples of pre-impressionist light and color
- (C) Examples of impressionist music
- (D) Examples of impressionist paintings

4. Fill in the blanks to complete the organizer.

Impressionist Movement

- first in _____ art, then _____
- focused on _____ of subject, not _____ depictions
- used _____ and _____ to express impact of feelings

Notes

	primarily *(adv)*: mostly; essentially
	carry *(v)*: to offer for sale; to have in stock
	relevant *(adj)*: important or related to a given topic
	postal *(adj)*: related to post office services
	bucks *(n)*: dollars

1. Is each of these post office services discussed in the conversation? Choose YES or NO.

	Yes	No
(A) Faxes		
(B) Envelopes		
(C) Stamps		
(D) Post Office Boxes		

2. Listen to part of the conversation. Then answer the question. ⌒
   What can be inferred about the student?
   (A) She is somewhat surprised.
   (B) She doesn't believe the man.
   (C) She wants him to check the information again.
   (D) She thinks the price may be wrong.

3. What will the woman probably do?
   (A) Sell stamps and envelopes
   (B) Go to the bank
   (C) Look for an off-campus post office
   (D) Go to the student union building

4. Fill in the blanks to complete the organizer.

   Student Union Post Office
   Opening hours:
   • Regular months: _____ to _____
   • Summer months: _____ to _____
   P.O. Boxes:
   • rent _____ a month.

READING | LISTENING | SPEAKING | WRITING | PRACTICE TEST

Notes

exposure *(n)*:
the condition of being subjected to an action or influence; the amount of light a film is subjected to

shutter *(n)*:
a device that can cover or uncover a lens or window

aperture *(n)*:
an adjustable opening, or hole, in a camera

reciprocity *(n)*:
the state of two or more things exchanging favors or privileges

appropriately *(adv)*:
accordingly; in a suitable way

1. Match each statement with the correct classification.

Aperture	Exposure	Shutter Speed

(A) The amount of light that falls on film
(B) The size of the hole through which light passes
(C) The length of time the hole is opened for

2. What can be inferred about the students?
(A) They are not very good at math.
(B) They are studying journalism.
(C) They will use cameras.
(D) They will take pictures of the professor.

3. What will the professor discuss next?
(A) Different exposures
(B) How to slow down shutter speed
(C) How to bypass reciprocity
(D) Video techniques

4. Fill in the blanks to complete the organizer.

Exposure: amount of _____ that falls on _____
• controlled by:
 - lens _____ (size of _____)
 - shutter _____ (amount of _____ hole is open)

Necessary Skills

Sequencing Steps

- Recognizing the organization of information in a lecture/conversation
- Recognizing the sequence of information
- Recognizing the main steps of a process
- Summarizing a process with the main steps
- Determining whether a sentence indicates a step of a process

Question Types

- In the lecture, the professor explains how _____. Put the steps in order. Click in the correct box for each step.
- The speaker describes the steps in _____. Put the steps in the correct order.
- The professor describes the process of _____. Indicate whether each of the following is a step in the process. Click in the correct box for each phrase.
- In the conversation, the speakers talk about _____. Summarize the conversation by putting the statements in the correct order.

Notes

grant **(v):**
to give; to provide

resolve **(v):**
to fix a problem; to create a
solution to an argument

convey **(v):**
to communicate; to show

perspective **(n):**
an opinion; a point of view

commit **(v):**
to promise to do; to pledge

---

1. In the dialog, the woman describes the steps in the process of roommate conflict resolution. Put the steps in order.

> Order: 1. _____ → 2. _____ → 3. _____ → 4. _____

(A) Hold a formal review
(B) Make a plan to solve the problems
(C) Get the roommates together to communicate their problems
(D) Each roommate commits to the plan

2. How does the man probably feel before he speaks to the woman?

(A) Misunderstood
(B) Tired
(C) Frustrated
(D) Satisfied

3. Why does the man say this: 🎧 ?

(A) To express uncertainty about where he should be
(B) To tell the woman where to go
(C) To indicate an example of his problem
(D) To indicate a difference between expectation and reality

4. Fill in the blanks to complete the organizer.

Conflict Resolution

1. _____ get together

2. discuss and plan

3. commit to a _____

4. hold review _____ later

5. if not resolved → apply for a _____

Notes

_____

_____

_____

_____

_____

_____

_____

input (n):
a piece or collection of information received from the senses

external (adj):
outside

process (v):
to evaluate; to deal with and organize

retain (v):
to keep within; to remember

selective (adj):
chosen according to importance or relevance

1. In the lecture, the professor explains filtering. Put the points in order.

> Order: 1. ____ → 2. ____ → 3. ____ → 4. ____

(A) Impossible to remember everything heard over an extended period
(B) Hear only what you want to hear
(C) Biological filter
(D) Psychological filter

2. What does the professor imply when she says this: 🎧 ?

(A) People can hear their psychological filters.
(B) People don't want to hear their psychological filters.
(C) People can't control their psychological filters.
(D) People can control their psychological filters.

3. What is an example the professor gives of a biological filter?

(A) A student not being able to remember everything in a lecture
(B) A person not hearing what he or she doesn't want to hear
(C) A piece of information coming from the outside world
(D) A professor using notes during her lecture

4. Fill in the blanks to complete the organizer.

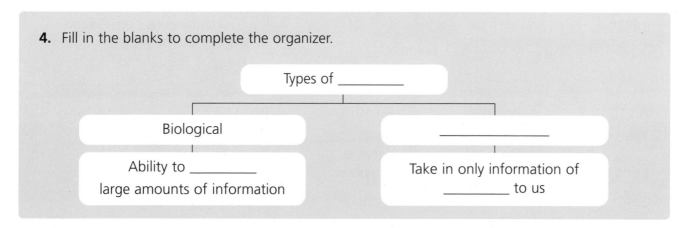

Types of _____

Biological   _____

Ability to _____ large amounts of information   Take in only information of _____ to us

Notes

_____

_____

_____

_____

_____

_____

_____

_____

parallel port (n phrase):
an interface between a computer and a printer through which information is passed on more than one wire

byte (n):
a sequence of eight bits (either 1 or 0) that computers process as information

transmit (v):
to send; to relay

relay (v):
to send; to transmit

confirmation (n):
the act of checking the truth or accuracy of information

1. The professor describes the process of a printer sending information to a computer. Indicate whether each of the following is a point in the lecture.

	Yes	No
(A) Some of the pins select the color of the print		
(B) 18-25 are grounding pins		
(C) One of the pins tells the printer that data is being sent		
(D) Pins 2-9 relay the confirmation signal		

2. What will the professor discuss next?
(A) The functioning of serial ports
(B) The popularity of inkjet printers
(C) Modern accounting principles
(D) Home computer market dynamics

3. According to the professor, which pins transmit the 8 bits of information?
(A) Pins 1-8
(B) Pins 2-9
(C) Pins 11-16
(D) Pins 18-25

4. Fill in the blanks to complete the organizer.

_____ ports: One bit at a time

_____ ports: simultaneous transmission

Example: _____ port of computer.

Pin 1:
Tells printer _____ is being sent

Pins 2-9:
Transmission of the _____

Pin 10:
Sends _____ signal to computer

Pins 11-17:
Various functions

Pins 18-25:
ground

Notes

permit *(n)*:
a card or sticker that signifies official permission

lottery *(n)*:
a selection made by a random choice

issue *(v)*:
to give officially; to publish

purchase *(v)*:
to buy

document *(n)*:
an official paper

1. The man describes the steps in getting a summer parking permit. Put the steps in the correct order.

   Order: 1. ____ → 2. ____ → 3. ____ → 4. ____

   (A) Pay for the permit
   (B) Show proof of enrollment to the parking office
   (C) Receive the permit
   (D) Enroll in a summer course

2. What will the woman probably do next?
   (A) Purchase a parking permit, then enroll in a summer course
   (B) Enroll in a summer course and ride her bike to school
   (C) Wait until they start selling parking permits and buy one then
   (D) Enroll in a summer course and return for her parking permit

3. Why does the woman say this: ∩ ?
   (A) To express relief
   (B) To express disappointment
   (C) To ask for more information
   (D) To tell him about an unmet expectation

4. Fill in the blanks to complete the organizer.

   _____ on campus

   Determined by _____ during regular school year.

   Restricted to students enrolled in summer _____ during the summer months

   $120 per year

   _____ per month

Notes

_____

_____

_____

_____

_____

_____

_____

_____

detrimental *(adj)*:
harmful; causing damage

toxic *(adj)*:
poisonous

break down *(v phrase)*:
to destroy; to disintegrate

eat away *(v phrase)*:
to damage; to cause to become smaller

overload *(v)*:
to put too much pressure or stress on

1. The professor describes the process of human pollution damaging the environment. Indicate whether each of the following is a step in the process.

	Yes	No
(A) The atmosphere breaks down the CFCs.		
(B) Humans produce CFCs.		
(C) CFCs destroy the ozone layer.		
(D) Humans produce a stable containable number of CFCs.		

2. What does the professor imply when she says this: 🎧 ?
   (A) Her students are not familiar with pollution.
   (B) People usually think pollution is detrimental.
   (C) Her students don't expect to hear about pollution in this course.
   (D) People don't usually hear about pollution.

3. What are the reasons that human pollution is detrimental to the environment? Choose 2 answers.
   (A) The ecosystem can't break down human pollution.
   (B) Human pollution overloads the environment.
   (C) Pollution is natural.
   (D) All organisms create waste.

4. Fill in the blanks to complete the organizer.

_____ is bad only when:

The _____ are too great.

The _____ can't break it down.

Example:
_____ are damaging the _____ because they can't be broken down.

Notes

	mean (v): to intend; to have an inexact plan **conduct (v):** to do; to perform **hand out (v phrase):** to distribute; to give to people **obligation (n):** a responsibility; a commitment **handle (v):** to manage; to be able to do without too much difficulty

1. In the conversation, the speakers talk about their plans. Summarize the conversation by putting the topics in the correct order.

   Order: 1. _____ → 2. _____ → 3. _____ → 4. _____

   (A) Applying for law school
   (B) Doing various kinds of volunteer work
   (C) Signing up with Blast
   (D) Volunteering every other week

2. Listen to part of the conversation. Then answer the question. ∩
   What does the speaker mean when he says this: ∩ ?
   (A) The woman will be too busy with schoolwork to volunteer with Blast.
   (B) The woman is having trouble with her studies.
   (C) The woman should do volunteer work if she wants to go to law school.
   (D) The woman should learn to hand out flyers.

3. What does the woman mean when she says this: ∩ ?
   (A) She is disappointed that she doesn't have enough time to do volunteer work.
   (B) She is disappointed that the program isn't enough to help her get into law school.
   (C) She is surprised that the man does volunteer work.
   (D) She is surprised that she has enough time to do volunteer work.

4. Fill in the blanks to complete the organizer.

   "Blast": An opportunity to _____ your time

   | Activities:
Conducting _____,
handing out flyers, making announcements | Benefits:
Develop _____ speaking skills, build confidence, and meet new people | Commitment:
_____ every other week |

Notes

at length *(adv phrase)*:
for a long period; in great detail

migration *(n)*:
a large movement of people or animals

entity *(n)*:
a thing that exists apart from other things

utopian *(adj)*:
relating to a perfect, harmonious life

incentive *(n)*:
a reason to act; an encouragement

1. In the lecture, the professor explains how times changed between the Roman Empire and the Renaissance. Put the points in order.

   Order: 1. ＿＿ → 2. ＿＿ → 3. ＿＿ → 4. ＿＿

   (A) The church told people of a heavenly afterlife.
   (B) People migrated to former Roman territories.
   (C) Society remained stable because of people's beliefs.
   (D) Life was very difficult.

2. What does the professor imply when she says this: ⌒ ?
   (A) The class has already studied the Roman Empire and the Renaissance.
   (B) The class is going to study the Roman Empire and the Renaissance next.
   (C) The class has already studied the Roman Empire and is going to study the Renaissance next.
   (D) The people of the Roman Empire lived Renaissance lives.

3. According to the professor, why didn't people of the Middle Ages fight to change their living conditions?
   (A) They were controlled by Roman armies.
   (B) They were waiting for the Renaissance.
   (C) Their living conditions were not difficult.
   (D) They believed in a utopian afterlife.

4. Fill in the blanks to complete the organizer.

   Events of the ＿＿＿＿ ＿＿＿＿

   | Fall of the ＿＿＿＿ ＿＿＿＿ | Large ＿＿＿＿ of people causing cultural changes | ＿＿＿＿ ＿＿＿＿ is unifying entity |

∩ Skill F **08** Biology

Notes

whereby *(adv)*:
by or through which

glucose *(n)*:
a sugar found in most plants and
animals

transform *(v)*:
to change completely

get rid of *(v phrase)*:
to eliminate; to throw away

take place *(v phrase)*:
to happen; to occur

1. The professor describes the process of photosynthesis. Indicate whether each of the following is a step in the process.

	Yes	No
(A) Carbon dioxide is transformed into water.		
(B) Carbon dioxide and water are transformed into glucose.		
(C) Glucose is transformed into starch.		
(D) Chlorophyll is produced as a waste.		

2. What does the professor imply when he says this: ∩ ?
   - (A) Many living things depend on oxygen.
   - (B) Plants waste a valuable resource.
   - (C) Animals engage in photosynthesis as well.
   - (D) Glucose is important for all living things.

3. What are the conditions necessary for photosynthesis to take place? Choose 3 answers.
   - (A) The presence of chlorophyll
   - (B) The presence of glucose
   - (C) The presence of water
   - (D) The presence of sunlight
   - (E) The presence of oxygen

4. Fill in the blanks to complete the organizer.

Photosynthesis: Occurs in _____ of plants.

Turns carbon dioxide and _____ into...   ▶   _____ and _____

Review A – F

Vocabulary Review

Instructions: Choose the best word or phrase to complete each sentence.

1. The Internet has become an important _____ of communication.
   - (A) medium
   - (B) senate
   - (C) pitch
   - (D) syllabus

2. She couldn't understand what he said because there was too much _____ on the phone.
   - (A) barter
   - (B) precipitation
   - (C) morality
   - (D) distortion

3. If your goal is to earn a high grade, it is _____ that you study every day.
   - (A) casual
   - (B) dense
   - (C) reluctant
   - (D) vital

4. My father is a _____ at the homeless center. He helps poor people without getting paid for it.
   - (A) volunteer
   - (B) contradiction
   - (C) position
   - (D) regime

5. He is studying medicine because he is an _____ doctor.
   - (A) external
   - (B) utopian
   - (C) aspiring
   - (D) aligned

6. Pacifists are quite _____ to use violence.
   - (A) reluctant
   - (B) literal
   - (C) relevant
   - (D) parallel

7. In certain situations, professors will _____ students an extended period of time to complete their assignments.
   - (A) grant
   - (B) retain
   - (C) transform
   - (D) portray

8. I have to _____ a survey of senior citizens for a project in my marketing class.
   - (A) overload
   - (B) conduct
   - (C) occur
   - (D) convey

Instructions: Choose the word or phrase closest in meaning to the underlined part.

9. With my old modem, I couldn't use the Internet and the phone <u>at the same time</u>.
   - (A) whereby
   - (B) primarily
   - (C) appropriately
   - (D) simultaneously

10. The store had <u>extra</u> stock, so it did not need to make a new order.
    - (A) eligible
    - (B) surplus
    - (C) ethical
    - (D) tremendous

11. Let's review the <u>chief</u> characteristics of the arctic tundra ecosystem.

(A) casual
(B) major
(C) dense
(D) flanked

12. The west coast receives the most rainfall <u>every year</u>.

(A) annually
(B) accurately
(C) automatically
(D) ultimately

13. Galileo <u>hypothesized</u> that the sun was the center of the universe, not the Earth.

(A) enforced
(B) portrayed
(C) retained
(D) postulated

14. My professor and I often have different <u>opinions</u> on the course material, but I have a great deal of respect for her.

(A) reciprocities
(B) obligations
(C) perspectives
(D) migrations

15. The promise of a wonderful afterlife acted as an <u>encouragement</u> to people to follow the teachings of the Bible.

(A) asset
(B) impact
(C) aperture
(D) incentive

Instructions: Write the missing words. Use the words below to fill in the blanks.

retain	selective	input
external	process	

(16) _____ includes all of the information coming at a person from the **(17)** _____ world. People use two kinds of filters to control this information: biological and psychological. Biological means a person can only **(18)** _____ and remember a certain amount of information at one time. For instance, a student cannot **(19)** _____ everything said in a lecture, so he or she takes notes on key points. The psychological filter is like **(20)** _____ attention, so information the listener is not interested in does not get processed.

Instructions: Choose the one word that does not belong.

21. shutter   exposure external aperture

22. convey   purchase relay   issue

23. detrimental relevant vital   instrumental

24. take place occur   enforce   happen

25. evolve   adjust   enclose   change

debate *(n):*
an argument

proponent *(n):*
a supporter

inherent *(adj):*
naturally a part of; innate

innate *(adj):*
naturally a part of; inherent

conversely *(adv):*
in contrast

slate *(n):*
an old-fashioned board used by
students to write on with chalk

predisposition *(n):*
a condition of being likely to be
some way

fraternal *(adj):*
relating to twins developed from
two separate eggs

sibling *(n):*
a brother or sister

variation *(n):*
a range of differences

mutually exclusive *(adj phrase):*
unable to exist or be true together

---

1. How does the speaker introduce twin studies?

(A) By discussing the nature vs. nurture debate

(B) By explaining the difference between identical and fraternal twins

(C) By pointing out that intelligence might be partly genetic

(D) By discussing the implications of genetic determinism

2. According to the professor, what is the difference between identical and fraternal twins?

(A) Identical twins share the exact same genetic makeup.

(B) Fraternal twins are more alike than identical twins.

(C) Fraternal twins are more intelligent than identical twins.

(D) Identical twins share the same interests, but fraternal twins usually don't.

3. Why does the woman say this: ∩ ?

(A) To support the professor's point

(B) To express uncertainty in her opinion

(C) To clarify the details of a theory

(D) To express certainty of her opinion

4. Based on the information in the talk, indicate whether each phrase below describes fraternal twins or identical twins.

	Fraternal Twins	Identical Twins
(A) Share 100% of genes		
(B) Come from the same egg and same sperm		
(C) Come from two eggs fertilized by two different sperm		
(D) Share about 50% of genes		
(E) More commonly have similar IQs		
(F) Are genetically the same as other pairs of siblings		

5. What does the professor imply when he says this: 🎧 ?
(A) Other studies may disagree.
(B) This course will follow a similar opinion.
(C) His research supports the findings of the study.
(D) Students should remember this information.

6. In the lecture, the professor describes the process of studying the intelligence of twins. Indicate whether each of the following is mentioned with respect to the research. Mark the correct box for each phrase.

	Yes	No
(A) Both identical and fraternal twins		
(B) Both IQ and EQ tests		
(C) Similar educations		
(D) Well-off families		

Notes

_____

_____

_____

_____

_____

_____

_____

_____

_____

_____

_____

show up *(v phrase)*:
to appear

specimen *(n)*:
a sample or example used for study

juvenile *(n)*:
an animal that has not reached adulthood

capture *(v)*:
to catch; to gain control of

prey *(n)*:
an animal hunted or caught for food

tentacle *(n)*:
a long, flexible arm or leg on a squid or octopus

footage *(n)*:
a series of photographed or videotaped images on a certain topic

lantern *(n)*:
a light and its protective case

dissect *(v)*:
to cut apart in order to study

corpse *(n)*:
a dead body

---

1. What aspect of the giant squid does the professor mainly discuss?

(A) Its migration patterns in different seasons
(B) Its behavior during mating season
(C) The difficulty in locating and studying it
(D) Its relationship with its enemy, the sperm whale

2. What are the two kinds of important evidence scientists have about giant squid? Choose 2 answers.

(A) Written accounts and paintings
(B) Dead specimens of the squid
(C) Video footage of live squid
(D) Live juvenile squid in captivity
(E) Photographs of full-grown squid

3. Why does the professor mention that the squid are common prey for sperm whales?

(A) To prove that the squid have a natural predator
(B) To prove that there are large numbers of squid
(C) To prove that the squid are not just a myth
(D) To prove that the squid are not poisonous

4. With what theory on squid movement are these points associated?

	Squid Constantly Move Around	Squid Don't Constantly Move Around
(A) Whales can find them easily.		
(B) They remain elusive to humans.		
(C) They must eat a lot of fish.		
(D) Whales eat a lot of squid.		

5. What does the professor imply when she says this: ◠ ?
(A) Not only do the whales eat the squid, but they are one of its primary food sources.
(B) The squid must be elusive because it needs to escape the sperm whales.
(C) The reason scientists can't find the squid is that the whale is detecting them by smell.
(D) The squid may not be that hard to find after all.

6. In the lecture, the professor explains different sources from which scientists have gathered information on giant squid. Put the sources in the order they are mentioned in the lecture.

Order: 1. _____ → 2. _____ → 3. _____ → 4. _____

(A) Dead specimens
(B) Body parts found inside the stomachs of whales
(C) Several juvenile specimens
(D) Stories and drawings

Chapter 2

Long Passage Skill Practice

Strategy

Main Ideas

- Listen carefully to the beginning of the lecture or talk (for a conversation, listen to the first few exchanges), where the speakers mention the topic.
- Pay attention to the expressions that indicate the topic:
  - ⇨ Today's talk is on...
  - ⇨ Today we are going to talk about...
  - ⇨ Now we are going to discuss...
- Listen to key words that can help you identify the main idea. Key words are usually emphasized or repeated.
- Keep in mind that two or more major ideas together may define the overall general topic.
- Do not choose an answer choice that is too general, not mentioned, or related to only part of the information.

Organization

- The organization of a lecture or talk is the way the speaker presents information. The information is organized in order to support the main idea, so understanding the main idea can help you predict the logical organization of information.
- Different types of organization may appear in the answer choices as follows:
  - ⇨ Classifying/categorizing
  - ⇨ Describing causes and effects
  - ⇨ Explaining causes/reasons
  - ⇨ Giving examples
  - ⇨ Showing contrast
  - ⇨ Summarizing a process
  - ⇨ Comparing
  - ⇨ Reminding
  - ⇨ Defining
  - ⇨ Contrasting
  - ⇨ Explaining in chronological order

Notes

_____

_____

_____

_____

_____

_____

_____

_____

_____

_____

meteorological *(adj)*:
related to weather and the study of weather

expedition *(n)*:
a journey organized to conduct scientific research

resuscitation *(n)*:
the act of bringing back to life

paramedic *(n)*:
a person trained to give medical treatment in emergency situations

pulmonary *(adj)*:
related to the heart

jumpstart *(v)*:
to start with a sudden jolt or push

juice *(n)*:
an informal word for energy or electricity

revive *(v)*:
to bring back to life

replenish *(v)*:
to refill a depleted supply

rhythmic *(adj)*:
in a regular pattern

hypothermia *(n)*:
a medical condition resulting from very low body temperatures

1. What is the woman trying to do?
   (A) Get into a good medical school
   (B) Sign up for special training
   (C) Apply for a job during the winter break
   (D) Have someone fix her car

2. What are the speakers mainly discussing?
   (A) The importance of all students learning first aid
   (B) Key points from a lecture that they both heard
   (C) The best way for the woman to impress her interviewer
   (D) When to take the course and how to sign up

3. How does the man explain CPR? Choose 2 answers.
   (A) He defines it.
   (B) He demonstrates the process with his friend.
   (C) He compares it to a similar procedure.
   (D) He describes the process with a diagram.
   (E) He summarizes three key points.
   (F) He describes his personal experience using it.

4. Listen again to part of the conversation and answer the question. 🎧
   What does the speaker mean when he says this: 🎧 ?
   (A) The training is better than the training at a competitor's schools.
   (B) It is always good to have the training in case of an emergency.
   (C) He hopes the student will not register too early in the year.
   (D) He needs to know what previous experience the student has.

Notes

_____
_____
_____
_____
_____
_____
_____
_____
_____
_____
_____
_____
_____

infrastructure (n):
the basic services and structures needed for society to function, such as electricity, roads, and water systems

coup d'etat (n):
a violent overthrow, or change, of government

apartheid (v):
a system of keeping different races separate, or apart, in South Africa

segregate (v):
to keep apart; to separate

protest (n):
a show of disagreement or disapproval

dismantle (v):
to take apart; to destroy

ethnic (adj):
related to members of a specific racial, religious, or cultural group

descent (n):
lineage; the condition of being derived through ancestors in a family line

breakdown (n):
an analysis of the parts of something

1. What is the professor talking about?
   (A) Economics in Africa
   (B) Political differences between two African countries
   (C) A particular country in Africa
   (D) The history of Dutch settlement in South Africa

2. What are the three main ideas in the lecture?
   (A) Social policy, the population, and the economy
   (B) Cities, famous places, and languages
   (C) Politics, economics, and education
   (D) Europeans, Indians, and Africans

3. Why does the professor want to avoid using the term "colored"?
   (A) This term is never used by Africans.
   (B) It may confuse students.
   (C) Nobody uses the term anymore.
   (D) The term is not actually accurate.

4. Why does the professor say this: 🎧 ?
   (A) To correct something he said earlier
   (B) To correct the student's answer
   (C) To give more information about a point introduced earlier
   (D) To introduce a new point related to the topic

Notes

| periodic table (n): |
| a chart displaying the known chemical elements |
| **in conjunction with (adv phrase):** |
| together; in connection |
| **recur (v):** |
| to happen repeatedly |
| **halfway (adj):** |
| at the middle point between two places or times |
| **devise (v):** |
| to create; to make |
| **octave (n):** |
| a group or series of eight units |
| **multiple (n):** |
| a number that may be divided evenly by another number |
| **predecessor (n):** |
| a person in a group or professional field who lived and contributed before |
| **periodically (adv):** |
| occasionally; repeatedly over time |
| **proton (n):** |
| a stable particle with a positive charge found in the nucleus of an atom |

1. What aspect of the periodic table does the professor mainly discuss?

   (A) The properties of the elements
   (B) The basis of the atomic number
   (C) The history of how it was developed
   (D) Its inventor, Dmitri Mendeleev

2. What is the speaker's main point?

   (A) The periodic table is a useful tool for chemists.
   (B) The periodic table is still imperfect.
   (C) Using atomic numbers solved the problems in the original table.
   (D) Using atomic mass was better than using atomic numbers.

3. How does the professor explain certain points about the periodic table? Choose 2 answers.

   (A) She shows the error related to a certain theory.
   (B) She explains what certain people did or thought.
   (C) She describes the process of an experiment.
   (D) She summarizes key properties of one group of elements.
   (E) She refers to a table in the book.

4. What does the professor imply when she says this: ∩ ?

   (A) The periodic table changed because people knew more about elements.
   (B) The periodic table is perfect now.
   (C) The periodic table was invented because new chemicals were discovered.
   (D) The periodic table is very useful for studying evolution.

Notes

---

deity *(n)*:
a god or goddess; a supernatural being

connotation *(n)*:
an implied or associated meaning separate from a literal meaning

incorporate *(v)*:
to include

suppress *(v)*:
to keep down; to ban

conceive *(v)*:
to become pregnant

pantheon *(n)*:
all of the gods for a certain culture considered as one group

solstice *(n)*:
a day of the year on which occurs the most or least hours of sunlight (depending on which hemisphere), usually June 21 and December 21

decree *(n)*:
an order by a figure of authority, making the order law

predominant *(adj)*:
having great importance; most common or prevalent

---

1. What is the topic of the lecture?

(A) The Roman Empire
(B) The spread of Christianity
(C) Roman Mythology
(D) Religion in the Roman Empire

2. What is the main idea of the talk?

(A) Rome was founded on Christian values.
(B) Deities were used to explain natural phenomenon.
(C) Roman religion incorporated many foreign beliefs.
(D) Christianity was based on the foreign cult of Mithras.

3. How does the professor emphasize his point about Christianity's appeal to the Romans?

(A) By reminding students of the most important gods in the Roman pantheon
(B) By contrasting Christianity to the Roman religion
(C) By listing examples of similarities between Roman and Christian traditions
(D) By describing the number of people who became Christians annually

4. Why does the professor say this: ⌒ ?

(A) To correct something he said earlier
(B) To explain the meaning of a term
(C) To explain what is wrong with a particular theory
(D) To summarize the main point of the lecture in a few words

Notes

| disturb (v): |
| to bother; to intrude upon |
| **available** (adj): |
| open for use; not occupied by other activities |
| **in return** (adv phrase): |
| in exchange; as a payment |
| **converse** (v): |
| to discuss; to talk |
| **accelerate** (v): |
| to increase the speed of |
| **reference** (n): |
| a letter of recommendation |
| **clarification** (n): |
| the act of explaining or making clear |
| **concept** (n): |
| an idea or theory |
| **ascertain** (v): |
| to discover; to find out |
| **adequate** (adj): |
| suitable; good enough for a given purpose |
| **make sense** (v phrase): |
| to be logical |
| **take advantage of** (v phrase): |
| to use some available service or opportunity |

1. What are the people mainly discussing?
   (A) Psychology
   (B) Scheduling
   (C) Safety procedures
   (D) Office hours

2. What is the professor's main point?
   (A) He does not like to be disturbed outside of class because he is busy.
   (B) Students should feel free to visit him during office hours, but they should come prepared.
   (C) All students participating in research must attend the meetings.
   (D) It is improper to speak to professors as if they are equals.

3. What does the woman learn from speaking to her professor?
   (A) She can gain a lot by making use of her professors' office hours.
   (B) Her professor welcomes visits from students any time, even if they just want to chat.
   (C) Most professors use their office hours as a time to prepare their lectures.
   (D) Her academic advisor does a similar job as her professor for this course.

4. What does the professor imply when he says this: ○ ?
   (A) He enjoys living the lifestyle of a professor.
   (B) He is compensated for his office hours.
   (C) He does not expect all students to own cars.
   (D) He prefers students to schedule an appointment.

🎧 Skill A 06 Business

Notes

symbol (n):	something that represents something else

symbol (n):
something that represents something else

logo (n):
a name or symbol designed for easy recognition

trademark (n):
an officially registered name or symbol that identifies a company or product

implement (v):
to put into use; to start using

differentiate (v):
to distinguish; to make different

precisely (adv):
exactly

unauthorized (adj):
without official permission

genericize (v):
to make generic, that is, not associated with a brand name

synonymous (adj):
the same in meaning

exert (v):
to put to use; to exercise

proprietorship (n):
the state of ownership of something

1. What is the topic of the lecture?
   (A) Famous brands and advertising
   (B) How companies create the names of their products
   (C) Uses and problems of trademarks
   (D) How to register a business with the trademark office

2. What is the main idea of the talk?
   (A) Companies must be careful to protect a product's name and identity.
   (B) Famous companies have an easier time marketing their products.
   (C) A good logo is useful for genericizing a company's products.
   (D) After a company registers a trademark, it can be sold worldwide.

3. How does the professor explain genericized trademarks? Choose 2 answers.
   (A) Eliciting examples
   (B) Describing causes and effects
   (C) Comparing products
   (D) Summarizing benefits
   (E) Contrasting two generic products

4. What does the professor mean when she says this: 🎧 ?
   (A) You surprised me.
   (B) Exactly.
   (C) Not quite.
   (D) Let's go over that again.

Understanding Main Ideas and Organization **295**

Strategy

- Since the answers to questions are generally found in order in the passage, it is helpful to take notes in the order of what you hear.
- Detail questions do not require inference. Choose what speakers actually say.
- There are questions that have more than one correct answer.
- There are negative questions that ask which answer choice is NOT true.
- In a lecture, detail questions are about the information related to the following: new facts, descriptions, definitions of terms/concepts/ideas, reasons, results, examples.
- Listen to the transitions that indicate emphasis, examples, cause and effect, etc.
- In a conversation, questions are about information such as the following: a speaker's problem in more detail, the cause of the problem, another speaker's suggestion, the reason for the suggestion, the reason for a speaker doing a certain thing.
- Incorrect choices may repeat some of the speakers' words but do not reflect information you have heard.
- Eliminate answers that are definitely wrong and choose the best answer(s) from the remaining choices.

Transitions and signal expressions

Illustration	for example, for instance, such (as), like, most, some, others, let's say, if...
Explanation	in this case, this is a __ that, there's a __
Emphasis	actually, in fact, you know, well, the way I understand it
Reason	because, since, for, due to, as a result of
Result	consequently, therefore, thus, hence, as a result, so
Contrast	but, however, although, even though, while, whereas, in contrast, on the other hand, despite, well
Addition	also, too, as well as, furthermore, moreover, in addition, not only __ but also
Time	in the 1820s, by the mid-1900s, for hundreds of years, until the mid-1800s, then
Process or Sequence	then, the next step is, after
Elaboration	in other words, that is, let me explain in more detail

Notes

restriction *(n)*:
a limitation; a rule that limits the use of something

clinic *(n)*:
a group session offering instruction on a particular skill

priority *(n)*:
a ranking of higher importance; precedence

consult *(v)*:
to ask someone or check some source for advice

face-to-face *(adv phrase)*:
in person; in close proximity

assume *(v)*:
to believe without evidence

critique *(n)*:
a critical review or commentary

constructive criticism *(n phrase)*:
a suggestion offered to improve something, as opposed to comments that merely point out flaws

instant *(adj)*:
immediate; right away

accountable *(adj)*:
answerable; liable to be called to account

---

1. What is the purpose of the conversation?
   (A) To find out about an online tutoring service
   (B) To learn about Internet connections
   (C) To find out information about the campus computer facilities
   (D) To submit coursework online

2. What are the main points in the conversation?
   (A) The service is free to anyone, but some students pay extra to purchase papers.
   (B) The free service runs 24 hours a day, but only current students can enroll.
   (C) The service is free, Internet access is necessary, and it runs Monday to Friday.
   (D) The free service is offered seven days a week, but tutors need two days to reply.

3. Which of the following must be true in order for the woman to use the service?
   (A) She must pay a registration fee.
   (B) She must wait 24 hours for the service to process her application.
   (C) She must be a member of the writing lab.
   (D) She must have a modem and Internet software.

4. Listen again to part of the conversation. Then answer the question. 🎧
   What does the man imply when he says this: 🎧 ?
   (A) He is not worried.
   (B) It would be easier for her to work during the day.
   (C) There is no problem.
   (D) The woman is correct.

Notes

---

underlay (v):
to be under; to be the foundation of

Middle Ages (n):
the period of European history from around 400 A.D. to 1450 A.D.

antiquity (n):
ancient times

classical (adj):
of or relating to ancient Greece or Rome, especially with regard to art, literature, and architecture

reconcile (v):
to make compatible; to resolve

theology (n):
the study of the nature of God and religious truth

clergy (n):
the people who are called to service in the Church

republic (n):
a nation whose head of state is usually elected, especially nations not ruled by monarchs

despotic (adj):
having the characteristics of a ruler with absolute power

fan the flames (v phrase):
to cause to increase or become more widespread

1. What is the professor talking about?
   (A) Greek and Roman Civilizations
   (B) Humanism
   (C) Renaissance philosophers
   (D) Italy

2. What is the main idea of the talk?
   (A) Humanism was the basis for the Renaissance.
   (B) Petrarch was a powerful leader in Italy during the Middle Ages.
   (C) Cicero was the first humanist.
   (D) Latin survived during the Middle Ages thanks to scholasticism.

3. Which two statements are true? Choose 2 answers.
   (A) Scholasticism was a rejection of humanism.
   (B) Humanism was a rejection of scholasticism.
   (C) Petrarch was from Florence.
   (D) Cicero did not agree with Petrarch's ideas.

4. Why does the professor say this: 🎧 ?
   (A) To help students make an obvious connection
   (B) To highlight a point of confusion for many students
   (C) To explain a term she just introduced
   (D) To present a question for the class to consider

Notes

---

capacity *(n):*
an amount that can be held or contained

arrive at *(v phrase):*
to find; to calculate

humble *(adj):*
low in quality; inferior

antiquated *(adj):*
very old; like an antique

floppy *(adj):*
flexible; able to be bent

measly *(adj):*
very small; worth little

obsolete *(adj):*
outdated; no longer useful

interface *(n):*
a point or place where two independent systems interact

astounding *(adj):*
astonishing; causing wonder

buzzword *(n):*
a word or phrase connected with a specialized field or group that usually sounds important or technical; a trendy or stylish word or phrase

---

1. What is the evidence that the professor discusses for changes in this field?

(A) Changes in terms related to computers
(B) New uses for computers in education
(C) Memory capacity
(D) Smaller hard drives

2. What is the main idea of the talk?

(A) Technology has grown amazingly and continues to do so.
(B) A human operator will always think more flexibly than a computer.
(C) The devices owned by members of the class are somewhat outdated.
(D) Steve Wozniak was a great figure and co-founder of Apple computers.

3. What is an example the professor gives of an obsolete device?

(A) A terabyte
(B) A memory stick
(C) A 3.5 inch floppy drive
(D) An external port

4. Listen again to part of the lecture. Then answer the question. 🎧

Why does the professor say this: ?

(A) To suggest another answer
(B) To help students imagine the device
(C) To ask the class for their opinion
(D) To confirm her understanding

Notes

---

fraternity (n):
a social organization of male students at a college or university

sorority (n):
a social organization of female students at a college or university

homecoming (n):
a celebration week at a college or university when students first return to school

dress up (v phrase):
to wear or put on formal/special clothes

authentic (adj):
real; conforming to fact

garb (n):
clothes

version (n):
a kind; a type

in mourning (adj phrase):
observing or respecting someone's death; saddened by someone's death

ornate (adj):
elaborate; flashy or showy

cast (n):
a group of people working to produce a theatrical production, including actors, directors, stage hands, etc.

---

1. What is the topic of the lecture?

(A) Costumes used in Roman theater
(B) A play that the class read
(C) Julius Caesar's life
(D) Roman fashion

2. What is a key point in the talk?

(A) The cloth should not be cut like a bed sheet.
(B) Most Romans did not really wear togas.
(C) The costumes for the show will be very expensive.
(D) Costumers need to have good imaginations.

3. According to the professor, what will the costumer need to make?

(A) White togas and black togas
(B) Togas for the men and dresses for the women
(C) Different *fivulates* for each character
(D) Purple togas for the senators and white togas for the slaves

4. Listen again to part of the lecture. Then answer the question. 🎧

What does the speaker mean when he says this: 🎧 ?

(A) The toga is very cheerful and festive but unfashionable for work.
(B) He wants the students to try working in a toga for practical experience.
(C) It is difficult to work in a toga because they are not very functional.
(D) The toga is more comfortable than pants or other kinds of work clothes.

Notes

	impact *(n)*: a significance; an influence
	revolve *(v)*: to go around; to spin around
	eureka *(interj)*: an exclamation of achievement similar to, "I have found it!"
	mundane *(adj)*: everyday; ordinary
	dispel *(v)*: to drive away
	misconception *(n)*: a wrong idea
	deduce *(v)*: to conclude; to infer
	inquisition *(n)*: a group of judges established to discover and suppress people and ideas that were in conflict with Church doctrine
	torture *(n)*: punishment involving severe pain in order to force information or a confession
	infinite *(adj)*: without end
	insecure *(adj)*: not confident; filled with anxiety

1. What aspect of the telescope does the professor mainly discuss?

(A) Its inventor, Galileo, and his books about astronomy

(B) The discoveries that Galileo made with the telescope

(C) The way the first one was built and how they are built today

(D) Scientists in history who have made discoveries with telescopes

2. What is the main idea of the talk?

(A) The Inquisition stood in the way of science.

(B) Galileo stood up for what he believed in.

(C) The telescope changed our understanding of our place in the universe.

(D) The discovery of Venus's phases changed science forever.

3. What was the evidence for the stars being further from Earth than the moon?

(A) The telescope showed that they were different colors.

(B) They moved more slowly across the sky than the moon.

(C) They looked small even through a telescope.

(D) More of them could be counted with the aid of a telescope.

4. Listen again to part of the lecture. Then answer the question. ⌒

What does the professor mean when he says this: ⌒ ?

(A) I won't go into that now.

(B) That topic will be covered at a later time.

(C) It's not true, so I won't discuss it.

(D) It's not important for students to learn about such things.

Notes

_____

_____

_____

_____

_____

_____

_____

_____

_____

_____

issue *(n)*:
a problem; a situation to be solved

statistics *(n)*:
data used to describe research

overall *(adj)*:
as a whole; all things considered

commit *(v)*:
to do; to carry out

category *(n)*:
a group to which things or information can be assigned

murder *(n)*:
to kill another person on purpose

rip off *(v)*:
to steal; to rob

massive *(adj)*:
huge; very large

as opposed to *(adj phrase)*:
compared with; in relation to

previous *(adj)*:
prior; occurring before

security *(adj)*:
related to safety or anti crime

soar *(v)*:
to rise quickly and steeply

resort to *(v phrase)*:
to use as an alternative or less desirable option

1. What is the topic of the conversation?
    (A) The crime rate in the US
    (B) Crime on American university campuses
    (C) The crime figures for one particular university
    (D) How to avoid crime

2. What is the main idea of the conversation?
    (A) There has been a big increase in all kinds of crime.
    (B) On the whole, crime is not a serious problem at the school.
    (C) The woman has been the victim of crime, whereas the man has not.
    (D) Crime is a problem on university campuses, but it is rarely reported.

3. What does the man say about thefts and burglaries over the past three years?
    (A) Both have decreased.
    (B) One has decreased, but the other has increased.
    (C) Both have increased.
    (D) One has increased, but the other has not been reported at all.

4. What does the woman imply when she says this: 🎧 ?
    (A) She feels uncomfortable with security cameras on campus.
    (B) Security cameras may have helped deter thefts.
    (C) She is glad that her school has cameras while other schools do not.
    (D) She thinks that the students should express their thanks for the new cameras.

Skill C — Determining Reasons, Purposes, and Attitudes

Strategy

Reason and Purpose

- Look at the overall organization of the passage and think about whether the purpose is to describe, explain, compare, or give an opinion.
- Consider the relationship between the speakers and the context in which the speakers meet.
- Use clues like intonation to help you understand the meaning behind the words.
- The following words are likely to appear in answer choices:
  - ⇨ complain, criticize, apologize, provide feedback
  - ⇨ offer, recommend, suggest, propose, inspire, encourage, request
  - ⇨ introduce, explain, describe, define, inform
  - ⇨ persuade, argue, discuss, support, emphasize
  - ⇨ clarify, illustrate, give an example of, verify
  - ⇨ compare, contrast, classify

Attitude

- Pay attention to adjectives and verbs of feelings. These may help you in recognizing words or phrases that indicate the speaker's feeling or opinion.
  - ⇨ Example: A: *The course Chemistry 204 was very helpful.*
    - B: *Yeah. I enjoyed the classes with Professor Jones very much.*
- Infer the speaker's attitude by the tone of voice, intonation, and the sentence stress that the speaker uses to show his or her feeling or opinion.
  - ⇨ Example: A: (With surprise) *You liked it?* (Speaker B does not agree with speaker A.)
    - or
    - A: (Pleased) *You liked it!* (Speaker A is happy with Speaker B's comment.)
- Consider the degree of certainty in what a speaker says.
  - ⇨ Example: *You want to know about when it was discovered? Hmm, well, let me think. Probably around 1600.* (The speaker is not sure of the information he is giving.)
- The following words are likely to appear in answer choices:
  - ⇨ knows, not sure, think/does not think, does not agree with

Notes

---

bizarre *(adj)*:
strange; unusual

deterrent *(n)*:
something that discourages a
certain behavior

hefty *(adj)*:
large

prank *(n)*:
a trick or joke

utter *(v)*:
to say; to speak

look up *(v phrase)*:
to find information from a list or
other source material

make sure *(v phrase)*:
to be certain; to ensure

situation *(n)*:
a circumstance; a problem

report *(v)*:
to tell authorities about

in progress *(adv phrase)*:
happening at the moment;
under way

immediate *(adj)*:
without a lag in time; very soon

1. What are the people mainly discussing?
   - (A) The response time of campus security
   - (B) What to do in an emergency
   - (C) How to operate the security system
   - (D) How to make a call on campus

2. What are the main things they can do?
   - (A) Call (9) 9-1-1, use the blue light, or call campus security's emergency line.
   - (B) Report it to the police, find a payphone, or call (9) 9-1-1.
   - (C) Find a campus phone and push the red button, go to campus security, or call for help.
   - (D) Find an emergency phone and press the blue button, call (9) 9-1-1, or call campus security.

3. Why is there a fine for using the blue light phones in non-emergency situations?
   - (A) Because the phones are expensive to run
   - (B) Because security personnel follow up on every call
   - (C) Because they're not meant for personal calls
   - (D) Because they cannot find you if you don't talk

4. Listen to part of the conversation. Then answer the question. ∩

   What can be inferred about the woman?
   - (A) She needs to pass in her history paper.
   - (B) She plans to use the non-emergency number.
   - (C) She is not being serious.
   - (D) She has been the victim of a crime.

⌒ Skill C **02** History

Notes

_____

regurgitate *(v)*:	to reproduce in an exact but uninteresting way
reject *(v)*:	to disbelieve; to dismiss as untrue
notion *(n)*:	an idea
commoner *(n)*:	a person of a lower class
outright *(adv)*:	completely; totally
tentative *(adj)*:	not fully agreed on; made with the possibility of future change
founder *(n)*:	the person who started or created an organization or place
devote *(v)*:	to concentrate on a specific topic or goal
reiterate *(v)*:	to say again in order to stress the importance of
take with a grain of salt *(v phrase)*:	to view with skepticism; to not believe completely

1. What is the talk mainly about?
   (A) Greek culture and its effect on international trade
   (B) Theories of people visiting America before Columbus
   (C) The mythology and rituals of Native American tribes
   (D) The traditional difficulties and dangers of overseas travel

2. What does the professor think of the contention that Columbus discovered the Americas?
   (A) He thinks it is the best conclusion from the facts.
   (B) He thinks it is a mistaken notion.
   (C) He thinks there needs to be more evidence before he can decide.
   (D) He thinks Columbus lied about his travels to the Americas.

3. Why does the professor mention that Peruvian sculptures resemble Medusa?
   (A) To show that Medusa is an archetype symbol in the universal psyche
   (B) To prove that a species of Medusa-like creatures used to live on the Earth
   (C) To show an example of the richness and beauty of Ancient Incan folklore
   (D) To indicate that Ancient Greeks may have visited Peru long ago

4. Why does the professor say this: ⌒ ?
   (A) To correct something he said earlier
   (B) To explain a term he just introduced
   (C) To explain what is wrong with the Chinese theory
   (D) To remind the students of his initial point

∩ Skill C **03** Literature

Notes

_____

_____

_____

_____

_____

_____

_____

_____

_____

_____

empathize *(v):*
to feel the same way as; to understand

standardize *(v):*
to make the same; to make standard

canon *(n):*
a group of books that represent a certain topic or time

righteous *(adj):*
correct in behavior; ethical

oeuvre *(n):*
an artist's work as a whole

emergence *(n):*
the act of taking form or becoming famous

prominence *(n):*
a position of respect, power, or fame

Eurocentric *(adj):*
concerned mostly with European matters

analects *(n):*
a collection of parts, or excerpts, from a literary work

eclectic *(adj):*
having many different styles or tastes

1. What is the talk mainly about?
   (A) The effects of globalization on traditions
   (B) Sources of ancient culture and their merits
   (C) Eurocentrism in the literature curriculum
   (D) The importance of English writers

2. What is the student's attitude toward the coursework list?
   (A) He is disappointed that there are too many books to read.
   (B) He is excited that there are only a few books to read.
   (C) He is disappointed that there are only European books.
   (D) He is excited that they will be reading Asian works of literature.

3. What reason is given for the nature of the course material?
   (A) It is required by Federal law, and the school could loose funding otherwise.
   (B) Students of other backgrounds are discouraged from keeping their traditions.
   (C) Translation difficulties excluded many fine texts from other languages.
   (D) It was based on the set of literature developed in the mid-twentieth century.

4. What does the professor imply when she says this: ∩?
   (A) That most maps nowadays are being drafted in Great Britain
   (B) That people from different countries use English to communicate
   (C) That fictional works are often written in English due to the language's flexibility
   (D) That the English language often prevents international disputes

READING LISTENING SPEAKING WRITING PRACTICE TEST

Notes

internship *(n):*
a period of service during which the worker learns a skill or trade

pay off *(v phrase):*
to give or produce a benefit

contact *(n):*
a person with whom a beneficial relationship exists

hang on *(v phrase):*
to wait briefly

pamphlet *(n):*
a small booklet of information

mandatory *(adj):*
necessary; compulsory

logistics *(n):*
the management of the details of an operation

counselor *(n):*
a person who supervises young people at a summer camp

vote of confidence *(n phrase):*
a compliment; encouragement

enthusiastic *(adj):*
showing energy and excitement

1. What are the people mainly discussing?
(A) A job fair
(B) Camp Ton-A-Wandah
(C) The graduation ceremony
(D) Making a resumé

2. What does the woman mean when she says this: ○ ?
(A) She already has definite plans for the summer.
(B) She has tentative summer plans, but they could change.
(C) She has no idea what she will do this summer.
(D) She is certain that she doesn't want to work in the restaurant.

3. Why does the man want to work at a summer camp?
(A) He loves kids.
(B) He loves nature.
(C) He wants teaching experience.
(D) He hopes to get in shape.

4. Listen to part of the conversation. Then answer the question. ○
What can be inferred about the woman?
(A) She needs to save her money this summer.
(B) Her career is her first priority.
(C) She'd like to do an internship, but she can't afford it.
(D) She already has a job that she's happy with.

Notes

_____

_____

_____

_____

_____

_____

_____

_____

_____

_____

_____

_____

transcribe *(v)*:
to write down on paper what is heard

routinely *(adv)*:
commonly; usually

branch *(n)*:
a section; a part

deductive *(adj)*:
related to logical reasoning

default *(adj)*:
standard; chosen unless specifically told not to

reverse *(v)*:
to change to the opposite

ultimate *(adj)*:
final; most important

pick up *(v phrase)*:
to observe and understand

myriad *(n)*:
a very large amount

subconscious *(adj)*:
without thinking purposefully

extrapolate *(v)*:
to estimate by extending known information

override *(v)*:
to counteract the normal operation of

1. What is the talk mainly about?

   (A) Robots
   (B) Artificial intelligence
   (C) Steven Spielberg
   (D) Mathematics

2. Why does the professor say this: ∩ ?

   (A) To remind the students of something discussed earlier
   (B) To explain a term she just introduced
   (C) To correct something she said earlier
   (D) To explain what's wrong with search AI

3. What are the four types of AI discussed in the lecture? Choose 4 answers.

   (A) Mathematical
   (B) Logical
   (C) Deductive
   (D) Search
   (E) Pattern recognition
   (F) Inference
   (G) Default

4. What is the professor's opinion of computer games?

   (A) She thinks they are a complete waste of time.
   (B) She thinks they can teach programmers a lot about AI.
   (C) She thinks they are not well developed.
   (D) She thinks they are fun.

Notes

---

atmosphere *(n)*:
the layer of air between the surface of the Earth and outer space

shift *(v)*:
to move; to change

generate *(v)*:
to produce; to create

aware *(adj)*:
knowing about; conscious of

correspond *(v)*:
to connect; to be related

deformation *(n)*:
an abnormal or unhealthy shape or form

coincide *(v)*:
to happen at the same time

link *(n)*:
a connection; a bond

radiate *(v)*:
to send out; to emit

thermal *(adj)*:
related to heat

supplement *(v)*:
to add; to increase

phenomenon *(n)*:
a happening; an occurrence

justified *(adj)*:
correct; supported by evidence

---

1. What is the talk mainly about?

   (A) Ocean tides
   (B) Air tides
   (C) Gravity
   (D) Sir Isaac Newton

2. Why does the professor say this: ∩ ?

   (A) To indicate a possible connection between weather and the moon
   (B) To review a theory taught in the lesson
   (C) To indicate a definite cause and effect relationship between two variables
   (D) To offer a justification for a digression

3. According to the professor, why is the Earth's atmosphere slightly warmer during a full moon?

   (A) Because of friction between the ocean and land
   (B) Because of higher tides
   (C) Because of light from the moon
   (D) Because of more hours of daylight

4. Listen again to part of the lecture. Then answer the question. ∩

   What does the professor imply about full moons affecting human behavior?

   (A) Full moons definitely alter the way people behave.
   (B) Full moons might alter the way people behave.
   (C) Full moons definitely do not alter the way people behave.
   (D) Only psychologists know for certain how full moons affect human behavior.

Review A – C

Vocabulary Review

Skill Review

Vocabulary Review

Instructions: Choose the best word or phrase to complete each sentence.

1. Thanks to the paramedic, the _____ of his heart was successful, and he survived the accident.
   - (A) expedition
   - (B) resuscitation
   - (C) hypothermia
   - (D) descent

2. Most developing countries don't have the money to build the _____ needed to keep the country running smoothly.
   - (A) coup d'etat
   - (B) octave
   - (C) infrastructure
   - (D) connotation

3. Part of what makes New York City interesting is its variety of different _____ groups. These different people bring their own music, food, and culture into one area.
   - (A) ethnic
   - (B) rhythmic
   - (C) adequate
   - (D) classical

4. Last year, she went to a school that _____ the girls from the boys. Before that, there were always boys in her classes.
   - (A) replenishes
   - (B) devises
   - (C) suppresses
   - (D) segregates

5. They have been trying to _____ for several years, but they still don't have any children.
   - (A) conceive
   - (B) incorporate
   - (C) converse
   - (D) accelerate

6. Catholicism is the _____ religion in Mexico. Most Mexicans go to church each weekend.
   - (A) adequate
   - (B) predominant
   - (C) antiquated
   - (D) astounding

7. The university has decided to _____ a new campus policy on alcohol, but many students disagree with it.
   - (A) differentiate
   - (B) reconcile
   - (C) revolve
   - (D) implement

8. At this point, improving my chemistry grade is my _____. I'm having the most difficulty in that class.
   - (A) capacity
   - (B) priority
   - (C) fraternity
   - (D) garb

9. The computer I used in high school is now _____. I'll have to buy a new one.
   - (A) astounding
   - (B) ornate
   - (C) obsolete
   - (D) mundane

10. We have to watch a film this weekend and write a _____ of it for homework.
   - (A) restriction
   - (B) critique
   - (C) buzzword
   - (D) clergy

11. Some dinosaurs grew to _____ sizes, much larger than animals living today.

(A) authentic
(B) astounding
(C) ornate
(D) insecure

12. If our first plan is unsuccessful, we may have to _____ our backup plan.

(A) resort to
(B) regurgitate
(C) look up
(D) pay off

13. You will have to increase the _____ of your hard drive in order to play this game. There isn't enough free memory now.

(A) cast
(B) contact
(C) capacity
(D) canon

14. The delegation's mission was aimed at transforming the country's government from a _____ system into a democracy.

(A) deductive
(B) despotic
(C) periodic
(D) thermal

15. The university is hoping that their strict new rules will act as a _____ against plagiarism and cheating.

(A) counselor
(B) myriad
(C) phenomenon
(D) deterrent

Instructions: Choose the word or phrase closest in meaning to the underlined part.

16. Her parents take trips to Europe <u>occasionally</u>.

(A) previously
(B) periodically
(C) precisely
(D) immediately

17. Modern Christianity <u>includes</u> many practices and beliefs borrowed from other faiths.

(A) suppresses
(B) disturbs
(C) consults
(D) incorporates

18. It is important to <u>talk to</u> your professors about any problems you might have with the course load.

(A) reconcile to
(B) converse with
(C) reiterate for
(D) deduce by

19. I didn't <u>exactly</u> understand that theory the professor introduced in class yesterday.

(A) precisely
(B) infinitely
(C) previously
(D) enthusiastically

20. The Shakespearian <u>type</u> of sonnet includes more parts than the Petrarchan type.

(A) atmosphere
(B) deformation
(C) interval
(D) version

21. Though a rare <u>occurrence</u>, an eclipse of the sun is a beautiful sight.

    (A) phenomenon
    (B) prominence
    (C) pamphlet
    (D) internship

22. It is <u>compulsory</u> for all freshman to enroll in Psychology 101.

    (A) hefty
    (B) pulmonary
    (C) mandatory
    (D) measly

23. Many ancient peoples believed a <u>god</u> controlled the weather.

    (A) garb
    (B) descent
    (C) multiple
    (D) deity

24. Our group has to <u>create</u> a plan of action for cleaning up the local ecosystem.

    (A) devise
    (B) dispel
    (C) accelerate
    (D) revolve

25. The earthquake caused a <u>huge</u> crack to open in the earth.

    (A) massive
    (B) bizarre
    (C) immediate
    (D) tentative

26. Ancient religious practices continue to have a strong <u>influence</u> on modern ways of life.

    (A) misconception
    (B) impact
    (C) inquisition
    (D) deterrent

27. Use the pattern of crime statistics from the past five years to <u>estimate</u> the numbers for next year.

    (A) correspond
    (B) supplement
    (C) revive
    (D) extrapolate

28. She's saving money to go on an archaeological <u>journey</u> next summer.

    (A) resuscitation
    (B) expedition
    (C) protest
    (D) connotation

29. I hate it when students use their MP3 players in the library. It always <u>bothers</u> me when I'm trying to study.

    (A) disturbs
    (B) converses
    (C) differentiates
    (D) genericizes

30. There are too many <u>limitations</u> on the use of campus tennis courts! I can never seem to play there for more than ten minutes.

    (A) rejections
    (B) situations
    (C) restrictions
    (D) inquisitions

Instructions: Write the missing words. Use the words below to fill in the blanks.

myriad	ubiquitous	ornate	breakdown	corresponding
version	categories	garb	mourning	prominence

The Roman people used to wear a **(31)** _____ of different types of **(32)** _____. The most common form was the toga. There were several different **(33)** _____ of toga, each **(34)** _____ to specific people and occasions. A **(35)** _____ of these different types of toga includes the *toga virilis*, or men's toga, which was worn by adult male citizens. Women, on the other hand, had their own **(36)** _____ of the toga called the *skola*. *Toga pulla*, or black togas, had two functions. People of the lower classes wore them regularly, and people of **(37)** _____ would wear them after the death of a loved one to show that they were in **(38)** _____. There was also a special kind of toga that featured a purple stripe and was worn by high-ranking officials and upper-class boys. Another special toga was the painted toga, which was very **(39)** _____ and worn on festive occasions by upper-class officials. The pure-white *toga candida,* so **(40)** _____ in media depictions of ancient Rome, was actually worn only by senatorial candidates.

Instructions: Choose the one word that does not belong.

41. republic   deity   theology   pantheon

42. obsolete   antiquated   authentic   outdated

43. massive   bizarre   hefty   large

44. symbol   logo   trademark   interface

45. revive   resuscitation   predecessor   paramedic

Instructions: Label each pair of words as similar (S) or opposite (O).

46. _____ justified   correct

47. _____ generate   dismantle

48. _____ correspond   coincide

49. _____ segregate   link

50. _____ adequate   sufficient

Notes

shuttle bus *(n phrase)*:
a bus that travels a regular route between two points

fixed *(adj)*:
set; unchanging

approximately *(adv)*:
about; close to

cater *(v)*:
to attend to the wants or needs of

circuit *(n)*:
a circular path or route

pick up *(v phrase)*:
to collect passengers for transport

adjacent *(adj)*:
next to; adjoining

doorstep *(n)*:
the front of one's home; the stairs leading up to a house

affiliated *(adj)*:
officially connected to

harsh *(adj)*:
severe; difficult

1. What does the woman need to know?

(A) The summer bus schedule
(B) The shuttle bus schedule
(C) The local bus schedule
(D) The way to the shuttle bus pick up point

2. What does the woman do on Fridays?

(A) Studies at home
(B) Takes a writing course
(C) Tutors students
(D) Works in the library

3. What is an example of the kind of information the student needs?

(A) How much a bus ride costs
(B) Where the local bus can be caught
(C) When the shuttle bus can be caught
(D) Where she can ride her bike

4. According to the man, at what time does the shuttle bus stop running?

(A) On Sundays

(B) At 8:00 a.m.

(C) At 8:00 p.m.

(D) At 12:15 a.m.

5. Which location is close to the library?

(A) The city bus stop

(B) Meany Hall

(C) The Communication building

(D) Garfield Lane

6. What does the man mean when he says this: ∩ ?

(A) Students have to work hard during the winter semester.

(B) Students become very tired during the winter semester.

(C) Bikes are forbidden on campus during the winter.

(D) The weather in winter makes it difficult to ride a bike.

Notes

vulnerable *(adj)*:
open to being hurt; susceptible to injury

diverse *(adj)*:
made up of many different parts

undergo *(v)*:
to experience; to endure

utilize *(v)*:
to use for

indicator *(n)*:
a gauge; a tool that measures

temperate *(adj)*:
mild; not overly hot

marine *(adj)*:
related to oceans and seas

habitat *(n)*:
an area in which an organism can live

outcrop *(n)*:
a group of rocks appearing above the surface of the surrounding land

core *(n)*:
an inner, base part

dramatic *(adj)*:
severe; very noticeable

estimate *(v)*:
to calculate an approximate number

chart *(v)*:
to follow the progress of; to monitor

1. What is the talk mainly about?

   (A) Ocean life
   (B) Coral reefs
   (C) Ocean temperatures
   (D) Marine scientists

2. How does the professor explain reefs? Choose 2 answers.

   (A) He brainstorms possible meanings.
   (B) He describes them.
   (C) He explains their chronological development throughout recent history.
   (D) He shows specimens to the class.
   (E) He gives two examples.

3. According to the professor, what are "polyps"?

   (A) Old skeletons or houses
   (B) Small simple tube-shaped water animals
   (C) Calcium carbonate skeletons
   (D) Changes in sea level

4. What reasons are given for changes in sea level?
   (A) Movements of the Earth's crust and the melting or freezing of the ice-caps
   (B) Coral coring and movements of the Earth's crust
   (C) Ice ages and meteors falling to Earth
   (D) Volcanic eruptions and tides

5. Why does the professor mention coring?
   (A) To tell how scientists protect fragile reefs
   (B) To explain how researchers study coral
   (C) To present an alternative to collecting pieces of coral
   (D) To help students understand the diversity of life around reefs

6. What does the professor mean when he says this: ⌒ ?
   (A) He thinks coral is hard to find, but informative.
   (B) He thinks that coral is beautiful, but tells us little about the world.
   (C) He thinks we can learn a lot from coral, and it is nice to look at.
   (D) He thinks people should take pictures of coral rather than take pieces of it out of the ocean.

Notes

baby boomer (n phrase):
a person born during a period of rapid population increase in North America during the 1940s and 1950s

oriented (adj):
tending to; likely to do

distorted (adj):
misshapen; altered beyond the normal form or shape

get a picture (v phrase):
to understand

privileged (adj):
given special advantages

cope (v):
to deal with a difficult situation; to endure

reliance (n):
the condition of needing, or depending on

extroversion (n):
the condition of not being shy

network (v):
to create a group of friends or contacts within a career-related environment

adept (adj):
effective at; skilled

---

1. What aspect of intelligence does the professor mainly discuss?
   (A) Reasons why intelligence is increasing in younger generations
   (B) How older people can retain their intelligence
   (C) Ways in which children can improve their intelligence
   (D) Theories that intelligence tests are inaccurate

2. How does the professor emphasize her point about how large the difference in intelligence is?
   (A) By stating the range of intelligence
   (B) By explaining the relationship between intelligence and earning power
   (C) By identifying the reasons why intelligence is highly regarded
   (D) By comparing intelligence to speed

3. According to the professor, how did researchers gather data on intelligence?
   (A) By observing parent-child interactions in a laboratory
   (B) By using statistics from consumer product purchases
   (C) By sending out questionnaires to over 4,500 participants
   (D) By comparing tests from the 1960s with today's tests

4. According to the speaker, why are younger people more extroverted?

(A) They have consumed more pesticides in their lifetimes.

(B) They spend more time outside of the family with others.

(C) They tend to watch more interactive television programs.

(D) They are better at using technology than their parents.

5. Why does the speaker mention cooking, cleaning, and doing laundry?

(A) To describe how doing these for others makes people more socially capable

(B) To explain that people are better at these tasks now because they are smarter

(C) To provide an example of how younger people are more self-reliant

(D) To introduce the topic of gender roles in the discussion

6. Why does the professor say this: ◯ ?

(A) To give an example of how life was less complex in the past

(B) To show how she suffered when she was a child

(C) To support the idea that children today are spoiled

(D) To convince her students to watch less TV

Notes

get down to *(v phrase)*:
to begin doing

primary *(adj)*:
first; most important

phylum *(n)*:
the largest category of living
things within each kingdom

catastrophe *(n)*:
a disaster; a terrible event

cycle *(n)*:
a repeated sequence of events

hardy *(adj)*:
strong; able to endure difficulty

weather *(v)*:
to endure; to survive difficulty

deem *(v)*:
to declare; to classify as

consistent *(adj)*:
reliable; steady

widespread *(adj)*:
occurring across a wide area

miraculously *(adv)*:
in an extremely surprising way

cease *(v)*:
to stop

wrap up *(v phrase)*:
to finish; to conclude

1. What is the talk mainly about?

   (A) Species that have remained unchanged
       for a long time
   (B) Species that went extinct long ago
   (C) Extinct species that scientists have
       brought back to life
   (D) Dinosaurs that are still alive today

3. According to the professor, how long, on
   average, do most species last?

   (A) 200 million years
   (B) 80 million years
   (C) 2 or 3 million years
   (D) 23 million years

2. How does the professor emphasize his point
   about the unexpected reappearance of
   lazarus taxons?

   (A) He tells the story of Lazarus.
   (B) He lists several important fossilized plants.
   (C) He gives details about the coelacanth.
   (D) He mentions several mysterious creatures.

4. What do the tuatara and the ginko tree have in common?

(A) They both belong to the lazarus taxon.
(B) They are both living fossils.
(C) They are both plants.
(D) They are both now extinct.

5. What is the professor's attitude toward animals that are called "living fossils"?

(A) He doubts that they truly exist.
(B) He thinks they get too much attention from the media.
(C) He thinks they have useful medical benefits.
(D) He thinks they are amazing.

6. Why does the professor say this: 🎧 ?

(A) To correct a mistake he has just made
(B) To give an example of a lazarus species
(C) To inform students not to focus on the point he just made
(D) To give students a clue about key information for their test

Matching Words and Categories

Strategy

- One of the questions is likely to be a categorizing question if a speaker discusses or mentions one of the following:

  ⇨ types   classes   categories   terms   methods   compare   contrast

- Questions with tables only appear after the listening is finished, so it is very important to take notes while you listen.

- When you take notes for this type of listening, pay special attention to the category words, their characteristics, and examples.

- In this type of question, you need to choose more than one answer. Some questions are worth more than one point.

- There are different types of tables you need to complete in the test. For one type of table, you need to click one of two boxes (Yes or No) for each phrase. For another type, you click in the box under the right category.

Notes

look down *(v phrase)*:
to appear sad or depressed

skate *(v)*:
to move or act with ease

disheartening *(adj)*:
depressing; taking away energy
or enthusiasm

vocation *(n)*:
a job

aptitude *(n)*:
a strong ability for

bomb *(v)*:
to do very poorly on a test or
piece of work

screw up *(v phrase)*:
to make a mistake

re-evaluate *(v)*:
to examine again; to think about
again and possibly change one's
mind

give a break *(v phrase)*:
to change the normal rules to
help someone

last resort *(n phrase)*:
a final choice; a last possible
action

appeal *(v)*:
to ask someone to change an
evaluation or decision

---

1. Is each of these courses of action discussed in the dialog? Mark the correct box.

	Yes	No
(A) Checking to see the grade isn't a mistake		
(B) Changing to a different major		
(C) Asking the professor to re-evaluate the grade		
(D) Appealing the grade with the department head		

2. What does the man advise the woman to do?
(A) Talk to her professor about her grade
(B) Admit her problems to her parents
(C) Apply to attend a different school
(D) Retake the course in which she received a low grade

3. What is the discussion mainly about?
(A) How to get revenge on a professor because of a low grade
(B) What factors should be considered when choosing a new major
(C) How to deal with receiving a low grade from a professor
(D) What actions should be taken if a professor intentionally gives a low grade

4. What does the man mean when he says this: ∩ ?
(A) He thought the woman wasn't trying hard at school.
(B) He thought the woman spent too much time having fun.
(C) He thought the woman was finding her classes easy.
(D) He thought the woman was exercising instead of studying.

READING

LISTENING

SPEAKING

WRITING

PRACTICE TEST

Notes

hype *(n)*:	an excessive amount of advertising
potentially *(adv)*:	possibly
garner *(v)*:	to get; to achieve
obvious *(adj)*:	easy to see or understand
convince *(v)*:	to make others agree with an idea
substandard *(adj)*:	of low quality; not good enough
expertise *(n)*:	a high level of ability or knowledge regarding a given topic
franchiser *(n)*:	a company that sells franchise businesses
franchisee *(n)*:	a person or group of people who buy a franchise business
diluted *(adj)*:	weakened
acumen *(n)*:	the ability to judge or reason correctly
tied down *(adj phrase)*:	committed to; obliged to

1. Match each word or phrase with the correct classification. Put one word in each box.

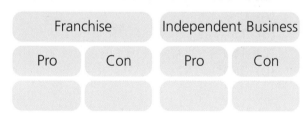

   (A) Established product
   (B) Creativity
   (C) Diluted market
   (D) Start-up capital

2. Why does the professor mention McDonald's restaurants?
   (A) To provide an example of a successful franchise
   (B) To give an example of a risky franchise
   (C) To show how certain business ventures require high start-up capital
   (D) To contrast a successful independent business with an unsuccessful franchise

3. What are the reasons for independent businesses being more successful than franchises? Choose 2 answers.
   (A) Independent businesses have an established brand loyalty.
   (B) Franchisers care more about selling their franchises than ensuring each one is successful.
   (C) Independent businesses allow for more creative ways to generate profit.
   (D) Franchise businesses start with a proven business model.
   (E) Independent businesses have higher start-up costs.

4. Why does the professor say this: ?
   (A) To correct something she said earlier
   (B) To explain a term she just introduced
   (C) To explain what is wrong with a particular theory
   (D) To remind students of something discussed earlier

Notes

| latitude *(n)*: |
| a measurement of distance north or south of the equator |
| **longitude** *(n)*: a measurement of distance east or west of the prime meridian |
| **hemisphere** *(n)*: a half of a sphere |
| **prime** *(adj)*: first; most important |
| **meridian** *(n)*: a line that divides something into two halves |
| **designate** *(v)*: to name; to label |
| **revolution** *(n)*: a complete 360° turn around an axis |
| **zone** *(n)*: an area |
| **nonetheless** *(adv)*: however; despite what might be expected |
| **equivalent** *(n)*: an equal thing |
| **predict** *(v)*: to guess what will happen in the future |

1. With which category are these things associated?

Latitude	Longitude

   (A) Poles
   (B) Run east-west
   (C) Run north-south
   (D) Equator
   (E) 49ᵗʰ parallel
   (F) Greenwich, England

2. What aspect of lines of longitude does the professor mainly discuss?
   (A) The rotation of the Earth at 15° per hour
   (B) The mapping of time zones
   (C) The problems associated with time zones
   (D) The origin of the Prime Meridian

3. According to the professor, how many degrees does the Earth spin in one hour?
   (A) 0°
   (B) 15°
   (C) 180°
   (D) 360°

4. What does the professor imply when he says this: ⌒ ?
   (A) People have to strictly follow the time zones.
   (B) Time zones usually cause a lot of inconvenience.
   (C) People who live in cities have fewer problems with time zones.
   (D) Time zones must be assigned after considering convenience to people.

Notes

_____

_____

_____

_____

_____

_____

_____

_____

_____

_____

_____

_____

policy *(n)*:
a course of action; a guiding principle; a rule

legally *(adv)*:
in accordance with the law

tick off *(v phrase)*:
to anger; to infuriate

rationale *(n)*:
a reason

cite *(v)*:
to claim; to present as a reason

compelling *(adj)*:
strongly affecting

have a good mind to *(v phrase)*:
to feel one has a strong justification for a potential action

sympathize *(v)*:
to feel the same as; to feel pity for

go overboard *(v phrase)*:
to act too extremely; to overreact

commute *(v)*:
to travel back and forth to work or school

sweep under the carpet *(expression)*:
to ignore or hide a problem

---

1. Are these statements true about the new university policies? Mark the correct box.

	Yes	No
(A) They are forbidding professors from drinking alcohol.		
(B) They are allowing alcohol to be sold only in the campus pub.		
(C) They are forbidding students from drinking in the dorms.		
(D) They are introducing a large tax on campus alcohol.		

2. What is the woman's opinion of the university's new alcohol policies?

(A) She does not mind them.
(B) She is angry about them.
(C) She is glad about the changes.
(D) She is suspicious of them.

3. What are the reasons for the university changing their alcohol policies? Choose 3 answers.

(A) Alcohol was becoming too expensive.
(B) Alcohol was causing students' grades to drop.
(C) Alcohol was causing violent behavior.
(D) Alcohol was causing too many students to move off campus.
(E) Alcohol led to the death of one student in the past.
(F) Alcohol was causing a rise in vandalism on campus.

4. According to the man, what may be a negative consequence of the new policy?

(A) It will make students drink stronger alcohol.
(B) It will increase the stress levels in students.
(C) It will force students to use harmful drugs instead of alcohol.
(D) It will increase the number of students driving drunk.

Notes

	come to mind (v phrase): to occur to; to strike with an idea
	typify (v): to be typical of; to be a normal characteristic of
	dissonant (adj): harsh and inharmonious
	cacophonous (adj): loud; noisy
	play around with (v phrase): to experiment with; to try different arrangements and combinations
	sheer (adj): considered separate from anything else
	precede (v): to exist or act before
	motivation (n): the reason for an action or belief
	approach (n): a way of thinking or acting
	distinct (adj): unique; different from others
	dramatically (adv): in a large, very noticeable way

1. Match each musical innovation with the appropriate category.

Baroque	Classical	Romantic

(A) Shorter symphonies
(B) Focus on clarity and simplicity
(C) Establishment of opera
(D) Themes from books, art, and myths
(E) Focus on emotions

2. What is the talk mainly about?

(A) The Romantic period in music
(B) The psychology of emotion
(C) The works of a composer
(D) Post-modern music

3. According to the professor, what was the musical period directly before the Romantic period?

(A) Classical
(B) Mozart
(C) Baroque
(D) Orchestral

4. Why does the professor say this: ⌒ ?

(A) To correct a student's mistaken idea
(B) To explain a term she just introduced
(C) To relate the topic to something most students are familiar with
(D) To remind the students of something discussed earlier

⌒ Skill D 06   Literature

Notes

	tuberculosis (n): a sickness that affects the lungs
	bar exam (n phrase): a qualification test for lawyers
	permanently (adv): in a way that affects things forever
	derivative (n): a thing that is taken from something else
	monstrosity (n): a thing that has an unusual and unattractive appearance or character
	base on (v phrase): to use as a starting point or foundation
	draft (n): a version of a written work
	sweeping (adj): large-scale
	two-facedness (n): the quality of behaving differently in front of different people
	remonstrance (n): an act of complaining or criticizing
	colonialism (n): the process of one nation exerting control over foreign lands

1. Match each title with the correct classification.

Novels	Other works

(A) "A Humble Remonstrance"
(B) *An Inland Voyage*
(C) *The Strange Case of Dr. Jekyll and Mr. Hyde*
(D) *In the South Seas*
(E) *Treasure Island*

2. What is the talk mainly about?
(A) A particular book
(B) The British Empire
(C) Societal change in London
(D) A famous author

3. According to the professor, where did Stevenson spend the last years of his life?
(A) Scotland
(B) Denmark
(C) Belgium
(D) Samoa

4. What does the professor imply when he says this: ⌒ ?
(A) He could not get the qualifications he needed to be a lawyer.
(B) He was a bad lawyer and had to quit.
(C) He quickly became famous as a lawyer without having to work hard.
(D) He was qualified, but worked very little as a lawyer.

Making Inferences and Predictions

Strategy

Inferences

- Watch for headphone icons indicating that you will listen to part of the conversation or lecture one more time.

- Try to guess the implied meaning of the given information. The correct answer is not directly stated.

- Relate what the speaker says to the topic or context in order to infer the meaning. For example, when a professor is giving suggestions on a student's essay and says, *"I'm not sure about this part,"* we can infer that the professor suggests changing some part in the essay.

- Use logic and think about how key points relate. For example, when a student says, *"I need to study more for my biology class, but my schedule is so tight,"* we can guess that "tight schedule" means the speaker doesn't have enough time to study for his biology class.

- Use clues such as vocabulary, word stress, intonation, or pace of what the speaker says. The same sentence can express different meanings when said in different ways.

  ⇨ Example: *Oh, you've never heard of that.* (I may need to explain more than I thought.)

    Oh, you've never heard of that? (I'm surprised that you've never heard of that.)

- Do not choose answer choices that are too general or vague.

Predictions

- Pay attention to the last part of a conversation. For example, if a speaker agrees with the other speaker's suggestion at the end, the speaker will probably do what is suggested.

- Listen for such expressions as the following:

  ⇨ I'd better   I will   then   I think I can   We'll discuss   We'll talk more about

- Pay attention to time expressions, such as *tomorrow*, *this evening*, and *next time/week/ semester*.

Notes

_____
_____
_____
_____
_____
_____
_____
_____
_____
_____
_____
_____
_____
_____
_____
_____
_____
_____
_____
_____

frustrated *(adj)*:
filled with a feeling of discouragement or dissatisfaction

due *(adj)*:
expected; scheduled to be given or returned

packed *(adj)*:
full; crowded

a mile long *(adj phrase)*:
very long

lounge *(n)*:
a room for relaxing

kick out *(v phrase)*:
to eject; to force to leave

check out *(v phrase)*:
to go and see

tip *(n)*:
a suggestion; a piece of advice

1. What can be inferred about the man?
   (A) He knows somebody who works in the library.
   (B) He has been to the copy room in Anderson Hall.
   (C) He lives off campus and uses a city bus to get home.
   (D) He is not very good with computers.

2. How does the woman feel about the lab in Anderson Hall?
   (A) She is often frustrated by it.
   (B) She thinks it should be closed.
   (C) She hopes to work there.
   (D) She likes it.

3. What will the man probably do?
   (A) Go with the woman the next time she visits the computer lab
   (B) Ask his professor to accept the paper a day late
   (C) Sign up for a business class so that he can use the computer lab
   (D) Use the computer lab in Anderson Hall

4. What does the woman imply when she says this: ∩ ?
   (A) Only certain people are allowed to use the lab.
   (B) The lab is not easy to find.
   (C) The lab is small and old.
   (D) The staff does not want students to use the lab.

READING | LISTENING | SPEAKING | WRITING | PRACTICE TEST

Notes

_____

_____

_____

_____

_____

_____

_____

_____

_____

_____

_____

_____

_____

_____

reunion *(n)*:
a celebration when family members come together after a long separation

disrupt *(v)*:
to break; to interrupt

foster care *(n phrase)*:
supervised care, usually in an institution or substitute home, for orphans or children who have been taken away from their parents

reliable *(adj)*:
dependable; trustworthy

census *(n)*:
an official study done by a country's government once every few years in which data about the population are collected

rule of thumb *(n phrase)*:
a useful principle that can be used most of the time, but may not give the proper results 100% of the time

surname *(n)*:
a family name; a last name

trendy *(adj)*:
in fashion; in accord with the latest fad

infancy *(n)*:
the youngest age of a child, before the child can walk

1. According to the speaker, what can be inferred about genealogical research?

   (A) It is very difficult, so only professionals can get reliable results.
   (B) The findings can never be trusted because the data is not reliable.
   (C) It can be useful for police investigations.
   (D) Some people do it for fun.

2. What would be considered the most reliable data in genealogical research?

   (A) A birth record from a city hospital
   (B) A personal letter signed by a family member
   (C) An individual's diary
   (D) A story told by a relative

3. What does the professor imply about women after they get married?

   (A) They live where their husbands choose to live.
   (B) They change their names.
   (C) They have great influence in choosing where to live.
   (D) They begin planning the names for their children.

4. Listen again to part of the lecture. Then answer the question. ⌒

   What does the professor mean when he says this: ⌒ ?

   (A) Two people referred to the record book.
   (B) Both of Mary's children were listed in the book.
   (C) Two copies of the record book were made.
   (D) Two names were recorded in the record book.

Notes

drawn out *(adj phrase):*
extended; going on and on

ample *(adj):*
available in a sufficient amount

hardy *(adj):*
physically strong and healthy

toxicity *(n):*
the degree to which something
is poisonous

metabolism *(n):*
the chemical processes of the
body in which food is broken
down in order to supply energy
to the body

indigestion *(n):*
an illness or discomfort resulting
from the inability to digest food

lethal *(adj):*
able to kill or cause death

buff *(n):*
an expert

corrupt *(v):*
to spoil or destroy the honesty or
integrity of

malfunction *(v):*
to not function properly

dose *(n):*
an amount of medicine prescribed
to be taken at one time

1. What does the professor imply about people who searched for wild plants to eat in the 1800s?
   (A) They lived in very poor countries.
   (B) They were doing what was normal at that time.
   (C) They knew about poisonous plants, so they rarely ate dangerous plants.
   (D) They were people who did not fit in society.

2. How does the professor feel about keeping plants inside the house?
   (A) She believes plants make a home healthier.
   (B) She is opposed to keeping plants inside the house.
   (C) She feels bad for the plants because they suffer when children damage them.
   (D) She thinks people should be more careful.

3. Which is true about hemlock?
   (A) It is a mineral.
   (B) It is an oxalate.
   (C) It is an alkaloid.
   (D) It is an extinct plant.

4. Listen again to part of the lecture. Then answer the question. ↷
   What does the professor imply about oxalates?
   (A) They are like weeds and irritate homeowners.
   (B) They are the most dangerous of the three categories of poisonous plants.
   (C) They can safely be consumed by animals, but not by people.
   (D) They do not have enough poison to kill a person.

Skill E 04 Drama

Notes

foremost *(adv):*
first; before other things

technical *(adj):*
having special skill or practical knowledge related to something mechanical

rehearsal *(n):*
a time of practice before a performance

down the road *(adv phrase):*
in the future

inspect *(v):*
to look at carefully

hazard *(n):*
a danger; a chance of being injured or hurt

extinguisher *(n):*
a device used to put out fires

privileged *(adj):*
having special benefits or privileges

bark *(v):*
to command loudly and quickly

delegate *(v):*
to divide responsibility among a group of people

rapport *(n):*
an emotional connection based on mutual trust and respect

1. What can be inferred about this lecture?

   (A) It was given on the first day of class.
   (B) It came just before a major exam.
   (C) It was meant to inform students about other courses in the drama department.
   (D) It was given on the last day of class.

2. How does the professor feel about the role of the stage manager?

   (A) It is more important than the role of the actors.
   (B) It is not as important as the role of the technical crew such as designers and lighting crew.
   (C) It is a very important role and should be taken seriously.
   (D) It is one of the least important roles among theater professionals.

3. What does the professor imply about assistant stage managers?

   (A) They should be responsible for keeping notes about rehearsals.
   (B) They usually quit, so it's not a good idea to depend on them.
   (C) They can serve as actors whenever members of the cast get sick.
   (D) They are not usually professionals.

4. Listen to part of the lecture again. Then answer the question.

   What does the professor mean when he says this: ?

   (A) Try not to remember.
   (B) That's OK.
   (C) Don't worry about the past.
   (D) Sometimes people forget things.

Notes

---

gross *(adj)*:
disgusting

deny *(v)*:
to take away a right; to refuse a request

vending *(adj)*:
for selling

prerogative *(n)*:
an exclusive right to decide

smokes *(n)*:
cigarettes

boulevard *(n)*:
a wide city street, usually with trees on either side

habitually *(adv)*:
as a routine or regular habit

hit the books *(v)*:
to start studying

inconvenience *(v)*:
to cause discomfort; to make unsuitable for one's needs

in favor of *(prep phrase)*:
for; supportive of

wise up *(v)*:
to become smarter

revolting *(adj)*:
disgusting

---

1. What can be inferred about the students?
   (A) They are outdoors.
   (B) They are in the library.
   (C) They are in a classroom.
   (D) They are sitting in a coffee shop.

2. How does the man feel about a completely smoke-free campus?
   (A) He doesn't like the idea because it denies students their freedom.
   (B) He is in full support of the idea.
   (C) He hopes the campus will become smoke-free after he quits smoking.
   (D) It would not bother him much.

3. What will the man probably do?
   (A) Buy a pack of cigarettes from a store on campus
   (B) Quit smoking in order to make the woman happy
   (C) Continue smoking unless the campus goes smoke-free
   (D) Move to a table outside in order to smoke

4. Listen to part of the conversation. Then answer the question. ⌒
   What does the woman mean when she says this: ⌒ ?
   (A) That is a bad idea.
   (B) That surprises me.
   (C) I forgot.
   (D) I didn't mention it before.

⋂ Skill E 06 Business

Notes

valuation *(n)*:
an assessed value or price

mismanagement *(n)*:
inappropriate or inefficient
management

solid *(adj)*:
strong; reliable

indicator *(n)*:
something used to predict future
trends

franchise *(n)*:
a business entity with the authority
to do business in a certain area or
region

commodity *(n)*:
an agricultural or mined product
that can be processed and sold

flexibility *(n)*:
the property of being adaptable
or responsive to change

face value *(n)*:
an apparent value; the value
printed on a bill or bond

count on *(v phrase)*:
to rely on; to depend on

minimize *(v)*:
to make as small as possible

cash in *(v phrase)*:
to settle one's account by
submitting for the present value

1. What does the professor imply about the investment decisions discussed in the lecture?

    (A) They are investments that managers consider at the end of the year.
    (B) They are related to personal investments.
    (C) They are decisions fund managers consider when investing other people's money.
    (D) They are only important for large investments made by corporations.

2. What can be inferred about a commodity-type company?

    (A) They have low franchise value.
    (B) They have high franchise value.
    (C) They set prices based on changes in their franchise value.
    (D) They are good investments for franchises.

3. According to the professor, what is possible to know about the stock market?

    (A) When something will happen
    (B) What will happen
    (C) Who will invest in a company
    (D) Where overvalued stocks are reported

4. Why does the professor say this: ⋂ ?

    (A) To correct something she said earlier
    (B) To explain a term she just introduced
    (C) To explain what is wrong with a particular theory
    (D) To remind the students of something discussed earlier

Placing Steps in a Sequence

Strategy

- One of the listening questions is likely to be a question about ordering or sequencing if a speaker discusses one of following:
  - ⇨ an experiment
  - ⇨ historical events that happened chronologically
  - ⇨ a biography
  - ⇨ instructions for making/doing something
  - ⇨ a natural/scientific phenomenon
  - ⇨ a mechanism of something
- When you take notes, pay special attention to what happens at each step in the process.
- Listen for the transitions that indicate the sequence:
  - ⇨ first, now, the first step is
  - ⇨ next, (and) then
  - ⇨ so now
  - ⇨ the last step is, finally
- One type of question asks whether each phrase or sentence in the answer choices is a step in a process or not. For this question, you need to click Yes or No for each answer choice.
- In this type of question, you need to choose more than one answer. Some questions are worth more than one point.

Notes

_____

_____

_____

_____

_____

_____

_____

_____

_____

_____

_____

eventual *(adj)*:
occurring at the end of a future
sequence of events

conscript *(n)*:
a person taken into the armed
forces by the will of the government

reservist *(n)*:
a person who volunteers to join
the armed forces in case of war,
not a full-time soldier

fleet *(n)*:
a large group of ships

disposal *(n)*:
the ability or power to use

compensate *(v)*:
to reward someone for work
done or damage caused

admiral *(n)*:
a high ranking official in the navy

subdue *(v)*:
to capture and control

spark *(v)*:
to start; to incite

foray *(n)*:
a military raid or expedition

foothold *(n)*:
a starting point; a place from
which troops can advance into
an area

---

1. The speaker explains a sequence of events. Put the events in the correct order.

> Order: 1. _____ → 2. _____ → 3. _____ → 4. _____

(A) Spanish rebellion
(B) Nelson defeats Napoleon in Egypt
(C) Trade war between Britain and France
(D) France seizes control of Belgium and the Netherlands

2. According to the professor, why couldn't the British invade France directly via land?

(A) The French had dug trenches.
(B) The British army was weak.
(C) The British lacked funding.
(D) The French had many allies.

3. What are the reasons for Britain having a strong navy? Choose 2 answers.

(A) They hired sailors from other European countries.
(B) A lot of British men volunteered to serve.
(C) They had a lot of experienced sailors from trade ships.
(D) Their enemies didn't know how to sail at the time.

4. How does the man probably feel when he says this: ⌒ ?

(A) Doubtful about what the professor just said
(B) Surprised by what the professor just said
(C) Frustrated by what the professor just said
(D) Depressed about what the professor just said

Notes

vague *(adj)*:
unclear; not exact

adapt *(v)*:
to change according to the situation

tighten up *(v phrase)*:
to make clear; to make more precise

attribute *(n)*:
a trait; a characteristic

food chain *(n phrase)*:
the system of energy movement between plants and animals

herbivore *(n)*:
an animal that eats plants

carnivore *(n)*:
an animal that eats meat

start off *(v phrase)*:
to begin

convert *(v)*:
to change the form of

1. How does the food chain work? Summarize the process by putting the steps in order.

   Order: 1. _____ → 2. _____ → 3. _____ → 4. _____

   (A) Herbivores get 100 units of energy by consuming plants.
   (B) One element of the system produces 100,000 units of energy.
   (C) One element of the system consumes herbivores.
   (D) Photosynthesis converts 10% of the energy.

2. What are the two reasons that students complained about systems theory? Choose 2 answers.

   (A) It is outdated for modern science.
   (B) Scientists need a versatile tool.
   (C) It is too vague.
   (D) It can be applied to almost anything.
   (E) It can't be applied to ecology.

3. What is an example the professor gives of a system that systems theory can be applied to?

   (A) The food chain
   (B) The solar system
   (C) The classroom
   (D) Photosynthesis

4. Why does the professor say this: ⌒ ?

   (A) To correct something he said earlier
   (B) To explain a term he just introduced
   (C) To explain the application of the theory
   (D) To remind the students of something discussed earlier

Notes

butter up (v phrase):
to flatter; to compliment someone in order to gain favor

hook up (v phrase):
to connect

shut down (v phrase):
to turn off

marvelous (adj):
very good; wonderful

access (v):
to go into; to start using

wealth (n):
an abundance; a large amount

inconvenience (n):
a situation that takes a lot of effort or time

sophisticated (adj):
modern; using advanced technology

replicate (v):
to copy; to reproduce

disguise (v):
to hide the true identity of

spy on (v phrase):
to secretly watch

bandwidth (n):
the capacity of an Internet connection to transfer data

---

1. The speakers discuss various computer problems. Summarize the conversation by putting the points in order.

   Order: 1. ____ → 2. ____ → 3. ____ → 4. ____

   (A) A firewall will be useful.
   (B) The Internet is useful, but problems can occur.
   (C) The man needs to clean his hard drive.
   (D) The computer may have a virus.

2. According to the woman, why should computer users install firewalls?

   (A) To gain access to other computers
   (B) To search the Internet
   (C) To prevent outside access to their computers
   (D) To get a faster connection

3. What does the woman advise the man to do? Choose 2 answers.

   (A) Remove his firewall program
   (B) Install an anti-virus program
   (C) Buy a faster computer
   (D) Stop downloading music files
   (E) Use a program to clean his hard drive

4. How does the man probably feel at the start of the conversation?

   (A) Tired
   (B) Happy
   (C) Frustrated
   (D) Amused

Notes

	bond *(v)*: to create a connection or relationship with
	procreate *(v)*: to reproduce; to make a baby
	fertilization *(n)*: the act of a sperm and an egg joining
	trigger *(v)*: to start into action; to set off
	labor *(n)*: the act of giving birth
	initiate *(v)*: to start; to act first
	prospective *(adj)*: potential; possible
	contraction *(n)*: a twitch, or flexing, of a muscle
	induce *(v)*: to force into action; to start
	mute *(v)*: to weaken; to make less
	counterintuitive *(adj)*: against common sense; contrary to what is expected
	nurture *(v)*: to show love for and take care of
	offspring *(n)*: a child or group of children

1. The speaker explains the process of parents bonding with children. Summarize the process by putting the following stages in order.

Order: 1. ____ → 2. ____ → 3. ____ → 4. ____

(A) Caring phase
(B) Preparatory phase
(C) Response phase
(D) Delivery phase

2. According to the professor, why is the parent-child bond stronger among species that have fewer children?

(A) Because males procreate with more than one female
(B) Because they must control behavior
(C) Because with fewer offspring, survival of each one is more important
(D) Because with fewer offspring, there is more food to go around

3. What is an example the professor gives of an animal that produces a litter of offspring?

(A) Rats
(B) Humans
(C) Bears
(D) Rabbits

4. What can be inferred about bears and rats?

(A) Mother bears take better care of their offspring than do mother rats.
(B) Mother bears have a more difficult labor than mother rats.
(C) Father rats are more involved with their children than father bears.
(D) Father rats have higher levels of blood prolactin than father bears.

Notes

assist *(v)*:
to help

financial *(adj)*:
related to money

take a nose dive *(v phrase)*:
to decrease rapidly

miserably *(adv)*:
in a large and negative way

malaise *(n)*:
a general feeling of poor health
and lack of energy

symptom *(n)*:
a sign or effect of a sickness

long shot *(n phrase)*:
a large amount or degree

come up with *(v phrase)*:
to create; to invent; to think up

refer *(v)*:
to send to for help

medical *(adj)*:
related to medicine and health

---

1. In the dialog, the two speakers discuss the man's problems. Put the problems in the correct order in which they were discussed.

   Order: 1. ____ → 2. ____ → 3. ____ → 4. ____

   (A) Health problems
   (B) Academic problems
   (C) Relationship problems
   (D) Financial problems

2. According to the man, in how many of his classes have his grades decreased?

   (A) One
   (B) Two
   (C) Five
   (D) All

3. What are the examples of necessities given by the woman? Choose 3 answers.

   (A) Tuition
   (B) Medication
   (C) Relationships
   (D) Books
   (E) Transportation
   (F) Jobs
   (G) Food

4. What does the woman imply when she says this: ∩ ?

   (A) The man has the worst symptoms she has ever seen.
   (B) Since he is very sick, nobody will want to come close to him.
   (C) Many other students feel the same way as the man.
   (D) The doctors will help him by giving him a new kind of medication.

READING
LISTENING
SPEAKING
WRITING
PRACTICE TEST

Notes

_____

_____

_____

_____

_____

_____

_____

_____

_____

_____

_____

_____

_____

component *(n):*
a part; an element

discipline *(n):*
an area of study or research

metaphysical *(adj):*
highly abstract; relating to
the nature of existence and
knowledge

framework *(n):*
the basic structure for a system
of thought

foretell *(v):*
to predict; to tell what will
happen in the future

static *(adj):*
unchanging

confirm *(v):*
to verify; to affirm the truth of

coin *(v):*
to give a name

underlying *(adj):*
underneath; basic

conundrum *(n):*
a difficult or unanswerable
problem; a paradox

dialectics *(n):*
the process of finding the truth
by examining opposite logical
arguments

1. The professor discusses different disciplines within cosmology. Put them in the order he discusses them.

Order: 1. ____ → 2. ____ → 3. ____

(A) Where are we going?
(B) Where did we come from?
(C) Why are we here?

2. Why does the professor mention the Big Bang?
(A) As an example of advancement in physical cosmology
(B) As an example of advancement in metaphysical cosmology
(C) To explain what is wrong with religious cosmology
(D) To disprove the cosmological argument

3. According to the professor, what does metaphysical cosmology use to understand the universe?
(A) Religious texts
(B) Scientific data
(C) Dialectics
(D) All of the above

4. What does the speaker mean when he says this: ∩ ?
(A) Physical cosmology is old-fashioned.
(B) Religious cosmology is correct.
(C) Scientists know less about the universe than they used to.
(D) Scientists know more about the universe than they used to.

Review A – F

Vocabulary Review

Skill Review

Vocabulary Review

Instructions: Choose the best word or phrase to complete each sentence.

1. After seeing this new evidence, I will have to _____ my opposition to this theory.

   (A) garner
   (B) re-evaluate
   (C) designate
   (D) predict

2. I don't know how to swim, so I'm going to try to _____ everyone to go to the mountains instead of the beach.

   (A) commute
   (B) convince
   (C) corrupt
   (D) confirm

3. One hour is the _____ of sixty minutes.

   (A) equivalent
   (B) policy
   (C) rationale
   (D) motivation

4. The university _____ campus crime statistics as the reason for increased spending on security guards.

   (A) typifies
   (B) re-evaluates
   (C) cites
   (D) appeals

5. The fall of the Roman Empire _____ the start of the Middle Ages by a short period of time.

   (A) preceded
   (B) disrupted
   (C) corrupted
   (D) delegated

6. Societies have many different _____ to government. Some believe in a government that controls most aspects of daily life, while others believe in a government that allows more individual freedom.

   (A) climates
   (B) metabolisms
   (C) indicators
   (D) approaches

7. Several of Shakespeare's works are _____ of earlier, Italian works.

   (A) drafts
   (B) derivatives
   (C) hemispheres
   (D) malfunctions

8. My term paper is _____ tomorrow, but I haven't started yet. I'm going to have to work all night!

   (A) reliable
   (B) due
   (C) ample
   (D) lethal

9. You should not take more than the _____ recommended by your doctor. You might get even more sick than you already are.

   (A) dose
   (B) policy
   (C) rapport
   (D) prerogative

10. "Thanks for driving me home. I hope I didn't _____ you at all." "No problem. It didn't take long."

    (A) deny
    (B) minimize
    (C) compensate
    (D) inconvenience

11. The president has a massive army at his _____. He can use it as he sees fit.

(A) admiral
(B) disposal
(C) foothold
(D) wealth

12. The government sometimes grants money to _____ soldiers who are injured in war.

(A) compensate
(B) subdue
(C) access
(D) replicate

13. _____ car buyers should closely examine all the possible cars on the market before spending a lot of money on one.

(A) Compelling
(B) Metaphysical
(C) Dissonant
(D) Prospective

14. Animal species that can best _____ to environmental changes have the best chance of surviving.

(A) adapt
(B) precede
(C) disguise
(D) bond

15. After the hurricane, the city needed a lot of _____ help to pay for repairs to roads and buildings.

(A) medical
(B) disheartening
(C) substandard
(D) financial

Instructions: Choose the word or phrase closest in meaning to the underlined part.

16. This new computer chip could <u>possibly</u> change the way people use their home computers.

(A) legally
(B) dramatically
(C) permanently
(D) potentially

17. Twentieth century developments in music theory offered a new and <u>unique</u> musical experience for audiences.

(A) diluted
(B) distinct
(C) dissonant
(D) derivative

18. The newspaper <u>predicts</u> heavy snowfall for the mountain regions this weekend.

(A) forecasts
(B) inspects
(C) counts on
(D) subdues

19. My uncle is a history <u>expert</u>, but he is not a professional historian.

(A) rehearsal
(B) buff
(C) boulevard
(D) admiral

20. A mother lion takes great care of her <u>children</u>.

(A) offspring
(B) malaises
(C) disciplines
(D) dialectics

21. The strange fossil remains found in Brazil were a real puzzle for paleontologists.

    (A) conundrum
    (B) component
    (C) vocation
    (D) acumen

22. The government named this coastal area a national wildlife reserve last year.

    (A) sympathized
    (B) based on
    (C) checked out
    (D) designated

23. Not everyone with the same last name is related.

    (A) framework
    (B) discipline
    (C) surname
    (D) symptom

24. The survey was intended to elicit descriptions of how parents care for children.

    (A) disguise
    (B) induce
    (C) nurture
    (D) compensate

25. The food in this cafeteria is disgusting. I recommend you eat elsewhere.

    (A) vending
    (B) underlying
    (C) revolting
    (D) disheartening

26. I made a mistake when hooking up my computer, and now it's going to cost me $500 to fix it!

    (A) garnered
    (B) screwed up
    (C) typified
    (D) kicked out

27. The fire alarm interrupted our math class this afternoon.

    (A) cashed in
    (B) corrupted
    (C) delegated
    (D) disrupted

28. One key characteristic of most carnivores is the presence of large, sharp teeth.

    (A) attribute
    (B) foothold
    (C) fleet
    (D) contraction

29. I never understood my brother's reason for leaving university to join the army.

    (A) malaise
    (B) remonstrance
    (C) rationale
    (D) reunion

30. My chemistry prof is so dependable. She's always on time for class and strictly keeps her office hours.

    (A) available
    (B) suitable
    (C) reliable
    (D) adaptable

Instructions: Write the missing words. Use the words below to fill in the blanks.

malfunction	hazard	indigestion	species	wise up
metabolism	lethal	revolting	procreate	toxicity

There are three main categories of **(31)** _____ in plants: extreme, moderate, and minimal. The severity of the poison in plants, however, depends on a host of factors, like the particular species and the **(32)** _____ of the person who consumes it. In fact, the term "poisoning" itself is also misleading. Poisoning does not only mean that the substance consumed is **(33)** _____ to humans. Poisoning can result in anything from **(34)** _____ and skin irritation to a major **(35)** _____ of internal organs. Poison can occur in plants as a by-product of one of the plant's natural life processes and sometimes the poison serves as a defense mechanism for the plant. Animals learn which plants represent a **(36)** _____ because the taste is **(37)** _____ or because they get sick after eating them. The animals then **(38)** _____ and avoid eating the plant in the future. Thus, the plant species will survive to **(39)** _____. This allows the population of the **(40)** _____ to flourish.

Instructions: Write the missing words. Use the words below to fill in the blanks.

on	up	down	out	overboard

41. Hi, John. You look _____. What's wrong?

42. I know your grade was lower than you expected, but don't go _____. You shouldn't quit university!

43. Newton's theory is based _____ the principle that light is a wave.

44. Hey, don't you know that you can get kicked _____ of the dorms for bringing in beer?

45. Maybe if you butter _____ your parents, they will buy you a new computer for Christmas.

Instructions: Write the letter choice for the opposite word in the blank.

46. _____ carnivore   (A) delete

47. _____ marvelous   (B) intensify

48. _____ replicate   (C) herbivore

49. _____ mute   (D) counterintuitive

50. _____ obvious   (E) terrible

Notes

Glossary
bare bones *(n phrase)*: the basic ideas; the fundamentals
silicate *(n)*: a compound with silicon as a part of it
exclude *(v)*: to not include; to leave out
plasma *(n)*: a state of matter found in lightning and stars
inorganic *(adj)*: not living or from a living organism
exemplify *(v)*: to stand as an example; to show
polymorph *(n)*: a substance that can appear in different forms
analogy *(n)*: a comparison based on similarity
grasp *(v)*: to understand
reverse *(adj)*: opposite
layman's terms *(n phrase)*: everyday language; not scientific words
suspended *(adj)*: supported within; not sinking

1. How does the professor explain the term "polymorph"? Choose 2 answers.
   - (A) She explains its chronological development throughout recent history.
   - (B) She defines it.
   - (C) She compares it to marble and statues.
   - (D) She brainstorms possible meanings.

2. According to the professor, why is it odd for people to think of ice as a mineral?
   - (A) We eat it too often.
   - (B) We forget that minerals take only one form.
   - (C) We have little experience.
   - (D) We usually only think about minerals that look like metal or rock.

3. Listen to part of the lecture. Then answer the question. ∩
   What can be inferred about the student?
   - (A) He isn't sure about the professor's exact words.
   - (B) He is confident that he has remembered correctly.
   - (C) He has no idea, but he is guessing.
   - (D) He is a good student.

4. Based on the information in the talk, indicate whether each phrase below describes a mineral or a non-mineral.

	Mineral	Non-mineral
(A) Exists in a liquid state		
(B) Is an organic compound		
(C) Always has the same composition		
(D) Can be a mixture of an element and a compound		

5. Listen again to part of the lecture. Then answer the question.

What will the professor discuss next?

(A) The uses of minerals
(B) Plasma forms of minerals
(C) The uses of ice
(D) Liquid chemical compounds

6. In the lecture, the professor describes the criteria for classifying something as a mineral. Put the criteria in the order in which they are mentioned.

Order: 1. _____ → 2. _____ → 3. _____ → 4. _____

(A) It must be inorganic.
(B) It must be either an element or a compound, not a mixture of the two.
(C) It must be naturally occurring.
(D) It must exist in a solid state.

Notes

_____

_____

_____

_____

_____

_____

_____

_____

_____

_____

_____

_____

go into *(v phrase)*:
to get a job or career in

women's shelter *(n phrase)*:
a place where women who are victims of domestic violence can stay safely

endeavor *(n)*:
a purposeful activity; an enterprise

hasty *(adj)*:
rushed; in a hurry

set down *(v phrase)*:
to create

catch up *(v phrase)*:
to move or work quickly enough to attain the same progress as others

hold off *(v phrase)*:
to wait; to delay

methodology *(n)*:
a set of procedures and rules used by people who work in a given field

enthusiastic *(adj)*:
showing great excitement and interest

slip *(n)*:
a piece of paper with written information; a form

1. Why does the woman go to see her professor?
   (A) She needs an extension on the deadline for her thesis abstract.
   (B) She wants some advice about changing her major.
   (C) She wants permission to take a class that is already full.
   (D) She needs to take a required prerequisite course that is full.

2. What are the two courses that the woman has already completed? Choose 2 answers.
   (A) Statistics
   (B) Chemistry
   (C) Introduction to psychology
   (D) Research methods and design
   (E) Developmental psychology
   (F) Social work

3. What is the professor's attitude toward the student?
   (A) He thinks she is not a good student.
   (B) He likes her enthusiasm.
   (C) He thinks she shouldn't study developmental psychology.
   (D) He is annoyed that she is wasting his time.

4. Are these statements true about the student? Click in the YES or NO column.

	Yes	No
(A) She wants to be a chemistry major.		
(B) She is in her third year at university.		
(C) She wants to help children in her future job.		
(D) She wants to specialize in developmental psychology.		

5. What does the speaker mean when he says this: 🎧 ?

(A) Most students decide their specializations before the third year.

(B) He is about to go home for the day.

(C) The student is too late to take his course.

(D) He is in a hurry to watch a football game.

6. The professor describes the steps the student should follow. Put the steps in the correct order.

Order: 1. _____ → 2. _____ → 3. _____

(A) Take a permission slip to the registration office

(B) Take a developmental psychology course

(C) Take statistics and research methods

proficiency (n):
the state of being able to do
something very well

neglect (v):
to forget to do; to not pay
attention to

notorious (adj):
famous for bad actions or
character; infamous

blow out of proportion (v phrase):
to exaggerate excessively

inefficient (adj):
slow and not effective

deconstruct (v):
to take apart for the purpose of
examination

economy (n):
the performance of an action
without spending too much energy

constitute (v):
to make up; to compose; to be
the parts of

get it (v phrase):
to understand

uniform (adj):
consistent; always the same

fluid (adj):
smooth; effortless

1. How does the coach explain the arm movements of the butterfly stroke? Choose 2 answers.

   (A) By demonstrating the movements herself
   (B) By telling a story about a swimmer
   (C) By contrasting them with the arm movements of other strokes
   (D) By classifying the movements into phases

2. According to the professor, what shape should the arms follow during the pull?

   (A) A straight line
   (B) A semicircle
   (C) A circle
   (D) An oval

3. Listen to part of the conversation. Then answer the question. ∩
   What is the instructor's opinion of the butterfly stroke?

   (A) She thinks the butterfly is a difficult stroke.
   (B) She thinks the butterfly is not as hard as people think.
   (C) She thinks the butterfly is an easy stroke.
   (D) She thinks children should not do the butterfly.

4. Match each motion with the correct phase.

Push	Recovery	Pull

(A) The palm catches the water.
(B) The arms swing sideways.
(C) The palms move backward through the water.

5. What will the students probably do next?

(A) Take a physical exam
(B) Study for a physical exam
(C) Practice the butterfly stroke
(D) Practice the breast stroke

6. The coach explains how to do arm movement for a certain stroke. Summarize the process by putting the steps in order.

Order: 1. _____ → 2. _____ → 3. _____ → 4. _____

(A) Repeat
(B) Pull
(C) Push
(D) Recovery

Notes

| constitutional *(adj)*: |
| related to a system of fundamental laws and principles |
| **impose** *(v)*: |
| to force upon |
| **principal** *(adj)*: |
| of great importance; chief |
| **candidate** *(n)*: |
| a person eligible for a certain position |
| **excommunicate** *(v)*: |
| to force out of a (usually religious) organization |
| **take hold of** *(v phrase)*: |
| to capture; to seize |
| **fed up** *(adj phrase)*: |
| tired of; unable to tolerate any longer |
| **vow** *(n)*: |
| a promise; an oath |
| **irrelevant** *(adj)*: |
| not related to the topic; unimportant |
| **contemporary** *(adj)*: |
| modern; current |
| **overrule** *(v)*: |
| to decide to rule against; to reverse the decision of another |
| **renounce** *(v)*: |
| to reject; to disown |

1. How does the professor explain the Magna Carta? Choose 2 answers.

   (A) She defines it.
   (B) She gives two examples.
   (C) She brainstorms two possible meanings.
   (D) She compares it to other forms of documents.
   (E) She explains its development.

2. According to the professor, how many times did King John fail as a king?

   (A) 1
   (B) 2
   (C) 3
   (D) 4

3. Why does the professor mention the nickname "Lackland"?

   (A) To show how English barons lacked respect for the king
   (B) To remind students of the king's family name
   (C) To illustrate a common practice of the 13th century
   (D) To demonstrate King John's characteristic sense of humor

4. In which century did these events occur?

	12ᵗʰ Century	13ᵗʰ Century
(A) John became king.		
(B) Richard the Lionheart died.		
(C) The Magna Carta was signed.		
(D) Henry became king.		

5. What does the professor imply when she says this: ( ) ?
(A) The barons were more powerful than the king.
(B) The barons feared the authority of the king.
(C) The king was more powerful than the barons.
(D) The barons agreed with all of the king's decisions.

6. The speaker explains a sequence of events. Put the events in the correct order.

Order: 1. ___ → 2. ___ → 3. ___ → 4. ___ → 5. ___

(A) King John lost a lot of land in Normandy.
(B) The barons forced King John to sign a document.
(C) John murdered Arthur.
(D) John was excommunicated by the Church of England.
(E) Article 61 was removed from the Magna Carta.

Chapter 3

Focus: Note-taking

Focus | Note-taking

Tips

When note-taking

- Use the organization of a lecture: introduction, body (point-by-point or comparison/contrast), and summary. Then, you can easily categorize the lecture for your notes.
- Pay special attention to the introduction to get an idea of the topic and the organization of the lecture. You can use this information as a road map to listen more effectively. The summary by the speaker is critical when checking for missed information.
- Think ahead. Anticipate what the speaker might say next.
- Take notes of the major points and connections. Try not to get lost in minor points and details.
- Do not try to write everything down. It may lead to distraction or confusion about the focus of the lecture.
- Try to take notes in your own words. It will help you summarize the lecture later.

Helpful techniques for note-taking

- Use margins to keep a key to important names, dates, formulas, etc. on one side and the outline on the other. Draw arrows for connecting or ordering ideas.
- Note the organization of the passage, whether it uses contrast, comparison, etc. It may be effective to use a column (just a vertical line between two categories) to group information.
- Create topic headings and indent subtopics.
- Listen for cues such as transitional words, repetition of certain phrases, changes in voice, or number of points.
- Use abbreviations and symbols for commonly occurring words and names. It will increase your note-taking speed.
- Use diagrams, pictures, or webs where necessary.
- Group related ideas with brackets and arrows.
- Make your notes neat and legible enough for your own reading. Do not be concerned about how they look to others.
- Develop your own system and your own abbreviations. You can even create abbreviations with your native language if it is more effective.

Focus A - Note-taking for Conversations  **01** Guided Practice

1. Campus Life

Directions: Listen and take notes on the important information in the conversation.

Woman	Man
situation:_____ _____	suggestion: _____ _____ benefits: _____ _____

Now use your notes to complete the summary.

The woman and the man talk about _____. The man suggests that the woman _____. One benefit of _____ is that the woman can _____. Another benefit is that _____. The woman says that she will _____.

2. Campus Life

Directions: Listen and take notes on the important information in the conversation.

Woman	Man
wants to:_____ _____ _____ _____ _____ _____	how: _____ can use: _____ submit papers: _____ receive feedback:_____ submit: _____ security: _____

Now use your notes to complete the summary.

The woman and the man talk about _____. One thing the man mentions is _____. For this service, students can _____. Students should _____ in order to _____. The woman plans to _____.

Focus A - Note-taking for Conversations

02 Self Practice

1. Campus Life

Directions: Listen and take notes on the important information in the conversation. 🎧

_____

_____

_____

_____

Now use your notes to complete the summary.

The woman and the man talk about _____. The first thing that the man should do is _____. Next, he should _____. Then, he needs to _____. The man should _____ in order to _____. The last step is to _____.

2. Campus Life

Directions: Listen and take notes on the important information in the conversation. 🎧

_____

_____

_____

_____

Now use your notes to complete the summary.

The woman's problem is that _____. The man suggests two things to the woman. First, he says she should _____. The woman thinks that _____. Next, he suggests that the woman _____ _____. The woman thinks that this is _____. She plans to _____.

Focus B - Note-taking for Lectures 01   Guided Practice

1. Geography

Directions: Listen and take notes on the important information in the lecture. ⌒

Topic: Effect of the _____ on the _____

I. _____
   A. _____   B. _____

II. _____
   A. _____   III. _____
   B. _____   A. _____
   C. _____   B. _____
        C. _____

Now use your notes to complete the summary.

This lecture is about the effect of the _____ on the _____. This idea was first suggested by _____, who also came up with _____. The professor talks about _____. These have been _____. They seem to cause _____. They might be related to _____, but _____. The professor also talks about the effect that _____ has on _____. He says _____ causes _____ _____. This is because _____.

2. Earth Science

Directions: Listen and take notes on the important information in the lecture. ⌒

The Five _____

1. _____
  - _____
2. _____
  - _____
3. _____
  - _____

4. _____
  - _____
5. _____
  - _____
Ex: _____!

Now use your notes to complete the summary.

In this lecture, the professor gives five _____. The first _____ is that it _____. The second _____ is that it _____. The third _____ is that it _____. The fourth _____ is that it _____. The fifth _____ is that it _____. The example of a _____ discussed in class is _____!

Focus B - Note-taking for Lectures 02   Self Practice

1. Biology

Directions: Listen and take notes on the important information in the lecture. 🎧

_____

_____

_____

_____

Now use your notes to complete the summary.

In this lecture, the professor talks about _____. She says that lots of people were _____ even _____, but _____.
The professor gives three _____, but she also says that _____. Three particular types of _____ mentioned in the lecture are _____. The professor explains something about the _____ in each type of _____ and _____.

2. Literature

Directions: Listen and take notes on the important information in the lecture. 🎧

_____

_____

_____

_____

Now use your notes to complete the summary.

This lecture is about _____. The professor begins by talking about _____ _____. Next, he explains that _____.
Each _____ in the book is followed by _____.
In order to write the book, _____, but he didn't _____.
Throughout history, people have _____ the book, including people like _____ and _____. However, in _____, the book _____ because _____.

Mastering Skills for the TOEFL® iBT

SPEAKING

SPEAKING Table of Contents

How the speaking section is organized

There are four main parts in the speaking section.

Introduction   Understanding what each section requires you to do
Chapter 1   Practicing organizing and synthesizing information
Chapter 2   Developing coherence
Chapter 3   Focusing on clarity of speech
Practice Test   Practicing with questions designed according to the real test format

Speaking

The prompts for speaking questions on the TOEFL® iBT can be categorized into six types:

Question	Time			
	Reading	Listening	Preparation	Speaking
Independent Q1			15 seconds	45 seconds
Independent Q2				
Integrated Q3	45 seconds	1-2 minutes	30 seconds	60 seconds
Integrated Q4				
Integrated Q5		1-2 minutes	30 seconds	60 seconds
Integrated Q6				

The purpose of the speaking section is to evaluate your ability to speak coherently both on your opinions and experiences as well as on information that you have read or have heard. The speaking questions fall into two categories, independent and integrated. For the two independent speaking questions, you should draw upon your own experience and knowledge. For the remaining four speaking questions, you will speak about what you read and/or hear. Your ideas need to be well-organized and the language you speak needs to be accurate enough to be easily understood.

In particular, each question type will require test-takers to organize their ideas and speak toward different goals:

Question	Task	Materials	Length	Tasks
1	Independent	none		Describe your experience.
2	Independent	none		Give your opinion and explain why you think this.
3	Integrated	Reading Conversation	100 words 200 words 60-90 seconds	Restate the opinion of the speaker and the examples used.
4	Integrated	Reading Lecture	100 words 200 words 60-90 seconds	Explain how the example from the lecture supports the passage.
5	Conversation-based	Conversation	300 words 90-120 seconds	Restate suggestions and tell which you think is better.
6	Lecture-based	Lecture	300 words 90-120 seconds	Summarize what you heard.

Study Tips for Speaking

- Master the North American English phonetic system as best you can. Pay special attention to difficult distinctions such as: b/v, f/p, r/l, s/th, j/z, s/sh, the vowel sounds in *bat/bet*, *it/eat*, and *shirt/short*. Also, practice pronouncing the diphthongs (combined vowels) as one short, continuous sound rather than two separate ones. These include the sounds in the following: *hey*, *bye*, *boy*, and *go*.
- Practice speaking with a North American inflection. This involves moving the lips and opening the mouth more and speaking more from the mouth and nose than from the back of the throat.
- Practice using the pauses and intonations you learn when studying for the listening section.
- Practice speaking at home. Use one of the independent writing topics as a speaking topic. Give yourself 15 seconds of preparation time. Use this time to think of your main idea and details/examples to support it. Speak for approximately 45 seconds on the topic. (Also practice with 30 seconds of preparation time and 1 minute of speaking time, as this will be the case for the integrated exercises.)

Test Management

You will speak into a microphone attached to a headset.

Independent Speaking questions come first.

You can take notes and then use your notes when preparing your response.

Check the time with the clock shown in the title bar.

How Speaking Will Be Scored

ETS graders will score test-takers' responses according to the following scale:

Score	General Description	Key Points
4	The response answers the question or prompt well. The speaker is easy to understand and there are only minor mistakes with grammar or pronunciation.	Fluent speech that is easy to understand and follow, appropriate use of grammar and vocabulary, ideas explained clearly
3	The response answers the question or prompt, but not all of the ideas are fully developed. The speaker can be understood, but there are some clearly noticeable mistakes in speaking.	At least two (2) of these problems: pronunciation, pace of speech, wrong word choice, limited use of grammar structures, or incorrect grammar
2	The response gives only a basic or minimal answer to the question or prompt. Most sentences can be understood, but some effort is required by the listener because speech is not fluent and pronunciation is not accurate. Some ideas are not clearly explained.	At least two (2) of these problems: speech is choppy (not fluent), mistakes in pronunciation, wrong word choice, only use basic grammar, poor use of grammar, only basic ideas are presented, explanation is absent or limited
1	The response is very short, does not show full understanding of the question or prompt, and is hard for the listener to understand.	At least two (2) of these problems: poor pronunciation, speech is choppy (not fluent), long or frequent pauses, poor grammar makes ideas difficult to understand, use of obviously practiced or formulaic expressions, lots of repetition of expressions in the prompt
0	There is no response or the response is not related to the question or prompt.	No response to grade or response is not related to the question or prompt

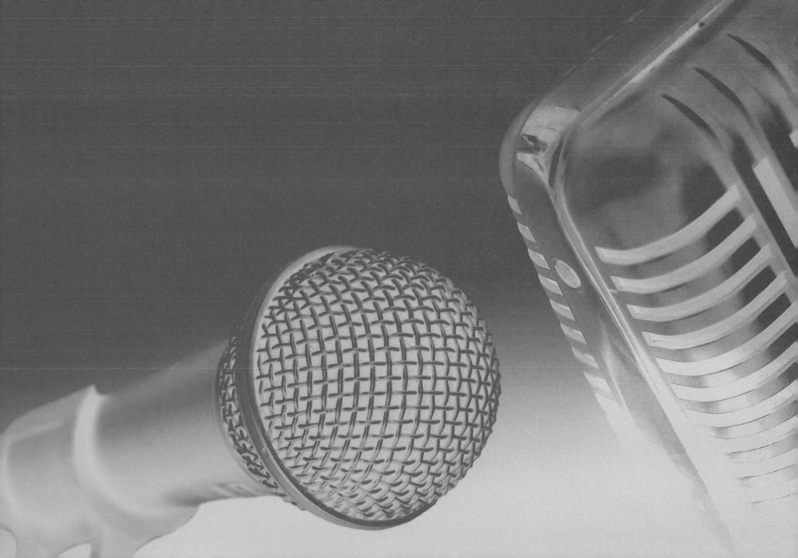

Chapter 1

Thinking and Speaking

Necessary Skills

- Describing a personal experience or expressing a personal preference
- Organizing ideas
- Expressing a clear topic statement and the supporting points
- Speaking clearly and accurately with knowledge of grammar, vocabulary, and pronunciation

Strategies

- Though preparation time is limited in the speaking portion of the test, it is nevertheless important to use this time in planning the organization of your response. In this way, your response will be more relevant and coherent. An organizational process for preparing your speech is detailed below. In each step, there are certain things that you need to keep in mind.

Process	Strategy
Read the question and understand the task	Be sure that you understand the question and what the question requires you to do.
Decide on the topic statement	Decide on the main idea or choose one of the positions. Use the relevant parts of the prompt in making up your topic statement.
Brainstorm and select supporting ideas	Quickly think of the supporting ideas from your experience. Choose those ideas that most clearly support your topic statement.
Organize the ideas	Arrange your ideas, putting them in order from most to least important.

Skill A Q1 Practice 1 – Personal Experience

Read the question. Write down your answer and related key points in the blanks.

> Tell about a person you admire who had an influence on your life. What specific characteristics do you admire in this person and in what ways has he or she influenced you?

The person I admire most is _____.

Many difficulties when He grew-up.

Characteristics I admire: _honest — working-hard—man—_
_____ he was a proffesional bycicle rider
_____ for almost 14 years he had many
_____ accidentes, but he always
Ways he/she has influenced me: _____ also _____
_____ perseverance.
_____

_____

Read the related ideas and expressions below. Add at least two of your own.

Related Ideas and Expressions

mentor:

guide, role model, hero, _____, _____

admire:

respect, esteem, revere, _____, _____

influence:

inspire, affect, compel, _____, _____

characteristics:

perseverance, dignity, virtue, _____, _____
Perseviriang-

mentor (n):
a respected person who guides and teaches

revere (v):
to admire greatly

compel (v):
to make somebody do something; to exert strong pressure or influence on

perseverance (n):
the quality of continuing to work at something despite difficulties and challenges

virtue (n):
the quality of moral excellence and righteousness; goodness

Step 2

Now create your own response using words and expressions from Step 1. Use the prompts below to help you.

_____ is my _____ for several reasons. First, he/she _____

_____. That, however, is not the only reason I _____. He/She also

_____. When _____, it

changed my life. He/She inspired me to _____.

His/Her qualities of _____ compelled

me to _____.

Step 3

Listen to the sample response and compare it with your response above. Make notes about the differences you hear.

Notes

Step 4

Review the response you wrote in Step 2 and your notes in Step 3. Then close your book and give a response to the question below. Say the response slowly and clearly. Try to speak for at least 60 seconds.

Tell about a person you admire who had an influence on your life. What specific characteristics do you admire in this person and in what ways has he or she influenced you?

Skill A Q1 Practice 2 – Personal Experience

Step 1

Read the question. Write down your answer and related key points in the blanks.

> Describe a specific instance in which technology has helped you in your schoolwork. Include details in your description.

Type of technology that helped me: _Computer, improve my studies_ _I send pictures, & technology_

Why I needed it: _to study, my daugther. find easy subject_

How it helped: _and my family._

What I would have to do without it: _I lived in ≠ country I can see my family_

Read the related ideas and expressions below. Add at least two of your own.

Related Ideas and Expressions

technology:

computers, gadgets, media, _____, _____

obstacle:

learning disability, dyslexia, hindrance, _____, _____

overcome:

beat, conquer, excel, _____, _____

help:

aid, assist, support, _____, _____

---

gadget (n):
a small tool or appliance, often electronic

learning disability (n phrase):
a disorder found in children of normal intelligence, causing difficulties in learning specific skills

dyslexia (n):
a disorder marked by difficulty in recognizing the order of written letters and words, thus making reading a challenge

hindrance (n):
a problem or impediment that slows the progress of

excel (v):
to perform better than others or better than expected

Step 2

Now create your own response using words and expressions from Step 1. Use the prompts below to help you.

One _____ that has helped me with schoolwork is _____. To begin,

I _____

The _____ was of great assistance to me. It _____.

I used it _____. Without it, I _____

_____. Because of my _____, I was able to _____.

Step 3

Listen to the sample response and compare it with your response above. Make notes about the differences you hear.

Notes

_____

_____

_____

_____

Step 4

Review the response you wrote in Step 2 and your notes in Step 3. Then close your book and give a response to the question below. Say the response slowly and clearly. Try to speak for at least 60 seconds.

Describe a specific instance in which technology has helped you in your schoolwork. Include details in your description.

Skill A Q1 Practice 3 – Personal Experience

Step 1

Read the question. Write down your answer and related key points in the blanks.

> Many children all over the world spend a great deal of time playing sports. Has your own experience with youth sports been positive or negative? Give specific reasons and details as to how playing sports has helped or harmed you.

Some sports I have practiced were: _____

_____

I feel that this has (helped/hurt) _____ me because:

Reason 1: _____

Details: _____

Reason 2: _____

Details: _____

Read the related ideas and expressions below. Add at least two of your own.

Related Ideas and Expressions

benefit:

gain, be better off, advantage, _____, _____

hurt:

hinder, negate, damage, _____, _____

important:

chief, crucial, integral, _____, _____

health:

endurance, strength, stamina, _____, _____

---

better off *(adj phrase)*:
in a better situation or condition

hinder *(v)*:
to impede; to slow the progress of

negate *(v)*:
to make ineffective; to counteract

chief *(adj)*:
main; principal

crucial *(adj)*:
very important; essential

stamina *(n)*:
the ability to perform exercise for a long period of time; endurance

---

Step 2

Now create your own response using words and expressions from Step 1. Use the prompts below to help you.

When I was a child, I used to _____. I feel that practicing

_____. The chief _____ was that competing in _____

_____. Playing _____

_____. _____, on the other hand, _____

_____. Developing a _____ when I was young

has _____.

Step 3

🎧 Listen to the sample response and compare it with your response above. Make notes about the differences you hear.

Notes

_____

_____

_____

_____

Step 4

Review the response you wrote in Step 2 and your notes in Step 3. Then close your book and give a response to the question below. Say the response slowly and clearly. Try to speak for at least 60 seconds.

> Many children all over the world spend a great deal of time playing sports. Has your own experience with youth sports been positive or negative? Give specific reasons and details as to how playing sports has helped or harmed you.

Skill A Q2 Practice 1 – Personal Preference

Step 1

Read the question. Write down your answer and related key points in the blanks.

> Do you agree or disagree with the following statement? High schools should allow students to study the courses that students want to study. Use specific reasons and examples to support your opinion.

I agree/disagree with _____

Reason 1: _____

Example: _____

Reason 2: _____

Example: _____

Read the related ideas and expressions below. Add at least two of your own.

Related Ideas and Expressions

allow:

permit, let, give permission, _____, _____

control:

select, in charge, destiny, _____, _____

enjoy:

crave, find diverting, be interested in, _____, _____

course:

subjects, curriculum, path, _____, _____

in charge (adj phrase):
in control; able to lead and make choices

destiny (n):
the events that will occur in one's life; fate

crave (v):
to want strongly

diverting (adj):
entertaining; fun

curriculum (n):
the group of subjects studied at school and their schedule of study

Step 2

Now create your own response using words and expressions from Step 1. Use the prompts below to help you.

In my opinion, _____.

This ensures _____. If, for example,

_____.

In the long run, _____.

Obviously, if _____.

Step 3

Listen to two sample responses and compare them with your response above. Make notes about the differences you hear.

Notes

_____

_____

_____

_____

Step 4

Review the response you wrote in Step 2 and your notes in Step 3. Then close your book and give a response to the question below. Say the response slowly and clearly. Try to speak for at least 60 seconds.

> Do you agree or disagree with the following statement? High schools should allow students to study the courses that students want to study. Use specific reasons and examples to support your opinion.

Skill A Q2 Practice 2 – Personal Preference

Step 1

Read the question. Write down your answer and related key points in the blanks.

> Some celebrities use their fame to influence society with their views. Some people are strongly affected by these celebrities, while other people believe the public should not pay attention to these views just because they come from rich and well-known members of society. With which opinion do you agree? Use specific reasons and examples to support your answer.

In my view, people _____ pay attention to the opinions expressed by celebrities.

Reason 1: _____

Example: _____

Reason 2: _____

Example: _____

Read the related ideas and expressions below. Add at least two of your own.

Related Ideas and Expressions

famous:

renowned, expert, erudite, _____, _____

opinions:

cynical, views, commentary, _____, _____

listen to:

pay attention to, heed, give credence to, _____, _____

influence:

sway, affect, persuade, _____, _____

expert (adj):
having great skill or knowledge

erudite (adj):
having or requiring a high level of knowledge or learning

cynical (adj):
skeptical; pessimistic

heed (v):
to listen to and follow the advice of

give credence to (v phrase):
to treat with respect and legitimacy; to believe and support

Step 2

Now create your own response using words and expressions from Step 1. Use the prompts below to help you.

Some celebrities _____, while others _____.

In my opinion, _____. After all,

_____.

Some _____.

However, _____.

Step 3

Listen to two sample responses and compare them with your response above. Make notes about the differences you hear.

Notes

Step 4

Review the response you wrote in Step 2 and your notes in Step 3. Then close your book and give a response to the question below. Say the response slowly and clearly. Try to speak for at least 60 seconds.

Some celebrities use their fame to influence society with their views. Some people are strongly affected by these celebrities, while other people believe the public should not pay attention to these views just because they come from rich and well-known members of society. With which opinion do you agree? Use specific reasons and examples to support your answer.

Skill A Q2 Practice 3 — Personal Preference

Step 1

Read the question. Write down your answer and related key points in the blanks.

> Do you agree or disagree with the following statement? Children should be required to help with household tasks as soon as they are able to do so. Use specific reasons and examples to support your answer.

I believe children _____.

Reason 1: _____

Details: _____

Reason 2: _____

Details: _____

Read the related ideas and expressions below. Add at least two of your own.

Related Ideas and Expressions

required:

obligated, made to, forced, _____, _____

household tasks:

chores, housework, domestic work, _____, _____

help out:

pitch in, lend a hand, lift a finger, _____, _____

responsibility:

competency, maturity, diligence, _____, _____

chore *(n)*:
a small piece of work often performed on a regular schedule

domestic *(adj)*:
related to the house or home country

pitch in *(v phrase)*:
to help others perform a certain task

lift a finger *(v phrase)*:
to work; to make an effort

maturity *(n)*:
the state of being responsible and adult-like

Step 2

Now create your own response using words and expressions from Step 1. Use the prompts below to help you.

Some children _____, while others _____.

I personally feel _____.

This _____ them _____. Children who _____

_____. Parents may think _____,

but in the long run, _____.

Step 3

Listen to two sample responses and compare them with your response above. Make notes about the differences you hear.

Notes

Step 4

Review the response you wrote in Step 2 and your notes in Step 3. Then close your book and give a response to the question below. Say the response slowly and clearly. Try to speak for at least 60 seconds.

Do you agree or disagree with the following statement? Children should be required to help with household tasks as soon as they are able to do so. Use specific reasons and examples to support your answer.

Skill A Independent Speaking: Organizing Speech

Q1 - Practice 1

Lance Armstrong is my role model for several reasons. First, he is a cyclist who has won the Tour de France seven times in a row. That, however, is not the only reason I respect this man. He also battled cancer. When I heard his story, it changed my life. Lance Armstrong inspired me to never give up on my dream of going to the Olympics, even though it may seem impossible. His qualities of endurance and perseverance compelled me to become a better athlete and a stronger person.

Q1 - Practice 2

One gadget that has helped me with schoolwork is my "reading pen." To begin, I have dyslexia, a learning disability that makes reading very difficult. The reading pen was of great assistance to me. It scans words on a page and reads them out loud to me. I used it every day to help me with my reading assignments. Without it, I would have spent hours reading my assignments and wouldn't have had time to study properly. Because of my reading pen, I was able to excel in school.

Q1 - Practice 3

When I was a child, I used to play soccer and baseball. I feel that practicing these sports helped me greatly. The chief benefit was that competing in these sports made my body healthy, instilling me with endurance and strength. Playing baseball developed my upper body strength for hitting and throwing. Soccer, on the other hand, provided me with lower body strength for kicking and stamina and endurance for playing full 90-minute games. Developing a strong, healthy body when I was young has been crucial in maintaining my health later in life.

Q2 - Practice 1

Opinion 1:

In my opinion, high school students should be required to follow a certain curriculum. This ensures students are exposed to a wide variety of subjects. If, for example, I had been permitted to select whatever courses I wanted, I would only have taken courses that I found diverting. In the long run, this would have limited my ability to pursue a medical career, which is what I'm doing now. Obviously, if I had been left to my own devices about choosing my courses, I would not be where I am today.

Opinion 2:

In my opinion, educators should let high school students decide which courses they want to study. This ensures that all students are in charge of their own destinies, and they should be permitted to determine their own academic paths. If, for example, a student prefers art to science, why should she waste her time studying science? In the long run, her efforts would be better spent on developing skills in a field that interests her. Obviously, if she has to direct part of her energy toward a course she doesn't like, she will have less time and energy to put toward her real interests.

Q2 - Practice 2

Opinion 1:

Some celebrities become rich and famous and then return very little to society, while others attempt to use their influence to raise public awareness of a special cause, such as environmentalism or human rights. In my opinion, we are all better off heeding the expert advice of professionals and officials. After all, how much can a pop star really know about solving problems in Africa? Some people say stars can do a lot if they get behind a particular cause, and there may be some truth to that. However, expecting an erudite opinion from a pop star about health issues in Nigeria is a different matter.

Opinion 2:

Some celebrities become rich and famous and then return very little to society, while others attempt to use their influence to raise public awareness of a special cause, such as environmentalism or human rights. In my opinion, the least the public can do is carefully consider these views. After all, a person living at the top of society probably has a much better view of it and can see problems that normal people cannot. Some cynics contend that people should ignore well-known artists when they express their thoughts on global issues. However, I attribute these views to jealousy.

Q2 - Practice 3

Opinion 1:

Some children begin helping out with household chores as soon as they are old enough, while others may never lift a finger. I personally feel that children should pitch in around the house as soon as possible. This teaches them the value of work and gives them a feeling of accomplishment and responsibility. Children who never have to assist around the house often become spoiled and grow up expecting others to do work for them. Parents may think they are helping their kids by doing their work for them, but in the long run, this is not the case.

Opinion 2:

Some children begin helping out with household chores as soon as they are old enough, while others may never lift a finger. I personally feel that childhood is a special time for learning and playing. This helps kids develop imagination, creativity, and social skills through interacting with friends. Children who have little time to enjoy childhood because they are doing work or chores are not given the opportunity to be young. Parents may think that they are teaching their kids responsibility, but in the long run, this lesson costs children more than it's worth.

Necessary Skills

- Understanding information in reading and listening passages
- Taking notes of important information and using this information in your spoken response
- Synthesizing background information with more specific information
- Synthesizing the information given in the reading and listening; using the points in the listening to highlight principles or differences in the reading
- Recognizing a speaker's purpose and attitude
- Paraphrasing information

Strategies

- An organizational process for responding to a prompt based on integrated material is detailed below. In each step, there are certain things that you need to keep in mind.

Process	Strategy
Read and listen	Take notes of the important information in the reading and listening passages.
Read the question and understand the task	Identify the relationship between the information from the listening passage and that from the reading passage. What aspects of each does the prompt want you to discuss?
Organize the ideas	Arrange the ideas from the listening and reading passages. Think of a topic sentence that reflects the information.

Step 1

Read the following information. Write 5 keywords or key phrases that would be useful in explaining this passage to someone else. While reading, try to guess what the conversation will be about.

CONSTRUCTION ANNOUNCEMENT

The construction of the new Science Center will commence on March 8th next to Clemens Hall. So that classes will not be disturbed by the noise and commotion, all classes in Clemens Hall will be relocated to other buildings on campus. All professors will receive a memo advising them of their new class location and should relay the information to their students. We regret any inconvenience this might cause, but feel confident that the new Science Center will be well worth the disruption.

commence (v):
to begin; to start

commotion (n):
a large, confusing amount of noise and movement

relocate (v):
to move; to change the place of

relay (v):
to pass information one has received on to another person or group; to tell

disruption (n):
a break from a regularly scheduled activity; an unpleasant interruption

keywords / key phrases

_____

_____

_____

_____

_____

Cover the passage and look at the keywords and key phrases only. Restate the passage in your own words.

Step 2

🎧 Now listen to a conversation related to the passage in Step 1. As you listen, take notes on important information. Write down 5 keywords or key phrases that would be useful in explaining this information to someone else.

notes / keywords

hold off *(v phrase)*:
to wait

distracting *(adj)*:
causing loss of focus and concentration

cacophony *(n)*:
a large amount of jarring, unpleasant sound

allay *(v)*:
to provide relief; to make better

figure out *(v phrase)*:
to make a final decision; to realize

Restate what you heard in the conversation using the notes or keywords you wrote above.

[handwritten: Although were wearing seed]

Step 3

Read the question. Circle the most important ideas in your notes, from both the reading and the listening. Write down the main points you need to speak about.

The woman changes her opinion about the construction of the new Science Center. State her original opinion and her reasons for it. Then state why she changes her mind.

Original Opinion: The woman thinks *is a bad idea, because classes will be* .

Reason: *noise and distract the classes, why they don't star in summer* .

Why she changes her mind: *she changed her mind when she knew they relocated would.*

[handwritten notes: would. when it was why they did didn't star in summer could. might why don't knew. noise would distrac changed was disagree Very]

Step 4

Now create your own response using the information from your notes in Steps 1, 2, and 3. Use the prompts below to help you.

The woman thinks that _____.

Her concern is _____.

However, _____.

When she learns this, _____.

Step 5

Listen to the sample response and compare it with your response above. Make notes about the differences you hear.

Notes

_____

_____

_____

_____

Step 6

Review the response you wrote in Step 4 and your notes in Step 5. Then close your book and give a response to the question below. Say the response slowly and clearly. Try to speak for at least 60 seconds.

> The woman changes her opinion about the construction of the new Science Center. State her original opinion and her reasons for it. Then state why she changes her mind.

Step 1

Read the following information. Write 5 keywords or key phrases that would be useful in explaining this passage to someone else. While reading, try to guess what the conversation will be about.

ANTI-SPAM POLICY

Commencing next week, a new anti-spam filter will scan all emails coming into the university network for unsolicited emails, a.k.a. spam. All emails sent to university accounts will be sorted into three categories: Spam, Potential Spam, and Safe. Naturally, safe email will go directly to the recipient's inbox. Conversely, if an incoming email is obviously spam, it will be blocked. Finally, if an email looks like it could be spam, it will be redirected to the recipient's bulk folder.

unsolicited (adj):
not requested; not asked for

a.k.a. (acronym):
also known as

recipient (n):
the person to whom an email or letter is sent; the person meant to receive something

redirect (v):
to change the direction of; to move to a place different from the originally intended place

bulk (adj):
being large in volume or quantity; related to mail sent to a large number of addresses simultaneously

keywords /
key phrases

_____

_____

_____

_____

_____

Cover the passage and look at the keywords and key phrases only. Restate the passage in your own words.

READING | LISTENING | SPEAKING | WRITING | PRACTICE TEST

Now listen to a conversation related to the passage in Step 1. As you listen, take notes on important information. Write down 5 keywords or key phrases that would be useful in explaining this information to someone else.

notes / keywords

implement *(v)*:
to put in; to start using

abhor *(v)*:
to hate

from time to time
(adv phrase):
occasionally

incertitude *(n)*:
a doubt; a feeling of uncertainty

misidentify *(v)*:
to make an incorrect conclusion about the nature of something

Restate what you heard in the conversation using the notes or keywords you wrote above.

Step 3

Read the question. Circle the most important ideas in your notes, from both the reading and the listening. Write down the main points you need to speak about.

> The woman expresses her opinion about the new anti-spam filter. The man expresses his concern about it. State the woman's opinion and the man's concern. Who changes his or her mind in the end and why?

Woman's opinion: The anti-spam filter is _____.

Reason: _____

Man's Concern: _____

_____ changes his/her mind.

Reason: _____

Step 4

Now create your own response using the information from your notes in Steps 1, 2, and 3. Use the prompts below to help you.

The man and the woman are discussing _____. The woman,

who hates _____, thinks it's _____ idea. The man, however,

_____.

The woman _____.

If an incoming email _____.

In the end, _____.

Step 5

Listen to the sample response and compare it with your response above. Make notes about the differences you hear.

Notes

Step 6

Review the response you wrote in Step 4 and your notes in Step 5. Then close your book and give a response to the question below. Say the response slowly and clearly. Try to speak for at least 60 seconds.

> The woman expresses her opinion about the new anti-spam filter. The man expresses his concern about it. State the woman's opinion and the man's concern. Who changes his or her mind in the end and why?

Step 1

Read the following information. Write 5 keywords or key phrases that would be useful in explaining this passage to someone else. While reading, try to guess what the conversation will be about.

SELWIDGE HALL LECTURE SERIES — JAMES BRENTWORTH

The Business and Information Technology faculties are proud to present this week's guest speaker, James Brentworth. James was only seventeen when he inaugurated his website, which has now grown into a multi-million dollar enterprise. James will speak on the topics of Internet business and the future of telecommerce from 7 p.m. to 8 p.m., Thursday night in Selwidge Hall. Students from all disciplines are welcome to attend, and the speech will be followed by a brief question-and-answer period.

faculty (n):
a branch of a university in charge of one field of study

inaugurate (v):
to begin; to launch

enterprise (n):
a business venture

telecommerce (n):
the field of business and banking done using telecommunications such as telephones or Internet

discipline (n):
a field of study; a major

keywords / key phrases

Cover the passage and look at the keywords and key phrases only. Restate the passage in your own words.

Step 2

 Now listen to a conversation related to the passage in Step 1. As you listen, take notes on important information. Write down 5 keywords or key phrases that would be useful in explaining this information to someone else.

notes / keywords

extra credit *(adj phrase)*: related to assignments outside the regular course assignments and exams that are designed to allow students to increase their grades

whiz kid *(n phrase)*: a teenager or child with exceptional intelligence or achievements

counsel *(n)*: a series of suggestions; advice

freebie *(n)*: an event or item that costs nothing

beforehand *(adv)*: prior to an event

Restate what you heard in the conversation using the notes or keywords you wrote above.

Step 3

Read the question. Circle the most important ideas in your notes, from both the reading and the listening. Write down the main points you need to speak about.

> The man asks the woman for some information about an assignment. What does the woman tell him, and how does he react?

The man wants information on: _____

The woman tells him he can: _____

The man's opinion of the assignment is that: _____

_____.

Reason 1: _____.

Reason 2: _____.

The man will: _____.

Now create your own response using the information from your notes in Steps 1, 2, and 3. Use the prompts below to help you.

First, the man _____.

The woman then _____.

The man is _____ about _____ for _____ reasons.

First, _____.

In addition, _____. Therefore, _____

_____.

■ **Step 5**

◯ **Listen to the sample response and compare it with your response above. Make notes about the differences you hear.**

Notes

■ **Step 6**

Review the response you wrote in Step 4 and your notes in Step 5. Then close your book and give a response to the question below. Say the response slowly and clearly. Try to speak for at least 60 seconds.

> The man asks the woman for some information about an assignment. What does the woman tell him, and how does he react?

kill B 4 Practice 1 — Reading and Lecture

tep 1

Read the following information. Write 5 keywords or key phrases that would be useful for explaining this passage to someone else. While reading, try to guess what the lecture will be about.

The Nash Equilibrium

One of the greatest contributions of renowned mathematician, John Nash, is the Nash Equilibrium. It describes situations in which competing parties maintain static strategies for success. Each competitor has a rational conception of the strategies of the other competitors, but no collusion takes place. Consequently, each competitor chooses a strategy for success based only on his or her best interests. Nevertheless, the continuation of each individual competitor's strategy also benefits the success of the competing parties. As a corollary, if one party decides to alter its strategy, all competing parties will suffer.

renowned *(adj)*: famous; well known

equilibrium *(n)*: a state in which things remain constant, or equal on two or more sides

static *(adj)*: unchanging

collusion *(n)*: the act of agreeing on a plan

corollary *(n)*: a consequence that follows logically

keywords / key phrases

_____

_____

_____

_____

_____

Cover the passage and look at the keywords and key phrases only. Restate the passage in your own words.

ntegrated Speaking: Synthesizing Information **407**

Step 2

Now listen to a lecture related to the passage in Step 1. As you listen, take notes on important information. Write down 5 keywords or key phrases that would be useful in explaining this information to someone else.

notes /
keywords

collision *(n)*:
the act of crashing, or colliding

oncoming *(adj)*:
moving towards

in essence *(adv phrase)*:
basically; essentially

delay *(n)*:
the condition of being later or
slower than expected or desired;
a postponement

pose *(v)*:
to put forward; to present

Restate what you heard in the lecture using the notes or keywords you wrote above.

Step 3

Read the question. Circle the most important ideas in your notes, from both the reading and the listening. Write down the main points you need to speak about.

The professor describes an example of how the Nash Equilibrium applies to daily life. Explain the example and how it relates to the Nash Equilibrium.

Nash Equilibrium: _____

Professor's example: _____

How they relate: _____

Step 4

Now create your own response using the information from your notes in Steps 1, 2, and 3. Use the prompts below to help you.

The reading passage describes _____.

The professor expounds on _____.

This example _____. If _____

_____, then _____. That is to say, _____

_____.

Step 5

🎧 Listen to the sample response and compare it with your response above. Make notes about the differences you hear.

Notes

Step 6

Review the response you wrote in Step 4 and your notes in Step 5. Then close your book and give a response to the question below. Say the response slowly and clearly. Try to speak for at least 60 seconds.

The professor describes an example of how the Nash Equilibrium applies to daily life. Explain the example and how it relates to the Nash Equilibrium.

Skill B Q4 Practice 2 — Reading and Lecture

Read the following information. Write 5 keywords or key phrases that would be useful for explaining this passage to someone else. While reading, try to guess what the lecture will be about.

The Black Plague

The Black Plague is the disease that swept through Europe in the 1300s, killing up to two thirds of the entire population. It would return once every generation or so for the next several hundred years. Eventually, the rise of germ theory found that this strain of the bubonic plague was caused by a bacterium called *Yersinia pestis*. This microorganism was spread from rats to humans via parasitic fleas. Improved public sanitation combined with the advent of antibiotics helped eradicate the disease in Europe.

sweep through *(v phrase)*:
to spread or move quickly across a given area

strain *(n)*:
a type

parasitic *(adj)*:
relating to living on another living thing without helping it

advent *(n)*:
the beginning; the coming of

eradicate *(v)*:
to destroy; to remove completely

keywords / key phrases

Cover the passage and look at the keywords and key phrases only. Restate the passage in your own words.

Step 2

 Now listen to a lecture related to the passage in Step 1. As you listen, take notes on important information. Write down 5 keywords or key phrases that would be useful in explaining this information to someone else.

notes / keywords

scrutiny (n):
the act of questioning and examining closely

culprit (n):
a guilty party; a cause

pandemic (n):
a widespread disease affecting many people

subsequent (adj):
following after in time

incubation (n):
the development of an infection from the time the microorganism enters the body until signs or symptoms first appear

Restate what you heard in the lecture using the notes or keywords you wrote above.

Step 3

Read the question. Circle the most important ideas in your notes, from both the reading and the listening. Write down the main points you need to speak about.

The professor explains new theories and evidence about the Black Plague. Explain how the new theories and evidence relate to the common understanding of the plague and how it spread.

Common understanding: _____

New evidence 1: _____

New evidence 2: _____

New theories:

1: _____

2: _____

Now create your own response using the information from your notes in Steps 1, 2, and 3. Use the prompts below to help you.

In the lecture, the professor _____

_____. The traditional theory _____

_____. First, _____

_____. Second, _____

_____. For these reasons, _____

_____.

■ **Step 5**

⌒ **Listen to the sample response and compare it with your response above. Make notes about the differences you hear.**

Notes

_____

_____

_____

_____

■ **Step 6**

Review the response you wrote in Step 4 and your notes in Step 5. Then close your book and give a response to the question below. Say the response slowly and clearly. Try to speak for at least 60 seconds.

> The professor explains new theories and evidence about the Black Plague. Explain how the new theories and evidence relate to the common understanding of the plague and how it spread.

Skill B Q4 Practice 3 — Reading and Lecture

Step 1

Read the following information. Write 5 keywords or key phrases that would be useful for explaining this passage to someone else. While reading, try to guess what the lecture will be about.

The Great Zimbabwe Civilization

Around 450 A.D., Shona-speaking herders migrated to the high Zimbabwe plateau to escape the ravages of the tsetse fly. Between 1100 and 1450, the plateau was the site of the Great Zimbabwe civilization, with cities, a king, and an impressive stone wall 800 feet long and 32 feet high. The civilization thrived on cattle and the gold trade but began to break up in 1450 for unknown reasons. It was badly plundered by the British during colonial times but is now a popular tourist attraction.

herder (n):
a person who raises livestock, such as cattle, sheep, or goats

migrate (v):
to move in large numbers from one area to another

plateau (n):
a large, flat area of land

ravages (n):
a series of problems or damage

thrive (v):
to live successfully

keywords / key phrases

Cover the passage and look at the keywords and key phrases only. Restate the passage in your own words.

Now listen to a lecture related to the passage in Step 1. As you listen, take notes on important information. Write down 5 keywords or key phrases that would be useful in explaining this information to someone else.

notes / keywords

undermine *(v):*
to destroy the foundation of

commission *(v):*
to hire officially

plunder *(v):*
to destroy and steal from

contradict *(v):*
to state the opposite of; to question the validity of

dispel *(v):*
to prove a belief or opinion is false

Restate what you heard in the lecture using the notes or keywords you wrote above.

Step 3

Read the question. Circle the most important ideas in your notes, from both the reading and the listening. Write down the main points you need to speak about.

The professor describes archaeological investigations of the ruins on the Zimbabwe plateau. Describe the archaeologists' conclusions about the ruins and how they relate to the accepted history of the site today.

First British investigation: _____

Conclusion and result: _____

Further investigation: _____

Conclusion and result: _____

Accepted idea today: _____

Step 4

Now create your own response using the information from your notes in Steps 1, 2, and 3. Use the prompts below to help you.

The lecture _____.

The reading _____.

This evidence _____.

British officials, on the other hand, _____

_____. Their hired archaeologists _____

_____. Finally, _____

_____.

Step 5

Listen to the sample response and compare it with your response above. Make notes about the differences you hear.

Notes

Step 6

Review the response you wrote in Step 4 and your notes in Step 5. Then close your book and give a response to the question below. Say the response slowly and clearly. Try to speak for at least 60 seconds.

> The professor describes archaeological investigations of the ruins on the Zimbabwe plateau. Describe the archaeologists' conclusions about the ruins and how they relate to the accepted history of the site today.

Skill B Independent Speaking: Synthesizing Information

Q3 - Practice 1

The woman thinks that the university ought to wait until summer before they start building the new Science Center. Her concern is that the classes in nearby buildings, specifically, her class at Clemens Hall, will be distracted by the noise from the construction. However, when she talks to the man, he tells her that the university is planning on relocating the classes in Clemens Hall to other buildings on campus. When she learns this, she is relieved, and changes her mind about waiting until summer to commence construction on the new building.

Q3 - Practice 2

The man and the woman are discussing a new anti-spam filter that will be installed at their university. The woman, who hates receiving spam, thinks it's a wonderful idea. The man, however, is concerned that the filter will make mistakes and accidentally block important mail. The woman assures him, though, that the filter has a safety feature. It only blocks mail that is obviously spam. If an incoming email looks suspicious, it is sent to the person's bulk folder. In the end, the man agrees that this system is probably safe and agrees with the woman that it is a good idea.

Q3 - Practice 3

First, the man asks the woman for information on an extra credit assignment for a Web Design class they are both in. The woman then refers him to an announcement about a guest speaker, reminding him that they can earn credit for attending the talk. The man is excited about the opportunity for two reasons. First, he thinks the guest speaker will provide useful advice for aspiring web designers. In addition, he is pleased that there's no charge for admission to the speech. Therefore, he will prepare some questions to ask the speaker and attend the speech to receive extra credit.

Q4 - Practice 1

The reading passage describes the Nash Equilibrium, a situation in competitions in which it is not in any competitor's interest to change strategy. The professor expounds on this idea by illustrating a real life example of the Nash Equilibrium. This example refers to drivers in rush hour traffic. If each driver is considered a competitor, and driving on one side of the road as the strategy, then it fits the Nash Equilibrium. That is to say, it is not in a driver's interest to change strategy, given that a collision could hinder the success of that driver, and coincidentally, the other drivers, too.

Q4 - Practice 2

In the lecture, the professor discusses new theories about the cause of the Black Plague, a disease that killed two-thirds of Europeans in the 14th century. The traditional theory that it was bubonic plague spread to people by fleas carried on rats does not match up with some new evidence. First, Iceland was severely affected despite the fact it had no rats. Second, the incubation period and spreading of the disease differed from those typical of bubonic plagues. For these reasons, some researchers are now proposing other diseases as the cause, such as pulmonary anthrax or the Ebola virus.

Q4 - Practice 3

The lecture discusses the rewriting of the history of the Great Zimbabwe civilization during the British Colonial period. The reading details the conclusions based on archaeological evidence. This evidence points to native Shona-speaking Africans as the founders of the civilization that boasted cities, royalty, and a monumental wall. British officials, on the other hand, put forth an official view that the civilization must have been built by foreigners from the north. Their hired archaeologists destroyed evidence and supported racist theories to justify imperialist ventures. Finally, after Zimbabwe gained its independence from Britain in 1980, the myth was dispelled and the truth became accepted.

Necessary Skills

- Understanding the key information in listening passages
- Taking notes on important information and using this information in your spoken response
- Paraphrasing information
- Expressing an opinion or preference
- Supporting an opinion with reasons or examples

Strategies

- An organizational process for preparing your speech is detailed below. In each step, there are certain things that you need to keep in mind.

Process	Strategy
Listen to a conversation or a lecture	Take notes on the points and important details.
Read the question and understand the task	Identify what you will need to discuss.
Organize the ideas	Decide on your topic sentence and the supporting details. Be sure to include reasons and examples for any personal opinions expressed.

Skill C Q5 Practice 1 — Conversation

Step 1

🎧 Listen to a conversation. As you listen, take notes on one person's problem and the solutions suggested by the other person.

Problem: _____

_____

Solution 1: _____

_____

Solution 2: _____

_____

frazzled *(adj)*:
feeling stress

take off *(v phrase)*:
to go away

monumental *(adj)*:
very large and important

shot *(n)*:
an attempt; a try

check out *(v)*:
to borrow; to officially remove from a library

Step 2

Read the question. Write down your opinion.

The students discuss two possible solutions to the woman's problem. Describe the problem. Then state which of the two solutions you prefer and explain why.

Problem: _____

Best solution: _____

Reason 1: _____

Reason 2: _____

Step 3

Now create your own response using words and expressions from Steps 1 and 2. Use the prompts below to help you.

The woman's problem is _____

_____. The man and the woman _____ two options. The first option

_____. The second option _____

_____. I think the _____ option _____. She _____

_____. Also, _____ , so _____

_____.

Step 4

Listen to the sample responses and compare them with your response above. Make notes about the differences you hear.

Notes

Step 5

Review the response you wrote in Step 3 and your notes in Step 4. Then close your book and give a response to the question below. Say the response slowly and clearly. Try to speak for at least 60 seconds.

> The students discuss two possible solutions to the woman's problem. Describe the problem. Then state which of the two solutions you prefer and explain why.

Skill C Q5 Practice 2 — Conversation

Step 1

Listen to a conversation. As you listen, take notes on one person's problem and the solutions suggested by the other person.

Problem: _____

_____

Solution 1: _____

_____

Solution 2: _____

_____

drive someone crazy *(v phrase)*: to make someone very upset

in jeopardy *(adj phrase)*: at risk; in danger

manipulative *(adj)*: tending toward using people for one's own selfish reasons

tough out *(prep phrase)*: to endure; to remain strong in a difficult situation

bicker *(v)*: to argue

Step 2

Read the question. Write down your opinion.

> The students discuss two possible solutions to the woman's problem. Describe the problem. Then state which of the two solutions you prefer and explain why.

Problem: _____

Best solution: _____

Reason 1: _____

Reason 2: _____

Step 3

Now create your own response using words and expressions from Steps 1 and 2. Use the prompts below to help you.

The woman is unhappy _____ .

The man admits _____ , but he recommends

_____ .

In my opinion, _____ . For one thing, _____

_____ . Also, _____

_____ .

Step 4

Listen to the sample responses and compare them with your response above. Make notes about the differences you hear.

Notes

Step 5

Review the response you wrote in Step 3 and your notes in Step 4. Then close your book and give a response to the question below. Say the response slowly and clearly. Try to speak for at least 60 seconds.

> The students discuss two possible solutions to the woman's problem. Describe the problem. Then state which of the two solutions you prefer and explain why.

Skill C Q5 Practice 3 — Conversation

Step 1

🎧 **Listen to a conversation. As you listen, take notes on one person's problem and the solutions suggested by the other person.**

Problem: _____

_____

Solution 1: _____

_____

Solution 2: _____

_____

dissect *(v):*
to cut open for the purpose of study

gross *(adj):*
disgusting; revolting

hold against *(v phrase):*
to think badly of someone because of some event; to resent

suck it up *(v phrase):*
to quietly endure a difficult situation

virtual *(adj):*
simulated on a computer

Step 2

Read the question. Write down your opinion.

> The students discuss two possible solutions to the man's problem. Describe the problem. Then state which of the two solutions you prefer and explain why.

Problem: _____

Best solution: _____

Reason 1: _____

Reason 2: _____

Step 3

Now create your own response using words and expressions from Steps 1 and 2. Use the prompts below to help you.

The man's biology class is _____

_____. The woman suggests that _____

and _____. The man expresses concern, though,

that _____. I believe the man should _____

_____. He will _____

_____.

Step 4

Listen to the sample responses and compare them with your response above. Make notes about the differences you hear.

Notes

Step 5

Review the response you wrote in Step 3 and your notes in Step 4. Then close your book and give a response to the question below. Say the response slowly and clearly. Try to speak for at least 60 seconds.

> The students discuss two possible solutions to the man's problem. Describe the problem. Then state which of the two solutions you prefer and explain why.

Skill C Q6 Practice 1 — Lecture

Step 1

🎧 Listen to a lecture. Fill in the missing information in the notes.

Falconry is: _____

Falconers must: a) _____

b) _____

Today, falconry is: _____

Historically, falconry was: _____

Nomadic people in the desert: _____

Falconry dates back to: _____

prey *(n)*:
an animal that is hunted

tame *(v)*:
to teach a wild animal to obey commands

custom *(n)*:
an accepted practice

ritual *(n)*:
a practice repeated and performed a specific way for religious purposes

context *(n)*:
the circumstances surrounding a situation

nomadic *(adj)*:
relating to people who constantly move, who have no fixed home

procure *(v)*:
to get

enlist *(v)*:
to get the help of; to recruit

subsistence *(n)*:
the act or state of surviving

assert *(v)*:
to claim strongly; to contend

Step 2

Read the speaking task related to the lecture you heard.

> Using points and examples from the lecture, explain the origins of falconry and how it is practiced today.

Now create your own response using words and expressions from Step 1. Use the prompts below to help you.

Falconry was originally _____.

Nomadic people _____.

Today, in contrast, _____.

Nonetheless, _____.

The falconer _____.

Step 3

Listen to the sample response and compare it with your response above. Make notes about the differences you hear.

Notes

Step 4

Review the response you wrote in Step 2 and your notes in Step 3. Then close your book and give a response to the question below. Say the response slowly and clearly. Try to speak for at least 60 seconds.

Using points and examples from the lecture, explain the origins of falconry and how it is practiced today.

Skill C Q6 Practice 2 — Lecture

Step 1

🎧 **Listen to a lecture. Fill in the missing information in the notes.**

An aura is _____

Example: _____

Common characteristics of migraines: — _____

— _____

— _____

— _____

Process of migraine: _____

→ _____

→ _____

Possible way to prevent migraines from occurring: _____

_____

migraine (n):
a severe form of headache

vomit (v):
to force material from the stomach up through the throat and mouth

can't stand (v phrase):
to hate; to not be able to tolerate

episodically (adv):
occurring occasionally, but in clusters or groups

blood vessel (n):
a vein or artery; a tube in the body through which blood can flow

stimulant (n):
a material or event that causes a reaction

contract (v):
to become smaller; to squeeze

compound (v):
to add to; to make stronger or more intense

compensate (v):
to make up for a shortcoming; to attempt to fix a problem

trigger (v):
to start; to set off

Step 2

Read the speaking task related to the lecture you heard.

> Using points and examples from the lecture, explain what migraines are and how they occur.

Now create your own response using words and expressions from Step 1. Use the prompts below to help you.

A migraine is a _____.

The migraine itself involves _____ and other symptoms, such as _____.

Doctors suspect a possible cause _____.

The brain then _____, which results in pain. Migraine sufferers should try

to identify _____.

Step 3

🎧 Listen to the sample response and compare it with your response above. Make notes about the differences you hear.

Notes

Step 4

Review the response you wrote in Step 2 and your notes in Step 3. Then close your book and give a response to the question below. Say the response slowly and clearly. Try to speak for at least 60 seconds.

Using points and examples from the lecture, explain what migraines are and how they occur.

Step 1

🎧 Listen to a lecture. Fill in the missing information in the notes.

Standard view of evolution: Species arise _____

Example: _____

Counter-evidence: Source: _____

Trend: Species _____ for long periods of time.

    New species _____.

New theory: _____

    — Large populations typically _____

    — Change occurs in _____

    — After the change, the new species might _____

    _____

The new theory _____ the standard view.

imperceptible *(adj)*:	too small to be noticed
punctuated *(adj)*:	occasionally interrupted
dilute *(v)*:	to make weaker; to decrease the ratio of
peripheral *(adj)*:	to the side; not part of the center
novel *(adj)*:	new; different from past examples
take over *(v phrase)*:	to become dominant; to seize control
exterminate *(v)*:	to kill; to destroy
predecessor *(n)*:	a person or thing that comes before
complement *(v)*:	to work well with; to improve the situation in combination with

Step 2

Read the speaking task related to the lecture you heard.

> Using points and details from the lecture, explain Punctuated Equilibrium and its relation to the standard, gradualist view of evolution.

Now create your own response using words and expressions from Step 1. Use the prompts below to help you.

The professor explains _____.

One example presented is _____.

This example supports _____. However, _____.

Punctuated Equilibrium is _____. It holds that _____

_____. On the other hand, _____

_____. The professor points out that the two theories _____

_____.

Step 3

Listen to the sample response and compare it with your response above. Make notes about the differences you hear.

Notes

Step 4

Review the response you wrote in Step 2 and your notes in Step 3. Then close your book and give a response to the question below. Say the response slowly and clearly. Try to speak for at least 60 seconds.

Using points and details from the lecture, explain Punctuated Equilibrium and its relation to the standard, gradualist view of evolution.

Skill C Integrated Speaking: Stating Opinions and Summarizing

Q5 - Practice 1

Opinion 1:

The woman's problem is that she does not have her university library card, but she needs to check out some books. The man and the woman discuss two options. The first option is that she just use the public library. The second option is that she try to find someone whose card she can borrow. I think the first option is better. She can go to the public library immediately without wasting any time looking for help. Also, there is no guarantee she would find anyone willing to be imposed upon, so the second option may be a waste of time.

Opinion 2:

The woman's problem is that she does not have her university library card, but she needs to check out some books. The man and the woman discuss two options. The first option is that she just use the public library. The second option is that she try to find someone whose card she can borrow. I think the second option is better. She can probably find a friend in her dorm who is more than happy to help her. Also, the public library may not have the resources she needs, so it may be a waste of time to go there.

Q5 - Practice 2

Opinion 1:

The woman is unhappy living with a friend who eats the woman's food and refuses to clean. The man admits the woman could just stick with the situation for a short time longer, but he recommends that she talk to her roommate about the problem. In my opinion, the woman should follow the man's recommendation. For one thing, it is not fair for her to have to do all the cleaning and pay for the food her roommate consumes. Also, if the woman convinces her roommate to start helping out, they will both be happier because there won't be any resentment between them.

Opinion 2:

The woman is unhappy living with a friend who eats the woman's food and refuses to clean. The man admits the woman could just stick with the situation for a short time longer, but he recommends that she talk to her roommate about the problem. In my opinion, the woman should follow her instincts and continue to live with her friend without complaint. For one thing, petty concerns are not worth losing a friend over. Also, if the roommate were to get upset and move out, the woman would be stuck paying all of the rent herself.

Q5 - Practice 3

Opinion 1:

The man's biology class is going to dissect a pig, and he does not want to take part because he believes that dissecting pigs is unethical. The woman suggests that he refuse to take part in the dissection and ask his teacher for an alternative project. The man expresses concern, though, that the teacher might be annoyed with him and lower his grade because of it. I believe the man should stick to his convictions and not take part in activities that contravene his beliefs. He will feel better about himself, and protesting might result in change.

Opinion 2:

The man's biology class is going to dissect a pig, and he does not want to take part because he believes that dissecting pigs is unethical. The woman suggests that he refuse to take part in the dissection and ask his teacher for an alternative project. The man expresses concern, though, that the teacher might be annoyed with him and lower his grade because of it. I believe the man should dissect the pig and not risk getting a poor grade. He will only have dissect the pig once, but a poor grade will cause him problems in the future.

Q6 - Practice 1

Falconry was originally employed as a tool to help people hunt food. Nomadic people in the desert tamed falcons in order to help them hunt for a larger variety of foods than they could acquire by themselves. Today, in contrast, people aren't as desperate to meet subsistence requirements. Nonetheless, falconry is still practiced as a sport. The falconer is highly skilled and must not only tame the falcon, but also teach it to hunt without killing the prey.

Q6 - Practice 2

A migraine is a severe headache that may be preceded by an aura, a symptom that signals the sufferer to the onset of a migraine. The migraine itself involves a headache and other symptoms, such as vomiting or intolerance for light or noise. Doctors suspect a possible cause is that restricted blood flow to the brain causes oxygen levels in the brain to decrease. The brain then tries to compensate by expanding the arteries in the brain, which results in pain. Migraine sufferers should try to identify what triggers their migraine to prevent further attacks.

Q6 - Practice 3

The professor explains two theories of evolution: one related to gradual evolution and the other related to rapid evolution. One example presented is the evolution of horses from cat-sized mammals to their much larger modern stature. This example supports the theory of gradual evolution. However, evidence in the fossil record indicates that species often remain unchanged for long periods, and then new species arise quite suddenly. Punctuated Equilibrium is a new theory that explains this. It holds that large populations dilute new mutations. On the other hand, beneficial mutations spread quickly in peripheral subpopulations. The professor points out that the two theories complement rather than contradict each other.

Vocabulary Review

Vocabulary Review 1

Instructions: Choose the best word or phrase to complete each sentence.

1. Her archaeology professor acted as her _____. He guided her through the difficulties of her master's program and helped shape the woman she is today.
   - (A) gadget
   - (B) curriculum
   - (C) mentor
   - (D) hindrance

2. She always _____ coffee in the morning. Without it, she can't work properly.
   - (A) craves
   - (B) hinders
   - (C) negates
   - (D) heeds

3. He developed a lot of _____ during his semester abroad. Afterwards, his parents trusted him with more responsibilities.
   - (A) destiny
   - (B) disruption
   - (C) incertitude
   - (D) maturity

4. There was a lot of _____ as crowds of people tried to see the famous actor walking through the mall.
   - (A) stamina
   - (B) discipline
   - (C) counsel
   - (D) commotion

5. After the air conditioning broke down, the students found the heat very _____. They just couldn't concentrate on the exam questions.
   - (A) diverting
   - (B) distracting
   - (C) crucial
   - (D) erudite

6. Because the government decided to construct a new highway through this land, they've decided to _____ the football stadium to another site.
   - (A) relocate
   - (B) relay
   - (C) allay
   - (D) abhor

7. We have decided to _____ on buying a car until we can save more money.
   - (A) figure out
   - (B) hold off
   - (C) redirect
   - (D) implement

8. Deciding what _____ to focus on in university can be a difficult decision.
   - (A) freebie
   - (B) mentor
   - (C) perseverance
   - (D) discipline

Instructions: Choose the word or phrase closest in meaning to the underlined part.

9. The huge snowstorm has <u>impeded</u> the progress of construction on the new library tower.
   - (A) excelled
   - (B) hindered
   - (C) revered
   - (D) relocated

10. A page listing your references is an <u>essential</u> component of your paper, so make sure you format it correctly.
    - (A) crucial
    - (B) diverting
    - (C) spoiled
    - (D) domestic

11. My friend is so <u>skeptical</u>. She never believes people are telling the truth.
   (A) domestic
   (B) erudite
   (C) crucial
   (D) cynical

12. Because our physics professor is attending a conference, Tuesday's lab session will <u>start</u> at 10:00 instead of 9:00.
   (A) commence
   (B) abhor
   (C) negate
   (D) heed

13. Could you please <u>pass</u> this information on to Dr. McCafferty?
   (A) inaugurate
   (B) relay
   (C) hold off
   (D) redirect

14. In general, a person's level of <u>doubt</u> increases as he or she encounters new information.
   (A) discipline
   (B) counsel
   (C) cacophony
   (D) incertitude

15. They have a good idea for a business <u>venture</u>. I think they're going to be quite successful.
   (A) dyslexia
   (B) stamina
   (C) expertise
   (D) enterprise

Instructions: Write the missing words. Use the words below to fill in the blanks.

diverting	gadget	better off
dyslexia	perseverance	

One **(16)** _____ that has helped me with school work is my "reading pen." To begin, I have **(17)** _____, a learning disability that makes reading very difficult. The reading pen not only made reading possible, it also made it quite **(18)** _____ for me. Without it, I would have spent tedious hours reading my assignments and probably would have given up. With **(19)** _____ and my reading pen, however, I was able to excel in school. I have been much **(20)** _____ because of it.

Instructions: Match the words that are opposites.

21. hinder   (A) ignore
22. heed   (B) love
23. commence   (C) pitch in
24. recipient   (D) sender
25. abhor   (E) hold off

Vocabulary Review 2

Instructions: Choose the best word or phrase to complete each sentence.

1. When the forces on an object are balanced, the object is in _____ .
   (A) collusion
   (B) equilibrium
   (C) collision
   (D) incubation

2. Because of the snowstorm, there was a _____ in my flight time. I had to spend an extra night in Norway.
   (A) corollary
   (B) plateau
   (C) culprit
   (D) delay

3. He has been trying to improve his grades, but instead, they have remained _____ . At least they haven't gotten worse.
   (A) static
   (B) oncoming
   (C) parasitic
   (D) virtual

4. Their hypothesis needs to be analyzed with more _____ . Experts have raised several questions about it that need answering.
   (A) ritual
   (B) subsistence
   (C) scrutiny
   (D) speciation

5. Nomadic tribes still wander across the Himalayan _____ in search of food.
   (A) plateaus
   (B) ravages
   (C) customs
   (D) migraines

6. Health officials are worried that a new _____ could spread across the planet, infecting millions of people with a serious, flu-like illness.
   (A) herder
   (B) prey
   (C) stimulant
   (D) pandemic

7. She has devised a _____ approach to measuring changes in ocean temperatures. Nothing like it has ever been employed before.
   (A) punctuated
   (B) nomadic
   (C) novel
   (D) manipulative

8. You will find that I manage in a manner quite different from my _____ . Nonetheless, I hope to maintain the standard of excellence they have set.
   (A) predecessors
   (B) migraines
   (C) rituals
   (D) ravages

Instructions: Choose the word or phrase closest in meaning to the underlined part.

9. The <u>famous</u> publisher, David Asper, will be speaking on campus next Saturday afternoon.
   (A) renowned
   (B) static
   (C) parasitic
   (D) subsequent

10. Hybrid automobiles use gas power to <u>work well with</u> electric power.
    (A) dilute
    (B) exterminate
    (C) compensate
    (D) complement

11. I find astrophysics difficult enough, but to <u>add to</u> the problem, my vision is getting worse. I'm going to need to get glasses in order to read what the professor writes on the whiteboard.

(A) contract
(B) compound
(C) assert
(D) enlist

12. Egyptians began constructing <u>large, important</u> structures thousands of years ago.

(A) frazzled
(B) parasitic
(C) monumental
(D) renowned

13. The problem, <u>basically</u>, is that American industry depends on oil imported from overseas.

(A) in a row
(B) in essence
(C) in charge
(D) in jeopardy

14. The local government has <u>officially hired</u> a group of investigators to help solve the city's traffic problems.

(A) commissioned
(B) plundered
(C) contradicted
(D) migrated

15. Since different continents have different <u>types</u> of flu viruses, it is important to be cautious when traveling overseas during winter.

(A) advents
(B) culprits
(C) customs
(D) strains

Instructions: Write the missing words. Use the words below to fill in the blanks.

imperceptible	asserts	peripheral
exterminate	dilute	

The traditional view of evolutionary theory **(16)** _____ that species develop slowly, in a series of small **(17)** _____ stages. Evidence from the fossil record, however, indicates that species often remain unchanged for long periods, and then new species arise quite suddenly. Punctuated Equilibrium explains that large populations **(18)** _____ new mutations. In contrast, small **(19)** _____ subpopulations occurring in new environments allow beneficial mutations to spread quickly. Furthermore, when new species evolve from this spread, they often **(20)** _____ older species.

Instructions: Choose the one word that does not belong.

21.	static	equilibrium	pandemic	unchanging
22.	thrive	undermine	plunder	exterminate
23.	dispel	contradict	bicker	enlist
24.	vomit	ravages	migraine	complement
25.	endure	tough out	surrender	suck it up

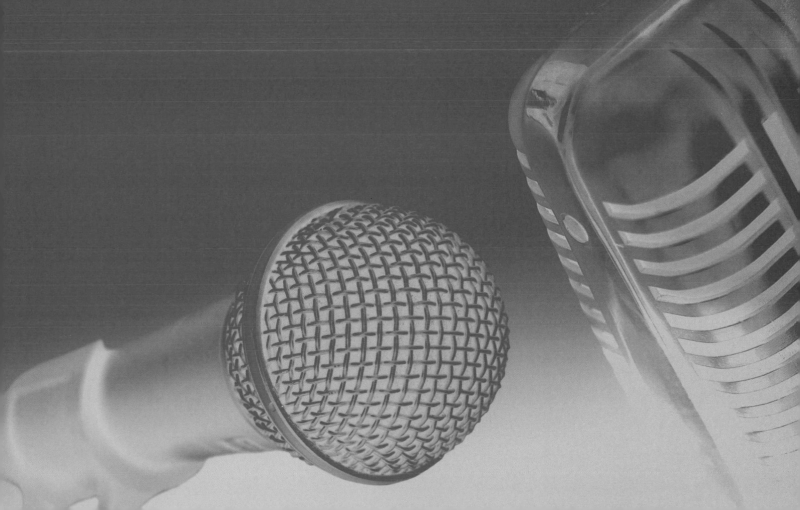

Chapter 2

Making Speech Coherent

A response to the independent speaking question usually has these components:

- An introduction to the general topic of the response—usually 1 sentence, but this can be skipped
- A statement of your opinion—generally 1 sentence
- Your reasons (2) + examples/details to support them—1 or 2 sentences each

Within 60 seconds, the time given to you for your response, you should be able to say about 8 sentences. These sentences would be similar in length to the following: "I often take my guitar to parties and play music for my friends there."

Before Speaking:

- Choose an opinion that is easily supported
- Organize the flow of your response in your mind
- Make sure that you have adequate reasons and examples

When Speaking:

- Make a clear statement of your opinion on the given topic
- State clear reasons for your opinion
- Use concrete examples
- Use transitions to order the flow of your speech

Skill A Q1 Practice 1 — Personal Experience

Step 1

Read and think about the question below.

> These days, the world is truly becoming smaller, allowing for greater communication between people from different countries. Describe how you have been able to communicate with someone from another country and how it has affected your life. Use specific details and examples to explain your answer.

The sentences below make up part of a response to the question above. Read the sentences, and underline any transitions you find.

(A) By now, we have become good friends, and we have both learned a lot.

(B) Every week, we chat for 30 minutes in English and 30 minutes in Chinese.

(C) Last year, I met a fellow language student on an Internet study forum when I was trying to practice for a Chinese class.

(D) Later, we developed a symbiotic relationship by helping each other practice our respective languages.

(E) Of course, among the things I've learned is the fact that Chinese culture is fascinating, and this experience has really broadened my view of the world.

(F) As it turned out, he was a Chinese student trying to practice English.

fellow *(adj)*:
belonging to the same group or engaged in the same activity

forum *(n)*:
a site at which people with similar interests can communicate

symbiotic *(adj)*:
beneficial to both parties

respective *(adj)*:
individually

broaden *(v)*:
to make wider

Look at the sentences again. Think of the role of each sentence in the response. Put the sentences in the right order.

			B		

Step 2

Do NOT look at the sentences in Step 1. Answer the following questions.

1. How did the speaker meet his new friend?

   _____

2. What do they do together now?

   _____

3. How did this experience affect the speaker?

   _____

Using the short answers you wrote above, try to speak for 60 seconds explaining the speaker's response. Use the words and phrases below while you are speaking. Time yourself and record the time below.

last year	when	later	every week	by now	of course	as it turned out

Response 1:   Speaking time: _____ seconds

Step 3

⌒ **Now, listen to a sample response. How is this response different from yours? What parts of the response can you use in your own? Write down any useful expressions the sample uses.**

Notes

⌒ **Listen again and repeat after the tape, paying attention to pronunciation, intonation, and word stress.**

Now write your own answers to these questions.

1. How have you communicated with someone from another country?

_____

2. Who was this person, and what was the nature of your correspondence?

_____

3. How has this experience affected you?

_____

Using the short answers you wrote above, give a spoken response to the prompt below. Try to incorporate additional parts of speech from Step 3, while also paying attention to your pronunciation and intonation. Record your time.

> These days, the world is truly becoming smaller, allowing for greater communication between people from different countries. Describe how you have been able to communicate with someone from another country and how it has affected your life. Use specific details and examples to explain your answer.

Response 2:   Speaking time: _____ seconds

Skill A **Q1** Practice 2 — Personal Experience

Step 1

Read and think about the question below.

> Describe a technological innovation that you have witnessed in your lifetime. Discuss how this invention has changed the way you live.

The sentences below make up part of a response to the question above. Read the sentences, underlining any transitions you find.

(A) After the Internet came into widespread use, however, I didn't have to go to the library at all.

(B) For example, I no longer had to make expensive, obligatory phone calls to my parents.

(C) One technological innovation I witnessed during my university days was the spread of the Internet.

(D) I could do all of my research from a computer in my dorm room, which saved a lot of time.

(E) Instead, I could send them updates via email for free.

(F) Before that, I spent hours in the library doing research.

(G) In fact, the Internet saved me a great deal of money, too!

> **widespread (adj):**
> common in many places
>
> **obligatory (adj):**
> done out of a sense of duty
>
> **innovation (n):**
> a new and improved technology or way of doing something
>
> **witness (v):**
> to see; to observe
>
> **update (n):**
> information about new events in a person's life

Look at the sentences again. Think of the role of each sentence in the response. Put the sentences in the right order.

   A

Do NOT look at the sentences in Step 1. Answer the following questions.

1. What was the speaker doing when Internet use became common?

_____

2. What is the first way the Internet changed the speaker's life?

_____

3. What is the second way the Internet changed the speaker's life?

_____

Using the short answers you wrote above, try to speak for 60 seconds explaining the speaker's response. Use the words and phrases below while you are speaking. Time yourself and record the time.

before that	for example	when	in fact	instead	which

Response 1:   Speaking time: _____ seconds

Step 3

Now, listen to a sample response. How is this response different from yours? What parts of the response can you use in your own? Write down any useful expressions the sample uses.

Notes

_____

_____

_____

_____

Listen again and repeat after the tape, paying attention to pronunciation, intonation, and word stress.

Step 4

Now write your own answers to these questions.

1. What were you doing when some form of new technology became common?

_____

2. Name one way in which this form of technology has changed your life.

_____

3. Name another way in which this form of technology has changed your life.

_____

Using the short answers you wrote above, give a spoken response to the prompt below. Try to incorporate additional parts of speech from Step 3, while also paying attention to your pronunciation and intonation. Record your time.

Describe a technological innovation that you have witnessed in your lifetime. Discuss how this invention has changed the way you live.

Response 2:   Speaking time: _____ seconds

Skill A **Q1** Practice 3 — Personal Experience

Step 1

Read and think about the question below.

> Unexpected weather can greatly affect our lives. Tell about a time when an unexpected storm or other weather event affected your life. Use specific details and examples to explain your answer.

A sample outline of a response is given below. Write down transition words or phrases that can be used in linking these ideas.

Unexpected weather event: snowstorm

- What happened: I was driving and I pulled over to help a stranded motorist.

- How it changed my life: I married the motorist.

Transition words:

_____   _____

_____   _____

_____   _____

Using this outline, give a spoken response to the prompt above. Time yourself and record the time.

Response 1:   Speaking time: _____ seconds

Step 2

🎧 **Now, listen to a sample response. How is this response different from yours? What parts of the response can you use in your own? Write down any useful expressions the sample uses.**

Notes

blizzard *(n)*:
a severe snowstorm

raging *(adj)*:
very strong and violent

stranded *(adj)*:
stuck; unable to move or escape

pull over *(v phrase)*:
to direct a moving vehicle to the side of a road and stop

lift *(n)*:
a ride somewhere

🎧 **Listen again and repeat after the tape, paying attention to pronunciation, intonation, and word stress.**

Step 3

Now, give a spoken response to the prompt without listening to the sample. Try to incorporate additional parts of speech from Step 2, while also paying attention to your pronunciation and intonation. Record your time.

Response 2:   Speaking time: _____ seconds

Step 4

Make up your own outline to the prompt. Try to incorporate transition words and useful phrases introduced earlier in the practice.

Unexpected weather event: _____

• What happened: _____

• How it changed my life: _____

Transition words:

_____   _____

_____   _____

_____   _____

Using this outline, give a spoken response to the prompt below. Time yourself and record the time.

> Unexpected weather can greatly affect our lives. Tell about a time when an unexpected storm or other weather event affected your life. Use specific details and examples to explain your answer.

Response 3:   Speaking time: _____ seconds

Skill A Q1 Practice 4 — Personal Experience

Step 1

Read and think about the question below.

> Groups or organizations are an important part of some people's lives. Tell about a group or organization that is important to you. Use specific reasons and examples to explain your answer.

A sample outline of a response is given below. Write down transition words or phrases that can be used in linking these ideas.

Organization in my life — The Optimists' Club

- Reason 1 — organized activities for me
  Example — youth basketball league
- Reason 2 — helped me with problems
  Example — advice on school

Transition words:

_____ _____

_____ _____

_____ _____

Using this outline, give a response to the prompt above. Time yourself and record the time.

Response 1:   Speaking time: _____ seconds

Step 2

🎧 **Now, listen to a sample response. How is this response different from yours? What parts of the response can you use in your own? Write down any useful expressions the sample uses.**

Notes

optimist (n):
a person who always looks on the positive side of an event or experience

enriching (adj):
causing improvement; making better

forge (v):
to create; to establish

lasting (adj):
enduring; remaining strong for a long time

on edge (adj):
nervous; feeling great stress

🎧 **Listen again and repeat after the tape, paying attention to pronunciation, intonation, and word stress.**

Step 3

Now, give a spoken response to the prompt without listening to the sample. Try to incorporate additional parts of speech from Step 2, while also paying attention to your pronunciation and intonation. Record your time.

Response 2:　　　　　　　　Speaking time: _____ seconds

Step 4

Make up your own outline to the prompt. Try to incorporate transition words and useful phrases introduced earlier in the practice.

Organization in my life — _____

- Reason 1 — _____
  Example — _____
- Reason 2 — _____
  Example — _____

Transition words:

_____　　_____

_____　　_____

_____　　_____

Using this outline, give a response to the prompt below. Time yourself and record the time.

> Groups or organizations are an important part of some people's lives. Tell about a group or organization that is important to you. Use specific reasons and examples to explain your answer.

Response 3:　　　　　　　　Speaking time: _____ seconds

Skill A **Q2** Practice 1 — Personal Preference

Step 1

Read and think about the question below.

> Do you agree or disagree with the following statement? The childhood years (the time from birth to twelve years of age) are the most important years of a person's life. Use specific reasons and examples to support your answer.

The sentences below make up part of a response to the question above. Read the sentences, and underline any transitions you find.

(A) Thus, it is crucial to have positive influences in childhood.

(B) Conversely, positive, nurturing experiences in childhood foster mental health and well-being in adulthood.

(C) For instance, a major trauma experienced at the age of six has a much more devastating effect than one experienced at age thirty.

(D) I believe that childhood is a critical period in a person's life.

(E) First, it is the time in which personality is developed.

(F) Second, a person's experiences in childhood affect the remainder of his or her life.

(G) Indeed, negative or traumatic experiences in childhood can lead to psychological problems in adulthood, such as depression and antisocial behavior.

> **remainder (n):**
> a part remaining; a part that is left
>
> **trauma (n):**
> an experience of great stress
>
> **antisocial (adj):**
> acting against society, i.e. criminal behavior
>
> **nurturing (adj):**
> caring and encouraging
>
> **foster (v):**
> to help develop

Look at the sentences again. Think of the role of each sentence in the response. Put the sentences in the right order.

☐ ▶ ☐ ▶ F ▶ ☐ ▶ ☐ ▶ ☐ ▶ ☐

Step 2

Do NOT look at the sentences in Step 1. Answer the following questions.

1. What is the speaker's view of childhood?

_____

2. What is one reason the speaker gives for this view?

_____

3. What is a second reason the speaker gives for this view?

_____

Using the short answers you wrote above, try to speak for 60 seconds explaining the speaker's response. Use the words and phrases below while you are speaking. Time yourself and record the time.

first	second	for instance	so	clearly

Response 1:   Speaking time: _____ seconds

Step 3

🎧 Now, listen to a sample response. How is this response different from yours? What parts of the response can you use in your own? Write down any useful expressions the sample uses.

Notes

_____
_____
_____

🎧 **Listen again and repeat after the tape, paying attention to pronunciation, intonation, and word stress.**

Now write your own answers to these questions.

1. What is your view of the importance of childhood?

_____

2. What is one reason why you have this view?

_____

3. What is a second reason why you have this view?

_____

Using the short answers you wrote above, give a spoken response to the prompt below. Try to incorporate additional parts of speech from Step 3, while also paying attention to your pronunciation and intonation. Record your time.

> Do you agree or disagree with the following statement? The childhood years (the time from birth to twelve years of age) are the most important years of a person's life. Use specific reasons and examples to support your answer.

Response 2:   Speaking time: _____ seconds

Skill A Q2 Practice 2 — Personal Preference

Step 1

Read and think about the question below.

> Some parents choose to home-school their children themselves rather than send them to public schools. In your opinion, which option is in the best interest of the child?

The sentences below make up part of a response to the question above. Read the sentences, underlining any transitions you find.

(A) These, I believe, are the most important skills learned at school.

(B) The skills I am referring to are social skills.

(C) Public schools, on the other hand, can and do provide this setting.

(D) Most parents are capable of teaching their children to read, write, add, and subtract, as well as many of the other basic skills children are taught at school.

(E) That's why I am of the opinion that children should learn in a social environment.

(F) However, there are some skills that cannot be taught sufficiently at home.

(G) Unfortunately, the home cannot provide an adequate social milieu for children to learn to live with a diverse group of people.

> **capable (adj):**
> able to do
>
> **sufficiently (adv):**
> well enough
>
> **adequate (adj):**
> sufficient, enough for a given purpose
>
> **diverse (adj):**
> many different
>
> **milieu (n):**
> a setting; an environment

Look at the sentences again. Think of the role of each sentence in the response. Put the sentences in the right order.

				E		

Step 2

Do NOT look at the sentences in Step 1. Answer the following questions.

1. What does the speaker think parents can teach their children?

_____

2. What does the speaker think parents cannot adequately teach their children?

_____

3. Where does the speaker think children should be educated?

_____

Using the short answers you wrote above, try to speak for 60 seconds explaining the speaker's response. Use the words and phrases below while you are speaking. Time yourself and record the time.

| that's why | however | I am referring to | unfortunately | on the other hand | these |

Response 1:   Speaking time: _____ seconds

Step 3

Now, listen to a sample response. How is this response different from yours? What parts of the response can you use in your own? Write down any useful expressions the sample uses.

Notes

_____

_____

_____

Listen again and repeat after the tape, paying attention to pronunciation, intonation, and word stress.

Step 4

Now write your own answers to these questions.

1. What do you think parents can teach children?

_____

2. What do you think parents cannot teach children?

_____

3. Where do you think children should be educated?

_____

Using the short answers you wrote above, give a spoken response to the prompt below. Try to incorporate additional parts of speech from Step 3, while also paying attention to your pronunciation and intonation. Record your time.

> Some parents choose to home-school their children themselves rather than send them to school. In your opinion, which option is in the best interest of the child?

Response 2:   Speaking time: _____ seconds

Skill A Q2 Practice 3 — Personal Preference

Step 1

Read and think about the question below.

> Do you agree or disagree with the following statement? A zoo has no useful purpose. Use specific reasons and examples to explain your answer.

A sample outline of a response is given below. Write down transition words or phrases that can be used in linking these ideas.

Possible purpose 1: educate visitors — useful? Yes

Possible purpose 2: provide entertainment — useful? Yes

Possible purpose 3: protect animals — useful? Yes

Transition words:

_____   _____

_____   _____

_____   _____

Using this outline, give a spoken response to the prompt above. Time yourself and record the time.

Response 1:   Speaking time: _____ seconds

Step 2

🎧 **Now, listen to a sample response. How is this response different from yours? What parts of the response can you use in your own? Write down any useful expressions the sample uses.**

Notes

_____

_____

_____

_____

_____

multitude *(n):*
a large number; several

indigenous *(adj):*
native; naturally occurring in

captivating *(adj):*
interesting; engrossing

venue *(n):*
a place for a specific purpose

endangered *(adj):*
threatened; facing possible extinction

🎧 **Listen again and repeat after the tape, paying attention to pronunciation, intonation, and word stress.**

Step 3

Now, give a spoken response to the prompt without listening to the sample. Try to incorporate additional parts of speech from Step 2, while also paying attention to your pronunciation and intonation. Record your time.

Response 2: Speaking time: _____ seconds

Step 4

Make up your own outline to the prompt. Think of other reasons to support the importance or lack of importance of zoos. Try to incorporate transition words and useful phrases introduced earlier in the practice.

Possible purpose 1: _____ useful? _____

Possible purpose 2: _____ useful? _____

Possible purpose 3: _____ useful? _____

Transition words:

_____   _____

_____   _____

_____   _____

Using this outline, give a spoken response to the prompt below. Time yourself and record the time.

> Do you agree or disagree with the following statement? A zoo has no useful purpose. Use specific reasons and examples to explain your answer.

Response 3: Speaking time: _____ seconds

Skill A Q2 Practice 4 — Personal Preference

Step 1

Read and think about the question below.

> In some countries voting is obligatory; that is to say, all citizens are required to vote by law. In other countries, voting is optional. Which system do you think is better for a society? Include details and examples in your explanation.

A sample outline of a response is given below. Write down transition words or phrases that can be used in linking these ideas.

Prefer system in which voting is: optional

a.   public interest more relevant

b.   freedom not to vote

c.   less authoritarian

Transition words:

_____   _____

_____   _____

_____   _____

Using this outline, give a spoken response to the prompt above. Time yourself and record the time.

Response 1:   Speaking time: _____ seconds

Step 2

Now, listen to a sample response. How is this response different from yours? What parts of the response can you use in your own? Write down any useful expressions the sample uses.

Notes

_____

_____

_____

_____

_____

turnout (n):
the level of participation in an activity

sway (v):
to convince; to change the opinion of

refrain (v):
to stop; to hold back

take part (v phrase):
to participate; to do something with others

constituent (n):
a person living in an area or district served by a politician

Listen again and repeat after the tape, paying attention to pronunciation, intonation, and word stress.

Step 3

Now, give a spoken response to the prompt without listening to the sample. Try to incorporate additional parts of speech from Step 2, while also paying attention to your pronunciation and intonation. Record your time.

Response 2:   Speaking time: _____ seconds

Step 4

Make up your own outline to the prompt. Think of other possible positive and negative factors for your choice. Try to incorporate transition words and useful phrases introduced earlier in the practice.

Prefer system in which voting is: _____

a. _____

b. _____

c. _____

Transition words:

_____ _____

_____ _____

_____ _____

Using this outline, give a spoken response to the prompt below. Time yourself and record the time.

> In some countries voting is obligatory; that is to say, all citizens are required to vote by law. In other countries, voting is optional. Which system do you think is better for a society? Include details and examples in your explanation.

Response 3:   Speaking time: _____ seconds

Sample Responses

Skill A Independent Speaking: Test Questions 1 and 2

Q1 - Practice 1

Last year, I met a fellow language student on an Internet study forum when I was trying to practice for a Chinese class. As it turned out, he was a Chinese student trying to practice English. Later, we developed a symbiotic relationship by helping each other practice our respective languages. Every week, we chat for 30 minutes in English and 30 minutes in Chinese. By now, we have become good friends, and we have both learned a lot. Of course, among the things I've learned is the fact that Chinese culture is fascinating, and this experience has really broadened my view of the world.

Q1 - Practice 2

One technological innovation I witnessed during my university days was the spread of the Internet. Before that, I spent hours in the library doing research. After the Internet came into widespread use, however, I didn't have to go to the library at all. I could do all of my research from a computer in my dorm room, which saved a lot of time. In fact, the Internet saved me a great deal of money, too! For example, I no longer had to make expensive, obligatory phone calls to my parents. Instead, I could send them updates via email for free.

Q1 - Practice 3

My life was changed by an unexpected blizzard. One day when I left my house to go to the airport, the weather was cool but clear. As I was driving to the airport, though, it started snowing. Within minutes, there was a raging blizzard. I knew my flight to Jamaica was going to be canceled, so I was terribly disappointed. Then, I noticed a stranded motorist, so I pulled over to help. I offered the man a lift so he could call a tow truck. Three years later, I married that man. If it weren't for that blizzard, we wouldn't have met.

Q1 - Practice 4

The Optimists' Club is an organization that has been very important in my life. They organize fun and enriching activities for kids in the city. For example, I had a great experience and forged lasting friendships while participating in their youth basketball league. In addition, they provide counselors who help troubled youths with problems. One time, I was on edge about my high school course work, and I did not have anyone to turn to for guidance. The Optimists' Club counselor provided me with some very useful advice I needed in order to select the appropriate classes to enroll in.

Q2 - Practice 1

I believe that childhood is a critical period in a person's life. First, it is the time in which personality is developed. Second, a person's experiences in childhood affect the remainder of his or her life. For instance, a major trauma experienced at the age of six has a much more devastating effect than one experienced at age thirty. Indeed, negative or traumatic experiences in childhood can lead to psychological problems in adulthood, such as depression and antisocial behavior. Conversely, positive, nurturing experiences in childhood foster mental health and well-being in adulthood. Thus, it is crucial to have positive influences in childhood.

Q2 - Practice 2

Most parents are capable of teaching their children to read, write, add, and subtract, as well as many of the other basic skills children are taught at school. However, there are some skills that cannot be taught sufficiently at home. The skills I am referring to are social skills. These, I believe, are the most important skills learned at school. That's why I am of the opinion that children should learn in a social environment. Unfortunately, the home cannot provide an adequate social milieu for children to learn to live with a diverse group of people. Public schools, on the other hand, can and do provide this setting.

Q2 - Practice 3

I believe zoos serve a multitude of useful purposes. For one thing, zoos educate visitors. If there were no zoos, children would grow up never witnessing species not indigenous to their area. With zoos, in contrast, children can learn about all kinds of different animal species and observe them up close. That's more captivating and educational than looking at pictures or reading texts. For that matter, zoos provide an entertainment venue for people of all ages. Additionally, they provide a safe home for animals whose survival is threatened in the wild. Animals that are endangered can be kept safe and well fed, as well as be encouraged to breed.

Q2 - Practice 4

In some countries, all citizens are required to vote, while in others, individuals are free to decide whether to vote or not. I prefer the system in which voting is optional. First, in this system, public interest is more important because it affects voter turnout. Therefore, governments and candidates for office must work harder to sway the opinions of voters. Second, people should be free to protest an election by refraining from taking part. Indeed, the very idea of forcing constituents to vote runs counter to the principles upon which free society is based.

Responses for the integrated speaking generally include the following parts:

Question 3

- A statement of the problem or situation, as expressed in the reading
- A statement of the speaker's opinion, as introduced in the conversation
- His or her reasons + additional information, as taken from the conversation

Question 4

- A statement of the main idea or topic of the reading and lecture
- Key points that are similar
- Key points that contrast

Before Speaking:

- Identify the topic and supporting details
- Organize the flow of your response in your mind
- Make sure that you have adequate reasons and examples

While Speaking:

- Begin your response by clearly stating the opinion/main idea of the reading and the conversation/lecture
- Give reasons or details from the conversation or lecture to support your opinion
- Make sure statements are clearly connected so that the scorer will more easily understand your points

Step 1

Read the passage below and underline important information.

STUDY ABROAD PROGRAM NOTICE

Trinity is pleased to announce that we are currently accepting applications for next year's Study Abroad Program. In the past three years, we have organized successful exchanges in over thirty-five different countries on every continent with the exception of Antarctica. This is an invaluable opportunity for students to gain exposure to another culture while receiving academic credit. Students with need-based scholarships will be permitted to use their grant money toward tuition abroad. The cost of a semester abroad is normally comparable to tuition here at Trinity, though some exceptions do apply. The rewards afforded by this opportunity, however, are unparalleled.

invaluable *(adj)*:
excellent

grant *(n)*:
a sum of money given to students to pay for tuition

comparable *(adj)*:
similar; approximately the same

afford *(v)*:
to produce; to create

unparalleled *(adj)*:
not equaled by others; the best

Write down the main idea and any important key points.

Notes

⌒ Now listen to a related conversation. Take notes on the man's opinion.

The problem: _____

Man's opinion of policy: _____

- Reason 1: _____

- Reason 2: _____

arbitrary *(adj)*:
chosen or created without justification

technically *(adv)*:
according to exact rules or definitions

fathom *(v)*:
to understand; to comprehend

preclude *(v)*:
to prevent; to forbid

merit *(n)*:
a quality deserving praise or respect

Step 2

Read and think about the prompt below.

> The man expresses his opinion of the policy regarding use of scholarships to pay for the study abroad program. State his opinion and explain the reasons he gives for holding that opinion.

WITHOUT looking at the original reading passage, review your notes from the reading and listening passages. Select the information you think is important. Fill in the blanks in the sample response below.

The man's opinion is that the school's policy _____

_____. To begin, _____

_____. Secondly, _____

_____. For these two reasons, he feels the woman _____

_____.

After you have filled in the blanks, read the response out loud. Pay attention to your pronunciation, intonation, and word stress. Record your time.

Response 1:   Speaking time: _____ seconds

Now listen to a sample response. How does it differ from your response? Write down any differences in information or phrasing.

Notes

Listen again and repeat after the tape, paying attention to pronunciation, intonation, and word stress.

Step 4

Now, give your own spoken response to the prompt. Try to incorporate additional parts of speech from Steps 1 and 3, while also paying attention to your pronunciation and intonation. Record your time.

Response 2:   Speaking time: _____ seconds

Step 1

Read the passage below and underline important information.

ANNOUNCEMENT: GRADUATE STUDENT HOUSING

We regret to inform all incoming first-year graduate students that due to renovations in the GS303 building, on-campus housing will be under limited availability during the upcoming academic year. All students are requested to sign up for the housing lottery by September 4th at www.dsu/administration/housing/lottery.htm. Arts and Humanities students as well as students in the Kurt Vonnegut Creative Writing Program will be given precedence. Students in the W. E. B. Dubois Sociology Program can sign up on the waiting list for housing in the undergraduate dorms. Partial tuition refunds will be proffered to students who do not receive a room assignment.

renovation (n):
a change to a room or building, usually for improvement

humanities (n):
the areas of study including literature, philosophy, and religion

precedence (n):
the opportunity to choose first; priority

partial (adj):
incomplete; in part

proffer (v):
to provide; to offer for acceptance

Write down the main idea and any important key points.

Notes

Now listen to a related conversation. Take notes on the woman's opinion.

Woman's opinion:

— lottery system is _____

Why:

— gives _____ but should be based on _____

— will cost her _____

— she won't be able to _____

What university should have done:

— _____

get by (v phrase):
to survive; to subsist

preferential (adj):
better; given more importance than others

prestige (n):
a level of high respect

pull in (v phrase):
to earn; to garner

give someone a piece of one's mind (expression):
to complain; to express anger

Step 2

Read and think about the prompt below.

> The woman expresses her opinion of the announced plan. State her opinion and explain the reasons she gives for holding that opinion.

WITHOUT looking at the original reading passage, review your notes from the reading and listening passages. Select the information you think is important. Fill in the blanks in the sample response below.

The woman is angry about _____.

First, she thinks it is _____.

Instead, she believes _____.

Second, she is upset because _____.

For example, she will pay more _____.

In the end, she _____.

After you have filled in the blanks, read the response out loud. Pay attention to your pronunciation, intonation, and word stress. Record your time.

Response 1:   Speaking time: _____ seconds

Step 3

Now listen to a sample response. How does it differ from your response? Write down any differences in information or phrasing.

Notes

Listen again and repeat after the tape, paying attention to pronunciation, intonation, and word stress.

Step 4

Now, make your own spoken response to the prompt. Try to incorporate additional parts of speech from Steps 1 and 3, while also paying attention to your pronunciation and intonation. Record your time.

Response 2:   Speaking time: _____ seconds

Step 1

Read the passage below and underline the important information.

MARINE BIOLOGY: FEEDING PATTERNS

When studying the feeding patterns of sea life, marine biologists classify animals into two categories: active and passive. An active feeder, such as a shark, hunts for food aggressively. In contrast, a passive animal, such as a jellyfish, simply drifts, letting its food come to it. Marine biologists can make inferences about an animal's feeding behavior based on the morphology of its body. For example, passive feeders are characterized by mechanisms that allow them to catch prey, such as net-like organs to entangle smaller organisms. Active animals, conversely, typically have sharp teeth or some form of claw-like appendage.

drift (v):
to move with the current of air or water

morphology (n):
a design or shape

mechanism (n):
a tool; a technique

entangle (v):
to capture as with a net; to twist together

appendage (n):
an attachment to a body, such as an arm or leg

Write down the main idea and any important key points.

Notes

_____

_____

_____

_____

Now listen to a related lecture. Fill in the missing information.

Morphology of giant squid:

length: _____

appendages: _____

suckers: _____

Theories on feeding behavior:

passive reason: _____

active reasons: i) _____

ii) _____

elusive (adj):
difficult to find or capture

in vain (adv phrase):
without success or purpose

glean (v):
to learn

carcass (n):
a dead body

specimen (n):
an example for scientific study

paradigm (n):
a model

Step 2

Read and think about the prompt below.

> The professor describes the physical morphology of the giant squid. Explain how this is related to the classification of the animal's feeding habits as active or passive.

WITHOUT looking at the original reading passage, review your notes from the reading and listening passages. Select the information you think is important. Fill in the blanks with this information in the sample response below.

The reading passage describes _____.

The lecturer examines _____.

First, the giant squid is _____.

Second, it has _____.

Some scientists have postulated that the _____.

Other scientists, in contrast, point to _____.

After you have filled in the blanks, read the response out loud. Pay attention to your pronunciation, intonation, and word stress. Record your time.

Response 1:   Speaking time: _____ seconds

Step 3

Now listen to a sample response. How does it differ from your response? Write down any differences in information or phrasing.

Notes

Listen again and repeat after the tape, paying attention to pronunciation, intonation, and word stress.

Step 4

Now, give your own spoken response to the prompt. Try to incorporate additional parts of speech from Steps 1 and 3, while also paying attention to your pronunciation and intonation. Record your time.

Response 2:   Speaking time: _____ seconds

Skill B Q4 Practice 2 — Reading and Lecture

Step 1

Read the passage below and underline the important information.

MELODY AND SCALES

Historical records note that traditional European music was governed by three complementary concepts: rhythm, melody, and harmony. The most important concept, melody, deals with the order of the musical notes. Musicians discovered that certain patterns of notes sound like they belong together. As a consequence, these patterns became the standard for composing music.

These melody patterns are called scales. The two most important scales are the major and minor scales. The major scale is used to express cheer and triumph, while the minor scale is used to express mystery and enchantment. These two scales have been widely used throughout history to convey a range of human emotions.

govern (v):
to control; to make rules for
complementary (adj):
working well together
triumph (n):
a feeling of victory or celebration
enchantment (n):
a feeling of something strange and intriguing
convey (v):
to express; to communicate

Write down the main idea and any important key points.

Notes

🎧 **Now listen to a related lecture. Fill in the missing information.**

Early 20th Century: _____

— reaction to _____

— music fans _____

— composers _____

Atonal music

— used _____ scale

— contained _____ notes

uproar (n):
a state of shock and loud disagreement
plug (v):
to fill a hole in order to stop anything flowing through it
mutter (v):
to speak quietly and unhappily
lambaste (v):
to criticize harshly
uncouth (adj):
crude; unrefined; not sophisticated
go out the window (expression):
to become irrelevant; to not be used

Read and think about the prompt below.

> The professor describes the beginnings of atonal music. Explain how this is related to the description of traditional music in the passage.

WITHOUT looking at the original reading passage, review your notes from the reading and listening passages. Select the information you think is important. Fill in the blanks with this information in the sample response below.

The professor begins by describing _____.

Listeners found the new style _____.

As the reading passage describes, traditional _____.

This music _____.

As the professor points out, atonal compositions _____.

The chromatic scale _____.

After you have filled in the blanks, read the response out loud. Pay attention to your pronunciation, intonation, and word stress. Record your time.

Response 1: Speaking time: _____ seconds

Step 3

Now listen to a sample response. How does it differ from your response? Write down any differences in information or phrasing.

Notes

Listen again and repeat after the tape, paying attention to pronunciation, intonation, and word stress.

Step 4

Now, give your own response to the prompt. Try to incorporate additional parts of speech from Steps 1 and 3, while also paying attention to your pronunciation and intonation. Record your time.

Response 2:   Speaking time: _____ seconds

Skill B Integrated Speaking: Test Questions 3 and 4

Q3 - Practice 1

The man's opinion is that the school's policy of only allowing students with need-based scholarships to use that money toward the Study Abroad Program is unfair. To begin, he contends that the woman earned her scholarship through academic merit rather than athletic skill or financial need. Secondly, the woman did qualify for a need-based scholarship but opted for the academic one, showing that she has the same financial need as students with need-based scholarships. For these two reasons, he feels the woman should be allowed to use her grant money to pay for tuition abroad.

Q3 - Practice 2

The woman is angry about the announced plan for a housing lottery for graduate students. First, she thinks it is unfair because students of certain majors are being given priority. Instead, she believes the housing should be assigned based on need. Second, she is upset because living off campus will be expensive and inconvenient. For example, she will pay more in rent and transportation and will not be able to study late on campus. In the end, she complains that they should have done the renovations during the summer or otherwise accommodated the needs of all students.

Q4 - Practice 1

The reading passage describes the morphological differences between marine animals that are active feeders and passive feeders. The lecturer examines the morphology of the giant squid and different theories about its feeding habits. First, the giant squid is a very large creature. Second, it has two tentacles that include sharp, claw-like components. Some scientists have postulated that the enormous size of the giant squid suggests it must be a passive feeder. Other scientists, in contrast, point to its tentacles and the model of smaller squid species as evidence suggesting that the giant squid is an active feeder.

Q4 - Practice 2

The professor begins by describing the negative response many early-20th-century audiences had to the advent of atonal musical forms. Listeners found the new style too unstructured in comparison to the traditional forms they were used to. As the reading passage describes, traditional European music was based on principles of melody. This music utilized the major and minor scales to produce the desired emotions. As the professor points out, atonal compositions utilized the chromatic scale rather than the major or minor scales. The chromatic scale includes 12 notes, all the notes a person can play on the piano.

Responses for the integrated speaking generally include the following parts:

- A statement of the problem or situation, as expressed in the conversation
- A statement of suggested solutions, as mentioned in the conversation
- Your opinion of these suggested solutions
- Your reasons + examples and details to support them
- A summary of the main points of the lecture

Before Speaking:

- Choose an opinion most easily supported
- Organize the flow of your talk in your mind
- Make sure that you have adequate reasons and examples

When Speaking:

- Make a clear statement of your opinion on the given topic
- State clear reasons for your opinion
- Use concrete examples
- Use transitions to indicate the flow of your speech

To Describe Problems:

- She/He is having a problem with _____.
- The problem is _____.
- She/He needs help with _____.
- She/He is having trouble _____.
- She/He can't figure out _____.

To Present Opinions/Solutions:

- She/He needs to _____.
- She/He should _____.
- One (Another) thing she/he can do is _____.
- The best thing she/he can do is _____.
- If I were her/him, I'd _____.

Skill C **Q5** Practice **1** — Conversation

Step 1

🎧 Listen to a conversation. Take notes on the problem presented and the possible solutions suggested.

Problem: _____

Solution 1: _____

    Advantages: _____

    Disadvantages: _____

Solution 2: _____

    Advantages: _____

    Disadvantages: _____

glitch *(n):*
a problem; an error

scanner *(n):*
a machine that reads the code on a card for information

find out *(v phrase):*
to discover; to learn

come through *(v phrase):*
to arrive

in training *(adj phrase):*
involved in a regiment of exercise; preparing for an athletic event

pain in the neck *(expression):*
an inconvenience; a nuisance

varsity *(n):*
a team representing a university or college

On your own, think of two or three additional possible benefits to each of the solutions suggested in the conversation. Write them in the spaces provided above.

Step 2

Read and think about the prompt below. Answer the following questions.

> The speakers discuss two possible solutions to the student's problem. Describe the problem. Then state which of the two solutions you prefer and explain why.

1. What is the problem? _____

2. What should the man do? _____

3. Why? _____

Step 3

Now create your own response to this topic using words and expressions from Steps 1 and 2. Use the prompts below to help you.

The man's problem _____ because _____.

The woman suggests two solutions to his problem. First, _____.

Second, _____. In my opinion, the _____

choice is preferable. To begin, _____.

In addition, _____.

🎧 **Now listen to a sample response. How does it differ from your response? Write down any differences in information or phrasing.**

Notes

_____

_____

_____

_____

🎧 **Listen again and repeat after the tape, paying attention to pronunciation, intonation, and word stress.**

Step 4

Now, give your own spoken response to the prompt. Try to incorporate additional parts of speech from Step 3, while also paying attention to your pronunciation and intonation. Record your time.

Response: Speaking time: _____ seconds

Skill C **Q5** Practice 2 — Conversation

Step 1

🎧 Listen to a conversation. Take notes on the problem presented and the possible solutions suggested.

Problem: _____

Solution 1: _____

    Advantages: _____

    Disadvantages: _____

Solution 2: _____

    Advantages: _____

    Disadvantages: _____

catch up *(v phrase)*:
to work fast enough to attain the same level as others

put one's nose to the grindstone *(expression)*:
to work very hard

from here on out *(adv phrase)*:
starting now and continuing until the end; from now on

pull off *(v phrase)*:
to do; to accomplish

extension *(n)*:
a delay in the date on which an assignment is due

dock *(v)*:
to subtract; to remove

suit *(v)*:
to please; to act according to preference

give something a shot *(expression)*:
to try; to make an attempt

heavy *(adj)*:
very serious; emotionally important

ASAP *(acronym)*:
as soon as possible

On your own, think of two or three additional possible benefits to each of the solutions suggested in the conversation. Write them in the spaces provided above.

Step 2

Read and think about the prompt below. Answer the following questions.

> The student has two possible choices in his current situation. Describe the situation. Then state which of the two choices you think is best and explain why.

1. What is the problem? _____

2. What should the man do? _____

3. Why? _____

Step 3

Now create your own response to this topic using words and expressions from Steps 1 and 2. Use the prompts below to help you.

The man's problem is that he wants _____ because

_____. In addition, _____.

The professor tries to _____.

In my opinion, he would be better off _____.

Even though he will _____, he will

_____.

Now listen to a sample response. How does it differ from your response? Write down any differences in information or phrasing.

Notes

Listen again and repeat after the tape, paying attention to pronunciation, intonation, and word stress.

Step 4

Now, give your own spoken response to the prompt. Try to incorporate additional parts of speech from Step 3, while also paying attention to your pronunciation and intonation. Record your time.

Response: Speaking time: _____ seconds

Skill C Q6 Practice 1 — Lecture

Step 1

🎧 Listen to a lecture. Take notes on the information presented.

Main topic of lecture: _____

    Origins of jazz and blues: _____

    _____

    Initial reactions: _____

    _____

    When became accepted: _____

    _____

    New forms today: _____

    _____

incarnation *(n)*:
a new form of a familiar idea

norm *(n)*:
a standard, or acceptable, behavior

mainstream *(adj)*:
accepted by the majority

intoxicating *(adj)*:
very fun and interesting; captivating

universally *(adv)*:
by all people around the world

infancy *(n)*:
the early years of; the period at the beginning

on the scene *(adv phrase)*:
within a certain sphere of activity

sample *(n)*:
an audio segment taken from an original piece and inserted, often repetitively, in a new recording

fusion *(n)*:
a mixture

myriad *(n)*:
a large number of different things

Step 2

Read and think about the prompt below. Answer the following questions.

> Summarize what you heard. Using points and examples from the talk, explain the development and innovations in music over the past one hundred years.

1. What development had the most influence on modern popular music?

_____

2. What changes did it bring to popular music?

_____

3. How did this music become accepted?

_____

Step 3

Now create your own response to this topic using words and expressions from Steps 1 and 2. Use the prompts below to help you.

According to the lecture, the advent of _____ had a significant influence

_____. To begin, it was developed _____

_____. In addition, _____

influenced the development of _____.

At first, these musical forms _____.

Later, however, they became _____.

Furthermore, _____.

🎧 **Now listen to a sample response. How does it differ from your response? Write down any differences in information or phrasing.**

Notes

_____

_____

_____

_____

🎧 **Listen again and repeat after the tape, paying attention to pronunciation, intonation, and word stress.**

Step 4

Now, give your own spoken response to the prompt. Try to incorporate additional parts of speech from Step 3, while also paying attention to your pronunciation and intonation. Record your time.

Response: Speaking time: _____ seconds

Skill C Q6 Practice 2 — Lecture

Step 1

🎧 Listen to a lecture. Take notes on the information presented.

Main topic of lecture: _____

    Traditional conception of family: _____

_____

    Those outside this conception: _____

_____

    Today's families: _____

_____

    Universal aspects of family: _____

_____

conjure (v):
to call or bring to mind; to evoke

pinpoint (v):
to define with exactness

regurgitate (v):
to reproduce exactly, without question or analysis

confines (n):
the limits; the scope

marginalize (v):
to put into a lower or outside group

pathological (adj):
relating to unhealthy behavior

dysfunctional (adj):
with abnormal or impaired functioning

adhere (v):
to stick; to conform

alarmist (n):
a person who exaggerates possible dangers in order to worry others

notion (n):
a belief; a conception

Step 2

Read and think about the prompt below. Answer the following questions.

> Summarize what you heard. Using points and examples from the talk, explain the traditional ideal of family, its current status in American society, and the role of the family in society.

1. What is the traditional conception of an ideal family?

_____

2. What happened to families in the past that differed from this ideal?

_____

3. What role does family serve in all societies?

_____

Step 3

Now create your own response to this topic using words and expressions from Steps 1 and 2. Use the prompts below to help you.

In this lecture, the professor examines _____.

The traditional ideal of _____.

Furthermore, _____ in the past.

These days, however, only _____.

In point of fact, the professor relates that _____.

Finally, the professor states that _____.

Now listen to a sample response. How does it differ from your response? Write down any differences in information or phrasing.

Notes

Listen again and repeat after the tape, paying attention to pronunciation, intonation, and word stress.

Step 4

Now, give your own spoken response to the prompt. Try to incorporate additional parts of speech from Step 3, while also paying attention to your pronunciation and intonation. Record your time.

Response: Speaking time: _____ seconds

Skill C Integrated Speaking: Test Questions 5 and 6

Q5 - Practice 1

The man's problem is that he cannot access the gym to work out because his student loans have not come through to pay his tuition. The woman suggests two solutions to his problem. First, he could find a student with access to accompany him to the gym. Second, he could talk to his coach and try to get a temporary ID. In my opinion, the first choice is preferable. To begin, his coach is away, so the man would have to wait. In addition, having a friend to work out with could help him maintain his exercise regime.

Q5 - Practice 2

The man's problem is that he wants to drop the professor's class because he is too far behind to earn a high grade. In addition, the deadline for dropping classes without penalty has passed. The professor tries to convince him to remain in the class and work hard to increase his grade. In my opinion, he would be better off dropping the class. Even though he will be penalized for dropping the class the same as if he had failed it, he will benefit by being able to concentrate his efforts on the courses of his major.

Q6 - Practice 1

According to the lecture, the advent of jazz music had a significant influence on the trajectory of popular music over the past 100 years. To begin, it was developed by African Americans combining African rhythms with European melodies. In addition, jazz influenced the development of blues, which added an extra note to the major scale, thus creating the blues scale. At first, these musical forms were met with resistance. Later, however, they became widely accepted after being incorporated into rock 'n' roll music by white musicians such as Elvis Presley. Furthermore, they have influenced the form of more recent popular music styles, such as hip-hop.

Q6 - Practice 2

In this lecture, the professor examines the idea of family. The traditional ideal of the family includes a working father, a domestic mother, and two or three children all living together in one home. Furthermore, families that differed from this ideal were marginalized and considered flawed or unhealthy in the past. These days, however, only a minority of families conform to this ideal. In point of fact, the professor relates that the ideal defined a generation or two ago is only one step on an ever-evolving sequence of ideals. Finally, the professor states that in all societies, the family helps define what is normal and natural.

Vocabulary Review

Instructions: Choose the best word or phrase to complete each sentence.

1. The shark and the lamprey have a _____ relationship. The lamprey keeps the shark's skin clean, and the shark provides the lamprey with food.
   (A) fellow
   (B) symbiotic
   (C) respective
   (D) widespread

2. In this country, a handshake is _____ when making a business agreement. Without it, the parties involved may not trust one another.
   (A) stranded
   (B) antisocial
   (C) diverse
   (D) obligatory

3. The school decided not to open because of the _____. Driving on the streets would have been too dangerous.
   (A) blizzard
   (B) forum
   (C) optimist
   (D) milieu

4. Most students find studying abroad for a year to be an _____ experience. I strongly recommend you try it.
   (A) enriching
   (B) endangered
   (C) adequate
   (D) indigenous

5. Moving to a different city can cause a lot of _____ for young children.
   (A) innovation
   (B) trauma
   (C) remainder
   (D) multitude

6. The _____ has changed for our meeting. Now, we're going to gather in Mac Hall room 201, not the library.
   (A) update
   (B) blizzard
   (C) lift
   (D) venue

7. They sampled a _____ range of foods on their travels and want to try some of their different recipes with us.
   (A) diverse
   (B) capable
   (C) nurturing
   (D) lasting

8. *Robinson Crusoe* is a novel about a man who gets _____ on a deserted island. He is stuck there for several years before getting rescued.
   (A) broadened
   (B) stranded
   (C) obligatory
   (D) captivating

9. Let's quit for the day. We can finish the _____ of this work in the morning.
   (A) remainder
   (B) optimist
   (C) innovation
   (D) forum

10. Childhood violence can lead to _____ behavior in adulthood. Therefore, it should be avoided at all costs.
    (A) endangered
    (B) adequate
    (C) capable
    (D) antisocial

11. The teacher demands that students
    _____ from chewing gum in class.
    (A) sway
    (B) refrain
    (C) fathom
    (D) proffer

12. The new law insists that government
    contracts be awarded on _____.
    Only the best proposals will be accepted,
    and no favoritism will be allowed.
    (A) merit
    (B) renovation
    (C) prestige
    (D) constituents

13. The professor's decision to give her an F
    seems completely _____! I can see
    no justification for it.
    (A) partial
    (B) preferential
    (C) unparalleled
    (D) arbitrary

14. The group from my university were able to
    _____ the opinion of the scientific
    community. Now, the validity of their theory
    is widely accepted.
    (A) sway
    (B) afford
    (C) complement
    (D) dilute

15. The _____ for the marathon for
    cancer research was higher than expected.
    Over 2,000 runners participated!
    (A) grant
    (B) humanities
    (C) turnout
    (D) prestige

Instructions: Choose the word or phrase closest in meaning to the underlined part.

16. Her strongest friendships were <u>established</u> in
    high school.
    (A) broadened
    (B) proffered
    (C) forged
    (D) precluded

17. You seem to be <u>feeling a lot of stress</u> these
    days. Is there something I can help you with?
    (A) preferential
    (B) on edge
    (C) arbitrary
    (D) captivating

18. The encouragement of her parents <u>helped
    develop</u> her skill as an artist.
    (A) fostered
    (B) fathomed
    (C) witnessed
    (D) refrained

19. A grade of C will be <u>sufficient</u> to pass to the
    next level; however, higher grades could earn
    you scholarship money.
    (A) endangered
    (B) respective
    (C) exclusive of
    (D) adequate

20. The palm tree is not <u>native</u> to California. It was
    introduced to the area by Spanish settlers.
    (A) stranded
    (B) indigenous
    (C) invaluable
    (D) partial

21. The police questioned seven people who <u>observed</u> the bank robbery.

(A) forged
(B) precluded
(C) compensated
(D) witnessed

22. People can suffer from a <u>large number</u> of fears. My strongest fear is of heights.

(A) remainder
(B) renovation
(C) constituent
(D) multitude

23. Many species of amphibian are becoming <u>threatened</u>. If we do not take action to save them, they may become extinct.

(A) adequate
(B) endangered
(C) invaluable
(D) preferential

24. That is an <u>engrossing</u> film. I couldn't take my eyes away from the screen when I watched it.

(A) captivating
(B) nurturing
(C) revolting
(D) manipulative

25. A <u>strong and violent</u> storm shut down most of the cities along the coast.

(A) partial
(B) punctuated
(C) raging
(D) symbiotic

26. This project gets <u>priority</u> over that one. We should complete it first.

(A) precedence
(B) turnout
(C) constituent
(D) merit

27. The school on the east coast <u>provided</u> her an athletic scholarship, but she declined the offer and attended a school on the west coast instead.

(A) pulled in
(B) proffered
(C) refrained
(D) swayed

28. The view of the ocean from this house is <u>the best</u>. I think you should buy it.

(A) exclusive of
(B) arbitrary
(C) imperceptible
(D) unparalleled

29. His injured leg <u>prevented</u> him from competing in the Olympic games.

(A) forged
(B) afforded
(C) precluded
(D) fostered

30. Her parents could never <u>understand</u> her decision to relocate overseas.

(A) fathom
(B) broaden
(C) exterminate
(D) compound

Instructions: Write the missing words. Use the words below to fill in the blanks.

fellow	symbiotic	fostered	unparalleled	forged
diverse	indigenous	invaluable	swayed	milieu

While searching for information on fishing in the Northwest, I encountered a website run by a
(31) _____ fishing enthusiast. As it turned out, he was a Korean student trying to practice
English on his website. Later, we met and developed a **(32)** _____ relationship by helping each
other. I **(33)** _____ his learning of English, while he showed me **(34)** _____ fishing spots
in our area. Through these interactions, we have **(35)** _____ a strong friendship. Over the time
we have known each other, he has introduced me to a **(36)** _____ range of places for fishing,
and I have also tasted a large variety of fish **(37)** _____ to this region of the country. I consider
our friendship to be **(38)** _____. In fact, my friend has **(39)** _____ me to join him on a
fishing expedition down south. He loves traveling and finds the cultural and natural **(40)** _____
of the US to be captivating.

Instructions: Choose the one word which does not belong.

41. innovation   forum   venue   site

42. sufficient   adequate   capable   endangered

43. stressed   diverse   frazzled   on edge

44. refrain   preclude   afford   stop

45. invaluable   obligatory   unparalleled   monumental

Instructions: Label each pair of words as similar (S) or opposite (O).

46. _____ symbiotic   parasitic

47. _____ widespread   common

48. _____ optimist   cynic

49. _____ foster   nurture

50. _____ foreign   indigenous

Vocabulary Review 2

Instructions: Choose the best word or phrase to complete each sentence.

1. An examination of the _____ of an animal's teeth can show if that animal is a predator.
   - (A) appendage
   - (B) carcass
   - (C) morphology
   - (D) triumph

2. She's been saving for a trip to Europe for three years. Unfortunately, reaching that goal is proving _____. She still needs a lot more money.
   - (A) elusive
   - (B) complementary
   - (C) uncouth
   - (D) mainstream

3. They celebrated in _____ after their country's team won the World Cup.
   - (A) extension
   - (B) incarnation
   - (C) fusion
   - (D) triumph

4. The cartoon mouse has gone through several different _____. The earliest drawings of him look much different from current ones.
   - (A) norms
   - (B) incarnations
   - (C) myriads
   - (D) confines

5. Societies all over the world have _____ individuals whose appearances differ from the norm. Slowly, however, many groups are trying to be more inclusive.
   - (A) marginalized
   - (B) conjured
   - (C) adhered
   - (D) suited

6. When my father was a young student, they were taught to memorize information and _____ it for exams. Thankfully, those teaching techniques have become outdated.
   - (A) pinpoint
   - (B) dock
   - (C) regurgitate
   - (D) catch up

7. The professor has given us all an _____ for the term papers. They're now due on Friday.
   - (A) incarnation
   - (B) extension
   - (C) infancy
   - (D) alarmist

8. The bottle _____ with the ocean current all the way to Japan.
   - (A) entangled
   - (B) drifted
   - (C) gleaned
   - (D) lambasted

9. Within the rainforest exist a _____ of plant and animal life forms.
   - (A) myriad
   - (B) notion
   - (C) scanner
   - (D) mechanism

10. The _____ of a dead great white shark washed up on shore last summer.
    - (A) carcass
    - (B) paradigm
    - (C) triumph
    - (D) enchantment

11. The fly _____ itself in the spider's web.
    (A) gleaned
    (B) entangled
    (C) governed
    (D) came through

12. If you don't want to take my advice, then _____ yourself. I think, however, that you will regret your decision.
    (A) dock
    (B) broaden
    (C) suit
    (D) witness

13. Because the team was _____ as a group, the management decided that a change in personnel was needed.
    (A) intoxicating
    (B) complementary
    (C) mainstream
    (D) dysfunctional

14. Ireland is famous for evoking pleasant feelings of mystery and _____ in its visitors.
    (A) infancy
    (B) extension
    (C) morphology
    (D) enchantment

15. Passionate Canadians everywhere were in a state of _____ upon learning of the cancellation of the hockey season.
    (A) uproar
    (B) appendage
    (C) paradigm
    (D) innovation

Instructions: Choose the word or phrase closest in meaning to the underlined part.

16. The Wright brothers set a <u>model</u> of powered aircraft that others would follow in the future.
    (A) specimen
    (B) paradigm
    (C) glitch
    (D) scanner

17. Many people find the <u>belief</u> that women should not have careers to be insulting and outdated.
    (A) notion
    (B) sample
    (C) varsity
    (D) uproar

18. Wolf behavior is <u>controlled</u> by the hierarchical structure of the pack.
    (A) plugged
    (B) muttered
    (C) conveyed
    (D) governed

19. There is some <u>error</u> with this program. It won't print what I want it to.
    (A) myriad
    (B) norm
    (C) glitch
    (D) varsity

20. Her boss <u>subtracted</u> fifty dollars from her pay every time she arrived for work late.
    (A) conjured
    (B) regurgitated
    (C) suited
    (D) docked

21. Due to recent events, professors are reminded that the <u>scope</u> of the teacher-student relationship does not allow for dating.
    (A) confines
    (B) fusion
    (C) infancy
    (D) extension

22. Unfortunately, we must <u>conform</u> to the company's rules for employee age. Therefore, your application has not been accepted.
    (A) pinpoint
    (B) adhere
    (C) marginalize
    (D) preclude

23. His mother believes that anyone who does not listen to Mozart on a daily basis is <u>uncivilized</u>.
    (A) preferential
    (B) unparalleled
    (C) endangered
    (D) uncouth

24. Darwin collected many <u>examples</u> of new plant and animal species for scientific examination.
    (A) specimens
    (B) carcasses
    (C) humanities
    (D) renovations

25. His wife <u>harshly criticized</u> him for arriving home from work at 1:00 a.m.
    (A) lambasted
    (B) pinpointed
    (C) broadened
    (D) forged

26. The <u>standards</u> of one culture may seem odd to people from another culture.
    (A) mentors
    (B) norms
    (C) stimulants
    (D) plateaus

27. The atmosphere at the festival was <u>exhilarating</u>. None of us wanted the day to end.
    (A) mainstream
    (B) intoxicating
    (C) peripheral
    (D) imperceptible

28. During its <u>early years</u>, the Internet was not used in most homes as it is today.
    (A) incarnation
    (B) varsity
    (C) morphology
    (D) infancy

29. The braking <u>tool</u> on my bicycle is broken, so I can't ride today.
    (A) appendage
    (B) mechanism
    (C) glitch
    (D) forum

30. The children <u>complain quietly</u> whenever their mother makes them study.
    (A) plug
    (B) convey
    (C) glean
    (D) mutter

Instructions: Write the missing words. Use the words below to fill in the blanks.

indigenous	elusive	myriad	in vain	specimens
lambaste	glean	convey	optimists	mainstream

The sasquatch, a large ape-like creature **(31)** _____ to North America has proven to be **(32)** _____. Over the past thirty years, a **(33)** _____ of expeditions have been launched in the attempt to capture a sasquatch. Unfortunately, these efforts have been **(34)** _____ as none have yet been captured. Because no actual **(35)** _____ have been captured for study, most scientists doubt its existence. Some go even so far as to **(36)** _____ colleagues who support the idea of its existence. Despite these cynical colleagues, researchers have discovered some evidence that helps science **(37)** _____ information about this mysterious animal. For example, sasquatch nests and droppings **(38)** _____ key details about its sleeping and eating habits. **(39)** _____ among the group of sasquatch researchers strongly believe the day will come when living examples of the animal will be discovered, and their theories will become accepted by **(40)** _____ science.

Instructions: Write the missing words. Use the words below to fill in the blanks.

off	by	in	in	over

41. If a police car turns on its sirens, you should pull _____ immediately.

42. We decided to take part _____ the protest against the war.

43. I depend on my student loans to get _____. Without them, I couldn't survive.

44. He tried _____ vain to find the information on the Internet. After three hours, he gave up and went to the library.

45. After a lot of hard work and constant study, she was able to pull _____ the highest grade in the class.

Instructions: Match the words that are opposites.

46. alarmist   (A) release

47. include   (B) marginalize

48. complementary   (C) forget

49. entangle   (D) optimist

50. glean   (E) dysfunctional

Chapter 3

Focus: Speaking Naturally

Focus A Sentence Stress

- Sentence stress on content words
- Sentence stress on function words

Focus B Stress and Intonation

- Changing pitch for emphasis
- Commas and series with *and* or *or*

Focus C Pausing

- Timing
- Pause and pitch

Focus | Speaking Naturally

Using the tips below, you can improve both your fluency and clarity of speech. These tips will also help you recognize your weak points in speaking.

When speaking:

- Open your mouth while speaking. Try not to mumble.
- Pay special attention to the pronunciation of content words and key terms.
  - Stress each syllable correctly and accurately.
  - Clearly pronounce both vowels and consonants.
  - Smoothly link sounds between words within a phrase and in consonant clusters.
- Change pitch between stressed and unstressed syllables.
- Speak in sentences or phrases, not word by word.
- Speak with appropriate speed, not too quickly.

When practicing:

- Practice speaking by writing down every word you say and marking each place where you pause or vary intonation.
- Examine this transcript of your speech and look for possible mistakes. Practice these parts again, focusing on correcting the previous mistakes.
- Record and listen to your speech. Note any areas that need improvement.

Sentence stress is very important in English. The rhythm of sentences spoken in English alerts listeners to the message presented. Words or phrases important to the content of the message tend to be stressed, whereas words or phrases that are not important tend to be reduced.

Focus A - Sentence Stress

Step 1 Sentence stress on content words

> Certain words within a sentence are given importance because of the meaning they communicate. These words are referred to as content words. Words with little or no meaning outside their grammatical function are usually not stressed within the sentence.
>
> — Content Words: nouns, verbs, adjectives, adverbs
>
> — Function Words: auxiliary verbs, *be* verbs, most pronouns, prepositions, articles
>
> Stressed syllables are pronounced longer, pitched higher, and spoken slightly louder.

Underline the content words and say the sentence. Be sure to stress the content words.

1. Before that, I spent hours in the library doing research.
2. My life was changed by an unexpected blizzard.
3. In addition, they provide counselors who help troubled youths with problems.
4. I believe that childhood is an integral period in a person's life.
5. Public schools, on the other hand, can and do provide this setting.
6. That's more captivating and educational than looking at pictures or reading texts.
7. I prefer the system in which voting is optional.
8. Instead, she believes the housing should be assigned based on need.

Now, listen and repeat.

Listen to the paragraph. Write only the words you hear most clearly.

Step 2 ## Sentence stress on function words

The normal pattern of sentence stress reduces function words. However, function words can be stressed when the speaker is expressing strong emotion, is disagreeing, or is clarifying mistaken information.

Ex. <u>Don't</u> you agree that English is easy?

I <u>do not</u> agree! (Non-contracted forms are often used to show stress.)

Say the sentences and indicate whether the underlined word is reduced (R) or stressed (S).

1. Technically, my scholarship isn't need-based, but I <u>do</u> need it.
2. If you put your nose to the grindstone from here on out, you <u>might</u> pull off a C.
3. After the Internet came along, I <u>could</u> do all of my research from a computer in my dorm room.
4. First, <u>it</u> is the time in which personality is developed.
5. However, there are some skills that <u>cannot</u> be taught sufficiently at home.
6. Public schools, on the other hand, <u>can</u> and <u>do</u> provide this setting.
7. In my opinion, the second choice <u>is</u> preferable.
8. Although no specimens have been found, there <u>is</u> a lot of evidence for scientists to examine.

Now, listen and repeat.

Circle any underlined words that should be stressed. More than one word may be stressed in each sentence.

Example. We didn't <u>have</u> a lot of rain last year, <u>but</u> we (do) this year.

1. That <u>isn't</u> <u>his</u> dog, <u>it's</u> <u>her</u> dog.
2. Most students <u>didn't</u> pass <u>the</u> exam, but John <u>did</u>.
3. She <u>likes</u> jazz music, <u>and</u> he likes blues music. I like jazz <u>and</u> blues music.
4. Kim <u>hasn't</u> paid <u>her</u> tuition fees, but Rick <u>has</u>.
5. The major scale <u>doesn't</u> have 12 notes, <u>but</u> the chromatic scale <u>does</u>.
6. Off-campus housing <u>isn't</u> just expensive; <u>it's</u> expensive <u>and</u> inconvenient.
7. <u>He</u> <u>didn't</u> get the need-based scholarship. <u>She</u> did.
8. You <u>can</u> take English 201 <u>or</u> English 205. You can't take both.

Now, listen and repeat.

Intonation is also very important in English. The pitch of the speaker's voice alerts listeners to the particular message being conveyed. By modifying the pitch of the voice to rise, fall, or do both, the speaker stresses certain words and meanings. When modifying the pitch, the speaker often lengthens the amount of time each word is pronounced.

Focus B - Stress and Intonation

Step 1 Changing pitch for emphasis

At the beginning of a conversation, the last content word in each sentence is usually the focus of meaning. Therefore, the primary stress in these sentences usually falls on the last content word. The sound of the speaker's voice rises on the focus word and then falls. If the sentence is a question, the sound of the speaker's voice rises but does not fall at the end of the sentence.

Ex. Is that a deer? No, it's a big dog.

However, the focus of a sentence can change. Thus, one sentence can have more than one intonation pattern. By noticing the word the speaker emphasizes, the listener can guess what will come next.

Ex. It's not a small dog. It's a big dog.

Listen to the first sentence and underline the focus word. Then choose the sentence that is most likely to come next.

1. Children should attend school.
   a. Adults should work.
   b. It's a good place to learn social skills.
2. This experience helped tremendously with my studies.
   a. I really learned a lot.
   b. Unfortunately, it didn't help with her studies.
3. Subsequent developments in pop music were generally met with the same disapproval.
   a. Hip-hop and reggae, for example, took a long time to reach the mainstream.
   b. Developments in classical music, on the other hand, were embraced in a short time.
4. Do you play on the varsity basketball team?
   a. No, I play on the hockey team.
   b. No, John plays on the basketball team.

Now, listen and repeat. Ensure your voice is rising on the stressed syllables and dropping afterwards.

Read the two sentences. Try to figure out how the second sentence relates to the first. Underline the focus word in the first sentence according to this context.

1. I don't abhor jazz music. I don't really enjoy it that much, though.
2. Her behavior is antisocial. He is actually a nice guy.
3. The squid doesn't have eight appendages. It has ten.
4. Jellyfish drift with ocean currents. Squid use their arms to swim.
5. There is a glitch with her computer. Her phone is working fine.
6. The campus renovations will begin in September. The campus celebrations begin in October.

Now, listen and repeat. Ensure your voice is rising on the stressed syllables and dropping afterwards.

Step 2 Commas and series with *and* or *or*

When there is a series of words with the conjunctions *and* or *or*, the intonation rises on all members of the series except the last. The last member has a rising-falling intonation.

  Ex. We went to the park, / (↗) the beach, / (↗) and the mountains. (↘)

    You can do it Monday / (↗) or Tuesday. (↘)

After the comma used between a sentence and an additional phrase, the intonation rises.

  Ex. It's three blocks from here, / (↗) near the supermarket. (↘)

    As for me, / (↗) I'll have the soup and salad. (↘)

Divide the sentences into thought groups by using slashes (/) and mark the intonation of each group with arrows (↗ or ↘).

1. Many of the most popular bands on the charts today are born from influences of rock, hip-hop, reggae, ska, and techno.
2. They were considered troubled, pathological, or dysfunctional.
3. I doubt it'll cover the cost of renting a place in this city, especially near the campus.
4. Most giant squid are smaller, growing to approximately ten meters.
5. European concert-goers were plugging their ears, walking out on performances, and muttering to themselves.
6. The chromatic scale simply means all the notes you can play on a piano, without any notes left out.

Now, listen and repeat.

Having appropriate pauses is also an important part of spoken English. Pauses are given after each message unit in order to provide listeners time to process the information. If a speaker speaks too rapidly or without thought to the grouping of the information presented, listeners may have difficulty distinguishing the important content of the message.

Focus C - Pausing

Step 1 Timing

Pausing, like stress and pronunciation, greatly adds to the clarity of speech.

There are several reasons for adding a pause:
- To make the meaning clear: When the wind blows [pause] the waves run high.
- For emphasis: Frankly [pause] I'm disappointed in you.
- To enable the speaker to catch a breath
- To give listeners time to understand complex sentences

Therefore, it is helpful to pause after commas, transitional words, and complicated ideas, such as lengthy subjects, prepositional phrases, and clauses in compound and complex sentences.

Look at the sentences and circle any slash (/) that indicates an appropriate pause.

1. The traditional ideal / of the family includes a working father, / a domestic mother, / and two or three children all living / happily in one home.
2. As it turned out, / he was a Chinese student / trying to practice English.
3. After the Internet / came into widespread use, / however, / I didn't have to go to the library at all.
4. Within minutes, / there was a raging / blizzard.
5. Some alarmists / contend that this is a fundamental societal problem, / a breakdown in values that will produce / immeasurable negative effects.
6. These, / I believe, / are the most important / skills learned at school.

Now, listen and repeat.

🎧 **Practice saying the sample response and write a slash (/) where you pause.**

1. The man's opinion is that the school's policy of only allowing students with need-based scholarships to use that money toward the Study Abroad Program is unfair.
2. To begin, he contends that the woman earned her scholarship through academic merit rather than athletic skill or financial need.
3. Secondly, the woman did qualify for a need-based scholarship but opted for the academic one, showing that she has the same financial need as students with need-based scholarships.
4. For these two reasons, he feels the woman should be allowed to use her grant money to pay for tuition abroad.

🎧 **Now, listen and repeat.**

Step 2 Pause and pitch

Every clause or thought group within a sentence contains a focus word. A rise and then a fall in pitch is used to mark this focus word. This change alerts listeners to the central meaning of the thought group. The fall in intonation, combined with pausing, helps listeners recognize the end of a thought group.

Ex.   I remembered to bring paper, / but I forgot my book.
When the water boils rapidly, / put the spaghetti in the pot.
When the water boils, / rapidly put the spaghetti in the pot.

🎧 **Practice saying the sentences. Be sure to use appropriate pauses and pitch.**

1. The reading passage describes the morphological differences between marine animals that are active feeders and passive feeders.
2. The lecturer examines the morphology of the giant squid and different theories about its feeding habits.
3. First, the giant squid is a very large creature.
4. Second, it has two tentacles that include sharp, claw-like components.
5. Some scientists have postulated that the enormous size of the giant squid suggests it must be a passive feeder.
6. Other scientists, in contrast, point to its tentacles and the model of smaller squid species as evidence suggesting the giant squid is an active feeder.

🎧 **Now, listen and repeat.**

Mastering Skills for the TOEFL® iBT

WRITING

WRITING Table of Contents

How the writing section is organized

There are four main parts in the writing section.

Introduction	Understanding what each section requires you to do
Chapter 1	Practicing the basic writing skills of brainstorming, organizing, and paraphrasing
Chapter 2	Developing writing skills by connecting and supporting ideas
Chapter 3	Focusing on sentence structure and word choice
Practice Test	Practicing with questions designed according to the real test format

The writing section of the test is designed to assess your ability to organize and support your ideas in essay format. You will have two writing tasks. One task is based on both a reading and a lecture. You will be required to summarize the information you have heard, and to relate the information heard in the lecture to the information in the passage. The second task requires you to generate an essay based on your own experience. In this second task, you will be given no material to work with; it will be based completely on your own ideas.

● **Question Types:**

Questions for the writing section of the TOEFL® test will appear in the following order:

Question	Type	Suggested Time	Response Length	Description
1	Integrated: 250-300 wd reading 250-300 wd lecture	20 minutes	150-225 wds	Contrast information presented in the reading passage with information presented in the lecture
2	Independent	30 minutes	300+ wds	Present a personal opinion or describe experience, including details and examples

Study Tips

- **Integrated Writing:**
  - ⇨ Look for magazine or newspaper articles that are about 300 words long. Time yourself as you read the articles. You should aim to read 300 words in less than three minutes. After reading, try to outline the article. Then, without looking back at the article, try to write a summary of the article from your outline.
  - ⇨ Practice listening to short reports given in English. There are many websites where such reports are available online. While you listen to a report, take notes. Try to summarize the report from your notes.
  - ⇨ Look for a variety of exercises in writing books that practice paraphrasing. Study the methods such books suggest for paraphrasing. Focus especially on exercises that practice the usage of synonyms and/or changing the grammar of given sentences in order to paraphrase them.
  - ⇨ Review useful phrases and expressions for citing sources. Pay attention to where these citation phrases can be placed in sentences and how the phrases should be punctuated.
  - ⇨ Practice your typing skills in English. You must type your essay for the TOEFL® iBT.

- **Independent Writing:**
  - ⇨ Practice writing TOEFL® essays. Get a list of sample topics at www.ets.org/Media/Tests/TOEFL/pdf/989563wt.pdf. Select a topic at random and write a 30-minute draft essay. Correct the essay, with the assistance of a teacher if possible, and rewrite it with the suggested corrections.
  - ⇨ When you are studying a group of writing topics, practice sorting them into "opinion" or "experience" topics. This will help you quickly determine the appropriate writing task you will have when you take the test.
  - ⇨ Practice outlining ideas before you write. You can do this by taking five or six topics for writing and making a short outline for each one. Don't write the essays; just write the outlines. You can also use different techniques for prewriting, such as making simple charts of information, drawing bubble diagrams, or creating lists of ideas.
  - ⇨ Look for a variety of exercises in writing books that practice writing introductions and conclusions. Study the methods that these books suggest for writing introductions and conclusions. Pay attention to tips for beginning and ending introductions and conclusions.
  - ⇨ Practice your typing skills in English. You must type your essay for the TOEFL® iBT.

Test management:

- In the integrated writing, you will read a passage and listen to a lecture afterwards. The reading passage disappears during the listening and reappears after the listening, so don't worry about taking notes about all of the key points in the reading. However, you will NOT be able to hear the listening again, so it is very important to take good notes while you listen.

- You have to type in your answers. You can use icon buttons at the top of the screen for editing. The editing tools include cut, paste, undo, and redo.

- Keep the style of essay writing in English in mind. First select a main idea, explain it clearly, then support and develop it using details and/or examples. Be sure your essay has a logical flow. There should be a reason for every sentence in your essay. Such reasons include introducing a new example or detail to support the main idea, or explaining or supporting an example or detail mentioned previously. Do not write any sentences that are unrelated to your main idea or that do not fit into the organizational structure of your essay just to increase your word count.

- Make every effort to use effective language and appropriate sentence structure and vocabulary. Try NOT to use vocabulary or constructions that you are not confident with, as these will increase your chances of making errors.

- Use a variety of language. English has a large number of synonyms and analogous constructions, so using the same construction repeatedly is considered poor style.

- Keep the 50-minute time limit for the entire writing section in mind. Remember that graders are expecting to read draft essays, not finely polished final products. If you find yourself stuck in a particular part of your essay, it is best to move on and complete the essay, then go back and fix the difficult area.

- Try to leave at least five minutes for revision. When revising, be sure to look for spelling or grammatical errors (remember, there is no spell checker on the test!) as well as ways to improve the structure and flow of your essay.

How Writing Will Be Scored

ETS graders will score test takers' essays for **integrated** writing tasks according to the following scale:

Score	General Description	Key Points
5	The essay includes important information from both the reading and the lecture and appropriately explains the information with regard to the prompt.	The essay is well organized; it include minor errors in grammar or word choice, but the errors do not make sentences difficult to understand.
4	The essay includes most of the key points from the reading and the lecture as they relate to the prompt. Some points may not be fully explained or the explanation may be vague.	There are several minor errors with language; some ideas may not seem connected, but there are no real problems with clarity.
3	The essay has one or more of the following problems: does not include a key point from the lecture or reading, shows only a limited understanding of the information, incorrectly explains a key point, problems with grammar or word choice make some sentences unclear.	Errors in sentence structure and word choice may make the meaning of some sentences unclear; transitions or connections between ideas are not always easy to follow; overall, the important ideas in the essay can be understood.
2	The essay has one or more of the following problems: does not include sufficient information from the reading, lecture or both, contains many problems with grammar or word choice so the reader cannot follow connections between ideas.	Errors in sentence structure and word choice make ideas in the essay difficult to understand in key points; readers unfamiliar with the reading and lecture may not be able to follow the essay.
1	The essay includes few or none of the key points from the reading, lecture, or both. The essay is poorly written and difficult to understand.	Frequent and serious errors in grammar and word choice make some sentences in the essay impossible to understand.
0	The essay only copies words from the prompt or is not related to the topic at all.	There is not enough of the student's writing available to score.

How Writing Will Be Scored

ETS graders will score test takers' essays for **independent** writing tasks according to the following scale:

Score	General Description	Key Points
5	The response answers the question or prompt well. The essay is easy to understand and well organized.	There is good use of language, correct choice of words and idioms to express ideas. Minor errors in grammar and word choice are acceptable.
4	The response answers the question or prompt, but not all of the ideas are fully developed. The essay can be understood, but there are some clearly noticeable mistakes in the writing.	There is good use of language, including a variety of sentence structures and appropriate range of vocabulary. There are some minor errors in sentence structure, word form, or the use of idioms, but these errors do not make comprehension difficult.
3	The essay gives a basic answer to the question or prompt, but not many examples or details are provided. Most sentences can be understood, but errors in grammar or word choice could make the meaning of some sentences unclear.	Little use of connectors to link ideas or show progression of thought. Sentence constructions are very simple or there are frequent errors in more complex sentence structures. Word choice and poor grammar may make some sentences vague or difficult to comprehend.
2	The essay is very short and not well organized. The ideas are not connected and examples are not explained.	Errors in grammar or word choice appear in almost every sentence. Overall, ideas are difficult to follow.
1	The essay is short and confusing. Little or no detail is given to support ideas, and irrelevant information is included. Some sentences cannot be understood by the reader.	There are serious errors in grammar and word choice.
0	The essay only copies words from the prompt or is not related to the topic at all.	Not enough of the student's writing is available to score.

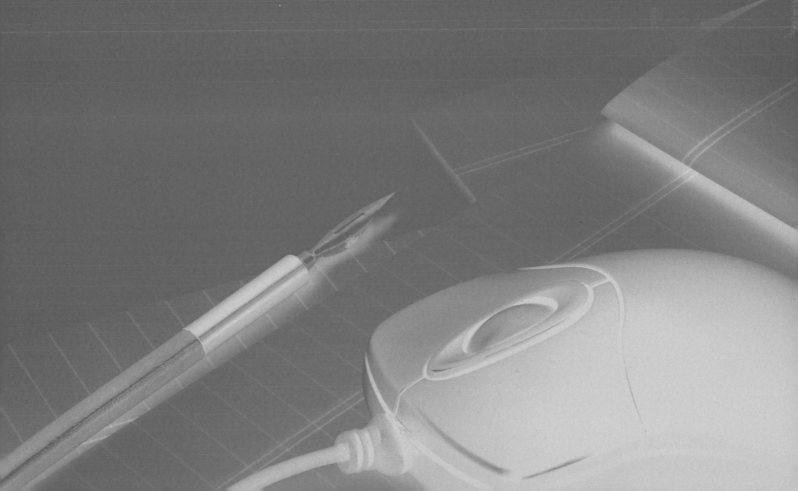

Chapter 1

Thinking and Writing

Integrated Writing: Organizing Information

Necessary Skills

- Understanding information from both reading and listening passages
- Taking notes on the reading and listening passages
- Using information from your notes in your writing
- Synthesizing the information taken from both the reading and listening passages

Process	Strategy
Read, listen, and take notes	You will not see the prompt until after you finish reading and listening, so taking notes is essential. Take notes on major points from both reading and listening.
Read the question and understand the task	Identify what kind of relationship between the reading and the listening the question asks you to discuss.
Select ideas from your notes	Choose the points that you need to discuss. Think about how the points in the lecture relate to the points in the reading. The listening passage will present details that will either challenge the information presented in the reading, present a counter example, or describe the consequences of an attempt to solve a problem presented in the reading.
Organize the ideas	Include information from both the reading and listening passages. Clearly show the relationship between the information presented in the listening and that presented in the reading passage. Limit the time for organizing to less than 2 minutes in order to give yourself more time for writing and editing.

Practice 1

Step 1

Read the following passage. Then, look at the note diagram and fill in the missing information.

Correlation studies are used to determine if two variables are related to each other. In this type of research, the researcher does not manipulate either variable, but instead measures the rates at which they occur naturally. If, for example, variable X increases in frequency as variable Y increases in frequency, X and Y are said to be positively correlated. If, on the other hand, Y decreases as X increases, X and Y are said to be negatively correlated.

For example, an investigation into the relationship between study time and grades earned might find that as the number of hours spent studying increases, exam scores also increase. This is an example of a positive correlation. An investigation into the relationship between TV time and grades earned might show a negative correlation; that is, as the number of hours spent watching TV increases, grades decrease.

Correlation studies, then, compare two or more variables and determine whether or not they have a relationship. This information is used to infer if a causal relationship exists between the variables. A causal relationship cannot always be inferred, however. For example, increased time spent watching TV may have a negative correlation with grades earned, but this does not necessarily indicate a causal relationship. It is probably the case that the more time a student spends watching TV, the less time that student will spend studying.

correlation *(n)*:
a connection or relationship between two things

variable *(n)*:
an aspect of an experiment that can be controlled or observed

manipulate *(v)*:
to change; to alter

positively *(adv)*:
in a direct relationship in which the rates of variables change in the same direction

negatively *(adv)*:
in an inverse relationship in which the rates of variables change in opposite directions

causal *(adj)*:
related to a cause or reason for an action

Correlation Studies: determine _____ two variables

— researchers don't _____ variables

— researchers _____ at which variables change naturally

Relationship types:

— Y increases when X increases: _____

— Y decreases when X increases: _____

— sometimes, a _____ can be inferred

Step 2

 Now listen to a lecture related to the topic in Step 1. Fill in the blanks of the note diagram below with the keywords or key phrases shown. Not all of the words or phrases will be used.

Main point: Correlation does _____ causation

— cannot be certain because investigators don't _____

— also, a _____ may be affecting the correlation

   ex. Eating ice cream and drowning have a _____

— but a third variable is _____

Correlations can _____ causal relationships, but more _____ is needed to prove it

   ex. A positive correlation between smoking and _____
   led to further research that proved a _____

component *(n)*:
a part of

assess *(v)*:
to evaluate; to analyze

validity *(n)*:
the state of accuracy or truthfulness

vital *(adj)*:
necessary; essential

cramp *(n)*:
a painful tightening of a muscle

indicate *(v)*:
to show; to state

**keywords /
key phrases**

| negative correlation | hot weather | research | not imply | causal relationship |
| positive correlation | third variable | suggest | cancer | manipulate variables |

Step 3

Review your notes from both the reading and the lecture. Pay attention to the main ideas and supporting details. Rewrite the ideas as complete sentences.

Reading:

Main idea: _____

Supporting idea: _____

Supporting idea: _____

Lecture:

Main idea: _____

Supporting idea: _____

Supporting idea: _____

Use the main ideas and details from Steps 1, 2, and 3 to complete the passage. Include information from both the reading and the lecture.

_____ are useful tools because they describe relationships between different _____ as they occur in the natural world. It is important, though, that researchers be careful not to make the common erroneous assumption that a _____.

Correlations indicate when two _____ are related somehow. This implies that researchers do not _____ either variable; they simply _____ events as they occur. For this reason, it is _____ to determine if one variable causes the other to change.

Furthermore, there is always the possibility of a _____ causing both to change. To demonstrate, the lecturer states that there is a positive correlation between ice cream consumption and _____. A _____ correlation means that as one variable increases, so does the other. So, in this example, as ice cream consumption increases, the rate of drowning _____ as well. It is a _____, though, to interpret these findings as indicating that ice cream consumption causes drowning. In this case, there is a third variable that is affecting both — the _____.

Sometimes, it is _____ to infer from a correlation study that one variable affects the other, such as in the example in the reading of increased study time being correlated to _____. It is very important, nonetheless, that one is careful to consider which _____ affects which, and that there is not a _____ affecting changes in both variables.

Skill A Q1 History

Practice 2

Step 1

Read the following passage. Then, look at the note diagram and fill in the missing information.

Historical Revisionism is the term used to describe a re-examination of historical data. Revisionists examine and update so-called historical "facts," arguing that as societies evolve, so do their histories. These historians believe that revisionism addresses imbalances in historical narratives that have ignored or discounted certain groups in societies. They update histories by re-examining facts and including new information.

Revisionist historians argue that despite the scientific methodology of historiography, history is biased. Like any other story of the past, history is a narrative, and narratives favor the elite within societies and help them maintain power. When these power structures change, revisionism becomes necessary in order to correct imbalances perpetrated through skewed historical writing.

This idea is best understood when illustrated by an example such as the notion that Christopher Columbus discovered America. Did he really discover America? If so, what about the many indigenous peoples that had populated both American continents for thousands of years? The word "discovered" actually displays a Eurocentric bias. It implies that a part of the world only becomes "real" when Europeans know about it.

Thanks to historical revisionism, we can now qualify this notion, and consequently, in modern historical texts, quotation marks are added when the word "discovered" is used.

imbalance (n):
a lack of fairness; an inequity

discount (v):
to ignore; to not pay sufficient attention to

methodology (n):
a body of practices, procedures, and rules used by those who work in a given discipline

historiography (n):
the body of practices, procedures, and rules used by historians

perpetrate (v):
to do; to commit an unethical act

skewed (adj):
not balanced; biased

indigenous (adj):
native to an area

Issue: Historical _____: A re-_____ of historical facts

Purpose: Corrects historical _____

Includes new _____

Motivation: Despite scientific _____, historiography is _____

History is a _____ that favors the _____ in society

Example/Argument: Did Columbus _____ America?

No. This is a _____ bias

🎧 Now listen to a lecture related to the topic in Step 1. Fill in the blanks of the note diagram below with the keywords or key phrases shown. Not all of the words or phrases will be used.

Key Issue: Historical Revisionism has come to be used _____

Why?

— Many _____ and crackpots pose as revisionist _____

— They present badly _____ papers, books, and _____ as fact

— Their writing _____ specific events in history

— They propagate a _____ bias

This is dangerous. Why?

Non- _____ are _____ to support an inaccurate perspective

Example: Denial of the _____

Solution: Legitimate researchers must _____ this trend by producing _____ research using verifiable _____

pejoratively (adv):
in a negative, disparaging way

tinged (adj):
colored; given a certain perspective or opinion

hacks and crackpots (n phrase):
people who make academic or scientific claims without any justification or proof

pose (v):
to pretend to be

controversial (adj):
causing many different strong emotional reactions

negate (v):
to work against; to counteract

condone (v):
to accept as valid

keywords / key phrases	political	experts	data	articles	pejoratively
	researched	combat	negates	historians	methodology
	imbalances	genuine	hacks	influenced	holocaust

Review your notes from both the reading and the lecture. Pay attention to the main ideas and supporting details. Rewrite the ideas as complete sentences.

Reading:

Main idea: _____

Supporting idea: _____

Supporting idea: _____

Lecture:

Main idea: _____

Supporting idea: _____

Supporting idea: _____

Step 4

Use the main ideas and details from Steps 1, 2, and 3 above to complete the passage. Include information from both the reading and the lecture.

In the reading, historical revisionism is presented in a _____ light. The writer explains that

revisionism is an attempt to correct _____ in biased versions of the past that _____

certain groups. The writer gives the example of the _____ Americans that are ignored when

historical texts refer to Columbus as having "discovered" America. The writer believes that

_____ is necessary because as societies change, so do the power structures that govern them.

Revisionism allows historians to include _____ information and re-examine the way history is

written, so that it is told not exclusively from the perspective of the elite, _____ ruling groups

in a society.

The speaker warns us that there is a particular kind of historical revisionism that is very dangerous and

negative. This form of revisionism is often practiced by individuals with no real _____ training

or expertise. These self-proclaimed revisionists make use of _____ theories and logical

_____ in their ill-researched writing on historical subjects. Such revision also often negates or

_____ that particular historical events, such as the _____, even took place. Their

work influences non-experts negatively and gives legitimate historians a _____ name. Such

revisionism must be _____ by authentic historians who use _____ data and

supportable documentation.

Practice 3

Step 1

Read the following passage. Then, look at the note diagram and fill in the missing information.

The Big Bang theory is the most dominant scientific explanation for how our universe came into existence. This theory states that the universe was created between ten and twenty billion years ago in a cataclysmic explosion that flung matter in all directions.

This theory was first postulated as long ago as 1927 by a Belgian priest named Georges Lemaître. He argued that the entire universe had been created via the explosion of a single atom. All matter, light, and energy came from this. In 1929, the influential astronomer, Edwin Hubble, discovered experimental evidence that supported Lemaître's theory. Hubble's studies indicated that galaxies and positive space matter are travelling away from one another at speeds proportional to their distance from us. This theory, called "Hubble's Law," also implies that our universe is still expanding.

One tenet of the Big Bang theory is that the universe contains a kind of radiation called "cosmic background radiation" caused by the original explosion of the primeval atom. In 1964, scientists Robert Wilson and Arno Penzias discovered the presence of such radiation. They were awarded a Nobel Prize for their work.

dominant *(adj)*: having the most influence or control

cataclysmic *(adj)*: causing great damage

postulate *(v)*: to suggest as true; to hypothesize

proportional *(adj)*: having the same ratio

primeval *(adj)*: having existed from the beginning; referring to the earliest times

Subject: How _____ was created.

Most _____ theory: _____ _____

Argument:

— Primeval _____ exploded, flung _____ in all _____

— All matter, _____, and energy came from this

— _____ found evidence to show universe is still _____

— "Cosmic background _____" discovered — 1964

Step 2

🎧 **Now listen to a lecture related to the topic in Step 1. Fill in the blanks of the note diagram below with the keywords or key phrases shown. Not all of the words or phrases will be used.**

Topic: 1. _____ holes in the Big Bang theory

2. _____ theories for how the universe originated

Argument: — Big Bang evidence is too general and _____

— Evidence also supports other _____

— Big Bang never proven beyond _____ doubt

— Theory, therefore, remains _____

_____ scenario argues two parallel _____ of matter _____

Supported by same _____ data as Big Bang

Conclusion: Await new _____ via technological advances

alternative (adj):
a different choice or possibility

verify (v):
to check and confirm the truth of

prestigious (adj):
well respected

entity (n):
a thing; something that exists

empirical (adj):
provable by observation, or using the senses

membrane (n):
a thin layer

precision (n):
the state of exactness

keywords / key phrases	hypothesis	information	vague	alternative	ekpyrotic	collided
	membranes	dominant	models	empirical	theoretical	reasonable

Step 3

Review your notes from both the reading and the lecture. Pay attention to the main ideas and supporting details. Rewrite the ideas as complete sentences.

Reading:

Main idea: _____

Supporting idea: _____

Supporting idea: _____

Lecture:

Main idea: _____

Supporting idea: _____

Supporting idea: _____

Use the main ideas and details from Steps 1, 2, and 3 above to complete the passage. Include information from both the reading and the lecture.

The reading explains that there is a _____ and dominant theory about how the _____ came into existence. It is called the Big _____ theory. This theory argues that the explosion of a primeval _____, _____ of years ago, caused all light, matter, and _____ to form. The reading informs us that the Big Bang theory is _____ by Hubble's evidence indicating that the universe is _____. The theory is also supported by the discovery made by two scientists in 1964 of cosmic _____ existing in space.

The lecturer believes that there are many theoretical _____ in the Big Bang theory. Actually, the theory has never been proven true beyond a _____ doubt, and the evidence supporting it also supports other theories of how the universe may have been created. As an example, the lecturer mentions the _____ scenario. This theory argues that the universe was created when two parallel _____ of space matter _____. This theory shares many elements of the Big Bang theory but also has some _____.

Practice 4

Step 1

Read the following passage. Then, look at the note diagram and fill in the missing information.

William Shakespeare, born in Stratford around the 23rd of April, 1564, is undoubtedly the world's most famous playwright. Some scholars argue, however, that the plays accredited to him were written by someone else. They believe a nobleman who lived at approximately the same time, named Edward De Vere, the 17th Earl of Oxford, wrote Shakespeare's plays. They claim the name William Shakespeare was a pseudonym used by Oxford to disguise his identity.

The arguments that support this viewpoint are multiple: A commoner, like the real Shakespeare, would not have had the classical education that the author of his plays and sonnets displays in his writing. The real author of Shakespeare's work would also have had to be familiar with aristocratic manners and sports. Access to such information was the privilege of the nobility. Oxford was not only such a nobleman; he was a writer as well.

There is also little documentation that links Shakespeare of Stratford to the stage. Therefore, there is scant proof that he worked as an actor in London at all. The six extant examples of Shakespeare's signature are all barely legible and are also very different looking. Three of the signatures are on his will, two are on other property documents, and one is a deposition. None of them, however, appears on any play or poem.

accredit (v):
to give credit for

pseudonym (n):
a false name used by writers or performers

aristocratic (adj):
from the ruling upper classes

documentation (n):
papers that authenticate

scant (adj):
little; weak; unconvincing

extant (adj):
in existence

Issue: Did _____ write the plays he is _____ with?

Answer: No. Some believe the Earl of _____ did

Shakespeare is a _____

Argument:

— No _____ education

— _____ with aristocratic _____ / sports

— Oxford was nobleman and was _____

— Little documentation Shakespeare worked as _____

— Extant _____ all _____-looking, none on plays/poems

🎧 **Now listen to a lecture related to the topic in Step 1. Fill in the blanks of the note diagram below with the keywords or key phrases shown. Not all of the words or phrases will be used.**

Key Issue: Shakespeare _____ debate:

Some _____ believe Edward De Vere wrote Shakespeare

Argument for Shakespeare:

— Little genuine _____ evidence for Earl of _____

— It is _____, poorly- _____ conspiracy theory

— Plays not considered _____ literature: reason for no name on play texts

— Numerous _____ documents refer to Shakespeare as actor and playwright

— Why would his contemporaries help nobleman? No _____

Conclusion: _____ wrote the plays

diligently (adv):
with dedication and hard work

sketchy (adj):
not clear

conspiracy (n):
an agreement to commit an illegal or deceitful act

genuine (adj):
real; authentic

categorically (adv):
without exception or doubt; absolutely

colleague (n):
a coworker; an equal

contemporary (n):
a person living at the same time

keywords / key phrases	Oxford	supportable	extant	playwright	researched	sketchy
	Shakespeare	Stratford	serious	motivation	authorship	scholars

Step 3

Review your notes from both the reading and the lecture. Pay attention to the main ideas and supporting details. Rewrite the ideas as complete sentences.

Reading:

Main idea: _____

Supporting idea: _____

Supporting idea: _____

Lecture:

Main idea: _____

Supporting idea: _____

Supporting idea: _____

Step 4

Use the main ideas and details from Steps 1, 2, and 3 above to complete the passage. Include information from both the reading and the lecture.

The reading claims that a _____ called Edward De Vere, 17th Earl of _____, actually wrote plays we accredit to William Shakespeare. He wrote them under a _____ to protect his _____. The plays _____ classical knowledge and information about aristocratic habits that Shakespeare wouldn't have been familiar with as a _____. Oxford was a nobleman with such experiences, and he was also a _____. According to the reading, there is also little documentary proof that Shakespeare worked as an actor, and his extant signatures all look _____ and, none appear on his plays or poems. All this evidence indicates that Oxford wrote Shakespeare's plays.

The speaker argues that Shakespeare did write Shakespeare. He believes that arguments favoring the Earl of Oxford are poorly _____ and states that there is a lot of _____ documentation referring to Shakespeare as an _____ and playwright. The speaker also argues that Shakespeare's name does not appear on his plays and poems because plays weren't considered important or serious _____ at that time. He believes Shakespeare's _____ had no reason to help an aristocrat like Oxford hide his true identity and that, therefore, Shakespeare did write his own plays. He thinks the theory about Oxford is a _____ theory.

Integrated Writing: Paraphrasing

Necessary Skills

- Understanding the original text accurately
- Using your own words to convey essential information and ideas from the reading and listening
- Being able to express the same information using different vocabulary and sentence structure

The Process of Paraphrasing

- Understand the full meaning of the original text.
- Take notes on the passage. Write down key information including a few phrases, major points, and important details.
- WITHOUT looking at the original passage, paraphrase the information in your own words, just by looking at your notes.
- Check the original passage for any missed key information.

Strategy

- Use related words and phrases, including synonyms and antonyms of words and concepts in the original passage.

  Example: The average daytime temperature in the Gobi desert does not often go below 38°C. → The average daytime temperature in the Gobi desert is usually at or above 38°C.

- Change word forms and rephrase to make things simpler.

  Example: for organization → in order to organize

  people at the age of thirty → thirty-year-old people

- Use different sentence structure.

  Example: Many Asian countries export rice to North America. →

  Rice is exported to North America by many Asian countries.

- Change the order of presentation of the information.
- Cite information from the original source by using signal words.

  Example: According to the professor/passage, →

  The speaker says/mentions/states/argues/believes/found that, etc.

Skill B Q1   Psychology

Practice 1

Step 1

Read the following passage. Underline the main idea. Predict how the listening passage may contrast with the reading.

One serious problem facing modern children is a lack of sleep. Experts claim that elementary school children should sleep nine hours each night. Studies show that children who get an inadequate amount of sleep can suffer in school and are at higher risk for accidental injury.

According to governmental agencies, about one third of all children do not get the minimum amount of sleep they require. Recent studies confirm this. After studying a group of 77 fourth and sixth-graders, Israeli psychologist Avi Sadeh reported that as little as one extra hour of sleep per night significantly improved academic performance. On tests assessing attention span and memory, students who received more sleep improved their performance by as much as two grade levels. Conversely, students who lost an hour of sleep showed no improvement on the memory and attention span tests. Indeed, on tests measuring reaction times, they performed significantly poorer than they had before being deprived of sleep.

An Italian study found that children under 14 who slept less than 10 hours a day were 86 percent more likely to be injured on the playground. Children between ages three and five who slept less than 10 hours a day also seemed to have a significant increase in injury risk. Studies such as these seem to support the old adage, "Early to bed and early to rise makes a man healthy, wealthy, and wise."

inadequate (adj):
not good enough for a given purpose; insufficient

minimum (adj):
related to the smallest amount necessary

confirm (v):
to check the truth of

attention span (n phrase):
the amount of time a person can mentally focus on a given task

conversely (adv):
in contrast; in an opposite way

deprive (v):
to keep from; to prevent from getting

adage (n):
a brief statement of truth; an aphorism

Step 2

Below is important information from the reading above. After each sentence are two possible paraphrases of it. Choose the best paraphrase for each sentence.

A. Conversely, students who lost an hour of sleep showed no improvement on the memory and attention span tests.

   1. In contrast, memory and attention span tests indicated that students who slept an hour less did not improve their scores.

   2. However, students who displayed no improvement on memory and attention span tests refused to lose an hour of sleep.

B. Children between ages three and five who slept less than 10 hours a day also seemed to have a significant increase in injury risk.

   1. Sleeping less than 10 hours led to a rise in injuries received by young children.

   2. Young children saw no significant increase in injury with less than 10 hours of sleep.

C. In the space below, write a paraphrase of the main idea that you underlined.

_____

Step 3

Now listen to a lecture related to the topic in Step 1. Fill in the blanks of the note diagram below with the keywords or key phrases shown. Not all of the words or phrases will be used.

Main idea:

— sleep deprivation is _____ in poor academic performance, but not the _____

Other important factors:

— _____ (ex. breakfast) important factor

— _____ such as warm coats and shoes

— home life; ex. _____ between parents

Recommendation:

— Educators must _____ other variables before _____ more sleep to students with _____

---

equation (n): a consideration of all the factors that produce a result

remiss (adj): careless; negligent

prescribe (v): to assign as a means of improving health or performance

knock-down, drag-out (adj phrase): very loud or violent

vis-à-vis (prep): in relation to; regarding

psyche (n): the part of the mind responsible for one's thoughts and feelings

primary (adj): of greatest importance

---

keywords / key phrases

| one factor | low grades | nourishment | consider | adequate |
| only factor | high grades | prescribing | clothing | fighting |

Step 4

Look at the phrases and sentences from the lecture notes. Try to think of synonyms for the words listed. Write correct sentences to paraphrase these notes using the synonyms that you thought of.

A. Sleep deprivation is one factor.

synonyms: deprivation - _____

             factor - _____

paraphrase: _____

B. Educators must consider other variables.

synonyms: educators - _____

             consider - _____

paraphrase: _____

A. Changing Keywords

Below are two incomplete paraphrases of key information from the lecture. Fill in the missing parts with words or phrases from the box. These words and phrases are synonyms or are similar in meaning to the actual words used in the lecture.

- how much / the amount of / the quantity of
- regarding / in relation to / concerning
- performance / achievement / development
- effect / ramification / significance
- paucity / deficiency / deficit
- greatly / largely / strongly

1. A child's _____ in school is _____ dependent on

   _____ sleep he or she gets.

2. What is the _____ of a _____ of sleep _____

   other factors?

B. Changing Sentence Structure

Try to complete the following paraphrases of the sentences from part A above.

1. The amount of sleep a child gets _____

2. With regard to other factors, _____?

Read the following sentences taken from the reading and the lecture. Create new sentences by combining the ideas in each pair of sentences.

1. **(A)** One serious problem facing modern children is a lack of sleep.

   (B) Experts claim that elementary school children should sleep nine hours each night.

   (A)+(B): _____

   _____

   _____

2. **(A)** Besides being well rested, children need to be well nourished.

   (B) They also need to be well clothed, and, most important of all, they need a stable, loving home life.

   (A)+(B): _____

   _____

   _____

Practice 2

Step 1

Read the following passage. Underline the main idea. Predict how the listening passage may contrast with the reading.

Throughout history, people wanting change have had a choice as to how to bring that change about. They could choose to take up arms and bring about change through violent actions, or they could choose to bring about change through civil disobedience, that is, non-violent means. An examination of history shows that non-violent means have not been as effective as violent means. Russian revolutionaries, for example, viewed non-violence as threatening to their cause. Similarly, opponents of racial oppression in the US considered non-violence unrealistic.

In Russia, Leon Trotsky argued that violence was an essential component of any revolutionary effort. In dealing with class struggle, he viewed non-violence as a way of imposing bourgeois morals and values on the proletariat. A disposition toward violent protest was, in his opinion, an essential tool for the emancipation of the proletariat. Indeed, the Russian proletariat achieved their desired change through violent upheaval.

Non-violence was also harshly criticized during racial equality movements in the US. George Jackson stated, "Non-violence is a false ideal." Malcolm X agreed with Jackson's perspective, stating, "It is criminal to teach a man not to defend himself when he is the constant victim of brutal attacks." Once again, the violent actions of these protesters helped effect the change they sought.

revolutionary (n):
a person closely involved in bringing about a revolution

oppression (n):
the act of using authority and force to deprive another group of freedoms

bourgeois (adj):
of the middle class

proletariat (n):
the working class

disposition (n):
a tendency toward a certain action or characteristic

emancipation (n):
the act of freeing people from oppression

upheaval (n):
a change or disturbance that greatly affects something

Step 2

Below is important information from the reading above. After each sentence are two possible paraphrases of it. Choose the best paraphrase for each sentence.

A. A disposition toward violent protest was, in his opinion, an essential tool for the emancipation of the proletariat.

1. He believed that a tendency toward violent protest was an integral ingredient in the freeing of the middle class.
2. The freeing of the middle class, he believed, was very important in the tendency toward violent protest.

B. George Jackson, stated, "Non-violence is a false ideal."

1. George Jackson contended that non-violence was not a realistic concept.
2. George Jackson falsely argued examples for non-violence.

C. In the space below, write a paraphrase of the main idea you underlined.

_____

🎧 Now listen to a lecture related to the topic in Step 1. Fill in the blanks of the note diagram below with the keywords or key phrases shown. Not all of the words or phrases will be used.

Key forms of non-violence are:

Civil Disobedience:

— _____ and government _____ each other

— principle of "_____" is the driving idea

— provides the _____ advantage of being _____

Passive Resistance:

— _____ break the law

— must expect to be _____ by _____

— should quietly _____ without _____

pioneer (v):
to invent something; to do some action first

boycott (v):
to not buy products from a company or country in protest

par excellence (adj phrase):
being the best or truest example; quintessential

martyr (n):
a figure respected for sacrificing him or herself for a cause

blockade (n):
a group of people or objects put in place to block the progress of something

get wind of (v phrase):
to hear about; to learn of

debilitate (v):
to injure; to damage something so that it can no longer function

keywords / key phrases	individual	authorities	resist	moral	peacefully
	attacked	don't support	retaliation	right	independence

Look at the phrases and sentences from the lecture notes. Try to think of synonyms for the words listed. Write correct sentences to paraphrase these notes using the synonyms that you thought of.

A. Principle of independence is the driving idea.

synonyms: principle - _____

independence - _____

paraphrase: _____

B. Should quietly resist without retaliation.

synonyms: resist - _____

retaliation - _____

paraphrase: _____

Step 5

A. Changing Keywords

Below are two incomplete paraphrases of key information from the lecture. Fill in the missing parts with words or phrases from the box. These words and phrases are synonyms or are similar in meaning to the actual words used in the lecture.

- successfully / effectively / efficiently
- autonomy / self-determination / independence
- finish / eliminate / give up
- government / control / power
- fair / just / right
- rule to follow / principle / guideline
- using / resorting to / utilizing
- reaching / achieving / accomplishing
- convinced / influenced / swayed
- hostility / aggression / bloodshed

1. _____ in mind and action is the guiding _____ for _____ what is

   _____ .

2. Without _____ to _____ , Gandhi _____ _____ the English

   to _____ colonial _____ in India.

B. Changing Sentence Structure

Try to complete the following paraphrases of the sentences from part A above.

1. The guiding principle for _____

2. Gandhi effectively persuaded the _____

Step 6

Read the following sentences taken from the reading and the lecture. Create new sentences by combining the ideas in each pair of sentences.

1. **(A)** Non-Violent forms of protest are ineffective.
   (B) Without resorting to violence, Gandhi effectively persuaded the English to end colonial rule in India.

   (A)+(B): _____

   _____

2. **(A)** Violence, in many ways, defines the revolutionary spirit.
   (B) Independence in mind and action is the guiding principle for achieving what is just.

   (A)+(B): _____

   _____

Skill B Q1 Chemistry

Practice 3

Step 1

Read the following passage. Underline the main idea. Predict how the listening passage may contrast with the reading.

Accepted views that only carbon-based chemical systems can support life are increasingly coming under attack. Theories on alternative biochemistry suggest that non-carbon-based forms of life could be possible in unusual environments. Two proposed alternatives include silicon-based and sulfur-based forms of life.

The possibility of silicon-based life as an alternative to carbon is real. The Earth is exceptionally silicon rich and carbon poor. Silicon-based life may be selected for survival in remote corners of our planet or especially in extra-terrestrial environments closer to the sun. Sulfur, like carbon, is water soluble and able to form the long molecule chains necessary for biological evolution. However, the possibilities of complex sulfur-based beings evolving are low. On the other hand, sulfur-based bacteria with metabolisms that break down hydrogen instead of oxygen have been found in exotic corners of the Earth.

All suggested forms of alternative biochemistry involve odd physical conditions uncommon or non-existent on Earth. This is because odd physical conditions may actually favor these alternative types of life. Arguably, these conditions are likely to result in the formation of non-carbon-based life.

biochemistry (n):
the study of the chemicals in living things

exceptionally (adv):
in a large or intense way

extra terrestrial (adj phrase):
not on Earth

soluble (adj):
able to dissolve, or break into small particles, in water

being (n):
a living thing

arguably (adv):
it can be logically argued though not proven

Step 2

Below is important information from the reading above. After each sentence are two possible paraphrases of it. Choose the best paraphrase for each sentence.

A. Two proposed alternatives include silicon-based and sulfur-based forms of life.

   1. Both silicon and sulfur-based organisms have been suggested as alternative life forms.

   2. Sulfur-based forms of life are proposed as alternatives to silicon forms.

B. Arguably, these conditions are likely to result in the formation of non-carbon-based life.

   1. The argument is that a non-carbon environment would probably result in carbon-based life.

   2. It can be argued that non-carbon-based life could probably result from these circumstances.

C. In the space below, write a paraphrase of the main idea you underlined.

_____

Step 3

Now listen to a lecture related to the topic in Step 1. Fill in the blanks of the note diagram below with the keywords or key phrases shown. Not all of the words or phrases will be used.

The argument against "carbon chauvinism"

— term _____ views that all life is _____

— all current _____ indicate carbon is _____ to life

— _____ is all carbon based

— we aren't able to test _____

— we have no _____ data about non-carbon _____

— _____ state of science not _____ of carbon chauvinism

chauvinism (n):
a prejudiced belief in the superiority of one's own group

discredit (v):
to create doubt about the integrity or validity of

pre-eminent (adj):
most important; most respected

abundant (adj):
many; plentiful

replicate (v):
to copy; to recreate

speculate (v):
to theorize; to explain based on incomplete evidence

sustain (v):
to maintain; to keep alive or functioning

keywords / key phrases					
discredits	data	necessary	empirical	alien environments	
guilty	present	biochemistries	terrestrial life	carbon based	

Step 4

Look at the phrases and sentences from the lecture notes. Try to think of synonyms for the words listed. Write correct sentences to paraphrase these notes using the synonyms that you thought of.

A. All current data indicate carbon is necessary to life.

synonyms: data - _____

necessary - _____

paraphrase: _____

B. Present state of science not guilty of carbon chauvinism

synonyms: state - _____

guilty - _____

paraphrase: _____

A. Changing Keywords

Below are two incomplete paraphrases of key information from the lecture. Fill in the missing parts with words or phrases from the box. These words and phrases are synonyms or are similar in meaning to the actual words used in the lecture.

> • present / actual   • make-up / composition   • have / contain
> • understand / recognize   • circumstances / environments   • essential to / required for
> • important / fundamental   • proof / facts

1. In fact, all _____ scientific _____ indicate(s) that carbon is _____ life

   as we _____ it.

2. The _____ point today is that all _____ for biological life "as we know it"

   _____ carbon in their _____.

B. Changing Sentence Structure

Try to complete the following paraphrases of the sentences from part A above.

1. That carbon is essential to _____.

2. That all circumstances for _____.

Read the following sentences taken from the reading and the lecture. Create new sentences by combining the ideas in each pair of sentences.

1. **(A)** Alternative biochemistry theories suggest that non-carbon forms of life could be possible in unusual environments.

   (B) But, the reality is we can't replicate and test such alien environments.

   (A)+(B): _____

   _____

   _____

2. **(A)** The Earth is exceptionally silicon rich and carbon poor.

   (B) Rare carbon has proven to be the successful life base on Earth, and not abundant silicon.

   (A)+(B): _____

   _____

   _____

Skill B Q1 Anthropology

Practice 4

Step 1

Read the following passage. Underline the main idea. Predict how the listening passage may contrast with the reading.

Native American legal claims to the remains of Kennewick Man stand in the way of science. If kinship can be proven, these human skeletal remains will be turned over to local Native American people for a traditional reburial. If allowed to continue, further study on the Kennewick Man's remains could radically alter current theories on early migration to the Americas.

Who exactly the Kennewick Man is and where he comes from are still not clear. None of the Native American groups involved in the ownership dispute have been able to establish proof of kinship. Initial studies reveal that the remains exhibit few of the skeletal features of Native American peoples. Some anthropologists now suggest his features most closely resemble those of Polynesian peoples. If this is true, it could reveal the existence of a wave of immigration across the Pacific to the Americas. Further tests, such as DNA analysis, could provide answers to these important anthropological questions. On spiritual grounds, however, Native American groups are demanding custody of the remains and oppose more scientific study.

All studies of the remains have now been halted as the ownership dispute rages on. If Native American groups are granted ownership, any further study will be impossible. This will represent a substantial loss to scientific progress.

remains *(n)*:
the body parts left after death

kinship *(n)*:
a family relationship to

reburial *(n)*:
the act of burying a dead body that has previously been buried

radically *(adv)*:
in a large, very different way

migration *(n)*:
the movement of people or animals in a large group

dispute *(n)*:
an argument; a disagreement

rage on *(v phrase)*:
to continue in an emotional or violent way

Step 2

Below is important information from the reading above. After each sentence are two possible paraphrases of it. Choose the best paraphrase for each sentence.

A. None of the Native American groups involved in the ownership dispute have been able to establish proof of kinship.

  1. The Native American groups that are part of the dispute over kinship have proven their rights to ownership.

  2. Of the Native American groups in the disagreement over ownership rights, none has successfully proven kinship.

B. If Native American groups are allowed to claim the Kennewick Man, any further study will be impossible.

  1. Any continued examination will be impossible if Native American groups are granted custody of the Kennewick Man.

  2. Native American groups will not be allowed to claim the Kennewick Man if further study is impossible.

C. In the space below, write a paraphrase of the main idea you underlined.

_____

Now listen to a lecture related to the topic in Step 1. Fill in the blanks of the note diagram below with the keywords or key phrases shown. Not all of the words or phrases will be used.

Native American claims don't mean stopping the progress of science:

— Some _____ take a _____

— Scientists argue _____ claims mean end of _____

— Native American groups not _____, just want to be consulted or involved

— Science can _____ while _____ Native American claims

— Many Native American groups involved in _____ projects

— Collaborative projects _____ and clarify scientific _____

take a hard line *(v phrase)*:
to leave no room for compromise when enforcing a rule or expressing an opinion

spell the end *(v phrase)*:
to signal the end of; to be a sign that something is about to end

accommodate *(v)*:
to make room for; to take into consideration

dignity *(n)*:
the condition of being worthy of respect

collaborative *(adj)*:
done by two or more people or groups

enlist *(v)*:
to get the help of; to recruit

enhance *(v)*:
to improve; to make stronger

keywords / key phrases	scientists	results	hard line	enhance	Native American
	research	respecting	anti-science	proceed	collaborative

Step 4

Look at the phrases and sentences from the lecture notes. Try to think of synonyms for the words listed. Write correct sentences to paraphrase these notes using the synonyms that you thought of.

A. Scientists argue Native American claims mean end of research

synonyms: argue - _____

mean - _____

paraphrase: _____

B. Science can proceed while respecting Native American claims.

synonyms: proceed - _____

respecting - _____

paraphrase: _____

Step 5

A. Changing Keywords

Below are two incomplete paraphrases of key information from the lecture. Fill in the missing parts with words or phrases from the box. These words and phrases are synonyms or are similar in meaning to the actual words used in the lecture.

- heart / root / core
- follow / continue / perform
- development / advancement / growth
- claims / privileges / demands
- ending / ceasing / preventing

- price / disadvantage / detriment
- traditions / beliefs / values
- remnants / vestiges / relics
- efforts / endeavors / undertakings

1. Respecting Native American _____ to archaeological _____ doesn't mean _____ the _____ of science.

2. _____ to freely _____ science at the _____ of Native American _____ are really the _____ of the debate.

B. Changing Sentence Structure

Try to complete the following paraphrases of the sentences from part A above.

1. Preventing the advancement _____ .

2. The core of the conflict _____ .

Step 6

Read the following sentences taken from the reading and the lecture. Create new sentences by combining the ideas in each pair of sentences.

1. **(A)** Native American legal claims to the Kennewick Man stand in the way of science.

   (B) That scientific study is impossible if Native American beliefs are honored is not true.

   (A)+(B): _____

   _____

2. **(A)** All studies of the remains are now halted as the debate rages on.

   (B) What the Kennewick Man conflict shows is more collaborative work is needed, not efforts to pursue science at all costs.

   (A)+(B): _____

   _____

C Independent Writing: Brainstorming

Necessary Skills

- Describing a personal experience
- Expressing an opinion on an issue and supporting it with concrete examples and details
- Organizing ideas in an effective way

Process	Strategy
Read the question and understand the task	Be sure that you understand the question and what the question requires you to do.
Brainstorm	Try to take less than 5 minutes to brainstorm. Write down all the ideas you can think of to support your opinion. Think of ways to express those ideas in English. Do not try to organize these points. You will select major ideas and organize them in the next step.
Organize ideas	Select major ideas that can be developed into topics. Do NOT include ideas that are unconnected to the task or main topics. Organize so that minor ideas act to support the major ideas. Select examples that clearly support the topics.

- Your organization may look like this:

Introduction	Body	Conclusion
Restatement of the question Thesis statement	Support idea 1 + examples Support idea 2 + examples Support idea 3 + examples	Restatement of the thesis

Skill C Q2 Opinion

Practice 1

Step 1

Read the question and think about possible responses. List some ideas in the blanks.

Imagine that you have received some land to use as you wish. How would you use this land? Would you use the land to earn a profit or to preserve nature? Use specific details to explain your answer.

For Profit:
sell natural resources from the land (eg. lumber)
build real estate and sell at a profit
clear land and make a golf course

_____

_____

_____

Nature Preserve:
create a wildlife reserve
grow a small crop for personal use
plant trees and other plant life

_____

_____

_____

Step 2

Read the sample response below and underline three sentences that are central to the organization of the passage.

> If I were so fortunate as to receive a piece of land, I would want to use it to do something positive that would not harm the land. Because I love plants and animals, and because I love nature, I would create a wildlife reserve. The survival of many woodland creatures is threatened because their natural habitats are being destroyed. I would want to create a place where these wild animals could live safely in a natural environment that is protected from development.
>
> Not only would this reserve create a home for animals, it would also create an opportunity for people to see the animals in their natural habitats. I think that is much more enjoyable than seeing animals in zoos. While I would charge a small admission fee, the money would go toward the care of the animals. I would not wish to make a profit off of the wildlife reserve. It would make me happy to see the land put to good use.
>
> Many land owners are selfish and see their land as a means of making money. They don't really care about the land; they only care about their investment. Some might sell the natural resources of the land, such as lumber. Others might build houses and develop the land in order to sell it later at a profit. Personally, if I had land handed to me for free, profit would be the last thing on my mind. I would take the opportunity to protect the land and all of the plants and animals on that land.

fortunate *(adj)*:
lucky

wildlife reserve *(n phrase)*:
an area in which animals are protected from hunting and other human dangers

woodland *(n)*:
an area with forests

habitat *(n)*:
the land in which a given species lives

admission fee *(n phrase)*:
an amount of money paid to gain access

investment *(n)*:
an amount of money spent in order to gain profits in the future

lumber *(n)*:
wood sold for construction

assuredly *(adv)*:
for sure; certainly

on one's mind *(adj phrase)*:
an idea or topic frequently thought about

Step 3

Answer the following questions in relation to the thesis and topic of the response in Step 2.

1. What is the thesis statement of the essay? (Write it.)

   _____

   _____

2. What is the topic sentence of the body paragraph? (Write it.)

   _____

   _____

Step 4

Answer the following questions in relation to the organization of the response in Step 2.

1. Which "side" of the prompt does this essay take?

   _____

   _____

2. What example does the writer give to support the thesis statement?

   _____

   _____

3. Does the writer present a comment or idea from the other side in the conclusion? If so, what is the comment or idea?

   _____

   _____

4. What is the main idea of the conclusion?

   _____

   _____

Read the sample response presenting another possible answer to the prompt from Step 1.

Receiving a plot of land free of charge would be an excellent opportunity to make some money. Of course, how to make the most money depends on the piece of land and its characteristics. If I were given a piece of land to use as I saw fit, I would carefully assess the land and consider all of my options.

There are many different ways to make a profit off of land. For example, if the land has a lot of trees, you could cut them down and sell the lumber. If the land doesn't have any resources that could be sold, you could develop the land. If the location is ideal, you could build a house on it and sell it to a family. An even more profitable venture would be to turn the land into a subdivision. Of course, that would depend on the size of the piece of land you were working with. Personally, I think I would try to develop the land and sell it. However, if I needed to cut down some trees in order to do that, I wouldn't object to selling them in the process.

A lot of people think that development projects like the one I am suggesting are a bad idea. They say that we humans are destroying the natural habitat of a lot of wildlife. While this is true, I don't think it would affect my decision. The way I see it, developing one more piece of land is not going to make a significant difference. In addition, if I didn't develop the land to make a profit, I'm sure someone else would once they had the opportunity.

plot (n):
a small piece of land

free of charge (adv phrase):
without costing money

see fit (v phrase):
to choose; to think wise or beneficial

resource (n):
a thing that can be used by people

venture (n):
a business enterprise involving some risk in expectation of gain

subdivision (n):
an area of real estate developed into smaller pieces for homes to be built on

Step 5

After studying the two sample responses, give your own opinion on the prompt. Brainstorm your own ideas below. Then, type your essay on a computer.

Brainstorming

Skill C Q2 Experience

Practice 2

Step 1

Read the question and think about your own experience. List some ideas about your experience in the blanks.

Decisions can be made quickly, or they can be made after careful thought. In your experience, are decisions made quickly better or worse than decisions made after careful thought? Use specific details and examples to support your answer.

Decisions I've made quickly:
small purchases like books and CDs
to leave a job
agreeing to get married

_____

_____

Decisions I've made after careful thought:
major purchases like my car
whether to take a job overseas
to study English in university

_____

_____

Step 2

Read the sample response below and underline three sentences that are central to the organization of the passage.

There are some types of decisions that require careful thought and other types that don't. For example, when I am at the supermarket trying to decide whether to buy orange juice or apple juice, I don't have to think very hard about it because it is not important. However, sometimes I make rash decisions about important things. When I make important decisions without thinking them through, I typically make the wrong choice. In my experience, it is always best to carefully consider my options when I make major life decisions.

Major life decisions include career choices, relationship choices, and money choices. When I was offered a job in another city, for example, I considered many factors before accepting it. I thought about the location, the salary, and the possibilities for career advancement as well as being in a new place and being away from my friends and family. In contrast, I once left a job without thinking about my decision. I was working for an insurance firm, and I became angry with my boss. Without thinking, I quit my job. A day later, I realized that I should have thought that decision through. As you can see, in my experience, major decisions that are made on the spur of the moment tend to be mistakes.

I know people who prefer to go with their instincts when they make decisions. When I was considering buying a certain car, a friend of mine asked me, "How did you feel in the car? Would you be happy driving it?" The truth was, I loved the car, but I would have been foolish to buy it because it probably wouldn't fit my needs as a student. Personally, I don't trust my instincts. I have to think about all of my important choices for a long time before I can make a final decision.

require (v):
to need

rash (adj):
without much prior consideration

major (adj):
very important; chief; principal

career advancement (n phrase):
the potential to improve one's job position

firm (n):
a company; a corporation

on the spur of the moment (adv phrase):
done suddenly, without prior consideration

instinct (n):
an inner knowledge or wisdom that is not gained from thought or experience

Step 3

Answer the following questions in relation to the thesis and topic of the response in Step 2.

1. What is the thesis statement of the essay? (Write it.)

_____

_____

2. What is the topic sentence of the body paragraph? (Write it.)

_____

_____

Step 4

Answer the following questions in relation to the organization of the response in Step 2.

1. Which "side" of the question prompt does this essay take?

_____

_____

2. What example does the writer give to support the thesis statement?

_____

_____

3. Does the writer present a comment or idea from the other side in the conclusion? If so, what is the comment or idea?

_____

_____

4. What is the main idea of the conclusion?

_____

_____

Read the sample response presenting another possible answer to the prompt from Step 1.

When making any kind of decision, whether major or minor, I prefer to trust my instincts. It's a lot faster, and, in my experience, just as wise as any decision that I spend a lot of time on. For me, in fact, the decisions that I have made on the spur of the moment have been the wisest decisions I've made. Usually, I find that when I take a lot of time to consider a decision before I make a final choice, I end up making the decision that coincides with my initial instinct anyway.

For most decisions, I believe the immediate emotional reaction is usually the correct one. One example was when I decided to go to university far from my hometown. Even though I would later receive good scholarship offers from schools closer to my friends and family, I am glad I chose to move away. In fact, after graduating, I found a great job and am still very happy here. Another example is when my husband asked me to marry him, and I said "yes" without even thinking about it. We had only been dating for a few months, but I knew we would have a happy marriage. At the time, my friends and family cautioned me to think it through, but I was confident in my immediate decision, and I was right. We have been happily married for fourteen years and we have three wonderful children.

My decision-making technique is not for everybody. Some people just aren't comfortable with a decision until they have thought it out carefully. Indeed, for some types of decisions, this might be a wiser method. However, for me and for most of my decisions, I typically go with my gut feeling. It's a lot faster, and I usually make the best decision.

coincide *(v)*:
to occur in connection with

initial *(adj)*:
early; at first

scholarship *(n)*:
an amount of money given to students to pay for tuition

caution *(v)*:
to warn against

technique *(n)*:
a method; a way of doing

gut feeling *(n phrase)*:
an impulse or motivation based on emotion and instinct rather than rational thought

Step 5

After studying the two sample responses, give your own opinion on the prompt. Brainstorm your own ideas below. Then, type your essay on a computer.

Brainstorming

Skill C Q2 Opinion

Practice 3

Step 1

Read the question and think about your own opinion. List some ideas about your opinion in the blanks.

What are the advantages and disadvantages of reading books vs watching movies? State your opinion and give specific reasons and details.

Advantages of Reading Books:

more engrossing

can learn more

more intimate experience

_____

_____

_____

Advantages of Watching Movies:

more exciting

doesn't take too long

more social experience

_____

_____

_____

Step 2

Answer the following questions about how you would organize a response to the prompt.

1. Which "side" of the prompt would your essay take? Briefly write your opinion.

   _____

   _____

2. What details would you list to support your "side" of the prompt?

   _____

   _____

3. Give one example for each detail you wrote above.

   _____

   _____

Step 3

Look at the two sample responses. Of the two, which agrees more with your response? Write down any keywords and key phrases that would be useful in your answer.

Since the advent of motion pictures, the use of books for entertainment has most certainly declined. Some contend that this trend produces negative effects on the individual as well as on society at large. Others defend movie watching, claiming that it is more entertaining, more convenient, and more geared to the accelerated pace of modern life. While I do enjoy watching movies, I feel that reading books provides more advantages to the reader than watching movies provides to the audience.

In my opinion, reading books has several advantages over watching movies. To begin, reading is a much more engrossing form of entertainment. Because reading involves an active, drawn-out process, the reader becomes more connected and involved with the text. Similarly, reading is a much more intimate activity than watching a movie. Of course, reading is done alone, which makes it an intimate activity, but it goes beyond that. The reader engages and relates to the setting, events, and especially the characters in a very personal way. Because a novel cannot visually present as many details as a movie, the reader creates his or her own interpretation and vision of these details. Furthermore, because the reader spends so much time connecting to the thoughts, dreams, and feelings of the characters, those characters become a part of the reader's personal experience, almost like a friend or family member. Finally, reading has the advantage of providing a source of learning. It endows the avid reader with a familiarity with literature, vocabulary, and grammatical structures, all of which boost his or her overall mental and linguistic faculty.

As the film industry has developed and expanded over the past century, fewer and fewer people have turned to reading as a source of entertainment. In my opinion, however, reading offers several advantages that movies cannot provide. These advantages include an engrossing, intimate experience, and a means of improving one's education.

advent *(n)*:
the invention or beginning of

motion picture *(n phrase)*:
a movie; a film

contend *(v)*:
to believe strongly; to argue

geared to *(adj phrase)*:
directed at; designed for

engrossing *(adj)*:
very interesting; able to hold one's attention

drawn-out *(adj)*:
taking a long time

engage *(v)*:
to interest; to involve

endow *(v)*:
to give; to provide

avid *(adj)*:
highly interested in

faculty *(n)*:
an ability

Keywords / Key phrases

_____   _____   _____

_____   _____

Since the advent of motion pictures, the use of books for entertainment has most certainly declined. Some contend that this trend produces negative effects on the individual as well as on society at large. Others defend movie watching, claiming that it is more entertaining, more convenient, and more geared to the accelerated pace of modern life. While I do enjoy reading books, I feel that watching movies provides the audience with a more exciting, intense, and social form of entertainment.

In my opinion, watching movies has several advantages over reading books. To begin, movies are a much more exciting and intense form of entertainment. Because films present a series of stunning, active, and visual stimuli combined with appropriately emotive auditory stimuli, the audience is brought into the story in a much more intense fashion than reading books can produce. In a similar vein, watching a movie is far more convenient as it only takes two hours or less. In contrast, reading a novel can take weeks without providing all the intense visual and auditory stimuli. Another advantage that movies have over books is that watching a film is a social activity. Whereas people read novels in the solitude of their homes, movie-goers are part of a large audience all engaged in the same activity. This helps movie watchers relate to and interact with others. Movies provide a common social experience through which people can connect with and relate to one another.

Though some literary types bemoan and lament the popularity of the film industry as compared to the book industry, I firmly believe that movies provide many advantages to society. First, films engage the senses in a much stronger way than books can. Second, they are more convenient. Finally, watching movies helps people share social experiences.

intense *(adj)*:
strong in emotion

stunning *(adj)*:
impressive; causing a strong emotional response

stimulus *(n)*:
an item or event that causes a reaction

emotive *(adj)*:
causing an emotional response

auditory *(adj)*:
related to sound and hearing

vein *(n)*:
a theme; a topic

solitude *(n)*:
the state of being alone

interact *(v)*:
to act and react to another person or thing

bemoan *(v)*:
to complain about

lament *(v)*:
to feel sad and complain about

Keywords / Key phrases

_____   _____   _____

_____   _____

Which response agrees with your answer and why?

_____

_____

_____

Skill C Q2 Experience

Practice 4

Step 1

Read the question and think about your own opinion. List some ideas about your opinion in the blanks.

Some people believe that art and music programs should be cut from schools. In your experience, has taking art and music when you were in school helped your adult life? Use specific details and examples to support your answer.

Art/Music programs in schools:
— Good Experiences

- Developed my general interest in education
- Developed my creativity and imagination
- Helped me think flexibly and approach school subjects in different ways

_____

_____

_____

Art/Music programs in schools:
— Bad Experiences

- Did not teach aspects relevant to my generation
- Forced to play trumpet, I wanted to play guitar
- Took my time away from more practical studies
- My teacher was not good

_____

_____

_____

Step 2

Answer the following questions about how you would organize a response to the prompt.

1. Which "side" of the prompt would your essay take? Briefly write your opinion.

   _____

   _____

2. What details would you list to support your "side" of the prompt?

   _____

   _____

3. Give one example for each detail you wrote above.

   _____

   _____

Look at the two sample responses. Of the two, which agrees more with your response? Write down any keywords and key phrases that would be useful in your answer.

Music and art programs have been mainstays in our public school system for generations. From my experience, though, I believe that neither program develops skills that the typical student will find relevant to his or her personal artistic goals or useful when entering the real world. What's more, these programs are very expensive, diverting funds from more practical studies such as computers and information technology.

When I joined my middle school band, I was forced to play the trombone, though I really wanted to learn guitar. In fact, I later ended up taking private guitar lessons years later on my own initiative. After six weeks in the band, I quit. This was partly because I found the instructor to be a bitter, hateful person, and partly because the music he was teaching us had no relevance to my personal music tastes. We studied outdated marching songs instead of more modern genres, like rock and hip hop. Again, I would later study these musical forms on my own time and with my own money.

My middle-school band teacher once told me that all of the instruments in the band room were worth more than all the equipment in the computer lab. In retrospect, I wish the school board had used this money on computer classes instead. Today, knowledge of computers and information technology is the single greatest asset people entering the workforce can have. If I'd had computer training in public school, I wouldn't have had to spend so much of my own time and money later in life to upgrade these skills.

All things considered, the art and music programs I experienced in school offered few practical benefits to my adult life. I think the money spent on these programs would have helped me more if it had been spent on computer classes instead.

mainstay (n):
a characteristic part of something over an extended period of time

relevant (adj):
important or significant to a given topic

real world (n phrase):
the period of life after schooling in which people get jobs and start families

divert (v):
to change the direction of; to take away from

initiative (n):
a decision to act

bitter (adj):
unhappy; angry

outdated (adj):
old-fashioned; no longer useful or relevant

genre (n):
a category; a type

in retrospect (adv phrase):
thinking back, or remembering, after an event is over

upgrade (v):
to improve; to modernize

Keywords / Key phrases

_____   _____   _____

_____   _____

Art and music programs are once again in danger of being cut from our public schools. In the past, this travesty has been averted time and again because people invariably remember the importance of these programs. I personally feel that art class increased the overall enjoyment of my educational experience and helped me develop the creativity and imagination I needed to further my career as an adult.

Usually, when I recollect my school years, I recall the hours of tedious memorization spent on subjects like mathematics and history. During these classes, I often found my mind wandering to thoughts of playing outside with my friends. The teachers of these subjects inspired little interest within me to progress academically. My art teacher, on the other hand, created a classroom experience full of creativity, energy, and encouragement. These art classes functioned as an anchor for me, fostering my interest in academics, thus allowing me to master the skills necessary to survive in the adult world. It sparked my interest in education by providing me with an hour of the day to look forward to.

The two greatest skills I learned in art class were creative thinking and imagination. Developing these skills in art class taught me to think flexibly. This enabled me to approach more rigorous subjects from multiple viewpoints, thus boosting my interest in them and providing me with an integral understanding of their theory and applications.

I do not currently work as an artist, even in the general sense of a performer or writer. In fact, my job is highly mathematical. Nevertheless, I use creative thinking every day to tackle problems from different directions and apply long-term strategies to development issues. Indeed, just as the three "R's" are fundamental to every education, art must also be considered indispensable to the development of the student's mind.

travesty *(n)*:
an unfair or illogical act

avert *(v)*:
to stay away from; to avoid

invariably *(adv)*:
always; without fail

recollect *(v)*:
to remember; to recall

tedious *(adj)*:
repetitive and boring

foster *(v)*:
to promote the development of

enable *(v)*:
to allow to do; to provide the necessary conditions or skills to do

rigorous *(adj)*:
strictly accurate; precise

integral *(adj)*:
very important; necessary

indispensable *(adj)*:
necessary; essential

Keywords / Key phrases

_____   _____   _____

_____   _____

Which response agrees with your answer and why?

_____

_____

_____

Independent Writing:
Writing Thesis Statements and Topic Sentences

Necessary Skills

- Stating your opinion or thesis clearly
- Stating clear and strong topic sentences that support the thesis

Strategy

- Make your thesis statement clear and concise.
- For your thesis, do not write, "I agree with this opinion." Restate the question when giving your opinion, such as "I agree with the statement that the government should tell people when to retire."
- Make your topic sentence a summary of all the points you will cover in the paragraph.
- Write clear topic sentences that will naturally lead into the rest of the information in the paragraph.

  Example:

  Weak topic sentence — I like dogs better than cats.

  Strong topic sentence — Having a dog as a pet is better than having a cat for three main reasons.

Skill D **Q2** Thesis Statements

Step 1

Read the following questions and sample thesis statements. Underline all of the words in the questions that are also in the thesis statements.

Question 1:

> Your school has received a gift of money. What do you think is the best way for your school to spend this money? Use specific reasons and details to support your choice.

Thesis statement 1:
If my school received a gift of money, I believe the money would be best spent in hiring more teachers.

Question 2:

> Many people visit museums when they travel to new places. Describe a time that you visited a museum while traveling. Was it an enjoyable experience? Why or why not? Use specific details and examples to support your answer.

Thesis statement 2:
Because of the multitude of interesting artifacts on display, I personally found my visit to the Museum of History and Anthropology while traveling through Mexico City to be a thoroughly enjoyable experience.

Question 3:

> Do you agree or disagree with the following statement? Television has destroyed communication among friends and family. Use specific reasons and examples to support your opinion.

Thesis statement 3:
I disagree with the contention that television has destroyed communication among friends and family; in fact, I believe the opposite to be true.

Question 4:

> Plants can provide food, shelter, clothing, or medicine. Tell about one kind of plant that you have found to be important to you or the people in your country. Use specific details and examples to explain your choice.

Thesis statement 4:
Because of its many uses, including shelter and food, the maple tree is an important plant to the people of my country.

Read each of the following questions. Decide if the question asks for your experience or your opinion. Then write the thesis statement that you would use in a short essay to answer each question.

Question 1:

> It has recently been announced that a large shopping center may be built in your neighborhood. Do you support or oppose this plan? Why? Use specific reasons and details to support your answer.

Does this question ask you to explain your opinion or your experience? Select one.

opinion ☐   experience ☐

Thesis statement: _____

_____

_____

Question 2:

> Some people prefer to plan activities for their free time very carefully. Others choose not to make any plans at all for their free time. Which strategy have you found to be more beneficial in your life? Use specific details and examples to describe your experience.

Does this question ask you to explain your opinion or your experience? Select one.

opinion ☐   experience ☐

Thesis statement: _____

_____

_____

Question 3:

> Some people believe that it is better for children to grow up in the countryside than in a big city. In which setting did you grow up? Tell about the positive and negative aspects you experienced growing up in that setting. Use specific details and examples to develop your essay.

Does this question ask you to explain your opinion or your experience? Select one.

opinion ☐   experience ☐

Thesis statement: _____

_____

_____

Question 4:

> Is the ability to read and write more important today than in the past? Why or why not? Use specific reasons and examples to support your answer.

Does this question ask you to explain your opinion or your experience? Select one.

opinion ☐   experience ☐

Thesis statement: _____

_____

_____

Skill D Q2 Topic Sentences

Step 1

Read the question and three sentences that could be used in a response to each question. One of the sentences is a thesis statement. One of the sentences is the topic sentence of the body paragraph. The other sentence is a support or example used in the body paragraph. Number the sentences as follows:

Thesis statement (1)
Topic sentence (2)
Support or Example (3)

Question 1:

> The twentieth century saw great change. What is one change that strongly affected your life? Use specific details and examples to illustrate your idea.

(   ) Having the Internet in my home allows me to communicate with people around the globe.

(   ) The advent of the Internet is one twentieth-century change that has strongly affected my life.

(   ) For instance, I send emails to friends, family, and work colleagues on a daily basis.

Question 2:

> Some people believe that a college or university education should be available to all students. Others believe that higher education should be available only to top students. Discuss these views. Which view do you agree with? Explain why.

(   ) Many people radically change their attitude and work ethic after high school, so their means of future success should not be limited by what they achieved during the high school years.

(   ) Many high school students, for example, may have difficulty earning top grades because of health or relationship issues.

(   ) In my opinion, some form of post-secondary education should be available to all students, not just top students.

Question 3:

> Many people believe that the Internet has destroyed the ability to communicate face to face. Is this belief true about your friends and family? Use specific details and examples to explain your experience.

(   ) In general, the Internet has not damaged my friends' and family's ability to communicate; however, it has negatively affected the social skills of one of my cousins.

(   ) When I was visiting his house during the holidays, he spent all of New Year's Eve alone in his room playing *Doom*.

(   ) He spends several hours each day playing online games and never comes out of his room to talk to others.

Question 4:

> Businesses should hire employees for their entire lives. Do you agree or disagree? Use specific reasons and examples to support your answer.

(   ) For instance, employees are more likely to work harder and take fewer breaks if they worry about their job status.

(   ) I disagree with the argument that businesses should hire employees for their entire lives.

(   ) Having workers who know that their employment can be terminated can help increase the company's productivity.

Step 2

Read each of the following questions. Complete the thesis statement. Then write three ideas you would use in a short essay to explain or support the thesis statement.

Question 1:

> What do you consider to be the most important room in your house? Why is this room more important to you than any other room? Use specific details and examples to support your idea.

The most important room in my house is _____.

    Reason 1: _____

    Reason 2: _____

    Reason 3: _____

Choose one of the ideas you listed above. Rewrite the idea as a full sentence that could be used as the topic sentence of a body paragraph.

Topic sentence: _____

_____

Question 2:

> Do you agree or disagree with the following statement? Parents should physically punish their children when they misbehave. Use specific reasons and details to support your opinion.

In my opinion, parents should _____.

Reason 1: _____

Reason 2: _____

Reason 3: _____

Choose one of the ideas you listed above. Rewrite the idea as a full sentence that could be used as the topic sentence of a body paragraph.

Topic sentence: _____

_____

Question 3:

> There are many reasons to work, including the need for money. Describe your reasons for choosing a job that you have had or would like to have. Use specific examples and details to support your answer.

I chose my current job for _____.

Reason 1: _____

Reason 2: _____

Reason 3: _____

Choose one of the ideas you listed above. Rewrite the idea as a full sentence that could be used as the topic sentence of a body paragraph.

Topic sentence: _____

_____

Question 4:

> Schools should ask students to evaluate their teachers. Do you agree or disagree? Use specific reasons and examples to support your answer.

In my opinion, asking students to evaluate their teachers is _____.

Reason 1: _____

Reason 2: _____

Reason 3: _____

Choose one of the ideas you listed above. Rewrite the idea as a full sentence that could be used as the topic sentence of a body paragraph.

Topic sentence: _____

_____

Vocabulary Review

Vocabulary Review 1

Instructions: Choose the best word or phrase to complete each sentence.

1. Scientists have to control many _____ in order to conduct an accurate experiment.
   - (A) cramps
   - (B) variables
   - (C) adages
   - (D) membranes

2. The politician _____ many crimes and dishonest acts before the people finally voted him out.
   - (A) discounted
   - (B) assessed
   - (C) manipulated
   - (D) perpetrated

3. Is this species of plant _____ to this area, or was it brought in from Europe?
   - (A) indigenous
   - (B) controversial
   - (C) primeval
   - (D) prestigious

4. Many scientists believe a(n) _____ event, probably a meteor strike, caused a great environmental change that led to the extinction of dinosaurs.
   - (A) cataclysmic
   - (B) empirical
   - (C) aristocratic
   - (D) soluble

5. She wrote under a _____ because women were not believed to be capable of producing worthy literature at the time.
   - (A) precision
   - (B) conspiracy
   - (C) colleague
   - (D) pseudonym

6. My professor said my research was _____. Therefore, I have to do the paper again in order to pass the course.
   - (A) bourgeois
   - (B) abundant
   - (C) inadequate
   - (D) fortunate

7. Her doctor _____ her a list of exercises and dietary changes to help her have more energy.
   - (A) confirmed
   - (B) debilitated
   - (C) prescribed
   - (D) sustained

8. The scientists from that university tried to _____ the work of scientists from my university, but the opposite happened. They validated their results instead.
   - (A) replicate
   - (B) pioneer
   - (C) accredit
   - (D) discredit

Instructions: Choose the word or phrase closest in meaning to the underlined part.

9. The term paper is the most important <u>part</u> of your grade for this course.
   - (A) component
   - (B) correlation
   - (C) imbalance
   - (D) methodology

10. It is <u>very important</u> that governments try to fight oppression in other places around the world.
   - (A) vital
   - (B) causal
   - (C) skewed
   - (D) proportional

11. Darwin <u>theorized</u> that animals evolve to adapt to new environments.
    (A) posed
    (B) verified
    (C) postulated
    (D) deprived

12. I can't <u>accept</u> your idea to cheat on the exam.
    (A) condone
    (B) confirm
    (C) prescribe
    (D) replicate

13. The Renaissance was an <u>extremely</u> interesting period of European history.
    (A) arguably
    (B) exceptionally
    (C) pejoratively
    (D) categorically

14. We have a <u>plentiful</u> supply of food for the picnic. Why don't you join us?
    (A) primary
    (B) inadequate
    (C) vital
    (D) abundant

15. Her father attended a <u>highly respected</u> university. She's going to attend the same school next year.
    (A) genuine
    (B) sketchy
    (C) prestigious
    (D) remiss

Instructions: Write the missing words. Use the words below to fill in the blanks.

precision	verify	membranes
postulated	empirical	

An idea that has recently been **(16)** _____ is called the ekpyrotic scenario. This theory argues that our universe was created when two thin layers or **(17)** _____ of space matter collided. While this theory has some elements in common with the Big Bang Theory, it also has many differences. In fact, the ekpyrotic scenario is supported by the same **(18)** _____ data gathered from experiments designed to **(19)** _____ the Big Bang Theory. At this point, scientists must continue to investigate the subject with care and **(20)** _____. Perhaps such carefully obtained data will one day prove how the universe came into being.

Instructions: Match the words that are opposites.

21.	proletariat	(A)	oppression
22.	inadequate	(B)	balanced
23.	emancipation	(C)	abundant
24.	confirm	(D)	aristocratic
25.	skewed	(E)	discredit

Vocabulary Review 2

Instructions: Choose the best word or phrase to complete each sentence.

1. The Native Americans living in the area today claim a _____ to the people who lived here thousands of years ago, though it is difficult to prove they are from the same family line.
   - (A) migration
   - (B) stimulus
   - (C) lumber
   - (D) kinship

2. I believe that all people should be treated with _____ until they prove they are not worthy of respect.
   - (A) dignity
   - (B) investment
   - (C) instinct
   - (D) solitude

3. The _____ of the flying squirrel is being destroyed by the expansion of cities.
   - (A) mainstay
   - (B) genre
   - (C) travesty
   - (D) habitat

4. I'm thinking about investing in a new business _____, but I'm not sure that the risks are worth the potential profits.
   - (A) advent
   - (B) faculty
   - (C) dispute
   - (D) venture

5. My _____ impression of the professor was not very positive, but now I look forward to her classes every day.
   - (A) initial
   - (B) avid
   - (C) emotive
   - (D) auditory

6. The _____ of the radio radically changed the way people communicated in the 20th century.
   - (A) faculty
   - (B) stimulus
   - (C) advent
   - (D) vein

7. The Rocky Mountains provide tourists with some truly _____ scenery. I recommend you visit them some day.
   - (A) relevant
   - (B) stunning
   - (C) outdated
   - (D) rigorous

8. That reporter has been a _____ on the 6:00 news for thirty years.
   - (A) mainstay
   - (B) travesty
   - (C) technique
   - (D) firm

Instructions: Choose the word or phrase closest in meaning to the underlined part.

9. We are lucky to live in a time when global communication is so readily available.
   - (A) collaborative
   - (B) fortunate
   - (C) rash
   - (D) initial

10. The armed forces need to recruit hundreds of soldiers each year for their military operations abroad.
   - (A) enhance
   - (B) require
   - (C) endow
   - (D) enlist

11. I believe in following my <u>gut feelings</u> when making a difficult decision.

    (A) solitudes
    (B) initiatives
    (C) instincts
    (D) subdivisions

12. The United Nations will attempt to solve the <u>disagreement</u> between the two countries.

    (A) dispute
    (B) migration
    (C) dignity
    (D) investment

13. The airline company is going to spend more money on food and comfortable seats in order to <u>improve</u> the in-flight experience for passengers.

    (A) enhance
    (B) accommodate
    (C) engage
    (D) coincide

14. That was a very <u>interesting</u> film. I want to see it again.

    (A) avid
    (B) emotive
    (C) engrossing
    (D) stunning

15. She was very <u>unhappy</u> about spending a lot of time and money on the course, only to receive a failing grade from the professor.

    (A) tedious
    (B) bitter
    (C) integral
    (D) auditory

Instructions: Write the missing words. Use the words below to fill in the blanks.

collaborative	invariably	contend
interacting	foster	

Last year, more than fifty Native American groups were **(16)** _____ with scholars on joint archaeological programs. To be sure, such **(17)** _____ work between scientists and Native American leaders is important. It shows the possibility for scientific progress not only to learn about the past, but to **(18)** _____ respect and positive feelings between the two groups in the present. Scientists involved in these programs **(19)** _____ report numerous advantages to conducting research with the participation of Native Americans. They **(20)** _____ that a deeper understanding of the scientific data is obtained.

Instructions: Choose the one word that does not belong.

21.	vital	initial	integral	indispensable
22.	endow	bemoan	lament	complain
23.	recall	recollect	require	remember
24.	plot	woodland	habitat	technique
25.	update	caution	improve	enhance

Chapter 2

Making Writing Complete

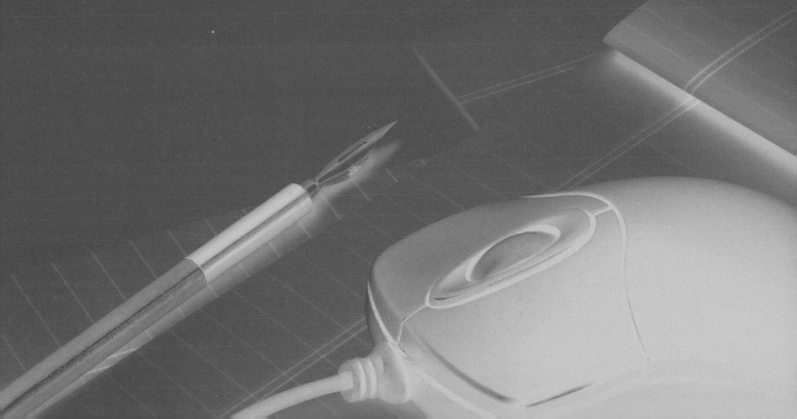

Strategies

- After determining the framework of your essay, further consideration must be given to the organization within the paragraphs themselves.

First paragraph contains:	Supporting paragraphs contain:
• the main idea of the whole response • one key point • examples and/or connection to the reading	• additional key points • examples and/or connection to the reading

- When developing your points, make sure that the statements are well connected so that the relationships between ideas can be seen clearly.
- Use transitional words and phrases to indicate the relationships among ideas.
- Use appropriate expressions to indicate when citing the source.

To Cite Information

- According to the lecture/passage,
- The reading states that
- In the reading, the author states that/discusses how
- In the author's/professor's opinion,
- According to the theory in the reading/lecture,
- The professor makes the point that
- The lecture supports/illustrates the idea that
- The lecture contradicts/refutes the idea that

To Compare and Contrast

- similarly, likewise, also, just as, both, by, by comparison, compared to, but, yet, although, in contrast, on the contrary, contrary to, on the other hand, however, conversely, is the opposite of, while, whereas, nevertheless, although, meanwhile, after all, although this may be true, in spite of, despite

To Show Cause and Effect

- because, since, for, thus, therefore, hence, as a result, accordingly, for the same reason

Practice 1

Step 1

Read the passage below and underline important information.

When most people think of great military strategists, the names Alexander the Great, Julius Caesar, or Napoleon Bonaparte come to mind. Spanish Conquistador Hernando Cortes, however, accomplished a feat that, arguably, outshines them all. Around 1520, Cortes conquered the 5-million-strong Aztec empire with only 600 men, twenty horses, and ten small cannons.

In 1519, Cortes sailed from Spain to Mexico with 11 ships and landed at various points along the Mexican coast. He easily subdued the small coastal tribes at what are now Tabasco and Veracruz. These people told him of the vast wealth of the Aztecs who lived inland. Cortes began to enlist the support of the smaller tribes he conquered as he made his way inland, a strategy that would serve him well. Since many of the tribes had no love for the Aztecs due to the Aztec policy of demanding costly tribute from them, they were often willing to join forces with Cortes.

Another circumstance that Cortes exploited was the fact that the Aztecs had a legend of a pale-skinned, bearded god, Quetzalcoatl, who they believed had once taught them agriculture and who would one day return to end their civilization. Cortes was believed to be this god by some Aztec citizens, most notably, the emperor Motecuhzoma. Additionally, the native Mexicans had never before seen horses, firearms, or the giant attack mastiffs the Spanish brought with them. Cortes exploited these two psychological advantages, the legend of the light-skinned god and the spectacle of his horses, dogs, and cannons, to conquer the entire Aztec empire largely through fear and negotiation. The brilliance of his approach leaves its mark, for better or worse, on the history of an entire nation today.

strategist (n):
a person who makes plans and strategies

come to mind (v phrase):
to be thought of

feat (n):
an accomplishment

outshine (v):
to appear or perform better than

subdue (v):
to capture and control

tribute (n):
a payment of money or goods demanded by the head of an empire from the nations under its control

firearm (n):
a gun

mastiff (n):
a large, powerful breed of dog

spectacle (n):
a large public performance or display

Step 2

🎧 **Now listen to a lecture and take notes on the important information.**

_____ was the secret to _____ 's success

1. Spaniards discover that she can _____ and use her

   _____

2. Cortes uses her to win _____ from _____

3. Unclear whether she was just an _____ or _____ as well

4. Independent _____ and _____ sources attest to

   _____

lingua franca (n phrase):
a second language spoken by people of many nations

entourage (n):
a group of people that accompany someone

concubine (n):
a woman responsible for bearing children to a man

campaign (n):
a military venture

cast doubt on (v phrase):
to make uncertain or doubtful

hierarchical (adj):
related to a ranking based on power or authority

Step 3

Read the question and understand your task.

Summarize the main points in the lecture, explaining how they cast doubt on points made in the reading.

Now read the passage and your notes again. Write down the parts of the reading and the lecture that disagree.

Reading	Lecture
_____	_____
_____	_____
_____	_____

Step 4

Read the sample response below. Identify the role of each statement and fill in the blanks with the appropriate words in the box.

The reading passage depicts Cortes as one of the greatest military strategists of all time and credits him with toppling an empire of millions with only 600 men and a few horses and cannons. **(1)** _____, it proposes he was a genius who exploited local politics, legends, and the spectacle of his small but advanced military to accomplish a nearly impossible feat. **(2)** _____, the speaker casts doubt on this version of history and credits Cortes's interpreter and concubine, Malintzin, as being the mastermind behind a significant part of his campaign. **(3)** _____, she asks us to ponder who was more likely the mastermind: the foreigner who had little to no knowledge of the politics, customs, or language, or the native who had knowledge of all of these and who was the one directly speaking with the leaders of the Aztecs and other nations. **(4)** _____, the speaker cites various sources, including accounts from Spanish soldiers and other conquistadors, as well as depictions in Nahua art, which support the case that Malintzin was much more than an interpreter and perhaps just as significant as Cortes himself.

in contrast / in addition to this / further / more specifically

Underline the main point, the example, and the final summary statement in the sample response. Then, change those sentences using your own words. Try to make your sentences as short and clear as possible.

Main Point: _____

Example Sentence: _____

Summary Sentence: _____

Step 5

Write your own response with the help of the sample and the words/phrases you wrote in Step 4.

Response word count: _____ (Suggested word count = 200)

Skill A Q1 Economics

Practice 2

Step 1

Read the passage below and underline important information.

The value of a professional sports team for a city's local economy is undeniable. The benefits begin with the construction of the stadium itself, providing thousands of local construction jobs. Once regular season play begins, an army of local workers is required to man the stadium facilities, for everything from concessions and ticket sales to security and administration. The economic benefits expand throughout the district of the stadium as fans pour into the area from far and wide. These fans support local parking decks, restaurants, bars, shops, and often hotel facilities. This contributes to the prosperity of local businesses and provides a general boost to the overall property value.

All of this revenue is of course taxed by the municipal authorities. Combine this with the millions of dollars in tax revenue that ticket sales can generate over the life of a sports team, and we have a clear benefit for all members of the community.

These benefits are easy to see, but the intangible benefits may be greater still. A professional sports team with regularly televised broadcasts is often the hallmark of what people generally perceive as a "major" city. Thus, the sports team becomes a kind of advertisement for the significance and prosperity of the city itself, attracting new business from the outside.

Some may say that the costs of new sports stadiums are an undue burden on cities, but all of the long-term benefits must be taken into account before passing hasty judgment on the economic effects of professional sports franchises.

concessions (n):
the food and drink sold in a stadium

prosperity (n):
the state of being successful

municipal (adj):
related to a city or town

intangible (adj):
not detectable by the physical senses

hallmark (n):
a characteristic sign of

undue (adj):
unnecessary; unjust; unwarranted

burden (n):
a source of stress or difficulty

hasty (adj):
done quickly, without careful consideration

Step 2

 Now listen to a lecture and take notes on the important information.

Sports stadium not _____

1. Jobs created _____ other jobs or _____ wages

2. Most money goes to _____

3. Tax revenue _____ compared to _____

4. Team's _____ to the city's _____ difficult to measure

federal (adj):
related to a nation

exempt (adj):
not applicable to; an exception to

infrastructure (n):
the structures necessary for a society to run smoothly, such as roads, schools, and hospitals

meager (adj):
small; insufficient

feasible (adj):
possible; able to be accomplished; plausible

top notch (adj phrase):
of high quality or level

Read the question and understand your task.

Summarize the main points made in the lecture, explaining how they cast doubt on points made in the reading.

Now read the passage and your notes again. Write down the parts of the reading and the lecture that disagree.

Reading	Lecture
_____	_____
_____	_____
_____	_____

Step 4

Now read the sample response below. Identify the role of each statement and fill in the blanks with the appropriate words in the box.

The reading states that a sports team greatly benefits a city in a number of ways, **(1)** _____ the lecture says the benefits do not justify the initial investment and that the sports team actually ends up taking money out of the community. The speaker implies that taxpayer money should not go to the stadium **(2)** _____ the sports team is a profit-seeking business, and they should not expect free money from the public. Further, the speaker argues that benefits such as jobs and tax revenues are not actually benefits if all relevant factors are taken into account, such as the kinds of jobs, and the comparison of the situation without the sports team. **(3)** _____, the reading proposes that the benefit to the city's image is invaluable, ultimately attracting new residents and businesses and contributing to the city's long-term growth. **(4)** _____ this fact, the speaker maintains that the city would benefit more from investing this money elsewhere, such as in education and infrastructure.

since / while / in spite of / however

Underline the main point, the example, and the final summary statement in the sample response. Then, change those sentences using your own words. Try to make your sentences as short and clear as possible.

Main Point: _____

Example Sentence: _____

Summary Sentence: _____

Step 5

Write your own response with the help of the sample and the words/phrases you wrote in Step 4.

Response word count: _____ (Suggested word count = 200)

Practice 3

Step 1

Read the passage below and underline important information.

In 1989, scientists in Utah made a controversial announcement. They claimed that they had carried out an experiment in which the results could only be explained by nuclear fusion. In their experiment, they filled a glass container with heavy water that had a small amount of salt dissolved in it. Into the container, they inserted two electrodes: one was platinum and one was palladium. The platinum electrode was connected to the positive charge of a car battery, while the palladium electrode was attached to the negative charge. This process created an excess amount of heat—more than could be explained by chemical reactions. Because it could not be explained by chemical reactions, the researchers jumped to the conclusion that nuclear fusion was the cause. This phenomenon is referred to as "cold fusion." It is not accepted by the scientific community, and it serves as an example of pseudoscience.

The scientific method demands that a claim be subject to peer review. The validity of any claim is based on reproducibility. Because no one has ever been able to reproduce the results of the first claim of cold fusion, it has been rejected. More importantly, the data does not coincide with current theories of nuclear fusion. It is well accepted that, when nuclear fusion takes place, neutrons are emitted. For one thing, no extra neutrons were detected. Secondly, if the number of neutrons necessary to support their claim had in fact been emitted, the researchers would have been killed. The only explanation for the experimenters' findings is that errors in measurement took place. This is supported by the fact that the methods they used to measure heat were highly specious.

carry out *(v phrase):*
to do; to perform

phenomenon *(n):*
an event; a happening

pseudoscience *(n):*
a false science; an unfounded claim of a scientific procedure

peer review *(n phrase):*
the process of having equals examine an academic work

reproducibility *(n):*
the ability to be repeated with the same results

emit *(v):*
to produce and give off

take place *(v phrase):*
to happen; to occur

specious *(adj):*
seeming to be true but actually false; deceptively attractive

Step 2

🎧 **Now listen to a lecture and take notes on the important information.**

• Cold fusion refers to _____

— _____

— _____

— _____

disdain *(n):*
a feeling of contempt for; a feeling of superiority in regards to

astound *(v):*
to surprise greatly

buy into *(v phrase):*
to believe

validate *(v):*
to prove true

deem *(v):*
to conclude; to state as

stance *(n):*
an opinion; a point of view

Step 3

Read the question and understand your task.

Summarize the main points made in the lecture, explaining how they relate to points made in the reading.

Now read the passage and your notes again. Write down the main points of the reading and the parts of the lecture that expand upon the points made in the reading.

Reading	Lecture
_____	_____
_____	_____
_____	_____

Step 4

Now read the sample response below. Identify the role of each statement and fill in the blanks with the appropriate words in the box.

The debate surrounding the possibility of cold fusion, **(1)** _____, nuclear fusion occurring at room temperature, is centered on the scientific process. The reading attacks the scientists' interpretation of their results. When they found that excess heat was generated in an amount that could not be explained by chemical reactions, the scientists concluded that nuclear fusion was taking place. The reading states that because such an interpretation does not concur with current theory, it should not be accepted. The speaker points out, however, that science relies on continual review of theories. Observations should not be ignored **(2)** _____ they are not explained by current theories. **(3)** _____ the statement in the reading that scientists have never been able to replicate the original experimenters' results, the speaker states that in the years that have passed, some indeed have found similar results. In sum, the reading states that cold fusion claims have not stood up to the scientific process, **(4)** _____ the speaker asserts that the scientific community was hasty in dismissing the notion before sufficient time was allowed to complete an analysis using the scientific process.

whereas / just because / that is / with regards to

Underline the main point, the example, and the final summary statement in the sample response. Then, change those sentences using your own words. Try to make your sentences as short and clear as possible.

Main Point: _____

Example Sentence: _____

Summary Sentence: _____

Step 5

Write your own response with the help of the sample and the words/phrases you wrote in Step 4.

Response word count: _____ (Suggested word count = 200)

Skill A Q1 Archaeology

Practice 4

Step 1

Read the passage below and underline important information.

Recent claims that the ancient Anasazi peoples engaged in cannibalism are unfounded. The practice of cannibalism does not coincide with the culture of the Native American groups who are descended from these people, that is, the Pueblo peoples of the American Southwest. Cannibalism is considered by Native Americans to be one of the most evil acts a person can engage in. It seems improbable, then, that their ancestors ate human flesh ritualistically. The speculation that the Anasazi people were human flesh eaters is based on skeletal remains that were found to have been broken and burned. It can be demonstrated from these findings that flesh was removed from the bones, but that does not prove that the meal was actually ingested. A more plausible explanation, and one that coincides with the beliefs of the Pueblo peoples, is that these are the remains of suspected witches who were put to death. The custom was to kill the suspected witch by burning the body and tearing apart the remains in order to remove and destroy the witch's "evil" heart. This explains the broken bones and burn marks. It also explains why the corpse was ripped apart. While the practice was brutal, it does not imply cannibalism. Any claim that the Anasazi people were cannibalistic is based not on fact, but on inference. The refusal of some to consider other plausible explanations is unscientific and irrational.

engage in (v phrase):
to do

unfounded (adj):
not supported by evidence

ancestor (n):
a relative that lived in the past; a person whom one is descended from

ritualistically (adv):
as part of a ceremony or ritual

ingest (v):
to eat; to consume

plausible (adj):
possible; able to be accomplished; feasible

brutal (adj):
violent; extremely harsh or cruel

Step 2

🎧 **Now listen to a lecture and take notes on the important information.**

• Evidence supports the claim that _____

_____

  — _____

  — _____

  — _____

touchy (adj):
causing strong emotions

revere (v):
to respect greatly

tag marker (n phrase):
a characteristic sign of

carcass (n):
a dead body

condemn (v):
to censure; to conclude as unethical or unworthy

tarnish (v):
to spoil; to lessen the value or purity of

Read the question and understand your task.

Summarize the points made in the lecture and state how they can be applied to the problem introduced in the reading passage.

Now read the passage and your notes again. Write down the main points of the reading and the parts of the lecture that expand upon the points made in the reading.

Reading	Lecture
_____	_____
_____	_____
_____	_____

Step 4

Now read the sample response below. Identify the role of each statement and fill in the blanks with the appropriate words in the box.

The dispute concerning whether or not the Anasazi people engaged in cannibalism is based on evidence obtained from the examination of human remains. These remains show that human skeletons were torn apart, cooked, and had the flesh removed from them. The reading states that this does not necessarily imply that cannibalism took place. **(1)** _____, they explain that these are the remains of suspected witches who were burned and had their bodies torn apart. The speaker, however, maintains that the evidence does suggest that ingestion took place. **(2)** _____, pot resin was found on the bones suggesting they were cooked. **(3)** _____, fossilized fecal matter shows traces of human flesh. While the reading states that Native American culture would not condone such activities, the speaker maintains that the evidence does not implicate anyone in particular in the act. She goes on to offer a plausible explanation that has been presented: that a group of foreigners engaged in cannibalism in order to terrorize the Anasazi. **(4)** _____, the peaceful reputation of this culture need not be tarnished by this evidence of cannibalism.

furthermore / thus / for example / instead

Underline the main point, the example, and the final summary statement in the sample response. Then, change those sentences using your own words. Try to make your sentences as short and clear as possible.

Main Point: _____

Example Sentence: _____

Summary Sentence: _____

Step 5

Write your own response with the help of the sample and the words/phrases you wrote in Step 4.

Response word count: _____ (Suggested word count = 200)

READING | LISTENING | SPEAKING | WRITING | PRACTICE TEST

Independent Writing: Making Ideas Flow

Strategies

Characteristics of a good introduction:

- is one (1) paragraph
- is an introduction to the general topic of the essay
- includes the thesis statement and a restatement of the question
- includes points that will be discussed or elaborated on in the body

- Do NOT try to say everything in the introduction; save details and examples for the body of your essay.
- Do NOT start with a statement that is too general; a more specific statement better sets up the information to follow.

Characteristics of a good body:

- can be several (1–3) paragraphs
- has a topic sentence for each paragraph that states the main idea of that paragraph
- has specific examples, reasons, or other details
- includes other sentences that link ideas or show transitions between ideas

- Write an accurate and clear topic sentence for each body paragraph.
- Make sure there are logical connections between statements.

Characteristics of a good conclusion:

- is one (1) paragraph
- has a restatement of your thesis in different words
- has a summary of your main points
- includes one or both of the following: a consideration of the opposite opinion, a recommendation

- Do NOT use the exact same words or expressions in your conclusion that you used in your introduction.
- Do NOT introduce new ideas or concepts that should belong in a new body paragraph.

Skill B **Q2** Independent

Practice 1

Step 1

Read the question and think of ideas to list in the blanks.

A gift (such as a camera, a soccer ball, or an animal) can contribute to a child's development. Some gifts produce positive effects on this development, while other gifts produce negative effects. What gift that you received as a child helped you develop into the person you are today? How? Use specific details and examples to describe your experience.

Gift: Produced positive development

- Books: Stimulate the imagination
      Develop language skills such as grammar, vocabulary, etc
      Encourage creativity
      Good for relaxation and de-stressing

_____

_____

Gift: Produced negative development

- Playstation: Very competitive
      Lack of exercise due to indoor activity
      Can make children antisocial and obsessive

_____

_____

Step 2

Now look at the sample response. Think of the role of sentences in each part of the essay. Look for any transitions that link the ideas and underline them. Then, put the sentences in the right order.

Introduction:

_____   _____   _____   _____

(A) It is thus, perhaps, no surprise that I ended up studying literature and finally became a language teacher and creative writer myself.

(B) Receiving my first storybook at the age of six was to change the course of my life.

(C) The gifts that really most affected my development as a child were books.

(D) I became an avid reader and developed a keen interest in literature and language studies.

Body:

_____   _____   _____   _____   _____   _____

(A) By developing a broad vocabulary through my writing, I was also able to excel in other academic subjects.

(B) I still find this benefit through reading today, in fact.

(C) I developed excellent language skills by doing a lot of reading and found reading to be creatively stimulating.

(D) I started to write my own stories and poems at a young age as a result.

(E) Furthermore, I found that reading relaxed me and helped me deal with stress more effectively.

(F) Reading books had a very positive influence on my life.

Conclusion:

_____   _____   _____   _____   _____

(A) Consequently, I hope to pass this love of books and reading on to my current students, so that they can gain the same benefits I did.

(B) Clearly, those books I received are part of the reason I am a language teacher today.

(C) Because books continue to stimulate my creativity and calm my nerves, I treasure them as much today as I did in childhood.

(D) Instead of indulging in television or computer games, I developed my imagination and critical faculties.

(E) I developed a passion for reading and writing simply because I received books as gifts from early on.

---

keen *(adj)*:
strong; intense

excel *(v)*:
to succeed at; to be good at

stimulating *(adj)*:
interesting; producing energy

indulge *(v)*:
to yield to desires; to do something fun but unproductive or unhealthy

critical faculties *(n phrase)*:
the ability to think analytically

Look back at the ideas you wrote in the blanks for Step 1. Write your own response to the prompt using one of your own ideas or another idea from Step 1.

Response word count: _____ (Suggested word count = 300)

Skill B **Q2** Independent

Practice 2

Step 1

Read the question and think of ideas to list in the blanks.

Having strong social programs in a country often means higher tax rates. In your opinion, is it better to live in a society that invests little money in social programs while keeping tax rates low, or would you prefer to live in a society where you are required to pay high taxes but reap the benefits of strong social programs?

High Taxes, Strong Social Programs

- ensure essential infrastructure (schools, roads, hospitals)
- ensure health care and education
- give security in case of illness, unemployment

_____

_____

Low Taxes, Weak Social Programs

- allow people more disposable income
- encourage responsible behavior
- allow freedom to choose services

_____

_____

Now look at the sample response. Think of the role of each sentence within the essay. Look for any transitions that link the ideas. Underline them. Then, put the sentences in the right order.

Introduction:

_____   _____   _____

(A) For this reason, I would have no qualms paying a higher portion of my income in taxes than I would if there were no social programs.
(B) I would prefer to live in a society that values social welfare over individual wealth.
(C) In short, I believe that it is the responsibility of the state to take care of those who cannot take care of themselves.

Body:

_____   _____   _____   _____   _____

(A) Within such economies, the opportunity of monetary success lies with the individual.
(B) This is an every-man-for-himself attitude that is based on a false premise, that is, that everyone has equal opportunities in a free-market economy.
(C) While it is possible for poor people to achieve great success, it is impossible for all poor people to do so.
(D) Some might argue that in a capitalist society, those who work hard enough can accrue wealth and thus won't have to rely on social welfare.
(E) However, such thinking fails to recognize the social conditions in place that allow the rich to get richer while simultaneously ensuring that the poor stay poor.

Conclusion:

_____   _____   _____   _____

(A) Further, it is not just the poor who benefit, as programs such as universal health care, day care, and social security are very important to the middle and upper middle classes as well.
(B) The success of a capitalist society depends on having a lower, middle, and upper class.
(C) In effect, paying taxes is not like giving money away to poor people, as everyone benefits from social programs.
(D) Therefore, because the middle and upper classes rely on the existence of a lower class for their continued comfort, I believe that it is their responsibility to take care of the poor with social welfare programs.

qualm *(n)*:
a feeling of uneasiness or worry; a reservation

portion *(n)*:
a part

welfare *(n)*:
the benefit and well being of

mentality *(n)*:
a way of thinking; a belief system

premise *(n)*:
a basic, fundamental idea or belief

accrue *(v)*:
to gain and increase

Step 3

Look back at the ideas you wrote in the blanks for Step 1. Write your own response to the prompt arguing for the opposite side to the response given.

Response word count: _____ (Suggested word count = 300)

Skill B Independent

Practice 3

Step 1

Read the question and think of ideas to list in the blanks.

The twentieth century saw great change. In your opinion, what is one change that should be remembered about the twentieth century? Use specific reasons to explain your choice.

Nuclear Fission: Good Development and Change in 20th Century

- Facilitated end of Second World War
- Fission research/splitting of atom led to other scientific development: Nuclear Power
- Brinkmanship: Threat of world destruction prevents superpowers going to war

_____

_____

Nuclear Fission: Bad Development and Change in 20th Century

- Nuclear bombs cause mass destruction
- Terrorists/rogue states develop weapons of mass destruction
- Nuclear capability causes world debates and power struggles

_____

_____

Step 2

Now look at the sample response. Think of the role of each sentence within the essay. Look for any transitions that link the ideas. Underline them. Then, put the sentences in the right order.

Introduction:

_____ _____ _____ _____

(A) For example, the use of nuclear fission in atomic weapons produced a meaningful impact on world politics.

(B) Let us investigate these two changes more closely.

(C) One of the greatest changes that occurred during the 20th century was the development of nuclear fission.

(D) In addition, nuclear fission greatly changed the way energy is produced.

Body:

_____ _____ _____ _____ _____ _____ _____

(A) To continue, the use of nuclear fission in reactors has had a great impact for two reasons.

(B) This effect was so severe, in fact, that atomic weapons became a powerful deterrent against the start of further large-scale wars.

(C) Nations were shocked and awed by the vast devastation they caused.

(D) In other words, they have brought about peace.

(E) To begin, atomic weapons were developed and used during World War II.

(F) Second, unlike the burning of wood or fossil fuels, nuclear reactors produce this energy with very little harm to the environment.

(G) First, they can produce a great quantity of electricity for a relatively low cost.

Conclusion:

_____ _____ _____ _____

(A) Thus, the development of nuclear fission forever changed energy production and the politics of war.

(B) Furthermore, the power generated by nuclear reactors makes for a cheaper, cleaner source of energy.

(C) The development of nuclear weapons and nuclear power were clearly very important in the 20th century, bringing about many fundamental changes to society.

(D) This is because nuclear weapons forever changed how war is practiced.

---

fission _(n)_:
the process of splitting into parts

meaningful _(adj)_:
important

reactor _(n)_:
a building or piece of equipment in which nuclear reactions take place

deterrent _(n)_:
a factor that influences against a given action

awed _(adj)_:
feeling an overwhelming emotion, such as fear

bring about _(v phrase)_:
to make happen; to effect

fundamental _(adj)_:
basic; essential

Look back at the ideas you wrote in the blanks for Step 1. Write your own response to the prompt arguing for the opposite side to the response given.

Response word count: _____ (Suggested word count = 300)

Skill B Q2 Independent

Practice 4

Step 1

Look at the prompt and try to figure out your task.

People usually learn from their elders; however, younger people can also sometimes teach those older than them. Tell about a time when you learned an important lesson from someone younger than you. Use specific details and examples to tell about your experience.

Read the two ideas for possible responses to the prompt. Write one more idea of your own.

1. Children remind us to use our imagination.

2. Children remind us of what's really important in life.

3. _____

Step 2

Read the sample introduction below. Then, in the space on the next page, try to write body paragraphs for 2 of the ideas above. Try to write 3-5 sentences for each body paragraph. Then read the sample conclusion paragraph.

Introduction:

Two years ago, I thought of nothing but work. My only interest was in things that would improve my resumé and my job prospects. One day, I was looking at my resumé and I realized that I needed to add some volunteer work to it. I decided to spend time with a young boy who had lost his parents in a car accident. I thought I would teach this boy, David, many valuable life lessons and give him a head start in the world. In the end, though, it was David who taught me something.

Body 1:

_____

_____

_____

_____

_____

Body 2:

_____

_____

_____

_____

_____

Conclusion:

Soon, my own imagination started running wild. When I got home, I started writing with no concern for structure or style. What's more, I had no intention of trying to have it published! I was having fun, and that was all that mattered. That is the lesson that David taught me. Now, I do things because I enjoy doing them, not because of how it will look on my resumé.

Now read the sample response on page 606. What similarities and differences do you see with the paragraphs you wrote?

Step 3

Write your own response to the prompt in Step 1. First, think of 2 or 3 ideas for body paragraphs. Then, try to write a response using your ideas.

Response word count: _____ (Suggested word count = 300)

Two years ago, I thought of nothing but work. My only interest was in things that would improve my resumé and my job prospects. One day, I was looking at my resumé and I realized that I needed to add some volunteer work to it. I decided to spend time with a young boy who had lost his parents in a car accident. I thought I would teach this boy, David, many valuable life lessons and give him a head start in the world. In the end, though, it was David who taught me something.

The first project David and I undertook together was to write a story. I thought I would teach him about grammar and how to structure a story the way my high school creative writing teacher had taught me. I imagined that David would grow up to be a great writer and dedicate his first book to me. When we began to write, I was amazed at how fast David came up with ideas. When I tried to slow him down to explain the finer points of composition, he wasn't interested. He had a story to tell, and he didn't care about structure and style. I decided to let him have free reign over the story, and I kept my mouth shut. In the end, it was the best story I'd ever read.

Soon, my own imagination started running wild. When I got home, I started writing with no concern for structure or style. What's more, I had no intention of trying to have it published! I was having fun, and that was all that mattered. That is the lesson that David taught me. Now, I do things because I enjoy doing them, not because of how it will look on my resumé.

prospect *(n)*:
a potential for improvement

head start *(n phrase)*:
an early start; an advantageous beginning

undertake *(v)*:
to do something that involves a lengthy process

structure *(v)*:
to organize

dedicate *(v)*:
to write a letter or page honoring someone

come up with *(v phrase)*:
to make; to create

free reign *(n phrase)*:
unrestricted permission; the permission to do whatever one wants

run wild *(v phrase)*:
to move or operate in an energetic, uncontrolled fashion

Practice 5

Step 1

Look at the prompt and try to figure out your task.

It is sometimes said that borrowing money from a friend can harm or damage the friendship. Has borrowing or lending money to a friend ever damaged one of your friendships? Use specific details and examples to explain your answer.

Now look at the outline of a possible response to this prompt. Fill in the blank for responding to this prompt.

Main Idea: Borrowing money can be dangerous to a friendship, but it is, in fact, possible under carefully controlled circumstances.

Details: Three dangers to guard against are resentment, superiority, and inability/failure to repay.

Conclusion: While it is probably best to avoid borrowing money in a friendship,

_____ .

Step 2

Read a sample body paragraph for an essay answering this prompt.

Body:

The first danger is feelings of resentment and/or superiority. A friendship is usually based on equality. As soon as one friend lends the other money, that equality is in jeopardy. The lender is in danger of feeling superior to the borrower and letting these feelings affect his or her behavior and the dynamic of the relationship. On the other hand, the borrower is in danger of resenting the lender for his or her financial position. This resentment can be just as detrimental to the friendship as the feelings of superiority.

Write a thesis statement to match this body paragraph.

_____

_____

Step 3

Now write an introduction and a conclusion for the prompt in Step 1. Use your thesis statement from Step 2. Try to write 3-5 sentences for each paragraph.

Introduction:

_____

_____

_____

_____

_____

Conclusion:

_____

_____

_____

_____

_____

Now read the sample response on page 610. What similarities and differences do you see with the paragraphs you wrote?

Step 4

Write your own response to the prompt. First, make a short outline like the example above. Then, try to write a response using your outline.

Response word count: _____ (Suggested word count = 300)

It is often said that a sure way to ruin a friendship is for one friend to lend money to another. While this aphorism may hold some truth, it is by no means unavoidably true. Most people probably know two friends from their lives who serve as a counter-example to this rule. The most useful discourse on the subject would be to identify the possible dangers involved in lending money to friends and discuss how to avoid them.

The first danger is feelings of resentment and/or superiority. A friendship is usually based on equality. As soon as one friend lends the other money, that equality is in jeopardy. The lender is in danger of feeling superior to the borrower and letting these feelings affect his or her behavior and the dynamic of the relationship. On the other hand, the borrower is in danger of resenting the lender for his or her financial position. This resentment can be just as detrimental to the friendship as the feelings of superiority.

A more tangible danger, of course, is inability, or worse, unwillingness, to repay. If the borrower has no clear means or no ultimate desire to get the money back to the lender, then the loan is more likely to function as a gift. In this case, the lender probably had not anticipated this eventuality and will be displeased, feeling that he or she has been taken advantage of.

In all, the dangers can be daunting, and certainly no one should loan or borrow a significant amount of money to and from a friend without careful consideration of the risks. However, under the right circumstances, when there is little risk of feelings of resentment or superiority and when the borrower appears to have the means and will for remuneration, there is no reason to rule out such pecuniary arrangements between friends.

aphorism *(n)*:
a brief statement of truth; an adage

discourse *(n)*:
a verbal exchange; a logical conversation

resentment *(n)*:
a feeling of anger or indignation

in jeopardy *(adj phrase)*:
in danger; vulnerable

dynamic *(n)*:
an interactive system or process; the workings and structure of a relationship

detrimental *(adj)*:
harmful

tangible *(adj)*:
noticeable; significant

anticipate *(v)*:
to predict and prepare for

daunting *(adj)*:
very challenging; fearsome

remuneration *(n)*:
the act of paying back a debt

pecuniary *(adj)*:
related to money and payment

Skill B **Q2** Opinion

Practice 6

Look at the prompt and try to figure out your task.

Do you agree or disagree with the following statement? Only people who earn a lot of money are successful. Use specific reasons and examples to support your answer.

Now look at the outline of a possible response to this prompt. Write one more idea of your own.

1. Society uses other factors to measure success, such as prestige, family, and position in the community.

2. For some professions, such as artist, writer, or actor, just making a living is considered success.

3. _____

Read the sample introduction below. Then, in the space on the next page, try to write body paragraphs for 2 of the ideas above. Try to write 3-5 sentences for each body paragraph. Then read the sample conclusion paragraph.

Introduction:

Money is typically considered the measure of success, but is it fair to say that it is the only true measure? Sociologically speaking, the perception of success can involve other factors as well, such as prestige, family, and importance within the community. Furthermore, some professions are highly coveted and difficult to enter. For these, just making a living may be viewed as success in and of itself. Finally, it is possible to think of a situation in which wealth does not translate into success.

Body 1:

_____

_____

_____

_____

_____

Body 2:

_____

_____

_____

_____

_____

Conclusion:

Finally, the reverse situation is sometimes true; that is, a wealthy person is not considered a success. Admittedly, this is the exception to the rule, but examples such as a business person or broker arrested for ethics violations provide a counterpoint. Though they may still be quite wealthy, it would be odd to consider them successful. In sum, money is neither necessary nor sufficient for success.

Now read the sample response on page 614. What similarities and differences do you see with the paragraphs you wrote?

Step 3

Write your own response to the prompt in Step 1. First think of 2 or 3 ideas for body paragraphs. Then, try to write a response using your ideas.

Response word count: _____   (Suggested word count = 300)

Money is typically considered the measure of success, but is it fair to say that it is the only true measure? Sociologically speaking, the perception of success can involve other factors as well, such as prestige, family, and importance within the community. Furthermore, some professions are highly coveted and difficult to enter. For these, just making a living may be viewed as success in and of itself. Finally, it is possible to think of a situation in which wealth does not translate into success.

The word "success" may call to mind a Wall Street stockbroker who earns half a million dollars per year, but other exemplars of success include a well-renowned professor, the head of a well-adjusted family, a chief of police, or a school principal. Any of these people may only make as much money as an unsuccessful stockbroker, but prestige, family, and community status all compensate in the perception of their success.

Other professions in fields such as art, acting, music, or writing may also garner success without money. Given the high percentage of failed artists, actors, and writers who have gone into other professions, anyone who succeeds in making a steady living in these professions is considered to be successful. Indeed, getting by and doing what one loves is a kind of success as well.

Finally, the reverse situation is sometimes true; that is, a wealthy person is not considered a success. Admittedly, this is the exception to the rule, but examples such as a business person or broker arrested for ethics violations provide a counterpoint. Though they may still be quite wealthy, it would be odd to consider them successful. In sum, money is neither necessary nor sufficient for success.

perception (n):
a belief; an opinion

prestige (n):
the condition of being highly respected

coveted (adj):
desired; sought after

translate into (v phrase):
to equal; to produce

exemplar (n):
a thing or person that stands as an example

renowned (adj):
famous

compensate (v):
to provide a benefit in exchange for work or suffering

garner (v):
to get; to achieve; to earn

violation (n):
an act against a rule or principle

sufficient (adj):
enough for a given purpose or need

Vocabulary Review

Vocabulary Review 1

Instructions: Choose the best word or phrase to complete each sentence.

1. The scientific achievements of Albert Einstein _____ those of almost every other scientist in history.
   - (A) deem
   - (B) emit
   - (C) astound
   - (D) outshine

2. Alexander the Great's army was able to _____ many nations as it swept across Europe.
   - (A) emit
   - (B) subdue
   - (C) validate
   - (D) ingest

3. The _____ taxes were increased in order to buy more buses for the city.
   - (A) municipal
   - (B) intangible
   - (C) meager
   - (D) specious

4. The money raised from this concert will go to a charity that helps build _____ such as hospitals and schools in developing countries.
   - (A) concessions
   - (B) burdens
   - (C) disdain
   - (D) infrastructure

5. The students are going to _____ an experiment to determine the melting point of cotton.
   - (A) buy into
   - (B) carry out
   - (C) rage on
   - (D) come to mind

6. All plants and animals rely on light _____ from the sun.
   - (A) emitted
   - (B) validated
   - (C) condemned
   - (D) outshined

7. Some scientists treat Native American claims to archaeological remains with _____, rather than honoring such claims.
   - (A) disdain
   - (B) tribute
   - (C) entourage
   - (D) burden

8. Her accusation that I cheated on the exam was _____. There was no truth to it whatsoever.
   - (A) plausible
   - (B) exempt
   - (C) federal
   - (D) unfounded

9. Over one thousand years ago, the _____ of modern-day Mexicans built some of the largest pyramids in the world.
   - (A) stances
   - (B) ancestors
   - (C) carcasses
   - (D) phenomena

10. Murder is one act that is _____ by almost all modern and ancient cultures.
   - (A) deemed
   - (B) bought into
   - (C) condemned
   - (D) revered

11. Genghis Khan is considered by many historians to be a great military _____. His plans helped the Mongols conquer much of Eurasia.
    (A) feat
    (B) firearm
    (C) strategist
    (D) deterrent

12. The Roman Empire demanded large _____ from the lands it conquered.
    (A) mastiffs
    (B) spectacles
    (C) concubines
    (D) tributes

13. The owners of the stadium are negotiating with the owners of the hockey team over rights to the _____ sold at hockey games.
    (A) concessions
    (B) hallmarks
    (C) infrastructure
    (D) entourage

14. They are relying on new investments to bring success and _____ to the company.
    (A) dynamic
    (B) pseudoscience
    (C) prosperity
    (D) reproducibility

15. My parents always recommend that I avoid making _____ decisions. They always want me to think things through.
    (A) feasible
    (B) hasty
    (C) top notch
    (D) touchy

Instructions: Choose the word or phrase closest in meaning to the underlined part.

16. Graduating from university was the greatest <u>accomplishment</u> of my life.
    (A) discourse
    (B) feat
    (C) disdain
    (D) premise

17. It is a <u>deceptively attractive</u> theory. It sounds logical, but it is based on incorrect assumptions.
    (A) brutal
    (B) hierarchical
    (C) intangible
    (D) specious

18. They are having a <u>national</u> election tomorrow. The voters will choose a new leader for the country.
    (A) meager
    (B) municipal
    (C) touchy
    (D) federal

19. If all the employees work a little overtime, it is <u>feasible</u> that the project be completed by next week's deadline.
    (A) meaningful
    (B) plausible
    (C) keen
    (D) undue

20. The annual migration of cranes is an <u>event</u> that occurs each fall in this region.
    (A) stance
    (B) portion
    (C) strategist
    (D) phenomenon

21. She was <u>very surprised</u> when she received an A on her paper. She had thought she had done very poorly.

(A) validated
(B) ingested
(C) tarnished
(D) astounded

22. His theory on the origins of corn farming has recently been <u>proven true</u> by further research.

(A) bought into
(B) revered
(C) validated
(D) condemned

23. Parents of babies just learning to crawl must be particularly careful to ensure they do not <u>consume</u> poisonous materials.

(A) ingest
(B) deem
(C) subdue
(D) cast doubt on

24. Many Native American peoples along the Pacific coast <u>greatly respected</u> the killer whale. In fact, they still do today.

(A) tarnished
(B) revered
(C) engaged in
(D) took place

25. The government is arguing about whether or not to ban all <u>guns</u> in the country.

(A) prospects
(B) campaigns
(C) firearms
(D) violations

26. Having large crowds of faithful fans is one of the <u>hallmarks</u> of a successful sports franchise.

(A) ancestors
(B) tag markers
(C) burdens
(D) spectacles

27. Unfounded conspiracy theories suggested by crackpots often garner <u>unnecessary</u> attention, while legitimate work gets ignored.

(A) exempt
(B) undue
(C) intangible
(D) hierarchical

28. Because of the snow storm, only a <u>very small</u> number of students attended class today.

(A) feasible
(B) federal
(C) top notch
(D) meager

29. The Spanish used <u>large attack dogs</u> to help conquer nations in the New World.

(A) phenomena
(B) burdens
(C) mastiffs
(D) concubines

30. She refuses to change her <u>point of view</u> despite all the evidence that it is incorrect.

(A) qualm
(B) stance
(C) carcass
(D) prosperity

Instructions: Write the missing words. Use the words below to fill in the blanks.

hierarchical	plausible	campaigns	ancestors	strategist
lingua franca	entourage	engaged in	validate	concubine

Though many historians contend that Hernando Cortes was the military **(31)** _____ behind the successful **(32)** _____ in the New World, a strong case can be made that Malintzin was the true conqueror of the Aztec Empire. Reportedly his **(33)** _____, she was definitely part of Hernando Cortes's **(34)** _____ as he made his way across modern-day Mexico. As a speaker of Nahua, the **(35)** _____ of Mexico at that time, it was Malintzin who actually **(36)** _____ negotiations with the powerful leaders of the nations standing between Cortes and the Aztecs. Indeed, because her **(37)** _____ were part of the noble class, she would have been familiar with the customs and **(38)** _____ nature of the culture. Nahua depictions of the couple, with Malintzin shown in the position of power, tend to **(39)** _____ the idea that she was in control. This evidence, in combination with Spanish reports of her importance in the conquest, makes the idea of Malintzin as conqueror a **(40)** _____ theory.

Instructions: Choose the one word that does not belong.

41.	undue	subdue	conquer	capture
42.	carry out	take place	ingest	engage in
43.	deem	tarnish	conclude	consider
44.	belief	condemn	opinion	stance
45.	welfare	campaign	firearm	strategist

Instructions: Label each pair of words as similar (S) or opposite (O).

46. _____ prosperity wealth

47. _____ hasty slow

48. _____ disdain revere

49. _____ astound surprise

50. _____ feasible unfounded

Vocabulary Review 2

Instructions: Choose the best word or phrase to complete each sentence.

1. She _____ at all subjects in school because she studies all the time.
   - (A) indulges
   - (B) accrues
   - (C) excels
   - (D) dedicates

2. The company decided to hire him because of his _____. They believed he'd be a useful asset when analyzing market trends.
   - (A) free reign
   - (B) critical faculties
   - (C) lingua franca
   - (D) tag markers

3. I've only completed a small _____ of my homework. I'll have to stay up all night in order to finish it.
   - (A) portion
   - (B) qualm
   - (C) welfare
   - (D) reactor

4. He doesn't have the right _____ to be a police officer. He always believes everything people say.
   - (A) fission
   - (B) prospect
   - (C) aphorism
   - (D) mentality

5. The city is building a nuclear _____ that will provide electricity to all the houses and businesses within 500 km.
   - (A) discourse
   - (B) reactor
   - (C) prestige
   - (D) premise

6. Many people contend that severe punishments act as a _____ against serious crimes.
   - (A) resentment
   - (B) perception
   - (C) dynamic
   - (D) deterrent

7. After completing a three-month training course, she now has many job _____ to choose from.
   - (A) prospects
   - (B) aphorisms
   - (C) remunerations
   - (D) exemplars

8. If we leave home at 6:00 a.m., we can get a _____ on the rush hour traffic.
   - (A) free reign
   - (B) dynamic
   - (C) head start
   - (D) deterrent

9. She _____ her first novel to the memory of her mother, who tragically died before the book was published.
   - (A) anticipated
   - (B) translated
   - (C) compensated
   - (D) dedicated

10. The professor has given us _____ to come up with our own essay topics, but I'm having trouble coming up with an idea without any restrictions.
    - (A) remuneration
    - (B) violation
    - (C) head start
    - (D) free reign

11. The _____ among students continued to grow after the professor inexplicably cancelled a third consecutive class.

(A) perception
(B) resentment
(C) prestige
(D) aphorism

12. Unless the government enacts laws limiting cars and factories, pollution will continue to have _____ effects on the environment.

(A) detrimental
(B) pecuniary
(C) sufficient
(D) fundamental

13. If we pay close attention to the clouds and the wind, we can often _____ the next day's weather.

(A) compensate
(B) anticipate
(C) garner
(D) accrue

14. Granting government contracts to family members is a _____ of rules on ethics.

(A) perception
(B) discourse
(C) violation
(D) premise

15. I don't have a _____ amount of money to pay for lunch. Could you lend me five dollars?

(A) sufficient
(B) renowned
(C) coveted
(D) daunting

Instructions: Choose the word or phrase closest in meaning to the underlined part.

16. I can't wait to go to archaeology class! Those lectures are always so <u>interesting</u>. Let's go!

(A) stimulating
(B) daunting
(C) astounding
(D) condemning

17. She's having some <u>reservations</u> about the trip to Africa. She's worried about being attacked by lions or elephants.

(A) perceptions
(B) violations
(C) qualms
(D) cramps

18. The <u>basic idea</u> behind that movie was too unbelievable. Therefore, I don't recommend you go see it.

(A) fission
(B) fusion
(C) prestige
(D) premise

19. Climbing Mount Everest can be a <u>challenging and fearsome</u> prospect.

(A) renowned
(B) sufficient
(C) cataclysmic
(D) daunting

20. Her new film is <u>earning</u> a lot of praise and attention from movie critics.

(A) garnering
(B) anticipating
(C) undertaking
(D) structuring

21. My grandfather is always repeating <u>adages</u> that he thinks will give us some wisdom about how to deal with life's problems. Actually, sometimes they are quite helpful.

(A) deterrents
(B) burdens
(C) aphorisms
(D) pseudonyms

22. Working hard and choosing a profession that one enjoys can <u>produce</u> a happy, satisfying life.

(A) run wild
(B) discourse
(C) translate into
(D) deprive

23. Einstein was <u>famous</u> for his work in the field of physics.

(A) detrimental
(B) renowned
(C) fundamental
(D) keen

24. Though widespread, the <u>belief</u> that baseball is the least interesting sport is not shared by the few true fans of the game.

(A) perception
(B) violation
(C) concession
(D) equation

25. Medicine and law are two of the most <u>sought-after</u> career choices among freshmen students.

(A) hierarchical
(B) pecuniary
(C) coveted
(D) collaborative

26. That diet and exercise plan my doctor prescribed has really made a <u>significant</u> difference in my energy level. I no longer fall asleep during my afternoon classes!

(A) tangible
(B) stimulating
(C) plausible
(D) tedious

27. A skilled novelist spends a lot of time and energy in <u>organizing</u> the sequence of actions in the story.

(A) undertaking
(B) dedicating
(C) diverting
(D) structuring

28. Many people argue that the government should spend money on <u>important</u> matters, like curing cancer, instead of on the exploration of space.

(A) meaningful
(B) keen
(C) unfounded
(D) rigorous

29. One of the <u>essential</u> characteristics of the Renaissance was the shift in focus from God to man.

(A) fundamental
(B) sufficient
(C) municipal
(D) initial

30. If you put money into a bank account, it will <u>gain</u> interest over time.

(A) indulge
(B) accrue
(C) excel
(D) deem

Instructions: Write the missing words. Use the words below to fill in the blanks.

| discourse | touchy | burden | pecuniary | undertake |
| dynamic | welfare | tarnish | exempt | remuneration |

One phenomenon that can **(31)** _____ or even destroy the **(32)** _____ of a friendship between two people is the entering into a **(33)** _____ relationship; that is, one friend lending money to the other. While it may be admirable for one friend to be concerned about the financial **(34)** _____ of the other, a detailed schedule for **(35)** _____ should be made before any money changes hands. Beforehand, it is wise for the two friends to **(36)** _____ a lengthy, detailed **(37)** _____ on the subject, discussing the dates and amounts to be repaid and any penalties that may occur if this schedule is not met. Many friends believe their relationships to be **(38)** _____ from the stress of lending and borrowing; however, money matters are generally a very **(39)** _____ subject. Outstanding debt between friends can become an undue **(40)** _____ and strain on the friendship. It is best, therefore, to avoid lending or borrowing if at all possible.

Instructions: Write the missing words. Use the words below to fill in the blanks.

| in | top | up | on | into |

41. We have to come _____ with an idea for our group project.

42. If I don't do well on the final exam, my passing this course will be _____ jeopardy.

43. Don't buy _____ everything a professor says. It's always a good idea to question what you are being taught.

44. The debate over property rights will rage _____ for decades to come.

45. She wants to go to a _____ notch graduate school in order to ensure a prosperous career in medicine.

Instructions: Match the words that are opposites.

46. compensate   (A) scant
47. discourse   (B) steal
48. undertake   (C) deprive
49. keen   (D) silence
50. indulge   (E) avoid

Chapter 3

Focus: Writing Grammar

Tips

When you review your essay, these tips can help you make it better:

- Check for errors in tense.
  Example If the train <u>come</u> on time, I will not be late. (comes)

- Check for word forms.
  Example The government's decision was very <u>disappointed</u>. (disappointing)

- Make certain each verb agrees with its subject.
  Example The <u>abuse</u> of diplomatic and economic sanctions against polluters <u>is</u> unreasonable and extreme.

- Avoid sentence fragments and run-ons.
  Example Fragment: I met Ann. But not John.
  (I met Ann but not John. OR I met Ann, but I didn't meet John.)
  Run-on: She lives in Canada her parents live in France.
  (She lives in Canada. Her parents live in France.)

- Make sure sentences are connected using the appropriate conjunctions or adverbs.
  Example Andrea wants to eat pizza, <u>so</u> Casey wants to eat chicken. (but/however)

Focus A - Word Forms and Uses

Verb forms and tenses

When you review your essay, consider common mistakes with verbs.

- The verb should agree with its subject.
  - Example   Watching certain television programs are a good way to educate children. (X)
  -            The man waiting for the campers were the park ranger. (X)

- *Be* verbs are used as helping verbs only in the passive voice and the continuous tense.
  - Example   Issues related to global warming are not easily resolved. (passive)
  -            They have been examining the damage of the hurricane. (continuous)
  -            He was met a very famous poet. (X)

- Auxiliaries and modals should reflect the correct tense/voice of the sentence.
  - Example   They had already fallen asleep when I came back. (past perfect)
  -            If she finds the answer, she will be really happy. (conditional)
  -            The teacher suggested that he do some research. (subjunctive)

- The summary of a lecture or reading should be written in the present tense.
  - Example   The professor argues that fossil fuels are relatively cheap.
  -            The professor argued that fossil fuels are relatively cheap. (X)

- The same modal verbs can have their own past forms and "have (has) + past participle" depending on how they are used.
  - Example   We must admit it. We had to admit it.
  -            It can't be the solution. It can't have been the solution.

Exercise 1

Find the eight (8) errors in tense in each of the paragraphs below. Correct the errors. There can be more than one incorrect word within a sentence.

1. The reading introduces the idea of supply and demand. In particular, the passage explains that a person's salary depended on public demand for his or her talent. In other words, a person with a rare talent should earns more according to this model because supply was limited while demand is high. The professor gives several specific examples of this theory in action. First, she talks about ordinary people who was made small salaries, such as bus drivers and fast-food workers. Then, she talked about people with special skills, and she points out that they earn significantly more per hour because of their skills. As extreme examples, the professor talks about movie stars and athletes. These people earned thousands or even hundreds of thousands of dollars per hour based on public demand for their rare talents.

2. I know a lot of people who treats their pets as family members. In fact, one of my close friends has have a cat since she was in elementary school. The cat was rather old now, but my friend takes good care of her. Actually, I think my friend spent too much time and money on her cat. Sometimes, I feel that she neglects her friends because she has to something for her cat, such as feed it or taken it to the veterinarian. In my opinion, it is unhealthy for people to focus so much attention on animals. If they focused this same energy and attention on people around them, it would to make a world of difference. They could spends the money wasted on pet food and toys on more useful pursuits like treating their friends or donating to charities!

READING
LISTENING
SPEAKING
WRITING
PRACTICE TEST

Exercise 2

Write the correct form of the verb.

A. The reading passage **(1)** _describes_ (describe) important space achievements in the 20th century, including NASA's lunar missions. In the lecture, the professor emphasizes the point that US astronauts are the only humans who have **(2)** _walked_ (walk) on the moon. He gives several interesting statistics related to lunar programs **(3)** _developed_ (develop) by other countries. In particular, the professor **(4)** _discusses_ (discuss) Russia's lunar program. He points out that although Russia has sent rockets to the moon, no Russian cosmonauts **(5)** _were_ (be) ever sent to land on the [have ever been] moon. He also mentions that China is **(6)** _developing_ (develop) plans to send humans to the moon, though those plans will not materialize for a long time.

B. In order to stay healthy, I walk whenever I can. This often means that I have to **(1)** _plan_ (plan) my day carefully so that I can leave enough time to get where I need to go. For example, if I **(2)** _take_ (take) the subway to my university, it takes about thirty minutes to get from my apartment to my classroom. However, if I get off the subway one stop early in order to walk for exercise, it **(3)** _takes_ (take) forty-five minutes to get to my classroom. Therefore, I **(4)** _have_ (have) to leave my apartment fifteen minutes earlier than normal so that I can exercise for fifteen minutes by walking to class. By walking to class, I can also enjoy the added benefit of relaxing in the fresh air rather than being **(5)** _cramp_ (cramp) and **(6)** _push_ (push) around on the crowded subway.

Word Forms and Uses

It is helpful to know word endings in order to use the correct word form. Some words have the same form for different parts of speech.

Noun	-acy, -nce, -ness, -ism, -ion, -ity, -ment, -ure, -al
Adjective	-able, -al, -ant, -ful, -ic, -ish, -ive, -less, -ing, -ed
Verb	-ate, -en, -ify, -ize

Same Form

practice (v=n), appeal (v=n), comment (v=n), cause (v=n), complete (v=adj), individual (n=adj), potential (n=adj)

Other examples

division / divisive / divide	affection / affected / affect	retirement / retiring / retire
validity / valid / validate	exposure / exposed / expose	offense / offensive / offend
failure / failed / fail	threat / threatening / threaten	benefit / beneficial / benefit
efficiency / efficient	disposal / disposable / dispose	responsibility / responsible

It is also helpful to know the position in which each part of speech can be used. Nouns cannot be used in the position of verbs. Adjectives are placed before the nouns that they modify or after a linking verb such as *be, become,* or *seem.*

Exercise 3

Choose the correct form of the word.

1. The group leader made an excellent _____B_____ for the new project.
   (A) suggest   (B) suggestion   (C) suggestive

2. Although the temperature was quite high, the _____A_____ was almost zero.
   (A) humidity   (B) humidify   (C) humid

3. The group's _____A_____ ensured that they won in the end.
   (A) competitiveness   (B) competitive   (C) compete

4. No one knew who was _____B_____ for the accident.
   (A) responsibility   (B) responsible   (C) responsibly

5. It was obviously a difficult situation, but he remained _____C_____.

    (A) optimism   (B) optimize   (C) optimistic

6. The company's _____A_____ to plan for changes in the market led to its bankruptcy.

    (A) failure   (B) failed   (C) fail

7. The newcomer was greeted with genuine _____A_____.

    (A) affection   (B) affective   (C) affected

8. Try to find a number that can _____B_____ both numeral A and numeral B.

    (A) division   (B) divide   (C) divisive

9. Many people in the audience found his jokes _____C_____.

    (A) offense   (B) offended   (C) offensive

10. Over the past few decades, the age of _____A_____ has actually risen.

    (A) retirement   (B) retire   (C) retired

11. Researchers in the US and Europe have yet to _____B_____ the findings reported by the Australian company.

    (A) validation   (B) validate   (C) valid

12. Until an environmentally safe method for the _____A_____ of nuclear waste can be found, construction of new reactors will continue to inspire debate.

    (A) disposal   (B) disposes   (C) disposable

13. Whenever skin is _____B_____ to direct sunlight, there is chance of damage to the skin.

    (A) exposure   (B) exposed   (C) exposable

14. Most people find the weather on the island more than _____C_____; they find it pleasant.

    (A) tolerance   (B) tolerate   (C) tolerable

15. Voters felt that she was not _____A_____ enough during her term as governor.

    (A) decisive   (B) decision   (C) decide

16. There are clear pros and cons related to the debate over whether or not to _____B_____ drugs.

    (A) legality   (B) legalize   (C) legal

Find the five (5) incorrect words in each of the paragraphs below. Correct the words. There can be more than one incorrect word within a sentence.

Both the reading and the lecture focus on the connect between poverty and single-parent families, in particularly, families headed by women. The reading describes a government study that looked at all families headed by women across the US. This study concluded that the number of families headed by women below the poverty line decreased from 1960 until the present. The lecture discusses a similarly study that found very different results. In the lecture, the professor says that researchers looked at only poor families headed by women. Between 1960 and the present, the number of poor families headed by women rose from 25 percent to over 50 percent. Thus, the professor correlation poverty to gender of household heads. In her words, the "feminization of poverty" is a real in modern society.

It is often said that the child years are the most important years of one's life. However, I think a person's young adulthood years are more important than the childhood years. As a child, a person spends time either in school or simply playing with friends. School may teach the child information or even certain skills necessity for life, but I think these are generic experiences for just about everyone. When a person becomes a young adult, on the other hand, he or she can truly individual himself or herself. In university, one has the opportune to make decisions without direction from parents or teachers. Of course, the actions each person decides to take can have a significance impact on the course of the rest of his or her life, unlike decisions typically open to children.

Focus B - Sentence Formation

Combining Sentences with Adjective Clauses

An adjective clause modifies a noun or pronoun. Adjective clauses are led by relative pronouns such as *who*, *which*, and *that*. For a noun of time or place, *when* or *where* can be used instead of the phrase *at which*.

When using adjective clauses, consider these common mistakes.

• When the subject noun is modified by an adjective clause, make sure the main verb of the independent clause agrees with the subject that comes before the adjective clause.

      Example A *person* who works part-time usually <u>receives</u> no benefits.

      People who work part-time usually <u>receive</u> no benefits.

• Use commas before and after an adjective clause if the noun it describes is a specific person or thing, for example, a proper noun.

      Example Rachel Kingsley, who writes mystery novels, is signing books at the bookstore.

      The writer who is signing books at the bookstore is Rachel Kingsley.

• If the noun is general, you may substitute *that* for *who* and *which*. Don't use commas if the adjective clause begins with *that*.

      Example The ticket that I needed in order to get onto the plane was not in the packet.

      The ticket, that I needed in order to get onto the plane, was not in the packet. (X)

• If the relative pronoun follows a preposition, the preposition can be in two positions: 1) before the relative pronoun or 2) at the end of the adjective clause.

      Example The speed <u>at which</u> the wheel turns is measured in revolutions per second.

      The speed <u>that</u> the wheel turns <u>at</u> is measured in revolutions per second.

• *Which* can refer to the whole previous sentence.

      Example He tried to apologize, which made her even angrier.

• Participle phrases can be formed by reducing adjective clauses.

      Example Adjective clauses → The audience, <u>which was</u> listening intently to the music, failed to notice the commotion that grew louder and louder in the theater's lobby.

      Reduced adjective clauses → The audience, listening intently to the music, failed to notice the commotion growing louder and louder in the theater's lobby.

For each sentence below, underline the incorrect part or parts of the sentence.

1. The designation of an individual's class, which can be based on a number of different factors, have been of key interest to sociologists for decades.

2. A child is only a few weeks old is capable of imitating a limited range of facial expressions that he or she observes from a care-giver.

3. Children who grow up in single-parent households typically do worse in school than children what are from two-parent households.

4. Diana Pearce who was an economist by profession suggested a theory that proved popular among sociologists.

5. The female lion, that is distinguished from the male by the lack of a mane, does the hunting.

6. A critical aspect of learning to read involves the integration of skills when develop at different stages of childhood, namely the ability to decipher sounds of a language and the ability to write.

7. One of the most influential theories related to cognitive development comes from Piaget who based his theory on observations of elementary-age children.

8. Paper products, that are made with at least 60% recycled fibers, consume 45% fewer raw materials than products made without recycled fibers.

9. The professor describes the Industrial Revolution as a time at when great strides were made in science and technology.

10. A utopian society is one in that citizens live in perfect fairness and harmony with each other.

11. Polaris, can be located easily on a clear night, is a reliable point in the sky to navigate by because it is located over the point of true north.

12. The claim that "laughter is the best medicine" are supported by research that shows laughter reduces stress, which contributes to a person's overall health and well-being.

Combine two simple sentences to make a complex sentence containing an adjective clause. Add commas if necessary. Then put parentheses around the relative pronoun and the verb IF they can be omitted.

1. The bowl was found in the cave. It was over 1,000 years old.

   _____.

2. A child knows he did something wrong. He will not look an adult in the eye.

   _____.

3. Cats were important in ancient Egyptian culture. Egyptian culture flourished in the Nile River Valley for thousands of years.

_____.

4. The desk was broken. It was removed from the classroom.

_____.

5. Columbus grew up in a large port city. This city was located on the coast of Italy.

_____.

6. The fossil was obviously a species of horse. The species is now extinct.

_____.

7. People grow up near the border. They usually learn to speak two languages.

_____.

8. The legal age of adulthood is 21. At the age of adulthood, a person can purchase alcohol.

_____.

9. Snoopy is a famous cartoon dog. Snoopy is a beagle.

_____.

10. Two critics reviewed the book. They did not agree.

_____.

11. The university has recently changed its admission policy. The policy used to prohibit women from studying there.

_____.

12. By definition, sunrise is a time in the morning. At this time, the sun first appears over the horizon.

_____.

Combining Sentences with Different Connectors

When writing sentences that are closely related, the writer must use certain techniques to combine the sentences. Various methods can be used to present the same meaning.

Example I did my best, but it was not good enough. (coordinating conjunction)
I did my best; however, it was not good enough. (coordinating adverb)
Although I did my best, it was not good enough. (subordinating conjunction)
Since arriving, we have visited many places. (participle phrase)

When connecting sentences and ideas, consider these common mistakes.

1. Sentence fragments:
We went home. And watched TV. (no subject)
→ We went home and watched TV.

They were happy with the program. But not the board. (no subject or verb)
→ They were happy with the program, but the board were not.

They agreed. Because it was more urgent. (dependent clause used independently)
→ They agreed because it was more urgent.

2. Run-on sentences:
They are happy with the program it is user friendly. (no connecting word or punctuation mark)
→ They are happy with the program. It is user friendly. OR They are happy with the program because it is user friendly.

Punctuation is also important. Look at the differences in punctuation in these sentences.
I was often late because I had to help her. (subordinating conjunction)
Because I had to help her, I was often late (subordinating conjunction + comma)
I had to help her, so I was often late. (comma + coordinating conjunction)
I had to help her. Therefore, I was often late. (coordinating adverb + comma)
I had to help her; therefore, I was often late. (semicolon + coordinating adverb + comma)
NOTE: I had to help her. So, I was often late. (informal, so best avoided in an essay)

Exercise 3

Indicate whether the sentence is correct (C) or incorrect (IC). Then correct the incorrect sentences.

_____ **1.** Musicians are only able to develop their technical skills through practice therefore they must devote long hours to exercises that develop particular techniques.

_____ **2.** Although Chaco Canyon has been declared a national park, the US government allows Native Americans to continue to live there.

_____ **3.** More and more families must rely on both parents working just to make ends meet because the cost of living continues to rise.

_____ **4.** Confucius did not begin teaching until very late in his life. But had a lasting impact on generations long after his death.

_____ **5.** Fresh fruits and vegetables are delivered to markets early in the morning, so shoppers who want the best quality produce do their shopping when the markets open.

_____ **6.** In 1963, Martin Luther King, Jr. was put in jail for a short time and that same year, his house was bombed.

_____ **7.** Because young children are being exposed to violence and sexually explicit material on television politicians are now debating a new law to censor some shows.

_____ **8.** Companies may directly email customers in order to alert them to special offers. Also, companies are now making use of banner ads on high-traffic Internet websites.

_____ **9.** Most people recall that Narcissus turned into a flower, however few remember what happened to his spurned lover, Echo.

_____ **10.** People can usually recall dreams they have just before they wake up. However, dreams occur throughout the entire night's sleep cycle.

_____ **11.** The researcher studied groups of men from various cultures interestingly he found that men's opinions were very similar across cultures.

_____ **12.** Parents usually don't think twice about letting their children go alone to a mall because they view malls as safe public spaces.

Exercise 4

Combine the sentences in two different ways using the words in parentheses.

1. In the past, you would have to pay for a stamp to send a message to a friend. Today, you can send messages for free using email. (but, whereas)

a. _____

b. _____

2. Many airlines are offering discount tickets for flights. More people are flying for weekend trips to scenic cities. (so, because)

a. _____

b. _____

3. The architect built many famous structures. He established a school of architecture in Arizona. (and, also)

a. _____

b. _____

4. My father did not hold a well-paying job. He enjoyed his job a lot. (although, but)

a. _____

b. _____

5. The epic work follows the lives of forty characters through the revolution. Readers often have trouble keeping track of who is who in the novel. (thus, so)

a. _____

b. _____

6. A driver caught operating a vehicle while intoxicated will be issued a ticket. The owner of the vehicle will receive a ticket as well. (additionally, and)

a. _____

b. _____

Exercise 5

Reduce the adverbial clause into a participle phrase.

Example <u>As they were too young to be left alone</u>, the young birds were taken from the nest and transported to a care facility.

<u>Being too young to be left alone</u>, the young birds were taken from the nest and transported to a care facility.

1. Since the building has been severely damaged by the storm, it has to be torn down.

_____

_____

2. The plastic melted and warped because it had been left in the car on a hot day.

_____

_____

3. We are only able to objectively view the core of the problem after we cut through all of the media hype.

_____

_____

4. Because the town wants to attract more companies, it will offer tax incentives to new businesses.

_____

_____

5. In the past, women were confined to the home by social pressure since they were primarily expected to bear and raise children.

_____

_____

Parallel Structure

In order to make a sentence clear and balanced, it is important to use parallel structures in all parts of the sentence. When words or phrases are connected, those words or phrases should be parallel in terms of their form, tense, and parts of speech. When using conjunctions, make sure the parts of the sentence are balanced or parallel.

- Forms

    I like to jog and lifting weights. (jogging and lifting)

- Tense

    They meet customers and are taking orders. (take)

- Parts of speech

    The plants grew over the walls and some were in the buildings. (over the walls and into the buildings)

Exercise 6

Indicate whether the sentence parts display parallel structure (P) or not (NP). Underline the parts that are or should be parallel.

_____ 1. A student who waits until the last minute to study for an exam and completes assignments in a careless manner will do poorly in the class.

_____ 2. Both by the way the couple dressed and by their interaction with each other, it was obvious they were on their honeymoon.

_____ 3. Job opportunities are increasing in fields related to Internet technology but have decreased in many traditional fields of engineering.

_____ 4. Learning how to write Chinese was harder for me than learning how to speak it.

_____ 5. My father taught me how to drive in reverse and how to parallel park.

_____ 6. Shakespeare wrote comedies, romances, tragedies, and plays based on real people from history.

_____ 7. She spent hours wandering around different floors of the library, enjoying her solitude, and discovering old, interesting books.

_____ 8. Learning to write well is important for business majors because employees at all levels may be required to write reports that are accurate and including important details.

Exercise 7

Underline the phrase that is not parallel to the rest of the sentence. Then change the phrase to make it parallel.

1. A child's voice is higher than an adult.

_____.

2. A family either learns to live within its budget or will risk sinking into debt.

_____.

3. I found most of the books required by the course interesting, informative, and they entertained me.

_____.

4. The violinist played with grace, incredible dexterity, and speed.

_____.

5. A shocking number of freshmen waste their first year of college not studying enough, doing things harmful to their health, and not utilizing the campus facilities available to them.

_____.

6. In the art appreciation course, students will learn to analyze important elements of art and recognizing styles of various art movements.

_____.

7. Most students expect three things out of university: to learn life skills, meeting new friends, and to prepare for their future careers.

_____.

8. The Hopi, the Navajo, and Zuni are three well-known Native American peoples of the southwest United States.

_____.

Read the sample paragraphs. Find four (4) mistakes in each paragraph and correct them.

The reading and the lecture both describe Chomolunga, which are the mountain better known as Mt. Everest. The reading introduces just the basic facts about the mountain, such as its location, height, and how much it snows there. The professor adds to this information by talks about all of the people who have tried to climb Mt. Everest. In particular, he explains that although thousands of people were trying to climb the mountain, only about 650 have succeeded. On top of that, 142 of those successful climbers died before they made it back down the mountain. Obviously, Mt. Everest is an incredible and dangerous mountain.

In my opinion, teamwork is a more valuable asset in a new employee than independence. Most jobs cannot be done alone therefore it is necessary for employees to be able to work both with colleagues what work within the same company as well as with individuals or teams from other companies. Employees must have the necessary skills to communicate effectively with others as well as cooperate in forming strategies or solutions for workplace tasks and problems. Although an independent employee might be able to do certain tasks without help or input from others, these are not the most efficient workers. Because the tasks he or she undertakes are smaller or more limited in nature than the tasks which can undertake by teams.

Mastering Skills for the TOEFL® iBT

PRACTICE TEST

Reading Section / Listening Section / Speaking Section / Writing Section

Reading

Reading Section

Directions

In this section, you will read three passages and then answer reading comprehension questions about each passage. Most questions are worth one point, but the last question in each set is worth more than one point. The directions indicate how many points you may receive.

You will have 60 minutes to read all of the passages and answer the questions. Some passages include a word or phrase that is underlined. For those words, you will see a definition or an explanation below the passage.

You can skip questions and go back to them later as long as there is time remaining.

When you are ready to continue, press **Continue** to go to the next page.

Herbs and Drugs

Herbs are different kinds of plants and plant parts that can be used for medicinal purposes. This can include the leaves, stems, roots, or seeds of the plant. Herbs have been important in traditional medicine for centuries, in both the East and the West. In Western medicine, they have largely been replaced by drugs. Herbal treatments are, however, still an integral part of Eastern medicine. In recent years, interest in traditional medicine has increased in the West. Many people are either using modern methods combined with traditional treatments or are turning to these treatments entirely. While traditional medicines can be helpful, they are not without their share of problems.

The main difference between herbs and drugs is that, while herbs are simply parts of plants, drugs are specific chemicals in a pure form. Many modern drugs are derived from chemicals found in plants. One example is aspirin, which is made from a chemical extracted from the bark of the willow tree. Other drugs are entirely synthetic. Even those drugs that are derived from natural sources are heavily processed in order to purify and concentrate them. This allows drugs to be administered in very precise amounts. Different kinds and degrees of illnesses often require dosages that differ only slightly. A little too much or not enough of a certain drug can have negative effects on the patient. Many drugs also produce negative effects even when taken in the recommended dosage. These undesired negative effects are called "side-effects."

The possibility of dangerous and unexpected side-effects from drugs has led many people back to traditional medicine. Herbal treatments seem more natural than modern drugs. Many feel that traditional medicine is more concerned with treating the underlying causes of disease instead of just the symptoms, though the truth of this claim is not yet clear. In any case, there is a certain comfort in taking natural herbal treatments instead of the processed, synthetic chemicals derived from them.

There are, however, disadvantages to herbal treatments, some of them serious. Few herbal treatments have been scientifically studied. While the active chemicals in the herb may be known, it may not be clear what they really do, or if they are really effective at all. Because the active chemicals are not used alone, it is very difficult to determine the proper amount for treatment, since the levels of the chemical are not constant throughout the plant. Therefore, the risk of under- and overdose is higher than with drugs. A more serious problem is that certain herbal treatments may have no real medicinal effect, thus giving the patient a false sense of security. This is particularly harmful when the patient refuses treatment with modern drugs that could be effective.

There are even certain herbs that can cause side-effects, just like a drug. ■ **A)** One of

these is ma-huang, also called ephedra, which is taken to increase energy. ■ **B)** It has been known to cause damage to the heart and nervous system. Garlic and ginger are common elements in food that are also taken as herbal treatments, but they can be dangerous for people with diabetes. ■ **C)** In general, herbs are most dangerous when they are taken along with common drugs. This may happen in two ways: a patient decides to supplement his or her regular treatment with herbs, or a dishonest manufacturer adds modern drugs to an herbal treatment. ■ **D)** In both cases, the results can be very serious. The herb St. John's wort is often used to treat depression, but if it is used along with conventional antidepressants, such as Zoloft, the combination can cause confusion, headaches, allergic reactions, and other problems.

Finally, because production of herbal treatments is seldom regulated, harmful substances can be present in herbal preparations. Herbs grown in polluted soil may contain lead, arsenic, or mercury. They may also be tainted with pesticides. It is for these reasons that herbs should not be treated as the perfect substitute for drugs. Although herbs appear to be quite distinct from modern drugs, it is important to use them with the same sort of care.

synthetic *(adj)*:
created artificially

dosage *(n)*:
the optimum amount of medicine for a patient for a particular disease or problem

1. The word "integral" in the first paragraph is closest in meaning to
   (A) harmful
   (B) important
   (C) famous
   (D) controversial

2. Which of the following is closest in meaning to "tainted" in paragraph 6?
   (A) Accompanied
   (B) Augmented
   (C) Substituted
   (D) Contaminated

3. The word "this" in paragraph 4 line 8 refers to
   (A) patients taking ineffective herbs instead of drugs
   (B) patients having a sense of security
   (C) the risk of under- and overdose of an herbal treatment
   (D) the patient's belief that modern drugs are bad for you

4. Why does the author mention that drugs are heavily processed?
   (A) To show that herbs cannot compete with modern medical techniques
   (B) Because many mistakes can occur in this processing
   (C) To illustrate that drugs are not natural
   (D) To point out that many countries cannot afford to produce drugs

5. What is the main difference between herbs and drugs according to the passage?
   (A) Drugs can cause side-effects, whereas herbs do not.
   (B) Drugs are at least partially synthetic, whereas herbs are natural.
   (C) Herbs are dangerous when taken in large amounts; drugs are safer.
   (D) Herbs can produce a false sense of security, whereas drugs do not.

6. According to the passage, when are herbs most dangerous?
   (A) When not taken under a doctor's supervision
   (B) When the patient refuses modern medicine
   (C) When the dosage is not administered precisely
   (D) When taken in combination with drugs

7. Which of the following best states the topic of the passage?
   (A) Patients are not educated enough to use herbal treatments.
   (B) Modern drugs are still a better choice than herbal treatments.
   (C) Modern medicine should use herbal treatments more in the future.
   (D) Herbal treatment can be helpful, but should be used with care.

8. According to the passage, who should not take ginger or garlic as herbal treatments?
   (A) Patients with diabetes
   (B) Patients with liver damage
   (C) Patients taking antidepressants
   (D) Patients with problems of the heart or nervous system

9. Which of the following is NOT mentioned in the passage?

(A) Some herbal treatments are not effective in fighting disease.

(B) Modern doctors often do not approve of using herbs.

(C) Herbal treatments can also produce side-effects.

(D) Some manufacturers add drugs to herbs.

10. It can be inferred from the passage that

(A) the drug industry is better regulated than the herb industry

(B) people who use drugs instead of herbs recover more quickly

(C) the popularity of herbal treatments will decrease in the future

(D) the side-effects of drugs are more serious than those of herbs

11. Look at the four squares [■] that indicate where the following sentence could be added to paragraph 5:

Certain herbs have also been known to be harmful for people suffering from asthma.

Where would the sentence best fit? Choose the square [■] where the sentence should be added to the passage.

(A) Line 1

(B) Line 2

(C) Line 5

(D) Line 7

12. Directions: *Complete the table by matching the phrases below. Select the appropriate phrases from the answer choices and match them to the type of treatment to which they relate. TWO of the answer choices will NOT be used.* **This question is worth 4 points.**

Drugs	Herbs
B	A
C	H
E	D

(A) Are most dangerous when use with other treatments

(B) Allow the dosage to be controlled precisely

(C) May contain harmful additives

(D) Treat the cause of the disease and not just the symptoms

(E) Are typically associated with side-effects

(F) Are gaining in popularity in the West

(G) Cause damage to the nervous system

(H) Undergo heavy processing

William Shakespeare

William Shakespeare was born in Stratford-Upon-Avon in Warwickshire, England on April 23, 1564. His mother, Mary Arden, had come from a fairly wealthy family. His father, John, was a glove maker and a leather merchant by trade. He also held the prestigious position of town bailiff in their community. In all, the Shakespeares had eight children, William being the third of these children and the first son. Three of William's brothers and sisters died during childhood.

Reportedly, Shakespeare did not have an extensive education. He did attend Stratford Grammar School, a school for the sons of prominent citizens, although it appears his family may not have paid for his education due to his father's status as a high-ranking town official. While it is not certain, it is believed that Shakespeare attended this school from age 7 to 14. The time he spent at this grammar school is assumed to be the only education he received, yet the literary quality of his works suggests a more advanced education. This matter has contributed to the debate concerning the authorship of his works.

On November 28, 1582, Shakespeare married Anne Hathaway, a farmer's daughter. ■ A) Anne was twenty-six years old when they married and was pregnant at the time. William was only eighteen. ■ B) Their marriage produced three children. ■ C) Shakespeare apparently abandoned his family and disappeared from 1585 to 1592. ■ D) No records of Shakespeare exist from this period of his life, and they are usually referred to as "the lost years." Some have speculated that he either became a schoolteacher, a butcher's apprentice, or was running from the law.

Shakespeare reappeared in London where he arrived with the goal of becoming an actor and playwright. Evidently, Shakespeare garnered envy for his talent early on. He even found a sponsor to help pay for his services. Shakespeare's work in the theaters came to a halt, however, when the theaters of London closed down due to the plague in January of 1593. This closing inspired Shakespeare and his company to move to the Globe Theater in the Bankside district, across the river from London's city limits.

Shakespeare's company, originally called "Lord Chamberlain's Men," changed their name to "The King's Men" after King James took over the throne in 1603. Because Shakespeare worked and performed for royalty, his company became the biggest and most famous acting company in the area. Consequently, Shakespeare became quite well-to-do as a director, writer, actor, and stockholder in The King's Men.

During his time, Shakespeare published and sold his plays in octavo editions. Also known as "penny copies," these were sold to the more literate members of his audience. It is noted that a playwright had never before enjoyed sufficient acclaim as to see his works published and sold as popular literature in the midst of his career. His 37 plays span the genres of tragedy, comedy, and history. While Shakespeare could not be considered wealthy by London standards, his success did allow him to purchase New House and retire in comfort in Stratford in 1611. He made a will on March 25, 1616, and died, as the legend has it, on his birthday, April 23, 1616. He was buried at Holy Trinity Church in Stratford on April 25th.

Shakespeare wrote his own epitaph to avoid the common tendency at the time of a person's grave being dug up after several years to accommodate another body.

"Good Friends, for Jesus' sake forbear,
To dig the bones enclosed here!
Blest be the man that spares these stones,
And curst be he that moves my bones."
To this day, no one has disturbed Shakespeare's grave.

In 1623, two working companions of Shakespeare from the Lord Chamberlain's Men, John Heminges and Henry Condell, printed the First Folio edition of his Collected Works, half of which were previously unpublished. The First Folio also contained Shakespeare's sonnets. Many argue that William Shakespeare's legacy is a body of work that will never again be paralleled in Western civilization. His words have endured for 400 years and still reach across the centuries as powerfully as ever.

epitaph *(n):*
an inscription on a gravestone
folio *(n):*
a book of a large size

13. As used in paragraph 2, what is the meaning of the word "prominent"?

(A) Feared
(B) Powerful
(C) Studious
(D) Hard-working

14. Which of the following could best replace the word "garnered" as used in paragraph 4?

(A) Discouraged
(B) Found
(C) Attracted
(D) Prevented

15. What does "this matter" in paragraph 2 refer to?

(A) Shakespeare going to a school for prominent families
(B) The surprisingly high quality of Shakespeare's works
(C) The uncertainty of whether he attended the grammar school
(D) His father's status as a high ranking town official

16. Why does the author mention that Shakespeare's father held the prestigious position of town bailiff in their community?

(A) To illustrate that his father was also quite talented and accomplished
(B) To show Shakespeare was not worried about the getting in trouble with the law
(C) To explain how his father could have married his mother, who was wealthy
(D) To explain why, although not wealthy, Shakespeare did enjoy some privilege

17. Look at the four squares [■] that indicate where the following sentence could be added to paragraph 3:

Two of Shakespeare's children were twins.

Where would the sentence best fit? Choose the square [■] where the sentence should be added to the passage.

(A) Line 1
(B) Line 3
(C) Line 3
(D) Line 4

18. According to the passage, why did Shakespeare stop performing in London?

(A) The audience in London did not enjoy his poetic style.
(B) King James forced him to leave the city in 1595.
(C) He began selling his own plays to literate audience members.
(D) All the theaters were closed due to the plague.

19. According to the passage, why were the years 1585 — 1592 called "the lost years"?

(A) No records of Shakespeare's life exist from this time.
(B) Shakespeare was unable to write during this time due to an illness.
(C) Shakespeare's plays from this period were burned in the Great Fire.
(D) Shakespeare refused to speak with his wife during these years.

20. Which of the sentences below best expresses the essential information in the highlighted sentence in the passage? *Incorrect* choices change the meaning in important ways or leave out essential information.

(A) The sale of Shakespeare's plays made him the most popular playwright of all time.

(B) London audiences were buying more plays then than ever before.

(C) Shakespeare was the first playwright who was famous enough to sell his plays while still producing them.

(D) Shakespeare's plays played an important role in this rise of literacy in the west.

21. All of the following are true EXCEPT

(A) Shakespeare spent time as a glove maker from 1585 to 1592.

(B) Shakespeare had three children with his wife.

(C) Shakespeare's company came to be called "The King's Men."

(D) Shakespeare is said to have died on his birthday.

22. What can be inferred from paragraph 2 about Shakespeare's works?

(A) Shakespeare must have gone to university at some point to write them.

(B) Some scholars today doubt that Shakespeare actually wrote them.

(C) They are viewed as the best example of what one person can accomplish.

(D) They have never been considered as having been written by just one person.

23. Why did Shakespeare write his own epitaph?

(A) He didn't want his grave to be dug up later.

(B) He didn't want it to be written by an inferior writer.

(C) It was the custom at the time to write one's own epitaph.

(D) To dedicate it to two former actors in Lord Chamberlain's Men.

24. Directions: *An introductory sentence for a brief summary of the passage is provided below. Complete the summary by selecting the THREE answer choices that express the most important ideas in the passage. Some sentences do not belong in the summary because they express ideas that are not presented in the passage or are minor ideas in the passage.* **This question is worth 2 points.**

First sentence: **William Shakespeare lived an interesting and accomplished life and is today regarded as the greatest English writer the world has ever known.**

(A) Shakespeare was the first playwright to enjoy such wide acclaim as to see his works published during his career.

(B) Shakespeare's acting company was originally called Lord Chamberlain's Men but later changed its name to The King's Men.

(C) Shakespeare's works are timeless and have endured for over 400 years.

(D) Shakespeare's father was a glove maker and the town bailiff of Stratford-Upon-Avon.

(E) Although he produced works of high quality, Shakespeare is not believed to have had an extensive education.

(F) Shakespeare's works have been translated into more languages than any other volume of literature, including the Christian Bible.

Pollination

Plants reproduce through a process called pollination. During this process, pollen must be introduced to the female portion of a plant of the same species. Many methods for pollination are discernible around the world. The most common methods are transport of the pollen by insects, animals, and non-living forces such as wind. Interestingly, plants seem to attract the living pollinators using methods most suited to that animal or insect. For instance, insects are attracted by different stimuli than birds or bats, so the plants that are pollinated by insects look and grow differently than ones pollinated by birds. The differences in plants may cater to the senses of sight and smell, to physical characteristics, or to the habits of particular pollinators.

Insects are the most common living pollinators. ■ **A)** Bees move from flower to flower to get nectar, a sweet, watery substance produced specifically to attract the bees. ■ **B)** Bees have a very good sense of smell, so flowers that are pollinated by bees have a sweet smell. Bees also have color vision, which makes yellow and blue flowers most attractive to them. ■ **C)** Bees have a short proboscis, which they can use like a straw to suck the nectar from a thin opening in the flower. ■ **D)** This means that some flowers pollinated by bees will have a flute-shaped blossom that is as long as the proboscis of the bee that pollinates it.

Bees are not the only insect to pollinate plants. Moths and butterflies also do this. Moths and butterflies may look similar, but they are different in a number of ways. Moths do not land while they feed on the sweet nectar of the flowers they pollinate. Therefore, they can feed on flowers that offer butterflies no place to land. This prevents other animals and insects from having access to the nectar. Butterflies do stop to feed, so the plants they pollinate generally have a larger blossom so the butterfly can land. Another difference between moths and butterflies is that moths fly at night and rely on their sense of smell more than their sense of sight. The flowers they pollinate are sweet smelling and fragrant. Because of the dim light at night, the flowers tend to be white or very light in color. Butterflies are active during the day, so they rely on their sense of sight. This makes them attracted to flowers that are brightly colored. Because they see well during the day, they don't have a well-developed sense of smell, and so many of the plants they pollinate have no smell, or the plant might even stink as a way of keeping other animals away. Both moths and butterflies have long proboscises, and, therefore, they can drink the nectar of a plant through a long, flute-like blossom. In fact, there are some moths that have proboscises as long as 30 centimeters!

Plants without flute-like blossoms have developed to accommodate pollinators without long proboscises, such as flies. Plants that are pollinated by flies must have more open and accessible nectar. Additionally, flies are attracted to rotting meat by their sense of smell, so many of the plants they pollinate smell like putrid flesh. The Malaysian raffelasia flower can have blossoms as broad as a meter in diameter. They are dusty red in color and smell like rotting meat. Because flies are attracted primarily by the smell of a flower, the color is usually light or dusty.

Birds can also pollinate plants, but they are much bigger, so they require plants with much more nectar than the insects do. They also have good eyes and are attracted to bright green, red, and yellow flowers. Birds do not have a very good sense of smell, so many of the plants they feed on do not have a strong smell. Birds that feed on nectar usually have beaks that match the shape of the flowers from which they eat. The hummingbird has a long, thin beak that fits into the thin, fluted shape of the flowers where they find nectar.

Because non-living methods of pollination are not attracted by smells or colors, plants pollinated by these methods appear simple or plain compared to plants with beautiful flowers. For instance, many grasses and conifers are pollinated by the wind. Instead of bright, sweet-smelling blossoms, the plants that are pollinated by the wind have <u>anthers</u> that are made to float on the breeze. On these plants, the anther is the part of the flower that holds the pollen.

proboscis *(n)*:
a flexible, elongated part of certain insects

anther *(n)*:
the part of a plant in which the pollen sacs are contained

25. The word "attracted" in paragraph 1 is closest in meaning to

(A) drawn to the attention of
(B) pulled by force
(C) drawn or taken away; diverted
(D) repulsed or caused to flee

26. Based on the information in paragraph 4, which of the following best explains the term "dusty"?

(A) Powdery or covered in dust
(B) Old and timeworn
(C) Having a white or gray tinge
(D) Smelling of mildew

27. The word "they" in paragraph 3 refers to

(A) blossoms
(B) moths and butterflies
(C) proboscises
(D) animals

28. Look at the four squares [■] that indicate where the following sentence could be added to paragraph 2:

Bees are probably the best known insect pollinators.

Where would the sentence best fit? Choose the square [■] where the sentence should be added to the passage.

(A) Line 1
(B) Line 2
(C) Line 5
(D) Line 6

29. In paragraph 3, the author states that

(A) moths and butterflies are exactly the same
(B) moths and butterflies look different, but act the same way
(C) moths and butterflies are very different than bees
(D) moths and butterflies look nearly the same but act differently

30. All of the following are mentioned as attracting specific pollinators to plants EXCEPT

(A) color
(B) location
(C) shape
(D) scent

31. According to paragraph 3, what do moths rely on to find nectar?

(A) Sight
(B) Smell
(C) Color
(D) Bees

32. Which of the following can be inferred from paragraph 2 about bees?

(A) Bees are a type of insect
(B) Bees make honey
(C) Bees are smaller than birds
(D) Bees fly at night

33. Why does the author mention "flowers that are brightly colored" in paragraph 3?

(A) Because butterflies are attracted to them
(B) Because moths are attracted to them
(C) Because bees are attracted to them
(D) Because they have a fragrant smell

34. Why does the author introduce the claim, "Plants that are pollinated by flies must have more open and accessible nectar"?

(A) Because flies like the smell of putrid flesh
(B) Because flies are attracted to sweet odors
(C) Because flies do not have long proboscises
(D) Because wind is not a living method of pollination

35. Which of the following best expresses the essential information in the highlighted sentence. *Incorrect* choices change the meaning in important ways or leave out essential information.

(A) Insects are not birds.
(B) Large plants require large birds that eat insects.
(C) Large birds need more nectar than insects.
(D) Birds pollinate more plants than insects.

36. **Directions:** *An introductory sentence for a brief summary of the passage is provided below. Complete the summary by selecting the THREE answer choices that express the most important ideas in the passage. Some sentences do not belong in the summary because they express ideas that are not presented in the passage or are minor ideas in the passage.* **This question is worth 2 points.**

First sentence: **Plant pollination can be accomplished by a number of animals and even by some natural processes.**

(A) Bees are one of the insects that pollinate plants.
(B) Nectar is a sweet water substance that attracts birds.
(C) Fluted blossoms control which insects can extract nectar.
(D) Wind and other non-living processes also pollinate plants.
(E) Birds are another animal that pollinate plants.
(F) Rodents pollinate plants by eating their leaves and fruit.

Listening

Section	Options		Time			Directions	Tools			
Listening	Pause	Section Exit	00 : 00 : 00	Hide		Continue	Volume	Confirm	Next	Help

Listening Section

Directions

In this section, you will listen to 2 conversations and 4 lectures. You will hear each conversation and lecture one time.

After each listening passage, you will answer some questions about it. Most questions are worth one point, but some questions are worth more than one point. The directions indicate how many points you may receive.

You will have 30 minutes to both listen and answer the questions. The questions ask about the main idea and supporting details. Some questions ask about a speaker's purpose or attitude.

You may take notes while you listen. You may use your notes to help you answer. Your notes will not be scored.

In some questions, you will see this icon: 🎧 . This means you will hear part of the conversation or lecture again.

When you are ready, press **Continue**.

Listen to part of a conversation between two students.

1. What kind of information does the man need?

    (A) Information on registering for classes
    (B) Information on where his lab class will meet
    (C) Information for using the school library
    (D) Information on the computer labs

2. When can the man use the facilities discussed in the conversation? Click in the correct box (Yes or No) for each time.

	Yes	No
(A) Monday at 7:30 a.m.		
(B) Wednesday at 8:00 p.m.		
(C) Saturday at 1:00 p.m.		
(D) Friday at 4:00 p.m.		
(E) Sunday at 2:00 p.m.		

3. Why does the woman mention the man's email account?

    (A) She plans to send him information via his email account.
    (B) It is necessary for getting a password.
    (C) Some students have been experiencing problems with their email accounts.
    (D) The labs don't have Internet access, so he won't be able to use it.

4. How does the woman feel about the registration process?

    (A) It is daunting.
    (B) It is complicated.
    (C) It is very time consuming.
    (D) It is simple.

5. What will the man probably do next?

    (A) He will visit the computer lab in the library.
    (B) He will go to a computer lab with the woman.
    (C) He will drop by the computer administration building.
    (D) He will buy a copy of the program at the student union.

6. Listen again to part of the conversation. Then answer the question. ( )

    What does the man imply when he says this: ( ) ?

    (A) He has time to go with her.
    (B) He will have time after 3:30.
    (C) This is not a good time for him.
    (D) He is surprised that it is already 3:30.

Listen to part of a lecture in an ecology class.

7. What is the talk mainly about?

(A) Methods for preventing pollution from affecting human populations

(B) Theories about how pollution spreads through an ecosystem

(C) The inefficiency of governments in responding to environmental problems

(D) Organisms that can signal harmful changes in the environment

8. What effects on various bio-indicators are mentioned in the lecture? Choose 3 answers.

(A) Babies dying before they are born

(B) Changes in chemical processes

(C) Deformities

(D) Fewer male babies

(E) Larger than normal babies

(F) Losing consciousness

9. Are these statements true about the student? For each statement, mark the correct box.

	Yes	No
(A) Humans do NOT use animals as bio-indicators.		✓
(B) Mines are given as examples of bio-indicators.	✓	
(C) Frogs are sensitive as bio-indicators because they absorb things through their skin.		
(D) Pets were a bio-indicator of problems at Love Canal.		
(E) Polluted water caused problems at Love Canal.		

10. What does the professor imply about human bio-indicators?

(A) That there is no such thing as a human bio-indicator

(B) That research involving human bio-indicators is illegal

(C) That humans are not sensitive enough to act as bio-indicators

(D) That they can also tell us about problems in our environment

11. How did the chemicals get into the city's water supply in Love Canal?

(A) From gases released in a nearby mine

(B) From frogs that carried pollution in their skin

(C) From rain water that fell over the city

(D) From buried chemical waste

12. Listen again to part of the lecture. Then answer the question.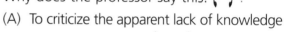

Why does the professor say this: ?

(A) To criticize the apparent lack of knowledge among young people today

(B) To express certainty that the example is unfamiliar

(C) To connect the lecture with a recent event in the news

(D) To suggest his uncertainty about how many students will understand the example

Listen to part of a lecture in a music class.

13. What aspect of 12-tone composition does the professor mainly discuss?

(A) The genius of Arnold Schoenberg
(B) The method of composing it
(C) How European instruments affected it
(D) Examples found in popular pieces

14. In the lecture, the professor describes several processes of transformation. Indicate whether each of the following is a transformation mentioned in the lecture. Click the correct box for each phrase.

	Yes	No
(A) Minor scale		✓
(B) Chromatic scale	✓	
(C) Prime row	✓	
(D) Retrograde	✓	
(E) Inverse	✓	
(F) Upside down and backwards		✓

15. Why does the professor mention the traditional scales in music?

(A) To show how atonal music differed from what was being done
(B) To show how atonal music improved upon a method already being used
(C) To show how traditional music sounds better than atonal
(D) To show how traditional music was easier than atonal

16. According to the lecture, how many times can the same note be played in a prime row?

(A) Once
(B) Twice
(C) Twelve times
(D) As many times as necessary

17. Listen again to part of the lecture. Then answer the question.

What does the professor imply about atonal composition?

(A) It should be quite simple to compose.
(B) It is hard to listen to because it doesn't follow any rules.
(C) It must include a planned structure.
(D) It can't be created from simply applying certain rules.

18. Listen again to part of the lecture. Then answer the question.

What does the professor mean when she says this: ?

(A) Count twelve notes back
(B) Use twelve fewer notes
(C) Play the twelfth lower row
(D) Hold the note for twelve beats

Listen to part of a lecture in a sociology class.

19. What is the talk mainly about?

    (A) The development of American culture

    (B) How conflicts between cultures develop

    (C) An introduction to the concept of culture

    (D) Communication with other cultures

20. What are two key features of culture mentioned in the lecture? Choose 2 answers.

    (A) Complex

    (B) Existing for many generations

    (C) Learned or taught

    (D) Passed down

    (E) Shared with animals

21. Why does the professor mention smiling?

    (A) To show that humans are basically good and not evil

    (B) To explain a key difference between Canadian and Indian culture

    (C) Because this is related to sexual taboos

    (D) To give an example of a cultural similarity

22. According to the professor, what does an Indian man choosing the woman he will marry demonstrate?

    (A) Borrowing from another culture

    (B) A difference between Indian and Canadian culture

    (C) Variation within Indian culture

    (D) Learned behavior

23. What does the professor imply about cultural change?

    (A) It happens faster with younger generations.

    (B) It does not occur until two cultures come into contact.

    (C) It will happen even if people resist it.

    (D) It makes it possible for the culture to spread.

24. Listen again to part of the lecture. Then answer the question.

What can be inferred about the professor?

    (A) He does not have a good opinion about the textbook.

    (B) He will stop talking and have students talk.

    (C) He knows more about Canadian culture than American culture.

    (D) He will use another example from Indian culture.

Listen to part of a conversation between a student and a tutor.

25. What does the man need from the woman?

(A) The answers to questions that he missed on the exam

(B) Suggestions for improving his essay

(C) Help understanding his lecture notes

(D) The names of authors he should read

26. Listen again to part of the conversation. Then answer the question. ◯

What does the woman imply about the man's problem?

(A) The theories do not relate to his problem.

(B) Lots of students have the same problem.

(C) She came across a theory that might help solve the problem.

(D) His problem confuses her.

27. Why does the man mention the sky and the ocean?

(A) As members of a particular category

(B) As empirical categories

(C) As experiences familiar to most people

(D) As objects that do not fit within Berkley's worldview

28. What does the man imply about Berkley's ideas?

(A) They are easier to explain than Locke's.

(B) They were not discussed in class.

(C) They will be a major part of the next exam.

(D) They are harder to grasp than Locke's.

29. What is an example the woman gives of idealism?

(A) Berkley's disappearance

(B) A magic chair

(C) Shapes with colors

(D) The chair that the man is sitting on

30. Listen again to part of the conversation. Then answer the question. ◯

What does the woman mean when she says this: ◯ ?

(A) Are you going to stay longer?

(B) Is that enough?

(C) Do you understand?

(D) Does that answer your question?

Listen to part of a lecture in a literature class.

31. What is the talk mainly about?

(A) A particular writer's style
(B) Ways stories can be written
(C) A novel with the title *Point of View*
(D) Writing stories with suspense

32. What are three ideas related to external narrators mentioned in the lecture? Choose 3 answers.

(A) Dramatized comments
(B) Position of characters
(C) Position of irony
(D) Position of suspense
(E) Rereading events
(F) The author's personality

33. What does the professor say about stories with third-person narration?

(A) Writers use this type of narration when they want to hide their opinions.
(B) A story written in third-person is more difficult to understand than a story written in first-person.
(C) This style of narration was more popular in the past than today.
(D) Many of the books for the course use this type of narration.

34. Listen again to part of the lecture. Then answer the question.
What does the speaker mean?

(A) The two terms refer to the same thing.
(B) The first term is not used a frequently as the second term.
(C) The second term is more precise than the first term.
(D) The terms refer to two different kinds of narrative.

35. Why does the speaker mention the book *Frankenstein*?

(A) It will be the first book that students read in this course.
(B) It is an example of a complex narrative form.
(C) It is one of the few books from the 1800s with a female narrator.
(D) It uses the position of suspense very effectively.

36. With what narration type are these details associated? Click in the correct column.

First person	Third person

(A) External narrator
(B) God's-eye-view
(C) Single character
(D) Gives reader more information than characters
(E) Uses "I" a lot

Speaking

Speaking Section

Directions

In this section of the test, you will demonstrate your ability to speak about a variety of topics. You will answer six questions by speaking into the microphone. Answer each of the questions as completely as possible.

In questions one and two, you will speak about familiar topics. Your response will be scored on your ability to speak clearly and coherently about the topics.

In questions three and four, you will first read a short text. The text will go away and you will then listen to a talk on the same topic. You will be asked a question about what you have read and heard. You will need to combine appropriate information from the text and the talk to provide a complete answer to the question. Your response is scored on your ability to speak clearly and coherently and on your ability to accurately convey information about what you read and heard.

In questions five and six, you will listen to part of a conversation or a lecture. You will be asked a question about what you heard. Your response is scored on your ability to speak clearly and coherently and on your ability to accurately convey information about what you heard.

You may take notes while you read and while you listen to the conversations and lectures. You may use your notes to help prepare your responses.

Listen carefully to the directions for each question. The directions are not shown on the screen.

For each question, you will be given a short time to prepare your response. A clock will show how much preparation time is remaining. When the preparation time is up, you will be told to begin your response. A clock will show how much time is remaining. A message will appear on the screen when the response time has ended.

If you finish before the allotted time, press **Continue** to go to the next question.

Question 1

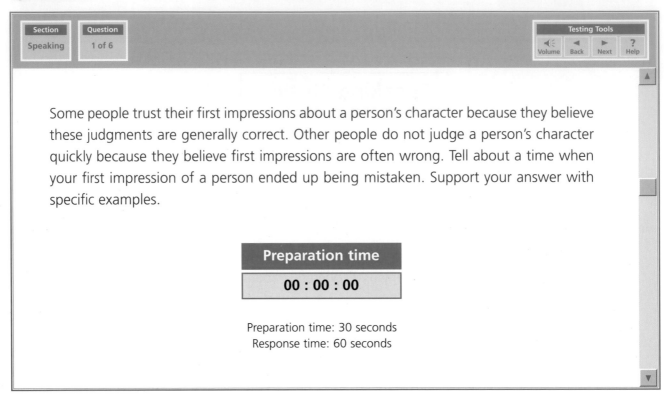

Section
Speaking

Question
1 of 6

Testing Tools

Volume Back Next Help

Some people trust their first impressions about a person's character because they believe these judgments are generally correct. Other people do not judge a person's character quickly because they believe first impressions are often wrong. Tell about a time when your first impression of a person ended up being mistaken. Support your answer with specific examples.

Preparation time

00 : 00 : 00

Preparation time: 30 seconds
Response time: 60 seconds

Question 2

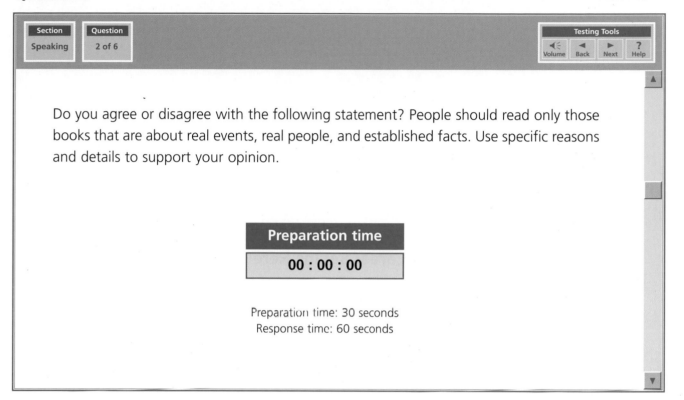

Do you agree or disagree with the following statement? People should read only those books that are about real events, real people, and established facts. Use specific reasons and details to support your opinion.

Preparation time

00 : 00 : 00

Preparation time: 30 seconds
Response time: 60 seconds

Question 3

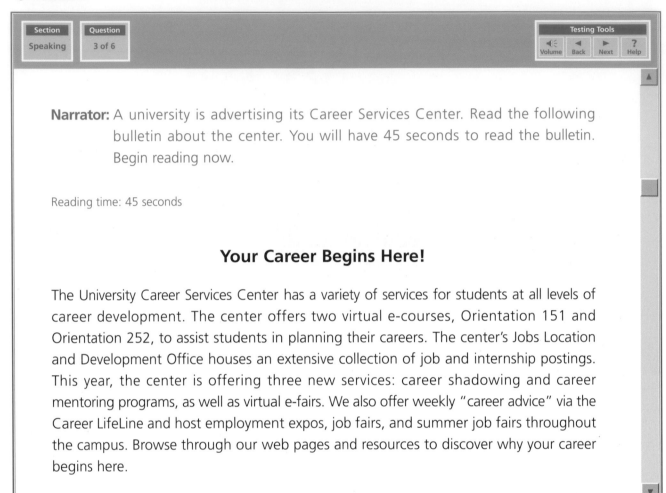

Narrator: A university is advertising its Career Services Center. Read the following bulletin about the center. You will have 45 seconds to read the bulletin. Begin reading now.

Reading time: 45 seconds

Your Career Begins Here!

The University Career Services Center has a variety of services for students at all levels of career development. The center offers two virtual e-courses, Orientation 151 and Orientation 252, to assist students in planning their careers. The center's Jobs Location and Development Office houses an extensive collection of job and internship postings. This year, the center is offering three new services: career shadowing and career mentoring programs, as well as virtual e-fairs. We also offer weekly "career advice" via the Career LifeLine and host employment expos, job fairs, and summer job fairs throughout the campus. Browse through our web pages and resources to discover why your career begins here.

Section	Question		Testing Tools
Speaking	3 of 6		Volume Back Next Help

Now listen to two students as they discuss the services described in the announcement.

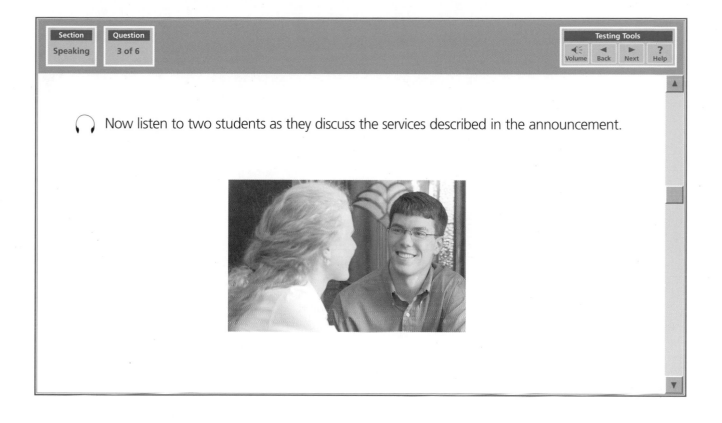

The woman expresses her opinion of the Career Services Center. State her opinion and explain the reasons she gives for holding that opinion.

Preparation time

00 : 00 : 00

Preparation time: 30 seconds
Response time: 60 seconds

Question 4

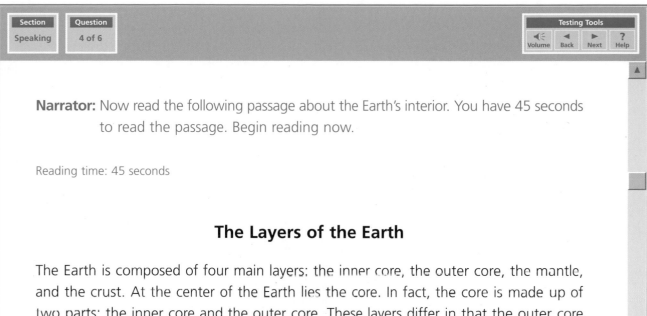

Narrator: Now read the following passage about the Earth's interior. You have 45 seconds to read the passage. Begin reading now.

Reading time: 45 seconds

The Layers of the Earth

The Earth is composed of four main layers: the inner core, the outer core, the mantle, and the crust. At the center of the Earth lies the core. In fact, the core is made up of two parts: the inner core and the outer core. These layers differ in that the outer core is molten, but the inner core is solid due to the extreme pressure at the center of the Earth. Above the core is the mantle, the layer in which most of the Earth's mass is found. The crust is much thinner than either the core or the mantle. The crust is rocky and brittle. Thus, it is susceptible to fracture, as happens during earthquakes.

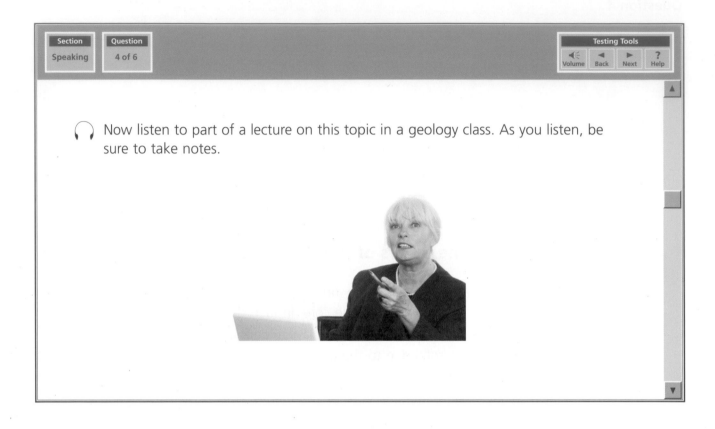

🎧 Now listen to part of a lecture on this topic in a geology class. As you listen, be sure to take notes.

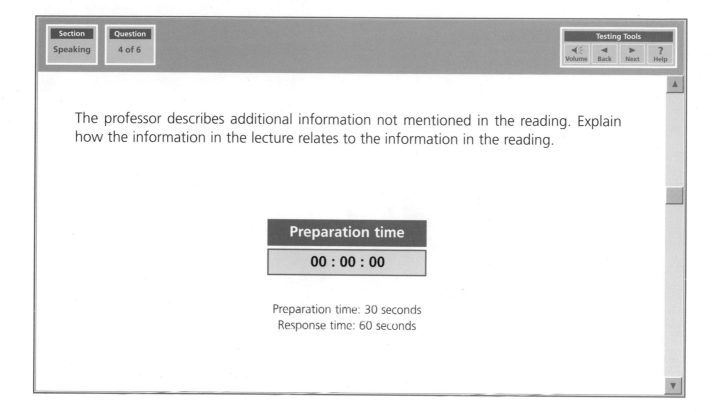

Section	Question		Testing Tools
Speaking	4 of 6		◄€ Volume ◄ Back ► Next ? Help

The professor describes additional information not mentioned in the reading. Explain how the information in the lecture relates to the information in the reading.

Preparation time

00 : 00 : 00

Preparation time: 30 seconds
Response time: 60 seconds

Question 5

Section
Speaking

Question
5 of 6

Testing Tools
Volume Back Next Help

🎧 Now listen to a conversation between two students.

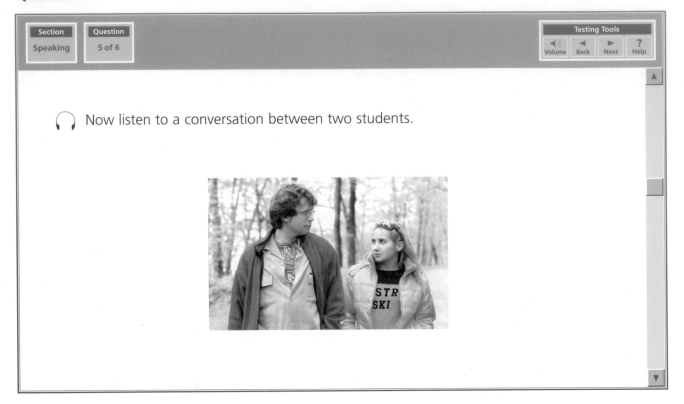

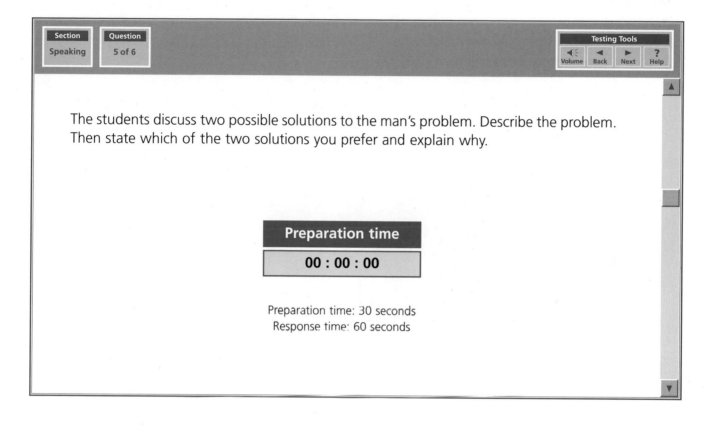

The students discuss two possible solutions to the man's problem. Describe the problem. Then state which of the two solutions you prefer and explain why.

Preparation time

00 : 00 : 00

Preparation time: 30 seconds
Response time: 60 seconds

Question 6

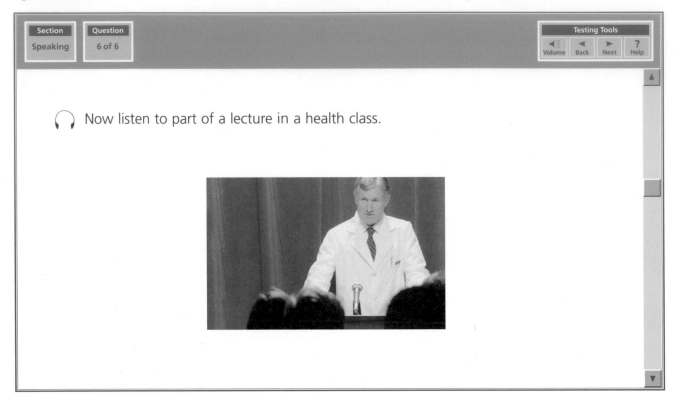

Using points and examples from the lecture, explain the basic theory behind Chinese medicine.

Preparation time

00 : 00 : 00

Preparation time: 30 seconds
Response time: 60 seconds

READING

LISTENING

SPEAKING

WRITING

PRACTICE TEST

Writing

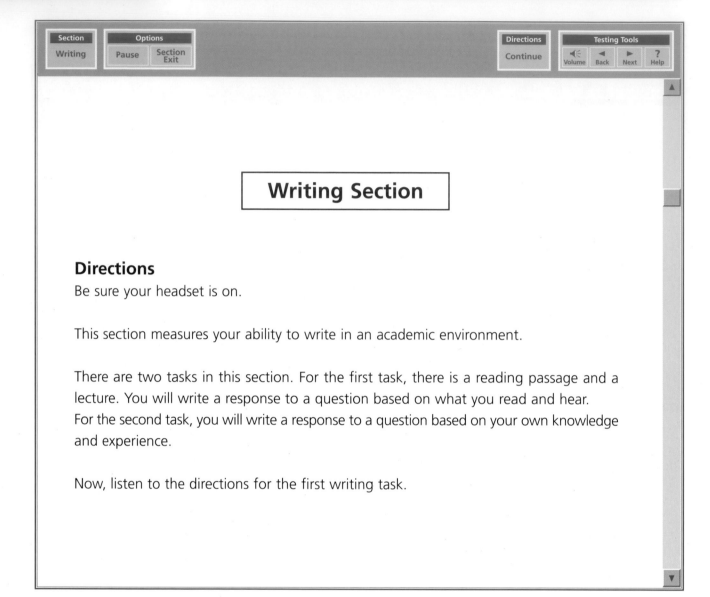

Section	Options			Directions	Testing Tools			
Writing	Pause	Section Exit		Continue	Volume	Back	Next	Help

Writing Section

Directions

Be sure your headset is on.

This section measures your ability to write in an academic environment.

There are two tasks in this section. For the first task, there is a reading passage and a lecture. You will write a response to a question based on what you read and hear. For the second task, you will write a response to a question based on your own knowledge and experience.

Now, listen to the directions for the first writing task.

Section	Options			Directions	Testing Tools			
Writing	Pause	Section Exit		Continue	Volume	Back	Next	Help

Integrated Writing Directions

For this task, you will have three minutes to read a passage about an academic topic. You may take notes while reading if you wish. The passage will then disappear and you will hear a lecture about the same topic. While listening, you may also take notes.

You will then have 20 minutes to write a response to a question related to the relationship between the lecture and the reading passage. Answer the question as completely as possible using information from both the reading passage and the lecture. The question will not ask you to express a personal opinion. The reading passage will appear again when it is time for you to start writing. You may use your notes from the lecture and the reading to help you answer the question.

Typically, an effective response for this task will be 150 to 225 words long. Your response will be graded on the quality of your writing and on the completeness and accuracy of the information you include in your response. If you finish your response before your time has run out, you may click **Next** to go to the second writing task.

Now, you will see the reading passage for three minutes. Remember that the passage will be available to you again while you are writing. Immediately after the reading time ends, the lecture will begin. Be sure to keep your headset on until the lecture has ended.

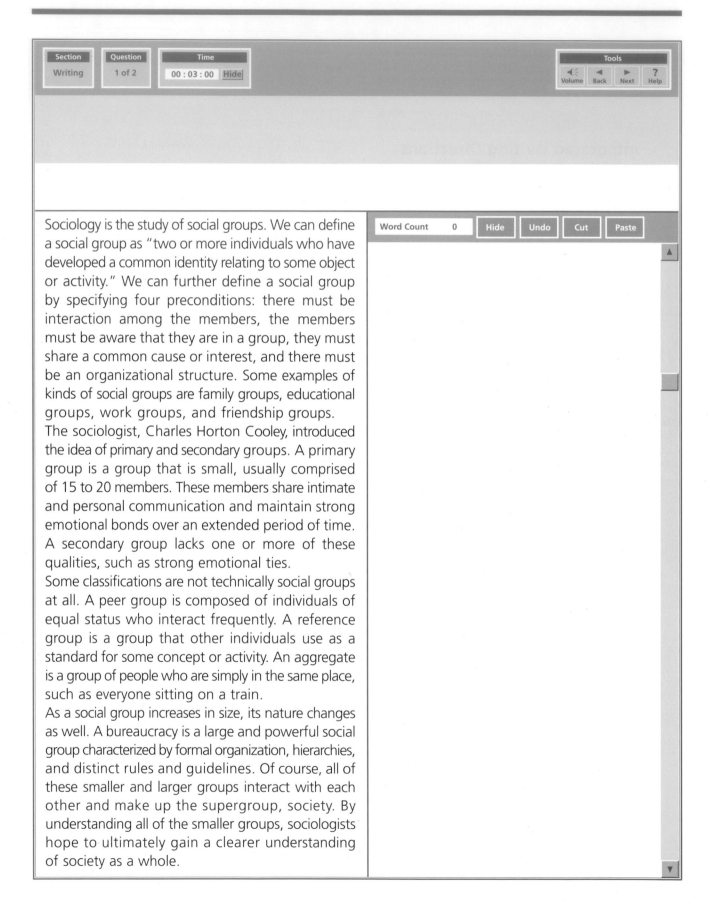

Word Count 0 Hide Undo Cut Paste

Sociology is the study of social groups. We can define a social group as "two or more individuals who have developed a common identity relating to some object or activity." We can further define a social group by specifying four preconditions: there must be interaction among the members, the members must be aware that they are in a group, they must share a common cause or interest, and there must be an organizational structure. Some examples of kinds of social groups are family groups, educational groups, work groups, and friendship groups.

The sociologist, Charles Horton Cooley, introduced the idea of primary and secondary groups. A primary group is a group that is small, usually comprised of 15 to 20 members. These members share intimate and personal communication and maintain strong emotional bonds over an extended period of time. A secondary group lacks one or more of these qualities, such as strong emotional ties.

Some classifications are not technically social groups at all. A peer group is composed of individuals of equal status who interact frequently. A reference group is a group that other individuals use as a standard for some concept or activity. An aggregate is a group of people who are simply in the same place, such as everyone sitting on a train.

As a social group increases in size, its nature changes as well. A bureaucracy is a large and powerful social group characterized by formal organization, hierarchies, and distinct rules and guidelines. Of course, all of these smaller and larger groups interact with each other and make up the supergroup, society. By understanding all of the smaller groups, sociologists hope to ultimately gain a clearer understanding of society as a whole.

Section	Question	Time		Tools
Writing	1 of 2	00 : 07 : 00 Hide		Volume Back Next Help

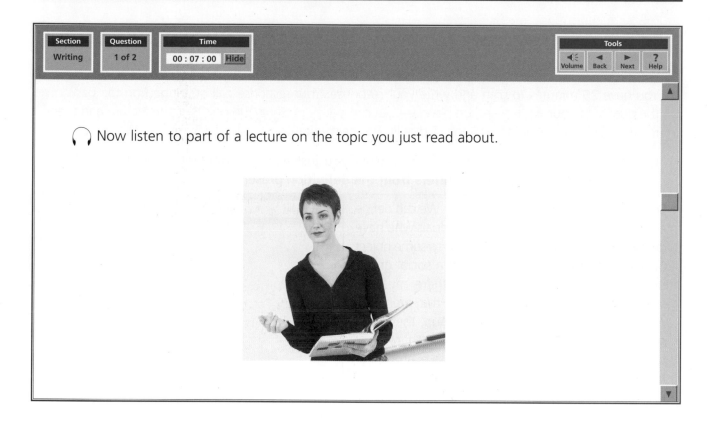

Now listen to part of a lecture on the topic you just read about.

You have 20 minutes to plan and write your response. Your response will be judged on the basis of the quality of your writing and on how well your response presents the points in the lecture and their relationship to the reading passage. Typically, an effective response will be 150 to 225 words.

Question: Summarize the points in the lecture you just heard, explaining how the speaker's definition of society differs from the definition presented in the reading.

Word Count   0   Hide   Undo   Cut   Paste

Sociology is the study of social groups. We can define a social group as "two or more individuals who have developed a common identity relating to some object or activity." We can further define a social group by specifying four preconditions: there must be interaction among the members, the members must be aware that they are in a group, they must share a common cause or interest, and there must be an organizational structure. Some examples of kinds of social groups are family groups, educational groups, work groups, and friendship groups.

The sociologist, Charles Horton Cooley, introduced the idea of primary and secondary groups. A primary group is a group that is small, usually comprised of 15 to 20 members. These members share intimate and personal communication and maintain strong emotional bonds over an extended period of time. A secondary group lacks one or more of these qualities, such as strong emotional ties.

Some classifications are not technically social groups at all. A peer group is composed of individuals of equal status who interact frequently. A reference group is a group that other individuals use as a standard for some concept or activity. An aggregate is a group of people who are simply in the same place, such as everyone sitting on a train.

As a social group increases in size, its nature changes as well. A bureaucracy is a large and powerful social group characterized by formal organization, hierarchies, and distinct rules and guidelines. Of course, all of these smaller and larger groups interact with each other and make up the supergroup, society. By understanding all of the smaller groups, sociologists hope to ultimately gain a clearer understanding of society as a whole.

Tools

Volume | Back | Next | Help

Independent Writing Directions

For this task, you will write a response to a question that asks you to present, explain, and support your opinion on an issue. You will have 30 minutes to write your response to the question.

Typically, an effective response for this task will be about 300 words long. Your response will be graded on the quality of your writing. Graders will consider various aspects of the response such as the development of your ideas, the organization of the content, and the quality and accuracy of the language used to express ideas.

If you finish your response before your time has run out, you may click **Next** to end this section.

When you are ready to begin, click on the **Dismiss Directions** icon.

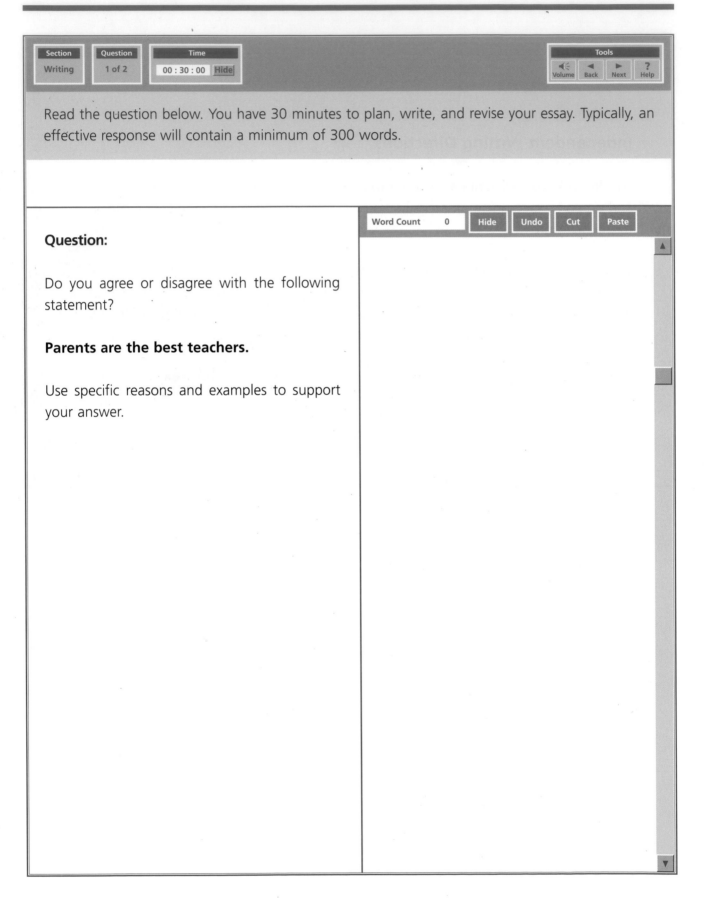

Section	Question	Time		Tools
Writing	1 of 2	00 : 30 : 00 Hide		Volume Back Next Help

Read the question below. You have 30 minutes to plan, write, and revise your essay. Typically, an effective response will contain a minimum of 300 words.

| Word Count 0 | Hide | Undo | Cut | Paste |

Question:

Do you agree or disagree with the following statement?

Parents are the best teachers.

Use specific reasons and examples to support your answer.

Mastering Skills for the TOEFL® iBT

TRANSCRIPTS

Listening Section / Speaking Section / Writing Section / Practice Test

Chapter 1

Skill A

01 Campus Life

W: Hey, I saw you guys playing softball. Could I join your team?

M: Well, we're full right now actually. Are you signed up in the intramural sports league?

W: No, how does that work?

M: Go to Withurst Hall room 304 and fill out a form to sign up as a free agent. Then, if a team needs a player, they can select you from a list. You just have to sign up and pay the fees.

W: Fees, huh? What are those like?

M: Well, they're 30 dollars per player for a season if you're on a team. I'm not sure about free agents.

02 Sociology

M: Could you explain the differences between preindustrial, early industrial, and mature industrial populations again?

W: Of course. A preindustrial population, like say, a tribe, has a high death rate and a high birth rate. Many people die, but many new babies are born, too. So, their population is stable. A mature industrial population, such as the US, has low birth and death rates, so the population is also stable in theory. On the other hand, an early industrial population, like India, can achieve low death rates but still have high birth rates, so it experiences a population explosion. Thus, it differs from the other two.

03 Literature

M: I noticed that many of you wrote in your term papers that Shakespeare invented the sonnet. This is a fallacy. Shakespeare did popularize the sonnet in England, but it had been in existence in Italy for two centuries before that. Sonnets were being written in Italian as pastoral love poems. If you recall from earlier lectures, it was Petrarch who refined the form and set the standard for the Italian sonnet, with two parts, the first part being eight lines and the second part six lines. Shakespearean sonnets, on the other hand, have four parts: three quatrains, or four-line parts, and one couplet, or two-line part.

04 Campus Life

M: What can I do for you?

W: I really wanted to take Chemistry 221 with you, but the class is full.

M: Is it a required course for you?

W: Yes, it is. I'm majoring in chemistry.

M: I presume you have the prerequisites, then?

W: Prerequisites?

M: Prerequisites are those courses that you need to have completed in order to enroll in any given class. The prerequisite for Chemistry 221 is Chemistry 100.

W: Oh, yes of course.

M: In that case, you can enroll in the class.

W: But the class is full. Don't I have to put my name on a waiting list or anything?

M: No, not for required courses. Anyone who needs to take a class to fulfill their course requirements is permitted to enter.

05 Geology

W: The two main types of glacial erosion are plucking and abrasion. Plucking occurs when blocks of rock are pulled away from the bedrock. The glacier works like a backhoe. Water flows into cracks in the rock. It then refreezes and expands, causing the chunk of rock to separate from the bedrock. A glacier can then pick up these loose chunks as it passes over the bedrock. This process creates a lot of loose debris, which causes abrasion. Now, abrasion works like sandpaper with the debris grinding away at the bedrock. If the debris is coarse, it will create long grooves in the bedrock called striations. On the other hand, if the debris is fine, it will create a smooth surface.

06 Health Science

M: One commonly pasteurized product is milk. By decreasing the amount of dangerous bacteria present, milk can be made safer to consume. It also lasts longer after it's been pasteurized. The most common pasteurization procedure is high temperature/short time (HTST) pasteurization. The milk is kept at 72° Celsius for at least 15 seconds. That is the high temperature — 72 degrees — for a short time — 15 seconds. This allows the milk to remain fresh for two or three weeks if refrigerated. For longer-lasting milk, the ultra high temperature (UHT) method is used. This milk is heated to 138° Celsius and held there for only two seconds. Milk pasteurized under the UHT method can remain fresh for up to two or three months.

07 Campus Life

M: Hey Josie! You assessed Peter's presentation didn't you?

W: Yep. I thought he did pretty well.

M: Me, too. How did you actually fill out the assessment form?

W: Well, I noted down the main ideas, the strengths, and then one thing that could be improved, like how Peter was chewing gum during the presentation.

M: (Laughs) OK. That's it?

W: No, then I graded him on several areas from 1 to 4, 4 being the best. Like, I gave Peter a 4 for eye contact because he didn't look at the floor at all.

M: I see. You know, I asked because I'm assessing you next Thursday.

08 Journalism

W: The scholarly method involves careful analysis and interpretation of information. Information must come from somewhere. These are the sources. There are three types of sources: primary, secondary, and tertiary. Primary sources come from documents created by people who witnessed events first hand. A person's diary is an example of a primary source. When information from primary sources is interpreted by others, it is called a secondary source. For example, if someone read that diary, compared it to newspapers from the same period and wrote about it, this would be a secondary source. If someone then read that secondary source and created a new document, that would be a tertiary source.

Skill B

01 Campus Life

M: I'd like to audition for the jazz band.

W: What is your name and instrument?

M: I'm Roger Watkins, and I play the trumpet.

W: OK, that's Roger Watkins on trumpet.

M: Do you have any pointers for how to prepare for the audition?

W: Well, you will be tested on style, tempo, dynamics, scales, tone, range, and sight-reading.

M: That's a lot of stuff. What is the most important?

W: You'd better have your scales memorized and be ready for sight-reading.

M: I know my scales. I've played the trumpet since middle school. So, I'll focus on my sight-reading.

W: On the day of the audition, be sure to arrive early and give yourself plenty of time to warm up. That's very important.

02 History

W: Alexander the Great began his quest to conquer the world at the age of twenty, when he became the king of Macedonia. That's probably the same age as many of you here. He and his army defeated the then-powerful Persian Empire and continued to acquire vast amounts of territory. At the time of his death, he ruled the largest Western Empire of ancient times. Some remember him as a charismatic leader whose purpose was to foster East-West relations. Others say he was a brutal killer who was only interested in personal glory. Most historians, though, do agree on one point: he was a brilliant military strategist and leader.

03 Paleontology

M: Fossils tell us about organisms that lived in the past. Actually, most people don't realize it, but fossil preservation is quite rare. So, we know very little about most of the organisms that came before us. The reason that fossil preservation is rare is that, in order to be fossilized, an organism must meet three specific requirements. First, it must be made of a substance that is preservable. Hard substances like bones or shells are highly preservable. Second, it must be buried in sediment, which protects it from decay. Third, the organism must have lived in a suitable environment, such as a shoreline. That's where dead animals would most likely be covered by sediment before they decay.

04 Campus Life

W: Sorry guys, this court is reserved from 3:00 to 4:00.

M: Reserved? For what?

W: Some other students registered to reserve this court over a week ago.

M: How do you do that?

W: You go to the gym office during office hours, tell them when you want to reserve the court, and then present your student ID card. Then, they'll authorize the reservation.

M: That's not very fair. We were here first, and someone can just reserve the court for whenever they want?

W: No, you can only reserve one hour per week and only one week beforehand. Otherwise, the court is on a first come first served basis.

M: Well, I appreciate the info. Let's go, guys.

05 Physics

W: We are all here to learn physics, but why?

M: Because it's a required course?

W: (chuckles) That's probably true for most of you. In truth, you can come here and just memorize the formulae and get a decent grade, but I want you to learn physics as an activity, like you would learn to ride a bike. If you have to jump a ravine, I want you to be able to calculate the required momentum to get across. If there is a fire in your house, I want you to know the best course of action based on principles of smoke and heat diffusion. Physics is actually quite useful.

06 Art

M: Masks have a long history in Western civilization, going as far back as the Greeks. They were first used in religious rituals to impersonate the god Dionysus. Obviously, rituals were not meant for entertainment, but these impersonations lead to full theatrical productions. Greek masks were made from painted leather or canvas. And like other masks you may be familiar with, these Greek masks exaggerated facial features. They also helped amplify the actor's voice, and allowed one actor to play multiple roles. Later, masks were important in medieval morality plays. Medieval masks were made from paper mache and represented demons, devils, and the seven deadly sins.

07 Campus Life

M: Why do we have to do a pre-lab report?

W: Well the reason we do pre-lab reports is to ensure we understand what we are studying and what we are about to do.

M: What does it involve?

W: Exactly that: we state the purpose and outline the procedure.

M: OK, so I start with the purpose.

W: That's right. Your purpose states what you are going to do and what you expect to find.

M: Should I talk about my — what was it called — my hypothesis?

W: Absolutely. Then outline the procedure in a flow chart.

M: So, I should write it in this order: purpose, hypothesis, and procedure.

W: Yes, and please do it all in your own words. Plagiarism will be punished harshly.

08 Drama

W: So, theater is a kind of art, but what kind is it?

M: Didn't you say it was a performing art?

W: That's right. Remember, we have three kinds of art: literary, visual, and performing. A performing art has two necessary and sufficient conditions. First, it requires a creator, interpreter, and an audience. And second, the audience and interpreter must be in the same place. Some examples of performing arts are dance, music, and opera. Film, as we discussed last time, contains facets of both visual and performing arts. So, in order to make a film, performing artists and visual artists work in collaboration.

Skill C

01 Campus Life

W: How do you always pull off such high grades in English, Harry?

M: I use a computer flash card program to remember the irregular forms. It makes studying kind of fun.

W: Huh? How does that help?

M: Well, it displays a verb, like "freeze" for example. Then, I have to type in the simple past and past participle forms.

W: That would be "froze" and "frozen," right?

M: Right. If I screw up, then it comes up again at the end of my list.

W: Wow, so it reinforces your shortcomings.

M: Yeah. It also provides adjectives with synonyms, phrasal verbs with definitions, and it has grammar exercises as well.

02 Sociology

M: Who was Mother Teresa, then?

W: The Indian nun?

M: Actually, she was not Indian, but Albanian. She grew up in modern day Macedonia, when it was encompassed within the Ottoman Empire.

W: But she did live in India, right?

M: That's right. She went there as a missionary with Irish nuns. She later started her own religious order to work with the poorest and sickest people. She even did special training with an American Medical Mission. She was truly a remarkable lady. She fed and taught abandoned children who lived in abject poverty, and she gave comfort to the dying. In 1979, she received the Nobel Peace Prize for her valuable work.

03 Ecology

M: What exactly are the problems with the intertidal pools on the California coast?

W: For one thing, intertidal pools were once some of the most bountiful reservoirs of marine life on the planet. It's now difficult to find a single animal in them, mainly due to poaching and a lack of education. People remove buckets of snails from the pools and use them as fishing bait. Or they pour chemicals in the pools to catch baby octopuses. It's shocking. Or they scrape pool rocks bare to collect barnacles. Most people are unaware that these areas are protected by law.

04 History

M: History can illuminate the value of tea. In the past, quality tea has been considered more valuable than gold. Tea has even been the impetus for war, like the American Revolution.

W: I thought that war happened because Americans didn't want to be ruled by the British. What did it have to do with tea?

M: One of the incidents that touched off the Revolutionary War was a shipment of tea being dumped into the ocean by a group of Americans. Haven't you heard about the Boston Tea Party? It wasn't a party at all. It was one of the first aggressive acts of the revolution.

05 Health Science

M: Pets actually bestow many benefits upon their owners. For example, studies have shown that with elderly people, having a pet nearby lowers their blood pressure and raises their spirits. So, for all of you with grandmothers or grandfathers living alone, maybe your next gift to them should be a puppy.
Another pertinent study from Britain showed that pets seemed to help fight disease. The study found that people cohabiting with pets had a lower risk of heart disease and recovered more quickly from heart attacks than those who didn't live with pets. The study also found that pet owners suffered fewer colds, headaches, and fevers than people who didn't own pets.

06 Campus Life

M: Did you hear the weather report, Jenny? It looks like the weather will clear up by Friday.

W: Awesome! That means we can take our class trip to the mountains after all. I was afraid our prof would have to cancel it.

M: I am really looking forward to the hike.

W: Yeah. This will be my first time hiking in the mountains.

M: Are you kidding? They're so close. I go up there most weekends with my friends.

W: I guess I'm just not the outdoors type. Are the trails on the mountain quite arduous?

M: Not really. Most of them are no sweat. Hiking on them is just like taking a nice long walk through the woods.

07 Paleontology

W: Sixty-five million years ago, dinosaurs were ubiquitous. Then, they all seemed to die very suddenly. So what happened?
Many scientists believe that the dinosaurs were wiped out by a colossal meteor. According to this theory, a meteor ten kilometers wide hurtled into the Earth. This collision propelled dust and dirt into the sky. Imagine a really cloudy summer day. It's a lot cooler, right? Well, every day was like that for a long time after the collision.
Because it was much darker and cooler, many species of plants began to die. Soon, there was no food source for plant-eating dinosaurs, and when they died, there was no food source for meat-eating dinosaurs. The only animals to survive were small ones able to subsist on many different kinds of food.

08 Campus Life

W: I'm having problems logging in to the Spanview system. It alleges my password is invalid.

M: Hmm, when was the last time you logged in?

W: Beats me — sometime last winter, maybe.

M: Well if you haven't logged in for 180 days, you need to procure a new password from the registrar's office. Try that first. If that doesn't help, then maybe someone else has gotten a hold of your username and password.

W: Ooh. What do I do if that's the case?

M: Use your secret question, probably your mother's maiden name, to regain control of your account. That should solve your problem.

Chapter 1

Skill Review

A-C

01 Campus Life

W: Good morning. I was wondering if you could give me some information about the Credit-by-Exam system.

M: Yes, of course. What would you like to know?

W: Well, first of all, I'm not really sure what credit-by-exam means.

M: OK. It is basically a combination of the tests administered by the departments of this university, the College Level Examination program, and other nationally recognized credit-by-exam programs.

W: Right. I know it's some kind of test, but I'm still not quite sure what exactly that means. Can you explain it in a little more detail?

M: The Credit-by-Exam system gives students a chance to take exams even if they are not registered in particular courses. For example, you want to take an exam in say, English composition, but you don't want to take an English composition class. You register for credit-by-exam, and if you pass the exam, you get the credit. So, you can demonstrate competence attained by educational experience, rather than university instruction.

W: So, I can take various exams, even if I didn't register for that course, or didn't attend any of the classes or lectures, and I can still get credits for taking those tests?

M: That pretty much sums it up.

W: Now, is it possible to get credits for graduate courses? I'd kind of like to combine my undergraduate degree and a master's degree at the same time, if that's possible. If I could get my BA and an MA at the same time, that would be great.

M: It would certainly save a lot of time, but I'm afraid that this is only for certain undergraduate courses.

W: Oh, well.

M: And of course, I hope you realize that guest matriculants are not eligible for credits.

W: I'm sorry? Guest matriculants?

M: I mean students who have been admitted to the university through an external program, but are not actually registered as full-time permanent students of this university.

W: Exchange students and that kind of thing?

M: They would fall under that category, yes, and extended studies students, too.

W: I'm a little worried about how the credits would appear on my transcript. Will there be anything on my transcript to indicate that I did not actually attend classes? I'm afraid that might affect my chances of being accepted to a graduate program if I have not actually attended the classes.

M: There will be nothing to show the credits were earned under the Credit-by-Exam system, but I don't think you need to worry. Each department has very strict eligibility criteria for students, and everyone taking a test is expected to have quite an extensive knowledge of the area to be tested. The credits you receive through testing are just as valid as credits received in the regular way. In any case, only a select few universities are being allowed to participate in the system, so academic standards are being tightly monitored.

W: Do you have a list of the courses for which students can receive credit by exam?

M: Yes. Why don't you take this information package, take a look, and give me a call if you have any more questions?

W: Great. Thanks.

02 Communications

W: You are giving a talk in front of a group of people. You've assembled all the relevant facts. You've planned it well, and your delivery is strong, but your audience doesn't respond or, even worse, they are giving you a negative response. What went wrong? Well, it is probably not what you are saying out loud that matters. The problem stems from what your body says, or in other words, your body language. By body language I mean things as simple as the way you stand, or, say, folding your arms across your chest. Body language includes the gestures and movements people make when they communicate. I can't stress enough how important this is. All too often, people just don't pay attention to their body language. If we go back to our earlier scenario of giving a talk for a moment, you might think you are communicating a clear message when you speak, but if your body is sending a different message, well, then your audience is just not going to react as you had hoped. You think you are a competent speaker, but if they see you slouching, not making eye contact, or pulling your earlobes, the audience will not feel confident that they can trust what you are saying. They may even stop listening.

You know, we start to read each other's body language from a very young age. Anytime we speak, the other person is checking our gestures and movements to see if they match what we are saying. You may not be aware of doing this, but we all do it. It comes naturally and is something we learn to do very well over time. If you think about your friends or your co-workers for example, after a while, you get to know their moods just by observing their body language or gestures. You know, your boss has a certain facial expression when he or she is upset, or maybe one of the guys in your office taps his fingers on his desk when he is feeling irritable.

An effective communicator will use what he or she sees in other people and take advantage of it. Even more important, however, is knowing and understanding your own body language. If you can exert a certain degree of control over the messages given by your body, you will be able to manipulate the responses of other people. You need to be aware of what your body is saying if you hope to succeed. Let me ask you a question. When we meet people and talk to them, they receive information from us. What percentage of that information comes from what we say, I mean the words we use when we speak? Any guesses? Yes?

M₁: Umm, maybe 75%?

W: Good guess, but I'm afraid not. Anyone else?

M₂: I'd say about 50%.

W: Wrong again. Would you believe that just 10% of the information is in the words? That means that 90%, the vast majority of information, is in our gestures, our expressions, our tone of voice, and — well, all of the other stuff.

Now, I'd like to give you some examples of body language that you might like to consider in your daily life. We don't have much time, so I'll focus on just a few aspects. Remember, I'm just giving you an introduction here. I'm sure you'll recognize a lot of these as things you often do yourself.

Eye contact. How do you feel when you are talking to someone, and they make very little or no eye contact? You feel they are disinterested, don't you? Or what if they make too much and they seem to be staring? Either way, you are not going to form a very good impression of that person.

Most of us do it all the time, but folding your arms across your body is very negative. It says "don't approach me, don't come any closer." That is not something you want to say at a job interview. Hold your body upright, keep it open and relaxed, and align yourself to place your body face to face with the other person. Then, they'll think you are honest and truthful. So, make a mental note to check your body language to make sure your body is saying the same thing as your mouth. With practice, you can send the desired message every time.

Skill D

01 Campus Life

M: Are you campaigning for the senate this year?

W: I hadn't thought about it. What does it involve?

M: Student senators decide what to do with the money we pay in student fees, and they deal with all of the organizations at the university. Stuff like that.

W: Who's eligible to run?

M: You have to be a full-time student and have at least a 2.0 GPA.

W: So, if you are elected, are you in until you graduate?

M: No, it's just a year. Then, you can be re-elected. You can be kicked out, too, if you don't attend the meetings.

W: Sounds interesting. I'll mull it over.

02 Economics

W: Money is something that can be exchanged for goods and services. It has several uses. One is that it is a medium of exchange. It is a lot easier to do business in a money-based economy than a barter-based one. Currency, or money, gives people a lot more flexibility in spending than trying to buy things with chickens or bags of grain. Money is also a way to measure value. When things are given a monetary value, we can compare their costs and values. Thirdly, money is an asset. We can put aside some money and use it at a later date.

03 Music

M: A chord is the sound created when three or more different notes or pitches are played simultaneously or relatively close together. Some combinations of notes are more popular than others, so normally only those three-note groups that are commonly used are called chords. On top of that, different genres of music tend to favor some chords over others. For example, power chords are often used in hard rock. They involve only two pitch classes. This is why power chords are common in this genre. Rock music involves a lot of distortion, and the power chords can avoid a lot of surplus noise.

04 Campus Life

M: Excuse me, sorry, how do I know which textbooks I need?

W: It's listed in the course schedule for some classes, but it's best to go to the first class and get the syllabus to be sure. Textbooks are pretty expensive. You don't want to buy one you don't need.

M: OK. Are there any used textbooks?

W: Usually. They're half off and are stacked next to the new ones. Look for the blue label. First come, first served.

M: Uh huh. If I get the wrong book, can I get a refund?

W: Yes, within seven days of purchase. However, you must bring back the receipt, and the book must be in the same condition as when you bought it.

05 Ecology

M: Three major biomes will be on the test: the tundra, the desert, and the grasslands. Let's go over them. The tundra is a polar desert — little precipitation, long cold winters, no trees, and a full range of daylight hours, from 0 to 24 hours. Grasslands are found inland, have hot summers and cold winters. Grasslands get 15-30 inches of rainfall annually. And remember that there are two types — tallgrass and shortgrass. Tallgrass grasslands have thick fertile soil. Shortgrass grasslands have thinner soil. Deserts are located within 20-30 degrees of the equator. They have hot days, cold nights, and little rainfall — only about 1-10 inches of rain per year.

06 Religious Studies

W: So, welcome to Religion and Morality. I hope you are all as excited to learn about this topic as I am to teach it! We will be spending a lot of time discussing what, if anything, the connection between religion and morality is. A lot of our moral vocabulary originally came from religious institutions. Religious groups today often make ethical prescriptions for their followers, take public stances, and participate in political activism on several key issues. God, of course, is a huge question. We will begin with the assumption that there is at least one God who is good. Later, we will examine the opposite assumption, that there is no God. The big question is what implications these assumptions have regarding morality.

07 Campus Life

W: Remember, these swimming drills are not for fitness. They are for recovery.

M: I understand. I'm not trying to get in shape.

W: That's right, and that's important because you don't want to overdo it.

M: So, I should swim slowly?

W: Yes. You should be very relaxed and keep your heart rate down.

M: So, what is the goal of these sessions?

W: The most important thing is getting your balance. The goal is to have perfect form throughout the session. Your neck and spine should be aligned at all times.

M: How is that possible?

W: Only your hips and your chin rotate.

M: OK, I'll try.

08 Botany

W: The fruit of a rose is called the hip. Most rosehips are red, but a few species, like *pimpinellifolia*, have dark purple or black hips. Each hip typically contains five to twenty-five seeds enclosed by stiff hairs. The hips of some species, particularly *canina* and *rugosa*, are very high in vitamin C, making them a vital food source for some birds. Now, I'm sure you are all well aware that most rose plants have thorns. They are usually hook-like and have evolved to help these plants hang on to other plants when growing over them. The *rugosa* and *pimpinellifolia* species, however, have tight clusters of straight spines instead — perhaps to inhibit sand erosion.

Skill E

01 Campus Life

M: Your English is really progressing, Maria.

W: It's all thanks to my language partner.

M: What do language partners do?

W: Well, they get together with foreign students for one or two hours a week and help them practice casual conversation.

M: Is that all?

W: No. Most partners explain Canadian culture and go to concerts and parties together. Mine has shown me some tremendous attractions here in Vancouver.

M: Isn't it kind of expensive?

W: No. The partners are all volunteers. It's a great way to make friends and practice English with a native speaker at the same time. My partner has really helped me adjust to life in Canada.

02 Physics

W: What is the truth about light wave theory? For many years, scientists were in disagreement. Newton hypothesized that light traveled faster in a denser medium, like a wave. On the other hand, Christian Huygens, in 1690, postulated that light waves slowed down in a denser medium, like particles. The problem was that it was impossible to measure the speed of light accurately. However, in 1850 Leon Foucault made the first accurate measurement. His result supported the wave theory for light. The theory was accepted until the late 19th century when Einstein discovered that light striking a surface caused particles to change their speed. This marked a return to contradiction and disagreement.

03 Geography

M: Did you know that the Mediterranean is part of the Atlantic Ocean? Though attached to the Atlantic, it is also a sea almost completely flanked by land — Europe to the north, Africa to the south, and Asia to the east. That is how it got its name. The name of this body of water comes from the Latin medi, which means middle, and terra, which means land. So even though it's a huge body of water, its name literally translates as "middle land." It has a long history of civilization and was instrumental in facilitating marine transportation in ancient times.

04 Campus Life

M: How do I register for a student union class?

W: Just head up to the 3rd floor of the student union building.

M: OK. Thanks.

W: Oh, wait. Is the course you want to take work related? If it is, you might want to register at the student employment office.

M: Actually, it is. I'm an aspiring bartender. I was hoping to get my bar skills certificate so I could apply for a position in a bar.

W: Is the bar here on campus?

M: Yes.

W: In that case, I would recommend registering at the student employment office. That way you can automatically apply for the bartending job when you register for the course.

M: That's great! Thanks a lot.

05 Political Science

M: After the first World War, the League of Nations was established for the purpose of settling conflicts between countries peacefully. As we know from the outbreak of World War II, they ultimately failed in their objective. The league lacked strength because it didn't have an army. It relied on its most powerful members to enforce its resolutions, but these countries were reluctant to do so. Britain and France, after World War I were largely pacifist and therefore reluctant to use force against Hitler's growing military regime. In the 1930s, the fascist powers left the league, and eventually World War II brought an end to the League of Nations. But the League did have one lasting effect…

06 Art History

W: Impressionism was a movement that began in the visual arts and then extended into music. Does that surprise some of you? Impressionist painters broke away from the tradition of creating life-like depictions. They used light and color to portray the impact or feeling of a subject. And soon after impressionism was established in art, musicians began applying its maxims to their compositions. They aimed to create the feeling of color and light in their music. Some impressionist musicians actually composed music as interpretations of paintings. Impressionism in both painting and music aimed to portray the impact or feeling of a subject rather than a literal depiction. So let's listen to a piece and analyze how a composer can do this.

07 Campus Life

W: Excuse me, could you tell me where the campus post office is located?

M: It's on the first floor of the student union building, next to the information desk.

W: Do you know its hours of operation?

M: 7:30 to 3:30, but during the summer, it opens later — at 8 a.m.

W: So, from next month it will open at 8 a.m. I see. Do they sell envelopes and stuff like a regular post office?

M: Yes. They primarily sell stamps and envelopes, but they carry other relevant postal products as well.

W: Do they have a post office box service?

M: Yes. P.O. boxes can be rented for $5 a month.

W: That's five bucks per month?

M: That's right. That's the same price you'll find at off-campus post offices, too.

W: Is that right? Then I might as well rent one on campus.

08 Photography

M: The process of taking a photograph involves exposing film to light. The amount of light that falls on the film is called the exposure. Hm. This is all something you'll have to do, so let me try to clarify that. Exposure is controlled by the lens aperture (the size of the hole letting in the light), and the shutter speed (the amount of time that the hole is opened for). Now, when planning exposure, a photographer considers reciprocity. This refers to the reciprocal relationship between aperture and shutter speed. For example, a slow shutter speed means that the film is getting more exposure to the light. Therefore, a smaller aperture is required. Similarly, a wide aperture requires a faster shutter speed. So, you must first determine the exposure and then adjust the aperture and shutter speed appropriately. Any guesses about how you can determine this?

Skill F

01 Campus Life

M: Umm, I need to apply for a room change. I'm having some problems with my roommate. Is this where I'm supposed to come?

W: Yes, it is. However, we don't grant room change requests except under special circumstances. If you have a roommate conflict you have to try to resolve it first using the conflict resolution procedure.

M: Oh, all right. What's the procedure?

W: Basically, you get all the roommates involved together and each one conveys their perspective. Then, you make a plan on how to resolve the problem, and each roommate commits to making the necessary changes. After one month, there's a formal review.

M: OK, thanks. I guess we'll try that then.

02 Communications

W: The most important element in communication theory is input. Input includes all of the information we receive from the external world. People have the ability to filter this information if there is too much of it. There are biological and psychological filters. Biological means a person can only process and retain so much information at a time. For instance, a student cannot remember everything said in a lecture, so he or she takes notes on key points. The psychological filter is like selective attention, or "you hear what you want to hear." So, information a person is not interested in doesn't ever get processed.

03 Computers

M: A computer communicates with a printer via a parallel port. This means that the 8 bits within the byte are all sent simultaneously, instead of one at a time. We call this serial communication, and it occurs through serial ports. The printer port has 25 pins. Pin 1 tells the printer that data is being sent. Pins 2-9 transmit the 8 bits of information in each byte. Pin 10 relays the confirmation signal to the computer. Pins 11 through 16 are for various functions such as printer error, out of paper, print job ready, etc. Pin 17 takes the printer offline. 18 through 25 are grounding pins. Let's compare that to another port on our computer.

04 Campus Life

W: I'd like to get a parking permit for the summer months. I know permits are normally issued through a lottery. Is that the case in the summer as well?

M: No, ma'am. There is a lot less demand in the summer. You can simply purchase a ticket.

W: Phew. That's just what I wanted to hear! I know it is $120.00 for the school year. How much for the summer?

M: $12.00 per month.

W: Can I buy it here?

M: Yes. I just need to see proof that you are enrolled in a summer course.

W: I haven't enrolled yet.

M: Well, you need to do that first and then come back here to the parking office with the documents. Then, we'll take your payment and give you the permit.

05 Ecology

W: Many of you may be surprised to hear that pollution is not necessarily a detrimental thing. In fact, it is perfectly natural. All organisms create waste. This is a basic part of life. It is not even a problem that the wastes are toxic. Many organisms also produce wastes that are toxic to themselves. There are, however, two problems with human pollution. First, it includes materials that the ecosystem cannot break down. For instance, we created CFCs, but nature cannot process them, so they float up and eat away at the ozone layer. Secondly, human pollution occurs in quantities that overload the ecosystem.

06 Campus Life

M: I just signed up for "Blast."

W: "Blast"? What's that?

M: It's a volunteering program.

W: Really? I've been meaning to do some volunteer work. What does it involve?

M: Helping freshmen students, conducting surveys, handing out flyers, making public announcements about events, and stuff like that. It's a good way to develop your public speaking skills.

W: It sounds great, but I don't have a lot of free time this year. I'm trying to get into law school.

M: Law school? Then it's perfect for you.

W: Yeah, I guess it would look good on my CV.

M: And it's not a big obligation — just 30 minutes every other week.

W: Is that all? I could handle that.

07 History

W: Today's topic is the Middle Ages. We've talked at length about the Roman Empire, and you're well-versed in Renaissance life, but what happened during the thousand years in between? The truth is, not much. There was a large migration of people into the former Roman territories, and this had a huge effect on society, law, culture, and trade. Life was arduous, which is perhaps why the one entity to survive the fall of the Roman Empire was the Christian Church. Since the Church promised a utopian afterlife to righteous followers, people had less incentive to fight to change their conditions here on Earth.

08 Biology

M: As you know, plants create oxygen. They do this through a process called photosynthesis. It is a chemical change occurring in the leaves of green plants whereby carbon dioxide and water are transformed into oxygen and glucose. Glucose can then be transformed into a starch and stored for later use. Oxygen is the "waste" of this process, but only in the sense that the plant gets rid of it. What is waste for the plant is an invaluable resource for the rest of us living creatures on Earth. In order for photosynthesis to take place, there must be chlorophyll, carbon dioxide, water, and sunlight.

Chapter 1
Skill Review

A-F

01 Sociology

M: Today, class, we're going to be continuing our examination of the nature versus nurture debate regarding human behavior. On the nature side of the argument, we have the belief that genes are more important than the environment in determining human behavior. Proponents of the nature argument believe that all human behavior is inherent and innate. This means that we are born sort of "pre-wired" to behave in a certain manner. Got it? OK, conversely, people on the nurture side believe that instead of being born pre-wired, the mind is a blank slate at birth. This means that we are born without any predispositions, that our genes do not influence our behavior. All of our behaviors are a result of experience and conditioning. What do you guys think?

W₁: Well, come on. Obviously, it can't all be in the genes. I mean, we have free will.

W₂: But then again, I don't really see how it could be all environment either. I mean, look at those twins you always hear about — you know — they're separated at birth and grow up in completely different environments, but then they turn out to have a lot in common.

M: I'm glad you brought that up, Ellen. Twins can tell us a lot about our genes. Think about it. Identical twins share 100% of their genes. In the womb, the egg splits in two after it has been fertilized by the father's sperm. Because the split happens after conception, the genes are the same. The twins come from the same egg and the same sperm, so they have the exact same set of genes. That's why they look exactly the same.

Fraternal twins, on the other hand, have a different set of genes. In this case, two eggs are released, before conception. Then, the two eggs are fertilized by two different sperm. Fraternal twins are no more alike, genetically, than any other pair of siblings. Normally, they share about 50% of their genes. So, by comparing the similarities and differences we see in identical twins with those in fraternal twins, we can learn about the influence that genes have on human behavior.

Think about intelligence. Some believe that people are born with a predisposition for intelligence. Others think that environmental factors influence how smart a child will grow up to be. So, researchers conducted a study that compared the intelligence of fraternal twins with that of identical twins. Now, all of these twins were from wealthy families, so we can assume that they had similar environmental advantages — good schools, good educational resources, etc. Now, they found that genetic predispositions accounted for most differences in intelligence. In other words, the studies found that with regards to intelligence, identical twins were more alike than fraternal twins. That means that genes do play a role.

W₁: So, you're saying that it is more common for identical twins to have similar IQs than it is for fraternal twins to have similar IQs?

M: According to this study, yes.

W₂: OK, but come on. Intelligence can't all be in the genes. Think about the implications. Surely there are studies that support the nurturists.

M: Indeed there are. Researchers looked at the IQs of both fraternal twins and identical twins who were raised in adequate conditions with those of twins raised in poor conditions. What they found was that when poverty is considered, environment is more important than genes.

W₁: Wait a minute! How did they figure that?

M: Well, twins raised in adequate conditions have less intellectual variation than those raised in poor conditions. Remember the first study when the environment was controlled, or kept the same? Identical twins were more alike than fraternal twins. All of these twins had the same educational advantages. What the next study found was that identical twins without educational advantages were not as similar as those who had them. Understand?

W₁: I think so.

M: So, as you can see, nature and nurture are not mutually exclusive. Human behaviors are a result of an interaction between genetics and the environment. Of course, nobody believes that human behaviors are entirely genetic, but research such as twin studies suggests that there is probably a role for the genes in shaping the people we become.

02 Biology

W: Everyone knows that the giant squid is, well, giant. It's extremely large, up to fourteen meters long. If it were swimming next to your boat, you'd definitely notice it. If it were swimming next to you in the ocean, you'd probably want to get out of the water as soon as possible. In any case, if there's a giant squid nearby, someone is going to see it, and obviously, people have reported first-hand accounts of giant squid sightings. The squid appears in all sorts of drawings and stories, dating back hundreds of years. It even appears in Herman Melville's classic, *Moby Dick*, published in 1851. However, even though it's easy to see when it shows up, it just doesn't seem to show up that often. This species has never been scientifically observed alive in nature. It has never been filmed, and there are no pictures of a full-grown specimen. Around fifteen dead ones are found every year, but there is not much we can learn from dead specimens. Several juveniles were caught near New Zealand in 2003, but very little was learned from them, since they all died soon after capture.

So, where are all the squid you may ask? They must be somewhere. After all, other animals eat them. They are common prey for sperm whales. Scientists have often found squid parts in the stomachs of sperm whales. Also, whales have been caught with scars on their bodies, which look like they were made by the suckers of squid tentacles. These suckers have rows of teeth, like oversized needles. If sperm whales often eat giant squid, then the squid must be fairly plentiful. In addition, the whales must know where the squid are. In fact, a recent attempt to find giant squid actually used sperm whales themselves. Scientists placed special video cameras on the whales. The scientists hoped that the whales would go looking for squid to eat, and in the process, would collect some useful video footage of the squid. This may have been a good idea. The whales did dive down to several hundred feet, so maybe this is where the squid live. Unfortunately, they found no squid, and the cameras only recorded black water.

What makes the giant squid so elusive? The most widely accepted theory is that the giant squid simply move around a lot. According to this hypothesis, the squid normally live about two thousand feet below the ocean's surface. This is where they do much of their feeding. We assume that these squid eat mostly fish. Fish parts, particularly lantern fish, have been found in the bellies of dissected giant squid corpses. Because they are so big, the giant squid must eat a lot of fish. This means they're going to have to spend much of their time looking for sufficient food supplies. They wouldn't stay in any one place for long. The animals are also going to be looking for food at different depths. This explains why squid have been seen on the surface of the ocean at certain times. It may even be that giant squid mate at higher depths. All of this makes finding giant squid very difficult.

There are some problems with this theory that the squid are always moving around, though. The most important one is that the squid, as I stated before, are frequently eaten by sperm whales. There are clearly enough giant squid to provide the whales with a lot of food, and the whales know where to find these squid in large numbers. If the squid really moved around so much that even one is difficult to find, how can sperm whales find and eat them so easily? It may be that the squid move to certain places at regular times. Sperm whales may know where these places are, and when the giant squid will be easy to find there. For the time being, there is no clear answer.

Chapter 2

Skill A

01 Campus Life

W: Hello, I'm one of students who needs to take the first aid certification course in order to go on the winter-break meteorological expedition.

M: OK, which course date did you want to sign up for? There are two courses offered every month, except for November, when we have three. The courses are all two weeks long.

W: What are the times?

M: Well, next month there are two courses. There's a morning and an evening course. The morning course is from 8:00 a.m. to noon, and the evening course from 5:00 to 9:00 p.m.

W: Huh, well you see I go to class during the day and work at night... There's no weekend course?

M: I'm afraid not. The expedition starts in January, right?

W: That's right, we leave January 3rd.

M: Well, you could take the course in December after your finals are over.

W: Huh, yeah I guess I'll have to. How much is this course?

M: It's 300 dollars, which includes all aspects of first aid, including CPR and mouth-to-mouth resuscitation.

W: Who's the course instructor?

M: Jeff Fulbright. He's a retired paramedic with over 35 years of experience. This is a nationally recognized qualification.

W: What is CPR exactly?

M: It stands for cardio-pulmonary resuscitation. Basically, it's what you perform on a patient who isn't breathing or whose heart isn't beating. It's like giving a car a jumpstart.

W: What do you mean?

M: Well, you know when you jumpstart a car, the battery is out of juice. So, you connect it to another car's battery using jumper cables and use the energy from the working car to revive the dead battery. After that, the battery should replenish itself and be OK.

W: Right.

M: Same principle. With CPR, the heart has stopped beating, so you kind of pump the heart back to life by applying pressure to the chest in rhythmic intervals. You're like the battery giving juice to the battery without juice. Hopefully, by doing CPR, you will get the heart to start beating on its own again.

W: That sounds like a handy skill.

M: Sure is. The course will also give you some useful procedures for your expedition, like how to treat hypothermia and frostbite.

W: That's good, though hopefully I'll never need it.

M: Hopefully, you'll never need any of the training, but it's better to have it and not need it than to need it and not have it.

W: Well, can I sign up for the morning course in December, then?

M: Sure, you can fill out this form and pay the 300 dollars in cash, by check, or debit card. Or, if you want to, you can register online at the website listed at the bottom of the form.

W: I see. Is there a registration deadline or anything?

M: The cut-off date for registration is one week prior to the start date, but it's best to register as far in advance as possible. It's rare, but sometimes the courses do fill up.

W: Well, OK, thanks for all your help!

M: No problem. Have a nice day.

02 Geography

M: Who can tell me which African country has the strongest economy? Of all the countries on the African continent, which one has the largest and most developed economy?

W₁: Kenya?

M: No, I'm sorry. Try again.

W₂: I would guess South Africa. It's probably got the most modern infrastructure of all the African countries.

M: And you would be right. Now, let me tell you a little bit about the place. First of all, South Africa is located at the southern tip of the African continent and is home to about 45 million people. One interesting tidbit is that it is one of the few countries in Africa that has never had a coup d'etat. A coup d'etat, of course, is when a group, such as the military, takes over the government. So, the South African government has never been overthrown. Today, it is one of the most stable democracies in that part of the world. Now, that's not to say that there haven't been problems in South Africa. I bet you can guess what I'm referring to.

W₂: Apartheid?

M: Very good. Who can explain apartheid?

W₁: Literally it means "apartness" or "separateness." I think it comes from Dutch, because the Dutch were the first European settlers there. Anyway, as I read somewhere, apartheid was the systematic segregation of the races. You know, like for example, non-whites had to use different toilets from white people.

M: Yes, under apartheid, the government maintained a policy of separating the white minority and the black majority. Keep in mind that we're talking about minority rule here. Early on, black people were barred from being members of parliament. It was a whites-only government. Now, apartheid was established in 1948 by the Nationalist Party. Effectively, black people in South Africa lived in a different world from that of the whites. They were required, by law, to live in certain areas called reserves and were denied the right to vote. There was a long struggle for democracy over the next fifty-odd years, and it was not just the black majority who wanted to bring an end to apartheid. There were other ethnic groups who suffered under apartheid as well. Just to give you an idea of the demographics, there are four major ethnic groups in South Africa. Under apartheid, they were classified legally as black, white, Indian, and "colored." Don't confuse the term colored with the old derogatory term for black people in the United States. In South Africa, it meant people of mixed race. The term is still used today, but since many don't like it, and since it has a different historical meaning in the US, I will use the term "mixed race" to avoid confusion. OK? Now, as I was saying, the demographics break down like this: 75% are black, 13.6% are white, 8.6% are mixed race, and then 2.6% are Indian. Now, like I said, the people of mixed race and of Indian descent supported the effort to bring down apartheid, and I should add that a few of the white people did as well. So, after a long and difficult struggle, apartheid was dismantled by F.W. De Klerk in 1990. Yes, do you have a question?

W₂: Does everyone speak English in South Africa?

M: No, not necessarily. Most people do, I think, but there are actually eleven official languages. English is one, and I'm sure you've all heard of Afrikaans? That's the language of the Dutch settlers. It sort of evolved into a new language over the centuries of Dutch settlement. The most commonly spoken language that's native to the area, I believe, would be Zulu. Then there are others, but I won't get into them right now... They should be in your book. Anyway, back to the different ethnic groups for a moment. You should be aware that South Africa has the largest population of people of European descent in Africa, and the largest Indian population outside of Asia. Not only that, it also has the largest mixed race community in Africa. Now, as I was saying earlier, South Africa has the largest economy of all the countries on the African continent. It has a labor force of more than 13 million people. If we look at a breakdown of those 13-million-or-so workers, we can see that 35% of workers are employed in services, 30% work in agriculture, 20% in industry, and 9% work in mining. The remaining 6% are employed in other fields. OK, so that's some general information about South Africa's demographics and economy. Now let's talk about their education system.

03 Chemistry

W: I know you are all very familiar with the periodic table, but do you know the history of it? That's what we are going to talk about today. OK, so as you know, the function of the periodic table is to organize chemical elements on the basis of their chemical properties. Over time, as we've learned more about the different elements, we've had to change the table. So, the table we know today has evolved over the years in conjunction with the science of chemistry. Originally, the elements were ordered according to their atomic mass in relation to the mass of a hydrogen atom, which is set at one atomic mass unit. Um, let me put that another way. The mass of a hydrogen atom is set at one. OK? And then using that as the standard weight, all other atomic masses are measured in relation to it. That was how things were done at first... how the table was ordered. Over time, certain recurring patterns were noticed with regards to the atomic mass of elements. For example, in 1817, Johann Dobereiner noticed that some elements could be grouped together in threes, and the grouping had to do with the relationship between the atomic masses. You see, he observed that for some groups of three elements, if you ordered them according to their atomic masses, you would find that the element in the middle would have an atomic mass that was halfway between that of the other two. In other words, the mass of the middle element was an average of the other two. Let's refer to the periodic table in the book. Look at the elements lithium, which is LI number 3, sodium,

which is NA number 11, and potassium, which is K number 19. If you add up the atomic masses of all three, which we don't have listed here on this table, then divide by three, your answer is the same as the atomic mass of sodium. That's the Law of Triads. Another pattern was observed in 1863 by John Newlands. He devised the Law of Octaves. As you might guess from the name, it involves sets of eight. This law states that elements behave similarly to elements whose mass differs from them by a multiple of eight. In other words, every eighth element, when grouped according to atomic mass, has similar properties.

Dmitri Mendeleev is considered the "father" of the modern periodic table. What he did was he wrote out the names, atomic masses, and other properties of each known element on separate cards. Then, he ordered them according to their atomic mass. He noticed, like his predecessors, that certain properties repeated periodically. Not all of the elements fit the pattern neatly, though, so Mendeleev had to move some elements into new positions, despite their atomic mass. Although some nice patterns had been observed, the table was not yet perfect. So Mendeleev didn't actually make the table we see in our book today, but he did put us on the path toward this table.

The problems Mendeleev had with his groupings were solved almost fifty years later when Henry Gwyn-Jeffries Mosely developed a system of assigning an atomic number to each element. Notice I said "atomic number" not "atomic mass." Try not to confuse those two. An element's atomic number is based on the number of protons within the nucleus of the atom of the element. So, the atomic number of an element is equal to the number of protons in the atomic nucleus. This proved to be a far more functional way to order the elements than by ordering them by atomic mass or by groupings. By ordering the elements according to their atomic number rather than their atomic mass, the problems with Mendeleev's table disappeared, and hence, a far more comprehensive periodic table was born.

So now, as you can see in your book, the table is organized into rows and columns. Each row is referred to as a period, and each column is referred to as a group. In some groups, all of the members of the group display similar properties. In general, we can say that elements share more similar properties with other elements in the same group than with other elements elsewhere in the table. However, there are a few periods — or rows — in which the elements share significant similarities. Does that make sense? What I mean is that any given element is a member of two things: a period, which is identified by the row it falls in, and a group, which is identified by which column it falls in. Got that? And in some of the periods the member elements have similar properties. Then the columns are the groups, and within the groups many of the elements share physical characteristics and chemical behavior.

04 History

M: We've talked about Roman mythology, which is adopted from Greek mythology when the Romans took over Greece. So, the Romans basically worshiped the same deities as the Greeks, but changed their names, right? There were various deities like Jupiter, who was known as Zeus to the Greeks, and the Roman god Mars, who was Ares in Greek mythology. I won't name them all right now. But basically, you should remember that the gods were typically associated with natural occurrences and other phenomena — kind of as a way to explain things that people saw around them. One example is this — in order to explain the movement of the sun across the sky, Romans believed, as did the Greeks, that a god rode a chariot across the sky, carrying the sun from east to west each day. This god the Romans named Sol, which is where we get the word sun.

Anyway, that was the state religion of the Roman Empire (before Christianity was established, that is). As the Empire expanded, the Romans came into contact with foreign people with different beliefs. Remember, the Roman Empire was huge. At its peak, it included all of the countries around the Mediterranean Sea, and much of northern Europe as well. So, the Romans encountered a lot of different cultures. Now, the state generally tolerated the people's beliefs in the other regions, so long as they didn't interfere with the power of the state.

Before we begin talking about the Roman cults, I want you to understand that the term cult, as we are using it here, does not have the same negative connotation that it has today. We are simply talking about worship. The foreign cults of Rome were groups that did not worship the deities that were the norm in Rome. The foreign cults worshiped different deities. Over time, some of these gods and goddesses were incorporated into the Roman religion, while others were suppressed. So, what began as tolerance for other religious beliefs led to the gradual incorporation of some aspects of those other belief systems.

Some of the more well known deities of the foreign cults included Isis and Mithras. Isis was the Egyptian goddess of fertility and motherhood. Mithras was the Persian sun god who emphasized strength and courage in the battle of good and evil. These are two examples of deities who were accepted into Roman mythology. Some time around the fourth century, things changed in the Roman Empire. The cults related to all the various gods pretty much disappeared in Rome. Christianity became the new state religion. It had been gaining in popularity up to that time, but it was still in competition with the earlier cults. Christianity became the official religion of Rome under the emperor Theodosius. At this time, all other forms of worship were banned, and as such, the other cults either disappeared or were practiced in secrecy. It is interesting to note, however, that quite a few elements of worship from these earlier faiths were incorporated into Christianity. Perhaps this was done in order to appeal to a wider range of people. For example, the standard day of worship for Jews — I mean those Jews who became known as Christians — their day of worship was the Sabbath, the last day of the week. But this day of worship for Christians shifted from the seventh day of the week to the first day, Sunday, which is named for Sol, the god we were talking about earlier, who, by the way, was the most important deity in the Roman pantheon. Another example of a borrowed tradition is the use of evergreen boughs and trees to decorate the home in winter. This was a long-standing tradition among many cultures to celebrate the winter solstice and the return of the sun's strength. Today's tradition of a decorated Christmas tree is a direct descendant of those earlier practices. And while we're on the topic of Christmas, there is the interesting choice of December 25th as the celebration of Jesus's birth. This was also the traditional day on which the earlier Roman cults celebrated the birthday of Mithras.

To recap, then, the rulers of the ancient Roman Empire allowed foreign religions, including Christianity, to exist as long as they did not interfere with their power. During the first few centuries A.D., Christianity became more and more popular in the empire, and in the fourth century, it became Rome's official religion by decree of then-emperor Theodosius. In order to gain acceptance from a wide base of the Roman population, Christianity adopted many aspects of other predominant religions of the time.

05 Campus Life

M: Come in.

W: Excuse me, Professor Altmann? Am I disturbing you? I have a question about the exam.

M: No, come in, come in. What is it with you students? Always worried about disturbing me. Why is that?

W: Well, I don't know. Aren't professors really busy preparing classes and doing research?

M: Yes, yes, that's true, but you see — forgive me, what was your name?

W: Emily.

M: Ah yes, Emily. You see Emily, these office hours are not my time to be making class preparations or doing my research. This is my time that is available for the students. This is why I am here now. Your tuition fees are paying for my house and car and the hot dog I ate for lunch. In return, I teach you about human behavior, if I can, and I hold office hours for you to converse with me. You see, it's an — economic exchange.

W: Really? So we can just come in anytime to chat?

M: Well, yes. During the office hours, basically, yes, but it's always nice to be a bit prepared of course.

W: What do you mean?

M: Well, as you know, there are many students, and only eight office hours per week, so we want to use this time wisely and efficiently.

W: Oh, like I should prepare a specific question.

M: Yes, that's always nice of course. Having a specific reason is a great start and can accelerate the process. Some students, you know, they want to get a good reference, so they come by all the time just to chat so that I know them well. Although I certainly want to get to know the students in my classes, that's too much, you know.

W: So, mainly these office hours are just if we're having problems in the course.

M: No, no, also if you would like some, aah, further clarification of some concept as well, but if you do come in for a problem, don't just come in and say, "Oh no! Oh help! I will never pass, it is hopeless, please help me professor." Then, I have to spend an hour asking questions to ascertain the specific problem, and sometimes, students want me to figure out an adequate paper topic for them and get them started on their research. That is OK, but you need to come with some ideas, something to start with.

W: OK, that all makes sense. Wow, thanks for taking the time to explain this to me. I should have been taking advantage of the office hours system a lot more over the past two years. They really should explain this to us when we start at the university.

M: Ah, yes, this would make perfect sense, but do they do it? No. It needs doing, though. Then, I have to do it. You don't have to tell me.

W: I wonder if there is some way to suggest it. Like is there someone in charge of freshman orientation who could be told about this problem?

M: That sounds like an excellent question for your academic advisor.

W: Oh, you're right. I'll have to ask her the next time I go see her.

M: Anyway, Emily, how can I help you today?

06 Business

W: TM. We are all used to seeing the symbol of a tiny T and a tiny M in the top right-hand corner of the name or logo of a company, but what does that TM really mean? Today, I'm going to explain just what a trademark is and what function it serves. Trademarks are an important part of brands and branding. I will start by defining trademarks, and then I will move on to explain different kinds of trademarks. OK. Generally speaking, a trademark can be defined as any word, name, phrase, design, logo, or picture implemented by a company to identify its goods and differentiate themselves and their products from the competition. That was a long definition, so let me repeat it for you. A trademark can be defined as any word, name, phrase, design, logo, or picture implemented by a company to identify its goods and differentiate themselves and their products from the competition. Trademarks are registered. That means companies notify a particular office in the country where they operate about the trademark. We could say that a trademark is a kind of ID badge, so to speak. Can anyone think of any examples of well-known trademarks?

M₁: Well, how about Coke?

W: Good example. That particular name can only be used by the Coca-Cola Company precisely because it is a trademark. When a company owns a trademark, it can enforce its use and protect its rights by preventing unauthorized use of the product's name or design. So, for example, no other company can call their drink "Coke" and no one can copy the Coca-Cola logo without permission. So, here we have the basics of trademarks. However, their use is not without problems, which brings me to genericized trademarks. Does anyone know what I mean by that?

M₂: I guess it must have something to do with generic products. Like, for example, Q-tips. The real name of the product is a cotton swab, but most people call them Q-tips.

W: You hit it on the nose. That's exactly what a genericized trademark is. Sometimes a trademark becomes synonymous with the generic name of the products or services to which it relates. It then replaces it in everyday speech and makes it difficult for the company to exert its proprietorship. Trademark owners need to be careful not to lose control of how their trademark is used. Like you said, Q-tip is a good example. Another one is the Bikini. I'm sure no one here today identifies "bikini" with any one particular company. To most people, a bikini is any two-piece swimsuit for women. Can you think of any other examples?

M₁: Is aspirin a genericized trademark?

W: Yes. Very good. Some other well known examples are kleenex and popsicles. Anyone surprised? I see that a few of you are. Next time you're in the store, you might recognize a few more. OK, so when a trademark becomes genericized, it's a problem. But what can a company really do? The best thing to do is to try to prevent it from happening. One way to prevent it is to avoid using the trademark as a verb or noun. A good example would be Rollerblade. Rollerblade can be used as a noun or as a verb. Someone might say, "I bought some new Rollerblades," referring to any new inline skates, or they might suggest going rollerblading. A good way for a company to prevent this from happening is to discourage generalization of that company's name in their marketing. That reminds me of another example. Do you remember the old Band-Aid commercial? "I am stuck on Band-Aid, cause Band-Aid's stuck on me!"? That's another example, isn't it? Band-Aid. What that company did was change their jingle to "I am stuck on Band-Aid brand, cause Band-Aid's stuck on me." That reinforced the idea that Band-Aid is a brand and not a product name. Another example is Xerox. Because that was the first brand of photocopiers, people started saying that they were "xeroxing" a document. Xerox then started an extensive marketing campaign to push the word "photocopying."

M₂: But, wouldn't it sort of be in the company's interest for generalization to happen?

W: Well, it certainly is a good sign for the company if their brand is genericized. That means it's popular, right? And it's true that many companies overlook the day-to-day use of their brand name to describe a product. However, there is a risk of losing control of your trademark. You see, it is possible to lose the rights and protection of the trademark if the name becomes too common. For example, Sony had registered the "Walkman" as a trademark, but the word became so commonly identified with the product, that they lost their rights to the brand name.

Skill B

01 Campus Life

M: Is there something I can help you with?

W: Yes, I have a few questions about that online tutoring service. I can't remember what it's called.

M: You mean Smartthinking.com? I think I can probably answer any questions you might have. What would you like to know?

W: Well, I'm thinking of enrolling, but there are a couple of things I'd like to know first. Like for one thing, are there any restrictions on log on times? I usually do my work late at night, so it won't be much use to me if it can only be accessed during regular working hours.

M: Not to worry. You are free to log on anytime, anywhere.

W: That's good to hear. I've also heard that there is some kind of writing clinic or something. What can you tell me about that?

M: Ah, you mean the writing lab. Yes, what that is is a tool to help you improve your writing. You can submit your writing to the online writing lab, and you will receive a critique with some constructive criticism to help you develop your writing skills. It's also open twenty-four hours a day, seven days a week.

W: That should be helpful. Will I get an instant reply?

M: It won't be instant, but you will receive a reply within 24 hours. We give priority to distance education students because it is impossible for them to consult their instructors face-to-face, but everyone using Smartthinking will get a fast response. Remember the 24-hour rule, though. If you have a paper due at eight o'clock the following morning, you probably won't get your response in time. Always submit your work at least two days before the paper is due. Be sure to leave yourself enough time to do revisions as well.

W: What about security? Is there any chance somebody could get a hold of my paper and copy it for themselves?

M: Absolutely not. Everyone who has access to submissions in the writing lab is accountable.

W: Oh! The papers go to a writing lab? So these aren't English professors who are giving feedback?

M: No. Your paper will be evaluated by a graduate student who works in our writing lab. Most of them are English majors. But even if they're not, they all have a strong background in writing.

W: I see. Now, I know that the tutoring program is free, but is there any kind of registration fee for first-time users?

M: No. There are no charges at all. However, only students currently enrolled at Citywide Community College can use Smartthinking. It has been set up to provide academic support for our students, so unfortunately, we can't offer the service to anyone else. Are you currently enrolled at this community college?

W: Yes.

M: Great. What kind of computer do you have?

W: I have a Mac. That won't be a problem, will it?

M: No, not at all. As long as you have Internet Explorer, you'll be able to log on to the online tutoring system with no difficulties. I assume that you have a modem?

W: Right, I have a 56K modem.

M: That's fine. Then all you need to do now is choose your subjects and sign up.

W: Can I sign up right now?

M: Of course. Those two computers right over there have Internet access. You can use either one to log on and sign up.

W: Great. Thanks.

02 History

W: I hope you'll all recall our lively discussion of Renaissance art from last week. We talked about such artists as Botticelli and DaVinci, who really characterized the Renaissance through their artwork. Art, however, is not created in a vacuum. Art is a reflection of the world, through the eyes of the artist. So, what was going on in the world to inspire such great art? Well, that's the topic of today's lecture. We're going to talk about the intellectual and social movement that underlay the Renaissance. The movement was called humanism. So, what is humanism? Let's go back to the word "Renaissance." As we talked about last time, the word means "re-birth," and that's just what humanism was. It was a revival of antiquity. Antiquity, in this case, refers to the classic civilizations of Greece and Rome. Now, following the fall of the Roman Empire, we had about a thousand odd years in which... well...nothing of note in the art world really happened. These we call the Middle Ages. Now, the dominant school of thought during the late Middle Ages was called scholasticism. That's "scholastic," like school related things, plus "ism" — scholasticism. A large part of humanism, the new idea in the Renaissance, was its rejection of scholasticism. The humanists felt that the scholastics were focusing too much on the Church. So, the humanists were rejecting the predominant, intellectual school in favor of the classics. The humanists studied the classical civilizations of ancient Greece and Rome and applied what they learned to their current society. It's not that the scholastics didn't know about the classics, they just tried to analyze them in such a way that the classics agreed with the Church. That was their whole purpose, to find ways to reconcile Greek and Roman philosophy with Christian theology. In the minds of the humanists, society had been going in the wrong direction since the fall of the Roman Empire. Not that they wanted to return to those times, but they felt that more could be learned from antiquity than from anything that had happened since. It was this revival of old ideas that changed the way that European people in the late Middle Ages thought. Humanist thinkers started to create new kinds of art and literature. They even changed the way societies thought about education, law, and, well, everything. Simply put, humanism was the basis of the Renaissance.

Now, as you may know, Renaissance thought started in Italy and spread to the rest of Europe. Most of the painters that we talked about yesterday, in fact, were Italian, but why Italy? The answer may surprise you. It was because of Latin. Remember, the humanists were looking back to the ancient civilizations. Much of the writings would have been done in Latin, right? Now, Italy was the only place where Latin was still studied outside of the church. As for the rest of Europe, only the clergy learned Latin because it was considered the language of the Church and didn't really have any other use. So, it seems only natural that these Italian Latin speakers would be the initiators of a review of classic literature. If we want to point to one person who began the humanist movement, it would have to be Petrarch. In case you don't know, Petrarch was an Italian poet who was influenced by Cicero. Cicero, of course, was a famous politician in the final years of the Roman Republic. So, what Petrarch did was translate a lot of Cicero's correspondence — letters to different people — and he also tried to imitate Cicero's style in his own Latin writing. Petrarch's revival of the teachings of Cicero was really what began the humanist movement, which of course, spread from Italy throughout Europe.

Now, some of the social factors that existed in Italy at this time are important to note. You see, Italy at this time consisted of two republics: Florence and Venice. However, there were neighboring states that were not republics but instead were under despotic rule. Some of these despotic states were interested in taking over the republics, so the people of Florence and Venice felt threatened. Petrarch was from Florence. Now, it's a common occurrence that when a state feels threatened, its people tend to feel patriotic. It's kind of like a defense mechanism. So, feeling threatened, the intellectuals in Florence followed Petrarch's lead and began to appreciate the past. Florence had a rich history, and people wanted to celebrate it. Those outside pressures were fanning the flames of patriotism.

03 Computers

W: OK, class, let's take a quick survey, shall we? Jake, what is the hard drive capacity of your home computer?

M₁: 80 gigs.

W: 80 gigabytes! That's 80 billion bytes, or 640 billion ones and zeros. How did I arrive at that answer? Anybody?

M₂: Well, a gigabyte is a billion bytes. So 80 gigabytes is 80 billion bites. Then, a byte is 8 bits. A bit, of course, is a one or a zero. So, if you've got 80 billion bytes, you multiply by 8 to get the number of bits. 80 times 8 is 640, so 80 billion bytes is 640 billion bits.

W: Well done. Now, that is no small amount of information on your personal computer, Jake. In fact, though, that is the current standard for home computers. We've come a long way, haven't we? Computer memory, as you probably know, actually had very humble beginnings, and I'm going to tell you about those beginnings today. We're going to look at the history of computer memory, have a look at how fast technology is improving, and consider what the future has in store. OK, does anyone here remember the early Altair and Commodore computers?

M₁: I've heard about them. I don't think I've ever seen one, though.

W: Never seen one? Great, well, I hate to give away my age here, but my first computer was actually a Commodore. Anyway, these antiques used paper tapes and cassette tapes, if you can believe that. To load a program, we would put the cassette in and press play! It took forever. That seems really antiquated to us now, but at the time, it seemed pretty high tech. Now we're used to tremendous capacity and high speeds. Anyway, the first big breakthrough was when Steve Wozniak, co-founder of Apple, introduced the floppy disk. These were originally five and a quarter inches across, and they stored a measly 160 kilobytes. Yes, Tom?

M₂: Why were they called floppy, anyway? I've always wondered that.

W: Because they were floppy. Many of you younger people may not remember these either, but these disks were actually floppy and bendable. You know, I think I may still have one in my attic.

I'll bring it to class next time. Anyway, the direct descendant of the floppy was the hard three-and-a-half inch disks you are probably more familiar with. Even though they were hard, they retained the name "floppy" so as not to be confused with hardware or hard drives. At first, both disks were sold, so people usually distinguished them by their size when they talked about them. So the three-and-a-half inch floppy came out in the mid-80s with a capacity of 1.44 megabytes, which seemed like an awful lot at the time. For a few years, home computers featured drives for both the five-and-a-quarter inch and for the three-and-a-half inch, but by the mid-90s, the older five-and-a-quarter diskette had become obsolete. In our current times, we are witnessing the extinction of the 3.5 inch disk, aren't we? Actually, Jake, could you tell us what kind of external memory interface your computer has?

M₁: It came with a CD/DVD read/write drive and two USB ports, where I can use my memory stick.

W: It doesn't have any floppy drive at all?

M₁: Nope. I didn't need it, and I didn't want it. My memory stick holds 512 megabytes. Why would I need to use disks?

W: I don't blame you. Not to mention that CDs have a capacity of 700 megabytes. DVDs can store 4.7 gigabytes, and you say your memory stick holds 512 megs? I just bought the latest model on the market, and it holds 140 gigabytes! So you're right, who needs disks anymore? While it is still possible to find a computer with a floppy disk drive, I predict that in the very near future, you won't be able to find them. Do you know what else is funny? These devices are only going to get better. Anyone reading a transcript of this lecture one year in the future would probably find these figures laughable, just as we were laughing at the five-and-a-quarter inch disks. And when we tell our grandkids about how we lived, they will think it's hilarious. The rate of technological improvement in this day and age is astounding. To demonstrate, have you heard the new buzzword, "terabyte lifestyle"? A terabyte equals 1,024 gigabytes. It is estimated that in five years, the home computer will have a five terabyte hard drive. Amazing, isn't it?

04 Theater

M: Are any of you guys members of a fraternity or a sorority organization? Quite a few of you. Good, uh, Luanne, what is the traditional party during homecoming?

W: You mean like the kind of party? The toga party, I guess. We all get dressed up in bed sheets.

M: Right, the toga, the traditional dress of ancient Rome. That's what we're going to talk about today. Since we're studying Julius Caesar, that would of course be the type of costume we need to design for the actors. So if we want to create authentic costumes, we have to know something about the history of this type of clothing. Now, in the beginning, the toga was a large woolen blanket. The ancient Romans would wrap it around their body for clothing.

W: Wasn't it just the upper class that wore the toga?

M: At first, no. What you may be thinking of is the law that non-citizens were not permitted to wear togas. It was actually forbidden for foreigners to wear togas. But pretty much all Romans wore the toga ubiquitously for all kinds of different occasions. That didn't last too long, though, because as you can imagine, or Luanne, as you probably know, the toga is a little awkward. It's OK to party in a bed sheet, but try farming or going to war in one. So, for activities that involved a lot of movement, the toga fell out of fashion in favor of more practical garb. Instead, the use of

the toga in Rome became more and more restricted to formal occasions. That's good news for us because the characters in Julius Caesar interact in mostly formal settings.

Now let me just tell you a bit about the actual toga itself. Historians believe togas were made from five and a half meter semi-circles of cloth. The cloth was cut in a big half-circle, not a rectangle like bed sheets. This cloth was, of course, wrapped around the body, and a sash was worn over the left shoulder and under the right arm. To keep the thing from falling off — and we certainly don't want the togas on our actors to slip off during a show — the toga was pinned up with pins. These were called *fivulate* in case you're interested. I have some pictures of authentic Roman *fivulate* on display in museums, so we can try to copy some of those designs for our costumes. Another option we have is to make a belt for some characters. Some Romans wore their togas with belts.

Now, when we think of togas, we picture everyone wearing pretty much identical outfits, right? Basically, white bed sheets for all. Not quite. There were actually many kinds. For example, the *toga virilis*, or men's toga, was worn by adult male citizens. Women, on the other hand, had their own version of the toga called the *skola*. *Toga pulla*, or black togas, had two functions. People of the lower classes wore them regularly, and people of the upper class would wear them after the death of a loved one to show that they were in mourning. That's important for us. We'll have to costume the slaves in our show in black togas. There was also a special kind of toga which featured a purple stripe and was worn by high-ranking officials and upper-class boys, or the painted toga, which was very ornate and worn on festive occasions by upper-class officials. Did anyone actually wear plain white togas? Actually, yes. The pure-white *toga candida* was worn by senatorial candidates. Guess what. That is actually what most of our actors will need! We'll take a look at the character list for our cast a little later, but for the most part, it looks like our costuming will be pretty easy. We'll need mostly plain white togas that are just big half-circles of cloth. That just means cutting and hemming. We'll also need to decide which characters to assign pins and sashes and which ones will get belts. Actually, the hardest job for the costumer in this show may be teaching all of the actors how to correctly put on their togas.

We haven't talked about footwear yet. Of course, our senators in this show aren't going to be running around the stage barefoot. So let's take a look at how authentic Roman sandals looked.

05 Astronomy

M: The invention of the telescope had a huge impact on our understanding of not only the universe, but also of our place in it. It changed the way that people viewed our world, and our world's place in the universe. Before the telescope allowed us to get a closer look at what was up in the sky, people believed that the Earth was the center of the universe, and everything else revolved around it. You can imagine why. The sun rises in the east and sets in the west. Why wouldn't people think that the sun was moving? It wasn't until the early seventeenth century, when Galileo invented the telescope and looked into the sky, that we found out this idea was wrong.

Galileo didn't just point his telescope up at the sky and say "Eureka!" He observed the sky by night and day for many years. The first discovery Galileo made with his telescope was that the moon had mountains and valleys. That may seem like a pretty mundane discovery to us. Even little kids know that today. But back then, it must have sounded pretty shocking. Another important thing he learned was that the stars are much further away from the Earth than the moon. And I'm sure there were plenty of people at that time who were uncomfortable with this idea. You see, it had been presumed that the stars were simply much smaller than the moon, but they were all part of this same sphere around the Earth. Galileo proved that assumption wrong. He noticed that when looking at the sky through a telescope, the moon seemed much bigger, but the stars were still tiny dots of light. How could that be if they were all part of the same sphere? Galileo concluded that the stars must be much further away. They appear smaller than the moon not because they are smaller, but because they are so far away. They don't look much bigger through a telescope because they're really, really far away!

His next major discovery was that Jupiter had four moons orbiting it. This dispelled another common misconception about objects and bodies in space. In Galileo's day, everyone thought that the Earth was the only body that had objects that orbited it. This assumption was based on the fact that everything that could be observed from Earth seemed to revolve around the Earth. They couldn't see anything that revolved around other bodies. So, the telescope not only gave people a better look at those bodies that they were familiar with, but it also allowed them to see things that they previously couldn't see at all. Galileo and other astronomers who were starting to follow his lead soon found more bodies in the solar system than anyone had thought.

Then, Galileo observed that Venus has phases, just like our moon. Through his telescope, sometimes Venus appeared as a crescent, and sometimes it was full. Now, by studying these phases, he deduced that Venus actually orbited the sun. Remember, people didn't know at the time that all of the planets orbited the sun. They firmly believed that everything orbited the Earth, so this was an important discovery leading to our current understanding of the solar system.

Galileo's discoveries and the notion that the Earth is not the center of the universe was a very difficult concept for people to accept. In fact, Galileo faced a great deal of opposition from the Church. During the Inquisition, he was arrested, threatened with torture, and put under house arrest for the last nine years of his life. Today, we consider Galileo one of the most important scientists of all time. We have to remember that people felt very threatened by science in early times. Many people felt that science was in opposition to religion. In fact, some people still feel that way today. But that's another story.

Today, we know that not only is the Earth not the center of the universe, it's not even the center of our own solar system, and our sun is not the center of the universe either. It's just one of millions of stars in an infinite universe. You can see why this kind of information made some people feel a little insecure. Galileo's ideas make the Earth seem pretty insignificant in the grand scheme of things, doesn't it?

06 Campus Life

W: Hey, what's that you're looking at there? Can I see?

M: What? Oh, hi Mara. Yeah, I'm just reading the campus newspaper.

W: The campus newspaper? Do people really read that? Is there anything interesting in it?

M: Yeah, actually. I was just reading an article in this issue on crime statistics for this university.

W: Campus crime? Surely crime isn't a problem here at our school?

M: If you had asked me ten minutes ago I would have said no...and... well...I guess overall it really isn't, although it would be interesting to compare the situation with a couple of other schools.

W: So, what does the article say about crime here? I didn't realize there was any. You never hear about anything.

M: Well, the article gives the figures for the past three years. Overall, the number of crimes committed has increased, but not in every category.

W: Oh? So, what kinds of crimes were committed? What kinds have increased?

M: Well, as you might expect, nothing too serious. I mean, there weren't any murders or anything like that.

W: Glad to hear it. I guess that's something we would have heard about.

M: But there were a lot of cases of theft.

W: Hmmm, I suppose I did hear of several people who had their laptops ripped off, actually, and wallets tend to disappear, too, don't they?

M: Right. I was shocked to find out that the number of thefts doubled from 34 to 70 during the first two years reported in this article.

W: Wow. That's a massive jump.

M: But then there was a decrease last year.

W: What are the figures for last year?

M: Still high, but only 60 as opposed to 70 for the previous year.

W: Perhaps we can thank the new security cameras.

M: Well, that's what I was thinking, but in fact, the number of burglaries soared from only 1 two years ago to 9 last year. Here's how I see it. Laptops have become more common, so that may explain the increase in theft in recent years. People started carrying valuable things around with them. Then, a lot of people had them stolen, and a lot of people heard about it. Then they started being more careful with their stuff as of last year, and because people were being more careful with their stuff when they were out and about, the thieves had to resort to burglary. That's just my guess.

W: That sounds reasonable. So, any other kinds of crimes?

M: There were two sex offenses in the first year reported in this article, but none in the next two years.

W: Well that's good. I hope it's not a case of them not being reported though.

M: Good point. There were also two cases of weapon possession last year. That's a new crime. There were no prior cases of that.

W: Do you mind if I borrow your newspaper after you finish with it? I'd like to read the rest of that article.

Skill C

01 Campus Life

W: What is that weird phone for, anyway?

M: The one with the blue lights?

W: Yeah.

M: That's an emergency phone. You just push the red button, and you get campus security.

W: I guess that's a good idea. It probably works more as a deterrent than a phone though.

M: What do you mean?

W: Well, I was just thinking that if you were going to attack somebody, you wouldn't do it anywhere near a blue light phone.

M: Yeah, I guess I never thought of that. It can also be used for other emergencies though—like, if you hurt yourself.

W: Does anybody ever use it even when they don't have an emergency?

M: I think there's a pretty hefty fine if you do. I mean, if you press that button and don't say anything, they know your location and will get there pretty fast.

W: They know your location? That's a good idea. Sometimes, you can't communicate in an emergency.

M: Yeah, that's why the prank calls are taken so seriously. They'll still come out here to verify that there isn't a problem, even if you don't utter a word.

W: So, what if you're inside, and you need help?

M: Same as anywhere else... you call 9-1-1.

W: But wouldn't it be better to call campus security? I mean, they're a lot closer.

M: Yeah, you can call campus security, and then they'll call 9-1-1. That's probably a better idea, actually.

W: Yeah, but then again, you're not going to take the time to look up the number during an emergency.

M: Yeah, It'd be a good idea to keep the number by your phone.

W: And what about those campus phones? For a normal call you have to dial 9 first. So, do you have to dial 9-9-1-1, or does 9-1-1 work automatically?

M: No, I think you do have to dial 9-9-1-1.

W: That's good to know.

M: Another thing, campus security has two numbers. You have to make sure you're calling the right one.

W: What's the other one for?

M: Non-emergency situations.

W: Non-emergency? Like what?

M: Like if you need to report a crime. You call 9-1-1 if there's a fire, or if you have a medical emergency...

W: Yeah, or a crime, right?

M: A crime in progress, yes. But suppose you're not in any immediate danger. Suppose you are the victim of a crime, then you would report it to campus security by calling the non-emergency number.

W: Like if someone stole your history paper?

M: Very funny. No, but if someone stole your CD player, you could report that.

W: I wouldn't go to the regular police for something like that?

M: For a CD player? No. That's something you'd report to the campus police.

W: I've been really lucky. I haven't had any emergencies or crimes in the past two years.

M: Except for that stolen history paper.

02 History

M: Good day students! I'm pretty jazzed about today's lecture topic, and I hope you all will be, too. If you find simply remembering and regurgitating names and dates a little dull, then this topic may be of interest to you. There are names and dates involved, but today I want you to engage, weigh, and analyze the information I present. Sound good? All right, let's continue.

In your textbooks and other various sources, you will encounter several contradictory theories regarding pre-Columbian discoveries of America. Can any of you clarify what I mean by "pre-Columbian"? Yes?

W: That means before Columbus arrived in the Americas, right? Before 1492?

M: Very good. That's correct. Most of us have learned that Columbus somehow "discovered" the continents, despite the fact that people were already living there... doesn't really make sense, now does it? The Native American people who had been living in the Americas for thousands of years aside, there are several claims that Europeans, Africans, or Asians had visited the Americas before Columbus. Historians typically either reject or accept these notions outright. A good historian, however, avoids both of these extremes. Since I want all of you to become good historians, then you too

should avoid both of these extremes. As I mentioned, you must engage, weigh, and analyze the available information before coming to a conclusion, and even then, such conclusions can be tentative at best.

Umm, OK, let's look at some examples. Let's begin with theories of early European contact. There are some sculptures of Peruvian gods that look nearly identical to Greek sculptures of Medusa. This has led to talk of an Ancient Greek presence in the Americas. In addition, people of the Hopi nation located in the southwestern US have stories about "Anasazi," or "ancient ones," who visited them. Some say the Hopi culture shows signs of Greek influence. Furthermore, the Aztec had a god called "Quetzalcoatl" who featured a white beard and was said to have come from the East. Could this god have been an Ancient Greek? Moving from Greece, now, there are also medieval Muslim reports from Moorish Spain. They speak of sailing across "the ocean of darkness and fog" and finding new populated lands there. While it is true that this ocean was the Atlantic, it is not clear if they landed in the Americas or just in some Atlantic islands. OK, so far we have some artistic similarities, some possible physical similarities with the white beard, and some textual clues from Europe. How do you feel about these? Are you convinced?

W: Well, not really.

M: OK. Why not?

W: Well, I've seen the pictures in the textbook of the Peruvian "Medusa" and well, I think the Peruvian people could have just invented their own god with a passing resemblance to the Greek Medusa. I don't think it's really the same deity. Also, like you said, the text could have just been referring to some islands in the Atlantic rather than a new continent.

M: Great job. As historians, we must approach evidence with a skeptic's mind. There is, though, one clear-cut case with solid evidence. Norse Vikings did explore and settle present-day Canada at least 500 years before Columbus. Leif Eriksson, son of Erik the Red, the founder of Greenland, discovered a new land that he called Vinland, which is now thought to be in Newfoundland, a Canadian province. There would be at least five additional Viking expeditions to Canada and even some temporary settlements. At first, we found textual evidence for these journeys in Norse sagas. Since then, we have strong physical, archaeological evidence to show this contact did take place. For example, there are the remains of Viking houses and villages, as well as old Viking tools found in the area. In fact, there are now three UNESCO world heritage sites in Canada devoted to Viking archaeological remains. So, to reiterate, this combination of historical texts detailing Viking trips to the New World with actual physical evidence left behind by the Vikings allows us to say with certainty that the Vikings "discovered" the Americas long before Columbus.

Now, there are numerous other claims relating to explorers from such places as Africa, Japan, and China. These are all very interesting and are fun to imagine, but all must be taken with a grain of salt. Accepting them without hard evidence would be just as irresponsible as dismissing them altogether.

03 Literature

M₁: Excuse me, professor. I have a question about the coursework listed here.

W: OK, what's up?

M₁: Well, umm, this course is called Introduction to World Literature, right, but everything on this syllabus list you handed out is European. I thought we'd be reading more international works.

W: Ah ha. Good point. Let's go ahead and address this. Largely, you are right, and this is unfortunate, so I empathize with your concerns. The reason for focusing on European literary works is that there was a big push in the mid-twentieth century to standardize what was called "The Western Canon," a set of great literary works that literature departments in several countries believed that all students should read. Of course, when I use the term "canon," I don't mean the kind you would find on a pirate's ship, I mean a group of books.

Now, this "Western Canon" is comprised of three eras. You see, literature departments wanted their students to gain exposure to literature from a wide variety of times as well as styles. The first of these three eras is the Theocratic Age, from the beginning until 1321. Can anyone tell me or guess at what "theocratic" means?

M₂: Umm... is it similar to "democratic"?

W: Well, in a way it is, they both end with "cratic," don't they? Who controls the power in a democratic system?

M₂: The voters... the people, right?

W: Exactly right, but in a theocratic system, it's a god or a supernatural authority that has the power. The Theocratic Age, then, was a time in which most nations were ruled according to religious laws. Books of the Western Canon from the Theocratic Age include the Sumerian *Epic of Gilgamesh*, Roman and Greek works like *The Odyssey*, and the Old English epic poem, *Beowulf*. I hope you'll notice that all of these works are epic tales with righteous heroes.

Now, umm, the second of the three ages covered in the Western Canon is The Aristocratic Age. The works of this age start with Dante's *Comedia Divina* and run up to Goethe's *Faust, Part Two* penned in 1832. Other works of this age include Cervantes's *Don Quixote,* Shakespeare's oeuvre, *The Canterbury Tales*, and so on. This period saw the emergence of comedy and shorter forms of poetry like sonnets and ballads. Is everyone keeping up? The Theocratic Age featured epics and heroic tales and the Aristocratic Age saw the emergence of other styles, like comedies and short poems.

Now, the third period covered in the Western Canon is the Democratic Age. We mentioned how people have the power in democratic systems. Well, in the Democratic Age, we saw writers from many different backgrounds get published and gain prominence. The works of this period mainly include English, French, and Russian writers, including Flaubert's *Madame Bovary*, Dostoyevski's *Crime and Punishment*, and Mark Twain's *Huckleberry Finn*. Those already familiar with these works will recognize that these works incorporate new and interesting voices that were not represented in past ages. Indeed, the major advances in the Aristocratic Age include the psychological novel, the antihero, and the new voices and perspectives I mentioned.

Now, admittedly, this is a very Eurocentric and, more particularly, very Anglo-centric grouping of literature. There is, of course, a wealth of literature from other areas of the world. East Asian literature, for example, was particularly rich, featuring works such as the *Tao* and *Analects of Confucius* among many others. The *Vedas* and *Bhagavad-Gita* of ancient India certainly deserve attention, as do the *Koran* and the writings of the Arab philosophers who guarded the torch of learning while Europe slept through the Dark Ages. Of course, there is also a wealth of oral tradition from many other places in the world. Hopefully, in the future, this European slant will give way to a more eclectic sampling. I certainly encourage all of you to seek out this literature as much as you can.

It is important to remember, however, that the 21ˢᵗ century world is, well, held together by the glue of English. Um, I mean that English is the universal language now and Anglo-American culture has the greatest influence throughout the world, for better or for worse. So, my point is, knowledge of this culture is useful for all of us.

04 Campus Life

M: Have you thought about what you're going to do this summer, Gloria?

W: Well, I can work full time at the restaurant if I want to.

M: That's where you worked last summer, right?

W: Yes, and I'm still working there part time.

M: Do they pay pretty well?

W: Yes, with tips the money is pretty good, but I'm graduating next year, so I'd like to get some experience in my field.

M: That's a good idea. Maybe you should try to get an internship.

W: An internship? I'd love to. It would mean a pay cut, but it'd be worth it.

M: Yeah, they don't pay very well, but in the long run, they sure do pay off. Not only do you get experience, you make all kinds of contacts.

W: Yes, it would be good to have some experience and some references under my belt when I start looking for work after graduation. I just have no idea how to go about finding a summer internship.

M: Why don't you go to the Summer Job/Internship fair?

W: I didn't know such a thing existed! When do they hold that?

M: Hang on, I've got the pamphlet in my backpack.

W: Great.

M: Here it is...let's see...it's actually next week, on the 16ᵗʰ. It starts at 9:30 a.m. and goes until 3:00 p.m.

W: Is it here on campus?

M: At the University Center Ballroom.

W: That's great. Is it casual, or should I dress as if I'm going to an interview?

M: It says here that it's business casual.

W: So, should I bring my resume?

M: Umm...it's not mandatory, but it's a good idea.

W: OK. Does it say there what kinds of internships are available?

M: You're into logistics, right?

W: Yup.

M: They've got something at Office Depot and at Wal-Mart.

W: Fantastic. Are you going, too?

M: Yes, I'm going to try to get hired on at a summer camp.

W: Oh, that sounds like fun.

M: It sure would be. It would be a good experience, too, since I'm studying to be a teacher.

W: Yeah, that would be excellent. Are there many camps listed on there?

M: There are three. One's at Camp Ton-A-Wandah, one's at Wesley Woods, and the other is at Camp Webb.

W: Camp Ton-A-Wandah? I went there when I was a kid! I had a horrible time. The camp counselors were awful.

M: Really? Well, I'll be different.

W: I'm sure you will. I'll give you a few pointers some time.

M: Let's just wait and see if I get the job.

W: You won't have any trouble. You're at the top of your class, and you do all that volunteer work.

M: Thanks for the vote of confidence. And good luck to you.

W: Thanks, I'll need it. Hey, do you want to go together?

M: Sure. We should go early.

W: Good idea. We'll look enthusiastic that way.

M: Let's meet at 9:15.

05 Computers

W: A few years ago, director Steven Spielberg made a movie called *AI*. It told the story of someone who looked and acted like a little boy, but wasn't a little boy. He was a robot, right? I can see some of you remember that one. Not the greatest movie ever made, but it's relevant to today's topic. Who can tell me what AI stands for? Yes.

M: Artificial intelligence, of course.

W: Right you are. I guess we're all familiar with this term these days from playing too many video games! Though video games relate to our topic of artificial intelligence, I do not recommend playing them as a means of studying for the course! Back on topic. We use artificial intelligence to produce not only video games to challenge us, but also useful machines that perform human tasks requiring intelligent behavior. We haven't yet produced the human-like robots seen in Spielberg's *AI*, of course, but we are getting closer.

In the meantime, we are using AI for some very important tasks. These include military applications, answering customer questions, and understanding and transcribing speech. AI systems are now routinely used by businesses and hospitals, and they are built into common home computer software such as Microsoft Office and the video games we all know and love.

Now, it's important to note that there are several different branches of AI. With one branch, called Logical AI, a machine uses deductive logic to decide how it should act. Information about the world, the machine's specific situation, and its goals are represented by logical mathematical language. The machine decides what to do by inferring that certain actions are appropriate for achieving its goals.

Another branch is Search AI. This program is able to rapidly examine a large number of possibilities and choose the best option. This is used, for example, in computers that play chess. A third branch of AI is called Pattern Recognition. We can program a machine to compare what it sees with a pattern. If a machine looks into a crowd of people, for example, it will match a pattern of eyes and a nose in order to find a face that it recognizes. Pattern recognition is also useful for understanding and transcribing human speech.

A fourth branch is Inference AI. With Inference AI, a machine is programmed for something called default reasoning. In default reasoning, when we hear of a bird, we infer that it can fly. However, if we learn the bird is a penguin, we have to reverse our conclusion about flight. Default reasoning allows the machine to change its original inference in situations like this. Now... yes, question?

M: Does AI want to make machines that are as intelligent as people?

W: Yes. The ultimate effort is to make computer programs that can solve problems and achieve goals in the world as well as humans.

M: How long before that happens?

W: Quite a while, I suspect. The Spielberg movie, remember, was set many years in the future. One problem is that common-sense reasoning is the area in which AI is furthest from the human level. Another problem is that machines presently cannot be programmed to learn the same way as a child does. Machines can't learn from physical experience like a child does, and they can't understand language well enough to learn much by reading. Furthermore, computers are not social beings as humans are. Where humans pick up on a myriad of tiny, often subconscious signals from the people around them, computers cannot.

OK, let's recap a bit. AI, or artificial intelligence, is the attempt to program computers to have human-like adaptability and intelligence. There are four main branches of artificial intelligence, including Logical AI, Search AI, Pattern Recognition AI, and Inference AI. Each branch focuses on one way in which human minds deal with the stimuli around us. Logic AI focuses on deductive reasoning using mathematical language, Search AI focuses on choosing appropriate actions from a list of possibilities, Pattern Recognition AI focuses on extrapolating a larger pattern from evidence of a smaller part of it. And finally, Inference AI focuses on using input to override default reasoning, like the example that birds fly, yet discovering that a bird is a penguin can override that default reasoning. As you know, computers and machines using artificial intelligence have numerous applications in homes, offices, factories, laboratories, and even in your video games. These applications can only grow in number and importance as our ability to program AI improves.

06 Geography

M: Good day everyone. Today, we're going to be looking at some of the effects the moon has on our lives. Can anyone tell me one such effect?

W1: Well, ummm, I've heard that full moons make people do crazy things.

M: Ha ha. Yes, I've heard that, too. Some statistics support that idea, but other studies refute it. In any case, you can debate that more in your psychology classes. But this is geography, so what physical effect does the moon have on our planet?

W1: Oh, OK then. Well, how about the tides? The moon's gravitational pull causes the tides, right?

M: Right you are. That's the information I was looking for, thank you. So, we know the moon causes tidal movement in the oceans, but can the moon cause rain? Do the moon and sun create tidal effects in the atmosphere as well as the oceans? In the past century, an air tide, or rather a kind of shifting of the atmosphere has been recognized. That, specifically, is what we're going to discuss today. As always, you are more than welcome to ask any questions you have as we go along.

The possibility of gravitational tides in the Earth's atmosphere was first suggested by Sir Isaac Newton. Newton is most famous for what discovery? Anyone?

W2: Wasn't he the gravity guy?

M: The gravity guy? Yes, I think you could say that. Newton was the first person to describe the force of gravity. Now, he came up with this theory on atmospheric tides while developing an explanation for ocean tides. Since 1918, scientists have been measuring air tides in the Northern Hemisphere, and although the changes in air pressure are small, their effects are not. Studies have shown that more cloudiness, rainfall, and storms are generated during certain lunar phases, such as the full moon.

In fact, even before Newton set down his theories on tides, people were aware that lunar phases corresponded with the rise and fall of the ocean tides. More recently, we have found that the moon is even able to cause deformations in the solid crust of the Earth. So, much in the same way the moon affects tidal movement in certain ways, it also pulls on the Earth's crust as well, causing it to move, too. Yes. Amazing, isn't it? The ground we walk on every day isn't necessarily as solid as it seems! Yes, there in the blue sweater?

W1: The textbook mentions that the moon can cause an atmospheric tide, and that it can create changes in air pressure. Is this an air tide, and is it true that these changes in air pressure can cause hurricanes?

M: Ah, as I was saying earlier, studies have shown an increase in storms corresponding to certain lunar phases. While we cannot yet explain this in full, it does appear that the moon has an influence on the weather. Whether they directly cause hurricanes or not, well, we'll have to wait for further research to determine that with any certainty, I'm afraid.

Let's look more at what happens during a full moon, though. Researchers at the University of Arizona discovered that at the time of a full moon, the temperature of the lower four miles of the Earth's atmosphere increases by a few hundredths of a degree. Now, a few hundredths of a degree may not sound like much to you, and you probably couldn't feel the difference yourselves, but it is significant. These researchers suggest that the moon warms our atmosphere in two ways. First, the moon's surface is heated by the sun and radiates thermal energy at the Earth. This energy is much less intense than the energy we get directly from the sun, but it is supplemented by a second phenomenon. The moon of course mirrors, or reflects, sunlight at the dark, or night, side of the Earth. However, the mirror effect is relatively slight because it reflects just 10 percent of the light of the sun. Nonetheless, as you all have experienced, I'm sure, that 10 percent is quite significant when compared to the zero percent reflected during a new moon. The difference is night and day, so to speak, if you'll forgive the pun. Anyhow, what I want you to take away from today's lecture is the fact that the moon can affect our weather. While we still have much to learn, we may well be justified in blaming the moon for a rainy day!

Chapter 2
Skill Review

A-C

01 Campus Life

W: Excuse me, I'm new here. Would you be able to give me some information about the Night Ride?

M: The shuttle bus? I sure can.

W: Great, when does it run?

M: Let's see...I think the schedule has changed since last year, so just let me have a look...okay...here it is. It runs from 8:00 p.m. until 12:15 a.m.

W: Is there a fixed schedule? Does it come at regular intervals?

M: It runs approximately every fifteen minutes.

W: OK. Is that going to change in the winter quarter?

M: No, that's the schedule for the fall, winter, and spring quarters. Since it's only here to cater to student needs, it runs on a less frequent schedule in the summer since there aren't as many students attending classes.

W: I see. So, now it runs Monday through Friday, right?

M: No no, the Night Ride only runs on school nights ...Sunday through Thursday.

W: Sundays, too? That's great.

M: That's right, but not Fridays.

W: I won't need it Fridays. That's when I review my lecture notes. I can do that at home. So, through the week, can I catch the Night Ride at the library? I usually study at the library.

M: Hmmm...the bus runs on a circuit through campus and the surrounding communities. The pick up points on campus are at Parrington Hall, the Communications Building, the HUB, Garfield Lane, and Meany Hall.

W: Isn't Meany Hall that old building adjacent to the library tower?

M: Yes, that's correct.

W: I see. So, I guess I could just catch it at Meany Hall. Where would I get dropped off?

M: There are no specific drop-off points. You just tell the driver where you want to go.

W: Really, he'll take me right to my doorstep?

M: Sure, as long as your doorstep is within a mile of campus.

W: A mile? Hmmm...I think my place is probably a little more than a mile.

M: Well, you could go in that direction on the shuttle and walk the rest of the way. Or, you could get let off at one of the local bus stops.

W: Hmmm...maybe I'll just take my bike. Can I take my bike on the shuttle?

M: Good question. I'm not sure. But maybe not. They haven't got bike racks. Maybe you could do this: take your bike to the bus stop, lock it up, take the bus to school, and then on your way home you could take the shuttle and get dropped off at the bus stop where you left your bike.

W: Do you think my bike would be safe there?

M: Well, of course, those stops are not affiliated with the university, so I can't really guarantee that. But I know other students haven't had any trouble.

W: I might as well just ride my bike to school and back.

M: That's another option. But then again, you can't really ride your bike in the winter.

W: Why not?

M: Well, the winters here can be pretty harsh.

W: Oh yeah. Well, I guess I can try the bus out and see how well it works for me. Thanks for all of your help. I really appreciate it.

M: My pleasure.

02 Oceanography

M: What exactly are reefs, and why are they so important? I hope this lecture will give you some answers to these two questions. Today, we will consider the history of reefs and the evolutionary changes they have gone through. It is important to understand the changing nature of a reef and how vulnerable it is to environmental influences.

A coral reef is a bank of coral, the top of which can sometimes be seen just above the sea. Reefs are some of the world's most diverse ecosystems. An ecosystem includes all the living things in an area and the way in which they affect each other and the environment. Coral reefs have been around for millions of years and have undergone numerous changes over time. We can utilize coral reef ecosystems as indicators of larger, global changes. This is especially important today in assessing the effects human activity may cause on the environment.

Reefs may be found in both tropical and temperate areas of the world. They are geological features that support a huge diversity of marine life and provide a habitat for sea life. The shape and form of a reef depend on where it is located and what type of forces the ocean subjects it to. Temperate reefs occur in colder waters where the temperature averages below 18°C. They usually form on existing rocky outcrops. Temperate reefs are not as well known as tropical reefs, but they are still home to a diverse range of species. Seaweeds such as coralline algae produce calcium carbonate that helps build up these rocky reefs. Tropical reefs, on the other hand, occur in warmer waters that average around 18°C and can reach into the high 20s. These reefs are built by the animals that live there, especially algae and corals. Over time, the reef grows by building on top of the calcium carbonate skeletons of polyps.

W: Excuse me sir, what exactly are polyps?

M: Polyps? Polyps are small simple tube-shaped water animals. The polyps divide and grow on top of their old skeletons or houses. Now, as I said earlier, we can use coral reef ecosystems as indicators of larger, global changes. All sorts of information about the past can be obtained from rocks and coral cores. Coral reefs can tell us things such as which times the Earth experienced a rise or fall in sea levels. They can even inform us about events such as ice ages, huge volcanic eruptions, and meteors falling to Earth causing mass extinctions by wiping out whole species. Modern corals grow in warm, clear, well-lighted and shallow water. Since coral reefs grow best from the low tide line to about a 20-meter depth, even relatively small changes in sea level can have very dramatic effects on coral reef growth. Reefs will always grow to the level of low tide. The location of fossils in a reef is very important because by observing fossils in a reef, we can accurately estimate sea level at the time the reef was formed. Therefore, fossils help us chart the various changes in sea level that have occurred over the years. Thanks to research by marine scientists, we know that sea level change has been going on continuously during the evolution of corals and reef organisms. There have been 17 cycles of sea level rise and fall in the last 2 million years.

So, how do marine scientists get their information? One method they use is called coral coring. By drilling a vertical core through the reef, it is possible to see periods of growth and decline in the reef. It is possible to date these periods of growth and decline by looking at fossils in the rock and measuring the types of atoms present in the rock. The type of atoms present in the rock can tell scientists lots about how old the rock is and what the climate was like at the time. Sea level rise and fall may be caused mainly by movements of the Earth's crust and changes in the amount of water locked up in the polar ice caps. As the polar ice caps melt or freeze, sea levels around the world change. So, coral is not just pretty to look at, it is also a great source of information.

03 Psychology

W: We hear a lot of criticism from the baby boomers about the younger generations. The stereotypical idea is that your parents' generation thinks that young people are lazier, less respectful, less goal-oriented, and so on. Now, perhaps this kind of criticism is common to generation pairs, but there's actually been some interesting research in this area. Let's take a look at what it shows. Is the younger generation really so bad, or are the baby boomers looking through distorted glasses, comparing their children to their adult selves instead of themselves at the same age?

How is it that we can research such a topic? Well, psychologists have been giving various psychological tests to samples of the adolescent population since the 1960s. By comparing the data from these tests for your generation against the data from your parents' generation, we can get a picture of what, if any, significant differences there are.

One major test was the IQ test. IQ stands for Intelligence Quotient. Intelligence is an idea that scientists use to describe why some people are better at academic tasks than others. The results of looking at IQ test scores from the past and from today show that the younger generation today is significantly more intelligent than their parents were in their adolescence. How significant? 10 points. This is a fairly large amount considering that IQ is only really measurable within a range of 70 to 130 points. This means that, on average, humans are increasing in intelligence by one IQ point every four years. Interesting, isn't it?

So, why would this be? Well, we have a few theories. First off, nutrition may be a key factor. More different kinds of food are more readily available today than ever before. This has been true for many, many years, so every new generation is privileged with better nutrition when developing in the womb. This is a critical period in the development of the brain. Nutrition makes a big difference during childhood as well. Think about what your parents used to eat for breakfast. Bacon, eggs, sausage, ham, steak...not a lot of vitamins!

Another theory is that as the world becomes more and more complex, our brains have to develop more in order to cope with it. The brain works just like a muscle. The more you use it, generally, the stronger it gets. A good example is computers. My daughter is six years old and has learned how to navigate the Internet, burn a CD, save files to folders, and a number of other tasks that her grandparents certainly can't do! You know, when I was six, all I had to learn how to do was turn on the TV and flip between 3 or 4 channels.

Your improved intelligence might also have something to do with your upbringing. Responsibility and self-reliance are both available and necessary at a much younger age than when I was a child. There are very few stay-at-home parents anymore. Many of you probably knew how to cook, clean, and do laundry by the time you were in high school. Sad to say, I never learned these things until I was in my mid-twenties.

So you're smarter. Is that it? Well, no. You've also scored higher than your parents on tests of extroversion. This means you are more outgoing, more open with yourself, and less shy in social settings. This is a great advantage in networking and getting desirable jobs. If you are socially adept, an employer is more likely to hire you.

So, why are you more extroverted? Well, once again, necessity is the mother of invention. You spend a lot more time outside of the family unit and with many different kinds of people. Also, you are much more likely to move away from your home town for university or for work, and you will probably move more times in your life than my generation did. This means you have to get out there and meet new people in order to maintain a network of social support.

There is one disadvantage though. The young generation today is more anxious and neurotic than their parents were at the same age, meaning that youth today worry more. I suppose this is understandable given the state of the world today, but it is also, of course, a negative factor for health and well-being in general.

04 Paleontology

M: All right, let's get down to living fossils. If you have any questions, please don't hesitate to ask. Uh...make sure you take notes because there's always a question about this on the primary exam. Where was I? Ah, yes living fossils.

Well...certainly, not all species on Earth have followed the usual pattern whereby species last about 2 to 3 million years before they are replaced. This number varies between different phyla, but that's an average figure. Evolution does its work, and older species often die out because of climate changes and natural catastrophes. Species that adapt well survive in the new conditions, and the cycle continues. Some hardy species, though, have weathered the ages and remain with us today. It's truly amazing to think that these plants and animals have adapted to so many changes. In some cases, perhaps, there has been stability in their environment, too. Nonetheless, these survivors are a scientific wonder because of their success.

First of all, it's important to realize that we have what are deemed "living fossils," but this isn't precisely the same as a "lazarus taxon." I'll explain that term soon. For now, let's stick with living fossils. A living fossil is a species of plant or animal that has existed since far back in the geological record and has never disappeared. These species haven't changed their form at all over an extensive period of time. What I mean is that they have lasted much longer than the average of 2 to 3 million years that I mentioned a few minutes ago. A great example of this is the tuatara lizard in New Zealand. This wonderful reptile has been around longer than the dinosaur. And we can find consistent evidence of its existence as far back as 200 million years ago. Tuataras are a single living species with no close living relatives, but which are the survivors of a large and widespread group in the fossil record. Another well-known example of this is the ginkgo tree. Ginkgo trees used to be part of a large group of plants, but, like tuataras, they're now one of a kind. Perhaps this has contributed to humanity's fascination with them, imbuing them with supposed healing properties. Anyway, that's beside the point, I suppose. The key thing is that, as with all true living fossils, at no point have ginkgo trees disappeared from the fossil record.

A lazarus taxon, or lazarus species, on the other hand, has done just that. Having disappeared from the fossil record for a long stretch, a living specimen is suddenly found. This is the case with the famous coelacanth. That's a tricky one to spell, so I'll write it on the board. Coelacanth: C-O-E-L-A-C-A-N-T-H. This fish was formerly thought to be long extinct. In fact, scientists can find no evidence of the coelacanth in the past 80 million years of the fossil record. Against all expectations, a living one was caught by fishermen near South Africa in 1938. Like the biblical character Lazarus, the species seemed to miraculously come back to life after everyone thought it was dead. It's a mystery why scientists can't fill in that missing fossil information. Of course, species do not just appear out of thin air, so all living lazarus species are nonetheless considered living fossils. They're merely in a special category. Should a more recent example of a coelacanth fossil be found, the missing link would be filled, and coelacanths would cease to be a lazarus taxon. They would be reclassified as just a regular living fossil.

OK, it's time to wrap this up, I'm afraid...in summary, a living fossil is a species that appeared long ago in the fossil record, and it is still around in the same form. It has survived against the odds, whereas most of its relatives have died out. Lazarus taxons share these characteristics, but they form a special class of living fossils because there is a gap in their fossil history. Because of this gap, scientists formerly thought these species had become extinct. Their sudden discovery on Earth today places them in the lazarus category. Until that fossil record gap is filled, they remain in that special category. I see we're almost out of time. Do any of you have questions?

Skill D

01 Campus Life

M: Hey Jill. You're looking down. What's wrong?

W: Hey Mike. Man, my whole academic career is in jeopardy. I don't know what to do anymore about my studies.

M: What do you mean? I thought you were skating through your classes and enjoying it.

W: That's the disheartening part. I was really enjoying my classes. I really thought social work was the vocation for me and that I had an aptitude for it.

M: So, what went wrong?

W: I just got my statement of grades back from last semester. I got a C- in one of my core classes. That means I can't take the next level. I don't know what to do.

M: How did you do in your other classes?

W: Fine — mostly A's and B's. I don't know how I ended up with a C-!

M: What do you mean? You didn't expect that grade?

W: No way! I had been doing quite well up until the final exam and term paper. In fact, it had been my best class.

M: Do you know the grade you earned on your exam and paper?

W: No, but I must have bombed them to drop my grade down to a C-.

M: Well, how did you feel about them? I mean, did you work hard on the paper? Did you find the exam really tough?

W: I worked really hard on that paper. Man, I did tons of research on it, but I guess I didn't write it that well. The exam was tough, but I didn't think I'd done so badly afterwards. I don't want to have to take that class again.

M: Well, retaking that class is one option if you really want to continue with social work, but there are other options. Have you spoken to your professor about your grade yet?

W: No, do you think she'll be willing to change it?

M: Well, first you make sure your grade isn't a mistake. I mean if you were doing so well and you felt your paper and exam went well, it could just be a simple mathematical slip by the prof. I mean they do have a ton of work to do with their own research and then grading exams and term papers and adding them up and entering them into the university computer system. I'm sure they make mistakes all the time. In fact, that very thing happened to a friend of mine last year.

W: Hmmm. I hadn't thought of that. I'd just assumed that I screwed up.

M: Another thing you can do is ask the professor to reevaluate your paper, if it did indeed receive a low grade. You said you worked hard on it, and if you really want to continue with your studies, the prof might give you a break on it.

W: Good idea. I hadn't thought of that, either.

M: As a last resort, you could appeal the grade with the department head, but you have to be really sure the professor has intentionally given you a lower grade than you deserve.

W: Wow, I don't think that'll be necessary, but I'm definitely going to see my professor and ask her some questions about my grade. Thanks for the advice.

M: No problem. Good luck.

02 Business Administration

W: Good afternoon, class. Today, we'll be discussing an aspect of business that is becoming more and more popular these days. We talked a little bit about this last class, and you should have read about it in your textbook, so you know that there is a lot of hype about franchising. Why do you think that is?

M: It's safe.

W: Exactly! When businesspeople buy a franchise, they are buying a business model that is tried and tested. People know that it works. When starting a new business from scratch, it takes a long time to learn that business, and it takes a significant amount of capital. What's more, it's potentially quite risky. With a franchise, on the other hand, someone else has done the learning already. A franchisee just has to apply that proven business model to garner success. Another thing, a franchisee is buying a product to sell that people not only recognize, but have an established brand loyalty to. Thus, the demand is already established. The most obvious example would be McDonald's restaurants. Everyone knows McDonald's. A new McDonald's franchisee doesn't have to convince consumers to buy the product because they already do. There is a ready-made, established market. Furthermore, franchises involve less start-up capital. The franchisee doesn't need to invest as much money in a franchise as he or she would to open up an independent business. Sounds pretty good, doesn't it? But what would you say if I told you that new franchises are actually less likely to survive than new independent businesses? Not only that, but they're less profitable as well.

M: If you weren't my business professor, I wouldn't believe you. So, with all of these benefits of franchises you just mentioned — the established brand recognition and demand, and lower start-up costs — why are they less likely to survive or turn a profit?

W: Well, like I said, franchising is great for some industries, like fast food. Now, the practice has become so successful that people are trying to apply it to other industries in which it just doesn't work. I'm talking, in particular, about service businesses. An example would be a chain of auto repair shops. Could anyone guess why it might be more difficult to run a repair shop franchise than a fast food restaurant?

M: Umm. Well, I used to work in a fast food joint. Flipping burgers is easy; anyone could do it. However, I don't even know how to change the oil in my car, let alone fix anything on it.

W: Excellent. Good reasoning there! So, in a service business, the business model itself is not as important as the business owner's knowledge and ability. So what you often have is substandard service providers relying on the expertise of the franchiser. Another problem is that franchisers earn their profits from franchising, while franchisees profit from the actual business. What I mean is that it is in the interest of the franchiser to sell more franchises. What do you suppose this means for the individual franchisees?

M: More competition?

W: Right on. The market may become diluted. What would happen if they opened ten new McDonald's restaurants here in town? The demand wouldn't increase; people would just have more options of where to go. So, let's say 500 people are going to eat at McDonald's today, here in town. Today, that means that the local McDonald's will have 500 customers. Open 10 more McDonald's, and each restaurant would only have about 50 customers each.

M: So you'd be better off opening your own restaurant?

W: That may be the case. Franchises do still have all the benefits I mentioned earlier. The potential franchisee has to look closely at the franchiser and analyze the potential demand for that proven product in the marketplace. He or she would also have to carefully analyze his or her own skills and acumen in business as well as the particular service being offered to the consumer. Of course, there are many factors involved. The nice thing about running your own business is that you have freedom. With a franchise, you are tied down by rules set by the franchiser. When running your own business, on the other hand, you can be creative in the ways you generate profit.

03 Geography

M: I'm sure many of you have experienced jetlag. You know, that tired, off feeling you get after traveling across time zones. Today, we're going to look a little more closely at time zones. You all know, from the readings and our previous lectures, about the lines of latitude and longitude, and how they help us locate a given location on a map. Just to review, we've got the equator at 0° latitude. Now, how does the equator divide the Earth again? Is it north-south or east-west?

W: The equator? It divides the Earth into northern and southern hemispheres.

M: Right you are. So, all of the lines of latitude run parallel to the equator all the way up or down to each of the poles. The equator is at 0°, and the poles are located at 90° north and south. Then, there are the lines of longitude, and the big one is the Prime Meridian. It runs from the North Pole, through Greenwich, England, to the South Pole, and is designated as 0°. On the other side, it goes back up to the North Pole at 180°. Each line of longitude measures the angle from the Prime Meridian going east or west to 180°. So, for example, let's take a point on the map — I don't know, how about New York City? New York City lies at 41°-north latitude and 74°-west longitude, but lines of latitude and longitude have more uses than just finding places on maps. Who can tell me another use?

W: Well, they act as borders sometimes, right?

M: Good point. Can you give us an example?

W: Umm. Well, most of the border between Canada and the US follows the 49th parallel, right? That's the latitude line of 49° north, and isn't the 38th parallel the border between North and South Korea?

M: Excellent. Those are some good examples of another way in which people use lines of latitude or longitude. There's another important use, though. Remember, I talked about jetlag and time zones? Let's look more at that.

Consider this: One day involves one revolution of the Earth on its axis or pole, right? So, one revolution is, naturally, 360°. OK, and a day is 24 hours. So, we can divide 360 by 24 to discover that the Earth spins at a rate of 15° per hour. How is this useful? Time zones, of course. Every 15° of longitude represents a one-hour time zone, more or less. Of course, this isn't exact. If you happened to live in a place with a time zone line running through it, you wouldn't want one side of town being in one time zone while you were in the other. Nonetheless, the lines of longitude give us a pretty good idea of how the time zones break down. This is how it works: When the sun is directly over a line of longitude, it is noon. East of this line, it is afternoon. West, it's morning. So, for example, if the sun is directly over Thailand, it is noon there. Go about 15° east to the Philippines, and it's 1:00 in the afternoon. Go west about 15° from Thailand to Sri Lanka and it's 11:00 a.m. So, let's say we are in Greenwich, England, and we want to call New York. Remember, Greenwich is at 0° longitude and New York is 74° west longitude. So, here in Greenwich it's 7:00 in the morning. So, what time is it in New York? Just divide 74° by 15. We divide by fifteen, remember, because that's how fast the Earth spins — 15° per hour. OK, so 74 divided by 15 is just about five. So, we are going five time zones west of Greenwich, which means we are going five hours back. Seven minus five is two. So, it's 2:00 in the morning in New York—probably not a good time to call. OK, just to reiterate, time zones are calculated based on the lines of longitude and the spin of the Earth. After doing the math work, we can see that one hour of time is the equivalent of 15° traveled by the Earth. You can use this 15° figure to calculate the time difference between two places, which can help you predict how bad your jetlag is going to be on a long trip!

04 Campus Life

M: Hey Nancy. Have you heard about the university's new alcohol policies? Man, it really ticks me off!

W: I haven't heard anything. What's going on?

M: They've decided to make it a dry campus!

W: Wow. That's a big step. I'm not so sure it's a bad idea, though. Why are you so mad about it?

M: What! Come on, we're all adults here. At least, the vast majority of students here are old enough to drink legally.

W: That's true. But they're not all mature enough to drink responsibly.

M: Well, who are you or even the university president to judge that? The law says it's OK for them to drink.

W: Yes, but I've seen enough people drink too much and get themselves in trouble. What is their plan to go dry anyway?

M: Well, they're not going to serve beer in the Bullpen anymore. They're also forbidding students to bring alcohol into their dorm rooms, and they're even assigning extra security guards to the fraternity houses to stop students from drinking.

W: Those are pretty extreme measures. Have they given their rationale for implementing them?

M: Yeah. Do you remember last spring? One student died of alcohol poisoning. I think his parents sued the university. These measures must be a reaction to that. They cite statistics on assaults, unruly behavior, and academic performance.

W: Those all sound like pretty compelling reasons to me. In fact, a friend of mine had some trouble last year after coming home from the Bullpen one Friday night. Now, she never walks alone on campus at night.

M: Well, those are good reasons, but it's still disrespectful to those of us who can drink responsibly. In fact, one of the big reasons I decided to live on campus was for the social life. Now, the school is killing that. I've got a good mind to sue them for my dorm fees back and get an apartment in a more exciting area off campus.

W: Hey, Derrick, I sympathize with you and all, but you're not really making any sense now.

M: (laughs) Yeah, I guess I was going overboard a little there. OK, I'm not about to sue the school, but I really might move off campus, and I probably won't be the only one.

W: All right, that's your choice. I think I'll still stay in the dorms. It'll still be a convenient place for attending classes, consulting with professors, and doing research in the library. I don't want to spend too much time commuting every day when I could be studying instead.

M: Yeah, you've got some good points there. Still, if we can't drink on campus, then a lot of students will be going to other areas of the city to drink and have fun. This means we'll likely see an increase in drunk driving charges, maybe even injuries and deaths. In the end, I'm not sure if they're improving the health of the student body or just sweeping the problem under the carpet so to speak.

W: That's a pretty strong argument. I think you should take it up with the president.

M: I just might write him a letter.

05 Music

W: What comes to mind when you think of "Romantic" music?

M: Love songs? Ballads?

W: Ah-ha, yes the term "romantic" now calls to mind images such as roses, candles, and flowers, but this is not the meaning of romantic music. It was not specifically music to listen to on a date. Remember, there are three periods of pre-20th century European classical music.

The first is Baroque, which occurred between the years 1600 and 1760. Baroque music is typified by Johan Sebastian Bach. Musical performances became larger and more complex during this period. Also, opera became established in the Baroque period. The second is the Classical period, typified by Mozart. It took place between the years 1730 and 1820. In general terms, Classical period music focused more on clarity and simplicity than Baroque period works.

The third period, which we'll be focusing on today, ran from about 1800 to 1900 and is called the Romantic period. The name implies that the expression of feeling or emotion through the music became more important than the structure, rules, or formal systems of the music. This trend actually continued into the 20th century in many respects as well.

So, how did they achieve this greater expressive power in the music? Well, we see many new chord forms appearing in the 19th century. These forms would have been regarded as dissonant, cacophonous, or simply as the incorrect form of a similar chord in previous times. However, as romantic composers proved, a strange chord in an appropriate context can be extremely expressive. Romantic composers also made much greater use of key changes, and they played around with the format of musical pieces. For example, the traditional third movement in a symphony is a sonata, a very soft relaxing piece. Many Romantic composers replaced this with the scherzo, a much more intense piece, in order to gain greater power of expression.

The sheer size of orchestras and the lengths of pieces saw a significant increase in the Romantic period. In fact, Gustav Mahler's 8th Symphony is also known as the "Symphony of a Thousand," because it took so many people to play it. Also, in the Classical period, a symphony lasted about 25 minutes. A Romantic symphony, however, often lasts up to 45 minutes. We also saw new instruments such as the piccolo become popular during this period.

Another major difference between the Romantic period and the Classical period that preceded it was the motivation behind the work. Nearly all Romantic pieces have a program, or theme, often based on a book, painting, myth, or folktale. For instance, Hector Berlioz created the theme of his *Symphonie Fantastique* himself. Through the symphony, Berlioz tells the story of how a young artist falls in love with a woman who doesn't return his love. You can probably guess the tragic end to this story told through music. "Character pieces" also came into being during the Romantic period. These are short pieces dedicated to a particular mood or feeling. They are usually played only on the piano. Composers such as Chopin and Schumann favored this approach. Opera was also affected. Many of the distinct movements began to blend together into a continuous flow of music.

To recap, then, the Romantic period of music had little to do with love, as we now associate with the word "romantic." It was a period of musical work that followed the Classical period and the Baroque period before that. Romantic period music stressed the importance of expressing emotion over careful attention to form and musical structure. New chords were added, and the arrangements of symphonies were altered. In addition, the length of symphonies and the number of instruments needed to play them both increased dramatically. Finally, Romantic pieces tended to have a theme or story expressed through the music. All in all, Romantic composers opened music up to a wide range of new possibilities, eventually leading to the atonal or serial movements of the 20th century.

06 Literature

M: OK, class. Today, we're going to continue our series of lectures looking at influential British authors. Today's topic is someone I'm sure you are all familiar with in one way or another. Who can tell me a bit about Robert Louis Stevenson?

W₁: Wasn't he the guy that wrote *The Ugly Duckling*, and several other short stories?

M: No, you're thinking of the Danish author, Hans Christian Andersen. The names are pretty similar, but Robert Louis Stevenson was from Scotland. He was also a famous author, though.

W₂: That name is really familiar. I'm sure I read one of his books as a kid. Did he write children's books?

M: You're getting closer. He didn't specifically write children's books, but one of his books became a famous tale that many children the world over have read. It's about pirates.

W₂: Oh! I know. He wrote *Treasure Island*, right?

M: Yes, that's right. You probably know him best for *Treasure Island* and *The Strange Case of Dr. Jekyll and Mr. Hyde*, but these are not his only works. In his time, he was known as a great author of travel books, short stories, and literary articles, in addition to fictional novels. Born in 1850 in Edinburgh, Mr. Stevenson had poor health right from his childhood. He suffered from tuberculosis, a disease affecting the lungs. This sickness would greatly affect the course of Stevenson's life as he moved from place to place trying to find a climate suitable for his condition. He first went to school to study engineering but later changed to law. He passed the Scottish Bar Exam in 1875 at the age of 25, but he never actually got around to practicing much law. Instead, he spent his time writing essays, short stories, and travel pieces. He published a book called *An Inland Voyage* based on his canoe tour of Belgium and France in 1878. On this trip, he also met his wife, Fanny Osbourne. They got married in 1880 and moved to California for a while. Then, they went back to Scotland but never really permanently settled there. They kept moving around in search of better climates for the rest of Stevenson's life.

Stevenson became famous with his pirate adventure novel, *Treasure Island*, published in 1883 when he was 33 years old. Three years later, he published *Kidnapped* as well as his most famous work, *The Strange Case of Dr. Jekyll and Mr. Hyde*. Who can tell me about this story? I'm sure you've all seen it in one form or another. There was even a version featuring Bugs Bunny and Porky Pig, if I recall correctly.

W₁: Sure, I know that one. That's the story of the scientist who drinks some chemical formula and becomes a big, mean monster... something like the Hulk, right?

M: Well, you're on the right track for sure. The Hulk is somewhat of a derivative of Stevenson's Hyde character. I find it interesting to note though, that in the book, the evil Hyde is actually physically smaller than the good Dr. Jekyll. Hyde's monstrosity was not in his muscular build, but in his selfish character.

In fact, *Jekyll and Hyde* was actually based on a nightmare Stevenson had. His wife woke him up from the dream, and he was angry that she had interrupted the story. He later wrote a draft of it and read it to his wife. She suggested expanding the idea into a novel. Originally, he was reluctant but finally agreed. Stevenson actually burned the first draft. He rewrote it in a mere three days, and after it was published, it soon became a sweeping success. Its main point was to criticize the two-facedness of people in society, especially upper-class Londoners. That is, the emphasis of appearances over substance and character.

Stevenson was also busy at this time writing a lot of articles for publication in various literary journals. The most famous one, "A Humble Remonstrance," first appeared in 1884, the year after the publication of *Jekyll and Hyde*. Stevenson's article was a response to "The Art of Fiction," an article published by his friend, the American philosopher, Henry James.

Stevenson spent the latter part of his life living on the South Pacific island of Samoa, where he wrote several works featuring aspects of Polynesian culture and criticizing European colonialism. In fact, his collection of essays on life on various Pacific islands is quite fascinating. It's called *In the South Seas* in case anyone is interested in it.

Skill E

01 Campus Life

W: What's the matter, John?

M: Oh, I'm just really frustrated at the moment. My midterm paper for my philosophy class is due at five o'clock, and I have to type it up, but the computer lab is always packed with people. No matter what time of the day I go there, there is always a waiting list a mile long to get on a computer.

W: Which computer lab do you go to?

M: What do you mean, which lab? The only computer lab I know of is the one in the basement of the library.

W: Actually, there are several computer labs around campus. The one in the basement of the library is the biggest, but that is probably why everyone goes there. That or, like you, they don't know about the others. Personally, I usually use the computers in Anderson Hall.

M: Anderson Hall? Isn't that the Business Administration building?

W: Yeah. They only have about a dozen computers in that lab, but it's pretty easy to find free ones there. I guess not many people know about it.

M: I had a business class there last semester, but I never saw a computer lab in that building.

W: It's kind of hidden away. My roommate's an accounting major. She spends most of her time in that building, and she told me about it.

M: So where is it then?

W: Do you know where the student lounge is in Anderson Hall?

M: It's on the second floor, right? The first room you come to at the top of the stairs — the stairs at the front of the building, I mean.

W: Right, and a couple of doors down from that is the copy room. Go in there, and you'll find another door that goes into the business computer lab.

M: Oh, I know what you're talking about. I always thought that door went into some kind of storage room. They should put a sign on it or something.

W: Maybe, but it's kind of nice that no one knows about it.

M: And anybody can use it? I mean, I'm not a business major. If I went in there and tried to use the computers, would anybody kick me out?

W: I don't think so. Even if they were reserved for business students, I don't think they'd care. I mean, like I said before, there are usually a couple of free computers. If there were people waiting, they might say something, but that's never happened to me. Any time I go there, no one even asks for my student ID or anything. I just sign in and start working, and I really don't think there's ever been a time when somebody was waiting for a computer to become free.

M: I think I'll go over to Anderson after my next class and check it out. Thanks for the tip. I might actually get this paper in on time.

02 History

M: There certainly seems to be a lot more interest in history these days, especially personal or family history. That's why I wanted to take some time in class to talk about non-academic historical research. You probably know this type of research better as genealogy. Genealogy is the investigation of family histories. Professional genealogists use written records and stories people tell in order to learn about where and when people lived and about their lifestyles. Aside from strictly personal interest, the information they gather can lead to reunions of families who have been disrupted by adoption, foster care, or immigration. This type of research could also lead to family reunions of distant relatives. But professionals as well as people who undertake genealogy as a hobby have to be careful. Genealogical investigations are not always based on reliable data. Well, before we talk about unreliable data, maybe we should list some different kinds of data that someone might look at when they do this kind of research. People might use census returns, birth, death, and marriage records, and even maps to determine when, where, and how relatives lived. But these records are not always accurate, as we shall see. Some types of information tend to be more accurate than others, so wary genealogists start with the most accurate information and then try to fill in whatever blanks they can't fill by using less reliable information.

Let's start at the top. The most accurate type of information is place names, so genealogists rely most on information containing the names of cities and towns. Place names are long lasting and seldom change. So, information related to the place of an event is often accurate. Are any of you interested in doing genealogy? Here is a rule of thumb for determining where someone was born — actually two rules because it is different for men and women. Historically, a woman would typically get married in the same place where she was born. So, if you find a marriage certificate, there is a good chance that the bride was born in the same place where the wedding took place. Not so for men. With men, actually, you look at where they were buried. Men were usually buried in the area in which they were born. This makes sense when you think about it. In old times, women worked in the home. Men usually took over the family business. So, while weddings traditionally took place in the bride's hometown, she would probably move with her new husband to his hometown after marriage, where he would probably take over the family business. In the old days, they would most likely stay there for the rest of their lives. So, if a man was buried in a town, there's a good chance he was born there, but for women, better to examine her marriage certificate to find out where she was born. Then we have names. Even names are not as reliable as you might think. Surnames, or what most people refer to as last names, are more reliable than first names, but not by much. Surnames have so many differences in spelling, it is difficult to tell whether people were related or not. Now, we wouldn't use first names to determine if people were related, but we still might be misled by first names. For one thing, they are really trendy. You get a lot of the same names recurring within each generation. Nicknames were common, too. In one village, for example, you might have three girls named Elizabeth. One goes by Beth, one by Lizzie, and one by Betty. On the census return, unfortunately, they are all Elizabeth, and they've all got brothers, Jack, John, and Jonathan. Another complication is that sometimes the same name will reappear in the same family...even in the same generation! This is because long ago, many children died in their infancy, and parents would often recycle the name when the next baby of the same gender was born. So, baby Mary died at birth, and then another baby Mary came along who survived. Both go into the record books.

The least reliable information of all is dates. You can't even trust the dates that were reported on census returns. For one thing, people lie about their age. And another problem in the past was that census takers weren't very accurate either. They didn't want to be bothered with lots of different data to manage, so they would round people's ages off to the nearest five!

03 Biology

W: Have you ever wondered how we know which plants are good to eat and which ones are poisonous? Well, it was simply a very long and drawn-out process of trial and error. Throughout history, people ate what they could find, kill, or otherwise get a hold of. When there was a lack of a traditional food source, people had to try new things. Over time, they started to figure out which plants made them sick and which didn't.

Now, I am not just talking about ancient times before farming became established. This trial and error with plants was going on well into the 18th and 19th centuries! In fact, historical records indicate that in the 1800s plant poisoning had become a serious issue. Since food wasn't as readily available then as it is today, people were forced to take more chances with what they ate. Rather than drop by the market at the end of the street, people would have to wander out into the fields or forests and find whatever looked edible. Today, because the food supply is rather ample and stable, we rarely have to go find our lunch or dinner out in the woods.

Nonetheless, we still need to be careful. Poisonous plants can be found all around us: in our homes as decoration, in our lawns, and in the general landscape. Of course, we don't generally go around putting random plants in our mouths. However, children do. Have any of you ever caught your baby brother or sister chewing on one of the plants in your house? Or maybe you were caught chewing on one! Considering the fact that a baby's body is smaller and less hardy than ours, we have to look out for them. A small amount of poison that might go unnoticed in an adult can cause more serious harm to a child. So, poisonous plants are dangerous to kids, but there are measures that can be taken to ensure safety. You can identify the plants in your surroundings by giving a call to your local garden center. You can describe the plant to them, and hopefully they can tell you whether or not it has poisonous properties. Alternatively, you can take the plant down to show them. Also, if you buy a new plant, it is wise to ask whether or not it is poisonous.

Now, there are three main categories of toxicity in plants: extremely toxic, moderately toxic, and minimally toxic. These names, however, are very misleading. You see, the severity of the poison depends on a host of other factors, like the particular plant and the metabolism of the person. The term "poisoning" itself is actually also misleading. Poisoning doesn't only mean a person dies from the poison. Poisoning can result in anything from indigestion and skin irritation to lethal brain damage or death.

Let's talk about a few categories of poisonous plants now. One category is the alkaloids. These are bitter-tasting plants with nitrogen compounds in them. A good example is hemlock. I mention it as an example because hemlock is famous. History buffs in the class may recall that it was the poison extracted from this plant that Socrates was forced to drink as his death sentence for corrupting the youth of Athens. That's just an interesting side note. Anyway, the effects of hemlock are similar to nicotine, but, obviously, much more severe as it can cause the nervous system to shut down, resulting in death. Plants with minerals in them form another category of poisonous plants. These plants build up a large amount of some mineral that is toxic in humans, such as lead or copper. The effects of eating these plants can include psychological malfunctioning and, in higher doses, death. Plants containing oxalates are the third category. Oxalates, spelled O-X-A-L-A-T-E-S, occur as small crystals in the plant and irritate the mouth. Not quite as serious as the other two, but poison nonetheless. Once again, those three categories of poisonous plants are the alkaloids, plants with minerals, and oxalates.

So, you may be wondering, why did poisonous plants evolve? What purpose does this serve? Well, there are many different sources of poison in different plants as we just heard, but in most cases, the poison is a by-product of one of the plant's natural life processes, and the poison serves as a defense mechanism for the plant. Animals learn which plants to stay away from because they get sick when they eat them. So, it follows that the plant will survive and reproduce because no one is eating it.

04 Drama

M: Welcome to Theater 351, Stage Management. Some of you may have worked as volunteer stage managers in the past. As such, you have probably developed your own habits, working practices, and manners of relating to the cast and crew, but, you are taking this class for a reason, correct? You want to learn how to do these things properly. If you thought you knew all there is to know about stage management, you wouldn't be here. So, you've got all that amateur experience. Forget it. Clear all of your old habits and techniques from your mind. The truth is, you most likely either didn't learn much at all, or you learned how to be a typical, amateur stage manager. I'm going to teach you to be an effective, professional stage manager.

OK, now the second thing I need you to do is to appreciate the responsibility of this position. A great deal of the success of the show depends on you. You are foremost responsible for every aspect of the performance of the technical crew and for the preparedness of the stage, set, and props. This includes every cue in the show. You must know exactly where in the script the cue occurs and ensure that the crew and equipment is prepared to make the necessary technical adjustments. This is important, too — keep records of all of the decisions made during rehearsals and meetings. This can prevent a lot of arguments and confusion down the road. For example, let's say it is decided that a certain cue will be changed, and then, a while later, an actor says that no one ever told him about the change. If you have a written record, you can get it out and show him the meeting or the rehearsal in which it was decided. I might add, too, that when people know that records are being kept, they tend to make more of an effort to be responsible and remember what's going on.

Another thing you are responsible for is the safety of the cast and crew. This is, of course, of paramount importance. You must arrive early to every rehearsal, without exception, in order to inspect the stage for safety hazards such as loose nails, weak boards, ramps, and stairs. You should also make sure that all exits are marked with glow tape so that actors and crew will be able to move around safely in the dark. Further, you must be aware of the location of the first aid kit and fire extinguishers, and you should be certified in CPR and first aid. Taking this course won't give you this certification, but I will be giving you information later in the semester about certification courses you can take. These are offered by paramedics at the fire station.

The third thing I need you to do is get rid of any ideas you may have about the stage manager being a privileged person — someone with lots of assistants and an attitude. If you come in late wearing sunglasses and barking orders at people, you are not doing your job effectively. You're also letting people know that you are not a professional stage manager. First off, a professional is polite and treats people with respect. Secondly, a professional always remains calm and never yells at others or panics. If people see the stage manager panicking at a performance, this panic can easily spread throughout the rest of the cast and crew. Needless to say, the overall performance will suffer. Thirdly, you have to learn to delegate authority as stage manager. As I've said, you have a tremendous responsibility. Don't think that you can do it all yourself. You have assistants, so use them, but always do so politely, especially if you are working with volunteers. After all, they're not getting paid. They're working because they want to have an enjoyable experience. If you treat them badly, they'll probably leave. At the same time, don't expect your assistants to do it all, and don't expect them to do all the menial tasks either, while you do the important ones. Get used to the idea that stage managers do make coffee, go on food runs, make photocopies, etc. It is of utmost importance that you maintain a good rapport with everyone. Part of your responsibility of making sure the performance comes off without a hitch is to make sure that everyone is content and feels like part of the team. The three most important things you'll learn, then, are preparation of cast and stage, workplace safety, and creating and maintaining a positive rapport with all the people involved in the production.

05 Campus Life

M: I'm kind of nervous about the test tomorrow. Want to sit down over here and go over the notes from class together?

W: OK, but do you mind if we sit somewhere else? People are smoking here.

M: Oh, sorry. I didn't know it bothered you so much. Let's go over there.

W: Thanks. Yeah, it really does bother me. Frankly, I think it's gross. I don't see why the campus just doesn't go totally smoke-free. All of the buildings are smoke-free now. Why don't they just put an end to smoking on campus altogether?

M: I don't know if they could. I mean, we're all adults here, and you're not really hurting anyone else by smoking outside. I guess they don't want to deny people their right to smoke if they want to.

W: Well, they're already denying smokers the right to buy cigarettes.

M: What do you mean?

W: None of the convenience stores or vending machines on campus sell cigarettes.

M: Well, I wouldn't really call that denying people their right to buy cigarettes. It's the university's prerogative whether they want to sell tobacco products or not. People are free to leave campus to buy a pack. Is that true, though? That you can't buy cigarettes on campus? I hadn't noticed that they didn't sell smokes on campus anymore.

W: Yeah, it's true. The closest place to buy a pack of cigarettes around here is the Speedy Mart across University Boulevard.

M: Yeah, that's where I always go to buy them.

W: You smoke? I had no idea. I've never seen you with a cigarette.

M: Well, I don't smoke habitually. Sometimes, I have a smoke when I want to take a break from studying. Of course, that means I have to go outside the library or outside my dorm building, but I don't mind so much. It gives me a chance to stretch my legs. The walk helps clear my mind, so I can focus better when I go back to hit the books.

W: So, if our campus ever did go completely smoke-free, I guess you'd be pretty upset.

M: Well, it would inconvenience me a little, but I wouldn't be that upset. I can quit anytime. I guess I just smoke now because the opportunity exists.

W: So, you're saying you would quit if the campus was smoke-free?

M: Yeah, I guess I probably would.

W: Well in that case, I think that's an excellent argument in favor of a fully smoke-free campus. Maybe there are lots of students like you who would actually give up smoking if there were no places to do it around here.

M: Yeah, I guess so, but I think most smokers are more addicted than I am. You sure are anti-smoking, aren't you? Why is that?

W: Well, I used to smoke in high school, but then I finally wised up and quit before I graduated. Now, I find the smell of smoke revolting.

06 Business

W: Investing money is risky. Naturally, you want to make money, not lose it. So any investment decision has to be carefully thought out. Once you have decided to invest some money, you need to decide how you are going to invest it. This is a big decision, and you need to learn about risk management. There are many factors to be considered in risk management, and I am going to go over three major ones today. They are business risk, valuation risk, and force of sale risk.

So, first you need to think about business risk. You are investing in a company, and in order for you to earn money, that company has to earn money. So, if its profits suffer due to competition or mismanagement, your earning power is decreased, too. So, how are you, as an investor, to know whether a company will be successful? Well, you need to look at the company's business plan and determine whether or not you think they have a solid plan for making a profit. But it doesn't have to be all guesswork. There are certain indicators that can give you a clue as to good or bad investments. One indicator is franchise value. Franchise value refers to the ability of the company to raise prices. You see, if some other factor contributes to loss of profits, like increased wages or increased costs of materials, the company needs to raise prices, right? Some types of businesses can do this easily. Those are the ones with franchise value. Other businesses, without franchise value, cannot increase prices because people will stop buying their products. These are called commodity-type businesses. Commodity-type businesses do not have the flexibility to raise prices because their sales are based on low prices, not on a factor like name recognition. So, if the economy is not doing well, a commodity-type business probably won't do well either because their costs will go up.

OK, so, once you have found a business that looks strong, you need to consider valuation risk. This is risk that is based on the relative value of different stocks. Just because a company looks like it is going to do well does not mean that you should invest. You have to consider the price of the stock relative to the price of other stocks. Remember what we talked about last time? Opportunity cost equals opportunity lost. As I mentioned before, this means that when you choose to invest in one opportunity, you are losing all kinds of other opportunities to invest, so it may come down to this: one company looks strong, but you have to invest a lot of money. Another company might not look quite so attractive, but the stock is not as expensive. In the end, you might make more money on the less attractive company because you can buy significantly more stock of that company. This is valuation risk. You see, a company might have an excellent business plan, and you might reasonably expect the company to grow. However, if their stock is overvalued, that means that they are basing the value on their forecasted growth and not on their current growth. Any number of events could occur that might prevent that projected growth from taking place. So, like I said, you might be better off buying a different stock that is being sold at face value. In essence, when assessing valuation risk, do not just ask, "Is this company a good investment?" but ask, "Is this company a good investment at this price?"

Now, once you find a company with both low business risk and low valuation risk, there is still one more risk to consider, and that is force of sale risk. This has to do with the time period in which you are expecting to see your investment turn into significant gains. If you are planning on making money by a certain date, you are taking a very big risk. Here is a good rule of thumb to follow: in the stock market, you might be able to know WHAT is going to happen, but not WHEN. Did you get that? You may know WHAT, but you don't know WHEN. You should never count on seeing your investment grow in a certain time period. So, ultimately, you are looking to minimize risk by investing in a company that is going to make money in good times and in bad. But you also want to buy stocks at a reasonable price in order to decrease valuation risk, and you want to be flexible about when you wish to cash in your stocks, minimizing your force of sale risk.

Skill F

01 History

W: We've looked quite a bit at Napoleonic-era France already. Today, we're going to look at its fiercest and strongest rival, England. There were many factors contributing to the strength of Britain in the early 19th century and its eventual victory over Napoleon. In spite of Britain's small population of only 10 million, it had a very large force of volunteers, conscripts, and reservists. By the time of the Napoleonic Wars, the number of British males serving in the armed forces was a startling 1 in 5.

A major source of Britain's power, oddly, came from its commercial activities. At this time, Britain was exporting its goods by sea across the world and importing goods by sea from other countries far and wide. This high volume of maritime trade ensured that there was a large supply of experienced and highly skilled sailors. This contributed to Britain having the largest and most powerful navy in the world. In 1792, the year Napoleon declared war on Great Britain, the British navy commanded a fleet of over 600 ships and 100,000 seamen, a fact that would prove to be a key factor in its success. Britain also had a highly efficient and developed banking and taxation system that placed a large amount of funds at the disposal of the government.

In this same year, 1792, France had seized control of Belgium and the Netherlands, in addition to various other minor kingdoms, and was just one step away from an invasion of England. The British army, unlike its navy, was weak compared to the French, and the British knew this. To compensate, they used their massive naval and economic advantage. They pulled most of their ships back for the defense of their island and attacked French trading ships on the open seas. They used their wealth to fund various allied armies on the continent, which at different times amounted to basically all of Europe besides France and its occupied nations. Yes? A question?

M: Yes, thanks. I just wanted to clarify — you mean that Britain actually paid soldiers of other countries to fight against France? I mean, they weren't fighting for nationalism or anything, just for the money?

W: Well, they might have been fighting in part for national pride, but essentially these armies were funded by Britain to fight against France in order to help Britain's position. It's an interesting concept, no? It's also an idea that has been used throughout history. Would it surprise you to know the US government did the same thing, funding armies in several Latin American countries in the 70s and 80s? Hmm, you don't look too surprised.

OK, moving on, when Napoleon went to take Egypt in 1789 with 35,000 men, Vice-Admiral Horatio Nelson and his fleet were sent to stop them. Napoleon did, in fact, take Cairo, but Nelson arrived soon thereafter and won a victory in the Battle of the Nile. This victory essentially gave Britain control over the Mediterranean while cutting off the supply lines of Napoleon's army in Egypt. Nevertheless, Napoleon eventually made it back to France, and by 1807, he had subdued Russia, Prussia, and Austria, the three largest continental powers at the time. This resulted in a trade war with Britain, in which Napoleon used his army to block trade between England and Europe, and Britain used its navy to block Napoleon's overseas trade.

Eventually, Napoleon's campaigns spread to Britain's long-time ally, Portugal. The seizure of Portugal, however, was hugely unpopular with France's ally, Spain. When the Spanish king protested, Napoleon replaced him with Joseph Bonaparte, Napoleon's brother. This sparked a rebellion and the opportunity for Britain to enter mainland Europe. The Spanish defeated Napoleon's army, which allowed the British to land their forces in Portugal.

OK, just to recap. France and England have been long-time rivals. This rivalry continued and even intensified during the rule of Napoleon. As Napoleon's forces spread across Europe, they cut off those markets to British trade. This, of course, was a large drain on Britain's economy. Britain, in turn, used its powerful navy to attack French trade ships, thus cutting them off to markets around the world. This, of course, was a large drain on France's economy. Britain also defeated France's foray into Egypt, further cutting them off from the rest of the world. Eventually, Spain went to war against France with assistance from Britain, which finally allowed British troops to gain a foothold on the continent, which eventually led to the downfall of Napoleon.

02 Ecology

M: So, many of you have sent me emails or visited me during office hours to complain about the material on systems theory. Some of your complaints are partly correct. The theory is vague, and it can be applied to almost anything. Rather than being frustrated by this fact, though, I want you to understand that this universality is the beauty of systems theory. Don't you see? Scientists need a tool that can be easily applied and adapted to describe any group of variables that interact in a predictable and recurring pattern. This tool is systems theory. Let's go over it again, because it will be on the exam. Who can tell me just what a system is? Anyone?

W: Isn't a system like the actual things in a relationship, and, like, what the things do together?

M: OK, that's a pretty accurate description, but let me just tighten up your definition a little. A system is defined as a process that is a result of its parts and their interactions. We call these parts "elements." So, every system has elements. Each element in the system has certain characteristics that are relevant to the functioning of the system. We call these "attributes." So, every element has attributes. Now, these elements and attributes have a cause and effect relationship with respect to one another. So, every system features relationships. Now, we have the three things that make up the system. We have the elements, the attributes, and the relationships. Now, what example did we discuss last time?

W: It was the food chain, right?

M: Right! OK, let's go through the example and apply these terms. The food chain system is the system of energy moving around in the ecosystem. So, the food chain has elements. We can distinguish four major ones: the sun, plants, herbivores, and carnivores. Those are the four elements of our system.

These elements have attributes, right? In this case, the attribute is energy. We start off with the sun, which has, say, 100,000 units of energy. The sun radiates this energy onto the Earth, where the plants are. Plants can then absorb this energy via photosynthesis. Who remembers what photosynthesis is?

W: That's the process that plants use to make food, I think. They breathe in carbon dioxide and breathe out oxygen, right? The opposite of us.

M: Good, that's right. Oxygen is indeed a waste product of photosynthesis. That, in fact, is another attribute in a larger system, but I don't want us to think about oxygen or carbon dioxide now. Let's stick to energy as our attribute.

OK, so we now have a relationship between the sun and plants on Earth. In photosynthesis, a plant takes light energy, water, and carbon dioxide and converts them into simple sugars and oxygen. These simple sugars are the plants' food and, thus, its source of energy. Plants can capture about one percent of the radiated energy from the sun. That one percent of energy is the plants' attribute. So, one percent of the sun's 100,000 units of energy leaves us with 1,000 units of energy being absorbed by the plants.

The next element in our system is the herbivores. This term means "plant eaters" in Latin, so these are plant-eating animals. The herbivores eat the plants — here we have another relationship — and from this, the herbivores are able to absorb 10 percent of the plants' energy. Remember, we started with 100,000 units of energy from the sun. The plants absorbed one percent, or 1,000 units of this energy. So, now we have the herbivores eating the plants and taking 10 percent of these 1,000 units of energy, which leaves 100 units of energy left at the herbivore level.

The final level is the carnivores, which is Latin for "meat eaters." These animals, in turn, can consume 10 percent of the energy from the herbivores. Remember, the herbivores ended up with 100 units of energy, therefore, we are finally left with 10 units of energy at the level of the carnivores. They make up the level furthest from the sun. So, this is our system, the attribute we followed is the energy starting from nuclear reactions in the sun and passing through the four elements in the system, from the sun, to the plants, and finally ending with the consumption of herbivores by carnivores.

03 Campus Life

M: Hey there, Betty.

W: Hi, John. What's up?

M: I wanted to talk to you. I'm having trouble with my computer, and you know more about computers than anyone I know.

W: You don't need to butter me up. I'd be glad to help you out. What seems to be the problem?

M: Well, ever since I got it hooked up to the Internet a month ago or so, it's been really slow, and sometimes, it just shuts down without warning. I lost half of a term paper the other week!

W: Aha, the Internet! A marvelous thing, don't you agree? We can now access a wealth of information from our homes, schools, and businesses, but, like any good thing, it has its problems.

M: Right. It's a great help for researching information for papers... and for downloading music files.

W: Anytime you surf the Web, your computer could get a virus, which might be a minor inconvenience, or it could pick up a virus that does serious damage. Hackers might get into your computer and delete important information, crash your computer, or even steal your credit card information.

M: Wow, do you think I might have a virus, then?

W: Yeah, that could be your problem. I'm sure you've heard news reports of computer viruses being spread through email. The two more serious types of viruses are worms and Trojan horses.

M: Worms?

W: Yeah, sounds funny, I know, but worms are a sophisticated type of virus that replicates itself and spreads to other computers without the user knowing what's going on. A Trojan horse is a type of virus that gets in to your computer by disguising itself as something useful or desirable, like a music file for example.

M: Uh oh.

W: Yeah. You also have to worry about spyware. As the name implies, it is a software program that basically spies on you. It gets into your computer and then gathers information about your activities that can then be sold to advertisers. Spyware can really use up your memory and bandwidth. This is probably what's slowing down your computer so much. Spyware can also lead to crashes.

M: Oh man! What should I do?

W: Don't worry, there is protection. One security device is called a "firewall." It sits between the computer and Internet, allowing the user to access the Internet, while preventing outside users from accessing your computer. So, basically, the firewall allows wanted traffic but stops unwanted traffic. It can be either a piece of hardware or a software program.

M: Great, so a firewall will solve my problems?

W: No. It will prevent you from getting problems in the future. You will also need an anti-virus program to prevent you from getting viruses.

M: I see.

W: I also have some programs that will search your computer for viruses and spyware and clean them from your hard drive. That's what we'll need to do first.

M: Wow, thanks a million!

04 Biology

M: Quick question: how many of you have children? Hmm, nobody yet, eh? All right then: how many of you have parents? (laughs) Right, you all have parents, of course. Today, we'll be looking at the bond that forms between parents and their children, or offspring. So, why do parents bond with their children?

W: I think they need to bond so parents will protect their children... you know, so the species will survive, right?

M: Very good. It is essential for the survival of the family and the species. But what actually happens when animals procreate? Well, there are a lot of hormones involved, and the bonding starts long before the baby is born.

The first phase of parental response is the preparatory phase. The fertilization of an egg signals the beginning of a series of hormonal changes in pregnant mothers. These hormonal changes cause lactation. Who can define "lactation" for me?

W: Isn't that when the mother starts making milk for the babies to drink?

M: Correct. Lactation is the production of milk in the mother. These hormones that trigger lactation also prepare the uterus for labor. The hormones also initiate changes in the prospective mother's behavior. Depending on the species, the mother might build a nest or otherwise find or prepare a safe space for the expected offspring. Pregnant mothers also tend to limit their social interactions when they are expecting, thereby limiting chances of trauma to herself and the babies she is carrying.

So, the first phase is the preparatory phase, and the second phase is the delivery. When the mother goes into labor, she has contractions. None of you have had your own children yet, but perhaps you know about contractions. What are they?

W: Aren't contractions when the mother's muscles start contracting, or flexing I guess, before the baby comes out?

M: Yes, that's right. When these muscles start contracting, a signal is sent to the brain that induces arousal, lactation, and maternal behavior. They also trigger the release of chemicals to reduce anxiety and mute pain responses. What all this does, hopefully, is cause an intense connection between mother and baby at birth. It is important that this occurs, because if the mother does not instantly bond with the baby, she may not take proper care of it.

Now, this brings us to the next phase: the parents' response following the birth. You might be surprised to discover that most mammals don't like babies. I see some surprised and skeptical-looking faces. It's quite a counterintuitive concept, isn't it? This is, however, another reason why the parent-child bond is so important. When an adult is exposed to a baby, one of two things can happen. More often than not, the adult will care for the baby. However, if the parents can't handle it, they have another option... it may be unthinkable, but it does happen... that second option is killing the baby. It's not very common, but sometimes parents will actually eat their young.

That's a rare occurrence, though. Usually, moms will care for their young and prepare them for adulthood. But what about the dads? We've seen how the body signals mothers to be nurturing, but what makes fathers help out? Well, the truth is that, among most species, they don't. In some species, however, fathers do help, and it turns out that among birds and mammals whose males engage in paternal behavior, the males actually have higher levels of blood prolactin, just like mothers. We also see changes in blood testosterone levels in these fathers.

Animals that have fewer children (for example bears) tend to be more committed to them than are animals that have litters (for example rats). Because mammals with fewer offspring procreate less, the survival of each one of their offspring is that much more important. It is also interesting to note that a species with fewer offspring can more easily influence the behavior of those offspring through reward and punishment to bring about desirable behavior. Of course, it's biologically important for parents and offspring to create a bond. That way, parents will support and protect the young so that they can grow to reproductive age and continue the species into the future. So, there are three basic phases that lead to this bonding. The first phase is the preparatory phase in which the mother's body prepares to nourish the child. The second phase is the delivery phase in which the mother's body prepares itself for the trauma of giving birth and the baby is actually delivered. The third phase is the parental response after birth in which emotional bonds are made between parents and offspring. It's also important to note that the fewer the offspring produced, the stronger the bond.

05 Campus Life

W: Yes, how can I assist you?
M: Hi. Ummm... I want to get some information.
W: OK, what kind of information would you like?
M: About the campus counseling. I think I might need some help.
W: I see. Well, that's what we are here for, to help students like you.
M: Good.
W: Now, I just need to ask you a few questions.
M: Sure, like what?
W: Well, first, what is the nature of your problem? Is it mainly academic? Is it a health issue? Is it financial, or is it perhaps related to a relationship problem?
M: Oh, OK. Hmmm. Well, it's kind of everything together.
W: OK. Let me ask some more specific questions.
M: All right.
W: Are your grades suffering? I mean, have they recently taken a nose dive?
M: Umm, yeah, in some classes they have.
W: OK, but not all classes?
M: No, not all.
W: OK, well that's a good sign. In how many classes have you noticed the change?
M: Two of the five I'm in now.
W: Well, that's not so bad.
M: Except that I'm now failing those classes miserably.
W: I see. Now, what about health problems? Are you feeling a specific pain or illness in some specific area, or is it more of a general malaise?
M: It's nothing specific really. It just seems that I never have any energy anymore. I never want to do anything. I don't want to talk to anyone or go out, and I sure don't want to hit the books when I should be. I can't even bring myself to go to classes much these days.
W: Aha. Those are actually really common symptoms at this time of year.
M: Really?
W: Oh yeah. The cold weather and short days can affect people that way, especially when combined with end-of-semester stress.

M: Wow. That's good to know.
W: Yeah. It's important for you to know that you're not alone in this — not by a long shot. Now, you also mentioned financial problems?
M: Yeah, well that's not the biggest problem, but I did quit my part-time job at the student union.
W: Do you have enough money for your basic necessities, like food, books, tuition?
M: Yeah. I just don't have enough to go out much anymore, which isn't such a big deal because I don't feel like going out much anymore.
W: All right, well hopefully we can turn that around. We can probably help you get your job back, too, if you so choose.
M: OK.
W: And what about your relationship problem?
M: Well, the problem is I don't have any relationships, though that's not a new thing. It's been like that for quite a while.
W: I see. OK, the next thing I need is your name and student number. Then, I can arrange an appointment to see a counselor for you. The counselor will talk more with you about your problems and will try to come up with a plan of action to get you back on track. He or she may even refer you to a medical doctor if they think you need medication. Any questions?
M: Umm, no, I guess not. Here's my student card.

06 Astronomy

M: You all know, of course, what astronomy is; this is Astronomy 205 after all, but do you know what "cosmology" is?
W: Hmmm. I know the Russians called "astronauts" "cosmonauts." Is cosmology just the Russian word for astronomy?
M: I like your reasoning on that, but no, I'm afraid you're not exactly correct. Cosmology is, in fact, quite similar to astronomy, but more specifically, cosmology is the study of the universe and its components. This includes how the universe was formed, how it has evolved, its future, and, by extension, man's place in it. You can think of cosmology in macro terms. Where astronomy also looks at every little planet and asteroid, cosmology is only concerned with the larger things, the cosmos as we say. Modern cosmology grew from the beliefs of ancient man and his ideas about the origin of the universe. Ever since people could think, they've sought to explain the existence and nature of the world around them. The search continues today for answers to the "big three" questions of life. One, where did we come from? Two, why are we here? Three, where are we going?

This quest has split cosmology into three main disciplines: religious cosmology, physical cosmology, and metaphysical cosmology. In religious cosmology, beliefs about the creation and destruction of the universe provide a framework for understanding man's role in the universe and his relationship to the creator of that universe — a god or gods, depending on the belief system. This view holds that the universe was consciously created, and that the creator has some purpose or design for everything in it, including man. In many cases, religious cosmologies also foretell the end of the universe. Many religions accept the findings of physical cosmology, arguing that science supports their conceptions. After religious cosmology, we have physical cosmology. Physical cosmology deals with the study of the physical origins of the universe and the nature of the universe on its very largest scale. It seeks to understand the universe through scientific observation and experiment. Modern scientific cosmology uses physics, astronomy, and mathematics to explain how the universe began and how it is growing. For hundreds of years, scientists thought the universe was static and unchanging, but in 1964, they confirmed that the universe began with an explosion, coined the "Big Bang." Recent technological advances in telescopes and space observatories have provided a wealth of new information about physical cosmology. We now have a much better understanding of not only what makes up the universe, but also its overall architecture. At the core of modern physical cosmology is an idea developed by the ancient Greeks, called geometric cosmology. Geometric cosmology is the belief that the underlying order of the universe can be expressed in mathematical form... but is mathematics a human invention, or does it have an independent existence?

W: Math is pure; it has an independent existence, doesn't it?

M: Well, that's what many people believe, but it's hard to prove. It's like the whole "if a tree falls in the forest and nobody is there to hear it, does it make a sound" conundrum. Mathematics may indeed have an existence independent from human invention, but as humans, we can only experience math as humans. This can be a tough concept to grasp, but let's move on now to the third type of cosmology: metaphysical cosmology. Who can tell me what metaphysics is? Any philosophy majors out there?

W: Yeah, metaphysics is the study of reality and the ways in which we can perceive it.

M: Very good, you must have taken a philosophy class or two. Thank you. So, metaphysical cosmology stands in between religious and physical cosmology. Metaphysical cosmology seeks to draw logical conclusions about the nature of the universe and man's place in it, addressing questions that are beyond the scope of science. Unlike religious cosmology, it approaches these questions using philosophical methods, such as dialectics, that is, examining opposite arguments in coming to a conclusion. For example, metaphysical cosmology might borrow presumed facts from religion or observation and compare it with scientific facts. One example is the cosmological argument, which is an argument for the existence of God based primarily on the point of view that the mere existence of a universe demands a creator.

So, just to review, the three types of cosmology are religious, physical, and metaphysical. Religious cosmology relies on religious texts and beliefs, physical cosmology uses science and math, and metaphysical cosmology uses philosophy to bridge the gap between religious and physical cosmology.

Chapter 2

Skill Review

A-F

01 Geology

W: Today, I'll begin with the basics about minerals. It's important that you supplement this information by reading chapter 3 in your textbook because I'm sticking only to the bare bones here. All right...it's essential to remember that both chemical composition and crystal structure together define a mineral. Some students find that surprising. They think that crystals are pure — just one element. That may be true for some crystals, but not all. Minerals range in composition from pure elements and simple salts to very complex silicates with thousands of known forms. So to define a mineral, we have to figure its composition. What all is in it? Now, here is a useful tip that may save you a point or two on the next exam. Organic compounds are usually excluded from the category mineral. Got that? If it's organic, don't classify it as a mineral. In fact, there are five main criteria for calling something a mineral. Let's go through those criteria. First of all, it must be in a solid state, not liquid, gas, or plasma. Minerals are solid. Second, it must be naturally occurring. In other words, it can't be man-made. Third, it has to be inorganic. Like I said, if it's organic, it's not a mineral. So third — oh, sorry — we're on number four now. Fourth, for something to be a mineral, it needs to have a fixed composition, which means the chemical composition is the same everywhere it is found and every time it is found. Mineral X found in my backyard is going to have the same composition as Mineral X found in Australia. Finally, our fifth criterion is that a mineral must be either an element or a compound; so it cannot be a mixture of a chemical compound and an element. Don't worry if that last one seems a bit vague at the moment. We'll talk a lot more about that over the next couple of classes.

Sometimes we get certain cases that satisfy all but one criterion. That's close, but not a mineral. These things are usually classified as mineraloids. Pearls would be a good example. Pearls are solid. They occur naturally. They have a fixed composition, and they're a compound. The only criterion they don't meet is the "inorganic test." Pearls are actually a mixture of organic and inorganic substances. So, because they have that extra organic stuff mixed in, we can't classify them as minerals. Pearls should be called mineraloids.

Now, here's another interesting case. Two or more minerals may have the same chemical composition, but differ in crystal structure. These are known as polymorphs. A good example of a polymorph pair is pyrite and marcasite, which are both iron sulfide. Let's create a simple analogy to help you grasp that concept in case you're confused. Let's say Michelangelo has one large piece of marble. He splits it in two. One piece, he carves into the shape of a horse, and the other piece into the shape of a woman. They are exactly the same in chemical composition, but nobody would really claim they're the same after he's finished. Think of pyrite and marcasite as two of nature's sculptures, both made of iron sulfide!

All right, let's see if you've been listening (laughs). Here's my question. How about frozen H_2O...or ice in layman's terms? Is it a mineral? Anybody? Yes, Sam?

M: Well, I'm not positive about this, but...in liquid state, it's just a chemical compound, right? But as ice it becomes a mineral.

W: We've got the five criteria for minerals, right? Tell me about each one in terms of ice and we can check.

M: OK. Ice is a solid with crystalline structure, and it's not a human-made substance. Ice isn't alive and never has been; it's...how did you put it?...exactly the same everywhere you find it and every time you find it, or whatever; it's a pure compound although it might have other elements suspended in it. Did I cover everything?

W: Well done, Sam. I'm glad somebody was listening (laughs). You're absolutely right. Ice is a mineral.

M: Kind of strange though. Before this class, I never would have thought of ice as a mineral.

W: I agree that it's odd to think of it as a mineral. That's because most of the minerals around us seem like metals or rocks. Most people forget that minerals come in many states of matter and forms. That's why we have those five criteria for determining whether or not a substance is a mineral. Also, we need to keep in mind that both chemical composition and crystal structure together define a mineral. OK, so now we can identify minerals. But what can we do with them?

02 Campus Life

W: Excuse me, Dr. Anderson?

M: You must be Maria, come in. What seems to be the problem?

W: Well, I've decided to change my major. I was majoring in chemistry, but now I've decided to major in psychology.

M: That's terrific. What area are you interested in?

W: Well, that's the problem. You see, because I was majoring in chemistry, I didn't take any psychology classes in my second year.

M: You're in your third year now, I presume.

W: That's right, and I'd like to take developmental psychology.

M: But it's a third-year course and you don't have the prerequisites.

W: Exactly.

M: So, just take some second-year courses this year, and next year you can take developmental. Unless you want to specialize in developmental...

W: That's just it. I want to go into child psychology.

M: Well, I'm sure you know that it's a little late in the game. Tell me, why the sudden change in plans?

W: Well, over the summer, I did some volunteer work at the women's shelter and spent a lot of time with the kids there. After working with children from violent homes, I really think I can make a difference in their lives.

M: A noble endeavor. Tell me, have you thought about your thesis topic yet?

W: No, not yet. I just made this decision a week ago, and I've only taken introductory psych.

M: I understand. That's why I think you shouldn't be too hasty in making this decision.

W: Why's that?

M: Well, like you said, you've only taken introductory psych. You may discover that you don't like developmental. To be honest, it sounds to me like you might be more interested in social work.

W: I suppose that's another option.

M: I'm not trying to discourage you. I'm just saying you should explore all of your options.

W: But this is my third year. I have to decide now.

M: OK. What I would suggest is this: first semester, you take a variety of psych courses. Get exposed to everything that the field has to offer.

W: That's a good idea.

M: Now, I want you to know that we do set down prerequisites for a reason.

W: Oh, I understand that, and I'll work extra hard to catch up.

M: I'm sure you will. Now, normally students take statistics in the first semester and research methods the next, but I want you to take both during the next semester. I'd like you to consider holding off on developmental until the semester after that, once you've got the methodologies down.

W: OK, I'll think about it, but I really would like to get started right away.

M: Well, it is nice to see such an enthusiastic student. Take this permission slip when you go to the office to register.

W: Oh, I really appreciate this, Dr. Anderson.

03 Phys. Ed.

W: Today, let's move on to the final stroke that I want you to practice — the butterfly. I hope you've all been working on freestyle, breast stroke, and back stroke in your scheduled pool time. On your physical exams, you'll have to show us that you can do them all with proficiency, so don't neglect any one of them. Umm...OK, now we come to the notorious butterfly. In my opinion, the difficulty of the butterfly has been blown all out of proportion. We just don't grow up doing it, and that's because it's a racing stroke. All right, I've been observing all of you during swimming practice, and... well... it's clear to me that your arm movement is inefficient. Today, let's review arm movement in the butterfly stroke.

Let's deconstruct it and look at its internal organization. Mastering the arms in the butterfly is all about economy and efficiency of movement. The butterfly stroke's arm movement has three major parts: the pull, the push, and the recovery. During the pull, the hands sink a little bit down with the palms facing outwards and slightly down at shoulder width. This is called catching the water. The pull movement follows a semicircle with the elbow higher than the hand and the hand pointing towards the center of the body and downward. The semicircle ends in front of the chest at the beginning of the ribcage. That constitutes the pull. Any questions about that? Sure, go ahead.

M: I get it, basically, but I have a problem. My arms get tired really fast.

W: And I'll tell you why, Greg. I was watching you this morning, and it's because your palms are too close together at the start of the pull.

M: Oh, I see, but I thought a wide entry was a bad thing.

W: Oh, it certainly is! The arms enter the water at shoulder width with the thumbs first. A wider entry loses movement in the next pull phase, and a smaller entry, where the hands touch, wastes energy. You need to find a happy medium. Got it?

M: Yes, thanks.

W: Next, the push. The swimmer pushes the palm backward through the water. The palm is underneath the body at the beginning of the push and at the side of the body at the end. The movement speeds up throughout the pull-push phase. Many swimmers make the mistake of thinking of the beginning of the pull as the focus. This leads them to neglect the push. In fact, that push should be fast and strong if you're going to make a good recovery. It's the only way to be truly efficient, looking at the arm movement as a whole, repeated process. Yes? Another question?

M: Is it the same as you said with freestyle? You said we should keep applying pressure until our hand leaves the water in freestyle.

W: It's not exactly the same. For the butterfly, you need to make sure you actually increase the speed throughout the pull-push phase. In freestyle, it's a uniform speed. We're running out of time here, so if anybody else has questions, I'll deal with them by the pool when I see you, but we need to talk about one point regarding recovery. As I said a few minutes ago, the speed at the end of the push is used to help with the recovery. Try not to use too much muscle during the recovery. The recovery swings the arms sideways across the water surface to the front, with the elbows slightly higher than the hands and shoulders. The arms have to be swung forward fast in order not to enter the water too early. If your arms enter the water too early, you lose a lot of momentum, forcing yourself to work a lot harder. A good rule of thumb is this: fly, don't jump. Get used to going in and out using a fluid motion. Don't jump in and out because that slows you down too much and tires you too quickly. Try to just skim the water. When you get used to it, it'll feel like you're just flying on top of the water. Pull, push, recovery, repeat. OK, that's all for now.

04 History

W: I would like to discuss some of the historical events that led to the signing of the Magna Carta. The Magna Carta is the most famous document of British constitutional history and is widely considered to be the first step in what was a long process leading to the establishment of a constitutional monarchy. The Magna Carta required the king to give up a number of rights. As a result, the king had to follow certain legal procedures and to accept that the will of the king was not absolute.

Let's take a look at the background to all this. By the end of the 12ᵗʰ century, that is the late 1100s, the English king had become the most powerful monarch ever seen in Europe. At that time, the king of England even controlled part of northern France, Normandy. All of England's possessions were controlled by barons, and the king ruled over the barons. However, when King John came to the throne in the early 13ᵗʰ century, he made a series of mistakes that led the barons of England to impose limitations on the king's power. The Magna Carta was the result of disagreements between King John and his barons over the rights of the king. We can identify three principal failures of King John. First, King John was not respected. This was due to the way he took power. There had been two candidates to take the place of the previous king, Richard the Lionheart, who died in 1199. One was John, and the other was his nephew, Arthur of Brittany. John captured Arthur and imprisoned him. Although there was no proof, it was believed that John murdered Arthur. This, of course, led people to have a very low opinion of John as someone who would kill members of his own family to be king.

His second failure occurred when he became involved in a dispute with the Church of England. John disagreed with the Church over who should be the next archbishop of Canterbury. The fight continued over several years, and in 1209, John was excommunicated. This meant he was no longer allowed to attend church services or be involved in the Church in any way. He finally had to give in to the Church in 1213.

His third failure was in 1214. Philip Augustus, the King of France, took hold of most of the land in France owned by the English. The English barons demanded that John retake the land. John did make an attempt, but failed. In the process, the English lost a large amount of land, and as a result, King John was given the nickname John "Lackland."

By 1215, the barons were fed up and stormed London. They forced John to agree to a document known as the "Articles of the Barons," and in return, the barons renewed their vows to be loyal to him. A formal document was created to record this agreement on July 15, 1215. This formal document was the original Magna Carta. The Magna Carta was composed of 63 different articles. Most of these were specific to society of the 13ᵗʰ century and thus irrelevant in contemporary times, but I would like to take a look at one of those articles, a very important article of the Magna Carta: Article 61.

Article 61 was the most significant clause for King John. It was known as the "security article" and was the longest portion of the entire document. Article 61 established a committee of 25 barons who could at any time meet, and, if they felt it was necessary, had the power to overrule the king. This could be done through force by seizing his castles and possessions if needed. In addition, the King had to take an oath of loyalty to the committee of barons. However, King John had no intention of honoring the Magna Carta, as he had been forced to sign it, and Article 61 basically took away his powers. In other words, it made him King in name only. John renounced the Magna Carta as soon as the barons left London, which threw the whole country into a civil war, known as the First Barons' War. John died in the middle of this war. His nine-year-old son was crowned King

Henry III in late October 1216, and the war then ended. On November 12, 1216, the Magna Carta was reissued with Article 61 omitted.

Chapter 3

Focus A 01

01 Campus Life

M: Have you thought about what you're going to do this summer, Gloria?

W: Well, I can work full time at the restaurant if I want to.

M: That's where you worked last summer, right?

W: Yes, and I'm still working there part time.

M: Do they pay pretty well?

W: Yes, with tips the money is pretty good, but I'm graduating next year, so I'd like to get some experience in my field.

M: That's a good idea. Maybe you should try to get an internship.

W: An internship? I'd love to. It would mean a pay cut, but it'd be worth it.

M: Yeah, they don't pay very well, but in the long run, they sure do pay off. Not only do you get experience, you make all kinds of contacts.

W: Yes, it would be good to have some experience and some references under my belt when I start looking for work after graduation. I just have no idea how to go about finding a summer internship.

M: Why don't you go to the Summer Job/Internship fair?

W: I didn't know such a thing existed! When do they hold that?

M: Hang on, I've got the pamphlet in my backpack.

W: Great.

M: Here it is...let's see...it's actually next week, on the 16ᵗʰ. It starts at 9:30 a.m. and goes until 3:00 p.m.

W: Is it here on campus?

M: At the University Center Ballroom.

W: That's great. Is it casual, or should I dress as if I'm going to an interview?

M: It says here that it's business casual.

W: So, should I bring my resumé?

M: Umm...it's not mandatory, but it's a good idea.

W: OK. Does it say there what kinds of internships are available?

M: You're into logistics, right?

W: Yup.

M: They've got something at Office Depot and at Wal-Mart.

W: Fantastic. Are you going, too?

M: Yes, I'm going to try to get hired on at a summer camp.

W: Oh, that sounds like fun.

M: It sure would be. It would be a good experience, too, since I'm studying to be a teacher.

W: Yeah, that would be excellent. Are there many camps listed on there?

M: There are three. One's at Camp Ton-A-Wandah, one's at Wesley Woods, and the other is at Camp Webb.

W: Camp Ton-A-Wandah? I went there when I was a kid! I had a horrible time. The camp counselors were awful.

M: Really? Well, I'll be different.

W: I'm sure you will. I'll give you a few pointers some time.

M: Let's just wait and see if I get the job.

W: You won't have any trouble. You're at the top of your class, and you do all that volunteer work.

M: Thanks for the vote of confidence. And good luck to you.

W: Thanks, I'll need it. Hey, do you want to go together?

M: Sure. We should go early.

W: Good idea. We'll look enthusiastic that way.

M: Let's meet at 9:15.

02 Campus Life

M: Is there something I can help you with?

W: Yes, I have a few questions about that online tutoring service. I can't remember what it's called.

M: You mean Smartthinking.com? I think I can probably answer any questions you might have. What would you like to know?

W: Well, I'm thinking of enrolling, but there are a couple of things I'd like to know first. Like for one thing, are there any restrictions on log on times? I usually do my work late at night, so it won't be much use to me if it can only be accessed during regular working hours.

M: Not to worry. You are free to log on anytime, anywhere.

W: That's good to hear. I've also heard that there is some kind of writing clinic or something. What can you tell me about that?

M: Ah, you mean the writing lab. Yes, what that is is a tool to help you improve your writing. You can submit your writing to the online writing lab, and you will receive a critique with some constructive criticism to help you develop your writing skills. It's also open twenty-four hours a day, seven days a week.

W: That should be helpful. Will I get an instant reply?

M: It won't be instant, but you will receive a reply within 24 hours. We give priority to distance education students because it is impossible for them to consult their instructors face-to-face, but everyone using Smartthinking will get a fast response. Remember the 24 hour rule, though. If you have a paper due at eight o'clock the following morning, you probably won't get your response in time. Always submit your work at least two days before the paper is due. Be sure to leave yourself enough time to do revisions as well.

W: What about security? Is there any chance somebody could get a hold of my paper and copy it for themselves?

M: Absolutely not. Everyone who has access to submissions in the writing lab is accountable.

W: Oh! The papers go to a writing lab? So these aren't English professors who are giving feedback?

M: No. Your paper will be evaluated by a graduate student who works in our writing lab. Most of them are English majors, but even if they're not, they all have a strong background in writing.

W: I see. Now, I know that the tutoring program is free, but is there any kind of registration fee for first-time users?

M: No. There are no charges at all. However, only students currently enrolled at Citywide Community College can use Smartthinking. It has been set up to provide academic support for our students, so unfortunately we can't offer the service to anyone else. Are you currently enrolled at this community college?

W: Yes.

M: Great. What kind of computer do you have?

W: I have a Mac. That won't be a problem, will it?

M: No, not at all. As long as you have Internet Explorer, you'll be able to log on to the online tutoring system with no difficulties. I assume that you have a modem?

W: Right, I have a 56K modem.

M: That's fine. Then all you need to do now is choose your subjects and sign up.

W: Can I sign up right now?

M: Of course. Those two computers right over there have Internet access. You can use either one to log on and sign up.

W: Great. Thanks.

Focus A 02

01 Campus Life

M: Excuse me?

W: Yes, may I help you?

M: I have a question about getting a book.

W: Sure, I can help you with that. Did you need help finding the book?

M: No, I found it. Or at least I found the listing on the computer, but it says the book is checked out. So, I wanted to ask if there was any way to put my name on a list or something so that I can come get the book once it is checked back in.

W: Oh, I see. You want to reserve the book.

M: I guess so. Do you have a reserve list or something?

W: Actually, you can reserve a book using the library computer. Let me show you. We can use this computer right over here. You can type in the information. I'll just tell you what you need to do at each step.

M: Great. Thanks.

W: Go ahead and type in the title of the book that you need.

M: So, I just do a regular search, like I want to find the book in the library? Like this?

W: That's right. Is that the book you were looking for?

M: That's it. See, it lists a due date next week.

W: OK. There is a button at the top of the screen that will allow you to request the next available copy as soon as it comes in.

M: Let me guess: this button that says "request next available copy"?

W: Right.

M: I feel dumb.

W: Not at all. I work with this system every day, so I know all of its features. Most students don't know half of the options available to them with our computer system. It can do a lot more than students use it for.

M: Now, it's asking me for my card number and PIN. I guess that means my student ID number since that's what I use as my library card.

W: Correct, and your PIN is the same as the PIN number you use when you access the university's online registration or other computer services.

M: Then, I just click this log in button down here?

W: Uh-huh, and after your log in information is confirmed, the request page should open. There it is. You can see that the box next to the "pick up" option is already checked. Just leave that checked, and when the book comes in, the circulation desk will email you that the book is here. Then, you can come in and pick it up.

M: What if I uncheck the "pick up" box. How can I get the book?

W: Then, the book will be mailed to the address we have on file with your student ID card, but mailing the book takes longer. If you need the book right away for class or for some research that you're doing, I would suggest just coming in and picking it up.

M: Yeah. I want the book as soon as possible, so I'll come pick it up.

W: Then you can just click the request button at the bottom of the screen and you're done.

M: OK. Request. Done. That was easy. Thanks for your help.

02 Campus Life

M: Donna? What are you doing? The cafeteria has closed for the afternoon. Why are you sitting here?

W: Oh. Nothing. I just didn't want to go back to my dorm room yet.

M: Uh oh. Roommate problems?

W: Kind of. Yes. I don't know, Rob. I just don't think I can live with her for the rest of the semester. I mean, she's not a terrible roommate. It's just the small things that irritate me, and recently there have been more and more small things.

M: Well, you can't spend the rest of the semester here in front of the cafeteria. You're going to have to talk to your roommate and let her know what's bothering you.

W: I can't do that.

M: Why not? I thought you were living with your old high school friend.

W: I am. That's why I can't tell her all the things that are bothering me. We've been friends for years. How can I tell her this long list of stuff that she does that drives me up the wall?

M: Are you afraid you'll offend her or something? Hey, better to talk about this and get things out in the open. You might offend her, but at least there is chance you can still be friends. If you don't talk to her about how you feel, you could end up going your separate ways at the end of the semester and never speaking to each other again.

W: The end of the semester. That seems so far away right now. Can't you think of anything else, Rob? Some other way, like a mutual friend of ours telling her for me? Do you think that would work?

M: And drag someone else in the middle of the problem? No, that is definitely not a good idea. But maybe there is something else you can do. You could tell your resident advisor about the problem. Then, she could act as a mediator for the two of you.

W: Hey, that's not a bad idea. I could talk to Beth. She's cool. I'm sure she'd understand.

M: That's really what resident advisors are there for, you know. When roommates are having problems, they try to solve things from an unbiased perspective.

W: Did you ever have to ask your resident advisor to mediate a problem with your roommate?

M: No. I never had a problem with my roommate. Actually, I never saw too much of my first roommate. Either I was too busy with stuff, or he was too busy with stuff. We were never in the room hanging out together. It was just the place where we both slept. And my roommate this semester works in a lab, so I never see him either.

W: Lucky you. My roommate is always in our room watching TV. That's one of the things that bugs me.

M: Hopefully, your resident advisor will help you work things out.

W: Yeah. I think I'll go talk to her right now.

Focus B 01

01 Geography

M: Good day, everyone. Today, we're going to be looking at some of the effects the moon has on our lives. Can anyone tell me one such effect?

W1: Well, ummm, I've heard that full moons make people do crazy things.

M: Ha ha. Yes, I've heard that, too. Some statistics support that idea, but other studies refute it. In any case, you can debate that more in your psychology classes. But this is geography, so what physical effect does the moon have on our planet?

W1: Oh, OK then. Well, how about the tides? The moon's gravitational pull causes the tides, right?

M: Right you are. That's the information I was looking for, thank you. So, we know the moon causes tidal movement in the oceans, but can the moon cause rain? Do the moon and sun create tidal effects in the atmosphere as well as the oceans? In the past century, an air tide, or rather a kind of shifting of the atmosphere has been recognized. That, specifically, is what we're going to discuss today. As always, you are more than welcome to ask any questions you have as we go along.

The possibility of gravitational tides in the Earth's atmosphere was first suggested by Sir Isaac Newton. Newton is most famous for what discovery? Anyone?

W2: Wasn't he the gravity guy?

M: The gravity guy? Yes, I think you could say that. Newton was the first person to describe the force of gravity. Now, he came up with this theory on atmospheric tides while developing an explanation for ocean tides. Since 1918, scientists have been measuring air tides in the Northern Hemisphere, and although the changes in air pressure are small, their effects are not. Studies have shown that more cloudiness, rainfall, and storms are generated during certain lunar phases, such as the full moon.

In fact, even before Newton set down his theories on tides, people were aware that lunar phases corresponded with the rise and fall of the ocean tides. More recently, we have found that the moon is even able to cause deformations in the solid crust of the Earth. So, much in the same way the moon affects tidal movement in certain ways, it also pulls on the Earth's crust as well, causing it to move, too. Yes. Amazing, isn't it? The ground we walk on every day isn't necessarily as solid as it seems! Yes, there in the blue sweater?

W1: The textbook mentions that the moon can cause an atmospheric tide, and that it can create changes in air pressure. Is this an air tide, and is it true that these changes in air pressure can cause hurricanes?

M: Ah, as I was saying earlier, studies have shown an increase in storms corresponding to certain lunar phases. While we cannot yet explain this in full, it does appear that the moon has an influence on the weather. Whether they directly cause hurricanes or not, well, we'll have to wait for further research to determine that with any certainty, I'm afraid.

Let's look more at what happens during a full moon, though. Researchers at the University of Arizona discovered that at the time of a full moon, the temperature of the lower four miles of the Earth's atmosphere increases by a few hundredths of a degree. Now, a few hundredths of a degree may not sound like much to you, and you probably couldn't feel the difference yourselves, but it is significant. These researchers suggest that the moon warms our atmosphere in two ways. First, the moon's surface is heated by the sun and radiates thermal energy at the Earth. This energy is much less intense than the energy we get directly from the sun, but it is supplemented by a second phenomenon. The moon of course mirrors, or reflects, sunlight at the dark, or night, side of the Earth. However, the mirror effect is relatively slight because it reflects just 10 percent of the light of the sun. Nonetheless, as you all have experienced, I'm sure, that 10 percent is quite significant when compared to the zero percent reflected during a new moon. The difference is night and day, so to speak, if you'll forgive the pun. Anyhow, what I want you to take away from today's lecture is the fact that the moon can affect our weather. While we still have much to learn, we may well be justified in blaming the moon for a rainy day!

02 Geology

W: Today, I'll begin with the basics about minerals. It's important that you supplement this information by reading chapter 3 in your textbook because I'm sticking only to the bare bones here. All right...it's essential to remember that both chemical composition and crystal structure together define a mineral. Some students find that surprising. They think that crystals are pure — are just one element. That may be true for some crystals, but not all. Minerals range in composition from pure elements and simple salts to very complex silicates with thousands of known forms. So to define a mineral, we have to figure its composition. What all is in it? Now, here is a useful tip that may save you a point or two on the next exam. Organic compounds are usually excluded from the category mineral. Got that? If it's organic, don't classify it as a mineral. In fact, there are five main criteria for calling something a mineral. Let's go through those criteria. First of all, it must be in a solid state, not liquid, gas, or plasma. Minerals are solid. Second, it must be naturally occurring. In other words, it can't be man-made. Third, it has to be inorganic. Like I said, if it's organic, it's not a mineral. So, third — oh, sorry — we're on number four now. Fourth, for something to be a mineral, it needs to have a fixed composition, which means the chemical composition is the same everywhere it is found and every time it is found. Mineral X found in my backyard is going to have the same composition as Mineral X found in Australia. Finally, our fifth criterion is that a mineral must be either an element or a compound; so it cannot be a mixture of a chemical compound and an element. Don't worry if that last one seems a bit vague at the moment. We'll talk a lot more about that over the next couple of classes.

Sometimes we get certain cases that satisfy all but one criterion. That's close, but not a mineral. These things are usually classified as mineraloids. Pearls would be a good example. Pearls are solid. They occur naturally. They have a fixed composition, and they're a compound. The only criterion they don't meet is the "inorganic test." Pearls are actually a mixture of organic and inorganic substances. So, because they have that extra organic stuff mixed in, we can't classify them as minerals. Pearls should be called mineraloids.

Now, here's another interesting case. Two or more minerals may have the same chemical composition, but differ in crystal structure. These are known as polymorphs. A good example of a polymorph pair is pyrite and marcasite, which are both iron sulfide. Let's create a simple analogy to help you grasp that concept in case you're confused. Let's say Michelangelo has one large piece of marble. He splits it in two. One piece, he carves into the shape of a horse, and the other piece into the shape of a woman. They are exactly the same in chemical composition, but nobody would really claim they're the same after he's finished. Think of pyrite and marcasite as two of nature's sculptures, both made of iron sulfide!

All right, let's see if you've been listening (laughs). Here's my question. How about frozen H₂O...or ice in layman's terms? Is it a mineral? Anybody? Yes, Sam?

M: Well, I'm not positive about this, but...in liquid state, it's just a chemical compound, right? But as ice it becomes a mineral.

W: We've got the five criteria for minerals, right? Tell me about each one in terms of ice and we can check.

M: OK. Ice is a solid with crystalline structure, and it's not a human-made substance. Ice isn't alive and never has been; it's...how did you put it?...exactly the same everywhere you find it and every time you find it, or whatever; it's a pure compound although it might have other elements suspended in it. Did I cover everything?

W: Well done, Sam. I'm glad somebody was listening (laughs). You're absolutely right. Ice is a mineral.

M: Kind of strange though. Before this class, I never would have thought of ice as a mineral.

W: I agree that it's odd to think of it as a mineral. That's because most of the minerals around us seem like metals or rocks. Most people forget that minerals come in many states of matter and forms. That's why we have those five criteria for determining whether or not a substance is a mineral. Also, we need to keep in mind that both chemical composition and crystal structure together define a mineral.

Focus B 02

01 Biology

W: Have you ever wondered how we know which plants are good to eat and which ones are poisonous? Well, it was simply a very long and drawn-out process of trial and error. Throughout history, people ate what they could find, kill, or otherwise get a hold of. When there was a lack of a traditional food source, people had to try new things. Over time, they started to figure out which plants made them sick and which didn't.

Now, I am not just talking about ancient times before farming became established. This trial and error with plants was going on well into the 18th and 19th centuries! In fact, historical records indicate that in the 1800s plant poisoning had become a serious issue. Since food wasn't as readily available then as it is today, people were forced to take more chances with what they ate. Rather than drop by the market at the end of the street, people would have to wander out into the fields or forests and find whatever looked edible. Today, because the food supply is rather ample and stable, we rarely have to go find our lunch or dinner out in the woods.

Nonetheless, we still need to be careful. Poisonous plants can be found all around us: in our homes as decoration, in our lawns, and in the general landscape. Of course, we don't generally go around putting random plants in our mouths. However, children do. Have any of you ever caught your baby brother or sister chewing on one of the plants in your house? Or maybe you were caught chewing on one! Considering the fact that a baby's body is smaller and less hardy than ours, we have to look out for them. A small amount of poison that might go unnoticed in an adult can cause more serious harm to a child. So, poisonous plants are dangerous to kids, but there are measures that can be taken to ensure safety. You can identify the plants in your surroundings by giving a call to your local garden center. You can describe the plant to them, and hopefully they can tell you whether or not it has poisonous properties. Alternatively, you can take the plant down to show them. Also, if you buy a new plant, it is wise to ask whether or not it is poisonous.

Now, there are three main categories of toxicity in plants: extremely toxic, moderately toxic, and minimally toxic. These names, however, are very misleading. You see, the severity of the poison depends on a host of other factors, like the particular plant and the metabolism of the person. The term "poisoning" itself is actually also misleading. Poisoning doesn't only mean a person dies from the poison. Poisoning can result in anything from indigestion and skin irritation to lethal brain damage or death. Let's talk about a few categories of poisonous plants now. One category is the alkaloids. These are bitter-tasting plants with nitrogen compounds in them. A good example is hemlock. I mention it as an example because hemlock is famous. History buffs in the class may recall that it was the poison extracted from this plant that Socrates was forced to drink as his death sentence for corrupting the youth of Athens. That's just an interesting side note. Anyway, the effects of hemlock are similar to nicotine, but, obviously, much more severe as it can cause the nervous system to shut down, resulting in death. Plants with minerals in them form another category of poisonous plants. These plants build up a large amount of some mineral that is toxic in humans, such as lead or copper. The effects of eating these plants can include psychological malfunctioning and, in higher doses, death. Plants containing oxalates are the third category. Oxalates, spelled O-X-A-L-A-T-E-S, occur as small crystals in the plant and irritate the mouth. Not quite as serious as the other two, but poison nonetheless. Once again, those three categories of poisonous plants are the alkaloids, plants with minerals, and oxalates.

So, you may be wondering, why did poisonous plants evolve? What purpose does this serve? Well, there are many different sources of poison in different plants as we just heard, but in most cases, the poison is a by-product of one of the plant's natural life processes, and the poison serves as a defense mechanism for the plant. Animals learn which plants to stay away from because they get sick when they eat them. So, it follows that the plant will survive and reproduce because no one is eating it.

02 Literature

M: OK, let's start with a bit of background on Plutarch before we get to his work. The particular work I mean is Plutarch's *Lives*. Plutarch lived from the year 46 to the year 120 in what had been (and at a later date continued to be) Greece. For many years, Plutarch served as one of the two priests at the temple of Apollo at Delphi (the site of the famous Delphic Oracle) twenty miles from his home. Greece, by the turn of the first millenium, was a sad ruin of its former glory. Mighty Rome had looted its statues and reduced Greece to a mere conquered territory. Despite these circumstances, Mestrius Plutarchus — that is actually Plutarch's given name — lived a long and fruitful life with his wife and family in the little Greek town of Chaeronea.

So, that is the man. Now, about his work. Plutarch's plan in his work *Lives* was to pair a philosophical biography of a famous Roman with the biography of a Greek who was comparable in some way. Plutarch's work includes short essays of comparison for each pair of lives, and after each essay, Plutarch pauses to deliver penetrating observations on human nature as illustrated by his subjects. This structure makes it difficult to classify *Lives* under a single genre — I mean to classify it as history, biography, or philosophy. Plutarch's announced intention was NOT to write a chronicle of great historical events, but rather to examine the character of great men, as a lesson for the living. I think — and I certainly hope you agree after you've had a chance to read it — that this is a fascinating work with applicable lessons for living for readers even today.

An interesting point about Plutarch's Greek heroes is that his subjects had been dead for at least 300 years by the time he wrote about their lives, around 100 A.D. That means Plutarch had to rely on old manuscripts, many of which no longer exist today. All we have left to rely on is Plutarch's work. But even ancient legends can yield some insight, as Plutarch says at the beginning of his life of Theseus. Plutarch himself had no faith in the accuracy of even the so-called factual materials he had to work with. He actually made a comment to this effect in his essay on the life of Pericles. To quote, he said, "It is so hard to find out the truth of anything by looking at the record of the past. The process of time obscures the truth of former times, and even contemporaneous writers disguise and twist the truth out of malice or flattery." That's something for you to keep in mind the next time you're reading your history textbook. Anyway, in spite of this problem, Plutarch managed to compare Roman and Greek heroes, and do it well enough that his work has survived the ages.

It is interesting that this work was very popular until the 20th century. Then, people pretty much forgot about it. Let's talk a little bit about why that happened. The Romans loved Plutarch's *Lives,* and enough copies were written out over the next centuries that a copy of most parts of *Lives* managed to survive the Dark Ages in different places. It's interesting to note the number of famous figures from history who have appreciated Plutarch's writing and wisdom. Beethoven, as he was growing deaf, wrote in 1801, and I quote: "I have often cursed my Creator and my existence. Plutarch has shown me the path of resignation. If it is at all possible, I will bid defiance to my fate, though I feel that as long as I live there will be moments when I shall be God's most unhappy creature ... Resignation, what a wretched resource! Yet it is all that is left to me." Beethoven read Plutarch's comparisons of the lives of Greek and Roman heroes and found wisdom there. There are many other examples of famous people finding inspiration in Plutarch. The poet Ralph Waldo Emerson was another fan of *Lives*.

So, you may be asking yourself, "If this book is so famous, why haven't I ever heard of it?" Well, despite all of the attention Plutarch's work got through the ages, by the 20th century, Plutarch's popularity began to fade. None of the literary scholars were putting out revitalized new editions of *Lives*. Probably because students were demanding more diversity in the reading curriculum, so a lot of classic works of literature were being pushed aside. Another factor could have been that *Lives* is a difficult book. Plutarch uses a complicated style of writing, so it's not an easy read.

Speaking

Chapter 1

Skill A

Q1 — practice 1
Sample response:
Lance Armstrong is my role model for several reasons. First, he is a cyclist who has won the Tour de France seven times in a row. That, however, is not the only reason I respect this man. He also battled cancer. When I heard his story, it changed my life. Lance Armstrong inspired me to never give up on my dream of going to the Olympics, even though it may seem impossible. His qualities of endurance and perseverance compelled me to become a better athlete and a stronger person.

Q1 — practice 2
Sample response:
One gadget that has helped me with schoolwork is my "reading pen." To begin, I have dyslexia, a learning disability that makes reading very difficult. The reading pen was of great assistance to me. It scans words on a page and reads them out loud to me. I used it every day to help me with my reading assignments. Without it, I would have spent hours reading my assignments and wouldn't have had time to study properly. Because of my reading pen, I was able to excel in school.

Q1 — practice 3
Sample response:
When I was a child, I used to play soccer and baseball. I feel that practicing these sports helped me greatly. The chief benefit was that competing in these sports made my body healthy, instilling me with endurance and strength. Playing baseball developed my upper body strength for hitting and throwing. Soccer, on the other hand, provided me with lower body strength for kicking and stamina and endurance for playing full 90-minute games. Developing a strong, healthy body when I was young has been crucial in maintaining my health later in life.

Q2 — practice 1
Sample response 1:
In my opinion, high school students should be required to follow a certain curriculum. This ensures students are exposed to a wide variety of subjects. If, for example, I had been permitted to select whatever courses I wanted, I would only have taken courses that I found diverting. In the long run, this would have limited my ability to pursue a medical career, which is what I'm doing now. Obviously, if I had been left to my own devices about choosing my courses, I would not be where I am today.

Sample response 2:
In my opinion, educators should let high school students decide which courses they want to study. This ensures that all students are in charge of their own destinies, and they should be permitted to determine their own academic paths. If, for example, a student prefers art to science, why should she waste her time studying science? In the long run, her efforts would be better spent on developing skills in a field that interests her. Obviously, if she has to direct part of her energy toward a course she doesn't like, she will have less time and energy to put toward her real interests.

Q2 — practice 2
Sample response 1:
Some celebrities become rich and famous and then return very little to society, while others attempt to use their influence to raise public awareness of a special cause, such as environmentalism or human rights. In my opinion, we are all better off heeding the expert advice of professionals and officials. After all, how much can a pop star really know about solving problems in Africa? Some people say stars can do a lot if they get behind a particular cause, and there may be some truth to that. However, expecting an erudite opinion from a pop star about health issues in Nigeria is a different matter.

Sample response 2:
Some celebrities become rich and famous and then return very little to society, while others attempt to use their influence to raise public awareness of a special cause, such as environmentalism or human rights. In my opinion, the least the public can do is carefully consider these views. After all, a person living at the top of society probably has a much better view of it and can see problems that normal people cannot. Some cynics contend that people should ignore well-known artists when they express their thoughts on global issues. However, I attribute these views to jealousy.

Q2 — practice 3
Sample response 1:
Some children begin helping out with household chores as soon as they are old enough, while others may never lift a finger. I personally feel that children should pitch in around the house as soon as possible. This teaches them the value of work and gives them a feeling of accomplishment and responsibility. Children who never have to assist around the house often become spoiled and grow up expecting others to do work for them. Parents may think they are helping their kids by doing their work for them, but in the long run, this is not the case.

Sample response 2:
Some children begin helping out with household chores as soon as they are old enough, while others may never lift a finger. I personally feel that childhood is a special time for learning and playing. This helps kids develop imagination, creativity, and social skills through interacting with friends. Children who have little time to enjoy childhood because they are doing work or chores are not given the opportunity to be young. Parents may think that they are teaching their kids responsibility, but in the long run, this lesson costs children more than it's worth.

Skill B

Q3 — practice 1
W: I heard they're going to start building that new Science Center soon.
M: That's right. They're starting on March 8th.
W: I don't know why they don't hold off until summer.
M: I think they want to have it finished before September when the new school year starts.
W: I know, but I teach a class in Clemens Hall like you. The cacophony from the construction is going to be really distracting.
M: Oh, didn't you see the announcement? They're going to relocate all of our classes.

W: Oh really? Well that allays my fears a bit. Maybe it's a wise decision after all. Where are we being moved to?

M: I don't know yet. We're supposed to get a memo once they figure it all out.

W: Well, I hope it's soon. It will take time to move all of our stuff.

Sample response:
The woman thinks that the university ought to wait until summer before they start building the new Science Center. Her concern is that the classes in nearby buildings, specifically, her class at Clemens Hall, will be distracted by the noise from the construction. However, when she talks to the man, he tells her that the university is planning on relocating the classes in Clemens Hall to other buildings on campus. When she learns this, she is relieved, and changes her mind about waiting until summer to commence construction on the new building.

Q3 — practice 2

M: Did you hear about this new anti-spam filter they're going to implement?

W: Yeah, I think it's tremendous. I abhor receiving spam. It wastes too much of my time.

M: My worry would be that it would block important mail, though. I mean, surely it will make mistakes from time to time.

W: Yes, of course, that's what your bulk folder is for.

M: Bulk folder?

W: Yes, according to the announcement, the anti-spam filter is only going to block mail that is obviously spam. If there's any incertitude, they will send it to your bulk folder.

M: Oh, so there's no chance that an email from a friend or from a potential employer will be misidentified as spam?

W: No, and it would be rare that something like that would be sent to your bulk folder.

M: OK. Well, if there's no risk involved, I think it's great, too.

Sample response:
The man and the woman are discussing a new anti-spam filter that will be installed at their university. The woman, who hates receiving spam, thinks it's a wonderful idea. The man, however, is concerned that the filter will make mistakes and accidentally block important mail. The woman assures him, though, that the filter has a safety feature. It only blocks mail that is obviously spam. If an incoming email looks suspicious, it is sent to the person's bulk folder. In the end, the man agrees that this system is probably safe and agrees with the woman that it is a good idea.

Q3 — practice 3

M: Hey June! Do you remember what the extra credit assignment was for our Web Design course?

W: Oh, yeah. Dr. Penrose said we could write a review of that guest speaker's presentation for 15 extra credit points.

M: Fifteen? Nice! Who's the speaker?

W: Oh, you know, James Brentworth, the high school whiz kid from San Diego who made a million dollars from his website.

M: Oh wow! THAT guy is gonna speak at our school? When?

W: There are announcements about it posted all over campus. It's gonna be Thursday night from seven to eight. I heard it's over in Selwidge Hall, next to the theater.

M: This should be a great opportunity. He probably has lots of useful counsel for future web designers. Plus, it's a freebie, right?

W: Yeah, and there's a question period afterwards, too.

M: Excellent! I'm going to prepare a few questions beforehand.

Sample response:
First, the man asks the woman for information on an extra credit assignment for a Web Design class they are both in. The woman then refers him to an announcement about a guest speaker, reminding him that they can earn credit for attending the talk. The man is excited about the opportunity for two reasons. First, he thinks the guest speaker will provide useful advice for aspiring web designers. In addition, he is pleased that there's no charge for admission to the speech. Therefore, he will prepare some questions to ask the speaker and attend the speech to receive extra credit.

Q4 — practice 1

W: You've all read about the Nash Equilibrium. Let's look at a real world situation to which a Nash Equilibrium might apply. Some seemingly insignificant choices in life become significant if people don't agree. For example, it doesn't matter if people drive on the left side of the road or on the right side, provided everyone agrees on one. Because of the risk of collision, it is in everyone's interest to adopt the same policy. Even during rush hour traffic, when drivers all want to get home as quickly as possible, and the left lane of oncoming traffic is empty, people will stay in the slow-moving right-hand lanes. In essence, these commuters are in competition with one another to get home as quickly as possible, yet each driver independently chooses the right side of the road because of the risk of failure or delay driving on the left side would pose.

Sample response:
The reading passage describes the Nash Equilibrium, a situation in competitions in which it is not in any competitor's interest to change strategy. The professor expounds on this idea by illustrating a real-life example of the Nash Equilibrium. This example refers to drivers in rush hour traffic. If each driver is considered a competitor, and driving on one side of the road as the strategy, then it fits the Nash Equilibrium. That is to say, it is not in a driver's interest to change strategy, given that a collision could hinder the success of that driver, and coincidentally, the other drivers, too.

Q4 — practice 2

M: The common view that the Black Plague was a strain of bubonic plague spread by fleas living on rats has come under renewed scrutiny in recent years. Several factors have led researchers to propose other microorganisms as the culprits for this pandemic. The first crucial piece of evidence comes from Iceland, where rats were not introduced until the 1800s. Despite this, Iceland was severely affected by the Black Plague long before 1800, but not by subsequent plagues known to have been spread by rats. Furthermore, the incubation period of the Black Plague (up to 30 days) and the rate at which it spread both point away from the bacterium *Yersinia pestis* as a logical cause. Some researchers have proposed pulmonary anthrax or the Ebola virus as more likely agents. Testing for these theories is still in its infancy, but forensic inspection of a 14th-century mass grave has revealed no traces of *Yersinia pestis*.

Sample response:
In the lecture, the professor discusses new theories about the cause of the Black Plague, a disease that killed two-thirds of Europeans in the 14th century. The traditional theory that it was bubonic plague spread to people by fleas carried on rats does not match up with some new evidence. First, Iceland was severely affected despite the fact it had no rats. Second, the incubation period and spreading of

the disease differed from those typical of bubonic plagues. For these reasons, some researchers are now proposing other diseases as the cause, such as pulmonary anthrax or the Ebola virus.

Q4 — practice 3

W: I trust that you've all read in your textbooks that the Great Zimbabwe civilization was founded around the year 450 by ancestors of modern-day Shona speakers. This, however, has not always been the accepted interpretation of the archaeological evidence. After the British "discovery" of the ruins, British Imperialist officials became concerned. You see, the idea of a "black" civilization undermined the justification behind British Imperialism, namely, that whites were superior and that it was their duty to civilize other, "savage" peoples. Government officials commissioned a number of British archaeologists, including Bent and Hall, to investigate the site. Unfortunately, these men destroyed and plundered much of the ruins and officially concluded that the civilization had been built by foreigners from the north. Fortunately, however, archaeologist Randall-MacIver investigated the site in 1905, and her findings contradicted the earlier theories. The British Empire responded by banning archaeologists from the site for nearly 25 years! The racist myth about the ruins was not fully dispelled until Zimbabwe's independence in 1980.

Sample response:
The lecture discusses the rewriting of the history of the Great Zimbabwe civilization during the British Colonial period. The reading details the conclusions based on archaeological evidence. This evidence points to native Shona-speaking Africans as the founders of the civilization that boasted cities, royalty, and a monumental wall. British officials, on the other hand, put forth an official view that the civilization must have been built by foreigners from the north. Their hired archaeologists destroyed evidence and supported racist theories to justify imperialist ventures. Finally, after Zimbabwe gained its independence from Britain in 1980, the myth was dispelled and the truth became accepted.

Skill C

Q5 — practice 1

M: Hey, Jill. You look a bit frazzled.

W: Yeah, well, I loaned my library card to a friend, and she's taken off for the holidays. Now, I have a monumental report due, and I need to borrow some books.

M: Gee, that's a tough one, but I guess there are a couple of things you can do.

W: Well, I thought I could just use the public library. That'd be quick, but they may not have all the books I need.

M: Yeah, that's one option. You could also try to find someone who'd let you use their library card.

W: Huh, I hadn't thought of that. Maybe I could ask around the dorms. There must be someone still around.

M: It might be worth a shot. I'd let you use mine, but I already have too many books checked out for research on my final presentation.

W: That's OK. At least I have a couple of ideas now.

M: Yeah, well, good luck with it. I'll see you around.

Sample response 1:
The woman's problem is that she does not have her university library card, but she needs to check out some books. The man and the woman discuss two options. The first option is that she just use the public library. The second option is that she try to find someone whose card she can borrow. I think the first option is better. She can go to the public library immediately without wasting any time looking for help. Also, there is no guarantee she would find anyone willing to be imposed upon, so the second option may be a waste of time.

Sample response 2:
The woman's problem is that she does not have her university library card, but she needs to check out some books. The man and the woman discuss two options. The first option is that she just use the public library. The second option is that she try to find someone whose card she can borrow. I think the second option is better. Chances are very good that she will find a friend more than happy to help her. Furthermore, the public library may not have the resources she needs, so it may be a waste of time to go there.

Q5 — practice 2

M: How's it going?

W: Not so good. My roommate is driving me crazy. She never cleans up after herself, and she always eats my food.

M: That's no good. You should talk to her about it!

W: The thing is, she's really sensitive, and I don't want to lose her as a friend.

M: You think complaining would put your friendship in jeopardy?

W: She can be really defensive. I wouldn't be surprised if she moved out and never spoke to me again.

M: Well, that sounds really manipulative to me. If you talk to her about it, I think you'll both be happier. Plus, you won't spend all your money feeding her.

W: But if she moves out, I'll have no help with the rent.

M: True. Well, if you can tough it out, graduation isn't that far off.

W: That's what I'm thinking. Then, I won't lose her friendship, and I won't have to spend the next two months bickering with her.

Sample response 1:
The woman is unhappy living with a friend who eats the woman's food and refuses to clean. The man admits the woman could just stick with the situation for a short time longer, but he recommends that she talk to her roommate about the problem. In my opinion, the woman should follow the man's recommendation. For one thing, it is not fair for her to have to do all the cleaning and pay for the food her roommate consumes. Also, if the woman convinces her roommate to start helping out, they will both be happier because there won't be any resentment between them.

Sample response 2:
The woman is unhappy living with a friend who eats the woman's food and refuses to clean. The man admits the woman could just stick with the situation for a short time longer, but he recommends that she talk to her roommate about the problem. In my opinion, the woman should follow her instincts and continue to live with her friend without complaint. For one thing, petty concerns are not worth losing a friend over. Also, if the roommate were to get upset and move out, the woman would be stuck paying all of the rent herself.

Q5 — practice 3

M: You took biology last year, right? Did you have to dissect a pig?

W: Yeah, it was gross.

M: I don't care if it's gross, I think it's wrong. I don't want to take part in it.

W: Why don't you explain your position to your teacher? Maybe he would give you an alternative project to do.

M: Yeah, but I'm scared he would hold it against me. You know, some teachers don't like troublemakers.

W: Well, I guess there's a chance that might happen. I guess you have to decide what is more important to you: your grades or your values. You can suck it up and do the dissection to ensure that you get a good grade, or you can stand up for what you believe in.

M: But you know that old saying about knowing when to stand and fight and knowing when to run.

W: You know what? There is power in numbers. If you can get your classmates to join your cause, you might actually bring about change. There's no reason why they can't do virtual dissections in biology class.

M: Hey, you know, you're right.

Sample response 1:

The man's biology class is going to dissect a pig, and he does not want to take part because he believes that dissecting pigs is unethical. The woman suggests that he refuse to take part in the dissection and ask his teacher for an alternative project. The man expresses concern, though, that the teacher might be annoyed with him and lower his grade because of it. I believe the man should stick to his convictions and not take part in activities that contravene his beliefs. He will feel better about himself, and protesting might result in change.

Sample response 2:

The man's biology class is going to dissect a pig, and he does not want to take part because he believes that dissecting pigs is unethical. The woman suggests that he refuse to take part in the dissection and ask his teacher for an alternative project. The man expresses concern, though, that the teacher might be annoyed with him and lower his grade because of it. I believe the man should dissect the pig and not risk getting a poor grade. He will only have to dissect the pig once, but a poor grade will cause him problems in the future.

Q6 — practice 1

M: So, today we're going to talk about falconry. This is a hunting method where the hunter, known as the falconer, trains a falcon to find and catch prey for him. Yes?

W: See, to me that's not hunting. It's like the fox hunt... you get another animal to do the hunting for you. Where's the skill in that?

M: OK, well, for one thing, taming a wild bird is no easy task. Indeed, part of that training lies in teaching the bird not to kill the prey. You see, in Arabia, where falconry still takes place, the prey must be killed according to Islamic customs and rituals. Therefore, it's not as if the falconer is passive during the hunt sequence. Now, let's talk about falconry in a historic context. While today it is a sport, when falconry began, it was an important means of survival. For example, nomadic people who traveled the desert needed to eat. The kinds of foods that they could procure for themselves were lacking in variety. Consequently, they enlisted one of the local hunters, the falcon, to help them add the dietary variety needed for subsistence. Some historians assert that falconry may have been the earliest hunting method developed by man. It was in use as far back as 2000 B.C. in China.

Sample response:

Falconry was originally employed as a tool to help people hunt food. Nomadic people in the desert tamed falcons in order to help them hunt for a larger variety of foods than they could acquire by themselves. Today, in contrast, people aren't as desperate to meet subsistence requirements. Nonetheless, falconry is still practiced as a sport. The falconer is highly skilled and must not only tame the falcon, but also teach it to hunt without killing the prey.

Q6 — practice 2

W: Any migraine sufferers here today?

M: I am.

W: Do you have auras?

M: Yes, I see flashing lights.

W: For those of you who don't know, "aura" refers to symptoms that precede an actual migraine. Sam says he sees flashing lights before his migraines set in. That's a common type of aura. So, Sam, what happens next?

M: Within about an hour, I'll have an incredible headache, and I'll start vomiting.

W: Does noise bother you?

M: Not as much as light. I have to find a dark room to rest in because I can't stand light.

W: That's common as well. So, that's what a migraine is . . . an intense headache accompanied by other symptoms. Not everyone gets them, but those who do get them episodically. Which leads us to the question "What causes migraines?" Well, medical science is not really sure, but we think it has something to do with blood flow in the brain. Basically, for some reason, some people's blood vessels respond in a weird way to certain stimulants. Arteries that bring blood to the brain contract and limit the blood supply, which means that less oxygen is getting to the brain. This problem is compounded because arteries in the brain will expand to compensate, and that expansion causes pain. So, the trick to preventing migraines is figuring out what triggers the arteries to contract in the first place.

Sample response:

A migraine is a severe headache that may be preceded by an aura, a symptom that signals the sufferer to the onset of a migraine. The migraine itself involves a headache and other symptoms, such as vomiting or intolerance for light or noise. Doctors suspect a possible cause is that restricted blood flow to the brain causes oxygen levels in the brain to decrease. The brain then tries to compensate by expanding the arteries in the brain, which results in pain. Migraine sufferers should try to identify what triggers their migraine to prevent further attacks.

Q6 — practice 3

M: You all should be familiar with the standard view of evolution. That is, that species change gradually over time as a result of natural selection until a new species is eventually formed. Who can give me an example?

W: Size?

M: OK, good. A species, like horses for instance, may grow from being the size of cats to the size of a modern horse over tens of thousands of years. The change in each particular generation is imperceptible, perhaps less than a nanometer. However, the fossil record holds evidence of another trend as well. This is the trend for populations to remain relatively unchanged over long periods of time, and then for new species to develop quite suddenly. A new idea in evolutionary theory attempts to account for this. It is called

Punctuated Equilibrium. In Punctuated Equilibrium theory, a large population typically dilutes advantageous mutations. According to this theory, the evolution of new species typically occurs in peripheral subpopulations, in smaller areas in which individuals are competing in novel ecosystems. In these populations, advantageous mutations can quickly take over. After this change, the new species may or may not compete with and exterminate its predecessor. I want to make it clear that this theory is not in conflict with the gradualist view of evolution. In fact, it complements it.

Sample response:
The professor explains two theories of evolution: one related to gradual evolution and the other related to rapid evolution. One example presented is the evolution of horses from cat-sized mammals to their much larger modern stature. This example supports the theory of gradual evolution. However, evidence in the fossil record indicates that species often remain unchanged for long periods, and then new species arise quite suddenly. Punctuated Equilibrium is a new theory that explains this. It holds that large populations dilute new mutations. On the other hand, beneficial mutations spread quickly in peripheral subpopulations. The professor points out that the two theories complement rather than contradict each other.

Chapter 2

Skill A

Q1 — practice 1
Sample response:
Last year, I met a fellow language student on an Internet study forum when I was trying to practice for a Chinese class. As it turned out, he was a Chinese student trying to practice English. Later, we developed a symbiotic relationship by helping each other practice our respective languages. Every week, we chat for 30 minutes in English and 30 minutes in Chinese. By now, we have become good friends, and we have both learned a lot. Of course, among the things I've learned is the fact that Chinese culture is fascinating, and this experience has really broadened my view of the world.

Q1 — practice 2
Sample response:
One technological innovation I witnessed during my university days was the spread of the Internet. Before that, I spent hours in the library doing research. After the Internet came into widespread use, however, I didn't have to go to the library at all. I could do all of my research from a computer in my dorm room, which saved a lot of time. In fact, the Internet saved me a great deal of money, too! For example, I no longer had to make expensive, obligatory phone calls to my parents. Instead, I could send them updates via email for free.

Q1 — practice 3
Sample response:
My life was changed by an unexpected blizzard. One day when I left my house to go to the airport, the weather was cool but clear. As I was driving to the airport, though, it started snowing. Within minutes, there was a raging blizzard. I knew my flight to Jamaica was going to be canceled, so I was terribly disappointed. Then, I noticed a stranded motorist, so I pulled over to help. I offered the man a lift so he could call a tow truck. Three years later, I married that man. If it weren't for that blizzard, we wouldn't have met.

Q1 — practice 4
Sample response:
The Optimists' Club is an organization that has been very important in my life. They organize fun and enriching activities for kids in the city. For example, I had a great experience and forged lasting friendships while participating in their youth basketball league. In addition, they provide counselors who help troubled youths with problems. One time, I was on edge about my high school course work, and I did not have anyone to turn to for guidance. The Optimists' Club counselor provided me with some very useful advice I needed in order to select the appropriate classes to enroll in.

Q2 — practice 1
Sample response:
I believe that childhood is a critical period in a person's life. First, it is the time in which personality is developed. Second, a person's experiences in childhood affect the remainder of his or her life. For instance, a major trauma experienced at the age of six has a much more devastating effect than one experienced at age thirty. Indeed, negative or traumatic experiences in childhood can lead to psychological problems in adulthood, such as depression and antisocial behavior. Conversely, positive, nurturing experiences in childhood foster mental health and well-being in adulthood. Thus, it is crucial to have positive influences in childhood.

Q2 — practice 2
Sample response:
Most parents are capable of teaching their children to read, write, add, and subtract, as well as many of the other basic skills children are taught at school. However, there are some skills that cannot be taught sufficiently at home. The skills I am referring to are social skills. These, I believe, are the most important skills learned at school. That's why I am of the opinion that children should learn in a social environment. Unfortunately, the home cannot provide an adequate social milieu for children to learn to live with a diverse group of people. Public schools, on the other hand, can and do provide this setting.

Q2 — practice 3
Sample response:
I believe zoos serve a multitude of useful purposes. For one thing, zoos educate visitors. If there were no zoos, children would grow up never witnessing species not indigenous to their area. With zoos, in contrast, children can learn about all kinds of different animal species and observe them up close. That's more captivating and educational than looking at pictures or reading texts. For that matter, zoos provide an entertainment venue for people of all ages. Additionally, they provide a safe home for animals whose survival is threatened in the wild. Animals that are endangered can be kept safe and well fed, as well as be encouraged to breed.

Q2 — practice 4
Sample response:
In some countries, all citizens are required to vote, while in others, individuals are free to decide whether to vote or not. I prefer the system in which voting is optional. First, in this system, public interest is more

important because it affects voter turnout. Therefore, governments and candidates for office must work harder to sway the opinions of voters. Second, people should be free to protest an election by refraining from taking part. Indeed, the very idea of forcing constituents to vote runs counter to the principles upon which free society is based.

Skill B

Q3 — practice 1

W: Darn! I really wanted to apply for the Study Abroad Program, but I can't afford it.

M: The tuition cost is no different from what you'd pay here.

W: Yeah, but I'm here on scholarship, and it can't be used toward tuition abroad.

M: I thought the announcement said that it could.

W: Only if it's need-based. Mine's academic.

M: That's so arbitrary and unfair.

W: I know. Technically, my scholarship isn't need-based, but I do need it.

M: I could fathom them precluding a person with an athletic scholarship from going, but you earned that scholarship.

W: There's not much I can do about it. They have their rules.

M: It doesn't make any sense, though. What difference does it make to them if your scholarship is based on academic merit or need? Why should a C student with poor parents have an advantage? I'm all for helping people out with university costs, but it's not fair that they can use their grant money and you can't.

W: Funny thing is, I qualified for a need-based scholarship, but I got more money with the academic one.

M: Well, there you go. There's no reason why you should be excluded from this program. You're an A student with financial needs.

Sample response:
The man's opinion is that the school's policy of only allowing students with need-based scholarships to use that money toward the Study Abroad Program is unfair. To begin, he contends that the woman earned her scholarship through academic merit rather than athletic skill or financial need. Secondly, the woman did qualify for a need-based scholarship but opted for the academic one, showing that she has the same financial need as students with need-based scholarships. For these two reasons, he feels the woman should be allowed to use her grant money to pay for tuition abroad.

Q3 — practice 2

M: I guess we'd better sign up for that lottery.

W: I can't believe this. It just doesn't seem fair. Why should people studying sociology get preferential treatment?

M: Who knows? I suppose they bring more prestige to the school. Maybe they pull in more research grant dollars. These things are usually all about the money.

W: It should be based on need. I'm just barely getting by on my grant as it is. Now, some kids whose parents have two houses are gonna get a dorm room and I'm not?

M: You might still get a room. Anyway, they said they'd give us a refund for living costs.

W: They said a partial tuition refund. I doubt it'll cover the cost of renting a place in this city, especially near the campus. Then, I'll have transportation costs on top of everything else, and I won't be able to stay at the library too late because I'll have to catch the last bus home.

M: Huh. I never thought about all that.

W: I should go give them a piece of my mind!

M: Yeah, but what can they do about it?

W: They should've done the renovations in the summer. Either that or made some other arrangements for their students.

Sample response:
The woman is angry about the announced plan for a housing lottery for graduate students. First, she thinks it is unfair because students of certain majors are being given priority. Instead, she believes the housing should be assigned based on need. Second, she is upset because living off campus will be expensive and inconvenient. For example, she will pay more in rent and transportation and will not be able to study late on campus. In the end, she complains that they should have done the renovations during the summer or otherwise accommodated the needs of all students.

Q4 — practice 1

W: The giant squid has proven a particularly elusive animal. In fact, marine biologists have tried in vain to conduct detailed studies of giant squid behavior for decades. The majority of what science knows about this species has been gleaned from the examination of dead squid carcasses washed up on shore.

Giant squid, as the name implies, are huge creatures. The largest specimen ever discovered measured fifteen meters in length. However, most giant squid are smaller, growing to approximately ten meters. They boast two large tentacles in addition to their eight arms. These tentacles have suckers, like that of an octopus, with sharp, claw-like components. They do not possess the stingers or net-like mechanisms for trapping prey commonly found on passive feeders.

Despite this, their enormous size has led some scientists to propose that giant squid are indeed passive feeders. Some theorists contend that, because of the energy requirements for such a large creature to move quickly enough to capture prey, it must, by necessity, be a passive feeder. Other theorists, needless to say, are not sympathetic to this view. Given the evidence presented by the physical morphology of the animal in conjunction with the feeding paradigm of its smaller cousins, it seems feasible that the giant squid may be an active feeder.

Sample response:
The reading passage describes the morphological differences between marine animals that are active feeders and passive feeders. The lecturer examines the morphology of the giant squid and different theories about its feeding habits. First, the giant squid is a very large creature. Second, it has two tentacles that include sharp, claw-like components. Some scientists have postulated that the enormous size of the giant squid suggests it must be a passive feeder. Other scientists, in contrast, point to its tentacles and the model of smaller squid species as evidence suggesting that the giant squid is an active feeder.

Q4 — practice 2

M: In the early 20th century, there was uproar in the musical world. European concert-goers were plugging their ears, walking out on performances, and muttering, "My Lord, what is that horrible, unstructured sound?"

That unstructured sound was the new, emerging style of European composition. It came to be known as atonal music. Basically, it was the beginning of a rebellion against the way music had always been. All the rules were going out the window, music fans were lambasting the composers, and the composers were replying that the fans were uncouth or needed more time and education to understand the new musical form.

So, how was their music so different? Well, let's think about the traditional way of arranging music. You use a scale, right? And you build the composition, or song, around that scale. The traditional scales were the major and minor scales. Well, these new composers started using the chromatic scale to structure their music. The chromatic scale means simply all the notes you can play on a piano, without any notes left out. The traditional scales had eight notes in total, and now they were using all 12 notes in the same composition!

Sample response:
The professor begins by describing the negative response many early-20th-century audiences had to the advent of atonal musical forms. Listeners found the new style too unstructured in comparison to the traditional forms they were used to. As the reading passage describes, traditional European music was based on principles of melody. This music utilized the major and minor scales to produce the desired emotions. As the professor points out, atonal compositions utilized the chromatic scale rather than the major or minor scales. The chromatic scale includes 12 notes, all the notes a person can play on the piano.

Skill C

Q5 — practice 1

M: Hi, is this the Student Administrative Services Center?

W: Yes, it is. What can I help you with?

M: Well, there seems to be some kind of glitch with my ID card. The scanner at the gym wouldn't read it, and they told me to come here to find out why.

W: Have you got your student ID on you?

M: Yeah, it's right here.

W: OK, let's get your record up on the computer...Bill Hailey, here it is. It seems you haven't paid your tuition yet.

M: Yeah, my loan hasn't come through yet.

W: Unfortunately, until you've paid in full, your status is not active.

M: Oh. Can I just pay the fee?

W: Sorry, you must have active status to use the facilities. If you know someone who does have access, you can go as his or her guest for five dollars.

M: Five dollars? OK, well, I guess I'll have to do that. I'm in training and I need to use the gym.

W: Keep in mind that your host has to be in the facility with you.

M: Gee, that's a pain in the neck.

W: You said you were in training; are you on a varsity team here?

M: Yeah, the basketball team.

W: Why don't you talk to your coach? Maybe you could get a temporary ID until your loan comes through.

M: Hmmm...my coach is away right now. Well, thanks for all you're help, anyway.

Sample response:
The man's problem is that he cannot access the gym to work out because his student loans have not come through to pay his tuition. The woman suggests two solutions to his problem. First, he could find a student with access to accompany him to the gym. Second, he could talk to his coach and try to get a temporary ID. In my opinion,

the first choice is preferable. To begin, his coach is away, so the man would have to wait. In addition, having a friend to work out with could help him maintain his exercise regime.

Q5 — practice 2

W: Richard. Long time no see.

M: Yeah, I've had some personal problems. I'm here to drop the class.

W: You know you've missed the deadline to drop a class without penalty?

M: I know, but I really don't see how I could catch up this late in the game.

W: Let me have a look... no term paper and a D on the midterm.

M: Like I said, I've had some personal problems.

W: Still, there's no advantage to dropping the class now. On the other hand, if you put your nose to the grindstone from here on out, you might pull off a C.

M: Hmm. Would you give me an extension on the paper?

W: Sorry. You'll be docked two points per day like everyone else.

M: Yeah, well, I think I'd rather just drop it.

W: Suit yourself, but dropping a course now is no different from failing it. Why don't you just give it a shot?

M: Well, I'll think about it. The thing is, if I drop this class, I can concentrate on the classes I'm taking for my major.

W: OK, but don't think too long. If you want to pass the class, you should turn in that paper ASAP.

Sample response:
The man's problem is that he wants to drop the professor's class because he is too far behind to earn a high grade. In addition, the deadline for dropping classes without penalty has passed. The professor tries to convince him to remain in the class and work hard to increase his grade. In my opinion, he would be better off dropping the class. Even though he will be penalized for dropping the class the same as if he had failed it, he will benefit by being able to concentrate his efforts on the courses of his major.

Q6 — practice 1

W: The most influential development in popular music history was undoubtedly the advent of jazz and its later incarnation, blues. Jazz and blues music originated in New Orleans, Louisiana, when African-American musicians broke free from the musical norms of that period. Jazz and blues artists combined faster, more powerful African rhythms with European melodies. They are also credited with the development of the "blues" scale, which uses the major scale with an extra note, the "blue" note. This music, however, was not widely accepted by mainstream America at the time. The wild, unstructured style of jazz was too much for them, just as later, the intoxicating beat of rock 'n' roll was met with disapproval. However, when white musicians such as Elvis Presley began incorporating these new styles into their music, it became wildly popular with the younger generations. As these generations grew up, rock 'n' roll eventually became universally accepted.

Subsequent developments in pop music were generally met with the same disapproval experienced by jazz, blues, and rock 'n' roll in their infancies. One example of this is hip-hop, which appeared on the scene in the early 1980s. It is based on poetic verses spoken over heavy backbeats, which include samples from other songs and repeated noises not produced by traditional instruments, such as police sirens and record scratches.

Pop music today is a fusion of a myriad of styles that did not exist 100 years ago. Many of the most popular bands on the charts today are born from influences of rock, hip-hop, reggae, ska, and techno, all of which met with resistance in their infancies.

Sample response:
According to the lecture, the advent of jazz music had a significant influence on the trajectory of popular music over the past 100 years. To begin, it was developed by African Americans combining African rhythms with European melodies. In addition, jazz influenced the development of blues, which added an extra note to the major scale, thus creating the blues scale. At first, these musical forms were met with resistance. Later, however, they became widely accepted after being incorporated into rock 'n' roll music by white musicians such as Elvis Presley. Furthermore, they have influenced the form of more recent popular music styles, such as hip-hop.

Q6 — practice 2

M: What images are conjured in people's minds when the word "family" is mentioned? It's difficult to pinpoint these days, isn't it? We can regurgitate the ideal family of our parents' generation, though, right? You know: Mom, Dad, and 2.5 children. Dad works nine to five. Mom takes Dad's family name, serves as his companion, and stays at home to cook, clean, and raise the children. They remain married until one of them dies. Sex only occurs inside the confines of marriage. Parents have the ultimate say in the lives of their children. Does that work for you?

In the past, families who did not conform to this paradigm were marginalized. They were considered "troubled," "pathological," or "dysfunctional." In the 1960s, about 70 percent of all families conformed to the ideal, leaving 30 percent in the "problematic" range.

Today, only 11-15 percent of families adhere to the above conditions for the ideal family. It appears this conception of family is disappearing. Some alarmists contend that this is a fundamental societal problem, a breakdown in values that will produce immeasurable negative effects. Is this true?

Well, let's look at it from another angle. There are myriad cultures around the world that have never held this ideal of the family. Even in the American past, the family has been defined differently depending on the time period. So, it seems that what was briefly the ideal family unit was just another phase.

We can cite a few aspects of family that apply universally. Family is the intersection between social reproduction, that is, making a society, and biological reproduction, that is, making new people. The concept of family is what provides a society with its notions of "normal" and "natural."

Sample response:
In this lecture, the professor examines the idea of family. The traditional ideal of the family includes a working father, a domestic mother, and two or three children all living together in one home. Furthermore, families that differed from this ideal were marginalized and considered flawed or unhealthy in the past. These days, however, only a minority of families conform to this ideal. In point of fact, the professor relates that the ideal defined a generation or two ago is only one step on an ever-evolving sequence of ideals. Finally, the professor states that in all societies, the family helps define what is normal and natural.

Chapter 3

Focus A

Step 1 — Sentence stress on content words
1. Before that, I spent hours in the library doing research.
2. My life was changed by an unexpected blizzard.
3. In addition, they provide counselors who help troubled youths with problems.
4. I believe that childhood is an integral period in a person's life.
5. Public schools, on the other hand, can and do provide this setting.
6. That's more captivating and educational than looking at pictures or reading texts.
7. I prefer the system in which voting is optional.
8. Instead, she believes the housing should be assigned based on need.

Paragraph:
I believe zoos serve a multitude of useful purposes. For one thing, zoos educate visitors. If there were no zoos, children would grow up never witnessing species not indigenous to their area. With zoos, in contrast, children can learn about all kinds of different animal species and observe them up close. That's more captivating and educational than looking at pictures or reading texts. For that matter, zoos provide an entertainment venue for people of all ages. Additionally, they provide a safe home for animals whose survival is threatened in the wild. Animals that are endangered can be protected, well-fed, and encouraged to breed.

Step 2 — Sentence stress on function words
1. Technically, my scholarship isn't need-based, but I do need it.
2. If you put your nose to the grindstone from here on out, you might pull off a C.
3. After the Internet came along, I could do all of my research from a computer in my dorm room.
4. First, it is the time in which personality is developed.
5. However, there are some skills that cannot be taught sufficiently at home.
6. Public schools, on the other hand, can and do provide this setting.
7. In my opinion, the second choice is preferable.
8. Although no specimens have been found, there is a lot of evidence for scientists to examine.

1. That isn't his dog, it's her dog.
2. Most students didn't pass the exam, but John did.
3. She likes jazz music, and he likes blues music. I like jazz and blues music.
4. Kim hasn't paid her tuition fees, but Rick has.
5. The major scale doesn't have 12 notes, but the chromatic scale does.
6. Off-campus housing isn't just expensive; it's expensive and inconvenient.
7. He didn't get the need-based scholarship. She did.
8. You can take English 201 or English 205. You can't take both.

Focus B

Step 1 — Changing pitch for emphasis
1. Children should attend school.
2. This experience helped tremendously with my studies.
3. Subsequent developments in pop music were generally met with the same disapproval.
4. Do you play on the varsity basketball team?

1. I don't abhor jazz music. I don't really enjoy it that much, though.
2. Her behavior is antisocial. He is actually a nice guy.
3. The squid doesn't have eight appendages. It has ten.
4. Jellyfish drift with ocean currents. Squid use their arms to swim.
5. There is a glitch with her computer. Her phone is working fine.
6. The campus renovations will begin in September. The campus celebrations begin in October.

Step 2 — Commas and series with *and* or *or*
1. Many of the most popular bands on the charts today are born from influences of rock, hip-hop, reggae, ska, and techno.
2. They were considered troubled, pathological, or dysfunctional.
3. I doubt it'll cover the cost of renting a place in this city, especially near the campus.
4. Most giant squid are smaller, growing to approximately ten meters.
5. European concert-goers were plugging their ears, walking out on performances, and muttering to themselves.
6. The chromatic scale simply means all the notes you can play on a piano, without any notes left out.

Focus C

Step 1 — Timing
1. The traditional ideal of the family includes a working father, a domestic mother, and two or three children all living happily in one home.
2. As it turned out, he was a Chinese student trying to practice English.
3. After the Internet came into widespread use, however, I didn't have to go to the library at all.
4. Within minutes, there was a raging blizzard.
5. Some alarmists contend that this is a fundamental societal problem, a breakdown in values that will produce immeasurable negative effects.
6. These, I believe, are the most important skills learned at school.

1. The man's opinion is that the school's policy of only allowing students with need-based scholarships to use that money toward the Study Abroad Program is unfair.
2. To begin, he contends that the woman earned her scholarship through academic merit rather than athletic skill or financial need.
3. Secondly, the woman did qualify for a need-based scholarship but opted for the academic one, showing that she has the same financial need as students with need-based scholarships.
4. For these two reasons, he feels the woman should be allowed to use her grant money to pay for tuition abroad.

Step 2 — Pause and pitch
1. The reading passage describes the morphological differences between marine animals that are active feeders and passive feeders.
2. The lecturer examines the morphology of the giant squid and different theories about its feeding habits.
3. First, the giant squid is a very large creature.
4. Second, it has two tentacles that include sharp, claw-like components.
5. Some scientists have postulated that the enormous size of the giant squid suggests it must be a passive feeder.
6. Other scientists, in contrast, point to its tentacles and the model of smaller squid species as evidence suggesting the giant squid is an active feeder.

Writing

Chapter 1

Skill A

Practice 1

01 Statistics

W: I hope you have all read the introduction to Correlation Studies in your textbooks. One component of that reading that I want to stress the importance of is that when assessing the validity of a correlation study it is vital to remember this rule: Correlation does NOT imply causation. It's easy, when you see a correlation, to assume that the changing rate of one variable is causing the changing rate of the other, but how do investigators determine which variable would be the cause and which the effect? Sometimes, it's common sense, but when the investigation itself is not manipulating either variable, it is difficult to know with certainty that one variable is causing the other to occur.

Another danger to be wary of is the possibility of a third variable. Consider this example. Ice cream consumption is positively correlated with drowning. Surprised? What might explain this correlation?

M: Well, maybe the ice-cream could give you a cramp while you're swimming.

W: Okay, maybe. But what if I told you that ice cream consumption is also positively correlated with boating accidents.

M: Okay, well, it's got something to do with the beach, or the water...

W: ...and when do people go to the beach or go boating?

M: In the summer.

W: Exactly — when it's hot. And when do people eat ice cream? When it's hot. The third variable here is the weather. So, just because two events are correlated, it doesn't mean that one event is causing the other. It might give us a hint that that might be the case, but further research has to be done to say conclusively that one event causes the other.

For example, smoking is positively correlated with cancer. This evidence alone does not indicate that smoking causes cancer. However, it was the basis for further research that has demonstrated a causal relationship between smoking and cancer.

So, correlation studies are valuable tools that provide a glimpse into how events are related, and they might indicate causal relationships, but alone they in no way determine that one event causes another.

02 History

M: Our topic today is the issue of historiography, specifically revisionist historiography. In many academic circles, the word "revisionism" has come to be used pejoratively. Why do you suppose that is? Well, the reasons are as follows: Whereas some academics still regard historical revisionism as a term simply referring to a re-examination of the past, many historians now believe that revisionism itself has become tinged with a political bias. They argue that many who call themselves "revisionist historians" are in fact hacks and crackpots posing as academics. Due to their own specific ideological leanings, these "revisionist" writers present poorly researched papers or publish controversial books and articles that negate or deny specific events in history. Such writings can be particularly dangerous when non-experts read them. This is because, without fully understanding the context, these readers are influenced to condone or support a controversial and often completely inaccurate historical perspective.

The best and most recent example of this form of historical revisionism is what has been dubbed, "Holocaust Denial." As most of you are aware, the term "holocaust" has come to refer to the war crimes perpetrated by the Nazi regime in Germany between 1933 and 1945 against, predominantly, the Jewish people. Holocaust deniers are those so-called revisionists who claim either that the holocaust never happened or that statistics surrounding the murders of Jews and other victims of the holocaust have been greatly exaggerated. Holocaust deniers and other revisionists deliberately misrepresent and manipulate historical evidence so as to propagate their political bias or to support an ideological bias. Their writing is usually full of logical fallacies and conspiracy theories and without much supportable documentation or verifiable data.

Such so-called revisionists are not only giving the term "historical revisionism" a bad name; they are coloring the entire field in a negative light through their biased and unscientific approach to the past. However, as long as legitimate students and scholars of history remain aware of this trend and work to combat it, genuine historical research and authentically revisionist enterprises can and should continue.

03 Astronomy

W: In today's astronomy lecture, I wish to discuss the theoretical holes that exist in the Big Bang theory. I also want to discuss alternative views of how the universe might have come into being. You have chosen a very tricky area of science to study, because we are dealing with subject matter that is often difficult to verify.

As most of you'll remember if you've read the assigned chapter, the Big Bang theory argues that our universe was created by an explosion that took place around 13.7 billion years ago. Such prestigious figures as Edwin Hubble, for whom the famous Hubble telescope is named, developed and supported this hypothesis. These scientists believed that our universe originated as a small, hot entity that inflated and expanded, then cooled, and now continues to expand.

I want to examine this theory more closely. What is the major evidence supporting it?

We know the universe had an origin, and we know galaxies are moving away from each other. Thanks to Wilson and Penzias, we've also discovered the existence of radiation in space as well as an abundance of Hydrogen and Helium gases that supports the idea that a big explosion occurred.

But this evidence is far too general and vague to be limited to the Big Bang theory. This empirical data also supports other models for how the universe came into being. It is important to remember that the Big Bang theory has never been proven beyond a reasonable doubt. It simply remains a popular and widely acknowledged hypothesis.

A new idea has recently emerged called the ekpyrotic scenario, that's E-K-P-Y-R-O-T-I-C. This theory argues, for example, that our universe was created when two parallel "membranes" of space matter collided. While this theory shares some elements with the Big Bang theory, it also has many differences. It is also supported by the same empirical data I have mentioned. All we can really do at this point, as scientists, is to keep investigating the subject with care and precision and wait for new technologies to uncover new information.

04 English Literature

M: Who wrote Shakespeare, students? The question sounds almost illogical, doesn't it?

You all want to shout out: "Duh, well, Shakespeare did of course. Who else could have written Shakespeare?" If only it were that simple. I'm afraid that in literary studies, things are never quite that simple. That is a good lesson for all of you to learn. Consequently, before we start our analysis of the *Hamlet* text you have so diligently brought along with you to class today, we are going to examine the authorship debate.

There are some literary scholars out there who believe an aristocrat called Edward De Vere actually wrote the plays we think of as Shakespeare's, under a pseudonym. The problem is that the arguments to support this claim are actually rather sketchy and poorly researched. Their notion is, in my opinion, a conspiracy theory with little genuine supportable evidence.

For example, it's true that not one single document categorically states that William Shakespeare of Stratford wrote *King Lear* or *Hamlet*, but then no such document exists for any other playwright of the time either. While the so-called "Antistratfordians" find it mysterious that Shakespeare's signature doesn't appear on the early quartos of his plays and that, in fact, no name appears on them at all, this is actually easy to explain. It is because at that time, contemporary plays weren't considered to be literature. Authorship was not considered particularly relevant or important since theater was considered to be popular art, not serious art. It was only after Shakespeare's death that his colleagues decided to collect his plays and publish them in the so-called "First Folio," in 1623.

There are also numerous extant documents referring to William Shakespeare as actor and playwright. These are easily accessible to the serious scholar. Why would Shakespeare's contemporaries, like playwright Ben Jonson, have referred to him so often by name had it really been a pseudonym? An entire group of artists wouldn't all agree to shield someone's identity without motivation. What could they gain from it? What would the purpose of such a deception have been?

Skill B

Practice 1

M: Psychologists are starting to acknowledge sleep deprivation as a vital factor in children's school performance. They tell us that just one or two more hours of sleep each night can make a substantial improvement in kids' grades. All parents have to do is make their children go to bed earlier. Hmm... Easier said than done, don't you think?

Well, as you read in the textbook, sleep no doubt plays an important role in how well a child performs at school. However, we need to remember that sleep is only one variable in the equation. Indeed, an educator would be remiss in merely prescribing more sleep for all students suffering from low grades. Besides being well rested, children need to be well nourished, too. It's tough to concentrate on an empty stomach. They also need to be well clothed, and, most important of all, they need a stable, loving home life.

If a child struggles at school, it may well be true that he or she did not get the recommended nine hours of sleep the previous night. The question we need to ask ourselves is, "Is that the only factor involved?" What about breakfast? Did the child have pancakes, eggs, toast, and orange juice . . . or just a piece of toast and a glass of water? Did he or she wear a warm coat? Were there holes in his or her shoes? If students have trouble with attention span, could it be because they're still thinking about the knock-down, drag-out fight between Mom and Dad last night? Furthermore, if they have an accident on the playground, were they too tired, too excited, or did they merely slip? What's the impact of lack of sleep vis-à-vis other factors?

The human psyche, especially in children, is fragile, complex, and mysterious. Sleeplessness is a valid concern. However, researchers must consider other variables before jumping to the conclusion that sleep deprivation is the primary cause of academic woes.

Practice 2

M: Today, we'll be talking about non-violent forms of protest. Can anyone give some other terms for this type of action?

W: I think the textbook called it "civil disobedience."

M: Ah, "civil disobedience" very good. Another form is passive resistance. So, you've read that some don't believe civil disobedience to be an effective means of protest, but others, of course, are more supportive.

Let's begin with civil disobedience. You saw that Henry David Thoreau pioneered the modern US theory on this form of non-violence. According to Thoreau, there is no need to physically fight the government as long as you and the government don't support each other in any way. Independence in mind and action is the guiding principle for achieving what is just. In this manner, Thoreau prescribes protesting through justice, rather than physical violence. Civil disobedience derives its power and value because it is "right." This is almost always the principle of peaceful demonstrations in the US today. People, or even nations, can use the principles of civil disobedience to protest companies or nations that they feel are involved in unethical behavior. Rather than using violence, they can boycott, or stop buying, products from that company or country, thus using economics rather than violence to effect change.

Passive resistance is the other form of non-violence we're looking at. Who's the main figure here?

W: Gandhi, right?

M: Good, Gandhi is the non-violent figure par excellence, isn't he? His method involved purposely breaking the law with the expectation of attack by the authorities and then quietly resisting without retaliation. In essence, he attempted to become a martyr. An example is his breaking of the salt tax. Gandhi's followers formed a peaceful blockade around the salt mines and allowed themselves, without resistance, to be brutally beaten by British soldiers. When people around the world, including Britain, got wind of this brutal behavior, they put pressure on the British government to change their ways. Thus, passive resistance was more debilitating than violence to the British colonial infrastructure. Without resorting to violence, Gandhi effectively persuaded the English to end colonial rule in India.

Practice 3

M: Have any of you heard of the term "carbon chauvinism"? Yes, this is science class, and chauvinism has found its way into science. The term, in fact, seeks to discredit views that all life forms are carbon based. But isn't the main question really whether science is being chauvinistic? The answer we'll discuss today is "probably not." In fact, all current scientific evidence indicates that carbon is necessary to life as we know it.

As you all have hopefully read, silicon-based life is one of the pre-eminent contenders to carbon. Yes, the Earth is silicon rich and carbon poor. Yes, tiny diatoms have silicate-based skeletons, but, do we actually have pure silicon life forms to study? We certainly do not. All terrestrial life is carbon based. Rare carbon, rather than the relatively abundant silicon, has proven to be the successful life base on Earth. What about non-terrestrial silicon life? Silicon bonds resist extreme heat better than carbon. This could provide it with the molecular stability for biological evolution on planets closer to the sun. However, the reality is we can't replicate and test such alien environments. Scientifically, we just can't say with certainty.

The other commonly speculated alternative biochemistry base is sulfur. Sulfur is similar to carbon because it's soluble in water. This is an important characteristic on Earth, where water is the medium for all biochemical life. We have, in fact, found some types of bacteria that use sulfur in their metabolism, but these bacteria are still carbon-based life forms, with sulfur playing a secondary metabolic role. Sulfur can form the long molecular chains required for biological evolution, but its high reactivity makes it too unstable to sustain complex, biological evolution here on Earth. We have no pure sulfur life forms on Earth to study! The point is that under conditions for life as we know it, we have no knowledge indicating this is possible.

The key point today is that all conditions for biological life "as we know it" include carbon in their chemistry. We have no empirical data about successful non-carbon biochemistries. So, I'd say the present state of science can't be held guilty of "carbon chauvinism." Alien environments or odd physical conditions are, for the most part, variables we either cannot study or for which there is no real data.

Practice 4

W: How many of you agree with Native American legal rights to archaeological remains? Think of such examples as the Kennewick Man! Wow!... I see the article you read raised some sympathy. Well, I also think scientific communities are taking a hard line with respect to Native American views. In fact, today we'll discuss this subject. Respecting Native American rights to archaeological remains doesn't necessarily mean stopping the progress of science. The problem is that many scientists argue Native American claims spell the end of all research. This is the case with the Kennewick Man, but are Native American claims really so threatening to science? I doubt it. As a matter of fact, I have here a comment from the Union of Confederate Tribes that suggests they are not! "We're not anti-science," they remark. "We just want a say in what happens to our ancestors." To accommodate scientific interests while respecting the dignity and importance of Native American beliefs — shouldn't that be the real goal? Well . . . many Native American groups already show their support of research on archaeological finds, if they are at least consulted or involved! Would you be surprised if I told you that at least 57 Native American groups currently work with scholars on joint archaeological programs? For sure, collaborative work between scientists and Native American leaders is important. It shows the possibility for scientific progress to not only respect Native American communities, but also enlist their participation. Scientists involved in these programs report a lot of advantages to conducting research with the participation of Native Americans. They say deeper understanding of these cultures is obtained by collaborative work. That's right, it enhances their knowledge and can even clarify their scientific results.

It is untrue to say that scientific study would not be possible if Native American beliefs were honored. Attempts to freely pursue science at the cost of Native American beliefs are really the root of the debate. What the Kennewick Man conflict shows is more collaborative work is needed, not efforts to pursue science at all costs.

Chapter 2

Skill A

Practice 1

W: We all know that Hernando Cortes conquered Motecuhzoma and the Aztec empire in the early 16th century, but a lesser known part of the conquest is the story of the secret behind Cortes's success. We know that he landed in Tabasco in 1519 and subdued the smaller nations there. According to the tales, the people of those nations told him of the Aztecs further inland, and he negotiated their support in the conquest. But how was this possible? How do you negotiate with a people whose language you have never heard?

The Spaniards had never set foot in that part of Mexico and had no prior contact with any of its peoples. Cortes did have a priest, Gerónimo, who could speak Yucatec Mayan, a language spoken far to the south. Coincidentally, they encountered a local woman who was bilingual in Mayan and Nahua, the language of the Aztecs, which also happened to be the lingua franca of central Mexico at that time. It was through Gerónimo and this woman, who the Spaniards called, Doña Marina, or Malinche, and who the Mexicans called Malintzin, that Cortes was able to communicate and negotiate with the various peoples he encountered. Cortes took Malintzin into his entourage as his interpreter-slash-concubine. Now, from this point on, his success strategy is clear. Via Malintzin, he wins the support of the many non-Aztec nations and makes his way toward Tenochtitlan, the Aztec capital. It would be difficult for modern historians to know who the real genius was behind the negotiations. Cortes presumably knew very little of local politics, history, and customs, and never communicated directly with any Mexicans, while on the other hand, Malintzin had knowledge of all these things. On top of this is the fact that she was the one who was actually speaking directly to the national leaders. The extent to which she was just repeating interpreted versions of Cortes's Spanish, or whether she was paraphrasing or speaking her own mind, will likely never be known.

By the time Cortes had reached Tenochtitlan, evidence suggests that Malintzin had begun to interpret directly between Spanish and Nahua without using the priest and the unrelated Mayan language as a go-between. Malintzin largely disappears from history after the fall of Tenochtitlan in 1521. We know she bore Cortes a son, who would later gain a high rank before being executed, and that she served as an interpreter again during Cortes's campaign in Honduras.

Some Spanish sources also indicate that she was much more than an interpreter. The soldier Díaz Castillo calls her a "great lady" who was indispensable to the expedition. Another conquistador quotes Cortes as saying that after God, Marina was the main source of his success. Nahua sources typically depict Cortes and Malintzin together, or even her alone as an authority in her own right.

Some sources also indicate that the Aztec would refer to Cortes as "Malintzin" as well, casting further doubt on the hierarchical nature of their relationship. So, the question that arises is "Was Malintzin the true conqueror of the Aztec empire and Cortes and his army merely the means she chose to do so?"

Practice 2

M: Most of you know that there is a new mega-dome being built in our city for our new football team, but did you know that you are helping pay for it? That's right. The federal government allows cities to sell tax-exempt bonds to produce capital to fund stadium construction. This means, on average, that about 70 million dollars in taxes are lost for a 225-million-dollar stadium. That's 70 million of your tax dollars being spent not on education or infrastructure, but on a sports team that makes millions a year in profit anyway.

Some will say that this 70 million dollars is an investment, from which we see returns in the form of local jobs, increased property value, a boost to the local economy, and national publicity for the city. On the surface, this appears to be true, but let's take a closer look at each of these points, one by one.

Does a stadium and sports team create jobs? Well, obviously. A better question is "What kind of jobs does it create?" Well, we have construction jobs to build the stadium and staffing jobs to run it. The construction workers would be employed elsewhere if not for the stadium, most likely at building something that serves a clearer public function, like roads, schools, residences, or business facilities. So, there's no gain here. The low level stadium workers are mostly part-time employees who earn meager wages. What about the players, coaches, and team managers? Well, they no doubt end up with most of the money, but most of these have little involvement in or attachment to the local community, and that money is typically invested elsewhere; or, as you might say, "sucked out of the community."

OK, then. What about all the visiting fans and tax revenue? Well, in theory that sounds nice, but if we look at the numbers...for instance, Baltimore's baseball stadium brings in the most outside fans, thanks to nearby D.C., which didn't have its own team until quite recently. Their annual revenue from that is about 3 million dollars per year. Sounds like a lot, but that's actually quite low for a 200-million-dollar investment. Also, most tax revenue from the stadium is not additional revenue; rather, it replaces tax revenue that would have gone through movie theaters, restaurants, and so on.

Finally, we have the idea that a sports team boosts a city's image, attracting businesses, and so on. Well, first off, this is not really feasible to measure. Also, we have to ask ourselves "Could that 70 million dollars be better spent on other projects that might do more to boost the city's image?" Like what? Well, like top-notch research facilities for the university. Like education and wi-fi infrastructure to attract businesses and families, or even in PR projects for the city. I mean, why not spend 10 million on PR and marketing for the city, rather than 70 million on a sports team that is a profit-seeking business?

Practice 3

W: When scientists in Utah announced they had discovered a way to create cheap energy with little waste, the media grabbed hold of the story. It seemed too good to be true. However, the claim was met with much disdain in the scientific community. The scientists claimed that in their experiment, they observed the creation of an amount of energy too great to be explained by chemical reaction. To explain this finding, they guessed that nuclear fusion was taking place and called it "cold fusion," as it was taking place at room temperature.

The scientific community was astounded and didn't readily buy into the "cold fusion" claim. For one thing, it didn't fit with current theory. Nuclear physicists will tell you that when nuclear fusion takes place, there are protons or neutrons emitted. According to theory, the researchers should have been killed when they did the experiment. However, they weren't. Further, they were unable to detect any extra neutrons or protons. If nuclear fusion necessarily involves the emission of protons and neutrons, and in this experiment they didn't see any excess protons and neutrons, then it couldn't possibly be nuclear fusion . . . unless, of course, the theory is incorrect. You cannot simply dismiss observations because they don't fit with a theory. That's how science works, isn't it? Theories are not facts. When evidence appears to contradict the theory, the theory needs to be reassessed. We cannot throw out observations because they don't fit with current theories. Science would not have progressed very far if we did. We'd still be wandering around thinking the sun and the planets revolved around the Earth!

The scientific method demands that findings need to be replicated in order to validate them. After all, human error can lead to some flawed findings. So, when the "cold fusion" scientists made their announcement, many scientists followed suit and tried to replicate their experiment. They failed. They could not, with measured predictability, reproduce the findings of the original scientists. Following this, the whole idea was dismissed. Some accused the scientists of fraud, while others maintained that there must have been errors in their measurements. Indeed, the equipment used to take the measurements was not very accurate. So, the whole idea of "cold fusion" was deemed by some to be a pseudoscience. It did not stand up to the scientific process.

There's a problem with this stance, though. The scientific process needs time. Just because results weren't replicated in the months following the initial experiment doesn't mean the findings are invalid. Fortunately, some have continued to pursue the idea, and many have, indeed, reproduced the original findings. The equipment used for taking measurements has improved greatly in this time, and is more reliable. While some continue to insist that any positive finding must be erroneous, (and indeed, some findings are erroneous,) no skeptic has been able to identify an error that could explain all of the positive results obtained.

Practice 4

M: The debate about whether or not cannibalism took place in Anasazi society is a touchy subject. The Anasazi are the ancestors of the Pueblo peoples, a collective name for various Native American groups in present-day New Mexico and Arizona. When we look at the more recent history of the Pueblo peoples, we revere them for their peaceful ways and their respectful relationship with the Earth. When evidence suggested that cannibalism took place between 900 and 1300 A.D. in these societies, people were naturally horrified and offended. How could such a peaceful and cooperative group of people have done such a thing? Well, the evidence is sound, and it effectively proves that cannibalism took place, but that does not mean that it was a culturally accepted practice. In fact, one of the leading researchers suggests that it was a method used by foreigners to terrorize the Anasazi.

Let's discuss the evidence. First of all, using basic tag markers of cannibalism, archaeologists have shown that certain skeletal remains of humans were indeed treated like the carcass of an animal. The bones were broken. They also showed signs of having been burned, and indentations from sharp instruments indicate that flesh was intentionally removed. Now, some say that this does not prove that the flesh was eaten and point to a witch slaughter to explain it. However, fossilized fecal matter from the same area shows that human flesh had indeed been digested. Again, this only proves that it happened once, and it doesn't rule out the witch slaughter explanation. Indeed, cannibalism has taken place at some point or another in many other cultures, whether it was due to starvation, criminal activity, or used as a means of social control. It could be that one particularly antisocial person engaged in cannibalism, and we should not condemn an entire group for the act of one person. However, there is one piece of evidence that is not explained by the witch slaughter theory. Resin from cooking pots was found on the bones. This definitively shows that the flesh was cooked, something that was not part of the witch slaughter ritual. Further, there are so many skeletal remains that have been treated like this, we cannot presume that it was a random criminal act, but that it was a quite significant occurrence.

I'd like to reiterate my point that the suggestion that cannibalism occurred among the Anasazi is not a direct attack on these people. We cannot, at this point, determine who ate whom. While the theory that it was a group of foreigners terrorizing the Anasazi people has not been proven, it is certainly a plausible explanation that does not tarnish our image of the Anasazi. Because cannibalism is so very taboo, even scientists are reluctant to consider evidence that points in that direction. However, science relies on objectivity, and in this case, the evidence is clear. Furthermore, the claim is not a direct implication of evil among the Anasazi.

Practice Test

Listening

01 Campus Life

W: Hey Miguel, how've you been lately?

M: Stressed. My global government prof just gave us a monster project. We have to do online research and make a presentation using some kind of computer program. I have no idea about how to use that program. I've never even heard of it before. Say, you don't know anything about how the computer labs work here, do you? I've never really had to do any assignments with computers before, so I've never been to the computer labs on campus.

W: Actually, I worked in one of the open labs for two semesters. What do you wanna know?

M: Wow, thanks, Jean. Where to begin... Well, first off, where are they?

W: Well the open labs are in the basement of the library, in the student union building, and then there are two more on campus. One in the science building and one in that other new building across campus, the building where they do freshman orientation.

M: Oh yeah. I know the one one you're talking about.

W: Anyway, the largest open computer lab is in the science building.

M: Oh, OK. Are they open 24 hours?

W: Unfortunately, no. They're open from 8 a.m. to 9 p.m. Monday through Thursday, and 9:00 to 5:30 on Friday. The good news is that during the fall and spring semesters, they're open Saturdays and Sundays as well. They're open 9:00 until 5:00 during the weekend.

M: Uh huh, and do they offer any kind of training on the computers? Like I said, I don't know much about computers.

W: Yes, they do actually. They hold computer training workshops twice a month. You can sign up for one in the library. There are also instructional tutoring sessions for students who need help with their course work in the science computer lab, and of course, individual assistance in all of the labs.

M: Can I just walk in and start using a computer, or do I need a password or something?

W: You don't need a password to walk in the door, but you will need one to log in and use a computer. You have a student email account, don't you?

M: Sure. Doesn't everybody?

W: Everybody could have one, but some people don't actually make use of the free service offered by this university. They'd rather pay an online company for some reason.

M: That's nutty.

W: I think so, too. Anyway, I was asking you about your email account because that's how you can get a password. You have to register with the computer administration office on campus. They're the ones who send you the password.

M: This is getting complicated.

W: It's not really. It just sounds daunting if you've never done it before. Hey, do you have some time right now? I can go with you and help you register for a password.

M: As a matter of fact, my next class doesn't start until 3:30.

W: How about going to the computer lab in the student union? That's the closest one.

M: Lead the way. I'm right behind you.

02 Ecology

M: I'm sure a lot of you in this class have your own car. Think about the dashboard of your car. There are some special indicator lights there, warning indicators. If something is wrong with your car, those indicator lights will come on to warn you. Well, today we're going to talk about a similar kind of indicator in nature. These are bio-indicators. A bio-indicator is an organism that can warn us about harmful changes in our environment. The typical example of a bio-indicator would be a miner's canary. Miners today don't use them, but anyway, it's a good example from history.

I'm not sure how much you know about mining. You might have heard about recent mining accidents in the news. Obviously, this is a dangerous occupation, but other than mine collapses or explosions, another danger for miners is gas. I mean natural gas in the air, that you can't see. Pockets of natural gas sometimes occur naturally in mine-shafts. These pockets of gas are difficult to detect and can suffocate and kill miners if they do not notice them. You might not realize it, but natural gas doesn't actually have a smell, or at least it doesn't smell like the stuff you put in your car at the gas station. So, when a miner is working in a cave where there is a lot of natural gas in the air — well, you can imagine it's not a good situation to be in. So, miners used to take canaries into the mines with them. A canary is quite small, and these birds will pass out long before a human in a gas pocket. So, if the miner notices that the canary passes out, the miner knows there is danger and that he has to get out of that part of the mine immediately. In this case, the canary is more sensitive to a problem in the environment — the mine in this case — than humans. Likewise, bio-indicators tell us about potential problems in our environment because they are more sensitive to it than we are. OK, quiz time. Can anyone think of another example of a bio-indicator? Yes, Carol?

W: Those frogs that were deformed because of the pollution?

M: Good example. Frogs breathe through their skin. This means that they directly absorb everything in the water and air they live in, making them much more easily affected by pollution than humans are. When we notice a population of frogs with lots of deformities, such as extra legs, missing body parts, or malformed parts, we know that the area has probably been polluted, that the appropriate testing needs to be performed, and the necessary precautions need to be taken. And, as Carol mentioned, we've seen this happen right here in the United States.

OK, so we see that pollution hurts frogs, but what about people? Is there any evidence to suggest this kind of pollution causes problems for humans, too? To answer this question, we need to take a look at human bio-indicators.

Who might be a human bio-indicator? People who are more sensitive to the environment. In particular, children and unborn babies, or fetuses, are more sensitive to pollution than full-grown adults. So, they can also tell us about our environment. We usually ignore bio-indicators like frogs because, well, they're just frogs, aren't they? But when there are health problems in human communities, that sure catches our attention!

Here's a good example. No doubt you guys are all too young to remember this, but when I was growing up, this was a big deal and everybody knew about it. In 1978, there was a serious health problem in Love Canal, a suburban neighborhood in upstate New York. There was a high rate of cancer among the children of the area, birth defects were increasing, and pregnant women were losing their babies. Because of the high rate of birth defects and pregnancy problems, people in the area began asking the government to find out why. There was actually a group of activists at the time who were using the slogan, "Our fetuses are our canaries."

So, what was it about Love Canal that made it different from healthy communities? Well, as it turns out, from 1920 until 1953, the site was used as a chemical dump, a place where a company buries its chemical waste! The dump was later filled in with dirt before it was sold as regular real estate. Of course, chemicals in the ground get washed into ground water supplies when it rains, and the ground water eventually finds its way into local city water systems.

03 Music

W: Let's think about the traditional way of arranging music. You use a scale, right? And you build the composition, or song, around that scale. The traditional scales are the major and minor scales. The major scale is C-D-E-F-G-A-B-C. I'm sure all of you know it well. The minor scale, again I am sure you all know, is A-B-C-D-E-F-G-A. But, I should point out, these only use the white keys on the piano. What if we played all the keys and don't skip any? These are C-C#-D-D#-E-F-F#-G-G#-A-A#-B-C.

Sounds strange, doesn't it? This is called the chromatic scale, and it includes all the notes that you can play on traditional European instruments. So, the major and minor scales include the eight notes everyone is familiar with, but the chromatic scale includes everything, a total of twelve notes. And strange as it sounds, this is what composers of the early 20th century were using to write new kinds of compositions.

OK, well, you might say, "Hey, that's easy, anybody can write a song like that." But it's not just a matter of putting together any notes that you want. In order to write compositions using the chromatic scale, composers worked with pretty strict rules. There was a lot more to it than just hitting all the keys.

Who made up the rules? A group of composers, led by Arnold Schoenberg, created the method that composers interested in this kind of writing used when they were working with the chromatic scale. As I mentioned, the method had strict rules. The most important rule was that you could not play any note twice until all the other notes had been played once. To the composers, this meant that the music was truly free of all of the old rules for composition. So, listeners had to hear all twelve notes once before they could hear any one of the notes repeated. This new kind of music got a special name. It was called "atonal" or "12-tone" music, and traditional music was then called "tonal" music.

So, now let's look at how they did it. Let's look at how to make a 12-tone composition. First, we take all twelve notes and arrange them in a particular order. Remember, each note is only used once, so writing twelve different notes one time each — we have what is called a tone row. I see some confused looks. OK, let's keep this really simple to start with. We know there are 12 tones in the chromatic scale, so let's number them tone one through tone twelve. So, one very simple tone row might be just our twelve notes in order from one through twelve. So, now we have a basic tone row for our composition. This will be called the prime row for our composition, but to make the composition interesting, we need to add some variation.

To get this variation, the atonal composers modified the prime row of their piece in particular ways called transformations. The simplest transformation is called the retrograde tone row. As you might guess from the word "retrograde," this transformation is just the prime row backwards, that is, in our example, from twelve to one. So, now we have two kinds of tone rows: the original, or prime, tone row, and the retrograde tone row.

There is also another, more advanced transformation called the inverse row. The inverse is a bit complicated and involves changing the relationships between the notes in a particular way. You take a particular note in your prime row and shift twelve notes backward. You do that for every note in the prime row. It is sometimes called the "upside-down" row. In our example, it's hard to see how an inverse row changes things because for us, the retrograde row and the inverse row look the same, but say you start your prime row with tone 3 and end with tone 2. So, it goes 3, 4, 5, 6, 7, 8, 9, 10, 11, 12, 1, 2. Our retrograde row is then 2, 1, 12, 11, 10, 9, 8, 7, 6, 5, 4, 3. But our inverse row, by doing a little math and saying that each note is equal to 12 minus x — our inverse row becomes 9, 8, 7, 6, 5, 4, 3, 2, 1, 12, 11, 10. You can see all three tone rows are different now.

So, now we have three rows: the original, or prime, row, the retrograde, and the inverse. Well, what do you think they did next? They took the inverse of the retrograde row and made the inverse retrograde row. So, that's three transformations: retrograde (or backwards), inverse (or upside-down), and the retrograde inverse (or upside-down and backwards).

So, a composer could then start putting together a piece with these kinds of transformations. He or she can combine these in any order. If I'm composing an atonal piece, I can play two prime rows, then an inverse retrograde row, then an inverse row. So, now we have an interesting composition!

04 Sociology

M: What exactly is culture? A definition that comes straight out of a textbook would be this: "Culture is the complex whole that includes knowledge, beliefs, arts, morals, laws, customs, and any other habits and capabilities acquired by human beings as members of society. Culture refers to all those ways of thinking, feeling, and behaving that are socially transmitted from one generation to the next." A bit long-winded, but a definition of culture really has to be. It's a big idea to cram into just a few words. In case you're having trouble grasping the idea of what our textbook definition actually means, I'll give you a paraphrased version. Culture is basically any aspect of human life that is learned and taught and then passed on to younger generations. OK, so culture is learned, and it is passed on. Culture is also typically thought of as existing in the minds of individuals, so people don't really mean sculptures or ethnic foods when they talk about culture. Those can be culturally understood, but the objects themselves are not "the culture." Anyway, back to my original point, on the one hand, culture is this collective and all-encompassing entity of knowledge, beliefs, art, and all that other stuff, and on the other hand, it is dependent on people like you and me for its existence. Now, here's a question that often gets tossed around: Do animals have culture? We generally think of culture as something that only humans have, even though strong arguments can be made that animals, particularly chimpanzees, certainly have some aspects of culture, such as learned use of tools or signals. However, it is only humans that exhibit all the phenomena that we associate with culture. Remember, we said culture was learned, passed on, and was in the mind. In addition, there were cultural creations such as art, laws, values, and traditions. The interesting thing is that wherever you go in the world and whatever people you come into contact with, you will find that their culture includes those kinds of creations. So, although some animals may exhibit a few traits that resemble culture, humans have culture in its fullest sense. It's not going to surprise anyone when I say that human cultures vary widely from one group of people to the next, and even within cultures, you can find variation. Take, for example, a culture in which marriage partners are selected by the individuals themselves and a culture in which they are selected by an authority figure or parent. When I suggested these cultures, what countries came to mind? Lots of countries could fit in either category, so I'll just choose two. Let's say Canada and India. It's pretty safe to say that the norm in Canadian culture is for individuals to choose their own marriage partners. In India, the norm is for parents to choose. Often, these arrangements are made when the couple are only children. An arrangement will be made for the two to marry at a certain future date. These marriages can be arranged to create a bond or tie between two families or for a number of other reasons. Now, notice that I said "norm" for both of these cultures. There are also plenty of people in both Canada and India who do things differently than the cultural norm dictates. Some Canadians have their marriage partners chosen by authority figures, and some Indians choose their own partners. So, cultures are different when you compare two cultures of different countries or groups, but also within a single group, culture can vary at the personal level.

Of course, it's fun to look at all the differences between cultures — to point out all the "strange" things other people do — but for all their differences, there are also many things that cultures have in common. Like, the vast majority of cultures have ceremonies for marriages, some kind of coming-of-age ceremony, birth and death ceremonies, not to mention taboos, especially taboos regarding nudity and sexual relations. Or smiles. A smile is a universally accepted gesture — or maybe I should say body language — anyway, a smile is universally accepted as meaning something good or friendly.

So far, I've given you a definition of culture, and I've talked a little bit about similarities and differences, but we haven't said anything about how cultures change or evolve. In fact, cultures are constantly in a state of flux in spite of people's tendency to resist change. A good example of this would be something like a culture that tries to resist changes in its language. Face it: if people use it, it's going to change, and people certainly use culture. Some people use it to form bonds within groups or to keep people out of groups. There are lots of ways we use culture, but using your own culture doesn't necessarily change it. Using someone else's culture within your own cultural context — now that can lead to change. In fact, that's one of the most common ways that cultures change — by borrowing from other cultures. Let's take a few minutes and brainstorm some features that American culture has borrowed from other cultures.

05 Campus Life

W: Hi. My name is Emily.

M: Hi, Emily. I'm Todd.

W: What course did you need tutoring for, Todd?

M: Philosophy. Man, that class is kicking my... uh, it's really hard.

W: I understand. The first time students come across some of those theories, it can be kind of confusing. So, what questions do you have about your class?

M: Um, in the last class, we were talking about John Locke and his theory, but I didn't get it.

W: All right, so let's look at John Locke. His big theory related to empiricism, but to start with, how about telling me what you know about Locke and his ideas?

M: OK. Well, he said our minds were a *tabula* uhhh... the blank slate.

W: OK, yes, a *tabula rasa*, a blank slate. What does that mean?

M: Our minds don't have any knowledge, they just organize our experiences; like by making categories.

W: Good, our minds make categories from our experiences. Can you think of an example of that?

M: In class, my professor talked about colors. The sky and the ocean go into the category of blue things.

W: Good, what else?

M: Could shapes be another category? Like oranges and soccer balls are both round things?

W: Right, so we have categories, like colors and shapes and numbers. So, our minds make categories from information that we get from our senses. Good. So, that's empiricism. Knowledge comes from the senses.

M: Wow. I guess I did learn something in class. What about Berkeley? He was an empiricist, right?

W: That's right. He called his worldview "idealism." What do you know about his theory?

M: That one is tough. I don't get it.

W: You said you didn't get Locke either, but you really did know something about him and his theory.

M: But Berkley — his ideas are out there. I really didn't get idealism. I mean, I can tell you what I have in my notes, but I just wrote it down. I don't understand what it means.

W: OK. What do your notes say?

M: Here it is. Berkley said that there are no things, that there is no world, that everything is just an idea. How can that be?

W: Well, Berkeley might ask: What is a chair to you? You can look at it, or touch it, or sit in it, but that's it, basically. He says we don't need to believe in "the real chair" because all we will ever know is "the experienced chair."

M: So what? The chair is just my experience of it?

W: Basically, yes.

M: That doesn't make any sense to me. It's a chair.

W: OK. Suppose we have two chairs. One is a normal chair, and one is magic.

M: A magic chair?

W: Bear with me. This magic chair disappears whenever you're not looking at it or touching it — when you're not perceiving it, when you're not experiencing it. So, Berkeley's question is, "How can you tell a normal chair from a magical disappearing chair?" You can't, can you? So Berkeley says, the question is irrelevant, and that's idealism. So Locke, the empiricist, believed that knowledge comes from the senses, our experiences, and is merely organized by the mind. Berkeley agreed with Locke, but he went a step further and said that there is no external world at all, and that there are no things underlying our experiences, only our experiences themselves. Are you still with me?

M: It's a little clearer for me.

06 Literature

W: One of the most important things to consider about literature is how the writer tells his or her story. There are numerous methods, aspects, and nuances in writing, and each combination can be used for different effects in the mind of the reader. First off, every story must have at least one narrator of some kind.

I want to start by giving you all an important cautionary note: The narrator and the author are not the same thing. Do not talk about the feelings of the author if you mean the feelings of the narrator. While these may often be one and the same, they may often not be as well. An author may give his or her narrator opinions, characteristics, political orientations, or predilections that are different from his or her own. He or she may be doing this to make a specific point. If you believe the narrator is in fact the author, then look for specific evidence in the text to support this belief. Do NOT start off by simply assuming it.

Moving on, the term "point of view" of the story gets used quite often and can be very vague. Usually, people mean one of two things. The first thing they might mean is the role of the narrator in the story itself. This is the distinction between first-person and third-person narrative. Also, is the narrator an all-knowing voice outside of the story, or is the narrator a character experiencing the story along with us? The second way people use the term "point of view" is to describe the way that the narrator treats the actions, characters, and issues in the story. Is the narrator rooting for the hero? Is the narrator sympathizing with the psychologically disturbed and misunderstood protagonist? Is the narrator making fun of the characters? These devices or methods could also be described as the narrator's point of view.

I guess I should mention for the sake of those who are unfamiliar with first- and third-person narratives just what these are. A first-person narrative is a story told by one character. So the narrative sections of the text have lots of "I said" or "I saw" or "I did" in them. In third-person narratives — well, since quite a few of the texts that we will read in this course are written as third-person narratives, I want to go into a bit more detail about this particular form of narrative. The basic third-person omniscient narrator is called the "external narrator." Another term that you might run across is the "non-focalized point of view." This narrator has access to all of the characters' minds and all of the events in the story, so there is no single focus or focal point. The reader gets a "god's-eye-view" of the action. This is often used to give the reader more knowledge than the characters have themselves, so readers can see things developing along a path — a path that they know something about the end of. Technically, this is called a position of irony — knowing and seeing things about a story that certain characters don't know. So, the external narrator puts the reader in a position of irony.

But the external narrator can also put the reader in a position of suspense. This means the narrator only gives the reader as much knowledge as the characters. This is useful for throwing a few surprises at the reader and also brings up the issue of the "second-reading" of the book. The reader can go back and reread a suspense novel with full knowledge of the story. So, you can see, a writer's intention for telling a story in a certain way may be short-circuited in some way by readers. It's an interesting problem. Anyway, since most of you will be reading the stories I've assigned for the semester for the first time, we'll be looking for examples of how writers utilize this position of suspense in their writing.

A third point about external narrators — we can characterize the external narrator with the concepts of drama and reactivity. A dramatized narrator puts in his or her own two cents. I mean, he or she comments on the story as it is happening: giving his or her opinions, hopes, grievances, etc. This, of course, can severely influence the reader and inhibit readers' abilities to see the story through their own eyes. However, this in itself may be a planned effect by the writer.

There are of course some more complicated techniques available in external narration, such as embedded narratives. A good example of that comes from Mary Shelley's *Frankenstein*. In *Frankenstein*, the narrator begins the story. Then, Dr. Frankenstein begins telling a story within that story. Later, the monster tells his story within Dr. Frankenstein's story.

Speaking

Question 3

M: Have you ever used any of the services offered by the Career Services Center?

W: I've never logged on to any of the e-fairs, but I have used the career mentoring program. It's great! I've been talking to this cool counselor at the Career Center, and he thinks I would be great in statistics or accounting.

M: Oh yeah? How does he know that?

W: He gave me a couple of tests to measure my interests and abilities. Then, he asked me lots of questions about the type of student I am, and what kind of lifestyle I want to have after I graduate. Then, he ran a computer cross-check that showed my skills and interests were most closely related to students who have majored in stats and accounting.

M: But what about finding a job when you graduate?

W: The Career Center also has a huge research database. The counselor told me there'll be lots of jobs in those two fields over the next 10 years.

M: It sounds good, but what if you declare one of those majors and then don't like it?

W: Well, the center can help me find an internship next summer. I can do volunteer work for a company in my major and see if I like it. If I don't, I can change my major. The counselor said the center will be glad to help. It's a great place. You should check it out!

Question 4

W: So, I think we've covered all there is to say about the core and the mantle. Those layers are quite familiar to students anyway. I want to take some time today to go into more detail about the Earth's crust. The description in the textbook is rather superficial. It basically describes the crust as a unified unit — I mean, you might get the impression that the crust is a homogenous layer, but it's not. The crust is actually better described as consisting of two parts: the continental crust and the oceanic crust. As you might guess from the names of these layers, the oceanic crust is the part under the oceans, and the continental crust is the part under the continents. Now, there are several interesting differences between these two parts of the crust, other than where they are located. One difference is the thickness. The continental crust is thicker than the oceanic crust. Also, the rocks found in the continental crust are older than the rocks found in the oceanic crust. Let's talk a bit about why this is the case.

Question 5

W: Hey, Ryan. What's new?

M: Hi, Jenny. Nothing much.

W: Everything OK? You seem kind of down.

M: I got this notice today. I'm on academic probation.

W: Probation?! Why? Your grades have been great!

M: Most of them are, but I failed geology.

W: Why?

M: Well, first I signed up for too many classes: 18 credit hours. Then, I got sick and fell behind in my economics class. That's my major. I had to write this big term paper. I also had to write another paper for my literature class, so I was concentrating on those. I just didn't have time to study geology.

W: Why didn't you drop it and take it again later?

M: I was going to, but like I said, I was sick for awhile, and I missed the deadline to drop classes. Man, I've never flunked a class in my life!

W: It'll be OK. Here's what you can do. You have two weeks to appeal to the college director. You can write him a letter and explain your circumstances. I'm sure when he hears what happened and looks at all your good grades, he'll take you off probation.

M: I could try, I guess, but I don't know ... I don't really have a good excuse. It IS my fault. And I was only taking geology to fulfill a stupid science credit!

W: Your second choice is just to take the class again. You have one year. If you pass it, the new grade will replace the "F" on your transcripts.

M: Well, I could try that, but . . . um, the thing is, I don't know if I CAN pass it. It was hard!

W: Sure you can! You're smart, and I'll help you. Next semester, just don't take so many hours so you have more time to study. But Ryan, you've gotta do something — unless you want that "F" on your permanent record!

Question 6

M: Herbal treatments are important in traditional Eastern medicine. There are different medical traditions in different Eastern countries, but the most well-known in the West is probably Chinese medicine. It is common to find Chinese herbs at health-food stores in North America, and there are Chinese medical clinics in some cities. However, Chinese medicine has not been completely accepted by most American doctors. This is not because some herbal treatments are ineffective, but because of the basic theory behind Chinese medicine.

Traditional Chinese medical theory states that there is a power in the body called "chi." This power moves through the body along specific paths. If these paths are blocked, pain or disease can result. Chi can be hot or cold, active or passive, but there should not be too much of one or the other. The healthiest person has chi that is balanced and flows freely. Chi can be blocked or unbalanced in various ways. Many things can affect chi movement, such as food and body position as well as a person's mental and emotional state. Different herbs have different effects on chi. Ginseng, for example, can stimulate active chi, hence warming the body, while other herbs have a cooling effect. Combinations of various herbs can have complex effects.

Traditional Chinese medicine tries to affect chi first, before treating the symptoms of an illness. Western medicine treats the symptoms first. Therefore, traditional Chinese doctors claim that their way is useful for treating continuing problems and preventing disease, while Western medicine is better for problems that need urgent help. While many Western doctors agree that Chinese herbal treatments can be beneficial, few believe in the idea of chi. Since chi is invisible and its effects cannot be measured, there is no direct evidence for it. Until chi can be proved or disproved, there will be no agreement about it.

Writing

W: The first and most fundamental step to take when studying an entity or phenomenon is to define it, right? Right. Starting with a definition ensures that there actually is something there to be studied and provides a certainty of what exactly it is being studied and, by extension, what is not being studied. Let's begin, then, by examining some of the aspects involved in the definition of society. A society involves a geographic area, like the United States or the world, for example, though a society can exist on a much smaller scale, like a local community. A society also involves a distinct identity. By this I mean that the individuals within the geographic area view themselves as a society. The people attending this university identify themselves as part of the student body here. Our common place of study gives us a common identity as members of this school. So, place is the first aspect we use to define a group — a social group. A big social group, we'll call a society. A society also involves a common government that sets and monitors rules under which the people in the society abide and coexist. At a national level, this is pretty easy to imagine. The society in any given country is under the rule of the national government. But there are also state governments, city governments, and our university even has a kind of governing body, doesn't it? As you might guess, things that we study in sociology are not always as cut-and-dry as you might think at first. So, going back to our definition of society, next we should talk about language. Members of a particular society share a common language through which they can communicate. It would be kind of hard for a society to function if its members couldn't communicate with each other. It is interesting to note that, in the US, we don't actually have an official national language. Most official business is conducted in English, so even though it's not the official language, it's the accepted common language here. And lastly, a society also shares common traditions, customs, and beliefs, though sociologists are beginning to question the accuracy and relevance of these last few aspects.

So, now that we have our definition, we can examine just what this force, society, actually does. For one, it organizes individuals into a system aimed at obtaining the things they need for survival. It does this by giving us guidelines for behavior, as mentioned in the definition. These guidelines serve two chief functions: first, they satisfy certain social needs, and second, they prevent conflict among the members of the society. Thus we have laws, some of which are unwritten taboos, that define and control relationships between women and men, adults and children, teachers and students, etc. In addition, we have laws against theft, violence, and other issues that could potentially create strife. Alright, with all of this in mind, I think we are ready to start thinking about society in a more systematic way.

Mastering Skills for the TOEFL® iBT

ANSWER KEY

Reading Section / Listening Section / Speaking Section /

Writing Section / Practice Test

Skill A

01

1. (C)   2. (D)   3. (D)
4. Children's eustachian tubes are smaller and straighter and their adenoids are larger. This means that the tubes do not drain as well, and the adenoids can block the tubes more easily.

02

1. (A)   2. (B)   3. (C)
4. a bridge = humankind's progress, the Titanic = the deadly outcome when man tries to do something too great (the fate of Icarus), the myth of Sisyphus = the futility of humankind's pursuits

03

1. (B)   2. (A)   3. (B)
4. The right to vote and the ability to enter into a legal contract

Skill B

01

1. (C)   2. (C)   3. (A)
4. which deviate from = in addition to, a variety of = other

02

1. (D)   2. (C)   3. (D)
4. (A) Why? Most of the information in the passage is about the rings, moons, and gaps. Also, Galileo did not know that Saturn's disc was really made of separate rings.

03

1. (A)   2. (A)   3. (C)
4. (A) Why? The passage includes information on crops used to make fabric, British control of materials for fabric, and things that colonists did with fabrics.

Skill C

01

1. (D)   2. (B)   3. (D)
4. (A) Why? The paragraph describes the main interest of each man. The answer cannot be (B) because the passage says nothing about how they felt about teaching.

02

1. (D)   2. (D)   3. (B)
4. "careful planning" + "useful" → support of ideas introduced by Sequoia example and provide a lead-in, or reason, for the following sentence on the frequency of planned fires.

03

1. (A)   2. (C)   3. (D)
4. (A) Why? The passage is about how babies communicate without speaking. Sentence (B) implies that the passage should describe why babies don't speak.

Skill D

01

1. (D)   2. (C)   3. (A)
4. First "its" — the water's; Second "its" — the lower Mississippi River's

02

1. (D)   2. (A)   3. (B)
4. it — information

03

1. (A)   2. (D)   3. (B)
4. Words in Anglo-Saxon, Old German, and Old Norse

Skill E

01

1. (D) 2. (C) 3. (C)
4. The passage states that Hemingway is most well-known for his novels, not his non-fiction pieces. Therefore, the answer is (C).

02

1. (C) 2. (B) 3. (A)
4. The passage states that the former, which refers to nodding, is communicated in Turkey by raising the eyebrows. Thus, someone in Turkey would not understand a nod from a person of another culture, so the answer is (B).

03

1. (B) 2. (C) 3. (A)
4. One night, a spirit wearing the jingle dress appeared to him in a dream. A spirit is a supernatural being and the Ojibwa man believed in it. Thus, the answer is (C).

Skill F

01

1. Native — (C), (D), (G); Non-native — (A), (E)
2. (A) 3. (A)
4. Neither (B) nor (F) is mentioned in the passage.

02

1. (A), (B), (D)
2. (B) 3. (A)
4. Sentences 2 and 3

03

1. Slang — (A), (C), (G);
   Mainstream Speech — (D), (E), (H)
2. (B) 3. (C)
4. Neither (B) nor (F) is mentioned in the passage.

Review A-F

Vocabulary Review

1. (D)	2. (C)	3. (B)
4. (D)	5. (D)	6. (C)
7. (D)	8. (A)	9. (D)
10. (A)	11. (D)	12. (C)
13. (C)	14. (A)	15. (C)
16. inability	17. distinguish	18. composing
19. contend	20. recite	21. perish
22. access	23. perish	24. proficient
25. preclude		

Skill Review

01

1. (C)	2. (A)	3. (A)
4. (D)	5. (A)	6. (C)
7. (B)	8. (A)	9. (C)
10. (A)	11. (C)	

12. Inflow — (B), (D), (H); Outflow — (A), (E), (F)

02

1. (B)	2. (D)	3. (A)
4. (B)	5. (C)	6. (A)
7. (D)	8. (B)	9. (A)
10. (B)	11. (A)	

12. (B), (E), (F)

Chapter 2

Skill A

01

1. (A) 2. (C) 3. (A)
4. (A)
5. England — (C), (E), (F), (G); France — (B), (D), (H)

02

1. (C) 2. (B) 3. (A)
4. (D)
5. Bit — (B), (G); Byte — (A), (C), (D)

03

1. (D) 2. (A) 3. (B)
4. (C) 5. (A), (E), (F)

04

1. (D) 2. (D) 3. (B)
4. (D)
5. Fear — (B), (C); Anxiety — (D), (E), (G)

05

1. (D) 2. (D) 3. (D)
4. (B) 5. (B), (C), (D)

Skill B

01

1. (B) 2. (C) 3. (D)
4. (C)
5. Flock in Florida — (D), (E);
Flock in Texas — (B), (C), (G)

02

1. (C) 2. (A) 3. (D)
4. (B) 5. (B), (D), (F)

03

1. (D) 2. (A) 3. (A)
4. (B)
5. Early jazz musicians — (C), (F), (G);
Armstrong's innovations — (B), (D)

04

1. (B) 2. (C) 3. (D)
4. (B) 5. (A), (C), (E)

05

1. (C) 2. (A) 3. (D)
4. (C)
5. Ideas Before 1300 — (C), (G);
Ideas After 1300 — (A), (B), (D)

Skill C

01

1. (D) 2. (C) 3. (B)
4. (B) 5. (A), (B), (C)

02

1. (D) 2. (B) 3. (B)
4. (C)
5. Herbs — (C), (D), (E), (H); Spices — (F), (G), (I)

03

1. (D) 2. (C) 3. (A)
4. (D) 5. (A), (D), (F)

04

1. (B) 2. (D) 3. (C)
4. (A) 5. (A), (B), (E)

05

1. (D) 2. (A) 3. (C)
4. (B) 5. (A), (C), (F)

Review A-C

Vocabulary Review

1. (B) 2. (C) 3. (A)
4. (C) 5. (A) 6. (D)
7. (B) 8. (B) 9. (D)
10. (B) 11. (C) 12. (A)
13. (D) 14. (A) 15. (A)
16. (C) 17. (D) 18. (C)
19. (A) 20. (B) 21. (C)

22. (A)	23. (B)	24. (A)
25. (D)	26. (B)	27. (D)
28. (B)	29. (C)	30. (C)
31. immigration	32. likelihood	33. occupation
34. social security	35. comprised	36. exposed
37. link	38. enables	39. misery
40. ensures	41. motivation	42. cite
43. descend	44. innovative	45. exclusively
46. (E)	47. (A)	48. (D)
49. (B)	50. (C)	

Skill Review

01

1. (D)	2. (C)	3. (C)
4. (C)	5. (B)	6. (B)
7. (D)	8. (C)	9. (C)

10. Causes of Isolation — (E), (H);
Effects of Isolation — (C), (D);
Ways to Prevent Isolation — (A), (F)

02

1. (B)	2. (B)	3. (D)
4. (B)	5. (A)	6. (C)
7. (D)	8. (A)	9. (A)

10. (B), (D), (F)

Skill D

01

1. (D)	2. (B)	3. (D)
4. (B)	5. (A), (D), (E)	

02

1. (D)	2. (D)	3. (A)
4. (C)	5. (A), (C), (F)	

03

1. (A)	2. (D)	3. (C)
4. (B)		

5. Traditional — (B), (E), (F); Non-traditional — (A), (C)

04

1. (B)	2. (C)	3. (B)
4. (A)	5. (A), (C), (E)	

05

1. (C)	2. (C)	3. (D)
4. (B)		

5. Classical Realism — (A), (D), (F);
Romantic Realism — (B), (C)

Skill E

01

1. (C)	2. (D)	3. (B)
4. (C)	5. (A), (C), (F)	

02

1. (B)	2. (A)	3. (D)
4. (B)	5. (A), (D), (E)	

03

1. (B)	2. (C)	3. (C)
4. (B)		

5. Imports — (B), (C), (G) Exports — (A), (D)

04

1. (A)	2. (C)	3. (C)
4. (B)	5. (A), (D), (F)	

05

1. (A)	2. (B)	3. (B)
4. (D)	5. (B), (D), (F)	

Skill F

01

1. (D)	2. (D)	3. (A)
4. (C)	5. (A), (C), (F)	

02

1. (C)	2. (C)	3. (A)
4. (B)		

5. Agents of Socialization — (A), (F), (H)
Types of Socialization — (B), (C), (G)

03

1. (B)	2. (B)	3. (B)
4. (C)	5. (B), (C), (E)	

04

1. (B)   2. (A)   3. (D)
4. (A)
5. Moving Plates — (B), (C), (E)
   Forming Mountains — (A), (G)

05

1. (A)   2. (B)   3. (C)
4. (C)   5. (B), (C), (E)

Review A-F

Vocabulary Review

1. (B)   2. (C)   3. (D)
4. (B)   5. (A)   6. (C)
7. (A)   8. (A)   9. (D)
10. (B)   11. (B)   12. (D)
13. (A)   14. (B)   15. (A)
16. (C)   17. (C)   18. (D)
19. (A)   20. (B)   21. (A)
22. (D)   23. (B)   24. (C)
25. (A)   26. (D)   27. (B)
28. (A)   29. (C)   30. (A)
31. advent 32. evolution   33. discredit
34. essence 35. Inevitably 36. interpret
37. diverse 38. adaptation 39. diverge
40. retain 41. obscurity   42. mechanical
43. prophetic 44. reverence 45. uniformity
46. (C)   47. (E)   48. (A)
49. (D)   50. (B)

Skill Review

01

1. (B)   2. (D)   3. (B)
4. (B)   5. (D)   6. (D)
7. (C)   8. (D)   9. (A)
10. (B)   11. (D)
12. Intensity — (A), (E), (G); Spread — (C), (D), (H)

02

1. (B)   2. (D)   3. (C)
4. (B)   5. (A)   6. (A)
7. (C)   8. (B)   9. (D)
10. (C)   11. (C)
12. (B), (C), (F)

Chapter 3

Focus A

Guided Practice

01 Acupuncture

Suggested underlined sentences:

In China, the practice of acupuncture has been traced back to approximately the 1ˢᵗ millennium B.C.

Acupuncture is understood to be a procedure for regulating the circulation of gi (vital energy) and blood.

Traditional Chinese medicine is not based on knowledge of modern physiology, biochemistry, nutrition, anatomy, or any of the known mechanisms of healing.

Though it has continued to be regarded with some level of skepticism and mistrust, acupuncture is gradually becoming accepted in the Western world as a form of medicine.

Summary

Suggested answer:

The technique of acupuncture has been used in China to help people recover from illness for at least 2,000 years. Acupuncture was originally used to control the flow of vital energy, called gi, and blood through the body. Because it is not founded in knowledge gained from modern health sciences, many medical experts in the western world do not accept the benefits of acupuncture. Despite this skepticism, more and more people are turning to acupuncture as a form of medicine.

02 Capitalism

Suggested underlined sentences:

Social stratification is the hierarchical arrangement of a society into social classes and strata that are very difficult for individuals to rise through.

By and large, individuals are locked into a socio-economic class from birth and are kept there by social limitations.

A key tenet of social stratification is that status is inherited.

The group can be defined by wealth and social status, but it is often also related to such factors as race, ethnicity, gender, age, and religion.

Summary

Suggested answer:

Social stratification is the hierarchical arrangement of a society into social classes and strata that are very difficult for individuals to rise through. One critical factor related to social class is that children can inherit this class from their parents. Additionally, those born into the higher strata of society use their power to maintain their wealth and position in society. Other birth factors that may determine a person's social class include the person's race, ethnicity, and gender.

Self Practice

01 Parts of Plot

Suggested underlined sentences:

Aristotle, in his *Poetics*, looks at the form of tragedy in drama.

By this, Aristotle indicates that the medium of tragedy is not narrative, but drama.

To be whole, the tragedy must have a beginning, middle, and an end.

The aim of the play is to bring out this catharsis within the audience.

Summary

Suggested answer:

In *Poetics*, Aristotle outlines the critical features of a tragedy. First, Aristotle claimed that tragedy should be shown rather than told. A tragedy must also have a logically connected beginning, middle, and end. Additionally, Aristotle believed that a tragedy should lead the audience to a catharsis.

02 Management

Suggested underlined sentences:

Several studies have identified key mistakes that can impede a talented manager's career.

The first key mistake is insensitivity.

Another somewhat related common flaw is arrogance.

Betrayal of trust is cited in the studies as a third common mistake.

The next mistake commonly linked to derailers is over-ambition.

The fifth key mistake identified in the research is that derailers do not effectively delegate.

Summary
Suggested answer:
Research indicates that potentially successful managers can derail their careers by making at least two of the following mistakes. They may be insensitive to their subordinates. They may be too arrogant and not listen to others who seem to have less skill or experience than they do. Another common problem is that derailers refuse to admit an inability to meet deadlines, thus betraying the trust of others they work with.

Focus B

Guided Practice

01 Anxiety

Fear	Anxiety
— normal, healthy	— unhealthy mental state
— source can be named	— not based on a describable source
	— wastes energy

Anxiety Disorders
- affects quality of life for sufferer
- panic attacks
- highest rate of effective treatment

Summary
Suggested answer:
Although many people think they are the same, psychologists differentiate between fear and anxiety. Fear is a normal, healthy reaction to a definable cause. Anxiety, in contrast, is an unhealthy mental state caused by an indescribable source. In severe cases, people may develop anxiety disorders which can negatively affect the quality of life of the sufferer.

02 Plea bargaining

Plea Bargaining: Disadvantages
- makes legal system bartering
- people may plead guilty to crimes they didn't commit
- criminals may not be punished for crimes they do commit

Plea bargaining: Advantages
- can save resources by avoiding trial
- can help convict high-level criminals
- can help convict criminals with insufficient evidence

Summary
Suggested answer:
Plea bargaining is a powerful tool for prosecutors, but there are both pros and cons related to this type of legal strategy. Critics contend that plea bargaining reduces the justice system to bartering and that dangerous criminals sometimes are not punished in exchange for testimony against others. On the other hand, plea bargaining allows the justice system to function fluidly by saving both the time and money that going to trial consumes. Finally, though some low-level criminals may not be punished for their crimes, their testimony helps keep more dangerous criminals in prison, thus protecting society on the whole.

Self Practice

01 Bits vs. Bytes

Bit: binary digit
- consists of 0s and 1s, on and off
- used by programmers to direct computer functions
- Kbps=kilobits per second

Byte: 8 bits
- single character of data on computer
- example: a letter in ASCII
- KBps=kilobytes per second
- kilo=1,024, NOT 1,000

Summary

Suggested answer:

Computers respond to data organized in two states, on and off, which are represented by 1s and 0s. Each of these 1s and 0s is called a bit and is used by computer programmers to direct the functions of a computer. These bits are arranged in groups of eight, which are referred to as bytes. A byte represents a single character of data on a computer, such as the letter A.

02 Technology in the Classroom

Use of technology in the classroom
- multimedia should provide framework, not too much detail
- teacher can become superfluous
- interaction can be reduced

Stages of lecture
- lecture should have beginning, middle, end
- beginning sparks student attention, provides overview of topic
- middle presents details
- should have breaks every 12-15 minutes to engage students
- end reviews key information, helps students assimilate info with own experience

Summary

Suggested answer:

A strong lecturer should use technology wisely and plan the stages of the lecture effectively. If technology presents too much information to students during a lecture, interaction will be reduced and the instructor may become unnecessary. The lecture should be divided into a beginning, middle, and end with appropriate content for each stage. Finally, the lecturer should plan a change of pace every 12-15 minutes in order to keep the students' attention and re-engage them with the material.

Listening Chapter **1** _____

Skill A

01
1. (D)   2. (B)   3. (C)
4. Go to room 304 in Withurst Hall / Fill out a FORM and pay a FEE. / The fee is THIRTY dollars for team players.

02
1. (B)   2. (B), (C)   3. (C)
4. Stage of Industrialization-Death Rate-BIRTH Rate-Population / Preindustrial-High-High-STABLE / Early Industrial-LOW-High-Explosion / Mature Industrial-Low-LOW-Stable

03
1. (A)   2. (D)   3. (C)
4. Petrarch's sonnets / 2 parts / 8 lines / 6 lines / Shakespeare's sonnets / 4 parts / 3 4-line parts / 1 couplet

04
1. (B)   2. (A), (C)   3. (C)
4. Enrolling in a class that is full / You may be able to enroll if it is a REQUIRED course. / You may be able to enroll if you have the PREREQUISITES. / You can be put on a WAITING list if the previous two conditions do not apply.

05
1. (C)   2. (D)   3. (A)
4. How glaciers erode bedrock / PLUCKING causes large chunks to be detached. / Abrasion / COURSE debris creates long grooves in the bedrock. / FINE debris creates a smooth surface.

06
1. (D)   2. (B)   3. (B), (C)
4. Pasteurization / HTST / — kept at 72°C for 15 seconds / — can last for two or three WEEKS / UHT / — kept at 138°C for 2 seconds / — can last for two or three MONTHS

07
1. (B)   2. (C)   3. (B)
4. Notes: MAIN ideas, strengths, one thing to IMPROVE / Grading: from 1 to 4; best score = 4

08
1. (D)   2. (C)   3. (D)
4. Where information comes from / PRIMARY / Ex: a diary / SECONDARY / Ex: a scholars interpretation of a PRIMARY source / TERTIARY / created from a SECONDARY source

Skill B

01
1. (C)   2. (C)   3. (B)
4. Jazz Band AUDITIONS / Memorize SCALES / Practice SIGHT-READING / Allow plenty of time to WARM UP

02
1. (B)   2. (B)   3. (A), (B), (D)
4. Alexander the Great / charismatic LEADER / a brutal KILLER / brilliant military STRATEGIST

03
1. (C)   2. (D)   3. (A), (D)
4. Needed for preservation / PRESERVABLE substance / BONE / SHELL / Buried in SEDIMENT / Suitable ENVIRONMENT / SHORELINE

04
1. (D)   2. (A)   3. (C)
4. Court policy: / The maximum limit is one HOUR, ONE time(s) per week. / RESERVATIONS are made one WEEK beforehand.

05
1. (A)   2. (A)   3. (C), (D)
4. Example: JUMPING over a ravine / FIRE in your house / Use of Physics: calculate necessary MOMENTUM / Use principles of (SMOKE AND) HEAT diffusion

06
1. (B)   2. (D)   3. (A)
4. MASKS / Greek / first used in (RELIGIOUS) RITUALS / theater masks made of painted LEATHER or canvas / MEDIEVAL / used in morality plays / made of paper mache

07

1. (A) 2. (A), (B) 3. (B)
4. The PRE-LAB report / Order of writing / PURPOSE / HYPOTHESIS / procedure

08

1. (C) 2. (A) 3. (B), (C)
4. ART / PERFORMING / Visual / Literary / THEATER, dance, opera, music / FILM / Painting, sculpture, illustration / Fiction, poetry

Skill C

01

1. (A) 2. (B) 3. (C)
4. Computer program / Shows a VERB (or WORD) / User TYPES in past form / Mistakes are REPEATED at the end

02

1. (D) 2. (D) 3. (A)
4. MOTHER TERESA / Albanian, not INDIAN / worked as a MISSIONARY / received NOBEL PEACE PRIZE in 1979

03

1. (B), (C) 2. (B) 3. (C)
4. Problem: Hard to find ANIMALS in intertidal pools / Cause 1: POACHING = taking animals from pools / SNAILS / octopuses / barnacles / Cause 2: People don't know LAW

04

1. (A) 2. (D) 3. (B)
4. AMERICAN Revolution / fought between US and BRITAIN / started over tea in Boston / Boston TEA Party : FIRST aggressive act of war

05

1. (A), (D) 2. (A) 3. (D)
4. Elderly people → pets → LOWERS blood pressure / RAISES spirits / Anybody → pets → LOWERS of heart disease / RAISES speed of recovery from heart attacks / LOWERS cases of colds, headaches, fever

06

1. (C) 2. (D) 3. (A)
4. The day of the trip: FRIDAY / The weather forecast: CLEAR / The location: MOUNTAINS / The student who went before: MAN

07

1. (B) 2. (D) 3. (A)
4. Meteor Theory / 1. 10 km meteor hit the Earth / 2. Earth became DARK and cold / 3. PLANTS died / 4. PLANT-eating dinosaurs died / 5. MEAT-eating dinosaurs died

08

1. (A) 2. (B) 3. (D)
4. Problem: PASSWORD isn't working / Possible cause: Hasn't logged in for 180 days / Another student is using her USERNAME and password / Solution: Go to REGISTRAR'S OFFICE and request a new one / Use SECRET QUESTION, probably mother's maiden name

Review A-C

Vocabulary Review

1. (D)	2. (B)	3. (A)
4. (A)	5. (D)	6. (B)
7. (D)	8. (B)	9. (D)
10. (C)	11. (A)	12. (C)
13. (C)	14. (A)	15. (D)
16. sufficient	17. facets	18. contend
19. collaboration	20. foster	21. (D)
22. (A)	23. (E)	24. (B)
25. (C)		

Skill Review

01

1. (B)	2. (A), (C)	3. (D)
4. (A)	5. (B)	6. (B)

02

1. (C)	2. (D)	3. (D)
4. (C)	5. (C)	6. (A)

Skill D

01

1. (B), (E)   2. (B)
3. Yes — (A), (C), (D); No — (B)
4. Student Senators / Eligibility: — FULL-TIME student /— 2.0 GPA / Responsibility: — decide what to do with STUDENT FEES (MONEY) / — deal with (UNIVERSITY) ORGANIZATIONS

02

1. (A), (B), (D) 2. (B)
3. Yes — (A), (B), (C); No — (D)
4. Uses of MONEY / 1. medium of EXCHANGE / 2. way to measure VALUE / 3. an ASSET that can be saved

03

1. (D)   2. (C)
3. Chord — (A), (D); Non-chord — (B), (C)
4. Chords / — combination of 3 or more different NOTES (PITCHES) played at same time / — only COMMONLY USED note groups called chords / — power chords involve only TWO pitch classes

04

1. (B), (C), (D) 2. (B)
3. Yes — (A); No — (B), (C), (D)
4. Required books: / — refer to SYLLABUS to be sure about titles / — used books are HALF OFF and have a BLUE label / — can be returned within 7 DAYS of purchase

05

1. (C), (D)   2. (C)
3. Yes — (B), (D); No — (A), (C)
4. Three Major Biomes / Tundra / —little RAINFALL / — cold WINTERS / — from 0 to 24 hours of daylight / Grasslands / — located INLAND / — receive 15-30 inches of rainfall / — two types: SHORTGRASS and TALLGRASS / Deserts / — located within 20 to 30 DEGREES of equator / — HOT days and COLD nights / — less than TEN inches of rainfall

06

1. (A)   2. (A)
3. First Part of Course — (C); Second Part of Course — (B); Entire Course — (A)
4. Class: RELIGION and MORALITY / — discuss CONNECTION between religion and MORALITY / assume EXISTENCE of God / later, examine OPPOSITE assumption

07

1. (D)   2. (A)
3. Fitness/Heart Rate — (C); Fitness/Swim Speed — (A); Recovery/Heart Rate — (D); Recover/Swim Speed — (B)
4. Goal of session: GET BALANCE / Form: neck and spine should be ALIGNED / Technique: rotate HIPS and CHIN

08

1. (A)   2. (C)
3. Rose hips — (B), (D); Rose thorns — (A), (C)
4. Rose Species / *Pimpinellifolia* / — dark PURPLE or black hips / — tight cluster of SPINES instead of thorns / *Canina* / — HIPS high in vitamin C / — RED colored hips / *Rugosa* / — HIPS high in vitamin C / — tight cluster of SPINES instead of thorns

Skill E

01

1. Yes — (A), (C); No — (B), (D)
2. (B)   3. (C)
4. Language Partners / — help foreign STUDENTS practice English / — are VOLUNTEERS, not paid / — explain language and CULTURE

02

1. Wave Theory of Light — (A), (C); Particle Theory of Light — (B), (D)
2. (A)   3. (C)
4. Light Theory / Wave: / — Newton: light travels FASTER in a dense medium / — FOUCAULT: measured speed of light / Particle: / — Huygens: light travels SLOWER in a dense medium / — EINSTEIN: light causes particles to change speed

03

1. Yes — (A), (B); No — (C), (D)
2. (D) 3. (C)
4. Location: bordered by Europe, AFRICA, and Asia. / Origin of name: from LATIN words / medi = MIDDLE, terra = LAND

04

1. Yes — (A), (D); No — (B), (C)
2. (B) 3. (D)
4. To register for student union class: / – go to THIRD floor of STUDENT UNION building / If course is WORK related: / – REGISTER at student EMPLOYMENT office

05

1. Yes — (B), (D); No — (A), (C)
2. (B) 3. (A)
4. League of Nations / when established: after WORLD WAR I / why established: to settle INTERNATIONAL CONFLICTS peacefully / why lacked strength: no ARMY / powerful member countries: BRITAIN and FRANCE

06

1. Impressionist — (B), (C); Pre-impressionist — (A)
2. (A) 3. (C)
4. Impressionist Movement / — first in VISUAL art, then MUSIC / — focused on FEELING of subject, not REALISTIC depictions / — used LIGHT and COLOR to express impact of feelings

07

1. Yes — (B), (C), (D); No — (A)
2. (A) 3. (D)
4. Student Union Post Office / Opening hours: / Regular months: 7:30 a.m. to 3:30 p.m. / Summer months: 8:00 a.m. to 3:30 p.m. / P.O. Boxes: /rent FIVE DOLLARS a month

08

1. Aperture — (B); Exposure — (A); Shutter Speed — (C)
2. (C) 3. (A)
4. Exposure: amount of LIGHT that falls on FILM / — controlled by: / — lens APERTURE (size of HOLE) / — shutter SPEED (amount of TIME hole is open)

Skill F

01

1. (C), (B), (D), (A)
2. (C) 3. (A)
4. Conflict resolution / 1. ROOMMATES get together / 2. discuss and plan / 3. commit to a PLAN / 4. hold review 1 MONTH later / 5. if not resolved → apply for a ROOM CHANGE

02

1. (C), (A), (D), (B)
2. (D) 3. (A)
4. Types of FILTERS / Biological / Ability to PROCESS large amounts of information / PSYCHOLOGICAL / Take in only information of INTEREST to us.

03

1. Yes — (B), (C); No — (A), (D)
2. (A) 3. (B)
4. SERIAL ports: One bit at a time / PARALLEL ports: simultaneous transmission / Example: PRINTER port of computer / Pin 1: Tells printer DATA is being sent / Pins 2-9: Transmission of the BYTE / Pin 10: Sends CONFIRMATION signal to computer / Pins 11-17: Various functions / Pins 18-25: ground

04

1. (D), (B), (A), (C)
2. (D) 3. (A)
4. PARKING on campus / Determined by LOTTERY during regular school year. / $120 per year / Restricted to students enrolled in summer COURSES during the summer months. / $12 per month

05

1. Yes — (B), (C); No — (A), (D)
2. (B) 3. (A), (B)
4. POLLUTION is bad only when: / The QUANTITIES are too great. / The ECOSYSTEM can't break it down. / Example: CFCs are damaging the OZONE LAYER (ATMOSPHERE) because they can't be broken down.

06

1. (C), (B), (A), (D)
2. (C)　　　　3. (D)
4. Blast: An opportunity to VOLUNTEER your time / Activities: Conducting SURVEYS, handing out flyers, making announcements. / Benefits: Develop PUBLIC speaking skills, build confidence, and meet new people. / Commitment: 30 MINUTES every other week

07

1. (B), (D), (A), (C)
2. (A)　　　　3. (D)
4. Events of the MIDDLE AGES / Fall of the ROMAN EMPIRE / Large MIGRATION of people causing cultural changes / CHRISTIAN CHURCH is unifying entity

08

1. Yes — (B), (C); No — (A), (D)
2. (A)　　　　3. (A), (C), (D)
4. Photosynthesis: Occurs in (GREEN) LEAVES of plants. / Turns carbon dioxide and WATER into / OXYGEN and GLUCOSE

Review A-F

Vocabulary Review

1. (A)	2. (D)	3. (D)
4. (A)	5. (C)	6. (A)
7. (A)	8. (B)	9. (D)
10. (B)	11. (B)	12. (A)
13. (D)	14. (C)	15. (D)
16. Input	17. external	18. process
19. retain	20. selective	21. external
22. purchase	23. detrimental	24. enforce
25. enclose		

Skill Review

01

1. (B)　　　　2. (A)　　　　3. (D)
4. Fraternal Twins — (C), (D), (F); Identical Twins — (A), (B), (E)
5. (A)　　　　6. Yes — (A), (C), (D); No — (B)

02

1. (C)　　　　2. (A), (B)　　　　3. (B)
4. Squid Constantly Move Around — (B), (C); Squid Don't Constantly Move Around — (A), (D)
5. (D)　　　　6. (D), (A), (C), (B)

Chapter 2

Skill A

01

1. (B)   2. (D)   3. (A), (C)   4. (B)

02

1. (C)   2. (A)   3. (B)   4. (C)

03

1. (C)   2. (C)   3. (B), (E)   4. (A)

04

1. (D)   2. (C)   3. (C)   4. (B)

05

1. (D)   2. (B)   3. (A)   4. (B)

06

1. (C)   2. (A)   3. (A), (B)   4. (B)

Skill B

01

1. (A)   2. (B)   3. (D)   4. (C)

02

1. (B)   2. (A)   3. (B), (C)   4. (A)

03

1. (C)   2. (A)   3. (C)   4. (D)

04

1. (D)   2. (A)   3. (A)   4. (C)

05

1. (B)   2. (C)   3. (C)   4. (A)

06

1. (C)   2. (B)   3. (C)   4. (B)

Skill C

01

1. (B)   2. (A)   3. (B)   4. (C)

02

1. (B)   2. (B)   3. (D)   4. (D)

03

1. (C)   2. (C)   3. (D)   4. (B)

04

1. (A)   2. (B)   3. (C)   4. (B)

05

1. (B)   2. (A)

3. (B), (D), (E), (F)   4. (D)

06

1. (B)   2. (A)   3. (C)   4. (B)

Review A-C

Vocabulary Review

1. (B)   2. (C)   3. (A)
4. (D)   5. (A)   6. (B)
7. (D)   8. (B)   9. (C)
10. (B)   11. (B)   12. (A)
13. (C)   14. (B)   15. (D)
16. (B)   17. (D)   18. (B)
19. (A)   20. (D)   21. (A)
22. (C)   23. (D)   24. (A)
25. (A)   26. (B)   27. (D)
28. (B)   29. (A)   30. (C)
31. myriad   32. garb   33. categories
34. corresponding 35. breakdown 36. version
37. prominence 38. mourning   39. ornate
40. ubiquitous 41. republic   42. authentic
43. bizarre   44. interface   45. predecessor
46. (S)   47. (O)   48. (S)
49. (O)   50. (S)

Skill Review

01

1. (B)   2. (A)   3. (C)
4. (D)   5. (B)   6. (D)

02

1. (B)   2. (B), (E)   3. (B)
4. (A)   5. (B)   6. (C)

03

1. (A)   2. (A)   3. (D)
4. (B)   5. (C)   6. (A)

04

1. (A)   2. (C)   3. (C)
4. (B)   5. (D)   6. (C)

Skill D

01

1. Yes — (A), (C), (D); No — (B)
2. (A)   3. (C)   4. (C)

02

1. Franchise: Pro — (A), Con — (C);
   Independent Business: Pro — (B), Con — (D)
2. (A)   3. (B), (C)   4. (B)

03

1. Latitude — (B), (D), (E); Longitude — (A), (C), (F)
2. (B)   3. (B)   4. (D)

04

1. Yes — (C); No — (A), (B), (D)
2. (A)
3. (B), (C), (E)   4. (D)

05

1. Baroque – (C); Classical – (A), (B);
   Romantic – (D), (E)
2. (A)   3. (A)   4. (B)

06

1. Novels — (C), (E); Other works — (A), (B), (D)
2. (D)   3. (D)   4. (D)

Skill E

01

1. (B)   2. (D)   3. (D)   4. (B)

02

1. (D)   2. (A)   3. (A)   4. (D)

03

1. (B)   2. (D)   3. (C)   4. (D)

04

1. (A)   2. (C)   3. (D)   4. (A)

05

1. (A)   2. (D)   3. (C)   4. (B)

06

1. (B)   2. (A)   3. (B)   4. (D)

Skill F

01

1. (D), (B), (C), (A)   2. (B)
3. (B), (C)   4. (B)

02

1. (B), (D), (A), (C)   2. (C), (D)
3. (A)   4. (B)

03

1. (B), (D), (A), (C)   2. (C)
3. (B), (E)   4. (C)

04

1. (B), (D), (C), (A)   2. (C)
3. (A)   4. (A)

05

1. (B), (A), (D), (C)   2. (B)
3. (A), (D), (G)   4. (C)

06

1. (B), (C), (A)   2. (A)
3. (D)   4. (D)

Review A-F

Vocabulary Review

1. (B)	2. (B)	3. (A)
4. (C)	5. (A)	6. (D)
7. (B)	8. (B)	9. (A)
10. (D)	11. (B)	12. (A)
13. (D)	14. (A)	15. (D)
16. (D)	17. (B)	18. (A)
19. (B)	20. (A)	21. (A)
22. (D)	23. (C)	24. (C)
25. (C)	26. (B)	27. (D)
28. (A)	29. (C)	30. (C)
31. toxicity	32. metabolism	33. lethal
34. indigestion	35. malfunction	36. hazard
37. revolting	38. wise up	39. procreate
40. species	41. down	42. overboard
43. on	44. out	45. up
46. (C)	47. (E)	48. (A)
49. (B)	50. (D)	

Skill Review

01

1. (B), (C)   2. (D)   3. (A)
4. Mineral — (C); Non-mineral — (A), (B), (D)
5. (A)   6. (D), (C), (A), (B)

02

1. (B)   2. (B), (C)   3. (B)
4. Yes — (B), (C), (D); No — (A)
5. (A)   6. (A), (C), (B)

03

1. (C), (D)   2. (B)   3. (B)
4. Push — (C); Recovery — (B); Pull — (A)
5. (C)   6. (B), (C), (D), (A)

04

1. (A), (E)   2. (C)   3. (A)
4. 12th Century — (A), (B); 13th Century — (C), (D)
5. (A)   6. (C), (D), (A), (B), (E)

Chapter 3

Focus A

Guided Practice

01

Woman	Man
situation: wants summer job	suggestion: look for internship at internship fair benefits: can submit resumé to lots of different companies ask questions to reps from companies

Summary

Suggested answer:

The woman and the man talk about summer jobs. The man suggests that the woman look for an internship at the internship fair. One benefit of attending the fair is that the woman can submit her resumé to lots of different companies. Another benefit is that she can ask questions to reps from different companies. The woman says that she will go to the fair with the man.

02

Woman	Man
wants to: get information about the online tutoring service	how: sign up online can use: 24 hours a day submit papers: to writing lab receive feedback: in 24 hours submit: 2 days early security: paper won't be stolen

Summary

Suggested answer:

The woman and the man talk about the college's online tutoring service. One thing the man mentions is the writing lab. For this service, students can submit papers and receive feedback in 24 hours. Students should submit their papers 2 days early in order to have time to get the paper back and make revisions. The woman plans to sign up for the service right away.

Self Practice

01

Man wants to:	Woman steps:
reserve a book	1) look up book on computer 2) click "request next available copy" button 3) type in student ID number and PIN 4) leave "pick up" box checked 5) click "request" button

Summary

Suggested answer:

The woman and the man talk about how to reserve a book at the library. The first thing that the man should do is look up the book on the computer. Next, he should request the next available copy by clicking a special button. Then, he needs to type in his student ID number and PIN. The man should leave the "pick up" box checked in order to get the book as soon as possible. The last step is to click the "request" button.

02

Man	Woman
	problem: roommate irritates her
solution 1: talk to roommate ⮕	bad idea — old friend, so hard to talk to
solution 2: talk to resident advisor ⮕	good idea — resident advisor is "cool"

Summary

Suggested answer:

The woman's problem is that her roommate bothers her. The man suggests two things to the woman. First, he says she should talk to her roommate. The woman thinks that this is not a good suggestion. Next, he suggests that the woman tell her resident advisor about the problem. The woman thinks that this is a good suggestion. She plans to talk to her resident advisor right away.

Focus B

Guided Practice

01
Topic: Effect of the moon on the atmosphere
- I. Newton
   - A. theory of gravity
   - B. theory of atmospheric tides
- II. air tides
   - A. measured since 1918 in N. hemisphere
   - B. more clouds, rain, storms
   - C. hurricanes? — not sure
- III. full moon
   - A. temp of lower atmosphere higher (few hundredths degree)
   - B. moon radiates thermal energy
   - C. moon reflects light (10%)

Summary

This lecture is about the effect of the moon on the atmosphere. This idea was first suggested by Newton, who also came up with the general theory of gravity. The professor talks about air tides. These have been measured since 1918. They seem to cause more clouds, rain, and storms. They might be related to hurricanes, but scientist are not sure yet. The professor also talks about the effect that the full moon has on the atmosphere. He says a full moon causes the temperature of the atmosphere to rise. This is because the moon radiates thermal heat and reflects light toward the Earth.

02
The Five Criteria for Minerals
1. solid
   - can't be gas or liquid
2. occur naturally
   - can't be man-made
3. inorganic
   - can't be organic
4. fixed composition
   - the same found anywhere at any time
5. element or compound
   - can't be mixture of chemical compound and element

Ex: ice!

Summary

In this lecture, the professor gives five criteria for minerals. The first criterion is that it must be a solid. The second criterion is that it must occur naturally. The third criterion is that it must be inorganic. The fourth criterion is that it must have a fixed composition. The fifth criterion is that it must be an element or a compound. The example of a mineral discussed in class is ice!

Self Practice

01
Poisonous Plants
- I. Which plants are edible?
   - A. trial and error
   - B. people in 1800s poisoned by plants
   - C. not as big a problem today
   - but houseplants could poison children
- II. Categories of toxicity
   - A. extremely
   - B. moderately
   - C. minimally
   - categories misleading, poisoning can be fatal or just indigestion
- III. Alkaloids
   - A. bitter, nitrogen compounds
   - B. hemlock
   - C. affects nervous system → death
- IV. Plants with minerals
   - A. build up lead or copper
   - B. affects mind → death
- V. Oxalates
   - A. crystals in plants
   - B. irritate mouth

Summary

In this lecture, the professor talks about poisonous plants. She says that lots of people were poisoned by plants even into the 1800s, but it is not such a big problem today. The professor gives three categories of toxicity for plants, but she also says that the categories can be misleading. Three particular types of poisonous plants mentioned in the lecture are alkaloids, plants with minerals, and oxalates. The professor explains something about the poison in each type of plant and how the poison affects people.

02

Plutarch's *Lives*

   I. the man
      A. lived 46 to 120 A.D.
      B. from Greece
   II. *Lives*
      A. paired biography of famous Greeks and Romans
      B. essay + observation about human nature
      C. history, biography, philosophy
      D. written from old manuscripts, Plutarch didn't really trust sources
   III. popularity
      A. Romans loved it, copied the manuscript many times
      B. Beethoven found wisdom in the book
      C. Ralph Waldo Emerson liked it
   IV. why not popular in 20th century?
      A. no new editions
      B. classic works pushed aside for diversity
      C. not easy to read

Summary

This lecture is about Plutarch's *Lives*. The professor begins by talking about when and where Plutarch lived. Next, he explains that this book presents paired biographies of famous Greeks and Romans. Each essay in the book is followed by Plutarch's observations about human nature. In order to write the book, Plutarch relied on old manuscripts, but he didn't really trust them. Throughout history, people have loved the book, including people like Beethoven and Emerson. However, in the 20th century, the book lost popularity because nobody wrote a new edition of the book, students wanted more diversity in books, and *Lives* is hard to read.

Skill B

Q3 – practice 1

Step 1

Suggested keywords:
construction, Science Center, Clemens Hall, relocated, location

Sample restatement:
Construction on the new Science Center will begin soon. Classes in Clemens Hall will be relocated. Professors will find out where the new class locations will be, and they should advise their students of the change.

Step 2

Suggested keywords:
Science Center, distracting, announcement, relocate, memo

Sample restatement:
The woman complains that the noise from the construction of the new Science Center will be distracting. The man tells her about an announcement saying the classes in their building will be relocated. She asks him where the classes will be relocated to, and he tells her that they will be informed through a memo.

Step 3
— Original Opinion: The woman thinks the university should wait until summer to begin construction on the new Science Center.
— Reason: The noise will be distracting to classes in Clemens Hall.
— Why she changes her mind: The man informs her that the classes in Clemens Hall will be relocated.

Q3 – practice 2

Step 1

Suggested keywords:
anti-spam filter, spam, inbox, potential spam, bulk folder

Sample restatement:
The university will install an anti-spam filter that will reject spam and send potential spam to bulk folders instead of inboxes, where non-spam emails will be sent.

Step 2

Suggested keywords:
Anti-spam filter, block important mail, mistakes, bulk folder, obviously spam

Sample restatement:
The man is concerned about the new anti-spam filter. He is worried that it will occasionally make mistakes and block important mail. The woman assures him that only mail that is obviously spam will be blocked. If there is any doubt, it will be sent to the man's bulk folder.

Step 3
— Woman's opinion: The anti-spam filter is great.
— Reason: She hates spam because it wastes her time.
— Man's concern: Important email will be blocked. The man changes his mind.
— Reason: The anti-spam filter doesn't block mail unless it is obviously spam. Suspicious mail gets directed to a bulk folder.

Q3 – practice 3

Step 1

Suggested keywords:
guest speaker, Internet business, telecommerce, all students welcome, question-and-answer period

Sample restatement:
A successful young Internet businessperson will speak from 7 p.m. to 8 p.m. Thursday night in Selwidge Hall. All students are welcome. There will be a question-and-answer period after the speech.

Step 2

Suggested keywords:
15 extra credit points, review of speech, Thursday night from 7 to 8, Selwidge hall, open to all students

Sample restatement:
The man asks the woman about their extra credit assignment. She tells him he can write a review of James's speech for 15 extra credit points. The speech is Thursday night from seven to eight in Selwidge Hall. The man is enthusiastic about learning from the guest speaker.

Step 3

- The man wants information on: the extra credit assignment.
- The woman tells him he can: write a review of the speech.
- The man's opinion of the assignment is that: it is a great opportunity.
- Reason 1: The speaker will have lots of useful advice.
- Reason 2: It's completely free.
- The man will: prepare some questions in advance.

Q4 – practice 1

Step 1

Suggested keywords:
the Nash Equilibrium, maintain static strategies, rational conception, no collusion, benefits competing parties

Sample restatement:
The Nash Equilibrium describes a competitive situation in which all competitors benefit from not changing their strategies. Also, each competitor decides to maintain his or her strategy independently of the others.

Step 2

Suggested keywords:
real world, agree, side of the road, risk of collision, rush hour traffic

Sample restatement:
The professor illustrates the Nash Equilibrium by giving the example of which side of the road cars drive on. The drivers only want to get home as quickly as possible. They don't communicate with one another to decide which side to drive on; nevertheless, everyone drives on the same side.

Step 3

- Nash Equilibrium: Each competitor cannot improve his or her odds by changing strategies.
- Professor's example: People wanting to get home quickly all drive on one side of the road.
- How they relate: Each driver is a competitor. They will not improve their chances of arriving more quickly by driving on the other side of the road and risking collision.

Q4 – practice 2

Step 1

Suggested keywords:
Black Plague, two thirds, germ theory, parasitic fleas, public sanitation

Sample restatement:
The passage is about the Black Plague, a disease that killed two-thirds of the population of Europe in the 1300s. Germ theory later discovered that it was caused by a bacterium spread to humans by parasitic fleas. Public sanitation and new medicine helped destroy the disease.

Step 2

Suggested keywords:
Yersinia pestis, Iceland, incubation period, pulmonary anthrax, Ebola virus

Sample restatement:
The professor talks about new theories that the Black Plague was not caused by *Yersinia pestis*. Some researchers now think it was pulmonary anthrax or the Ebola virus. Iceland was affected by the first plague, even though there were no rats. The incubation period of the disease also makes some people think this disease was NOT spread by fleas on rats.

Step 3

- Common understanding: The Black Plague was a bubonic plague caused by the bacterium *Yersinia pestis*, which was spread by fleas on rats.
- New evidence 1: There were no rats in Iceland, yet it was affected by the Black Plague.
- New evidence 2: The Black Plague had a longer incubation period and spread more quickly than *Yersinia pestis*.
- New theories: 1: Pulmonary anthrax
             2: Ebola virus

Q4 – practice 3

Step 1

Suggested keywords:
450 A.D., Shona-speaking herders, Zimbabwe plateau, 1100-1450, great civilization

Sample restatement:
The passage discusses the Great Zimbabwe civilization. It was founded by Shona-speakers in 450 and reached its peak between 1100 and 1450, when it had a king and a monumental wall.

Step 2

Suggested keywords:

British Imperialism, foreigners from the north, archaeologists, destroyed and plundered, racist myth

Sample restatement:

British officials felt threatened by the idea of a civilization founded by Black Africans. It undermined their justifications for imperialism. They hired archaeologists who destroyed and plundered the ruins and then concluded that foreigners from the north had founded the civilization. After another archaeologist contradicted the official theory, the site was closed off. Eventually, people recognized the reality behind the racist myth.

Step 3

— First British investigation: archaeologists destroyed and plundered site

— Conclusion and result: foreigners from the north built the ruins

— Further investigation: archaeologists studied site again in 1905

— Conclusion and result: contradicted earlier findings, archaeologists banned from site

— Accepted idea today: ruins built by local Shona-speakers

Skill C

Q5 – practice 1

Step 1

Suggested answers:

Problem:	The woman needs to get some books but does not have her university library card.
Solution 1:	Use the public library
Solution 2:	Try to borrow someone else's card

Step 2

Problem:	She needs to get some books but does not have her university library card.
Best solution:	Use the public library
Reason 1:	This is the quickest solution.
Reason 2:	The other solution will impose on someone.

Problem:	She needs to get some books but does not have her university library card.
Best solution:	Try to borrow someone else's card
Reason 1:	She will probably find someone to help her.
Reason 2:	The public library may not have adequate resources.

Q5 – practice 2

Step 1

Suggested answers:

Problem:	The woman's roommate is untidy, and she eats her food.
Solution 1:	Talk to her about it.
Solution 2:	Say nothing and wait until the school year is over. Then, she won't have to live with her anymore.

Step 2

Problem:	The woman's roommate is untidy, and she eats her food.
Best solution:	Talk to the roommate and ask her to be more considerate.
Reason 1:	She will be happier if they resolve the problem.
Reason 2:	The woman will save money on food.

Problem:	The woman's roommate is untidy, and she eats her food.
Best solution:	Tolerate the roommate's behavior for two more months.
Reason 1:	Don't risk having her roommate move out.
Reason 2:	Keep her roommate as a friend.

Q5 – practice 3

Step 1

Problem:	The man doesn't want to dissect a pig in biology class.
Solution 1:	Refuse to take part
Solution 2:	Dissect the pig

Step 2

Problem:	The man doesn't want to dissect a pig in biology class.

Best Solution: Refuse to take part
Reason 1: Won't have to do something that he is morally opposed to
Reason 2: May bring about change in the school's practice

Problem: The man doesn't want to dissect a pig in biology class.
Best Solution: Dissect the pig
Reason 1: Stay on the teacher's good side
Reason 2: Won't risk getting a bad grade

Q6 – practice 1

Step 1

Falconry is: a way to hunt prey using a trained falcon
Falconers must:
    a) tame the falcon
    b) train the falcon not to kill the prey
Today falconry is: a sport
Historically, falconry was: a means of survival
Nomadic people in the desert: used falconry to add variety to their diets
Falconry dates back to: China in 2000 B.C.

Q6 – practice 2

Step 1

An aura is a symptom or set of symptoms that precede a migraine.
example: perception of flashing lights
Common characteristics of migraines:
    — bad headache
    — vomiting
    — bothered by noise
    — bothered by light
Process of migraine: Arteries bringing blood to the brain constrict → Less oxygen getting to the brain → Arteries in brain expand causing pain
Possible way to prevent migraines from occurring: Identify the triggers that cause the arteries to constrict and avoid them.

Q6 – practice 3

Step 1

Standard view of evolution: Species arise gradually over time due to natural selection.
Example: Horses used to be the size of small cats.
Counter-evidence: Source: Fossil record
Trend: Species remain unchanged for long periods of time.
    New species arise quickly.
New theory: Punctuated Equilibrium
    — Large populations typically dilute advantageous mutations.
    — Speciation occurs in peripheral subpopulations because they are smaller and are located in novel ecosystems.
    — After the change, the new species might compete with and exterminate the old species.
The new theory is not in conflict with the standard view.

Vocabulary Review

Review 1

1. (C)	2. (A)	3. (D)
4. (D)	5. (B)	6. (A)
7. (B)	8. (D)	9. (B)
10. (A)	11. (D)	12. (A)
13. (B)	14. (D)	15. (D)
16. gadget	17. dyslexia	18. diverting
19. perseverance	20. better off	21. (C)
22. (A)	23. (E)	24. (D)
25. (B)		

Review 2

1. (B)	2. (D)	3. (A)
4. (C)	5. (A)	6. (D)
7. (C)	8. (A)	9. (A)
10. (D)	11. (B)	12. (C)
13. (B)	14. (A)	15. (D)
16. asserts	17. imperceptible	18. dilute
19. peripheral	20. exterminate	21. pandemic
22. thrive	23. enlist	
24. complement	25. surrender	

Chapter 2

Skill A

Q1 — practice 1

Step 1

Transitions: by now, every week, last year, later, of course, as it turned out

Sentence Order: C, F, D, B, A, E

Step 2

Suggested answers:

1. They met on an Internet site for students studying languages.
2. They practice Chinese and English together.
3. It helped him appreciate Chinese culture and broadened his view of the world.

Step 3

Sample response:

Last year, I met a fellow language student on an Internet study forum when I was trying to practice for a Chinese class. As it turned out, he was a Chinese student trying to practice English. Later, we developed a symbiotic relationship by helping each other practice our respective languages. Every week, we chat for 30 minutes in English and 30 minutes in Chinese. By now, we have become good friends, and we have both learned a lot. Of course, among the things I've learned is the fact that Chinese culture is fascinating, and this experience has really broadened my view of the world.

Q1 — practice 2

Step 1

Transitions: after, however, for example, instead, before that, in fact

Sentence Order: C, F, A, D, G, B, E

Step 2

Suggested answers:

1. The speaker was studying at university when the Internet became commonly used.
2. The Internet allowed the speaker to do research from her dorm room.
3. The Internet allowed the speaker to communicate with her parents for free.

Step 3

Sample response:

One technological innovation I witnessed during my university days was the spread of the Internet. Before that, I spent hours in the library doing research. After the Internet came into widespread use, however, I didn't have to go to the library at all. I could do all of my research from a computer in my dorm room, which saved a lot of time. In fact, the Internet saved me a great deal of money, too! For example, I no longer had to make expensive, obligatory phone calls to my parents. Instead, I could send them updates via email for free.

Q1 — practice 3

Step 2

Sample response:

My life was changed by an unexpected blizzard. One day when I left my house to go to the airport, the weather was cool but clear. As I was driving to the airport, though, it started snowing. Within minutes, there was a raging blizzard. I knew my flight to Jamaica was going to be canceled, so I was terribly disappointed. Then, I noticed a stranded motorist, so I pulled over to help. I offered the man a lift so he could call a tow truck. Three years later, I married that man. If it weren't for that blizzard, we wouldn't have met.

Q1 — practice 4

Step 2

Sample response:

The Optimists' Club is an organization that has been very important in my life. They organize fun and enriching activities for kids in the city. For example, I had a great experience and forged lasting friendships while participating in their youth basketball league. In addition, they provide counselors who help troubled youths with problems. One time, I was on edge about my high school course work, and I did not have anyone to turn to for guidance. The Optimists' Club counselor provided me with some very useful advice I needed in order to select the appropriate classes to enroll in.

Q2 – practice 1

Step 1

Transitions: thus, conversely, for instance, first, second, indeed

Sentence Order: D, E, F, C, G, B, A

Step 2

Suggested answers:

1. The speaker's view is that childhood is the most important time of a person's life.
2. One reason is that childhood is when basic personality develops.
3. Another reason is that experiences in childhood affect the rest of a person's life.

Step 3

Sample response:

I believe that childhood is a critical period in a person's life. First, it is the time in which personality is developed. Second, a person's experiences in childhood affect the remainder of his or her life. For instance, a major trauma experienced at the age of six has a much more devastating effect than one experienced at age thirty. Indeed, negative or traumatic experiences in childhood can lead to psychological problems in adulthood, such as depression and antisocial behavior. Conversely, positive, nurturing experiences in childhood foster mental health and well-being in adulthood. Thus, it is crucial to have positive influences in childhood.

Q2 – practice 2

Step 1

Transitions: on the other hand, that's why, however, unfortunately

Sentence Order: D, F, B, A, E, G, C

Step 2

Suggested answers:

1. The speaker thinks parents can teach their kids academic skills, like reading, writing, and math.
2. The speaker thinks that parents cannot adequately teach their children social skills.
3. The speaker thinks children should be educated in a social setting, i.e. in schools.

Step 3

Sample response:

Most parents are capable of teaching their children to read, write, add, and subtract, as well as many of the other basic skills children are taught at school. However, there are some skills that cannot be taught sufficiently at home. The skills I am referring to are social skills. These, I believe, are the most important skills learned at school. That's why I am of the opinion that children should learn in a social environment. Unfortunately, the home cannot provide an adequate social milieu for children to learn to live with a diverse group of people. Public schools, on the other hand, can and do provide this setting.

Q2 – practice 3

Step 2

Sample response:

I believe zoos serve a multitude of useful purposes. For one thing, zoos educate visitors. If there were no zoos, children would grow up never witnessing species not indigenous to their area. With zoos, in contrast, children can learn about all kinds of different animal species and observe them up close. That's more captivating and educational than looking at pictures or reading texts. For that matter, zoos provide an entertainment venue for people of all ages. Additionally, they provide a safe home for animals whose survival is threatened in the wild. Animals that are endangered can be kept safe and well fed, as well as be encouraged to breed.

Q2 – practice 4

Step 2

Sample response:

In some countries, all citizens are required to vote, while in others, individuals are free to decide whether to vote or not. I prefer the system in which voting is optional. First, in this system, public interest is more important because it affects voter turnout. Therefore, governments and candidates for office must work harder to sway the opinions of voters. Second, people should be free to protest an election by refraining from taking part. Indeed, the very idea of forcing constituents to vote runs counter to the principles upon which free society is based.

Skill B

Q3 – practice 1

Step 1

Suggested answers:

The problem: woman can't use scholarship to study abroad

Man's opinion of policy: arbitrary and unfair

- Reason 1: woman earned her scholarship (not athletic or need-based)
- Reason 2: woman qualified for need-based, but chose academic scholarship instead

Step 3

Sample response:

The man's opinion is that the school's policy of only allowing students with need-based scholarships to use that money toward the Study Abroad Program is unfair. To begin, he contends that the woman earned her scholarship through academic merit rather than athletic skill or financial need. Secondly, the woman did qualify for a need-based scholarship but opted for the academic one, showing that she has the same financial need as students with need-based scholarships. For these two reasons, he feels the woman should be allowed to use her grant money to pay for tuition abroad.

Q3 – practice 2

Step 1

Suggested answers:

Woman's opinion:

- lottery system is unfair

Why:

- gives preferential treatment but should be based on need
- will cost her a lot of money for rent and transportation
- she won't be able to study late at the library

What university should have done:

- done construction in summer or made arrangements for students

Step 3

Sample response:

The woman is angry about the announced plan for a housing lottery for graduate students. First, she thinks it is unfair because students of certain majors are being given priority. Instead, she believes the housing should be assigned based on need. Second, she is upset because living off campus will be expensive and inconvenient. For example, she will pay more in rent and transportation and will not be able to study late on campus. In the end, she complains that they should have done the renovations during the summer or otherwise accommodated the needs of all students.

Q4 – practice 1

Step 1

Suggested answers:

Morphology of giant squid:

- length: 10-15 meters
- appendages: 8 arms, 2 tentacles
- suckers: have sharp, claw-like components

Theories on feeding behavior:

- passive reason: large body requires too much energy to move quickly
- active reasons: i) tentacles have claw-like parts suggesting capture of prey
  ii) smaller squid species are active feeders

Step 3

Sample response:

The reading passage describes the morphological differences between marine animals that are active feeders and passive feeders. The lecturer examines the morphology of the giant squid and different theories about its feeding habits. First, the giant squid is a very large creature. Second, it has two tentacles that include sharp, claw-like components. Some scientists have postulated that the enormous size of the giant squid suggests it must be a passive feeder. Other scientists, in contrast, point to its tentacles and the model of smaller squid species as evidence suggesting that the giant squid is an active feeder.

Q4 – practice 2

Step 1

Suggested answers:

Early 20th Century: uproar in music world
— reaction to new style of music
— music fans criticized composers
— composers called fans uncouth

Atonal music
— used chromatic scale
— contained 12 notes

Step 3

Sample response:

The professor begins by describing the negative response many early-20th-century audiences had to the advent of atonal musical forms. Listeners found the new style too unstructured in comparison to the traditional forms they were used to. As the reading passage describes, traditional European music was based on principles of melody. This music utilized the major and minor scales to produce the desired emotions. As the professor points out, atonal compositions utilized the chromatic scale rather than the major or minor scales. The chromatic scale includes 12 notes, all the notes a person can play on the piano.

Skill C

Q5 – practice 1

Step 1

Suggested answers:

Problem:	The man needs to use the gym, but won't have access until his student loan arrives.
Solution 1:	use the gym as a guest of a friend
Advantages:	can continue training
Disadvantages:	costs money each time; is inconvenient
Solution 2:	talk to coach and arrange a temporary card
Advantages:	save money and don't need a host
Disadvantages:	the coach is away

Step 2

Suggested answers:

1. The man cannot access the gym to work out because his student loan has not come through yet.
2. He should find a friend with access to the gym to act as a host.
3. His friend can give him access to the gym, and they can work out together.

Step 3

Sample response:

The man's problem is that he cannot access the gym to work out because his student loans have not come through to pay his tuition. The woman suggests two solutions to his problem. First, he could find a student with access to accompany him to the gym. Second, he could talk to his coach and try to get a temporary ID. In my opinion, the first choice is preferable. To begin, his coach is away, so the man would have to wait. In addition, having a friend to work out with could help him maintain his exercise regime.

Q5 – practice 2

Step 1

Suggested answers:

Problem:	The man wants to drop a class, but he has missed the deadline.
Solution 1:	drop the class
Advantages:	can concentrate on other subjects
Disadvantages:	dropping is same as failing
Solution 2:	don't drop the class
Advantages:	with hard study, could earn an OK grade
Disadvantages:	will be difficult and distract from other classes

Step 2

Suggested answers:

1. The man is behind in a class and wants to drop it, but dropping now would be the same as failing the class.
2. He should drop the class.
3. It would be better to concentrate on getting strong grades in the courses of his major.

Step 3

Sample response:

The man's problem is that he wants to drop the professor's class because he is too far behind to earn a high grade. In addition, the deadline for dropping classes without penalty has passed. The professor tries to convince him to remain in the class and work hard to increase his grade. In my opinion, he would be better off dropping the class. Even though he will be penalized for dropping the class the same as if he had failed it, he will benefit by being able to concentrate his efforts on the courses of his major.

Q6 – practice 1

Step 1

Suggested answers:

Main topic of lecture: changing music of the 20th century

— Origins of jazz and blues: in New Orleans; African Americans mixed African rhythms with European melodies

— Initial reactions: not accepted by most Americans; too wild, unstructured

— When became accepted: after white musicians used it in rock 'n' roll

— New forms today: still meet resistance; ex. hip-hop

Step 2

Suggested answers:

1. The advent of jazz had the most influence on modern popular music.
2. It brought new rhythms and scales to popular music.
3. It became accepted when white musicians used these forms in rock 'n' roll music.

Step 3

Sample response:

According to the lecture, the advent of jazz music had a significant influence on the trajectory of popular music over the past 100 years. To begin, it was developed by African Americans combining African rhythms with European melodies. In addition, jazz influenced the development of blues, which added an extra note to the major scale, thus creating the blues scale. At first, these musical forms were met with resistance. Later, however, they became widely accepted after being incorporated into rock 'n' roll music by white musicians such as Elvis Presley. Furthermore, they have influenced the form of more recent popular music styles, such as hip-hop.

Q6 – practice 2

Step 1

Suggested answers:

Main topic of lecture: the changing definition of the family

— Traditional conception of family: included man, woman, and 2.5 children, with man working outside the house and woman inside

— Those outside this conception: were marginalized and considered sick or unstable in some way

— Today's families: only 11-15 percent conform to traditional definition

— Universal aspects of family: intersection between making a society and making new people; it provides ideas of normal and natural

Step 2

Suggested answers:

1. The traditional conception of the family includes a working father, a domestic mother, and two or three children all living together in one home.
2. In the past, families that differed from this ideal were marginalized and considered flawed or unhealthy.
3. In all societies, the family helps define what is normal and natural.

Step 3

Sample response:

In this lecture, the professor examines the idea of family. The traditional ideal of the family includes a working father, a domestic mother, and two or three children all living together in one home. Furthermore, families that differed from this ideal were marginalized and considered flawed or unhealthy in the past. These days, however, only a minority of families conform to this ideal. In point of fact, the professor relates that the ideal defined a generation or two ago is only one step on an ever-evolving sequence of ideals. Finally, the professor states that in all societies, the family helps define what is normal and natural.

Vocabulary Review

Review 1

1. (B)	2. (D)	3. (A)
4. (A)	5. (B)	6. (D)
7. (A)	8. (B)	9. (A)
10. (D)	11. (B)	12. (A)
13. (D)	14. (A)	15. (C)
16. (C)	17. (B)	18. (A)
19. (D)	20. (B)	21. (D)
22. (D)	23. (B)	24. (A)
25. (C)	26. (A)	27. (B)
28. (D)	29. (C)	30. (A)
31. fellow	32. symbiotic	33. fostered
34. unparalleled	35. forged	36. diverse
37. indigenous	38. invaluable	39. swayed
40. milieu	41. innovation	42. endangered
43. diverse	44. afford	45. obligatory
46. (O)	47. (S)	48. (O)
49. (S)	50. (O)	

Review 2

1. (C)	2. (A)	3. (D)
4. (B)	5. (A)	6. (C)
7. (B)	8. (B)	9. (A)
10. (A)	11. (B)	12. (C)
13. (D)	14. (D)	15. (A)
16. (B)	17. (A)	18. (D)
19. (C)	20. (D)	21. (A)
22. (B)	23. (D)	24. (A)
25. (A)	26. (B)	27. (B)
28. (D)	29. (B)	30. (D)
31. indigenous	32. elusive	33. myriad
34. in vain	35. specimens	36. lambaste
37. glean	38. convey	39. Optimists
40. mainstream	41. over	42. in
43. by	44. in	45. off
46. (D)	47. (B)	48. (E)
49. (A)	50. (C)	

Chapter 3

Focus A

Step 1   Sentence stress on content words

Suggested answers:
1. <u>Before</u> that, I spent <u>hours</u> in the <u>library</u> doing <u>research</u>.
2. My <u>life</u> was <u>changed</u> by an <u>unexpected</u> <u>blizzard</u>.
3. In addition, they provide <u>counselors</u> who help <u>troubled</u> <u>youths</u> with <u>problems</u>.
4. I believe that <u>childhood</u> is an <u>integral period</u> in a <u>person's life</u>.
5. <u>Public schools</u>, on the other hand, <u>can</u> and <u>do</u> <u>provide</u> this <u>setting</u>.
6. That's more <u>captivating</u> and <u>educational</u> than looking at <u>pictures</u> or <u>reading texts</u>.
7. I prefer the <u>system</u> in which <u>voting</u> is <u>optional</u>.
8. <u>Instead</u>, she believes the <u>housing</u> should be assigned <u>based on need</u>.

Suggested clear words in **bold:**
I believe zoos serve a **multitude** of **useful purposes**. For one thing, zoos **educate** visitors. If there were no zoos, children would grow up **never witnessing** species **not indigenous** to their area. With zoos, in contrast, **children** can **learn** about **all kinds** of **different** animal species and **observe** them up close. That's more **captivating** and **educational** than looking at **pictures** or **reading texts**. For that matter, zoos provide an **entertainment** venue for people of **all ages**. Additionally, they provide a **safe home** for animals whose survival is **threatened in the wild**. Animals that are endangered can be **protected, well-fed**, and **encouraged** to breed.

Step 2   Sentence stress on function words

1. (S)	2. (S)	3. (R)
4. (R)	5. (S)	6. (S), (S)
7. (R)	8. (S)	

1. That **isn't his** dog, <u>it's</u> **her** dog.
2. Most students **didn't** pass <u>the</u> exam, but John **did**.
3. She <u>likes</u> jazz music, <u>and</u> he likes blues music. I like jazz **and** blues music.
4. Kim **hasn't** paid <u>her</u> tuition fees, but Rick **has**.

5. The major scale **doesn't** have 12 notes, <u>but</u> the chromatic scale **does**.
6. Off-campus housing **isn't** just expensive; <u>it's</u> expensive **and** inconvenient.
7. **He** <u>didn't</u> get the need-based scholarship. **She** did.
8. You <u>can</u> take English 201 **or** English 205. You can't take both.

Focus B

Step 1   Changing pitch for emphasis

1. <u>Children</u> should attend school.
   a. Adults should work.
2. This experience helped tremendously with <u>my</u> studies.
   b. Unfortunately, it didn't help with her studies.
3. Subsequent developments in <u>pop</u> music were generally met with the same disapproval.
   b. Developments in classical music, on the other hand, were embraced in a short time.
4. Do you play on the varsity <u>basketball</u> team?
   a. No, I play on the hockey team.

1. I don't <u>abhor</u> jazz music. I don't really enjoy it that much, though.
2. <u>Her</u> behavior is antisocial. He is actually a nice guy.
3. The squid doesn't have <u>eight</u> appendages. It has ten.
4. <u>Jellyfish</u> drift with ocean currents. Squid use their arms to swim.
5. There is a glitch with her <u>computer</u>. Her phone is working fine.
6. The campus <u>renovations</u> will begin in September. The campus celebrations begin in October.

Step 2   Commas and series with *and* or *or*

1. Many of the most popular bands on the charts today are born from influences of rock, /(↗) hip-hop, /(↗) reggae, /(↗) ska, /(↗) and techno. (↘)
2. They were considered troubled, /(↗) pathological, /(↗) or dysfunctional. (↘)

3. I doubt it'll cover the cost of renting a place in this city, /(↗) especially near the campus. (↘)
4. Most giant squid are smaller, /(↗) growing to approximately ten meters. (↘)
5. European concert-goers were plugging their ears, /(↗) walking out on performances, /(↗) and muttering to themselves.(↘)
6. The chromatic scale simply means all the notes you can play on a piano, /(↗) without any notes left out.(↘)

Focus C

Step 1   Timing

1. The traditional ideal of the family includes a working father, / a domestic mother, / and two or three children all living happily in one home.
2. As it turned out, / he was a Chinese student trying to practice English.
3. After the Internet came into widespread use, / however, / I didn't have to go to the library at all.

4. Within minutes, / there was a raging blizzard.
5. Some alarmists contend that this is a fundamental societal problem, / a breakdown in values that will produce immeasurable negative effects.
6. These, / I believe, / are the most important skills learned at school.

1. The man's opinion is that the school's policy / of only allowing students with need-based scholarships to use that money toward the Study Abroad Program / is unfair.
2. To begin, / he contends that the woman earned her scholarship through academic merit / rather than athletic skill or financial need.
3. Secondly, / the woman did qualify for a need-based scholarship / but opted for the academic one, / showing that she has the same financial need as students with need-based scholarships.
4. For these two reasons, / he feels the woman should be allowed to use her grant money to pay for tuition abroad.

Writing Chapter 1

Skill A

Practice 1

01

Step 1

Correlation Studies: determine RELATIONSHIP BETWEEN two variables
- researcher doesn't MANIPULATE variables
- researchers MEASURE RATE at which variables change naturally

Relationship types:
- Y increases when X increases: POSITIVE CORRELATION
- Y decreases when X increases: NEGATIVE CORRELATION
- sometimes, a CAUSAL RELATIONSHIP can be inferred

Step 2

Main point: Correlation does NOT IMPLY causation
- cannot be certain because investigators don't MANIPULATE VARIABLES
- also, a THIRD VARIABLE may be affecting the correlation
  ex. Eating ice cream and drowning have a POSITIVE CORRELATION
- but a third variable is HOT WEATHER
- Correlations can SUGGEST causal relationships, but more RESEARCH is needed to prove it
  ex. A positive correlation between smoking and CANCER led to further research that proved a CAUSAL RELATIONSHIP

Step 3

Reading:
- Main Idea: Correlation studies can determine a connection between two variables.
- Supporting Idea: If the rate of one event increases when the rate of another event increases, they have a positive correlation.
- Supporting Idea: If the rate of one event decreases when the rate of another event increases, they have a negative correlation.

Lecture:
- Main Idea: Correlations found from correlation studies do not necessarily mean a causal relationship exists.
- Supporting Idea: Other, "third" variables may be affecting the relationship between the two variables in a correlation study.
- Supporting Idea: Correlations found from correlation studies can suggest the need for further study to discover if a causal relationship truly exists.

Step 4

CORRELATION STUDIES are useful tools because they describe relationships between different PHENOMENA as they occur in the natural world. It is important, though, that researchers be careful not to make the common erroneous assumption that a CORRELATION IMPLIES CAUSATION.

Correlations indicate when two VARIABLES are related naturally. This implies that researchers do not MANIPULATE either variable; they simply OBSERVE events as they occur. For this reason, it is IMPOSSIBLE to determine if one variable causes the other to change.

Furthermore, there is always the possibility of a THIRD VARIABLE causing both to change. To demonstrate, the lecturer states that there is a positive correlation between ice cream consumption and DROWNING. A POSITIVE correlation means that as one variable increases, so does the other. So, in this example, as ice cream consumption increases, the rate of drowning INCREASES as well. It is a FALLACY, though, to interpret these findings as indicating that ice cream consumption causes drowning. In this case, there is a third variable that is affecting both — the WEATHER.

Sometimes, it is ACCEPTABLE to infer from a correlation study that one variable affects the other, such as in the example in the reading of increased study time being correlated to HIGHER GRADES. It is very important, nonetheless, that one is careful to consider which VARIABLE affects which, and that there is not a THIRD VARIABLE affecting changes in both variables.

Practice 2

02 History

Step 1

Issue:
- Historical REVISIONISM: A re-EXAMINATION of historical facts

Purpose: - Corrects historical IMBALANCES
- Includes new INFORMATION
Motivation: - Despite scientific METHODOLOGY, historiography is BIASED
- History is a NARRATIVE that favors the ELITE in society
Example / Argument:
- Did Columbus DISCOVER America?
- No. This is a EUROCENTRIC bias

Step 2

Key Issue: - Historical Revisionism has come to be used PEJORATIVELY
Why? - Many HACKS and crackpots pose as revisionist HISTORIANS
- They present badly RESEARCHED papers, books, and ARTICLES as fact
- Their writing NEGATES specific events in history
- They propagate a POLITICAL bias
This is dangerous. Why?
- Non- EXPERTS are INFLUENCED to support an inaccurate perspective
Example: - Denial of the HOLOCAUST
Solution: - Legitimate researchers must COMBAT this trend by producing GENUINE research using verifiable DATA

Step 3

Reading:

- Main Idea: Historical Revisionism attempts to re-examine the past.
- Supporting Idea: Revisionism combats historical bias that favors the powerful.
- Supporting Idea: This helps correct existing imbalances in historical narratives.

Lecture:

- Main Idea: Revisionism is now often regarded in a negative light.
- Supporting Idea: Non-experts often present badly researched work as fact.
- Supporting Idea: Such work often reveals a political or ideological bias.

Step 4

In the reading, historical revisionism is presented in a POSITIVE light. The writer explains that revisionism is an attempt to correct IMBALANCES in biased versions of the past that EXCLUDE certain groups. The writer gives the example of the INDIGENOUS Americans that are ignored when historical texts refer to Columbus as having "discovered" America. The writer believes that REVISIONISM is necessary because as societies change, so do the power structures that govern them. Revisionism allows historians to include NEW information and re-examine the way history is written, so that it is told not exclusively from the perspective of the elite, POWERFUL ruling groups in a society.

The speaker warns us that there is a particular kind of historical revisionism that is very dangerous and negative. This form of revisionism is often practiced by individuals with no real SCIENTIFIC training or expertise. These self-proclaimed revisionists make use of CONSIPIRACY theories and logical FALLACIES in their ill-researched writing on historical subjects. Such revision also often negates or DENIES that particular historical events, such as the HOLOCAUST, even took place. Their work influences non-experts negatively and gives legitimate historians a BAD name. Such revisionism must be COMBATED by authentic historians who use VERIFIABLE data and supportable documentation.

Practice 3

03 Astronomy
Step 1
Subject: How UNIVERSE was created.
Most DOMINANT theory: BIG BANG
Argument:
- Primeval ATOM exploded, flung MATTER in all DIRECTIONS
- All matter, LIGHT, and energy came from this
- HUBBLE found evidence to show universe is still EXPANDING
- "Cosmic background RADIATION" discovered — 1964

Step 2

Topic: 1. THEORETICAL holes in the Big Bang theory

2. ALTERNATIVE theories for how the universe originated

Argument:

- Big Bang evidence is too general and VAGUE
- Evidence also supports other MODELS
- Big Bang never proved beyond REASONABLE doubt
- Theory, therefore, remains HYPOTHESIS

EKPYROTIC scenario argues two parallel MEMBRANES of matter COLLIDED

- Supported by same EMPIRICAL data as Big Bang

Conclusion:

- Await new INFORMATION via technological advances

Step 3

Reading:

- Main Idea: The Big Bang theory states that the Universe was created when an atom exploded.
- Supporting Idea: Evidence of expanding universe supports this.
- Supporting Idea: Discovery of cosmic radiation supports this.

Lecture:

- Main Idea: There are theoretical holes in the Big Bang theory.
- Supporting Idea: The evidence is vague and also supports other theories.
- Supporting Idea: The Big Bang theory has never been proven.

Step 4

The reading explains that there is a POPULAR and dominant theory about how the UNIVERSE came into existence. It is called the Big BANG theory. This theory argues that the explosion of a primeval ATOM, BILLIONS of years ago, caused all light, matter, and ENERGY to form. The reading informs us that the Big Bang theory is SUPPORTED by Hubble's evidence indicating that the universe is EXPANDING. The theory is also supported by the discovery made by two scientists in 1964 of cosmic RADIATION existing in space.

The lecturer believes that there are many theoretical HOLES in the Big Bang theory. Actually, the theory has never been proven true beyond a REASONABLE doubt, and the evidence supporting it also supports other theories of how the universe may have been created. As an example, the lecturer mentions the EKPYROTIC scenario. This theory argues that the universe was created when two parallel MEMBRANES of space matter COLLIDED. This theory shares many elements of the Big Bang theory but also has some DIFFERENCES.

Practice 4

04 English Literature

Step 1

Issue: - Did SHAKESPEARE write the plays he is ACCREDITED with?

Answer:

- No. Some believe the Earl of OXFORD did
- Shakespeare is a PSEUDONYM

Argument:

- No CLASSICAL education
- UNFAMILIAR with aristocratic MANNERS/sports
- Oxford was nobleman and was WRITER
- Little documentation Shakespeare worked as ACTOR
- Extant SIGNATURES all DIFFERENT-looking, none on plays/poems

Step 2

Key Issue:

- Shakespeare AUTHORSHIP debate: Some SCHOLARS believe Edward De Vere wrote Shakespeare

Argument for Shakespeare:

- Little genuine SUPPORTABLE evidence for Earl of OXFORD
- It is SKETCHY, poorly RESEARCHED conspiracy theory
- Plays not considered SERIOUS literature: reason for no name on play texts
- Numerous EXTANT documents refer to Shakespeare as actor and playwright
- Why would his contemporaries help nobleman? No MOTIVATION

Conclusion:

- SHAKESPEARE wrote the plays

Step 3

Reading:

- Main Idea: Oxford wrote Shakespeare's plays under a pseudonym.
- Supporting Idea: Shakespeare had no classical education and was unfamiliar with aristocratic manners and sports.
- Supporting Idea: Little documentation proves Shakespeare worked as an actor.

Lecture:

- Main Idea: Shakespeare wrote Shakespeare.
- Supporting Idea: The evidence supporting Oxford is sketchy and poorly researched.
- Supporting Idea: There is no motivation for Shakespeare's contemporaries to hide Oxford's identity.

Step 4

The reading claims that a NOBLEMAN called Edward De Vere, 17th Earl of OXFORD, actually wrote plays we accredit to William Shakespeare. He wrote them under a PSEUDONYM to protect his IDENTITY. The plays DISPLAY knowledge and information about aristocratic habits that Shakespeare wouldn't have been familiar with as a COMMONER. Oxford was a nobleman with such experiences, and he was also a WRITER. According to the reading, there is also little documentary proof that Shakespeare worked as an actor, and his extant signatures all look DIFFERENT, and none appear on his plays or poems. All this evidence indicates that Oxford wrote Shakespeare's plays.

The speaker argues that Shakespeare did write Shakespeare. He believes that arguments favoring the Earl of Oxford are poorly RESEARCHED and states that there is a lot of EXTANT documentation referring to Shakespeare as an ACTOR and playwright. The speaker also argues that Shakespeare's name does not appear on his plays and poems because plays weren't considered important or serious LITERATURE at that time. He believes Shakespeare's CONTEMPORARIES had no reason to help an aristocrat like Oxford hide his true identity and that, therefore, Shakespeare did write his own plays. He thinks the theory about Oxford is a CONSPIRACY theory.

Skill B

Practice 1

Step 1

Main idea: One serious problem facing modern children is a lack of sleep.

Step 2

A. 1   B. 1

C. Sample answer: Receiving an inadequate amount of sleep is a serious problem for children today.

Step 3

Main idea: - sleep deprivation is ONE FACTOR in poor academic performance, but not the ONLY FACTOR

Other important factors:

- NOURISHMENT (ex. breakfast) important factor
- CLOTHING such as warm coats and shoes
- home life; ex. FIGHTING between parents

Recommendation:

- Educators must CONSIDER other variables before PRESCRIBING more sleep to students with LOW GRADES

Step 4

A. Sleep deprivation is one factor.
    synonyms: - deprivation — neglect, lack of
                    - factor — variable, aspect
    paraphrase: - Lack of sleep is one variable.

B. Educators must consider other variables.
    synonyms: - educators — teachers, instructors, professors
                    - consider — contemplate, take into account
    paraphrase: - Teachers must take other factors into account.

Step 5

A. 1. A child's DEVELOPMENT in school is LARGELY dependent on THE AMOUNT OF sleep he or she gets.

2. What is the SIGNIFICANCE of a DEFICIENCY of sleep IN RELATION TO other factors?

B 1. The amount of sleep a child gets HAS A GREAT SIGNIFICANCE ON HIS OR HER PERFORMANCE IN SCHOOL.

2. With regard to other factors, WHAT EFFECT DOES A DEFICIT OF SLEEP HAVE?

Step 6

1. One problem that children face today is getting less than the recommended nine hours of sleep each night.

2. In addition to getting enough sleep, children need a healthy diet, suitable clothing, and a happy life at home.

Practice 2

Step 1

Main idea: An examination of history shows that non-violent means have not been as effective as violent means.

Step 2

A. 1   B. 1

C. Sample answer: It can be seen from history that violence is an effective tool of social change.

Step 3

Key forms of non-violence are:

Civil Disobedience:
- INDIVIDUAL and government DON'T SUPPORT each other
- principle of "INDEPENDENCE" is the driving idea
- provides the MORAL advantage of being RIGHT

Passive Resistance:
- PEACEFULLY break the law
- must expect to be ATTACKED by AUTHORITIES
- should quietly RESIST without RETALIATION

Step 4

A. Principle of independence is the driving idea.
synonyms: - principle — concept, rule
- independence — self-reliance, self-sufficiency
paraphrase: - The concept of self-reliance is the main point.

B. Should quietly resist without retaliation.
synonyms: - resist — endure, defend
- retaliation — fight back
paraphrase: - Should quietly endure and not fight back.

Step 5

A. 1. INDEPENDENCE in mind and action is the guiding PRINCIPLE for ACHIEVING what is JUST.

2. Without RESORTING to HOSTILITY, Gandhi SUCCESSFULLY CONVINCED the English to ELIMINATE colonial GOVERNMENT in India.

B. 1. The guiding principle for ACHIEVING WHAT IS JUST IS INDEPENDENCE OF MIND AND ACTION.

2. Gandhi effectively persuaded the BRITISH, WITHOUT USING VIOLENCE, TO END COLONIAL GOVERNMENT IN INDIA.

Step 6

1. Although violent forms of protest are considered ineffective, Gandhi successfully achieved the independence of India without resorting to violence.

2. Achieving what is right and just can be possible through independence of mind and action, rather than carrying out revolution through violence.

Practice 3

Step 1

Main idea: Theories on alternative biochemistry suggest that non-carbon-based forms of life could be possible in unusual environments.

Step 2

A. 1   B. 2

C. Sample answer: Some theories on alternative biochemistry contend that abnormal conditions could be home to non-carbon-based life forms.

Step 3

The argument against "carbon chauvinism"
- term DISCREDITS views that all life is CARBON BASED
- all current DATA indicate carbon is NECESSARY to life
- TERRESTRIAL LIFE is all carbon based
- we aren't able to test ALIEN ENVIRONMENTS
- we have no EMPIRICAL data about non-carbon BIOCHEMISTRIES
- PRESENT state of science not GUILTY of carbon chauvinism

Step 4

A. All current data indicate carbon is necessary to life.
    synonyms: - data — information
                - necessary — essential
    paraphrase: - Carbon is essential to life according to current information.

B. Present state of science not guilty of carbon-chauvinism
    synonyms: - state — circumstance
                - guilty — blame
    paraphrase: - Carbon chauvinism can't be blamed upon present scientific circumstances.

Step 5

A. 1. In fact, all ACTUAL scientific PROOF indicates that carbon is ESSENTIAL TO life as we UNDERSTAND it.
    2. The FUNDAMENTAL point today is that all CIRCUMSTANCES for biological life "as we know it" HAVE carbon in their MAKE-UP.

B. 1. That carbon is essential to LIFE AS WE KNOW IT IS A FACT SHOWN BY ALL ACTUAL SCIENTIFIC PROOF.
    2. That all circumstances for BIOLOGICAL LIFE HAVE CARBON IN THEIR MAKE-UP IS THE FUNDAMENTAL POINT BEING MADE TODAY.

Step 6

1. Although alternative biochemistry theories suggest non-carbon forms of life could be possible in unusual environments, in reality, such alien environments cannot be replicated or tested.

2. Despite the fact that the Earth is exceptionally silicon rich and carbon poor, it is carbon, not silicon, that has proven to be the successful life base on Earth.

Practice 4

Step 1

Main idea: Native American legal claims to the remains of Kennewick Man stand in the way of science.

Step 2

A. 2
B. 1
C. Sample answer: Native American groups are interfering with the progress of science by attempting to claim the Kennewick Man.

Step 3

Native American claims don't mean stopping the progress of science:
- Some SCIENTISTS take a HARD LINE
- Scientists argue Native American claims mean end of RESEARCH
- Native American groups not ANTI-SCIENCE, just want to be consulted or involved
- Science can PROCEED while RESPECTING Native American claims
- Many Native American groups involved in COLLABORATIVE projects
- Collaborative projects ENHANCE and clarify scientific RESULTS

Step 4

A. Scientists argue Native American claims mean end of research
    synonyms: - argue — claim, believe
                - mean — represent, signify
    paraphrase: - Native American claims are believed by scientists to signify the end of research.

B. Science can proceed while respecting Native American claims
    synonyms: - proceed — continue, go on
                - respecting — regarding, honoring
    paraphrase: - Native American claims can be honored while scientific study continues.

Step 5

A. 1. Respecting Native American CLAIMS to archaeological REMNANTS doesn't mean ENDING the ENDEAVORS of science.

   2. EFFORTS to freely CONTINUE science at the DETRIMENT of Native American BELIEFS are really the ROOT of the debate.

B. 1. Preventing the advancement OF SCIENCE DOESN'T RESULT FROM HONORING NATIVE AMERICAN CLAIMS TO ARCHAEOLOGICAL FINDINGS.

   2. The core of the conflict IS ENDEAVORS TO UNDERTAKE SCIENCE AT THE DETRIMENT OF NATIVE AMERICAN VALUES.

Step 6

1. The belief held by many scientists that scientific progress will be halted by honoring Native American beliefs and respecting their claims to the Kennewick Man is unfounded.

2. The raging debate surrounding the remains of the Kennewick Man shows that more collaborative efforts on both sides are required.

Skill C

Practice 1

Step 2

If I were so fortunate as to receive a piece of land, I would want to use it to do something positive that would not harm the land. Because I love plants and animals, and because I love nature, I would create a wildlife reserve. The survival of many woodland creatures is threatened because their natural habitats are being destroyed. I would want to create a place where these wild animals could live safely in a natural environment that is protected from development.

Not only would this reserve create a home for animals; it would also create an opportunity for people to see the animals in their natural habitats. I think that is much more enjoyable than seeing animals in zoos. While I would charge a small admission fee, the money would go toward the care of the animals. I would not wish to make a profit off of the wildlife reserve. It would make me happy to see the land put to good use.

Many land owners are selfish and see their land as a means of making money. They don't really care about the land; they only care about their investment. Some might sell the natural resources of the land, such as lumber. Others might build houses and develop the land in order to sell it later at a profit. Personally, if I had land handed to me for free, profit would be the last thing on my mind. I would take the opportunity to protect the land and all of the plants and animals on that land.

Step 3

1. If I were so fortunate as to receive a piece of land, I would want to use it to do something positive that would not harm the land.

2. Not only would this reserve create a home for animals; it would also create an opportunity for people to see the animals in their natural habitats.

Step 4

1. The writer of the essay prefers to use the land as a nature preserve rather than using it to earn a profit.

2. The writer states that he or she would use the land to create a wildlife reserve, which is an example of something positive that would not harm the land.

3. Yes, the writer points out that many people prefer to use land to make a profit by either selling natural resources or developing the land to sell for more money.

4. The main idea that the writer concludes with is that he or she would prefer to protect wildlife than earn a profit on his or her land.

Practice 2

Step 2

There are some types of decisions that require careful thought and other types that don't. For example, when I am at the supermarket trying to decide whether to buy orange juice or apple juice, I don't have to think very hard about it because it is not important. However, sometimes I make rash decisions about important things. When I make important decisions without thinking them through, I typically make the wrong choice. In my experience, it is always best to carefully consider my options when I make major life decisions.

Major life decisions include career choices, relationship choices, and money choices. When I was offered a job overseas, for example, I considered many factors before accepting it. I thought about the location, the salary, and the possibilities for career advancement as well as being in a new culture and being away from my friends and family. In contrast, I have left a job without thinking about my decision. I once worked for an insurance firm, and I became angry with my boss. Without thinking, I quit my job. A day later, I realized that I should have thought that decision through. As you can see, in my experience, major decisions that are made on the spur of the moment tend to be mistakes.

I know people who prefer to go with their instincts when they make decisions. When I was considering buying a certain house, a friend of mine asked me, "how did you feel in the house? Would you be happy there?" The truth was, I loved the house, but I would have been foolish to buy it, because it probably wouldn't increase in value as much as some of my other options. Personally, I don't trust my instincts. I have to think about all of my important choices for a long time before I can make a final decision.

Step 3

1. In my experience, it is always best to carefully consider my options when I make major life decisions.
2. Major life decisions include career choices, relationship choices, and money choices.

Step 4

1. The writer takes the stance that it is better to think about important decisions carefully.
2. The writer tells about his or her experience of quitting his or her job without thinking carefully about the decision and later realizing that it was a mistake.
3. Yes, the writer gives an example of a friend who thought he or she should choose a house based on how he or she felt inside it.
4. The writer concludes that he or she prefers to think carefully before making important decisions.

Practice 3

Step 3

Suggested answers:
Keywords / key phrases:
engrossing, active, intimate, source of learning, interpretation
Keywords / key phrases:
exciting, stimuli, intense, convenient, social skills

Practice 4

Step 3

Suggested answers:
Keywords / key phrases:
information technology, relevance, practical, outdated, workforce
Keywords / key phrases:
creativity, anchor, indispensable, imagination, flexibility

Skill D

Thesis Statements

Step 1

Question 1: If my school received a gift of money, I believe the money would be best spent in hiring more teachers.

Question 2: Because of the multitude of interesting artifacts on display, I personally found my visit to the Museum of History and Anthropology while traveling through Mexico City to be a thoroughly enjoyable experience.

Question 3: I disagree with the contention that television has destroyed communication among friends and family; in fact, I believe the opposite to be true.

Question 4: Because of its many uses, including shelter and food, the maple tree is an important plant to the people of my country.

Step 2

Question 1: opinion

Sample thesis statement: I believe that the construction of a large shopping center would cause several serious problems for my neighborhood; therefore, I oppose this plan.

Question 2: experience

Sample thesis statement: From my experience, I have found that carefully planning my free-time activities provides me with the opportunity to get the most enjoyment out of life.

Question 3: experience

Sample thesis statement: There were numerous positive and negative aspects to my childhood in a big city.

Question 4: opinion

Sample thesis statement: Because communication is a larger part of daily life today than in the past, I believe that the ability to read and write is more important in our times than in past times.

Topic Sentences

Step 1

Question 1

(2) Having the Internet in my home allows me to communicate with people around the globe.

(1) The advent of the Internet is one twentieth-century change that has strongly affected my life.

(3) For instance, I send emails to friends, family, and work colleagues on a daily basis.

Question 2

(2) Many people radically change their lives after high school, so their means of future success should not be limited by what they achieved during those years.

(3) Many high school students, for example, may have difficulty because of health or relationship issues.

(1) In my opinion, some form of post-secondary education should be available to all students, not just top students.

Question 3

(1) In general, the Internet has not damaged my friends' and family's ability to communicate; however, it has negatively affected the social skills of one of my cousins.

(3) When I was visiting his house during the holidays, he spent all of New Year's Eve alone in his room playing *Doom*.

(2) He spends several hours each day playing online games and never comes out of his room to talk to others.

Question 4

(3) For instance, employees are more likely to work harder and take fewer breaks if they worry about their job status.

(1) I disagree with the argument that businesses should hire employees for their entire lives.

(2) Having workers who know that their employment can be terminated can help increase the company's productivity.

Vocabulary Review

Review 1

1. (B)	2. (D)	3. (A)
4. (A)	5. (D)	6. (C)
7. (C)	8. (D)	9. (A)
10. (A)	11. (C)	12. (A)
13. (B)	14. (D)	15. (C)
16. postulated	17. membranes	18. empirical
19. verify	20. precision	21. (D)
22. (C)	23. (A)	24. (E)
25. (B)		

Review 2

1. (D)	2. (A)	3. (D)
4. (D)	5. (A)	6. (C)
7. (B)	8. (A)	9. (B)
10. (D)	11. (C)	12. (A)
13. (A)	14. (C)	15. (B)
16. interacting	17. collaborative	18. foster
19. invariably	20. contend	21. initial
22. endow	23. require	24. technique
25. caution		

Chapter 2

Skill A

Practice 1

Step 1

When most people think of great military strategists, the names Alexander the Great, Julius Caesar, or Napoleon Bonaparte come to mind. <u>Spanish Conquistador Hernando Cortes, however, accomplished a feat that, arguably, outshines them all.</u> Around 1520, Cortes conquered the 5-million-strong Aztec empire with only 600 men, twenty horses, and ten small cannons.

In 1519, Cortes sailed from Spain to Mexico with 11 ships and landed at various points along the Mexican coast. He easily subdued the small coastal tribes at what are now Tabasco and Veracruz. These people told him of the vast wealth of the Aztecs who lived inland. <u>Cortes began to enlist the support of the smaller tribes</u> he conquered as he made his way inland, <u>a strategy that would serve him well. Since many of the tribes had no love for the Aztecs</u> due to the Aztec policy of demanding costly tribute from them, <u>they were often willing to join forces with Cortes.</u>

<u>Another circumstance that Cortes exploited was the fact that the Aztecs had a legend of a pale-skinned, bearded god, Quetzalcoatl, who they believed</u> had once taught them agriculture and who <u>would one day return to end their civilization.</u> Cortes was believed to be this god by some Aztec citizens, most notably, the emperor Motecuhzoma. Additionally, <u>the native Mexicans had never before seen horses, firearms, or the giant attack mastiffs the Spanish brought with them.</u> <u>Cortes exploited these two psychological advantages,</u> the legend of the light-skinned god and the spectacle of his horses, dogs, and cannons, <u>to conquer the entire Aztec empire</u> largely through fear and negotiation. <u>The brilliance of his approach leaves its mark,</u> for better or worse, <u>on the history of an entire nation today.</u>

Step 2

MALINTZIN was the secret to CORTES's success

1. Spaniards discover she can SPEAK BOTH NAHUA AND MAYAN and use her TO INTERPRET
2. Cortes uses her to win SUPPORT from the NON-AZTEC NATIONS
3. Unclear whether she was just an INTERPRETER or A LEADER as well
4. Independent SPANISH and MEXICAN sources attest to HER IMPORTANCE

Step 3

Reading

- Cortes was a brilliant military strategist
- Cortes was a great negotiator
- Cortes's brilliance changed Mexican history

Lecture

- Malintzin was the main source of Cortes's success
- It is not certain who the real negotiator was
- Sources lend equal importance to Malintzin

Step 4

The reading passage depicts Cortes as one of the greatest military strategists of all time and credits him with toppling an empire of millions with only 600 men and a few horses and cannons. **(1)** <u>Further/In addition to this</u>, it proposes he was a genius who exploited local politics, legends, and the spectacle of his small but advanced military to accomplish a nearly impossible feat. **(2)** <u>In contrast</u>, the speaker casts doubt on this version of history and credits Cortes's interpreter and concubine, Malintzin, as being the mastermind behind a significant part of his campaign. **(3)** <u>More specifically</u>, she asks us to ponder who was more likely the mastermind: the foreigner who had little to no knowledge of the politics, customs, or language, or the native who had knowledge of all of these and who was the one directly speaking with the leaders of the Aztecs and other nations. **(4)** <u>In addition to this/Further,</u> the speaker cites various sources, including accounts from Spanish soldiers and other conquistadors, as well as depictions in Nahua art, which support the case that Malintzin was much more than an interpreter and perhaps just as significant as Cortes himself.

Practice 2

Step 1

<u>The value of a professional sports team for a city's local economy is undeniable.</u> The benefits begin with the

construction of the stadium itself, <u>providing thousands of local construction jobs</u>. Once regular season play begins, an army of local workers is required to man the stadium facilities, for everything from concessions and ticket sales, to security and administration. <u>The economic benefits expand throughout the district of the stadium</u> as fans pour into the area from far and wide. These fans support local parking decks, restaurants, bars, shops, and often hotel facilities. <u>This contributes to the prosperity</u> of local businesses and provides a general boost to the overall property value.

<u>All of this revenue is of course taxed</u> by the municipal authorities. Combine this with the <u>millions of dollars in tax revenue that ticket sales can generate</u> over the life of a sports team, and we have a clear benefit for all members of the community.

These benefits are easy to see, but <u>the intangible benefits may be greater still</u>. A professional sports team with regularly televised broadcasts is often the hallmark of what people generally perceive as a "major" city. Thus, <u>the sports team becomes a kind of advertisement</u> for the significance and prosperity of the city itself, <u>attracting new business from the outside</u>.

Some may say that the costs of new sports stadiums are an undue burden on cities, but <u>all of the long-term benefits must be taken into account</u> before passing hasty judgment on the economic effects of professional sports franchises.

Step 2

Sports stadium not A GOOD INVESTMENT
1. Jobs created REPLACE other jobs or PAY LOW wages
2. Most money goes to MANAGERS AND PLAYERS
3. Tax revenue VERY SMALL compared to THE INVESTMENT
4. Team's BENEFIT to the city's IMAGE difficult to measure

Step 3

Reading
• Stadiums create jobs
• Stadiums produce tax revenue
• Boosts city's image

Lecture
• Does not create new jobs, takes money out of city
• Revenue gains are small compared to investment
• PR benefit is vague claim, funds better spent elsewhere

Step 4

The reading states that a sports team greatly benefits a city in a number of ways, **(1)** <u>while</u> the lecture says the benefits do not justify the initial investment, and that the sports team actually ends up taking money out of the community. The speaker implies that taxpayer money should not go to the stadium **(2)** <u>since</u> the sports team is a profit-seeking business, and they should not expect free money from the public. Further, the speaker argues that benefits such as jobs and tax revenues are not actually benefits if all relevant factors are taken into account, such as the kinds of jobs, and the comparison of the situation without the sports team. **(3)** <u>However</u>, the reading proposes that the benefit to the city's image is invaluable, ultimately attracting new residents and businesses and contributing to the city's long-term growth. **(4)** <u>In spite of</u> this fact, the speaker maintains that the city would benefit more from investing this money elsewhere, such as in education and infrastructure.

Practice 3

Step 1

In 1989, scientists in Utah made a controversial announcement. They claimed that they had carried out an experiment in which the results could only be explained by nuclear fusion. In their experiment, they filled a glass container with heavy water which had a small amount of salt dissolved in it. Into the container, they inserted two electrodes: one was platinum and one was palladium. The platinum electrode was connected to the positive charge of a car battery, while the platinum electrode was attached to the negative charge. <u>This process created an excess amount of heat—more than could be explained by chemical reactions. Because it could not be explained by chemical reactions, the researchers jumped to the conclusion that nuclear fusion was the cause. This phenomenon is referred to as "cold fusion".</u> It is not accepted by the scientific community, and it serves as an example of pseudo science.

The scientific method demands that a claim be subject to peer review. <u>The validity of any claim is based on reproducibility. Because no one has ever been able to reproduce the results of the first claim of cold fusion, it has been rejected.</u> More importantly, the <u>data does not coincide with current theories of nuclear fusion</u>. It is well accepted that, when nuclear fusion takes place, neutrons are emitted. For one thing, no extra neutrons were detected. Secondly, if the number of neutrons had have been emitted to support their claim, the researchers would have been killed. <u>The only explanation for the experimenters' findings is that errors in measurement took place.</u> This is supported by the fact that the methods they used to measure heat were highly specious.

Step 2

Cold fusion refers to <u>a debatable claim that nuclear fusion can take place at room temperature</u>.

- <u>scientists must not dismiss observations that don't concur with current theory</u>
- <u>in time, scientists have reproduced the original findings</u>
- <u>measurement equipment has become more reliable</u>

Step 3

Reading

- "Cold fusion" claims do not fit current nuclear fusion theories
- Scientists were unable to reproduce the results of the original experiment
- Positive results can only be explained as error

Lecture

- Science relies on reexamination of theories when evidence is presented to contradict them
- While results weren't reproduced immediately after the announcement, in time, scientists have reproduced the same results
- No skeptic has been able to identify an error that explains all positive results

Step 4

The debate surrounding the possibility of cold fusion, **(1)** <u>that is</u>, nuclear fusion occurring at room temperature, is centered on the scientific process. The reading attacks the scientists' interpretation of their results. When they found that excess heat was generated in an amount that could not be explained by chemical reactions, the scientists concluded that nuclear fusion was taking place. The reading states that because such an interpretation does not concur with current theory, it should not be accepted. The speaker points out, however, that science relies on continual review of theories. Observations should not be ignored **(2)** <u>just because</u> they are not explained by current theories. **(3)** <u>With regards to</u> the statement in the reading that scientists have never been able to replicate the original experimenters' results, the speaker states that in the years that have passed, some indeed have found similar results. In sum, the reading states that cold fusion claims have not stood up to the scientific process, **(4)** <u>whereas</u> the speaker asserts that the scientific community was hasty in dismissing the notion before sufficient time was allowed to complete an analysis using the scientific process.

Practice 4

Step 1

Recent claims that the ancient Anasazi peoples engaged in cannibalism are unfounded. The practice of cannibalism does not coincide with the culture of the Native Americans who are descended from these people, that is, the Pueblo peoples of the American Southwest. <u>Cannibalism is considered by Native Americans to be one of the most evil acts a person can engage in.</u> It seems improbable, then, that their ancestors ate human flesh ritualistically. The speculation that the Anasazi people were human flesh eaters is based on skeletal remains that were found to have been broken and burned. It can be demonstrated from these findings that flesh was removed from the bones, but <u>that does not prove that the meat was actually ingested</u>. A more plausible explanation, and one that coincides with the beliefs of the Pueblo peoples, is that <u>these are the remains of suspected witches who were put to death</u>. The custom was to kill the suspected witch by burning the body and tearing apart the remains in order to remove and destroy the witch's "evil" heart. This explains the broken bones and burn marks. It also explains why the corpse was ripped apart. While the practice was brutal, it does not imply cannibalism. Any claim that the Anasazi people were cannibalistic is based not on fact, but on inference. The refusal of some to consider other plausible explanations is unscientific and irrational.

Step 2
Evidence supports the claim that cannibalism took place in Anasazi society.
- Evidence does not implicate anyone in particular
- Fossilized fecal matter proves ingestion took place
- Pot resin on bones rules out witch slaughter explanation

Step 3
Reading
- Evidence may be explained by witch slaughter
- It cannot be proven that human flesh was eaten
- Native American culture denounces cannibalism

Lecture
- Human carcasses were torn apart and cooked
- Fossilized feces and pot resin on bones prove that human flesh was cooked and eaten
- Evidence does not indicate who engaged in cannibalism

Step 4
The dispute concerning whether or not the Anasazi people engaged in cannibalism is based on evidence obtained from the examination of human remains. These remains show that human skeletons were torn apart, cooked, and had the flesh removed from them. The reading states that this does not necessarily imply that cannibalism took place. **(1)** Instead, they explain that these are the remains of suspected witches who were burned and had their bodies torn apart. The speaker, however, maintains that the evidence does suggest that ingestion took place. **(2)** For example, pot resin was found on the bones suggesting they were cooked. **(3)** Furthermore, fossilized fecal matter shows traces of human flesh. While the reading states that Native American culture would not condone such activities, the speaker maintains that the evidence does

not implicate anyone in particular in the act. She goes on to offer a plausible explanation that has been presented: that a group of foreigners engaged in cannibalism in order to terrorize the Anasazi. **(4)** Thus, the peaceful reputation of this culture need not be tarnished by the evidence of cannibalism.

Skill B

Practice 1

Step 2
Introduction: (C), (B), (D), (A)
Transitions: thus, finally

Body: (F), (C), (D), (A), (E), (B)
Transitions: by, also, in fact, as a result, furthermore

Conclusion: (E), (D), (B), (C), (A)
Transitions: because, consequently, clearly, instead of

Practice 2

Step 2
Introduction: (B), (A), (C)
Transitions: for this reason, in short

Body: (D), (B), (A), (E), (C)
Transitions: that is, while, however

Conclusion: (B), (D), (A), (C)
Transitions: further, in effect, therefore

Practice 3
Step 3
Introduction: (C), (A), (D), (B)
Transitions: for example, let us, in addition

Body: (E), (C), (B), (D), (A), (G), (F)
Transitions: to continue, in fact, in other words, to begin, second, first

Conclusion: (C), (D), (B), (A)
Transitions: thus, furthermore

Vocabulary Review

Review 1

1. (D)	2. (B)	3. (A)
4. (D)	5. (B)	6. (A)
7. (A)	8. (D)	9. (B)
10. (C)	11. (C)	12. (D)
13. (A)	14. (C)	15. (B)
16. (B)	17. (D)	18. (D)
19. (B)	20. (D)	21. (D)
22. (C)	23. (A)	24. (B)
25. (C)	26. (B)	27. (B)
28. (D)	29. (C)	30. (B)
31. strategist	32. campaigns	33. concubine
34. entourage	35. lingua franca	36. engaged in
37. ancestors	38. hierarchical	39. validate
40. plausible	41. undue	42. ingest
43. tarnish	44. condemn	45. welfare
46. (S)	47. (O)	48. (O)
49. (S)	50. (O)	

Review 2

1. (C)	2. (B)	3. (A)
4. (D)	5. (B)	6. (D)
7. (A)	8. (C)	9. (D)
10. (D)	11. (B)	12. (A)
13. (B)	14. (C)	15. (A)
16. (A)	17. (C)	18. (D)
19. (D)	20. (A)	21. (C)
22. (C)	23. (B)	24. (A)
25. (C)	26. (A)	27. (D)
28. (A)	29. (A)	30. (B)
31. tarnish	32. dynamic	33. pecuniary
34. welfare	35. remuneration	36. undertake
37. discourse	38. exempt	39. touchy
40. burden	41. up	42. in
43. into	44. on	45. top
46. (B)	47. (D)	48. (E)
49. (A)	50. (C)	

Chapter 3

Focus A - Verb Forms

Exercise 1

The reading introduces the idea of supply and demand. In particular, the passage <u>explains</u> that a person's salary <u>depends</u> on public demand for his or her talent. In other words, a person with a rare talent should <u>earn</u> more according to this model because supply <u>is</u> limited while demand is high. The professor gives several specific examples of this theory in action. First, she talks about ordinary people who <u>make</u> small salaries, such as bus drivers and fast-food workers. Then, she <u>talks</u> about people with special skills, and she <u>points out</u> that they earn significantly more per hour because of their skills. As extreme examples, the professor talks about movie stars and athletes. These people <u>earn</u> thousands or even hundreds of thousands of dollars per hour based on public demand for their rare talents.

I know a lot of people who <u>treat</u> their pets as family members. In fact, one of my close friends <u>has had</u> a cat since she was in elementary school. The cat <u>is</u> rather old now, but my friend takes good care of her. Actually, I think my friend <u>spends</u> too much time and money on her cat. Sometimes, I feel that she neglects her friends because she has <u>to do</u> something for her cat, such as feed it or <u>take</u> it to the veterinarian. In my opinion, it is unhealthy for people to focus so much attention on animals. If they focused this same energy and attention on people around them, it <u>would make</u> a world of difference. They could <u>spend</u> the money wasted on pet food and toys on more useful pursuits like treating their friends or donating to charities!

Exercise 2

The reading passage <u>describes</u> important space achievements in the 20th century, including NASA's lunar missions. In the lecture, the professor emphasizes the point that US astronauts are the only humans who have <u>walked</u> on the moon. He gives several interesting statistics related to lunar programs <u>developed</u> by other countries. In particular, the professor <u>discusses</u> Russia's lunar program. He points out that although Russia has sent rockets to the moon, no Russian cosmonauts <u>were</u> ever sent to land on the moon. He also mentions that China is <u>developing</u> plans to send humans to the moon, though those plans will not materialize for a long time.

In order to stay healthy, I walk whenever I can. This often means that I have to <u>plan</u> my day carefully so that I can leave enough time to get where I need to go. For example, if I <u>take</u> the subway to my university, it takes about thirty minutes to get from my apartment to my classroom. However, if I get off the subway one stop early in order to walk for exercise, it <u>takes</u> forty-five minutes to get to my classroom. Therefore, I <u>have</u> to leave my apartment fifteen minutes earlier than normal so that I can exercise for fifteen minutes by walking to class. By walking to class, I can also enjoy the added benefit of relaxing in the fresh air rather than being <u>cramped</u> and <u>pushed</u> around on the crowded subway.

Exercise 3

1. (B)	2. (A)	3. (A)
4. (B)	5. (C)	6. (A)
7. (A)	8. (B)	9. (C)
10. (A)	11. (B)	12. (A)
13. (B)	14. (C)	15. (A)
16. (B)		

Exercise 4

Both the reading and the lecture focus on the <u>connection</u> between poverty and single-parent families, in <u>particular</u>, families headed by women. The reading describes a government study that looked at all families headed by women across the US. This study concluded that the number of families headed by women below the poverty line decreased from 1960 until the present. The lecture discusses a <u>similar</u> study that found very different results. In the lecture, the professor says that researchers looked at only poor families headed by women. Between 1960 and the present, the number of poor families headed by women rose from 25 percent to over 50 percent. Thus, the professor <u>correlates</u> poverty to gender of household heads. In her words, the "feminization of poverty" is a <u>reality</u> in modern society.

It is often said that the <u>childhood</u> years are the most important years of one's life. However, I think a person's young adulthood years are more important than the childhood years. As a child, a person spends time either in school or simply playing with friends. School may teach the child information or even certain skills <u>necessary</u> for life, but I think these are generic experiences for just about everyone. When a person becomes a young adult, on the other hand, he or she can truly <u>individualize</u> himself or herself. In university, one has the <u>opportunity</u> to make decisions without direction from parents or teachers. Of course, the actions each person decides to take can have a <u>significant</u> impact on the course of the rest of his or her life, unlike decisions typically open to children.

Focus B - Sentence Formation

Exercise 1

1. The designation of an individual's class, which can be based on a number of different factors, <u>has</u> been of key interest to sociologists for decades.
2. <u>A child who is</u> only a few weeks old is capable of imitating a limited range of facial expressions that he or she observes from a care-giver. OR A <u>child only</u> a few weeks old is capable of imitating a limited range of facial expressions that he or she observes from a care-giver.
3. Children who grow up in single-parent households typically do worse in school than children <u>who</u> are from two-parent households.
4. Diana <u>Pearce, who</u> was an economist by <u>profession, suggested</u> a theory that proved popular among sociologists.
5. The female lion, <u>which</u> is distinguished from the male by the lack of a mane, does the hunting. OR The female <u>lion, distinguished</u> from the male by the lack of a mane, does the hunting.
6. A critical aspect of learning to read involves the integration of skills <u>that</u> develop at different stages of childhood, namely the ability to decipher sounds of a language and the ability to write.
7. One of the most influential theories related to cognitive development comes from <u>Piaget, who</u>

based his theory on observations of elementary-age children.
8. Paper <u>products that</u> are made with at least 60% recycled <u>fibers consume</u> 45% fewer raw materials than products made without recycled fibers.
9. The professor describes the Industrial Revolution as a <u>time when</u> great strides were made in science and technology.
10. A utopian society is one in <u>which</u> citizens live in perfect fairness and harmony with each other.
11. <u>Polaris, which can</u> be located easily on a clear night, is a reliable point in the sky to navigate by because it is located over the point of true north.
12. The claim that "laughter is the best medicine" <u>is</u> supported by research that shows laughter reduces stress, which contributes to a person's overall health and well-being.

Exercise 2

1. The bowl (that was) found in the cave was over 1,000 years old.
2. A child who knows he did something wrong will not look an adult in the eye.
3. Cats were important in ancient Egyptian culture, which flourished in the Nile River Valley for thousands of years.
4. The desk that was broken was removed from the classroom.
5. Columbus grew up in a large port city (that was) located on the coast of Italy.
6. The fossil was obviously a species of horse (that is) now extinct.
7. People who grow up near the border usually learn to speak two languages.
8. The legal age of adulthood, at which/when a person can purchase alcohol, is 21.
9. Snoopy, (who is) a famous cartoon dog, is a beagle.
10. Two critics who reviewed the book did not agree.
11. The university has recently changed its admission policy, which used to prohibit women from studying there.
12. By definition, sunrise is the time in the morning at which/when the sun first appears over the horizon.

Exercise 3

_IC_ 1. Musicians are only able to develop their technical skills through practice. Therefore, they must devote long hours to exercises that develop particular techniques.

_C_ 2.

_C_ 3.

_IC_ 4. Confucius did not begin teaching until very late in his life, but he had a lasting impact on generations long after his death.

_C_ 5.

_IC_ 6. In 1963, Martin Luther King, Jr. was put in jail for a short time, and that same year, his house was bombed.

_IC_ 7. Because young children are being exposed to violence and sexually explicit material on television, politicians are now debating a new law to censor some shows.

_C_ 8.

_IC_ 9. Most people recall that Narcissus turned into a flower; however, few remember what happened to his spurned lover, Echo.

_C_ 10.

_IC_ 11. The researcher studied groups of men from various cultures. Interestingly, he found that men's opinions were very similar across cultures.

_C_ 12.

Exercise 4

1. a. In the past, you would have to pay for a stamp to send a message to a friend, but today, you can send messages for free using email.

   b. In the past, you would have to pay for a stamp to send a message to a friend, whereas today, you can send messages for free using email.

2. a. Many airlines are offering discount tickets for flights, so more people are flying for weekend trips to scenic cities.

   b. Because many airlines are offering discount tickets for flights, more people are flying for weekend trips to scenic cities.

3. a. The architect built many famous structures, and he established a school of architecture in Arizona.

   b. The architect built many famous structures. Also, he established a school of architecture in Arizona.

4. a. Although my father did not hold a well-paying job, he enjoyed his job a lot.

   b. My father did not hold a well-paying job, but he enjoyed his job a lot.

5. a. The epic work follows the lives of forty characters through the revolution. Thus, readers often have trouble keeping track of who is who in the novel.

   b. The epic work follows the lives of forty characters through the revolution, so readers often have trouble keeping track of who is who in the novel.

6. a. A driver caught operating a vehicle while intoxicated will be issued a ticket. Additionally, the owner of the vehicle will receive a ticket as well.

   b. A driver caught operating a vehicle while intoxicated will be issued a ticket, and the owner of the vehicle will receive a ticket as well.

Exercise 5

1. Having been severely damaged by the storm, the building has to be torn down.

2. Having been left in the car on a hot day, the plastic melted and warped.

3. We are only able to objectively view the core of the problem after cutting through all of the media hype.

4. Wanting to attract more companies, the town will offer tax incentives to new businesses.

5. In the past, women were confined to the home by social pressure, being primarily expected to bear and raise children.

Exercise 6

_P_ 1. A student who <u>waits until the last minute to study for an exam</u> and <u>completes assignments in a careless manner</u> will do poorly in the class.

_P_ 2. Both <u>by the way the couple dressed</u> and <u>by their interaction with each other</u>, it was obvious they were on their honeymoon.

NP 3. Job opportunities <u>are increasing in fields related to Internet technology</u> but <u>have decreased in many traditional fields of engineering</u>. (are decreasing)

P 4. <u>Learning how to write Chinese</u> was harder for me than <u>learning how to speak it</u>.

P 5. My father taught me <u>how to drive in reverse</u> and <u>how to parallel park</u>.

NP 6. Shakespeare wrote <u>comedies</u>, <u>romances</u>, <u>tragedies</u>, and <u>plays based on real people from history</u>. (historical dramas)

P 7. She <u>spent hours wandering around different floors of the library</u>, <u>enjoying her solitude</u>, and <u>discovering old, interesting books</u>.

NP 8. Learning to write well is important for business majors because employees at all levels may be required to write reports that are <u>accurate</u> and <u>including important details</u>. (include)

Exercise 7

1. A child's voice is higher than an <u>adult</u>. (adult's)
2. Either a family learns to live within its budget or <u>will risk sinking into debt</u>. (risks sinking into debt)
3. I found most of the books required by the course interesting, informative, and <u>they entertained me</u>. (entertaining)
4. The violinist played with grace, <u>incredible dexterity</u>, and speed. (dexterity)
5. A shocking number of freshmen waste their first year of college not studying enough, <u>doing things harmful to their health</u>, and not utilizing the campus facilities available to them. (not taking care of their health)
6. In the art appreciation course, students will learn to analyze important elements of art and <u>recognizing styles of various art movements</u>. (to recognize styles of various art movements)

7. Most students expect three things out of university: to learn life skills, <u>meeting new friends</u>, and to prepare for their future careers. (to meet new friends)
8. The Hopi, the Navajo, and <u>Zuni</u> are three well-known Native American peoples of the southwest United States. (the Zuni)

Exercise 8

The reading and the lecture both describe Chomolunga, which <u>is</u> the mountain better known as Mt. Everest. The reading introduces just the basic facts about the mountain, such as its location, height, and <u>climate/weather conditions</u>. The professor adds to this information <u>by talking</u> about all of the people who have tried to climb Mt. Everest. In particular, he explains that although thousands of people <u>have tried</u> to climb the mountain, only about 650 have succeeded. On top of that, 142 of those successful climbers died before they made it back down the mountain. Obviously, Mt. Everest is an incredible and dangerous mountain.

In my opinion, teamwork is a more valuable asset in a new employee than independence. Most jobs cannot be done <u>alone. Therefore, it</u> is necessary for employees to be able to work both with colleagues who work within the same company as well as with individuals or teams from other companies. Employees must have the necessary skills to communicate effectively with others as well as cooperate in forming strategies or solutions for workplace tasks and problems. Although an independent employee might be able to do certain tasks without help or input from others, these are not the most efficient workers <u>because</u> the tasks he or she undertakes are smaller or more limited in nature than the tasks which can <u>be undertaken</u> by teams.

Reading

Herbs and Drugs

1. (B)	2. (D)	3. (B)
4. (C)	5. (C)	6. (D)
7. (D)	8. (A)	9. (B)
10. (A)	11. (C)	

12. Drugs — (B), (E), (H); Herbs — (A), (C), (F)

William Shakespeare

13. (B)	14. (C)	15. (B)
16. (D)	17. (C)	18. (D)
19. (A)	20. (C)	21. (A)
22. (B)	23. (A)	

24. (A), (C), (E)

Pollination

25. (A)	26. (C)	27. (B)
28. (A)	29. (D)	30. (B)
31. (B)	32. (A)	33. (A)
34. (C)	35. (C)	

36. (A), (D), (E)

Listening

Campus Life

1. (D)

2. YES — (B), (C), (D), (E); NO — (A)

3. (B)	4. (D)	5. (B)	6. (A)

Ecology

7. (D)   8. (A), (C), (F)

9. YES — (C), (E); NO — (A), (B), (D)

10. (D)	11. (D)	12. (B)

Music

13. (B)

14. YES — (D), (E), (F); NO — (A), (B), (C)

15. (A)	16. (A)	17. (C)	18. (A)

Sociology

19. (C)	20. (C), (D)	21. (D)	22. (C)
23. (C)	24. (B)		

Campus Life

25. (C)	26. (B)	27. (A)	28. (D)
29. (B)	30. (C)		

Literature

31. (B)	32. (A), (C), (D)
33. (D)	34. (A) 35. (B)

36. First person — (C), (E); Third person — (A), (B), (D)

Speaking

Question 1

Some people trust first impressions, while others prefer to get to know someone before making judgments. I used to trust first impressions, but now I do not. When I was working as a waiter at a cafe, I saw a man with worn-out clothes and really messy hair. He looked like a beggar, but then he sat down at a table. I told him I was sorry but he couldn't rest in the restaurant. It turned out that the man was a famous artist waiting for the director of a local museum. I was very embarrassed, and now I do not trust first impressions.

Question 2

Sample response 1:
I agree with the statement that people should only read books about real events, real people, and established facts. First, reading about legends or unproven claims only creates confusion and argument between people. Second, reading works of fiction only uses up time that could be spent learning about the world or real things. After all, there is more than enough to learn about the real world to keep people busy. Finally, getting too involved in works of fiction can damage a person's social skills and interest in interacting with others.

Sample response 2:
I disagree with the statement that people should only read books about real events, real people, and established facts. For one thing, it is not always clear which books are about real events and which are not. For instance, a religion may consider its holy book to be objective fact, or a country might consider its history books to be objective fact, while others, of course, do not. In addition, works of fiction spark the imagination and help people develop and grow in a way that non-fiction simply cannot.

Question 3

In the woman's opinion, the Career Services Center is a great place. She describes several ways that the center has helped her. First, she details how a counselor there helped her choose her major area of study. By using a series of tests of interests and abilities, he advised her to major in statistics or accounting. Second, she tells how the center can help students find jobs after graduation. They maintain a database of job and internship listings that students can read in order to find career opportunities. In the end, she recommends the man visit the center.

Question 4

Both the reading and the lecture are about the Earth's layers. The reading says that there are four layers. Those are the core, the mantle, the crust — uh, the core actually has two parts: the inner core and outer core. But the woman says that there are extra parts of the crust. I mean, the crust should really be thought of as having two parts, not just one. Those two parts are the continental crust and the oceanic crust. Then, she also goes on to explain some of the differences between the two parts of the crust. She mentions things like where they are located, how thick they are, and what they are made of. Anyway, the key point that she adds to the information in the reading is that the crust really has two parts.

Question 5

Sample response 1:
The two students discuss the man being put on academic probation. Because he chose to take too many courses and then became sick, he failed a geology class. Two possible solutions to his problem are discussed. The first option is to appeal the probation. The second option is to take the class again. In my opinion, the first option is the better of the two. Since the man does have extenuating circumstances surrounding his low grade, I think there is a good chance he could have the probation revoked. Thus, his failure would not appear on his records.

Sample response 2:
The two students discuss the man being put on academic probation. Because he chose to take too many courses and then became sick, he failed geology class. Two possible solutions to his problem are discussed. The first option is to appeal the probation. The second option is to take the class again. In my opinion, the second option is the better of the two. Since the man doesn't have a good excuse for his failure, he should retake the course within a year and work hard to earn a high grade. Thus, his failure would not appear on his records.

Question 6

In the lecture, the professor explains traditional Chinese medicine. First, he describes the theory of "chi," a form of energy that flows through paths in the body. In addition, he states that chi can be hot or cold. Chinese medicine contends that a healthy body maintains clear paths for the flow of chi as well as a balance between hot and cold forms. Unhealthy blockages or imbalances can arise through diet, body position, and mental stress. The professor also explains how Chinese medicine seeks to treat the cause of the problem rather than the symptoms. One form of treatment is the use of different herbs to manipulate chi.

Writing

Sample Responses

Task 1

The reading and the lecture define society in different ways. They both talk about groups of people, but the way each talks about groups is very different. In the reading passage, groups are categorized by size and type. For example, there are small social groups and large social groups, and both these small groups and large groups interact with each other. All of the small groups and large groups together make a supergroup, society.

In the lecture, the speaker does not define society in this way. Instead, she gives several common aspects that can be used to define society. Among these aspects, she lists a common place, a common government, a common language, and common traditions. According to the speaker, society is not necessarily a large supergroup. In her view, a relatively small group of individuals within a relatively small area can be defined as a society. She points to the student body of a university as an example. As long as the group of individuals has the aspects she lists, it can be considered a society.

Task 2

In life, a number of sources contribute to one's learning and development: parents, teachers, friends, television, books, and movies. Each source is essential to human development in some way. It is my belief, however, that parents are the best and most important teachers for a number of reasons.

First, parents are the first teachers that each individual encounters. Even before birth, mothers and fathers "teach" babies by talking and singing to them. After birth, parents teach by talking, reading, and introducing their children to the world around them. Scientists contend that children's brains grow rapidly between ages one and five — the period spent almost exclusively with Mom and Dad.

Second, parents teach children not only how to talk, read, and write, but also how to behave correctly. Infants, of course, do not know anything about other people. Parents instruct them how to be polite, how to show respect, how to handle emotions, whom to trust, and whom not to trust. In other words, they teach their children how to survive and thrive in society.

Third, and most important, parents teach by example. Because children spend so much time with their parents when they are young, they learn by observation and imitation. This can be both positive and negative. For example, children can learn harmful behaviors, like violence or smoking, if their parents exhibit such actions. Children, therefore, learn what they live. If their parents are kind, the children will be, too. If the parents are selfish, so will be the children.

The final aspect is the longevity of the relationship. Since parents act as teachers for 18 or more years before the child leaves home, they have a much stronger impact than a school teacher whom students may know for as little as one year. Indeed, even after graduating from university and starting a family of their own, children often turn to their parents for guidance.

Though there are numerous people and media through which children can learn, the lessons and examples received from parents shape personalities and influence lives the most. For these reasons, I think parents are the most important teachers in a person's life.